PUBLICATION HISTORY

Most of the material in this volume is being published for the first time. The only exceptions are parts of the "Reconstruction" chapter found in the 1975 edition of The Traffic Accident Investigation Manual (Volume 1) and the Traffic Institute publication "Estimating Vehicle Stopping Time and Distance," which also covered certain material used in this book. Otherwise, the topics found in this volume represent new material.

First Edition, 1990

Copyright 1990 by Northwestern University Traffic Institute

Evanston, Illinois 60204

ISBN 0-912642-07-6

Library of Congress Catalog Number 90-60196

Printed in the United States of America

Traffic Accident Reconstruction

Volume 2 of The
Traffic Accident
Investigation Manual

Lynn B. Fricke

NORTHWESTERN TRAFFIC INSTITUTE
UNIVERSITY

ACKNOWLEDGMENT

The development and publication of this volume has been made possible by grants from:

The Anheuser-Busch Charitable Trust

The James S. Kemper Foundation, the Corporate Foundation of the Kemper Group

Allstate Insurance Companies

The Northwestern University Traffic Institute is deeply grateful to these organizations for their generosity and continued support.

Noel C. Bufe, Ph.D.
Director

Foreword

This book, Volume 2 of *The Traffic Accident Investigation Manual*, is a collection of 17 topics dealing with the major issues that arise in traffic accident reconstruction. The concepts presented here should not prove difficult for engineers or for people with technical education. Those learning how to reconstruct traffic accidents will find this volume especially useful. Individuals with less technical background, however, may find certain topics difficult. Clearly, as one progresses from data collection to the reconstruction phase of accident investigation, more mathematics are needed to help interpret how an accident occurred.

Traffic Accident Reconstruction represents a considerable expansion of the "Reconstruction" chapter found in the 1975 edition of the *Manual*. It is the product of numerous individuals who have taught and practiced accident reconstruction at the Northwestern University Traffic Institute. In the future, no doubt, additional revisions to the topics covered in this book will be necessary.

As their respective titles would indicate, Volume 1, *At-Scene Investigation and Technical Follow-Up*, deals mainly with data collection and, to a lesser degree, data interpretation; *Traffic Accident Reconstruction*, the present volume, emphasizes interpretation, with little discussion of data collection.

The topics covered in this volume are also covered in The Traffic Institute's two traffic accident reconstruction courses. Much of this material has therefore been "tried out" on students at the Institute. Whenever practical, the authors have included real-world accident cases in each topic. Indeed, some of our former students may recognize a case that was used in a class they took.

Nearly all the material in this volume is being published for the first time. The only exceptions are parts of the 1975 "Reconstruction" chapter cited above and the TI publication "Estimating Vehicle Stopping Time and Distance," which also covered certain material used in this book. Otherwise, the topics found in this volume represent new material.

Arrangement

As in Volume 1, each topic has been written to stand separately. Thus, the pages for each topic are numbered independently of the rest of the book.

The first digit in all topic numbers is "8." (The 800 series has been assigned to accident investigation/reconstruction topics.) Any topic number 850 or higher is found in Volume 2; any topic number lower than 850 applies to Volume 1. For clearer pagination, the first digit of the topic number (always 8) has been dropped from the page numbers. For example, the third page of Topic 852 is 52-3.

As with Volume 1, there are gaps between topic numbers. This allows room for adding further related topics at a later date. The topics are placed in the book in numerical sequence.

Metric System

In most of Volume 2, both metric and U.S. units are given. Not all example problems are worked in both sets of units, only when confusion might otherwise result.

International Symbols

New students of accident reconstruction are often surprised and confused by the many different symbols used to represent the same quantity. The authors have made a significant effort to have the units used in *Traffic Accident Reconstruction* conform to the standard symbols recommended by the International Standards Organization (ISO). This may disappoint some people and please others, depending on the symbols they are accustomed to using.

Contributors

It has taken approximately five years to complete this revision and expansion of the 1975 "Reconstruction" chapter. J. Stannard Baker wrote two topics for the present volume, and both represent the excellent work traditionally associated with him. Other topics, formerly bearing his name, have been revised by others who have made every effort to maintain the high quality of Mr. Baker's original work.

Many people have contributed to the creation of this book. Everyone in TI's Accident Investigation Division has made many sacrifices to produce it. Extremely heavy teaching and consulting loads were often assumed by others so that those writing the book could complete their task, the latter often working nights and weekends. Without the help of Thad Aycock, Ken Baker and Gary Cooper, this book would have taken much longer to produce.

In addition, each topic represents the collective effort of many. Every manuscript was subjected to an internal Accident Investigation Division review before being turned over to our editor, Steve Hillyer, who made a considerable effort to ensure that a clear, consistent format was followed. We are indeed grateful to him. In nearly all cases, Gary Cooper, of the Accident Investigation Division, produced the final drawings. His patience in working with the authors to make camera-ready illustrations is gratefully acknowledged. Photographic enhancements were done by Paul Lane of Photo Source, Inc. Vernon Lockhart, Dick Detzner and Diana Gondek, of TI's Graphics Department, produced the final pasteup copy. Alex Weiss, director of the Publications Division, coordinated the production effort and was a great source of support during the whole project.

A final acknowledgement must go to Dr. Noel Bufe, director of The Traffic Institute, and TI deputy directors Paul Chylak and Diane Stolle-Tye for their abiding support, understanding and encouragement throughout the production of this book.

Lynn B. Fricke is the primary author and technical editor of *Traffic Accident Reconstruction* and was co-author of *At-Scene Investigation and Technical Follow-Up*. He has been with The Traffic Institute since 1975, and became director of its Accident Investigation Division in 1981. Mr. Fricke has B.S. and M.S. degrees in engineering and is a member of the Society of Automotive Engineers' Accident Investigation Practices Committee. He has testified as an expert in several state and federal courts.

CONTENTS

Topic 861
UNDERSTANDING VEHICLE BEHAVIOR IN COLLISIONS

Topic 862
DRAG FACTOR AND COEFFICIENT OF FRICTION IN TRAFFIC ACCIDENT RECONSTRUCTION

Topic 864
PERCEPTION AND REACTION IN TRAFFIC ACCIDENTS

Topic 866
SPEED ESTIMATES FOR VEHICLES THAT FALL, FLIP, OR VAULT

Topic 876
UNDERSTANDING OCCUPANT BEHAVIOR IN VEHICLE COLLISIONS

Topic 877
VEHICLE-PEDESTRIAN ACCIDENT RECONSTRUCTION

Topic 878
RECONSTRUCTION OF HEAVY TRUCK ACCIDENTS

Topic 890
DERIVATIONS OF EQUATIONS FOR TRAFFIC ACCIDENT RECONSTRUCTION

Topic 892
THE USE OF COMPUTERS IN TRAFFIC ACCIDENT RECONSTRUCTION

PROCESS OF TRAFFIC ACCIDENT RECONSTRUCTION

Topic 850 of the *Traffic Accident Investigation Manual*

by
J. Stannard Baker
and
Lynn B. Fricke

NORTHWESTERN UNIVERSITY TRAFFIC INSTITUTE

PROCESS OF TRAFFIC ACCIDENT RECONSTRUCTION

Traffic accident reconstruction is the effort to determine, from whatever information is available, *how* the accident occurred. Reconstruction is not determining *why* an accident occurred. In Topic 810 the five levels of traffic accident investigation were discussed. They are repeated here:

1. Accident reporting
2. At-scene extra data collection
3. Technical follow-up
4. Professional reconstruction
5. Cause analysis

The beginning levels, such as reporting, at-scene data collection and technical follow-up, tend to be routine activities. As the effort moves into the technical follow-up and reconstruction, the tasks become more analytical and less routine, as suggested by Exhibit 1. The purpose of this topic is to suggest a process to analyze problems in traffic accident reconstruction. By their very nature, however, analytical processes do not lend themselves to a foolproof approach that will always guarantee answers.

1. RECONSTRUCTION GOALS

Objectives

Describing the events of the accident, in more or less detail, is the aim of accident reconstruction. This involves at-

PROPORTION OF ROUTINE AND ANALYTICAL EFFORT

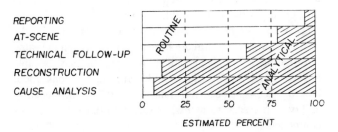

Exhibit 1. As the level of activity moves from the basic levels of investigation to the higher levels, the effort becomes less routine and more analytical.

tempting to determine, for each vehicle or pedestrian involved, such particulars as

- Position on the road
- Facing or heading direction
- Speed
- Direction of travel
- Acceleration or deceleration
- Rotation

A requirement of reconstruction may be to determine these details at a time or place, such as at the moment of first contact in a collision, or at a series of short intervals — for example, every tenth of a second — before or after the first harmful event. Such work may result in time, space, velocity, and acceleration diagrams.

Driving strategy and evasive tactics may be inferred in reconstruction from descriptions of position and movement. This is done by relating velocity and position of one vehicle (or pedestrian) to another, or relating velocity and position to features of the surroundings, such as view obstructions, grades, curves, and traffic control devices.

Traffic law violations are mainly a matter of driving strategy, for example, position on the road, speed, and signalling intent to turn or stop. Laws specify what drivers and pedestrians must do or not do in using roads. Therefore, when one has determined by accident reconstruction *how* the road was used, determining whether the use violated some law follows naturally, but often inconclusively. The reason that accident reconstruction is often inconclusive is that accident reconstruction is limited with respect to accuracy. Suppose, for example, that the reconstruction problem is to determine whether a vehicle's speed was more than the legal limit of 25 mph where the accident occurred. Speeds estimated by reconstruction are usually expressed as a range — for example, "30 to 40 mph." That range would be clearly above a legal limit of 25 mph and the driver in question would definitely have violated the law. But if the limit was 35 mph (within the range), the matter would be inconclusive and one could not say whether there was a violation.

Who was driving may also be a problem in accident reconstruction. Sometimes the question of which vehicle occupant was at the wheel when the accident occurred is in dispute or is not sufficiently answered by reports of informants. Then an analysis of injuries, positions of bodies, and even vehicle damage can lead to useful conclusions.

Injuries. Describing exactly how injuries were received may also require some form of accident reconstruction. For example, an opinion may be needed as to how injuries might have been different had restraint devices (belts, airbags) been in use at the time of collision.

Causes. Reconstruction does not try to explain *why* an accident happened. That would require describing the entire combination of conditions which would produce another identical accident. Describing why an accidednt happened is cause analysis rather than reconstruction. Cause analysis is briefly discussed in Topic 852. However, reconstruction does often suggest circumstances or conditions that were contributing factors; that is, had they been different, the accident would not have occurred.

Results of Reconstruction

Opinions or conclusions are the products of accident reconstruction. To the extent that reports of direct observations are available and can be depended on as facts, reconstruction is unnecessary. But if there were no eyewitnesses of the occurrence, reconstruction can sometimes form useful conclusions about how the accident happened from the results of the accident, such as marks on the road and damage to vehicles.

When two or more eyewitness informants differ importantly in reports of their observations, reconstruction can be very helpful in deciding which of their reports to believe or, in some cases, whether to believe any of their reports.

Also, when the statement of an informant appears to be his opinion or belief rather than a reliable report of his observations, reconstruction from what facts are available may be helpful in corroborating or discrediting the informant's opinions.

Always remember that the results of reconstruction are opinions. Like any conclusions, they are more or less accurate and more or less credible depending on the information on which the reconstruction is based, on who does the reconstruction, and on the circumstances under which they are made.

Reports of some kind usually express the opinions formed in accident reconstruction. The kind of report depends on who wants the opinion and for what purposes. Sometimes the report is a simple "Yes" or "No" over the telephone in reponse to a very specific question. Sometimes the report is a deposition or testimony in court in response to a series of questions asked by an attorney. Usually the report is written. It may be a brief letter, or it may be a formal engineering report summarizing conclusions, listing the data on which the conclusions were based, explaining any scientific princi-

ples involved, describing, at least in a general way, the reasoning leading from the data to the conclusions, and finally evaluating the accuracy and reliability of the conclusions expressed. Such a formal report may include maps, drawings, and photographs to direct attention to the facts available and to explain more fully the conclusion.

Limitations

Do not think for a minute that every accident can be reconstructed, because there are always very definite limitations on the effort to reconstruct an accident. There are essentially four kinds of limitations:

1. Quantity and quality of information available
2. Ability of people doing the reconstruction
3. How much reconstruction is required
4. Time and money available

1. *Quantity and quality* of information is the most important element in traffic-accident reconstruction. With enough good information, the facts speak for themselves and there is need for only the simplest inferences. On the other hand, information may be so scarce and so unreliable that practically no solid facts on which to base conclusions are available. Then reconstruction turns out to be speculation.

In some instances a single bit of information is missing. For example, an opposite-direction collision made tiremarks in the snow. Photographs of these marks indicated well where the vehicles collided; but the center line and roadway edges, being covered by snow, did not appear in the pictures. Therefore, it was impossible to determine which vehicle was across the center of the roadway on the wrong side when they collided. The bit of information missing was where the center line was in the pictures.

In other cases, the information is not good enough for reconstruction. For example, some measurements were made to locate final positions of vehicles; but these measurements were neither recorded accurately nor sufficiently related to permanent landmarks to permit locating the vehicles on an after-accident situation map made later.

Hence, if data are adequate, little special training is necessary to do the reconstruction required; but if adequate data are lacking, nobody can assemble pieces to give a satisfactory picture of what actually happened.

2. *Ability of persons* reconstructing the accident is the next most important limitation on that work. Given the same information about the accident, one person may be able to form much more reliable and complete opinions about how the accident occurred than another. The difference in ability is not easy to assess. It seems to have three major components:

1. Aptitude for recognizing relevant results of the accident, such as marks on the road and damage to vehicles, either at the site of the accident or in photographs

2. A working knowledge of basic sciences, especially some aspects of physics, dynamics, psychology, optics, and mathematics
3. A proclivity for recognizing the important difference between fact and opinion in the investigator's thinking and also in what others have to say.

Sometimes, the person attempting reconstruction encounters vital questions for which he has no answer. Then he must seek the help of someone else who does have the needed knowledge and skill — if such a person can be found. Consequently, some attempts to reconstruct an accident may require a panel or team of experts, each especially qualified to do some part of the whole job. If you are not qualified yourself, don't try to "wing it." Sooner or later this will lead to your lack of credibility.

3. *How much reconstruction is required*, in practice, usually determines the extent of reconstruction. A *complete* description of how the accident happened is rarely necessary. As a rule, whoever requests the work done has specific issues in mind — for example, speed of a vehicle, which vehicle was across the center line, or whether a taillight was on or off.

For law enforcement purposes, the essential need is to determine whether a specific law has been violated — for example, the speed of a vehicle, or which of two vehicles was over the center line. In some cases, it may be necessary to determine which of the occupants of a vehicle was driving.

For liability lawsuits, the requirements for reconstruction may be the same as those for law enforcement purposes but, in addition, may involve analysis of driver behavior and vehicle performance.

The most thorough reconstruction is required by research teams seeking clues to the causes of accidents.

For all purposes, data collection at the scene, which involves little in the way of conclusions, is about the same. Technical preparation for litigation by collection of additional information later, however, varies substantially with the requirements of reconstruction.

Therefore, the first step in accident reconstruction is to state the problem. That means defining as exactly as possible what issues are to be resolved and what questions must be answered. Stating the issues initially saves time and effort by reducing collection of unnecessary data and pursuit of irrelevant lines of thinking.

4. *Time and money* available also limit the extent to which accidents can be reconstructed. The cost is usually of little consequence if a lamp is examined to determine whether it was on or off before a collision; but if the problem involves special road tests, disassembly of vehicles, or extensive drawings and calculations, the opinions resulting may not be worth the effort they would entail, and reconstruction may have to be curtailed. Often the results of reconstruction are needed on a few hours' notice — for example, for a trial which has already begun; but if no satisfactory reconstruc-

tion can be accomplished in that time, the issues involved must be simplified or reconstruction must be abandoned.

2. GENERAL PROCEDURES

Before discussing specific methods of accident reconstruction, it is useful to consider for a moment just what kind of activity is involved in trying to describe in detail the series of events that constitute a traffic accident.

Thinking

From the description of accident reconstruction, it should be plain that accident reconstruction is not so much a matter of collecting information about an accident as it is of *thinking* about information that has been collected. Reconstruction essentially interprets data gathered in lower levels of investigation.

Definite procedures can be set up for most information gathering. These have been described in earlier topics. Indeed, many items of information actually are specified by the forms used to record them. So, while some effort is required to get most of the needed information, little thought is involved. If similar adequate step-by-step procedures could be developed to interpret the information gathered, little special thinking would be needed for reconstruction.

But reconstruction involves so much imagination, so much matching of one bit of information with another, and so much application of basic science to available data in such a variety of circumstances, that definite rules or formulas can be written for only certain limited reconstruction situations.

Professional people trying to reconstruct accidents often need information which is available but not at hand. Lacking a skilled investigator to send for it, such professionals themselves often have to go out to get measurements, look up published data in books, or try to find people who can tell them what they need to know. Data for reconstruction may even have to come from specially conducted tests. But the fact that professionals doing reconstruction have to obtain additional data does not necessarily make the collection of such data a part of accident reconstruction.

The thinking required is essentially disciplined and purposeful study of available data, always keeping in mind two quite different ideas: 1) the issues to be resolved, and 2) applicable principles of basic sciences.

The Puzzle Analogy

Reconstructing an accident is like assembling a jigsaw puzzle to see what the picture looks like. The data available correspond to the pieces of the puzzle. With a simple puzzle having only a few pieces that all match easily, assembling the picture is child's play. But when many pieces are missing and there are pieces that do not belong (perhaps false information intended to mislead), the problem can be difficult or even impossible.

When you have fitted together all the pieces you can, and have put aside all those you are sure do not belong, you may or may not have a picture sufficiently complete to reveal what you want to know about the accident. If not, you must try to determine, from the facts you have assembled, what the missing pieces of the picture must have been like. This involves a basic understanding of what the objects pictured were like. For example, if a piece you have shows only the head of a dog, you know that the missing pieces may have shown the body of a dog, its four legs, and its tail. In a similar way, you have photographs of tiremarks on the roadway. These do not tell you directly what you want to know — for example, the speed of the vehicle that made them — but an understanding of how tires leave marks on the road enables you to recognize these marks as braking skidmarks left by locked wheels. Then, knowing the distance the vehicle slid and the kind of surface on which it slid, a basic knowledge of the mechanics involved enables you to calculate how fast the vehicle would have had to be going to slide to a stop in that distance. Thus, from bits of information fitted together — the character of the mark on the road, the length of that mark, and the nature of the surface — you can form a useful opinion about something that was not apparent before: the minimum speed of the vehicle.

Unfortunately there is no recipe or simple set of rules that tells you how to solve puzzles; otherwise they would not be puzzles. Likewise, there are no simple rules for reconstructing accidents.

Approaches to the Problem

Although few specific rules can be set down for reconstructing traffic accidents, certain useful approaches to the problem have been developed. Such approaches are applicable in many typical cases, but it would be ridiculous to try to force these approaches to apply universally. Many accident investigations have such special requirements that an appropriate approach has to be invented. Some of the steps described below apply to every accident reconstruction problem; others are less generally applicable.

1. *State the problem or problems.* Get clearly in mind the issues to be resolved. This immediately sets limits on the work you have to do.

2. *Review data available.* Put aside any data which appear to be irrelevant — for example, descriptions of injuries when the issue is which vehicle was on the wrong side of the road. Reviewing the data reveals what information you have to go on and enables you to sort out information which may be useful from that which clearly will not be. Data normally can be sorted into the three groups shown in Exhibit 2. Thus, the material to be handled is reduced to more manageable proportions.

3. *Consider the need to obtain more data.* From the examination of data at hand, it may appear at once that additional useful material might be available — for example,

RELEVANT   QUESTIONABLE   IRRELEVANT

EVALUATE

Exhibit 2. *Sort the data into the three groups in order to have a more manageable case.*

certain photographs, statements of informants, or measurements. Or it might seem desirable — or even necessary — to try to secure additional data, such as weights of vehicles, further details from witnesses, or locations of traffic control devices. Sometimes development of additional data involves tests or experiments — for example, skid tests to measure friction of road surfaces or experiments to establish visibility at the accident site. If additional data are necessary and reconstruction is urgent, direct every effort at once to obtaining that information; but otherwise plan to obtain the information while other work is going forward, perhaps with estimated values or assumed facts always subject to revision and reassessment when the desired information is obtained.

4. *Prepare a working after-accident situation map* as described in Topic 834. Sometimes the map is not needed — for example, when the only issue is whether taillights were on or off. But more often it is indispensable — for example, when the major issue is the position of vehicles on the road in angle or opposite-direction collisions. In cases where the issues to be resolved need accurate maps and no measurements were taken, consider using photogrammetric techniques to obtain measurements, so that an after-accident map can be drawn. Topic 830 discusses very simple techniques and more complicated mathematical approaches.

5. *Work back.* With issues to be resolved firmly in mind and available data sorted out, try to work back from the results of the accident. This procedure is outlined in Exhibit 4. For cases that have such results as marks on the road, damage to vehicles, final positions of vehicles or bodies, and injuries to persons, ask yourself what would have produced each reported result. This usually means matching contact damage on one vehicle with that on another to learn how the vehicles were related during collision, and then matching marks on the road with tire patterns or abrasion on vehicles to learn the position of the vehicle on the road at a particular point. This procedure is discussed in considerable detail in Topic 861, *Understanding Vehicle Behavior in Collisions.* Calculation of speed from a braking skidmark or a turning yaw-mark is a form of working back. In such cases, the mark on the road is the result of the accident from which you begin to work back. First, you must clearly recognize just how this mark was made. Then the length of slide or radius of turn

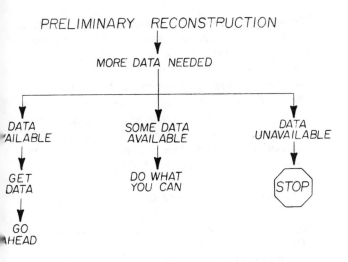

PRELIMINARY RECONSTPUCTION

MORE DATA NEEDED

DATA AVAILABLE — GET DATA — GO AHEAD

SOME DATA AVAILABLE — DO WHAT YOU CAN

DATA UNAVAILABLE — STOP

Exhibit 3. *Consider the need for additional data. If data is incomplete, the issues to be resolved may be intermediate or partially determinate.*

must be determined. Next, the resistance of the surface to sliding must be estimated. Finally, principles of mechanics are applied to discover what speed would have been required to slide to a stop in that distance or to turn that sharply.

6. *Testing theories (hypotheses)* as shown in Exhibit 5 may adequately resolve issues if working back does not yield satisfactory solutions to problems. Assume, as a theory, a set of circumstances before the accident: positions of vehicles, their speeds, accelerations, and directions of travel. Then, according to laws of mechanics, project these movements to test the theory. If observed results would have been produced, the assumptions made in the theory are supported; if observed results would not have occurred, the assumptions are refuted. Often it is convenient to take the statement of an informant as a theory. Reconstruction from his statement may corroborate or refute that statement. Several theories may have to be tested. It may be that none can be satisfactorily supported or that more than one is possible, especially

when descriptions of the results are not precise. Both working back from results and testing theories may be employed in the same reconstruction effort.

7. *Consider whether all reported results of the accident are satisfactorily accounted for.* Some results of the accident may be accounted for by conclusions reached as a result of reconstruction, but other reported results which do not contribute to the conclusions must also be satisfactorily explained. Otherwise, confidence in the conclusions can be undermined. For example, in Exhibit 6 the gouges, G, are good indicators of the maximum engagement area of two colliding vehicles. But tiremarks A and B help to explain how the vehicles travelled to their first contact positions. If the tiremarks are not fully explained, it can be argued that the reconstruction is inadequate because it neglects these conspicuous marks at the site of the accident.

8. *Test the conclusions reached.* Can the same conclusions be reached by two different approaches (Exhibit 7)? For example, if an opinion has been reached about the positions of two vehicles in an opposite-direction collision based on marks on the road, try to reach an opinion about their positions based on the damage to the vehicles *without* reference to the marks on the road. If the two approaches lead to the same or nearly the same conclusion, they confirm each other. Another test is to have another qualified person form an opinion concerning the issues involved using the same basic information. If two people separately arrive at the same opinion from the same data, the opinion is supported. If not, the observations and reasoning of each should be compared with those of the other to see where they differ. Also, consider alternate possibilities. Especially when facts are few and information may be unreliable, there may be two or more possible explanations of what happened. Do not be satisfied with the first one that comes to mind, but search for others. Out of several possibilities one may be more credible than the others; some of these possibilities may be tested as hypotheses.

WORKING BACK

OBSERVED RESULTS
▼
WHAT RESULTS INDICATE
▼
SCIENCE INVOLVED
▼
CONCLUSIONS

Exhibit 4. *The results of the accident allow you to work back to develop conclusions on how the accident occurred.*

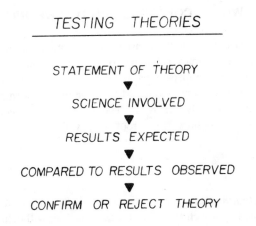

TESTING THEORIES

STATEMENT OF THEORY
▼
SCIENCE INVOLVED
▼
RESULTS EXPECTED
▼
COMPARED TO RESULTS OBSERVED
▼
CONFIRM OR REJECT THEORY

Exhibit 5. *The process of testing theories (hypotheses) is important. This will allow you to evaluate possible scenarios for an accident.*

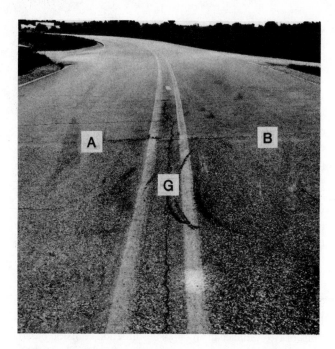

Exhibit 6. *All of the marks on the road that are a result of the accident should be fully explained in an accident reconstruction.*

9. *Prepare diagrams, charts, and tables* to illustrate and explain your conclusions. These may be supplementary maps showing sequences of vehicle positions before and after the first harmful event, tables showing estimates if different possible values are used, or any other appropriate exhibit. Technology today can produce three-dimensional models that can be used to videotape the sequence of a collision. Computer models can display the motion of vehicles from their pre-collision positions to their final positions. In many cases the cost of these technologies may not be warranted. If required, these exhibits are embodied in whatever kind of report is wanted.

3. WHY RECONSTRUCTIONS GO WRONG

Mistakes in accident reconstruction are often not easy to discover. Sometimes solutions to accident reconstruction problems are so transparent as to leave little doubt; but often there is no good way to judge whether the opinion formed is really true or only seems so. The fact that one *believes* strongly in an opinion is no proof of its validity.

Pitfalls

Evaluating an opinion, as one of the steps in the suggested approach to accident reconstruction, will help uncover errors. But enumerating some of the pitfalls that have been found to increase the chance of mistakes in accident reconstruction will help to avoid them.

Starting with a conclusion is a common way to take a wrong turn in accident reconstruction. The investigator starts with some preconceived solution to a problem at issue. This is very easy to do:

- Someone desperately urges that conclusion. For example, an attorney, a claim adjuster, a driver involved, or a spouse or parent of a driver hopefully suggests or even confidently asserts how the accident happened and, without opposition, the idea takes root and grows in the investigator's mind. This is called "accepting a ready-made theory".
- Long before all available information is at hand, the investigator starts to speculate about what happened, discovers a logical possibility, and gets carried away by it. This is called "jumping to conclusions".
- The investigator has picked up some rote thinking that partly closes his mind to inquiry. For example, he has been lead to believe that hard braking with a flat tire throws a car out of control; or he has heard so often that rear-end collisions result from following too closely that he does not imagine other circumstances; or he has accepted the idea that tire friction marks on the roadway all are skidmarks and result from braking. Such stereotypes may be true sometimes, but the danger is that they may not *always* be true.
- Bias may lead to false conclusions. For example, the investigator is prejudiced against long-haired boys, blacks, women, or whatever. In the investigator's mind, such a driver is likely to be responsible for the accident. People are not the only subject of bias; it may also involve motorcycles, trucks, sports cars, and many other things.

Forming conclusions to start with has unfortunate results:

- The investigation stops there. The issue is resolved. No further information needs to be sought. The mind is made up.
- The investigator accepts only those facts which fit the conclusion and rejects those which do not. Once you have a theory about how the accident happened, it is easy to accept any statements, signs, or facts that seem to confirm that theory and overlook completely any which do not. It then becomes more difficult to discover the truth.

However, this warning about starting an investigation with a conclusion should not discourage you from thinking about various possibilities or testing any hypothesis that comes to mind. There is an important difference between a conclusion and a hypothesis. A conclusion is opinion which more or less ends the matter by settling the issue; a hypothesis, on the other hand, is a tentative theory to be examined. Whatever hypothesis best stands testing may become the most acceptable conclusion.

Failure to distinguish fact from opinion is a form of uncritical thinking. Critical thinking is a matter of separating, in the mind, information and ideas of which one can be very

TWO SUPPORTS ARE BETTER

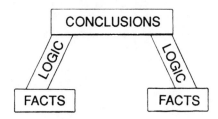

Exhibit 7. *If two different approaches to a reconstruction issue are used and the same conclusions are reached, this makes your conclusions more creditable.*

sure from those which are less certain, and those which are guesswork or speculation. Too often the "facts" which have been relied on as the basis for some aspect of accident reconstruction turn out to be only speculation or even a falsehood. Courts try to make this important distinction with respect to testimony permitted by witnesses. An investigator can easily slip into the notion that his own opinion, which he has come to believe in, is a fact. It may indeed be a fact, but if not, it is an insecure basis for further attempts to find out what actually happened in a motor-vehicle accident.

Expecting someone to explain what happened. The investigator believes that if he just asks enough questions, somebody will tell him all he needs to know about what happened. He has never really learned to look and think for himself. Sometimes an investigator carries his questioning to the point of forcing a *theory* about what happened from a person who does not remember what *actually* happened. Having received such a theory, right or wrong, the investigator is satisfied.

Faulty interpretation of accident results may be a reason why a reconstruction is wrong. Yaw marks, for example, are interpreted to be skids, which will then yield incorrect speed estimates. Underbody debris is used to determine the location of first contact positions of two vehicles when the debris has moved a considerable distance from those positions. In situations such as these the conclusions are based on a poor or incorrect interpretation. Thus, nearly any conclusion based on these will give erroneous answers.

Assuming inappropriate values can lead to some absurd conclusions. If a tire-pavement coefficient of friction is equal to 0.80, there is no guarantee that a car after a collision will decelerate with a drag factor of 0.80. This is a common error seen in some reconstructions. In many cases the person doing the reconstruction should use a range of values when calculations are made. At times the final result — speed, for example — may vary a little or a lot. By doing this type of analysis, the reconstructionist can determine how *sensitive* the answer is to the input variables. If the answer changes radically with a small change in the inputs, this suggests that the methodology being used may not be reliable.

Incorrect application of science occasionally occurs to those with little experience in reconstructing accidents. One of the most common mistakes for a beginner is to add velocities. Say, for example, a car slides over a hard surface, then slides on a gravel shoulder, and finally slides on grass. Many people would calculate a slide to stop speed for each of these three surfaces and simply add them together. This is wrong.

Indeterminate cases do occur. This is often because of poor data collection in the first place. Occasionally people become too personally involved in the case and start believing that the available data tells them more than is really there. For example, this occurs when someone wants to see something (tire mark, etc.) in a photograph that really isn't there. Be careful not to become overzealous in the analysis.

Routines

No detailed rules for accident reconstruction have been published. It would require a large volume embracing certain aspects of a number of scientific disciplines. Several A.I. Topics describe in more or less detail certain phases of accident reconstruction — for example, the mechanics of automobile collision (Topic 890) and the examination of automobile lamps (Topic 823).

Commonly used routines of accident reconstruction can be represented by equations or tables for easy reference. These are handy for investigators who need to make quick preliminary judgments as to whether a law has been violated or whether the accident warrants further investigation. Some of these routines are explained in other A.I. Topics. These explanations apply only to *simple* cases. Situations which require more complex considerations frequently appear. A well-qualified expert in accident reconstruction must have a considerably broader understanding, especially of the scientific principles involved, than is presented here. The simple routines described should not be applied to any set of circumstances that differ materially from those enumerated for that routine. Some special problems have been mentioned in connection with the explanation of some of the methods, but no attempt has been made to suggest detailed procedures for resolving these difficulties.

4. SOURCES

Authors

J. Stannard Baker is a traffic engineer specializing in accident investigation. He was Director of Research and Development at the Northwestern University Traffic Institute from 1946 to 1971 and is a guest lecturer for the Institute.

Lynn B. Fricke is a traffic engineer specializing in accident investigation. He has been with The Traffic Institute since 1975. In 1981, he became director of the Institute's Accident Investigation Division.

Exhibits

The following are the sources of the exhibits used in this topic:

Baker, J. Stannard, San Diego, CA
  Charts: 1, 3, 4, 5
  Diagrams: 2, 7
Fricke, Lynn B., Lincolnshire, IL
  Photo: 6

CAUSES AND CONTRIBUTING FACTORS IN TRAFFIC ACCIDENTS

Topic 852 of the *Traffic Accident Investigation Manual*

by
J. Stannard Baker

NORTHWESTERN UNIVERSITY TRAFFIC INSTITUTE

CAUSES AND CONTRIBUTING FACTORS IN TRAFFIC ACCIDENTS

There is widespread expectation that traffic accident investigation will reveal the true causes of traffic accidents; but when statistics compiled from investigations are examined for that purpose, the result is generally disappointing. Even information obtained by investigation of a particular accident is usually inadequate to answer important questions about *why* that accident happened.

It is important, therefore that a traffic accident investigation manual consider the problems of determining causes of such accidents.

This topic treats traffic accident causes and contributing factors under six headings:

1. Nature of causes
2. Operational factors
3. Condition factors
4. Predisposing circumstances
5. Conventional concepts
6. Cause analysis.

A more complete discussion has been published elsewhere.[1]

1. NATURE OF CAUSES

Discussion about causes is often too vague to be useful. It should be helpful, therefore, to begin by trying to reach an understanding of what we mean when we speak of "causes."

Events and Conditions

There is general agreement that a *cause* is whatever is required to produce a *result*.

Ordinarily, more than one circumstance is required. For example, for an electric lamp to emit light 1) the lamp must be whole (neither broken nor burned out); 2) it must be connected in an electric circuit; 3) the circuit must be supplied with power; and 4) the circuit must be closed by some means. None of these four circumstances, by itself, will result in light from the lamp, so none alone can be its cause.

Yet we usually think that flipping the switch (closing the circuit) causes the light to come on, that is, until the lamp burns out, power fails, or a fuse blows. The cause that results in light is the *entire* combination of circumstances necessary to produce it, not just one circumstance. Each contributing circumstance is a *factor* or element of the cause, but none, by itself, is capable of producing the result. It may be a simple matter to find one factor that contributes to the cause, such as flipping a switch, but it is often quite difficult or even impossible to discover some of the others.

Simultaneous conditions. Usually several factors (circumstances) must exist at the same time (simultaneously) to produce the result. In the foregoing example, two simultaneous conditions are necessary: 1) the lamp must be whole; and 2) it must be connected in a circuit.

Usually, when conditions function simultaneously as factors causing an occurrence, the degree of each condition involved is important. The same result may ensue when one condition is at quite different levels, provided other conditions are at appropriate levels at the same time. For example, consider two drivers, A and B, in a car after dark. Driver A can see better in dim light than Driver B. Without headlights, neither has sufficient visual capacity to read a certain sign. With high-beam headlights, both have sufficient visual capacity. With low-beam lights, Driver A can perceive the sign and Driver B cannot. Thus, a high degree of illumination combined with his poor visual ability, causes Driver B to perceive; but low illumination combined with a high degree of visual ability causes Driver A to perceive. If Driver B is involved in an accident because he cannot see the sign, a cause analysis of the accident must try to determine whether it was because of low illumination or low visual ability or both. Of course, when three or more condition factors interrelate, evaluation of the combination becomes considerably more complicated.

Sequential events. In many cases, an event results in conditions or factors that produce another event and so on, one leading to the next. Sometimes a sequence or chain of this kind is called the "domino" phenomenon, referring to a row of dominoes standing on end and so closely spaced that if one tips over, it strikes the next and tips that over, eventually making the last domino in the row fall.

In the electric-lamp example, in addition to the two *conditions* mentioned, two *events* must occur: 1) power must be supplied to the circuit and 2) the circuit must be closed.

As in the case of conditions, the nature and extent of each event in a series must be appropriate or else subsequent events will not necessarily be triggered.

Combinations of events and conditions are closely interwoven. Each event in a series depends on certain conditions and each condition usually depends on certain previous events. Some of the conditions and events may be obvious, but many are obscure. Hence, valid combinations are difficult to determine. For example, suppose that gasoline leaks from a damaged fuel pump in motor-vehicle crash. The chain of events and combination of conditions creating the fuel leakage are not difficult to explain. Then a fire starts. The exact events and conditions which ignited the fuel are difficult to ascertain; a number of speculative possibilities come to mind, but which of these possible factors actually contributed cannot readily be determined.

Definitions

Cause. The foregoing brief explanation yields a definition of cause, namely, the combination of simultaneous and sequential factors without any one of which the result could not have occurred.

Factor may then be defined as any circumstance contributing to a result without which the result could not have occurred. Each factor is an element which is necessary to produce the result, but not, by itself, sufficient.

It is useful to distinguish between causes and factors. One cause produces the result. That cause is a combination of factors which may be difficult, if not impossible, to describe in detail because some factors may be obscure.

So, in discussing why results occur, we will be less vague if we limit the word *cause* to meaning all of the combined circumstances necessary to effect a result, whether known or not known, and use the word *factor* to mean any one of the circumstances, especially one that is recognizable.

The term *contributing factor* is sometimes used. It means the same thing as factor alone, because if a circumstance did not contribute to the cause it would not be a factor.

"Primary cause" is a meaningless expression if we hold the view that the result has only one cause, a combination of factors. If there is only one, there is no primary or secondary.

Exhibit 1. *Accidents often occurred at this sharp turn in a road, especially at night and in bad weather. The road situation is a factor in the accidents, but, by itself, would not cause accidents; otherwise all who pass that turn would have accidents. Driver and car factors are also necessary to cause accidents at this place.*

To use "primary factor" instead of "primary cause" is also meaningless when "primary" signifies "most important," because, if all factors are necessary, none is most important. In the example of night visibility described above, was Driver B's failure to perceive primarily a matter of low illumination or of low visual ability? Either more illumination or more visual ability would have permitted him to see the sign. Factors of a cause are like links of a chain; all are necessary, but none is more important than any other. One factor in a cause may be more conspicuous or more easily controlled than others, but it is not more necessary and so cannot be considered primary in any sense of that word.

Traffic Accident Causes

So far, causes have been considered in general as producing any kind of result, either desirable or undesirable. Rereading the foregoing explanation and substituting the word *accident* for the word *result* makes the discussion applicable to accidents, which are a special kind of result, and also, of course, applicable to traffic accidents which are a special kind of accident.

To illustrate how these ideas about cause and factors apply to a traffic accident situation, consider the right angle turn of a state route in a northern city (Exhibit 1). In one direction, the roadway was lower on the outside of the turn than on the inside (reverse) because of the crown on the roadway. The turn warning sign was accompanied by an advisory speed limit of 15 mph. During a year, more than 20 cars failed to negotiate this turn and ran into the guardrail or trees. What caused these accidents? The sharp turn was undoubtedly a factor, but if it were the cause, *every* vehicle traversing the curve would have had an accident. The reverse bank was a factor in some but not all the accidents because, after it was corrected, there were still accidents, but fewer of them. More accidents occurred during darkness and when the pavement was wet or snowy than at other times; hence, these conditions were also factors in some but not all accidents. Even under the least favorable combination of road conditions, most vehicles had no difficulty; consequently when an accident did occur, there must also have been some inadequacy of the vehicle-driver combination. Exactly what these vehicle-driver deficiencies were could not be determined, but it is more likely that they were driver rather than vehicle deficiencies because the driver has so much control over the sequence of events that he can compensate for unfavorable conditions. Each of these accidents doubtless had a different combination of factors as a cause, but probably some of these combinations differed only slightly.

Examining conditions and events that may have contributed to a traffic accident is not the only way to try to understand why a traffic accident occurred. There is another more systematic approach. Think of *successful* highway travel as a result. Then the cause of a successful trip is the combination of events and conditions that produce that result. An accident makes a trip unsuccessful, so seeking what factors were lacking to make the trip a success leads to an understanding of why the accident made the trip unsuccessful. The next section of this chapter will take that approach.

2. OPERATIONAL FACTORS

The Trip

Highway transportation produces trips which move people or goods from one place to another over a path constructed for that purpose. A traffic accident spoils a trip; then that product of highway transportation is defective.

To produce a trip without accident, the road-vehicle-driver system must successfully perform one set of operations after another from start to finish of the trip. The object of these operations is to keep the vehicle (or pedestrian) moving along the *available path* toward a destination.

Breakdown of operations. A useful way to think about traffic accidents and their causes is to consider accidents as malfunctions in the series of operations necessary to make a trip on a highway without damage or injury.

Operations which fail and lead to accidents are then operational factors in those accidents.

The available path is more than the part of the trafficway which a traffic unit is permitted by law to use. It is the entire area in which a vehicle or pedestrian may maneuver in an emergency. Ordinarily the available path includes both halves of a two-way undivided road, shoulders of the road if they will support a vehicle, and unoccupied parking lanes. The available path is *not* limited to the road space to which a traffic unit is legally entitled; it may be much more. However, any part of the road which is occupied by a traffic unit or other subject is not available for maneuver. Then, the path is restricted, and its alignment may be modified as shown in Exhibit 2.

Situation hazards are continually encountered along the traveler's path. There are a great variety of them to be avoided, for example

- The edges of the roadway, especially at curves
- Obstacles in the roadway, mainly stopped vehicles
- Moving vehicles (or pedestrians) on a collision course, usually at roadway intersections
- Occasional irregularities in the roadway surface.

Evasive Tactics

Whenever a driver or pedestrian is confronted by a situation hazard, something has to be done to try to avoid it. The action is an evasive tactic. All three elements of the highway transportation system (road, driver, and vehicle) are involved in one way or another in most evasive tactics. Every

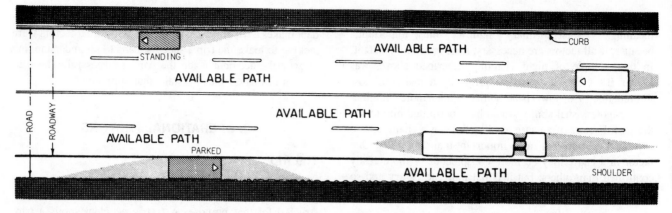

Exhibit 2. *The path available for evasive tactics is all of the road which is not occupied. It is much more than laws ordinarily permit a traffic unit to use.*

evasive tactic involves a sequence of three acts:

1. Perception of the situation hazard
2. Decision concerning how to avoid it
3. Performance of the evasive tactics decided on.

Each of these three acts will now be discussed more fully.

1. *Perception* is apprehending a situation, such as a hazard, by means of the senses and the mind. Therefore perception is a human factor in highway transportation; it is comprehending the risk of starting or continuing a movement. It is a person who perceives, but the road also participates in perception in a number of ways such as

- The degree to which roadway configuration is visible
- The artificial illumination provided, if any
- Information supplied by traffic control devices

The vehicle likewise participates in such ways as

- Providing visibility through window areas and mirrors
- Headlighting the roadway
- Enhancing the vehicle's visibility by external lighting
- Signalling the driver's intent to change velocity.

Delays in perception are common in evasive tactics. The driver or pedestrian fails to become aware of the situation hazard as soon as he might have because of lack of attention or diversions. Falling asleep results in an indefinite delay in perception. Perception delay can sometimes be offset by quick and violent maneuvers, but attempts to do so are often unsuccessful. If perception delay persists beyond the point of no escape, a collision ensues.

Misunderstanding a hazard may also result in faulty perception. For example, an object stopped in the roadway is mistaken for a moving one, or a sign is misread. Experienced drivers are less likely to fail to comprehend a hazard than inexperienced ones.

2. *Decision,* also a human factor, follows perception and is based on it. Faulty or delayed perception impairs decisions.

A driver's choices among evasive tactics are generally limited to six:

1. Decelerate (slow down or stop)
2. Accelerate (speed up)
3. Steer right
4. Steer left
5. Back up
6. Do nothing.

Reaction time is the time required to decide what to do and commence to do it. The length of reaction time depends on how clear perception is and what choices have to be made in deciding what to do (See Topic 864). Usually quickness of reaction is not so important as correctness; if the wrong thing is done it does not make much difference how quickly it is done. Reaction distance is the distance traveled during reaction time. It depends, of course, on speed.

3. *Performing the operation* decided on is partly a matter of skill, another human factor developed by practice. Performance is usually satisfactory if the decision is correct. Nevertheless, performance can fail in many ways, especially if the time available for it is short due to delay in perception or prolonged reaction. For example

- A decision to brake forcibly sometimes goes wrong so that the accelerator pedal rather than the brake is pushed downward.
- The driver overreacts to the discovery that his vehicle is about to leave the roadway or overreacts to some other contingency. He turns the steering wheel far more than is necessary to correct his course and precipitates a yaw. Tiremarks from overreaction are not difficult to find on expressways. (See Topic 817).
- The driver flinches when he experiences the unaccustomed sensations of rapid slowing. He releases the brake, sometimes producing a gap skid. (See Topic 817).
- In an emergency, a timid driver applies his brakes much too gradually, thereby requiring a much greater distance in which to stop than he might have.

52-6

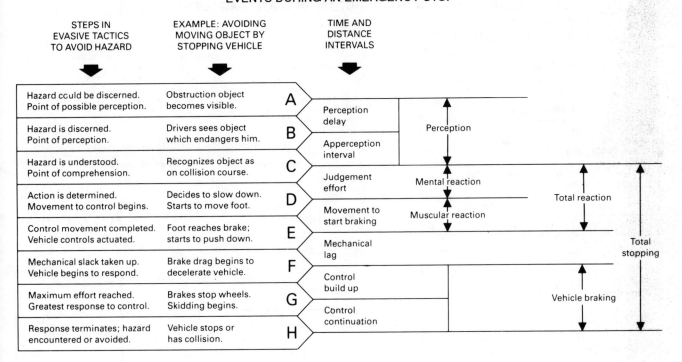

Exhibit 3.

EVENTS DURING AN EMERGENCY STOP

STEPS IN EVASIVE TACTICS TO AVOID HAZARD	EXAMPLE: AVOIDING MOVING OBJECT BY STOPPING VEHICLE		TIME AND DISTANCE INTERVALS
Hazard could be discerned. Point of possible perception.	Obstruction object becomes visible.	A	Perception delay
Hazard is discerned. Point of perception.	Drivers sees object which endangers him.	B	Apperception interval
Hazard is understood. Point of comprehension.	Recognizes object as on collision course.	C	Judgement effort
Action is determined. Movement to control begins.	Decides to slow down. Starts to move foot.	D	Movement to start braking
Control movement completed. Vehicle controls actuated.	Foot reaches brake; starts to push down.	E	Mechanical lag
Mechanical slack taken up. Vehicle begins to respond.	Brake drag begins to decelerate vehicle.	F	Control build up
Maximum effort reached. Greatest response to control.	Brakes stop wheels. Skidding begins.	G	Control continuation
Response terminates; hazard encountered or avoided.	Vehicle stops or has collision.	H	

(Time and distance intervals: Perception; Apperception interval — Perception; Mental reaction; Muscular reaction — Total reaction; Total stopping; Vehicle braking)

A driver is generally unaware of failure to execute the maneuver decided on. Often part of the operation is an unconscious reflex reaction. (See Topic 815). The result of the reaction is sudden, unexpected, and even terrifying. Afterwards, the driver remembers his decision, what he *intended* to do, but is quite unaware of his response, what he *actually did*.

Success and failure. In ordinary driving, some evasive tactic is necessary every few seconds. Nearly all of these are habitual, unhurried, and completely successful. They result in no accident; no harm is done, and the trip continues. Of the few evasive tactics that are critical, nearly all are also successful, resulting at most in near misses.

In the relatively few instances in which an evasive tactic is unsuccessful, an accident results; more or less harm is done, and the trip is interrupted if not terminated. Even when evasive tactics end in accidents, the tactics are usually not completely ineffective; they frequently serve to reduce severity of the crash. However, there are instances in which inept evasive tactics actually increase the severity of the accident, for example, when misjudgment and faulty performance increase the speed of a vehicle rather than decreasing it.

When two traffic units are on collision courses, each becomes a hazard to the other. Successful evasive tactics on the part of either avoids collision. Then the other, in spite of any faulty operations, is spared the accident. Hence, inept tactics do not necessarily involve a driver in an accident.

The most common evasive tactic is steering, mostly minute adjustments of the direction of the vehicle to keep in on the available path. The most common critical evasive tactic is emergency braking, which locks the wheels (unless the vehicle is equipped with anti-lock brakes). The series of operations involved in emergency braking is described in detail in Exhibit 3.

How evasive tactics fit into the whole process of motor-vehicle operation in the road-vehicle-driver system is summarized in the lower left part of Exhibit 4. This chart is worth careful study in connection with the present discussion of traffic accident causes and factors. As an outline, the chart is especially useful for review purposes.

Situation Hazard

Sometimes a situation hazard confronting a traffic unit on a trip is such that the best possible perception, decision and performance in evasive tactics cannot possibly be successful in avoiding a crash.

Two elements constitute a situation hazard: 1) conditions existing at the location, especially restricted sight distances, reduced visibility, and slippery pavements; and 2) speed and position of traffic units.

The first of these elements is not under the control of the traffic unit; one must expect and be able to cope with conditions on his trip as he finds them. However, the second element, speed and position, is at least partly under the driver's control because ordinarily he governs his own speed and position.

Exhibit 4.

OPERATIONAL AND CONDITION FACTORS IN TRAFFIC-ACCIDENT CAUSES

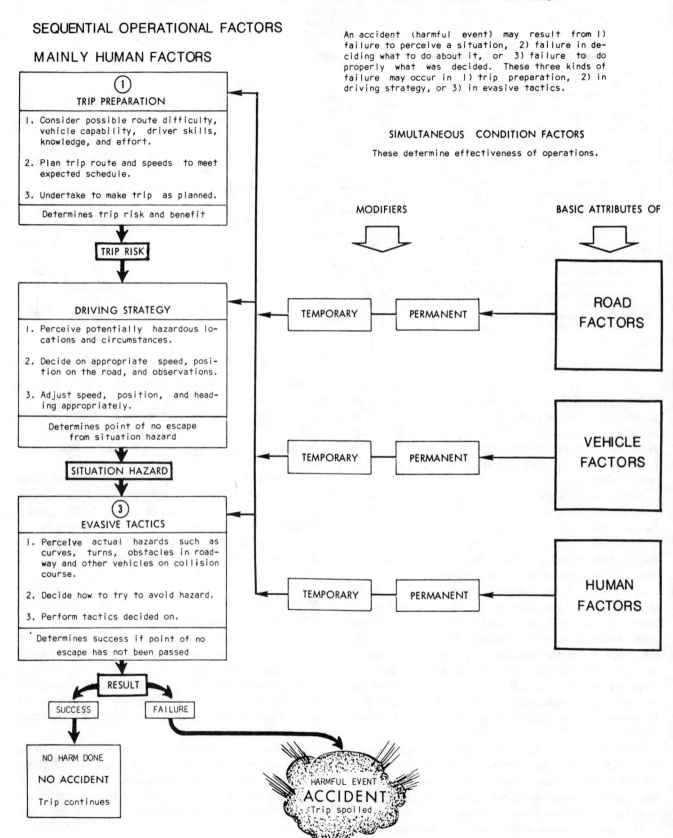

SEQUENTIAL OPERATIONAL FACTORS

MAINLY HUMAN FACTORS

①
TRIP PREPARATION

1. Consider possible route difficulty, vehicle capability, driver skills, knowledge, and effort.

2. Plan trip route and speeds to meet expected schedule.

3. Undertake to make trip as planned.

Determines trip risk and benefit

TRIP RISK

DRIVING STRATEGY

1. Perceive potentially hazardous locations and circumstances.

2. Decide on appropriate speed, position on the road, and observations.

3. Adjust speed, position, and heading appropriately.

Determines point of no escape from situation hazard

SITUATION HAZARD

③
EVASIVE TACTICS

1. Perceive actual hazards such as curves, turns, obstacles in roadway and other vehicles on collision course.

2. Decide how to try to avoid hazard.

3. Perform tactics decided on.

Determines success if point of no escape has not been passed

RESULT

SUCCESS   **FAILURE**

NO HARM DONE

NO ACCIDENT

Trip continues

An accident (harmful event) may result from 1) failure to perceive a situation, 2) failure in deciding what to do about it, or 3) failure to do properly what was decided. These three kinds of failure may occur in 1) trip preparation, 2) in driving strategy, or 3) in evasive tactics.

SIMULTANEOUS CONDITION FACTORS

These determine effectiveness of operations.

MODIFIERS   **BASIC ATTRIBUTES OF**

| TEMPORARY | PERMANENT | **ROAD FACTORS** |

| TEMPORARY | PERMANENT | **VEHICLE FACTORS** |

| TEMPORARY | PERMANENT | **HUMAN FACTORS** |

HARMFUL EVENT
ACCIDENT
Trip spoiled

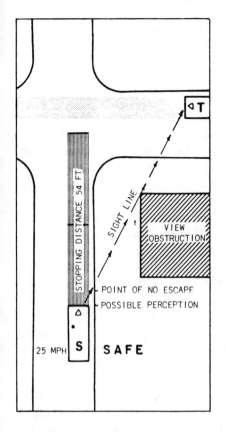

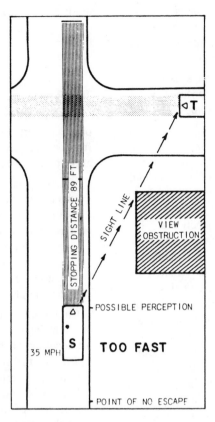

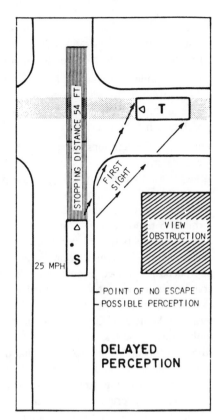

Exhibit 5. *A safe situation. Driver of Unit S, moving at 25 mph, sees Unit T on a cross street just as it appears from behind a building on the right. Unit S is 50 ft from the intersection and its speed will permit it to stop just short of Unit T's path. Unit S has not passed the point of no escape, so he puts on his brakes and stops. Speed is safe; perception is as prompt as possible; and evasive tactics are correct. The driver tried to, could, and did yield the right of way. He avoided a collision.*

Exhibit 6. *Speed unsafe. Driver of Unit S, moving at 35 mph, sees Unit T on a cross street just as it appears from behind a building on the right. The driver has passed his point of no escape. He tries to stop, but does not have space enough to do so and slides into the vehicle on the cross street. Perception was prompt; the evasive tactic was the best; but speed was too great to permit stopping in time. The driver of Unit S tried to yield the right of way but could not.*

Exhibit 7. *Perception delayed. Driver of Unit S, moving at 25 mph, does not see Unit T on the cross street when it appears from behind the building on the right. He first sees it when he is 25 ft from it and he is 25 ft beyond the point of no escape. He puts on brakes but cannot stop from the safe speed of 25 mph. Unit S crashes into Unit T. Delayed perception is at fault. Speed is safe; evasive tactic is correct. Driver of unit S tried to yield the right of way but could not.*

Strategy

It is by adjusting his speed and position that a driver or pedestrian is able to cope with situation hazards, especially to avoid collisions with other traffic units. This is a human factor called *driving strategy* which can be defined as any action, while a driver or pedestrian is on a trip, which increases the probability of successful evasive tactics by that unit.

Strategy involves recognition of a general situation in terms of the probability of a hazard appearing; it appraises the probability of two or more hazards appearing almost simultaneously with the consequent necessity of choosing an evasive tactic for one which may create or prolong another; and it considers the physical environment and capabilities of the traffic unit to cope with them. As a result of strategic decisions, therefore, a driver or pedestrian continually does things that puts him in a better position for evasive tactics. For want of appropriate appraisal, however, he may do

something which puts him in a less advantageous position. To favor himself, by a greater margin of safety or smaller total disposition to an accident, he reduces speed in a business district, for example, and keeps as far to the right as possible when approaching a hill crest.

Margin of Safety

Under the same conditions two drivers may not do the same thing to prepare themselves to meet a hazard. Risk perception will not be the same among drivers. For example, one may drive faster on the same street than the other. This may be because each evaluates the possibility of a hazard differently, but it is also because one driver is willing to take more chances. The same driver may be willing to take more risk at one time than another. If he is in a hurry, he may think the time saved worth the greater risk involved. Thus, different people have different margins of safety based on many considerations, and the same driver may give himself a greater margin of safety at one time than at another.

The set of three operations involved in driving strategy correspond closely to the three for evasive tactics:

1. Perception of a *potential* hazard of some kind
2. Decision as to what speed and road position will be most favorable if an actual hazard develops
3. Executing the decision.

This cycle of operations is repeated continually when driving. It determines a driver's margin of safety. The success of strategy usually determines the possibility of success in subsequent tactics. A simple example of a common situation will illustrate the relation between strategy and tactics. In Exhibits 5 to 10, Vehicle S approaches a junction at which its path intersects that of any vehicle on a cross street. The driver cannot see Vehicle T on the cross street which, as it approaches, is on a collision course. Driver of Vehicle T will continue at a constant speed without evasive tactics. These exhibits illustrate what happens with various driving patterns for Vehicle S. Obviously, if driver of Vehicle T also took evasive tactics, results would differ. If Vehicle T stopped short of Vehicle S's path, what the driver of Vehicle S did would make no difference.

The place driving strategy occupies in the process of motor-vehicle operation is also summarized in Exhibit 4.

All but a few of the laws relating to the operation of a motor vehicle are intended to require beneficial driving strategy, for example, requirements to

- Limit speed
- Driver on the right half of the roadway
- Stop before entering roadways at certain places
- Signal intent to stop or turn
- Follow at a proper distance
- Not overtake where view is obstructed.

Impending Impact Zone

Sometimes the area ahead of a vehicle which will be occupied by it in braking to a stop from the vehicle's speed is called the impending impact zone.[2] The driver cannot avoid a collision with any object in this zone. At low speeds, the zone extends only a little way ahead of the vehicle; at high speeds it may stretch much more than a hundred feet ahead.

In Exhibits 5, 6, 7, 9, and 10, this stopping distance area is shown by a shaded area ahead of Car S.

Describing Operational Factors

Consideration of operational factors related to a particular accident is on the border line between accident reconstruction and cause analysis. Describing the events of the accident, including mistakes in evasive tactics and strategy, is within the scope of reconstruction; but attempting to evaluate road, vehicle, and especially driver conditions which induced or permitted these events is definitely a matter of cause analysis.

Always remember that an error in reconstruction will inevitably start cause analysis off in the wrong direction.

Trip Risk

Circumstances related to the trip either facilitate or obstruct efforts to make strategy and tactics always successful. For example, a trip on a tight schedule requires continual effort to save time which has results such as these:

- Hasty operations which are more likely to be mistakes than ones that are unhurried
- With greater speed, the point of no escape is always farther from the situation; more time and space are required for evasive tactics
- Fast turns are more likely to result in sideslipping because centrifugal force approaches tire-road traction more closely.

Circumstances other than speed can modify the difficulty of maintaining a comfortable margin of safety, for example, the condition of the vehicle and the road and the amount of traffic on the road. The combined effect of such circumstances determines the *trip risk*.

Like the situation hazard, trip risk is more or less under the control of the driver or pedestrian. If the trip is altogether too dangerous, it may be abandoned or postponed. In any case, trip preparation modifies the level of trip risk. The driver prepares for the trip in three steps similar to those employed for driving strategy and evasive tactics:

1. Contemplates possible difficulties and compares difficulties of the road, vehicle, and driver; considers the purpose and urgency of the mission to decide whether it should be undertaken
2. Plans the route and schedule
3. Undertakes to make the trip as planned.

There may be difficulties in following a trip plan, such as getting lost, encountering delays due to traffic, and having trouble with the vehicle. Such difficulties may require changes in the trip plan, perhaps a tighter route and schedule which tends to reduce freedom in strategy, or perhaps adjusting the time for completion.

It is possible to imagine still earlier circumstances that influence trip planning, driving strategy, and evasive tactics, for example driver training. However, their effect is so diffuse that their consideration is not likely to be fruitful.

The outline that has just been completed of the operation of the road-vehicle-driver system in producing trips for travel and transportation is, of course, much simplified, perhaps even oversimplified. Nevertheless, it does provide a useful framework for considering where in a series of operations the failure occurred, a failure which becomes a factor in the cause of an accident. Thus, it helps to understand *how* an accident happened.

In the past, operational factors of traffic accidents have

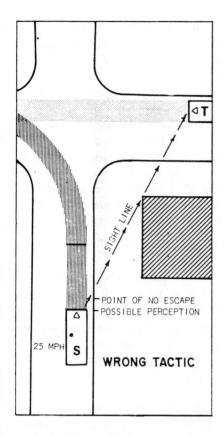

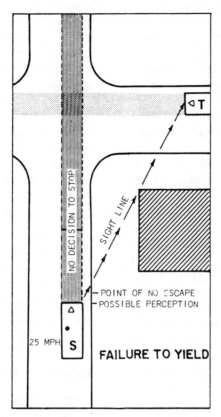

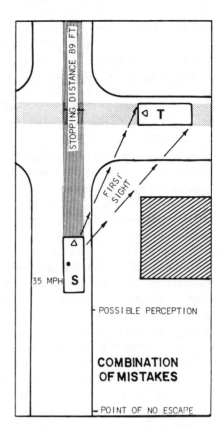

Exhibit 8. *Wrong evasive tactic. Driver of Unit S, moving at 25 mph, sees Unit T on a cross street just as it appears from behind a building on the right. He has not passed the point of no escape. However, instead of braking, he turns left as sharply as he can. The turn could not be sharp enough to prevent a collision with Unit T. A wrong choice of evasive tactic was at fault. The driver could have yielded the right of way but did not because he chose the wrong evasive tactic.*

Exhibit 9. *Faulty evasive tactic. Driver of Unit S, moving at 25 mph, sees unit T on a cross street just as it appears from behind a building on the right. He has not passed his point of no escape. He decided that if he kept on going that Unit T would employ evasive tactics to avoid collision. In other words, he decided not to yield the right of way. Driver of Unit T did nothing and there was a collision. Lack of evasive tactic was at fault; speed was safe; perception was prompt.*

Exhibit 10. *Combination of contributing operational factors. Driver of Unit S, moving at 35 mph, did not see Unit T on a cross street until Unit S was 25 ft from Unit T's path. Unit T had passed its point of no escape when the driver perceived the hazard. He tried to yield the right of way but could not. Evasive tactic was correct; speed was unsafe and perception was delayed. Under these circumstances, no evasive tactic could be successful.*

been called "direct causes," but this terminology no longer seems appropriate.

3. CONDITION FACTORS

Knowing *how* an accident happened does not explain *why*; but before you can explain why, you must understand how the accident occurred.

If traffic accidents are to be prevented, changes must be made in one or more of the elements that constitute the highway transportation system: the road, the vehicle, or human beings using the trafficway. Operational analysis, by reconstruction of traffic accidents, indicates *where* and *how* failure occurred but not *why*. To learn why operations fail, contributing *conditions* of road, driver, and vehicle must be sought. Regardless of whether one is thinking of a road, a driver, or a vehicle, qualities or characteristics which are necessary to avoid accidents must be considered.

Take, for example, the simple task of avoiding an object which has been detected in the vehicle's path. Among other things, the *driver* must have strength enough to apply brakes, the *vehicle* must have a brake system of suitable capacity for the driver's strength and the car's weight, and the *road* must have a surface with proper friction characteristics. These attributes and others, in various degrees, determine the performance or behavior of the traffic unit after a decision to stop has been reached.

Attributes

An attribute is any inherent characteristic of a road, a vehicle, or a person that affects the probability of a traffic accident. Attributes may be present in varying degrees. Thus, friction characteristics of the road surface are not always the same, but differ from place to place and time to time.

It is unnecessary to refer to a specific accident to describe an attribute. Attributes are not events like leaving the assigned path; they are not behavior like evasive tactics. Attributes are characteristics which explain behavior or events. For example, if we were considering attributes of a vehicle, without reference to an accident, we would observe and describe its size and shape, measure its power, evaluate its stopping ability, and note how readily it might be recognized on the road by other drivers. The vehicle would not have to be in an accident to permit description of these attributes. When a vehicle is bought, its attributes are appraised. If we inspect a highway, we consider its attributes, for example, its width, slope, curvature, surface slipperiness, markings, control devices, information signs, and many other inherent characteristics. A partial list of such attributes of roads, of people, and of vehicles is given in Exhibit 11. Do not think of these lists or other lists of this kind as complete and authoritative. They are useful now for classifying condition factors relating to traffic accidents, but experience with the study of accidents has not yet reached the point where anyone can say that this or any other list represents *all* of the possible attributes, or that the words used in the lists to name attributes are sufficient to describe them.

Each of these attributes may affect the probability of an accident, and each has several aspects. Consider, for example, the vehicle attribute, recognizability. What characteristics make a vehicle easy or difficult to perceive and so affect the probability of its prompt recognition as a hazard? Size is one; a large object is more easily seen than a small one. Another, of course, is shape; a familiar shape can be more quickly identified than an unfamiliar one. Color also contributes to recognizability, and so, at night, do lights on the vehicle. Still more aspects of recognizability which could be subdivisions of this general attribute can be imagined.

Relation of attributes to operations. Attributes representing conditions of vehicles, roads, and drivers. All may explain, to some degree, *why* certain operations failed. We may note that some attributes apply to one phase of the cycle of operations while other attributes are related to other phases, that is, some attributes affect perception, some decision, and some performance. Take a specific example, the amount of light, which is one characteristic of the road situation. Light would have little if anything to do with how quickly and surely a driver stopped after he had decided that reducing speed was the best evasive tactic; light would not contribute much to the quality of the decision to slow; but light is immensely important to seeing and hence to perceiving a hazard. Therefore, light, as a road attribute, generally relates to recognition as indicated in Exhibit 11. Road illumination, as a function of headlamps, contributes to recognition at all levels of actual hazards at the tactical level of operation; it contributes to recognition of potential hazard at the strategy level, and it may even be a factor at the preparation level.

An attribute may be a condition factor in an accident,

if tactics, strategy, or planning involve that particular attribute of road, vehicle, or driver. This relationship is suggested in Exhibit 4.

Evaluating attributes. In evaluating the contribution of an attribute to a specific accident, try to determine its level or quality at the time of the accident. This may be difficult because by the time the driver, road, or car is examined, the condition may have changed in important respects. It may also be difficult to establish the logical relationship of an attribute as it was at the time of the accident and the failure of an operation. For example, at the time and place of an accident there was not much light. Thus at least three questions arise:

1. How much more light would have enabled the driver to perceive?
2. Could the driver have perceived with existing light if he had better vision, and how much better vision would be required?
3. Would the driver have failed to perceive even with good light and good vision, and if so, why?

Modifiers of Attributes

Variability of attributes. Were we to measure or observe attributes — let us say those of a driver — at different times, we would find that most of them change more or less from one time to another. Some changes occur in a short time, for example, those occurring with consumption of alcoholic beverages. Others might be quite gradual like the increase and later decline of strength with age. After some of the changes, the person, vehicle, or road returns to its previous condition; but after other changes, it does not.

If attributes of the road, people using the road, and the vehicles with which they travel change from time to time, we must seek circumstances which produce these changes because they would also be factors contributing to traffic accidents. These circumstances which change attributes are *modifiers* of the attributes.

Temporary and permanent modifiers. The point has been made that some modifiers act quickly and some slowly. The effect of some is permanent and of others temporary. Ice on a road, for example, melts soon; but a chuck hole in the pavement remains until repaired. The distinction is perhaps one which may be detected by asking whether the attribute could be expected to return to normal of its own accord. This difference seems to be worth noting. We can appropriately call these contrasting classes of modifiers *temporary* and *permanent*.

Relationship of modifiers to attributes. The distinction between attributes and modifiers is not a sharp one. For example, smoothness or evenness of a road is an attribute. An object on the road or holes in it modify its smoothness.

Exhibit 11.

SUMMARY OF CONDITION FACTORS CONTRIBUTING
TO TRAFFIC ACCIDENT CAUSES

ATTRIBUTES	**MODIFIERS**

HUMAN FACTORS

Relating to Recognition	Observing habits Sensory abilities Signaling habits Recognizability (mainly pedestrian) Knowledge	Temporary	Sun exposure Glasses, etc. Emotional upset Pressure, stress, hurry Preoccupation Weather Irritants Ingestion, inhalation Fatigue, boredom Temporary illness Injury Clothing Things carried Prosthetic devices
Relating to Decision	Intelligence, judgment Attitudes Emotional stability Alertness, Concentration		
Relating to Performance	Operating skill, habits Size, weight, strength Freedom of movement	Permanent	Deterioration, age Chronic illness Permanent injury Experience, training Customs, tradition Authority, enforcement

ROAD FACTORS

Relating to Recognition	Light, illumination Visibility View obstructions Recognizability Recognizability aids Distractions, monotony Confusion, Standardization Warning signs Guide signs	Temporary	Weather, atmospheric conditions Natural light Temporary devices Temporary roadside activities Roadside objects Objects on the road Loss of alignment Social and legal symbols Surface deposits, ruts Road damage, holes
Relating to Decision	Signals Traffic signal controls Regulatory signs and markings		
Relating to Performance	Alignment Surface character Dimensions Restraining devices	Permanent	Wear Deterioration, age

VEHICLE FACTORS

Relating to Recognition	Recognizability Recognizability aids Headlights Sensory aids View obstructions Distractions Instruments Signalling devices Control feedback	Temporary	Glare Weather Surface deposits Cargo Passengers Social and legal symbols Adjustment loss Damage, contamination
Relating to Decision	Comfort Symbolism Automatic controls	Permanent	Deterioration, age Irreparable damage Wear
Relating to performance	Control arrangement, function Operating space Dimensions Weight Performance Stability		

In general, modifiers are those circumstances, which change the road, car, or driver, from an originally normal or expected condition and make it more or less hazardous at least for the time being. Modifiers must directly affect the object modified. Thus, we might say that enforcement of laws relating to brake performance would produce better brakes; but we would not be accurate. Enforcement will not directly change the vehicle at all. It changes owners and drivers, perhaps, but not the road or the vehicle.

The general relationship of modifiers to attributes is shown schematically in Exhibit 4. A listing of attributes of roads, people, and vehicles is given in Exhibit 11. Any factor contributing to an accident may be fitted into these classifications either as an operational factor or as a condition factor with or without modification. More than 800 operational and condition factors have been suggested as contributing to traffic accidents.[3] There are possibly many which have not been identified and described. At one time, condition factors, especially modifiers, were called "mediate causes" of accidents, but this no longer seems appropriate.

Remote Condition Factors

All who have considered the subject seriously have recognized that, in the long run, prevention of automobile accidents may involve changing the cultural "climate" in which the attributes and their modifiers develop. Economic, social, legal, and even moral and religious influences affect the beliefs, desires, symbolisms, and values, not only of automobile drivers and pedestrians but also of the automobile manufacturers, the highway designers, and the many kinds of public officials concerned with the control of traffic accidents.

Remote condition factors were at one time called "early causes." Such a remote factor is an act or negligence on the part of some person or organization that contributes in a general way to conditions unfavorable to safety in highway transportation. These remote factors explain condition factors directly associated with accidents. Because of their intricate and tenuous connection with accidents, these remote factors will not be described here in detail.

Summary

In a traffic accident the sequential factors contributing to cause are malfunctions in one or more of three operations (perception, decision, and performance) in one or more of three operational phases (trip preparation, driving strategy, and evasive tactics) performed by the road-vehicle-driver system in producing trips for highway travel and transportation. The simultaneous factors are conditions in the form of attributes of the road, vehicle, and driver modified permanently or temporarily which determine, at various operational phases, the success or failure of the functions performed.

4. PREDISPOSING CIRCUMSTANCES

Everybody realizes that there are circumstances which increase the risk of accidents, injury, illness and death. An example of this is the limited seeing ability of Driver B in the example described earlier in this topic. His disability increases the risk of having an accident. In the last 20 years, smoking has come to be recognized as predisposing to illness and shortening life but it is not by itself something that will cause death or immediately produce illness.

Alcohol in body fluids definitely increases the risk of traffic and other accidents. Small amounts, for example 0.03 percent, seem to have no perceptible detrimental effect. Large amounts, such as 0.50 percent, are likely to be fatal. Between these extremes, combination with other unfavorable circumstances will determine whether alcohol in the blood may result in trouble.

The insidious aspect of these predisposing circumstances is that an individual may be exposed to them repeatedly for years without difficulty. That convinces him that they are not dangerous. Indeed, many are harmless when experienced singly or in low degrees. It is when several predisposing circumstances occur at the same time, especially if one or more are severe, that real trouble results. This situation is illustrated by the tricky road curve cited earlier.

Thus a predisposition is not usually a factor in a traffic accident until it combines with one or more other predispositions.

Many predispositions can be controlled or overcome by the driver. Their management is part of accident prevention strategy. Some, like weather, cannot be controlled but may be avoided in trip planning.

Speed

A vehicle's velocity is the most common predisposing accident factor. It is always present in some degree. Without motion there would be very few traffic accidents. Therefore speed may be considered a factor in almost every traffic accident.

As a predisposing accident factor speed is easily and almost continuously controlled by the driver: adjusting speed is a usual driving strategy — it is the object of legal speed limits; slowing is the most common evasive tactic.

Too much speed makes it *impossible to follow the desired curve*. Each curve or turn has a radius or degree of sharpness, a superelevation or amount of banking on the outside of the curve, and a drag factor or slipperiness of the road surface. In combination, these determine how fast a vehicle can travel around the curve without sliding off the roadway. Some vehicles, especially trucks, have a high center of mass compared to their track width on the road and so may roll over on a curve rather than slide off if the speed is too high.

Too much speed also makes it *impossible to take successful evasive tactics* even if a hazard is perceived as soon as possible. When a vehicle appears on a cross street from behind a blind corner (Exhibits 5 to 10) or a pedestrian runs from behind a parked car, the driver may see the hazard instantly, but he cannot stop or swerve instantly. The faster he is going the longer it takes him to stop or the less sharply he can turn. In a place where hazards may appear suddenly, therefore, speeds must be slow if accidents are to be avoided. At night the distance at which a hazard can be seen is definitely limited by the light given by headlamps, and so safe speed is limited by such light.

Unusual speeds surprise other road users. High speeds, low speeds, or sudden changes of speed can all, under certain circumstances, present such unexpected problems to other drivers or pedestrians in that they do not have time to solve them successfully by evasive tactics. A driver does not expect a vehicle to come from behind a view obstruction at a very high speed or a pedestrian to run as fast as he can from between parked cars. However, on a road on which nearly everybody travels fast and where there is no apparent reason for slowing or stopping, a slow moving vehicle presents an unexpected problem, especially at night or beyond a hill crest or obscured corner. Sudden slowing, especially where there is no apparent reason for it, may also present an element of surprise.

In other words, speed can put the driver beyond the point of no escape at his point of perception. This is a simple statement of an operational situation and does not suggest reasons for it. Such reasons would be factors in a resulting accident.

Safe speed is quite different from speed limits established by law. At any time or place safe speed may be more or less than the legal speed limit. A *safe speed* is one adjusted to the *potential* or possible hazards of the road and traffic situation *ahead*. It is such that if the potential hazard develops into an actual one, and is perceived promptly, the traffic unit can avoid the accident by practical evasive tactics.

Safe travel speed is usually determined by such things as the curves in the road, the frequency of access to the road, the use being made of the roadside by people, and the amount and kind of traffic. Safe speed is especially affected by visibility which is reduced by darkness, fog, or smoke and by slipperiness. Even for normal conditions, a safe speed will vary considerably along a road.

Where there are cross roads or side roads with view obstructions, approach speed must be reduced for potential hazards. *Safe approach speed* is the safe speed in preparation for entering or crossing a road or intersection. Sometimes the safe approach speed is zero. That means that vehicles or pedestrians must stop for safety before entering or crossing. Travel speed can sometimes be so high that a driver or pedestrian cannot reduce his speed soon enough for a safe approach after recognizing the curve, cross road, or side road ahead. The travel speed is then, of course, unsafe.

Average speeds. Most drivers travel most of the time at safe speeds. Otherwise there would be far more accidents than there are. Hence, the speeds below which most people drive may be considered maximum safe speeds under most ordinary circumstances. Traffic engineers, in establishing speed zones, often consider 15 percent of the drivers as going too fast for safety and, therefore, use the 85 percentile speed as a guide for setting speed limits. The *85 percentile speed* is the speed at or below which 85 percent of vehicles travel. Sometimes this is a fair guide to safe speed, but by no means always. A little snow and ice making the road slippery can create a condition under which many drivers — sometimes even most of them — drive too fast and get into trouble.

The chain reaction accidents in fog on heavily traveled roadways are examples of conditions in which a whole group of drivers are caught in a great multiple accident because all but a few have not reduced speed sufficiently for the low visibility and more than half of them are driving too fast for conditions. Therefore, the speeds at which most people drive can be used as only a rough guide to safe speed, especially under unusual conditions.

Evaluation

In traffic accident reconstruction, the extent to which predispositions are a factor is usually not a major issue. Reconstruction aims only at describing the *events* of the accident, not the contributing factors.

But evaluating predisposing circumstances is always a part of cause analysis, often the most important part, and usually the most troublesome. In cause analysis, one must try to explain, for example, how the blood alcohol level contributed. Would the same accident have occurred had there been no alcohol in the body or less alcohol, and if less, how much less? And what other circumstances combined with the influence of alcohol resulted in the "breakdown" of the highway transportation system, in an event known as a traffic accident? What effect did alcohol have on a driver's judgment in controlling other predisposing circumstances such as speed?

Available techniques of traffic accident investigation are not yet adequate to evaluate the contribution of most predispositions to *individual* accidents. Attempts at such refinements usually result in speculation, imaginative of course and interesting, but scarcely dependable enough to be of much real use.

Statistics

It is possible to evaluate the effect of some predisposing circumstances on traffic accidents in general. Special studies of large samples of traffic accidents have often been used for this purpose. For example, a number of studies have been made to determine the risk increase at various levels of alcohol in the blood (Exhibit 12).[4] Efforts to evaluate the effect of speed, however, have been much less successful.

Such statistical studies are very helpful in guiding highway safety programs. If any predisposing circumstances can be mitigated, the results will be beneficial.

5. CONVENTIONAL CONCEPTS

Some ideas about causes of traffic accidents have been borrowed by one "authority" from another so often and for so long that they have come to be unquestioned. These ideas have merit, but, as stereotypes, they fail to accommodate rigorous examination of accidents for the sets of factors that constitute causes.

Carelessness, Negligence, and Recklessness

General ideas such as "carelessness" and "recklessness," are ancient explanations of accidents. As "causes" of motor-vehicle accidents they focus on the driver's failure to cope with some situation.

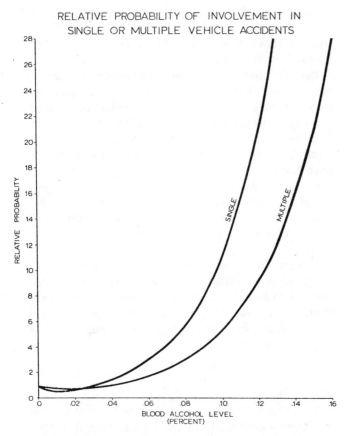

RELATIVE PROBABILITY OF INVOLVEMENT IN SINGLE OR MULTIPLE VEHICLE ACCIDENTS

Exhibit 12. *Statistical studies can evaluate the relative risk of various degrees of a predisposing circumstance, in this case alcohol in the blood. But such studies are rarely helpful in evaluating the contribution of this factor to a particular accident.*

Carelessness essentially connotes a breakdown of strategy or preparation and refers more often to decision than to recognition or performance. It suggests that observations of the general situation, which should have been made, were not or that performance was not as skillful as the driver could have made it. It implies that decisions were not reached or if reached, were delayed in execution.

In trip preparation, carelessness usually refers to not doing what apparently needed to be done to ready the vehicle for the trip, especially with respect to its safety equipment. But carelessness can also be an attribute of the individual. As such it is indefinite. Sometimes it is applied to lack of skill, but mainly it refers to an attitude that certain strategic operations are unimportant or to a general lack of alertness or vitality by which the traffic problem to be solved fails to get the attention it deserves.

Negligence is a more formal and legal way of expressing almost the same idea as carelessness. In legal practice, negligence has become closely associated with law violation because law violations are generally *prima facie* negligence, while other forms of negligence, such as inattention, are very difficult and often impossible to prove. Within the general classification of causes, negligence can be treated the same as carelessness without being far wrong.

Recklessness is quite a different thing. It assumes that a driver, or perhaps a pedestrian, has perceived the situation and has decided on strategic action which gives only a minimum margin of safety. He places a low value on the possible consequences of underestimating the risk. Hence, as an operational factor, recklessness is in the decision phase of the strategic cycle. Recklessness can also be an attribute of an individual. As such, it may be under one or more of several attribute headings. It may be an aspect of attitude, judgment, or emotional instability. It may be some of two or all three of these. Legally, it involves the concept of willful or wanton disregard for the safety of persons or property, and consequently does not involve lack of perception or performance.

Law Violations as "Causes" of Accidents

Many of us have been accustomed to thinking of law violations as causes of accidents. Indeed traffic laws are written to prescribe exactly how people shall behave in using and sharing the highways so as to avoid accidents. There are officially listed about 60 rules governing the behavior of drivers and an additional 15 for pedestrians.[5] Most unconventional behavior of the vehicle is also a law violation by the driver, but some unconventional behavior is not specifically against the law. Skidding is an example. A few traffic laws relevant to accident prevention relate to the condition of the vehicle (brake performance, etc.), and one or two to the condition of the driver (driving while intoxicated); but the greater number of them relate essentially to strategic action (speed, stop signs, position on the road, signalling intent, etc.) that puts the driver in a favorable situation to take evasive action if a hazard develops.

Law violations tend to be the legal and police concept of causes of traffic accidents. If you seek contributing factors in a police traffic-accident report you will find it mainly in terms of law violations.

Violation of law in connection with an accident does not necessarily mean that the behavior or condition represented by the violation was a factor in the particular accident. For example, a vehicle may well be in an unlawful condition that has no bearing on the accident. It may lack proper registration or it may be without headlamps which, by daylight, although illegal, would make no difference. Driver intoxication is often a factor contributing to an accident, but a driver may be guilty of driving while intoxicated without that circumstance being a factor in his accident. For example, an intoxicated driver waiting at a traffic light is run into by the following car. He would have had the same accident had he been quite sober. Even unlawful behavior at the time of an accident may not contribute to the accident. For example, a car leaves and enters the left half of the roadway in making a left turn at an intersection. This is unlawful. But the car is going so fast that an accident occurs because it cannot even make the turn with the larger radius provided by "cutting" the corner. It strikes a curb on the right side of the street it enters. The law violation tends to increase the radius of the curve and so lessen the tendency to strike the curb. It helps the situation rather than makes it worse, unless some other road user is involved by being crowded.

Speed too fast for conditions is a way of indicating that driving strategy is faulty. It may make successful evasive tactics impossible. Speed has been discussed separately.

Failure to yield right-of-way, willfully, cannot properly be considered more than a very rare factor in an accident. The designation "failure to yield right-of-way" usually only indicates that one arbitrarily designated traffic unit of two on a collision course failed to perform a successful evasive tactic. Such a generalized designation obscures operational factors, such as too much speed, failure to communicate, delayed perception, or failure of performance due to road or vehicle conditions. Failure to yield right-of-way is, therefore, nearly impossible to fit satisfactorily into any operational scheme of traffic accidents. It can only be classified as some kind of failure in an evasive tactic.

Does vehicle behavior violate law? A vehicle, not being a person, cannot violate a law. Its behavior may be unsafe, but any violation of the law that this represents is imputed to the driver. The law says always that no person shall drive his vehicle in the prohibited manner or that all drivers shall drive their vehicles in the prescribed maner. It would be possible to have vehicle behavior cause an accident against the will of the operator. For example, a car runs a red light. If the driver took a chance on running the red light there would be a law violation on his part. Also, if he failed to see the red light, he would violate the law requiring him to stop for it. The behavior of the vehicle would be the same in either case but the explanations of this behavior might be quite different. The condition of the driver in the first instance would probably be one of attitude and the second a lack of attention. Now, suppose that the brakes fail when they are applied and the driver does his best to stop the car. *He* has not violated the law by driving through the red light; *he* has not failed to stop although the vehicle has. The trouble is with the *vehicle*. It might be that the driver's law violation was one of driving a vehicle which would not perform as specified by law. In practice, enforcement agencies make no such fine distinction between behavior of the driver and of the vehicle. In accident investigation, the distinction is important.

Delayed perception is not a specific law violation in most places. It is embodied in the general provisions of many laws which prohibit *careless* or *reckless* driving or *driving so as to endanger.* Such general rules are intended to cover behavior which is not otherwise specifically prohibited. In civil litigation, delayed perception is embraced by the general idea of negligence or failure to take the last clear chance to prevent an accident. Delayed perception and faulty evasive action are not behavior that is sufficiently observable to permit effective enforcement action even if they were specifically against the law. They are much different — with respect to detecting them for enforcement purposes — from driving on the wrong side of the road or running a red light.

Proximate Cause

The word *proximate* means close or near. Used with *cause,* it implies that there are other causes; that the event, for example a traffic accident, has other causes than the "proximate" one, perhaps a simultaneous contributing factor of some kind. The idea of multiple causes is contrary to the concept that an event has a single cause which is a combination of contributing factors required to produce the resultant event.

Proximate cause is a legal rather than a scientific concept. It corresponds roughly to what we have been calling a contributing factor.

Proximate, meaning near, seems to signify necessary and understandable. Hence, for our purposes, you might reword *proximate cause* as *demonstrable contributing factor.*

Law books devote many pages to discussing the fine points of what is meant by proximate cause. To. . ."be held criminally responsible for injury or homicide arising from his neglegent operation of a vehicle or in violation of law, it is uniformally held that it must be shown that such. . . was the *proximate cause* of such death or injury. This means that there must have been a *causal connection* between the act and the resulting harm."

"'*Proximate cause*' is a phrase frequently encountered...Its meaning is somewhat elastic and there is no simple or mechanically precise method by which the difference between *proximate* and *remote* causes can be made clear..."

"...For centuries, the phrase proximate cause, has been understood as indicating a cause of which the law will take notice. It means substantially the same as 'efficient cause' or 'legal cause'. 'Legal cause' is perhaps a more accurate phrase..."

"One usually reliable test in such matters is whether the act or omission assigned as the cause constituted a *substantial factor* in bringing about the particular harm. This is on the theory that law does not concern itself with trifles."[7]

6. CAUSE ANALYSIS

What is Cause Analysis?

Cause analysis has been identified as Level 5 of traffic-accident investigation, the final level. Cause analysis has been defined as the effort to determine, from whatever information is available, *why* an accident occurred, that is, the complete combination of factors that caused the highway transportation system to malfunction at the time and place of the accident with resultant injury and damage. If the complete cause of the accident could be reproduced, including the chance arrangement of moving traffic units, another identical accident would result.

By cause analysis, one seeks to find out *why* an accident happened as contrasted to reconstruction which aims to find out *how* it happened. By cause analysis, one seeks explanations of why preparations, strategy, and, finally, tactics were not successful in avoiding particular hazards of a particular trip.

Cause analysis is certainly more than naming some driver condition, such as intoxication, or a road condition, such as slipperiness, which was present or may εven have contributed to the accident. It is more than discovering law violations in connection with accidents. Although such circumstances may, indeed, contribute to accidents, they rarely, perhaps never, by themselves produce an accident. A slippery pavement, for example, may be negotiated successfully by a thousand drivers before one arrives whose condition prevents him from coping with the slippery surface. To analyze that accident, we must know not only that the paving was slippery but also what the condition of that particular driver or his vehicle was that differed from other traffic units which were not involved in an accident at that spot. An intoxicated driver in an accident may have driven successfully many times before with the same degree of intoxication. To analyze his accident for causes, we must,

therefore, know what other circumstances were also present when he had an accident that had not been present when he drove under the influence before without an accident.

Methods of Analysis

Even if all the facts can be determined, discovering the combination of factors after an accident is always difficult and often impossible. The severe damage done by collision often obscures slight vehicle defects which made the difference between an accident and no accident. The experience of the accident itself immediately modifies subtle attitudes of the driver which may have made the little difference in the factor of safety he allowed himself at the moment.

Trying to find these contributing conditions involves a number of general steps. The first, of course, is accident reconstruction to determine what behavior (operational factors) was involved. The second general step is to study carefully the road situation, the driver or pedestrian, and the vehicle to try to find out what qualities or attributes of each are required completely to explain the accident behavior.

If a mistake is made in reconstruction to determine what operation failed, conclusions about what conditions explain the behavior are almost sure to be wrong. For example, let us consider a common situation. Two traffic units approach a road intersection on a collision course. Our immediate concern is with one of these. The fact is that it was going so fast that, when the driver was able to perceive that the other unit was on a collision course, he was already beyond his point of no escape. Now, suppose that we mistakenly conclude that our traffic unit had decided to bluff the other into taking any evasive action required. This means that we believe that it was failure to yield the right-of-way and not speed that prevented our driver from stopping before reaching the path of the other vehicle. Then, if we seek driver attributes to explain his failure to yield right-of-way, whatever we conclude is almost sure to be wrong because we should be seeking driver attributes to explain speed. We imagine reasons why the driver decided not to take evasive action when, in fact, he made no such decision. Instead, we should be wondering what there was about the driver that made him go so fast, because speed, not failure to yield right-of-way, is the behavior which we should be trying to explain.

But even if reconstruction is correct, study of the road, driver or pedestrian, and vehicle is not without its pitfalls. It brings up questions which we may not have the facts or the wisdom to answer properly. Study of the road is easiest. Its attributes are not much changed by the accident; it is static. Even so, it is not easy to evaluate road factors, for example, the effect on a specific accident of an unbanked road at a sharp turn. How much bank on the turn would have prevented this particular accident?

The vehicle is more difficult to study and the driver most difficult of all. At least, the vehicle can be dismantled for study. But unless the driver is dead, this cannot be done; and even if the coroner does a postmortem examination, what he can discover is limited to physiological conditions. To measure psychological condition of a living driver may take many hours of testing and examining by highly trained people. But even when the trained people and the necessary time are available, we do not have sufficiently sensitive tests for driver attitude and skill, for example.

The costs of complete cause analysis for most accidents would exceed the cost of repairs to the vehicle and the medical expenses resulting from the injuries.

Assuming that reconstruction is possible and has been correctly done, there are then two general approaches to cause analysis. Both should be used. If conclusions reached by the two approaches are similar, confidence in the conclusions is enhanced. On the other hand, if the two approaches give different results, there is much less confidence in the opinions formed as a result of analysis.

The first approach is to examine the road situation, the driver or pedestrian, and the vehicle to list every condition or deficiency that might conceivably contribute to any accident. Then decide what part of the operational cycle of trip preparation, driving strategy, and evasive tactics might be affected by each of these conditions in such a way as to produce the behavior as determined by reconstruction of the accident.

The second approach is to start with the points at which reconstruction indicates failure in some phase of the operational cycle. Then try to determine what conditions of the elements of the road-driver-vehicle system might have produced the failure. Finally, in this approach, examine the road, person, and vehicle to determine whether the suspected conditions did, indeed, exist at the time of the accident.

Certainty of Conclusions

Opinions, in the form of conclusions, are the result of the analysis of causes. Because facts are often missing, there may be important gaps in the information available about an accident. Therefore, we may not be entirely sure of our conclusions. Some conditions in some accidents can be determined to be contributing factors beyond any doubt. Other conditions can be ruled out as possible contributing factors from certain accidents. For example, intoxication or a slippery surface might be considered in connection with many accidents, but upon investigation be ruled out as factors in most of them. In many investigations, so many facts are wanting that truly satisfactory analyses are impossible. Then, pressing for conclusions inevitably leads to speculation. Speculation about possible condition factors is useful so long as we do not deceive ourselves about accuracy or completeness of our conjectures.

Because cause analysis expresses conclusions, the investigator should indicate the degree of certainty of these conclusions. It is not practical to attempt to do this with numerical probabilities, as one does in statistics. The following descriptive degrees of certainty are useful for this purpose:

1. *Certain* (The conclusion may be "proved" by clear reasoning from established fact.)
2. *Probable* (The conclusion explains the circumstances better than any other that comes to mind. All available facts point to it but are not sufficient to "prove" the conclusion. Additional facts or futher insight might prove the conclusion false.)
3. *Possible* (The conclusion is a plausible explanation, but one of several which is suggested by the facts.)

Forms and Procedures

The demand for evaluating contributing factors for a particular accident has been insistent. In some cases, this leads to requiring a report of "causes" on an official traffic-accident report form. The result of such crude attempts to discover "causes" was usually misinformation. In reporting accident causes police and drivers are prepared for little more than guesswork usually colored by personal bias.

For example, for a long time, statistics compiled from such reports suggested that perhaps ten percent of drivers involved in fatal accidents were under the influence of alcohol. It was not until blood of drivers killed in such accidents was tested for alcohol that it appeared that the true figure was close to five times as great.

In reporting causal factors, there is a strong tendency to attribute accidents to vehicle malfunction. Statistics from some official traffic-accident reports indicated that ten to fifteen percent of single vehicle accidents involved blowouts or other tire disablements. More careful data collection on high-speed roads developed the information that only about 2.5 percent of accidents followed tire disablements.

Because of such misleading experience with cause reporting, two steps were recommended by those most concerned:

1. Omit opinion data from official traffic-accident report forms. That would remove a large element of speculation in the data collected.
2. Provide a separate supplementary form for "cause analysis," a form that would require more careful reasoning.

Considerable progress has been made in eliminating cause and other guesswork from official reports. But the separate supplementary cause form was not successful.

At the request of a traffic records committee, a form was designed. It had one page for "direct cause" analysis and a second for "mediate cause analysis." When pub-

published[6] with directions for its use, this form excited interest and even some admiration. But when it was tested experimentally in three police departments, the form proved to be woefully unreliable. Using the form, the same accident was often attributed by separate investigators to quite different combinations of contributing factors. Publication of the form was discontinued and its use discouraged.

Example of Cause Analysis

Attempts to describe and evaluate the numerous factors causing a traffic accident often require a score or more of pages. Explaining accident reconstruction, on which cause analysis is based, may take many pages more. It is not feasible, therefore, in a manual of the scope of this one, to give detailed examples of accident reconstruction and cause analysis. Accidents differ so much that it would take scores of examples to serve as patterns for reconstruction and cause analysis of even the more common varieties of traffic accidents.

7. SOURCES

Author

J. Stannard Baker is a traffic engineer specializing in traffic accident investigation. He was Director of Research and Development at the Northwestern University Traffic Institute from 1947 to 1971. Thereafter he became a consultant and guest lecturer at the Traffic Institute.

References

Superscript numbers in the preceding pages refer to the following publications:

1. Baker, J. Stannard and H. Laurence Ross, *Concepts and Classification of Traffic Accident Causes* (SN 1109), 1960, Traffic Institute, Northwestern University, Evanston, IL 60204 (119 pages)
2. Barzelay, Martin E., and George W. Lacy, "Auto-Pedestrian Accidents" (Chapter 14) in *Scientific Automobile Accident Reconstruction,* 1983, Matthew Bender, New York NY (Chapter 14, 119 pages)
3. Baker, J. Stannard and Leroy R. Horn, *An Inventory of Factors Suggested as Contributing to Traffic Accidents* (SN 1111), 1961, Traffic Institute, Northwestern University, Evanston, IL 60204 (56 pages)
4. Borkenstein, Robert F. and four others, *The Role of the Drinking Driver in Traffic Accidents,* 1964, Department of Police Administration, Indiana University, Bloomington IN
5. *Uniform Vehicle Code and Model Traffic Ordinance,* National Committee on Uniform Traffic laws and Ordinances, Washington DC (Order from P.O. Box 1409, Evanston IL, 60204)
6. Baker, J. Stannard, *Traffic Accident Investigator's Manual for Police,* 1957, The Traffic Institute of Northwestern University, Evanston IL (617 pages) 7. Fisher, Edward C. and Robert H. Reeder, *Vehicle Traffic Law,* 1974, Northwestern University Traffic Institute, Evanston IL 60204 (339 pages)

Exhibits

The following are the sources of the exhibits used in this topic:

Baker, J. Stannard, San Diego CA
Photo: 1
Chart: 2
Table: 11
Diagrams: 3,4,5,6,7,8,9,10
Borkenstein, Robert L, Indiana University, Bloomington IN
Chart: 12

MATHEMATICS AND PHYSICS REVIEW FOR TRAFFIC ACCIDENT RECONSTRUCTION

Topic 856 of the *Traffic Accident Investigation Manual*

by
Lynn B. Fricke
and
Gary W. Cooper

NORTHWESTERN UNIVERSITY TRAFFIC INSTITUTE

MATHEMATICS AND PHYSICS REVIEW
FOR TRAFFIC ACCIDENT RECONSTRUCTION

This topic is a *review* of much of the mathematics and elementary physics used in traffic accident reconstruction. If you have a strong math/physics background (for example, if you are an engineer), you should skip this topic; presumably your mathematical skills do not need to be reviewed. If you have had a good mathematical preparation but have not used it for years, you may find this topic useful; review of the material covered here may be just what you need. If you have little or no mathematical background, you may find this topic too difficult, and we suggest that you enroll in an algebra course at a local junior college. References 1 through 4 list books that would be helpful for self-study.

1. ARITHMETIC OPERATIONS

Symbols used for arithmetic are commonly known. A plus sign ($+$) is used for addition; a minus sign ($-$) for subtraction; ($\div$) or (/) for division; and an "$\times$," parentheses ( ), or dot ($\bullet$) for multiplication. There is little confusion of symbols with addition or subtraction. For division, the symbol $\div$ is not used in this manual. Sometimes that symbol is confused with a minus sign. Multiplication can have several symbols. For example, when 2 is multiplied by 2 it can be expressed as

$$2 \times 2$$
$$2 \bullet 2$$
$$(2)(2)$$
$$(2)2$$
$$2(2)$$

Any of the above can be used. An $\times$ is not used to indicate multiplication in this manual because it can be confused with a variable x.

For expressing v times t, the most common method is vt. Two times a is simply $2a$.

The *order of operations* is always multiplication, division, addition and subtraction. For example,

$$2 + 3 \bullet 4 - 1/4 = 2 + 12 - 1/4$$
$$= 14 - 1/4$$
$$= 13\ 3/4$$

If parentheses are used, the operations inside the parentheses are always done first.

$$(2 \bullet 4)(6 - 3)(4/2) - 4 = (8)(3)(2) - 4$$
$$= 48 - 4$$
$$= 44$$

If there are several terms in the numerator and/or the denominator, these operations are done first.

$$\frac{(4)3 - 2}{(4)(5) - 10} = \frac{12 - 2}{20 - 10}$$
$$= 10/10$$
$$= 1$$

Positive and negative (signed) numbers are part of arithmetic that often result in accident reconstruction problems. The rules for addition, subtraction, multiplication and division of signed numbers are simple.

For adding numbers with like signs, their absolute values are simply added and the same sign is prefixed:

$$(+7) + (+6) = +13$$
$$(-7) + (-6) = -13$$

For subtraction of a positive number from a positive number, the opposite negative is added:

$$(+9) - (+6) = (+9) + (-6) = +3$$

To subtract a negative number, add its opposite positive:

$$(+7) - (-6) = (+7) + (+6) = 13$$

The rule for multiplication of signed numbers is relatively simple. If the signs of the two numbers are the same, the resulting product (answer) is positive; if the signs of the two numbers are different, the resulting product is negative.

$$(+7)(+3) = +21$$
$$(-7)(-3) = +21$$

$$(+7)(-3) = -21$$
$$(-7)(+3) = -21$$

The rule for division of signed numbers is essentially the same as that for multiplication. If the two numbers (numerator and denominator) have the same sign, the quotient (answer) is positive; if the two numbers have different signs, the quotient is negative.

$$(+6)/(+3) = +2$$
$$(-6)/(-3) = +2$$

$$(-6)/(+3) = -2$$
$$(+6)/(-3) = -2$$

If more than two numbers are multiplied, do the multiplication by grouping in order to get the correct sign. For example,

$$(-3)(+2)(-4) = (-6)(-4)$$
$$= +24$$

A similar situation may come up in division:

$$\frac{(+3)(-2)+8}{(+16)(-2)+31} = \frac{(-6+8)}{(-32+31)}$$
$$= +2/(-1)$$
$$= -2$$

The *square root* of a positive number is a number that, multiplied by itself, gives the positive number. Thus, the square root of 9 would be $+3$ or -3. This is indicated by the radical: $\sqrt{9} = \pm 3$. In more complicated expressions, the operations are done under the radical before the square root is taken.

$$\sqrt{4 \cdot 3 - 3} = \sqrt{12 - 3}$$
$$= \sqrt{9}$$
$$= \pm 3$$

Square root can also be written as a fractional exponent, like this: $\sqrt{(4 \cdot 3 - 3)}$ or $(4 \cdot 3 - 3)^{0.5}$. We will not be using this method.

2. SIGNIFICANT FIGURES

There is often a misunderstanding of the term *significant figures*. Make sure that after doing several calculations re-

garding such things as time, distance, and velocity relationships, your final answer is not "more accurate" than the data used in the first place. An example may serve to explain this better. Suppose that the given data were the length of a braking skid equal to 40.0 feet (12.2m) and a rate of deceleration of 20.2 ft/sec/sec (6.16 m/sec/sec). The initial velocity can be calculated to be 40.1995 ft/sec (12.2599 m/sec). This "accuracy" is calculated to the nearest $1/10,000$th, but the initial data was rounded to the nearest $1/10$th for the U.S.A. unit.

Significant figures refer to the quantity of significant digits in a number. For example, 20.2 has three significant figures. Thus, if this number is used to calculate something, the final answer should be rounded to three significant digits. For the previous example, 40.1995 would be rounded to 40.2.

Significant digits do *not* mean the number of decimal places. The number 20.2 has three significant figures. The number 0.202 also has three significant figures. The number 0.0202 has three significant figures but it is carried to the nearest $1/10,000$th.

As a practical matter, do not calculate anything to more significant figures than can be measured. For example, if four people went out separately and measured the length of one skidmark, no one would measure it more accurately than one-tenth of a foot (2cm). In real life, it is extremely doubtful that four people would measure the skid to the same distance (e.g., 40.0 feet or 12.2 meters). Therefore, it would be rather silly to calculate the velocity to any measurement more accurate than one-tenth of a foot per second.

Time to skid to a stop could be calculated to three significant figures. In the previous example, where the length of skid was 40.0 feet (12.2m) and the rate of deceleration was 20.2 ft/sec/sec (6.16 m/sec/sec), the time to stop calculates to be 1.99 sec. In this case, carrying the answer to two decimal places is acceptable because there are three significant figures. In practice, however, this would normally be rounded to 2 seconds.

3. ELEMENTARY ALGEBRA

Algebra is a small step past basic arithmetic. Certain rules are agreed upon and must be followed. This section briefly reviews the basic rules of algebra which are helpful in traffic accident reconstruction problems.

Definitions used in algebra may be useful for review. A *term* is a number or the product of numbers. For example, 5, $5x$, $5x^2$ are each different terms. The number 5 is a *coefficient* of the terms $5x$ and $5x^2$. An *expression* consists of one or more terms. For example, $5x + 5x^2$, is an expression.

When like terms are added or subtracted, their coefficients are added or subtracted. This is the use of the "distributive law" in algebra.

$$12x^2 - (-4x^2) = 12x^2 + 4x^2$$
$$= 16x^2$$

$$10x + (-6x) = 10x - 6x$$
$$= 4x$$

An *equation* (or formula) is a statement that has symbols (letters) that take the place of specific quantities (numbers).

Often it is necessary to rearrange the equation so that it can be solved for another quantity. If the equation is

$$x = y + 2$$

and it is necessary to rewrite the equation for y in terms of x, the inverse operation is performed. That is, the value 2 is subtracted from both sides of the equation.

$$x - 2 = y + 2 - 2$$

$$x - 2 = y$$

Because we read left to right, the equation is rewritten:

$$y = x - 2$$

If the equation is

$$x = y - 2$$

and the equation must be solved for y in terms of x, the inverse of subtraction (addition) must be used:

$$x + 2 = y - 2 + 2$$
$$x + 2 = y$$
$$y = x + 2$$

When an equation has multiplication, the same basic procedure is followed. The inverse of multiplication is division.

$$x = 6y$$

In order to solve for y, both sides of the equation must be divided by 6.

$$\frac{x}{6} = \frac{6y}{6}$$

$$\frac{x}{6} = y$$

or

$$y = \frac{x}{6}$$

If an equation has division, then the inverse (multiplication) is used.

$$x = \frac{y}{4}$$

Multiply both sides by 4.

$$4x = \frac{y}{4}(4)$$

$$4x = y$$

or

$$y = 4x$$

Multiple Operations are often required to separate a variable. If multiplication (or division) and addition (or subtraction) are involved, it is usually easier to do the addition (or subtraction) first. Consider the equation

$$x = 28 + 7y$$

First, isolate the $7y$ term by subtracting 28 from both sides of the equation.

$$x - 28 = 28 - 28 + 7y$$
$$x - 28 = 7y$$

Now divide both sides of the equation by 7. Note that the whole quantity $x - 28$ is divided by 7.

$$\frac{x - 28}{7} = \frac{7y}{7}$$
$$\frac{x - 28}{7} = y$$
$$y = \frac{x - 28}{7} = \frac{x}{7} - 4$$

A more difficult way to solve for y in the equation (or at least the potential for error is higher)

$$x = 28 + 7y$$

is to first divide both sides by 7 and then do the subtraction.

$$\frac{x}{7} = \frac{28}{7} + \frac{7y}{7}$$

Note that both 28 and $7y$ must be divided by 7.

$$\frac{x}{7} = 4 + y$$

$$\frac{x}{7} - 4 = 4 - 4 + y$$

$$\frac{x}{7} - 4 = y$$

$$y = \frac{x}{7} - 4$$

Two equations with two unknowns often occur when problems are solved. As long as the number of unknowns do not exceed the number of equations, the unknowns can be solved. The form of two equations and two unknowns may be as follows:

$$ax + by = c$$
$$dx + ey = f$$

where a, b, c, d, e and f are constants and x and y are variables.

Two methods to solve for two unknowns with two equations are the *addition-subtraction* method and the *substitution* method. In some cases, one method may be easier to use than the other.

The *addition–subtraction* method requires that the two equations either be added or subtracted in order to eliminate one of the unknowns.

$$2x + 3y = 11$$
$$3x - 3y = -6$$

If these two equations are added together (i.e., the quantities left of the equal sign are added and the quantities to the right of the equal sign are added), then the y terms drop out.

$$\begin{aligned} 2x + 3y &= 11 \\ + \underline{3x - 3y} &= \underline{-6} \\ 5x &= 5 \end{aligned}$$

Now solve for x by dividing both sides by 5.

$$\frac{5x}{5} = \frac{5}{5}$$
$$x = 1$$

The value for x is substituted into either of the two original equations, and then the value of y is determined.

$$2x + 3y = 11$$
$$(2)(1) + 3y = 11$$
$$2 + 3y = 11$$
$$2 - 2 + 3y = 11 - 2$$
$$3y = 9$$
$$3y/3 = 9/3$$
$$y = 3$$

Thus the solution is $x = 1$ and $y = 3$. This can be checked by substituting these values into the second equation.

$$3x - 3y = -6$$
$$(3)(1) - 3(3) = -6$$
$$3 - 9 = -6$$

The answers are correct.

A second example follows, where the coefficients of a and b are not equal. The value k is simply a constant.

$$2a + 4b = 10 + k$$
$$a + 3b = 12 - k$$

In this case it is necessary to multiply either equation by some quantity such that the two equations can be subtracted or added, resulting in one of the terms (either a or b) dropping out. Multiply the second equation by 2 so that the two equations can be subtracted which will cause the a term to drop out.

$$2(a + 3b = 12 - k)$$
$$2a + 6b = 24 - 2k$$

Note that 2 is multiplied times each term. Now subtract this equation from the first one.

$$\begin{aligned} 2a + 4b &= 10 + k \\ - \underline{(2a + 6b} &= \underline{24 - 2k)} \\ 0 - 2b &= -14 + 3k \end{aligned}$$

Solve for b.

$$-2b = -14 + 3k$$
$$\frac{-2b}{-2} = \frac{-14}{-2} + \frac{3k}{-2}$$
$$b = 7 - 3k/2$$

Solve for a using either of the two original equations.

$$2a + 4b = 10 + k$$
$$2a + 4(7 - 3k/2) = 10 + k$$
$$2a + 28 - 6k = 10 + k$$

Subtract 28 from both sides and add $6k$ to both sides so that $2a$ will be by itself on the left side of the equation.

$$2a + 28 - 28 - 6k + 6k = 10 - 28 + k + 6k$$
$$2a = -18 + 7k$$
$$\frac{2a}{2} = \frac{-18}{2} + \frac{7k}{2}$$

Therefore, the solution is $a = \dfrac{7k}{2} - 9$ and $b = 7 - \dfrac{3k}{2}$.

The *substitution method* may sometimes be easier for solving equations than the addition–subtraction method. In this method the value of one variable is inserted into the other equation. Then only one unknown is present in the resulting equation.

$$2x + 5y = 19$$
$$7x + 2y = 20$$

Choose one of the equations and solve for one of the variables.

$$2x + 5y = 19$$

Solve for x.

$$2x + 5y - 5y = 19 - 5y$$
$$2x = 19 - 5y$$
$$2x/2 = 19/2 - 5y/2$$
$$x = 19/2 - 5y/2$$

Substitute the value for x in the second equation.

$$7x + 2y = 20$$
$$7(19/2 - 5y/2) + 2y = 20$$
$$133/2 - 35y/2 + 2y = 20$$

Multiply both sides of the equation by 2 in order to eliminate the fractions.

$$2(133/2) - 2(35y/2) + 2(2y) = 2(20)$$
$$133 - 35y + 4y = 40$$
$$133 - 31y = 40$$

Subtract 133 from both sides of the equation.

$$133 - 133 - 31y = 40 - 133$$
$$-31y = -93$$

Divide both sides by -31.

$$\frac{-31y}{-31} = \frac{-93}{-31}$$
$$y = 3$$

Substitute $y = 3$ into

$$x = 19/2 - 5y/2$$
$$x = 19/2 - 5(3)/2$$
$$x = 19/2 - 15/2$$
$$x = 4/2$$
$$x = 2$$

Therefore the solution to the two equations is $x = 2$ and $y = 3$.

4. MULTIPLICATION AND DIVISION OF ALGEBRAIC EXPRESSIONS

When two algebraic expressions are multiplied, a new term or new terms result. For example, $2x^2$ multiplied by $3y$ gives

$$3y(2x^2)$$
$$= (3)(2)x^2y$$
$$= 6x^2y$$

The numbers are multiplied to get 6. Then x^2 times y is simply x^2y. Thus the whole product is simply $6x^2y$.

An algebraic equation can be classified as monomial, binomial or polynomial. A *monomial* is an algebraic expression with only one term. Examples are $3x$, $3x^2y$, $2xy$. A *binomial* is an algebraic expression with two terms. Examples are $x - y$, $3x + 2b$, $x^2 + 3b$. A *polynomial* is an algebraic expression with three or more terms. Examples are $x^2 + 2xy + 6y$, $a^2 + 2ab + b^2$.

If $3y$ is multiplied times a group of terms (polynomial), it is multiplied times *each* term. For example,

$$3y(2x^2 + 3x + 4)$$
$$= 3y(2x^2) + (3y)(3x) + (3y)(4)$$
$$= 6x^2y + 9xy + 12y$$

Division of two algebraic expressions is similar to multiplication. Divide $6x^2y$ by $3y$.

$$\frac{6x^2y}{3y}$$

Cancel the y terms and numbers to get

$$\frac{2\cancel{6}x^2\cancel{y}}{\cancel{3}\cancel{y}}$$

$$= 2x^2$$

If a group of terms (polynomial) is divided by a term, each term must be divided. For example,

$$\frac{(6x^2y + 9xy + 12y)}{3y}$$

$$= \frac{6x^2y}{3y} + \frac{9xy}{3y} + \frac{12y}{3y}$$

Then cancel:

$$= 2x^2 + 3x + 4$$

Products of Binomials

A *binomial* is an algebraic expression with two terms, such as $(x + y)$ or $(2x - 3)$. Frequently, binomials are multiplied times each other. The general form of two binomials multiplied times each other is as given below:

$$(ax + by)(cx + dy)$$

You must multiply each term of $(ax + by)$ times $(cx + dy)$. Simply do as follows:

$$(ax + by)(cx + dy)$$
$$= (ax)(cx) + (ax)(dy) + (by)(cx) + (by)(dy)$$

A more typical example you will encounter is

$$(2x - 3)(x + 4)$$

$$= (2x)(x) + (2x)(4) - 3x - 3(4)$$
$$= 2x^2 + 8x - 3x - 12$$
$$= 2x^2 + 5x - 12$$

Factoring Binomials

Factoring can be considered the reverse of multiplication of binomials. You certainly understand the number 6 could be the product of 3 times 2. Thus, 6 could be factored as $(3)(2)$.

If a polynomial (group of more than one term) is multiplied by a monomial (one term), each term of the polynomial is multiplied by the monomial.

Therefore, any term that is common to each term in the monomial can be factored. For example,

$$5x^2 + 10x - 15$$

has the number 5 as a factor of each term. Therefore, the expression can be factored as

$$5(x^2 + 2x - 3)$$

A more complicated example is

$$6x^2y + 9xy + 12y$$

The common factor is $3y$:

$$3y(2x^2 + 3x + 4)$$

Factoring trinomials of the type $x^2 + rx + s$ is slightly more difficult than factoring out a monomial from a polynomial. In the earlier discussion on multiplying binomials it was shown that if you have to multiply $(x + a)$ times $(x + b)$, the answer is

$$(x + a)(x + b) = x^2 + (a + b)x + ab$$

Thus, for the general equation

$$x^2 + rx + s$$

$$r = a + b$$
$$s = ab$$

If these numbers can be found, then the desired factors are $(x + a)$ and $(x + b)$. An example will help to illustrate this:

$$x^2 + 7x + 12$$

The above expression can be factored as

$$(x + 3)(x + 4)$$

Thus, $a = 3$ and $b = 4$.

Another example is $x^2 - 10x + 24$

You can see that $(-6) + (-4) = -10$ and $(-4)(-6) = 24$. Thus, the expression is factored as

$$x^2 - 10x + 24 = (x - 4)(x - 6)$$

5. QUADRATIC EQUATION SOLUTIONS

If something is multiplied by itself, it is *squared*, or raised to the second power. For example,

$$x \cdot x = x^2$$
$$3 \cdot 3 = 3^2$$

If you have a polynomial equation in which the highest power of the unknowns is 2, you have a *quadratic* equation. The following equations are quadratic equations:

$$x^2 = 49$$
$$y^2 + 2y - 3 = 0$$

The general (standard) form of a quadratic equation is

$$ax^2 + bx + c = 0$$

where a, b and c are constants. A *complete* quadratic is one where neither a nor b is equal to zero. A *pure* quadratic occurs when b equals zero.

For a pure quadratic it is relatively easy to solve for the unknown. Isolate the square of the unknown on one side of the equation and take the square root of both sides.

$$6x^2 = 216$$
$$\frac{6x^2}{6} = \frac{216}{6}$$
$$x^2 = 36$$
$$\sqrt{x^2} = \sqrt{36}$$
$$x = \pm 6$$

The answer is $+$ and -6 because (-6) times (-6) is also equal to 36.

For quadratic equations that are complete, i.e., those with the bx term, the solution is not as easy. Two methods can be used to do this: factoring or the quadratic equation.

Quadratic Equations Solved by Factoring

This method makes use of the property of real numbers that if the product of two of them equals zero, then at least one of them has to equal zero. Using symbols $xy = 0$, then either $x = 0$ or $y = 0$ or both x and y equal zero.

If you have the equation

$$x^2 + 7x + 12 = 0$$

this can be factored into

$$(x + 4)(x + 3) = 0$$

Because $(x+4)$ and $(x+3)$ represent real numbers and their product equals zero, it follows that

$$x+4=0 \qquad\qquad x+3=0$$
$$x+4-4=0-4 \qquad x+3-3=0-3$$
$$x=-4 \qquad\qquad x=-3$$

Therefore, two possible answers for x are $x=-4$ and $x=-3$.

Quadratic Equation

Sometimes it is not as easy to factor an equation as was done in the previous example. Use of the quadratic equation would then simplify the process. First, reduce the equation to the standard quadratic form:

$$ax^2+bx+c=0$$

Then the equation can be solved by using the quadratic equation:

$$x=\frac{-b\pm\sqrt{b^2-4ac}}{2a}$$

The following example illustrates this process.

Given:

$$3x^2=2x+8$$

Subtract $2x+8$ from both sides of the equation:

$$3x^2-2x-8=2x-2x+8-8$$
$$3x^2-2x-8=0$$

Now the equation is in the standard form $(ax^2+bx+c=0)$ where

$$a=3$$
$$b=-2$$
$$c=-8$$

Substitute into the quadratic:

$$x=\frac{-b\pm\sqrt{b^2-4ac}}{2a}$$
$$x=\frac{-(-2)\pm\sqrt{(-2)^2-4(3)(-8)}}{2(3)}$$
$$x=\frac{2\pm\sqrt{4+96}}{6}$$
$$x=\frac{2\pm\sqrt{100}}{6}$$
$$x=\frac{2+10}{6} \text{ and } x=\frac{2-10}{6}$$
$$x=2 \text{ and } x=-4/3$$

If you are concerned that you may have made a mistake, simply substitute the two solutions into the original equation and check.

$$3x^2-2x-8$$
$$3(2^2)-2(2)-8$$
$$12-4-8$$
$$0=0$$

$$3x^2-2x-8$$
$$3(-4/3)^2-2(-4/3)-8$$
$$16/3+8/3-8$$
$$24/3-8$$
$$8-8$$
$$0=0$$

Clearly, both solutions are correct answers to the mathematical equations. However, if you are working on a problem that has to relate to a real-world situation, only one answer may be reasonable. For example, if you have a positive and negative answer for time, only the positive one applies.

6. ELEMENTARY PLANE GEOMETRY

In accident reconstruction there are times when a general knowledge of plane geometry is helpful. The many books on this subject can be consulted for more detail. Some of the principles of geometry used in reconstruction are presented in this section. Many of these principles are applied in derivations of the equations used in accident reconstruction. Topic 890 gives these derivations.

Law of Pythagoras

The law of Pythagoras (or the Pythagorean theorem) states that the square of the hypotenuse of a right triangle equals the sum of the squares of the legs. A *right triangle* is a triangle where only one of the angles is 90 degrees. In Exhibit 1, the angle at C is 90 degrees. The *hypotenuse* is defined as the side opposite the 90-degree (right) angle of the triangle. In Exhibit 1, side c is the hypotenuse. The legs of the right triangle are the sides (a and b in Exhibit 1) that are not the hypotenuse. Therefore the law of Pythagoras stated mathematically (and referring to Exhibit 1) is

$$c^2=a^2+b^2$$

To solve for the hypotenuse you simply take the square root of both sides of the equation:

$$c=\sqrt{a^2+b^2}$$

Sides a and b can also be solved:
$$a=\sqrt{c^2-b^2}$$
$$b=\sqrt{c^2-a^2}$$

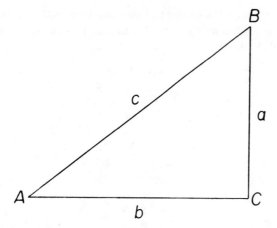

Exhibit 1. *The Law of Pythagoras states the square of the hypotenuse (side c) of a right triangle (angle C = 90 degrees) equals the sum of the square of the two sides (side a and b). In equation form, $c^2 = a^2 + b^2$.*

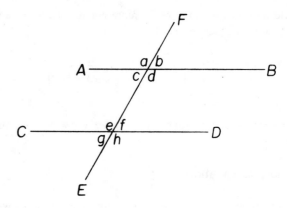

Exhibit 3. *Line EF is a transversal of the two parallel lines AB and CD.*

The proof of the law of Pythagoras can be found in typical plane geometry books. If you have further interest in this, you should consult one of those references.

Parallel Lines

Parallel lines are straight lines that lie in the same plane and do not intersect, regardless of how far they are extended. Exhibit 2 shows two parallel lines *AB* and *CD*. The lines are in the same plane of the paper, and they do not intersect when extended.

A *transversal* of two or more lines is a line that crosses the lines. Thus in Exhibit 3, *EF* is a transversal of *AB* and *CD*. The angles formed by two lines cut by a transversal are labelled in Exhibit 3. If *AB* and *CD* are parallel, it can be proven by plane geometry that angles *a, d, e* and *h* are equal and that angles *b, c, f* and *g* are equal.

Parallelograms

A parallelogram is a *quadrilateral* (four-sided figure in a plane) whose opposite sides are parallel. Thus in Exhibit 4, *AB* is parallel to *CD* and *AD* is parallel to *BC*. Other properties of parallelograms:

- Opposite sides are equal; $AB = CD$ and $AD = BC$
- Opposite angles are equal; angle $A =$ angle C and angle $B =$ angle D

Principles of Similar Triangles

By definition two triangles are similar when

1) corresponding angles are equal;
2) corresponding sides are in proportion.

Thus in Exhibit 5, angles C and C' are equal, as are angles A and A' and B and B'. If the sides are in proportion, then the ratios of corresponding sides are also equal. Again referring to Exhibit 5,

$$a/a' = b/b' = c/c'$$

Similar triangles occur in many plane geometry problems. A case that is useful to know is shown in Exhibit 6. The two triangles shown are similar. Side $A'B'$ is perpendicular to

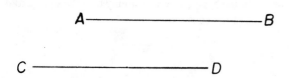

Exhibit 2. *Lines AB and CD are in the same plane and do not intersect. They are parallel.*

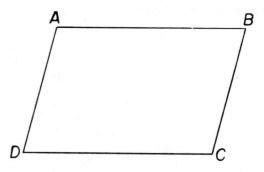

Exhibit 4. *This quadrilateral (four-sided figure in a plane) is a parallelogram with side AB parallel to side CD and side BC parallel to side AD.*

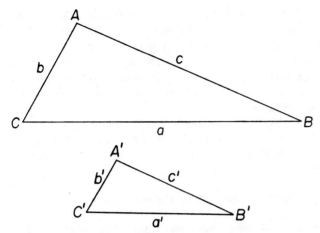

Exhibit 5. *The two triangles ABC and A'B'C' are similar. This allows proportions to be developed for the sides of the triangles.*

side *AC*. Side *B'C'* is parallel to *AC*. When these conditions occur, the two triangles are *similar*. Thus, angle Θ is equal to angle Θ'. For these two similar triangles the rules of proportion clearly would apply.

7. INTRODUCTION TO VECTOR ADDITION

Quantities can be categorized as *scalar* and *vector* quantities. A *scalar* quantity has only magnitude (how much). For example, volume (quart or liter), time (seconds), and money (dollars, pesos) have a magnitude. Scalar quantities can be added like any algebra problem (2sec + 3sec = 5sec).

A *vector* quantity has *both* direction and magnitude. Some examples are

Force—the parked car was pushed eastward by the striking car.

Displacement—the car traveled a distance of 15 ft. in the westbound direction.

Velocity—the car traveled with a constant velocity of 50ft/sec going northbound.

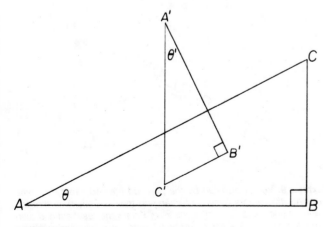

Exhibit 6. *Triangle ABC is similar to triangle A'B'C'.*

The most commonly used forms of vectors in accident reconstruction are to add two *momentum* vectors and to divide a momentum vector into two parts. *Momentum* is the product of mass times velocity and is discussed in detail in other parts of the *Manual*. The sum of two (or more) vectors is called the *resultant*. Parts of vectors are called *components*. A component of a vector is its effective value in any direction.

Graphical Vector Addition by Parallelograms

The resultant of two vectors can be obtained by drawing the diagonal of a parallelogram with the two vectors as sides. First, the tails of both vectors must be placed at the same origin, *O*, as in Exhibit 7 (step 1). Through the head (arrow)

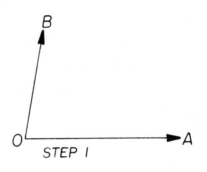

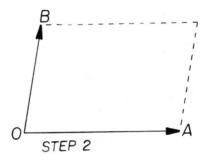

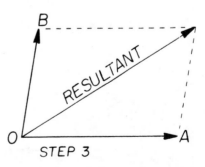

Exhibit 7. *The steps shown illustrate how two vectors are added by the parallelogram method. A parallelogram is drawn and the diagonal line represents the resultant vector.*

of each vector, draw a line parallel to the other vector as the dotted lines show (step 2). Where these lines intersect is one corner of the parallelogram. Techniques to draw parallel lines are shown in Topic 834. The diagonal line from O to the intersecting dotted lines is the resultant of vectors A and B (step 3).

A more complex case is shown in Exhibit 8. The angle between the two vector tails is *obtuse* (greater than 90 degrees and less than 180 degrees.). The three steps are identical to those of Exhibit 7.

Graphical Vector Addition by Polygons

This method is no more difficult than the parallelogram technique. All that is necessary is to place a head to a tail of consecutive vectors. Start at a convenient spot as the origin. Place each vector head to tail (to scale). For vector addition only the length and direction must be maintained. That is, you can "move" vectors around but you must keep them in the same direction and make them the same length. The resultant of the vector addition is a vector drawn from the origin to the last vector head.

The polygon procedure is shown with two examples in Exhibits 9 and 10. These are the same vectors used in Exhibits 7 and 8. Note how the resultants are the same for Exhibits 7 and 9 and for Exhibits 8 and 10.

Vector Components by Parallelograms

A vector component is its effective value in any specified direction. For example, the vector A in Exhibit 11 has hori-

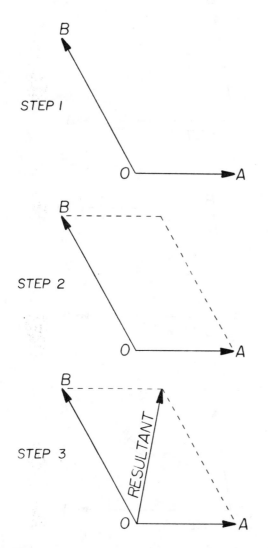

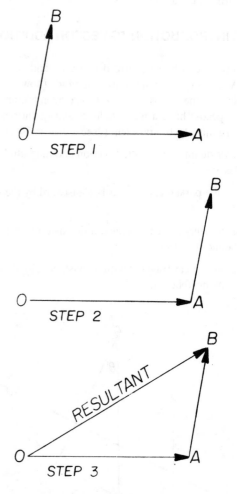

Exhibit 8. *The same three steps, as illustrated in Exhibit 7, are shown again for the vector addition of two vectors that are positioned at an obtuse angle.*

Exhibit 9. *Vector addition by the polygon method simply involves moving the vectors (while not changing their direction) so that the head of one lies on the tail of the next. Finally the resultant is drawn from the origin to the last vector head. Note this is the same problem as Exhibit 7.*

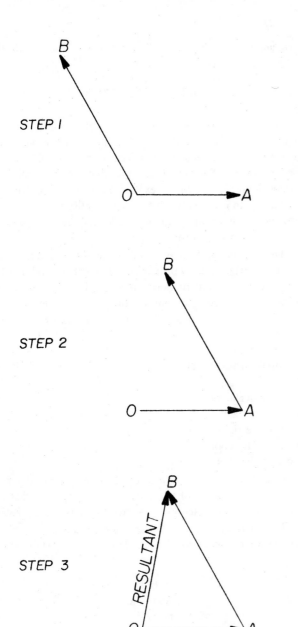

STEP 1

STEP 2

STEP 3

Exhibit 10. *The same procedure as shown in Exhibit 9 applies to the case shown here. Note this is the same problem as Exhibit 8.*

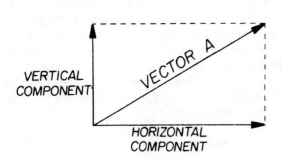

Exhibit 11. *Horizontal and vertical components of a vector can always be determined using a parallelogram as shown.*

zontal and vertical components as shown. In some momentum problems in accident reconstruction it is desirable to know components of a vector that are not horizontal and vertical. This can be done by drawing parallelograms.

In a typical vector component problem, the direction of the components and the length and direction of the vector are known, as shown in Exhibit 12. As shown in step 2 of Exhibit 12, draw a line parallel to each component through the tail of vector *A*. Refer to Topic 834 if you have problems drawing

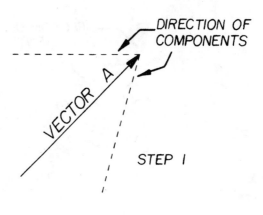

STEP 1

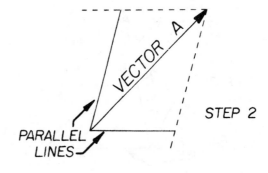

STEP 2

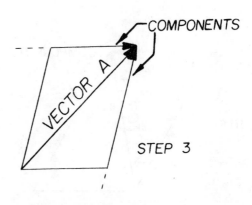

STEP 3

Exhibit 12. *Components of a vector do not have to be at right angles to each other. The three steps to graphically determine components by parallelograms are illustrated above.*

parallel lines. Then the actual components are the resulting two sides of the parallelogram along the component directions. Another, more complicated example is shown in Exhibit 13.

Vector Components Using Trigonometry

The use of parallelograms is a graphical technique to solve for vector components. This can also be done using

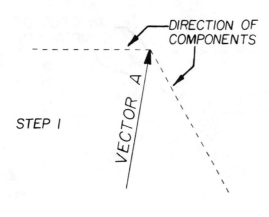

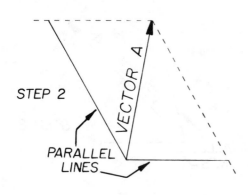

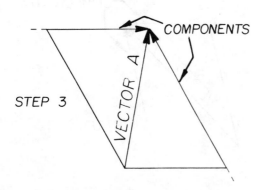

Exhibit 13. *In this example the components of vector A come together at an obtuse angle. Use the same three steps as shown in Exhibit 12 to determine vector A's components.*

trigonometry. This method is discussed further in the trigonometry section of this topic.

8. TRIGONOMETRY

For traffic accident reconstruction problems the use of trigonometry is usually not necessary. In nearly all cases where trigonometry is used, similiar triangles would give the same answer. Students often ask that the principles of trigonometry be used to explain accident reconstruction problems. In many cases this would simplify the task of the instructor. Unfortunately, many students do not have a good working knowledge of trigonometry.

This section has been included for those who want a quick review of trigonometry principles that may be useful in solving accident reconstruction problems. This in no way is meant to be a complete discussion of trigonometry. Other texts on this subject should be consulted if this is one of your weak areas.

Coordinate System

Consider a coordinate system as shown in Exhibit 14. At the origin (center), $x = 0$ and $y = 0$. The coordinate x is positive to the right of the origin and negative to the left of the origin. The coordinate y is positive above the origin and negative below the origin.

In Exhibit 14, a point with the coordinates x and y is a straight-line distance of r from the origin. The angle that the line r is rotated counterclockwise from the x axis is Θ (theta).

The basic definitions of *sine, cosine* and *tangent* (abbreviated sin, cos and tan) of the angle Θ are (see Exhibit 14):

$$\sin\Theta = y/r$$
$$\cos\Theta = x/r$$
$$\tan\Theta = y/x$$

The values for sin, cos and tan are given in many mathematical or engineering handbooks. Many calculators have these trigonometric functions built in. As long as the angle Θ is between 0 and 90 degrees, the sin, cos and tan of the angle are positive. In Quadrant II (Θ is between 90 and 180 degrees) the sin is positive but the cos and tan are negative. In Quadrant III (Θ is between 180 and 270 degrees) both the sin and cos are negative, but the tan is positive. In Quadrant IV (Θ is between 270 and 360 degrees) the sin and tan are negative, but the cos is positive. Most hand-held calculators today take care of the sign of the trig functions, which simplifies the problem.

Solving for *x* and *y*

Assume that the values of r and the angle are known. In order to solve for x and y simply take the basic relationships.

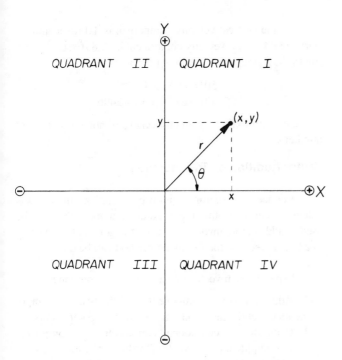

Exhibit 14. *A rectangular coordinate system is shown above. Note the positive directions for x, y, and Θ.*

$$\sin \Theta = y/r$$

$$\cos \Theta = x/r$$

and solve them for x and y.

$$\sin \Theta = y/r$$

Multiply both sides by r

$$r \sin \Theta = r(y/r)$$
$$r \sin \Theta = y$$

or

$$y = r \sin \Theta$$

The same can be done to solve for x:

$$x = r \cos \Theta$$

For example:

If $r = 10$ and $\Theta = 30°$

From tables or a calculator

$$\sin 30° = .500$$
$$\cos 30° = .866$$

Then

$$y = r \sin \Theta$$
$$= (10)(.500)$$
$$y = 5$$

and

$$x = r \cos \Theta$$
$$= 10 \,(.866)$$
$$x = 8.66$$

Exhibit 15 shows a point with the coordinates $x = 8.66$ and $y = 5.00$. The distance (r) from the origin is 10 and the angle that r makes, measured counterclockwise from the x axis, is 30 degrees.

As can be seen in Exhibit 15, a right triangle is formed with the hypotenuse (opposite the 90-degree angle) equal to 10, the side opposite Θ equal to 5, and the side adjacent to Θ equal to 8.66. For simple trigonometric problems the definition on the basic trig functions are sometimes given as

$$\sin \Theta = \frac{\text{side opposite}}{\text{hypotenuse}}$$

$$\cos \Theta = \frac{\text{side adjacent}}{\text{hypotenuse}}$$

$$\tan \Theta = \frac{\text{side opposite}}{\text{side adjacent}}$$

where definitions of the sides are shown in Exhibit 16.

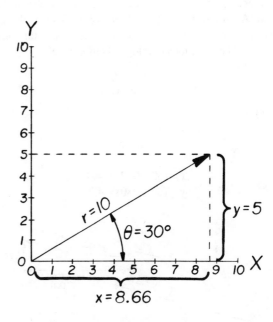

Exhibit 15. *The vector r = 10 at an angle 30 degrees counterclockwise to the positive x-axis has an x– component of 8.66 and a y– component of 5.*

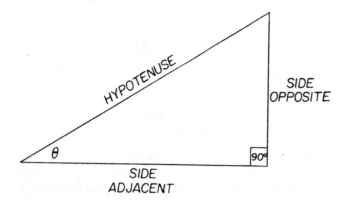

Exhibit 16. *The trigonometric functions of the angle θ can be defined as ratios of the side adjacent, side opposite and the hypotenuse.*

Example of x and y Components

An example of how trigonometry may be used to calculate components in the x and y direction may help illustrate the use of trigonometry. Suppose a vehicle is traveling up an eight-percent grade and then starts a fall. If the vehicle's velocity at takeoff was 50 feet per second, what are the vertical and horizontal components of velocity at takeoff?

What angle has a tangent equal to 0.08? Simply look in a set of tables for the answer or use the arc tan button on a calculator. Arc tan θ simply means "what is the angle that has the tan value of"–in this case, 0.08. The answer is $\theta = 4.57$ degrees.

The takeoff of the vehicle is shown in Exhibit 17. The angle of takeoff is $\theta = 4.57$. Therefore, the center of mass of the vehicle is traveling at an angle of 4.57 relative to the horizontal. As in Exhibit 15, the velocity of 50 ft/sec is the same as r. The vertical component is y and the horizontal component is x. The equations developed before were

$$x = r \cos \theta$$
$$y = r \sin \theta$$

Therefore,

$$x = 50 \cos 4.57°$$
$$y = 50 \sin 4.57°$$

$$x = (50)(.997) = 49.8$$
$$y = (50)(.080) = 4.0$$

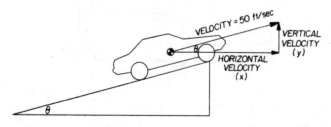

Exhibit 17. *A vehicle before it starts to fall may have both vertical and horizontal velocity components if it is on a grade.*

Thus, the vertical velocity component is 4.0 ft/sec and the horizontal vertical velocity component is 49.8 ft/sec. According to the Pythagorean theorem ($c^2 = a^2 + b^2$)

$$50^2 = 49.8^2 + 4.0^2$$
$$2,500 = 2,480 + 16 = 2496$$

This is approximately equal because of some rounding of numbers.

Vector Addition by Trigonometry

The concept of vector addition by graphical method was discussed earlier in this topic. Another method that can be used to add vectors involves the use of trigonometry. In order to add two vectors, the following method can be used.

1. Separate each vector into $x-$ and $y-$ components.
2. Add the two $x-$ components and the two $y-$ components to get the new vector's $x-$ and $y-$ components.
3. Using the $x-$ component sum and the $y-$ component sum, compute the new vector R value ("r" value).
4. Calculate the vector's angle based on the $x-$ component sum and the $y-$ component sum (R_x and R_y)

An example of this procedure will help to illustrate the four steps. As discussed earlier in this topic, the two vectors must start at the same origin. One vector, B, is 35 units long and has an angle of 30 degrees measured counterclockwise from the positive x axis. The second vector, A, is 25 units long and is 60 degrees counterclockwise from the positive $x-$ axis.

Step 1
Separate each vector into its $x-$ and $y-$ components. Remember $x = r \cos \theta$ and $y = r \sin \theta$

Vector A
$$x = 25 \cos 60°$$
$$y = 25 \sin 60°$$

$$x = (25)(0.50) = 12.5$$
$$y = (25)(.866) = 21.7$$

Vector B
$$x = 35 \cos 30°$$
$$y = 35 \sin 30°$$

$$x = (35)(.866) = 30.3$$
$$y = 35 (.50) = 17.5$$

Step 2
Add the vector $x-$ and $y-$ components to get the resultant R (vector) components

$$R_x = 12.5 + 30.3 = 42.8$$
$$R_y = 21.7 + 17.5 = 39.2$$

Step 3

Compute the new vector. Using the law of Pythagorus (see earlier discussion in this topic), the sides of a right triangle are R_x, R_y and R as shown in Exhibit 18. Thus R is computed by taking the square root of the sum of R_x squared and R_y squared:

$$R = \sqrt{R_x^2 + R_y^2}$$
$$R = \sqrt{42.8^2 + 39.2^2}$$
$$R = 58$$

Step 4

Calculate the angle, Θ_R.

$$\tan \Theta_R = R_y/R_x$$
$$= 39.2/42.8$$
$$= 0.916$$

Consult tables or use your calculator to find the angle that has a tan of 0.916. This is

$$\Theta_R = 42.5°$$

Therefore the sum, R, of the two vectors A and B, has an angle of 42.5 degrees counterclockwise of the positive $x-$ axis and is 58 units long.

9. FORCES AND THEIR EFFECTS

A *force* may be considered as an action that produces a pushing or pulling effect on a body. This implies that a force

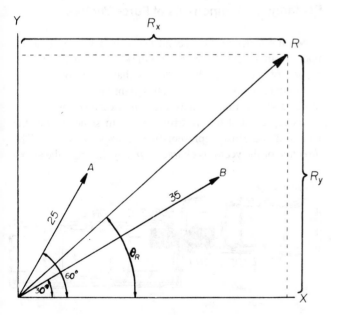

Exhibit 18. *Vectors A and B can be added using trigometric functions to obtain the resultant vector R.*

exists through the action of one body on another. A force that is produced by direct contact between two bodies is an *applied force*. An example of an applied force is the slowing force produced by friction when the tires on an automobile are sliding across a road surface. A *nonapplied force* is an action produced without direct contact; for example, the gravitational pull (force) of the earth on the moon.

A more formal definition of force is an action on a body that tends to change the body's state of motion. In the example of a vehicle sliding on a road surface, the slowing force (frictional force) is changing the motion of the vehicle by reducing its velocity. How much a force influences the motion of a body can be predicted from certain physical laws governing the effect of forces on motion.

Three natural laws relate force and motion. These laws were first stated by Sir Isaac Newton (1642-1727).

Newton's First Law of Motion

Newton stated in his first law of motion that a body will remain at rest, or if in uniform motion (constant velocity in a straight line) remain in motion, unless it is acted upon by an unbalanced force. The definition of force can be seen in this law. An unbalanced force must exist to change the motion of a body. Therefore, force is an action which tends to change the motion of a body.

Newton's Second Law of Motion

Newton's first law stated what must exist to change the motion of a body. Newton stated in his second law what the change in the motion would be. His second law describes in two steps the effects of an unbalanced force. First, he stated what occurs when an unbalanced force exists; second, he quantified the result of the unbalanced force on the body.

Newton's second law of motion first states that, if the net force acting on a body is not zero, the body will be accelerated in the direction of the force. The definition of force can also be seen in this statement. Acceleration is a body's change of velocity with respect to time, therefore its change in motion. The second part of the law states that the magnitude of the acceleration (change in motion) will be directly proportional to the net force and inversely proportional to the mass of the body. It also states how much the motion would change and what the change was dependent upon.

The amount of acceleration depends on the amount of unbalanced force and the mass of the body the force is acting upon. A given unbalanced force acting upon a body with a certain mass will be accelerated (A in Exhibit 19). If the mass of the body is doubled and the force remains the same, the acceleration will be only half what it originally was (B in Exhibit 19). However, if the mass remains constant and the force is doubled, the acceleration will also double (C in Exhibit 19).

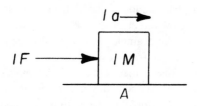

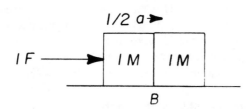

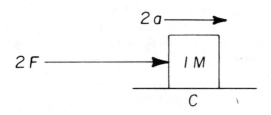

Exhibit 19. *Newton's second law of motion relates acceleration of a body to the force applied to the body and the body's mass.*

Newton's second law of motion can be written in equation form as follows:

$$a = F/m$$

In this equation a is acceleration, F is force, and m is mass. This equation can be rewritten in a more common form by solving it for force, F:

$$F = ma$$

Mass

This discussion indicates that the acceleration experienced by a body resulting from an unbalanced force depends on a property of the body known as mass, m. Mass may be defined as the amount of matter of which an object is made. Mass can be related to the more common term, *weight*.

On earth, if an object is dropped in free fall, it is accelerated by gravity due to its weight, w. Therefore, the unbalanced force is the object's weight and the acceleration is

gravity, g. This relationship can be expressed in equation form. First, from Newton's second law of motion:

$$a = F/m$$

Solving this equation for mass:

$$m = F/a$$

In a free fall, the unbalanced force, the weight of the object, and the acceleration produced by the weight are due to gravity. Thus:

$$F = w \text{ and } a = g$$

Substituting these relationships into the equation reveals the relationship between mass and weight:

$$m = w/g \text{ or } w = mg$$

Newton's Third Law of Motion

Newton's third law of motion states that whenever one body exerts a force upon a second body, the second body exerts a force upon the first. These forces are equal in magnitude and opposite in direction. This law is often referred to as the action-reaction law. It indicates that forces exist in pairs, not singularly, and are equal but in opposite directions. When two vehicles collide, the force exerted by each vehicle on the other is equal in magnitude but opposite in direction. In Exhibit 20, the force of vehicle 1 on vehicle 2 is equal to the force of vehicle 2 on vehicle 1. However, they are coming from opposite directions.

Rectangular Components of Force Vectors

Newton stated in his second law that if a body is acted upon by an unbalanced force, it will be accelerated in the direction of the force. This indicates that force not only has magnitude, but direction as well. Quantities that have magnitude and direction, such as force, are called *vectors*. A vector is represented by an arrow drawn to scale so that the length of the arrow represents the vector's magnitude. The *direction* of the vector is characterized by the angle the arrow

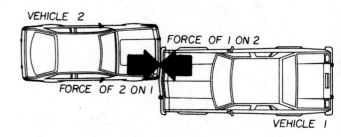

Exhibit 20. *Newton's third law of motion explains how two vehicles in a collision push on each other with an equal and opposite force.*

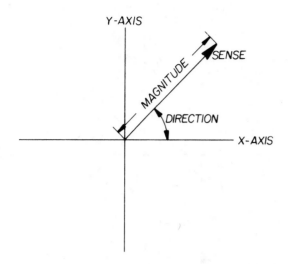

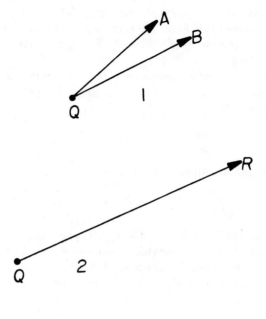

Exhibit 21. *A force vector can be illustrated graphically by an arrow. The* length *indicates the magnitude and the* sense *is the direction in which the arrow points.*

forms with some fixed axis, and the *sense* of the vector is the direction toward which the arrowhead points (Exhibit 21).

Resultant

Two forces acting upon a body may be replaced by one single force that has the same effect on the body. This single force is called the *resultant* of the two separate forces. In Exhibit 22, part 1 shows the two forces A and B acting on point Q. Part 2 shows the resultant force, R, acting on point Q. Force R will tend to change the motion of point Q by itself in the same manner as forces A and B would together.

The resultant force R may be found, as shown in part 3 of Exhibit 22, by drawing a parallelogram, using A and B as the sides. The diagonal that passes through point Q is the resultant, R.

It should be clear from this discussion that vector quantities do not add according to the rules used in ordinary arithmetic. For example, two forces acting at a right angle to each other, one of magnitude 3 lbs and the other of 4 lbs, have a resultant magnitude of 5 lbs, not 7 lbs.

Rectangular Components

A single force can be replaced by two separate forces that have the same effect as the original one. These two forces are called the *components* of the single force. When the two components are perpendicular to each other, the forces are called the *rectangular components* of the original force.

Normally, the rectangular components are along the $x-$ axis and $y-$ axis of a rectangular coordinate system. Exhibit 23 shows the single force, F; the $x-$ axis component, F_x; the

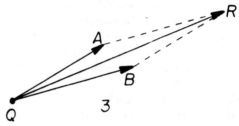

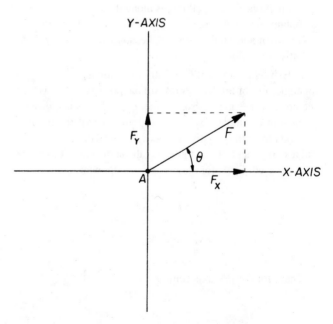

Exhibit 22. *Components of a force vector can be determined by using parallelograms. This is, in essence, the same as was shown in Exhibits 7 and 8.*

Exhibit 23. *Force vector components can be determined using trigonometry.*

$y-$ axis component, F_y; and the angle, Θ, between the $x-$ axis and the single force. The parallelogram drawn to obtain the two components is a rectangle. Hence, the components are rectangular.

The rectangular components may be found mathematically. The equation for the magnitude of the $x-$ axis component is

$$F_x = F \cos \Theta$$

And the magnitude of the $y-$ axis component is

$$F_y = F \sin \Theta$$

In Exhibit 23 a force, F, of 100 lbs is applied to point A at an angle, Θ, of 30 degrees to the positive $x-$ axis. To determine the rectangular components of the force, F, the equations given are used. First, for the $x-$ axis component:

$$F_x = F \cos \Theta$$
$$F_x = (100)(\cos 30°)$$
$$F_x = 86.6 \text{ lbs}$$

Then, for the $y-$ axis component:

$$F_y = F \sin \Theta$$
$$F_y = (100)(\sin 30°)$$
$$F_y = 50 \text{ lbs}$$

In problems with more than one force, each force is first resolved into its rectangular components. Then all forces along the $x-$ axis are added to obtain the total force in the $x-$ direction. Finally, all forces along the $y-$ axis are added to obtain the total force in the $y-$ direction. Care must be taken when adding these forces, because some may be in the negative direction.

In Exhibit 24 a force, F_1, of 100 lbs is applied to point A at an angle, Θ_1, of 50 degrees toward the positive $y-$ axis from the positive $x-$ axis. Also, a force, F_2, of 50 lbs is applied to point A at an angle, Θ_2, of 25 degrees toward the negative $y-$ axis from the negative $x-$ axis. To determine the rectangular component of the force, F_1, the same equations as before are used. First, for the $x-$ axis component:

$$F_{1x} = F_1 \cos \Theta_1$$
$$F_{1x} = (100)(\cos 50°)$$
$$F_{1x} = 64.3 \text{ lbs}$$

Then, for the $y-$ axis component:

$$F_{1y} = F_1 \sin \Theta_1$$
$$F_{1y} = (100)(\sin 50°)$$
$$F_{1y} = 76.6 \text{ lbs}$$

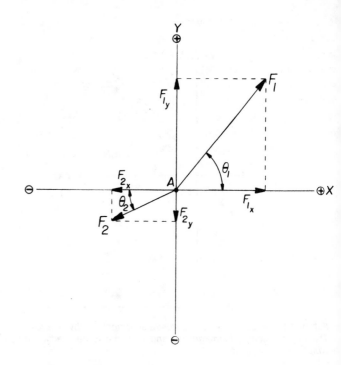

Exhibit 24. Force vectors F_1 and F_2 can be added by using trigonometric equations.

The same is done for the force, F_2, for the $x-$ axis:

$$F_{2x} = -F_2 \cos \Theta_2$$
$$F_{2x} = -(50)(\cos 25°)$$
$$F_{2x} = -45.3 \text{ lbs}$$

The $x-$ axis component is negative because it is in the negative $x-$ axis direction. Now, the $y-$ axis component:

$$F_{2y} = -F_2 \sin \Theta_2$$
$$F_{2y} = -(50)(\sin 25°)$$
$$F_{2y} = -21.1 \text{ lbs}$$

The $y-$ axis component is also negative because of its direction.

The total component on the $x-$ axis is the sum of the $x-$ axis components:

$$F_x = F_{1x} + F_{2x}$$
$$F_x = (64.3) + (-45.3)$$
$$F_x = 19 \text{ lbs}$$

The total component on the $y-$ axis is the sum of the $y-$ axis components:

$$F_y = F_{1y} + F_{2y}$$
$$F_y = (76.6) + (-21.1)$$
$$F_y = 55.5 \text{ lbs}$$

As was stated before, these two forces can be replaced by one single force having the same effect. Before, this was done by drawing a parallelogram. It may also be done mathematically using the Pythagorean Theorem and trigonometry. Because the $x-$ and $y-$ components are at a right angle to each other, the sum of their squares is equal to the square of the resultant. For example, given the $x-$ component of 19 lbs and the $y-$ component of 55.5 lbs. found before, the resultant would be:

$$R = \sqrt{F_x^2 \times F_y^2}$$
$$R = \sqrt{(19)^2 + (55.5)^2}$$
$$R = 58.7 \text{ lbs}$$

This is only half the answer. The direction must also be known. Trigonometry can be used to determine the angle the resultant is to the $x-$ axis:

$$\tan \Theta = F_y/F_x$$
$$\tan \Theta = 55.5/19$$
$$\tan \Theta = 2.92$$

Therefore: $\Theta = 71.1$ degrees counterclockwise toward the positive $y-$ axis from the positive $x-$ axis.

Moment of a Force

The moment of a force, M, is a measure of how much a force tends to make a body rotate about an axis. The *moment of a force* is defined as the product of an applied force, F, and the length of the moment arm, d. The *moment arm* is the perpendicular distance from the pivot point, A, to the line of action of the force. In equation form:

$$M = Fd$$

Exhibit 25 shows the force, moment arm distance, and pivot point.

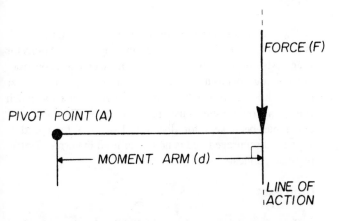

Exhibit 25. *A moment is defined as the force times the moment arm, which is the perpendicular distance to the line of force measured from the pivot point.*

The moment of a force has magnitude as well as direction. The magnitude depends on the force and its perpendicular distance from the pivot point. The direction depends on the position of the force to the pivot point and the direction of the force. The moment of a force will tend to rotate the body clockwise or counterclockwise.

In Exhibit 25, if the force, F, is 20 lbs and the moment arm, d, is 3 ft, the moment will be:

$$M = Fd$$
$$M = (20)(3)$$
$$M = 60 \text{ ft lbs clockwise}$$

Equilibrium

Newton's first law of motion states that a body will tend to remain in a state of rest or in uniform motion unless acted upon by an unbalanced force. If the forces are balanced, then the body is in equilibrium. This means that neither the body's translation nor rotational motion is changing.

Two conditions must exist for a body to be in equilibrium. The first condition for equilibrium is that the algebraic sum of all forces acting upon the body must be zero. This condition may be written:

$$\Sigma F = 0$$

The Greek letter Σ (sigma) means "the sum of". This may be still further broken down into the three dimensional components.

The first condition of equilibrium ensures that the translational motion of a body will not change. *Translational motion* refers to the movement of a body's center of mass (that is, rotation about the center of mass is not considered for translational motion). The second condition of equilibrium ensures that rotational motion is unchanged. This second condition of equilibrium is that the algebraic sum of the moments of all the forces acting upon a body is zero. This condition may be written

$$\Sigma M = 0$$

Usually, forces acting upward or to the right are positive, and forces acting downward or to the left are negative. Similarly, counterclockwise moments are usually positive, and clockwise moments are negative.

The two conditions of equilibrium can be useful for solving certain problems in *statics*. Static conditions occur when the body in question has no motion. In Exhibit 26, a box that weighs 2,000 lbs is placed 2 ft from the right end of a 10-ft beam (that is assumed for this example to have zero weight). To find out how much weight each end of the beam is supporting, the two conditions of equilibrium are used. First, a diagram, called a *free body diagram*, is drawn showing the

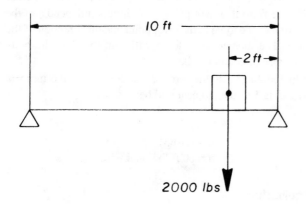

Exhibit 26. *The forces that must be applied to the beam to support the 2,000 lb object can be calculated using elementary statics.*

forces and distances (Exhibit 27). Second, the equations of translational equilibrium (up and down and sideways) are written:

$$\Sigma F_x = 0 \text{ (No forces in the } x- \text{ direction)}$$
$$\Sigma F_y = 0 = F_1 + F_2 - 2,000$$

or:

$$F_1 + F_2 = 2,000$$

Then the equation for rotational equilibrium is written using the left end as the pivot point:

$$\Sigma M_1 = 0 = (F_2)(10) - (2,000)(8)$$

or:

$$(F_2)(10) = (2,000)(8)$$

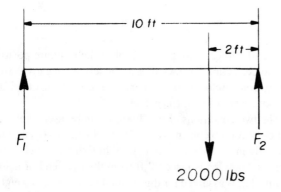

Exhibit 27. *A free body diagram of what is depicted in Exhibit 26 is illustrated above. The two supporting forces, F_1 and F_2, can be calculated by summing the forces and moments.*

solving:

$$F_2 = 1,600 \text{ lbs}$$

Going back to the first condition of equilibrium:

$$F_1 = 2,000 - F_2$$
$$F_1 = (2,000) - (1,600)$$
$$F_1 = 400 \text{ lbs}$$

10. STANDARD SYMBOLS

The *Traffic Accident Investigation Manual* has been well-received in the Western world. It has been used by engineers, police officers, attorneys, insurance adjusters, and others. The symbols for equations presented in the *Manual* in the past have followed neither U.S.A. nor international standards. A major effort has been ongoing at The Traffic Institute to move the accident reconstruction community toward the U.S.A. standard. It seems appropriate that a more standardized set of symbols be used. This would make it easier for individuals to understand other people's work. It clearly would make it easier for the beginning student in accident reconstruction, because everyone would be using the same symbols to mean the same thing. In addition, this would mean that equations would look the same.

In the U.S.A., the American National Standards Institute (ANSI) sets standards for many things. The American Society of Mechanical Engineers sponsored and published the standard entitled *Letter Symbols for Mechanics and Time-Related Phenomana.*[5] This is the ANSI and an International Standards Organization (ISO) standard that applies to symbols used in accident reconstruction. Exhibit 28 gives the uses for symbols recommended by ANSI that apply to accident reconstruction. The *Manual* follows nearly all these standard symbols. The exceptions are as follows:

Distance

The standard symbol for distance moved or length of path is *s*. This has been used in physics and engineering books for years. Also occasionally used is *d*. The accident reconstruction community has used *S* as a symbol for speed in miles per hour or kilometers per hour. It was decided that too much confusion could result in using *s* for distance. Thus, the symbol *d* has been kept for distance. Use of *S* for speed is strongly discouraged and is no longer used in current Traffic Institute publications.

Drag Factor

Drag factor, *f*, is not listed in Exhibit 28, and the ANSI standard has no mention of this quantity. It is defined in Topic 890. The standard does allow *f* to be used for coeffi-

Quantity	Symbol	SI Units		U. S. Units		ISO number
		Name	Symbol	Name	Symbol	
time, interval, duration	t	second	s	second	s	1-6.1
length, longest dimension	l	meter	m	foot	ft	1-3.1
breadth, width, short dimension	b	meter	m	foot	ft	1-3.2
height, vertical dimension	h	meter	m	foot	ft	1-3.3
thickness	d	meter	m	foot	ft	1-3.4
radius	r	meter	m	foot	ft	1-3.5
diameter	D	meter	m	foot	ft	1-3.6
length of path, distance moved	s	meter	m	foot	ft	1-3.7
velocity, speed	v	meter per second	m/s	feet per second	ft/s	1-9.1
acceleration	a	meter per second squared	m/s²	feet per second squared	ft/s²	1-10.1
angular velocity	ω	radian per second	rad/s	radian per second	rad/s	1-7.1
angular acceleration	α	radian per second squared	rad/s²	radians per second squared	rad/s²	1-8.1
angle, plane angle	αβτθ Δ	radian degree	o	radian	o	1-1.1
acceleration due to earth gravity	g	9.8 m/s²		32.2 ft/s²		1-10.2
mass	m	kilogram	kg	pound	lb	3-1.1
momentum	p,mv	kilogram meter per second	kg.m/s	pound feet per second	lb·ft/s	3-7.1
angular momentum	L	kilogram meter squared per second	kg m²/s	pound feet squared per second	lb·ft²/s	3-8.1
force	F	Newton kilogram-force	N kgf	pound-force	lbf	3-10.1
work, energy	$E (W)$	kilogram-force meter	kgf·m	foot pound-force	ft·lbf	3-24.1
coefficient of friction	μ					3-20.1
weight	W	Newton kilogram-force	N kgf	pound-force	lbf	3-10.2

Exhibit 28. *The American National Standards Institute has adopted the above symbols that apply in accident reconstruction problems.*

cient of friction. The symbol, *f, never* means coefficient of friction in the *Manual*.

Momentum and Weight

For these two quantities a change in upper and lower case is made. The symbol p is used for momentum and W is used for weight in Exhibit 28. In the *Manual* the upper case P is used for momentum and the lower case w is used for weight. W is used for work, which is the standard given in Exhibit 28.

11. SOURCES

Authors

Lynn B. Fricke is a traffic engineer specializing in traffic accident reconstruction. He has been with The Traffic Institute since 1975. In 1981, he became the director of the Institute's Accident Investigation Division.

Gary W. Cooper has been on the Traffic Institute staff since 1984 in the Accident Investigation Division. Formerly a member of the Indiana State Police, he graduated from Purdue University with an A.A.S. degree in Mechanical Engineering Technology.

References

1. Spiegal, Murray R., *College Algebra*. Schaum's Outline Series, McGraw-Hill, Inc., New York, NY.
2. Beiser, Arthur, *Applied Physics*. Schaum's Outline Series, McGraw-Hill, Inc. New York, NY.
3. Ayres, Frank Jr., *Trigonometry*. Schaum's Outline Series, McGraw-Hill, Inc. New York, NY.
4. Rich, Barnett, *Plane Geometry*. Schaum's Outline Series, McGraw-Hill, Inc. New York, NY.
5. American Society of Mechanical Engineers, *Letter Symbols for Mechanics and Time-Related Phenomena*. ASME, New York, NY.

Exhibits

The following are the sources of the exhibits used in this topic:

Baker, J. Stannard, San Diego, CA
  Table: Exhibit 28
Cooper, Gary W., Northwestern University Traffic Institute, Evanston, IL
  Figures for Exhibits 19 through 27
Fricke, Lynn B., Northwestern University Traffic Institute, Evanston, IL
  Figures for Exhibits 1 through 18

BASIC MOTION EQUATIONS USED IN TRAFFIC ACCIDENT RECONSTRUCTION

Topic 860 of the *Traffic Accident Investigation Manual*

by
Lynn B. Fricke

NORTHWESTERN UNIVERSITY TRAFFIC INSTITUTE

BASIC MOTION EQUATIONS USED
IN TRAFFIC ACCIDENT RECONSTRUCTION

1. INTRODUCTION

Kinematics

This topic is a discussion of the application of the basic equations of motion to traffic accident reconstruction problems. The branch of engineering mechanics which deals with the motion of particles, lines and bodies without consideration of the forces required to produce or maintain motion is called *kinematics*. Thus, this topic could be called the application of kinematics to accident reconstruction.

The equations discussed in this topic are derived from Topic 890. In some cases it may be useful for you to consult that topic.

Basic Three Equations

Essentially this topic illustrates the application of three equations.

$$a = \frac{v_e - v_i}{t}$$

$$d = v_i t + 1/2\, at^2$$

$$v_e^2 = v_i^2 + 2ad$$

where a = acceleration in ft/sec/sec
(or m/sec/sec)

d = distance in ft (or m)

t = time in sec

v_i = initial velocity in ft/sec
(or m/sec)

v_e = end velocity in ft/sec
(or m/sec)

Each of the three equations has four variables. Therefore, by algebraic manipulation, each of the variables can be solved for each equation. Experience in teaching this subject has shown that the equations given in Exhibit 1 provide the basis to solve many problems found in accident reconstruction. This topic illustrates the application of these 12 equations to various accident reconstruction problems.

2. FIVE BASIC QUANTITIES

Previously, the five quantities acceleration (a), time (t), distance (d), initial velocity (v_i) and end velocity (v_e) were presented. The subject of kinematics applied to traffic accident reconstruction issues is often limited to these variables. Understanding their relationships is essential in answering most accident reconstruction issues.

Distance

Distance is a linear measurement from some point. For reconstruction problems distance is measured relative to a coordinate system fixed on the earth. Depending on the issue, this may be, for example, from the point where a vehicle started to accelerate or decelerate. In U.S.A. units the dimension for distance is always feet. In the metric system distance is measured in meters.

Time

Time for both the metric and U.S.A. system is measured in seconds. There are instances where it may be useful to know the distance that could be traveled during an hour. However, the values for time in the equations listed in Exhibit 1 are always in seconds.

Velocity — Initial and End

Velocity is a rate of change of distance with respect to time. Thus velocity has the units of distance per time. The

TO FIND	WHEN GIVEN	EQUATION TO USE
ACCELERATION a (feet per second^2 or meters per second^2)	$t \quad v_i \quad v_e$	1. $a = \dfrac{v_e - v_i}{t}$
	$t \quad v_i \quad d$	2. $a = \dfrac{2d - 2v_i t}{t^2}$
	$v_i \quad v_e \quad d$	3. $a = \dfrac{v_e^2 - v_i^2}{2d}$
INITIAL VELOCITY v_i (feet per second or meters per second)	$t \quad a \quad v_e$	4. $v_i = v_e - at$
	$t \quad a \quad d$	5. $v_i = \dfrac{d}{t} - \dfrac{at}{2}$
	$a \quad v_e \quad d$	6. $v_i = \sqrt{v_e^2 - 2ad}$
END VELOCITY v_e (feet per second or meters per second)	$t \quad a \quad v_i$	7. $v_e = v_i + at$
	$a \quad v_i \quad d$	8. $v_e = \sqrt{v_i^2 + 2ad}$
DISTANCE d (feet or meters)	$t \quad a \quad v_i$	9. $d = v_i t + \frac{1}{2}at^2$
	$a \quad v_i \quad v_e$	10. $d = \dfrac{v_e^2 - v_i^2}{2a}$
	$t \quad v_i \quad v_e$	11. $d = \dfrac{t(v_i + v_e)}{2}$
TIME t (second)	$a \quad v_i \quad v_e$	12. $t = \dfrac{v_e - v_i}{a}$

NOTE: $a = gf$ where $g = 32.2$ fps^2 in USA and 9.81 mps^2 in Metric

Exhibit 1. Basic motion equations — use of only these 12 equations reduces the confusion that beginning students often have.

values used in the U.S.A. system are *ft/sec* and in the metric system are *m/sec*. If a vehicle is traveling at *constant velocity*, then

$$v = d/t$$

Clearly, the other two equations that apply for constant velocity are

$$d = v\,t$$
$$t = d/v$$

Do not make the mistake of using these three equations when velocity is not constant. If this is done you can expect that your answer will be wrong.

If velocity changes from one velocity to another, the first velocity is designated as initial velocity (v_i) and the second velocity is called end velocity (v_e). The change in velocity takes place over a time period, t.

Acceleration

Just as velocity is a rate, acceleration is also a rate. Acceleration is the rate of change of velocity with respect to time. Because velocity has the units of ft/sec (m/sec) and time has the unit of seconds, the units for acceleration are

$$\frac{velocity}{time} \quad \frac{ft/sec}{sec} \text{ or } \frac{m/sec}{sec}$$

This is often simply written as *ft/sec/sec* (*m/sec/sec*) or ft/sec^2 (m/sec^2). The ft/sec^2 (m/sec^2) term is the algebraic equivalent of *ft/sec/sec* (*m/sec/sec*).

An example of uniform acceleration may by useful to understand this concept. Consider the particle shown in Exhibit 2 to be accelerated at 5 ft/sec/sec. This means that after every second its velocity has increased by 5 ft/sec. At time equal to zero the velocity equals zero. After one second the velocity has increased from zero to five ft/sec. At time equal to two seconds the velocity has increased to 10 ft/sec.

Then clearly after three seconds of acceleration from zero ft/sec, its velocity equals 15 ft/sec. This is an example of positive acceleration, which simply means the velocity is increasing.

If a vehicle is slowing, then negative acceleration occurs. Exhibit 3 shows a vehicle slowing from an initial velocity of 80 ft/sec to an end velocity of 25 ft/sec during a time period of 2 seconds. The value for acceleration can be calculated from Equation (1) listed in Exhibit 1.

$$a = \frac{v_e - v_i}{t} = \frac{25 - 80}{2} = -27.5 \text{ ft/sec/sec}$$

The -27.5 ft/sec/sec means that after every second 27.5 ft/sec in velocity is lost. Thus after one second the velocity is reduced to 52.5 ft/sec (80 − 27.5 = 52.5). In the next second the velocity will again be reduced by 27.5 ft/sec to give 25 ft/sec (52.5 − 27.5 = 25).

3. PROBLEM SOLUTION APPROACH

There are more equations that can be used to solve time, distance, acceleration and velocity problems than those listed in Exhibit 1. It is, however, strongly recommended that beginning students, in particular, limit their confusion by only using those equations listed in Exhibit 1.

Drag Factor

In many problems you may be given drag factor, *f*, instead of acceleration. The first thing you should do is change this to acceleration. Drag factor is related to acceleration by the following equations:

$$a = fg$$
$$f = a/g$$

See Topic 890 for these derivations. In U.S.A. units g = 32.2 ft/sec/sec and in metric units g = 9.81 m/sec/sec. The quantity, *g*, is the acceleration of gravity.

$$a = \text{ft/sec/sec}$$

●	●	●	●
$t = 0$ sec	$t = 1$ sec	$t = 2$ sec	$t = 3$ sec
$v = 0$ ft/sec	$v = 5$ ft/sec	$v = 10$ ft/sec	$v = 15$ ft/sec

Exhibit 2. *The particle is accelerated at 5 ft/sec/sec. Each second the distance traveled is greater than the previous second.*

Drag factor does not have a positive or negative sign associated with it. Thus, you will have to remember, if you have deceleration (decreasing velocity), to add the negative sign to the accleration rate.

Units for Velocity

In many problems you may be given values for velocity (speed) in *mi/hr* or *km/hr*. Because the equations given in Exhibit 1 are for velocity in *ft/sec* for U.S.A. units or *m/sec* for metric units, it is important to change the *mi/hr* or *km/hr* immediately to *ft/sec* or *m/sec*.

To change from/to *mi/hr* to/from *ft/sec* requires multiplication or division by 1.47. The value 1.47 is simply 5,280 ft (the feet in a mile) divided by 3,600 sec (the seconds in an hour). This relationship is

$$ft/sec = (1.47)\,(mi/hr)$$

$$mi/hr = (ft/sec)\,/\,1.47$$

The change from/to *km/hr* to/from *m/sec* requires multiplication or division by 0.278. The value 0.278 is simply 1,000 m (the meters in a kilometer) divided by 3,600 sec (the seconds in an hour). These equations are

$$m/sec = 0.278\,(km/hr)$$
$$km/hr = (m/sec)\,/\,0.278$$

Analysis Procedure

You will notice that in Exhibit 1 the center column always has three known variables. To use any of the equations you need to know three variables. If you know three variables you can always solve for the other two. Remember there are only a total of five variables: a, v_i v_e, t and d. If you are given f, convert that to a. If the velocity (speed) is given in *mi/hr* or *km/hr* change that to *ft/sec* or *m/sec*.

The first thing you should do is summarize the known quantities. Do this in the correct units using the appropriate symbols (e.g., a, v_i, etc.). Secondly, decide what is required. This makes it easier to use the equations listed in Exhibit 1. After you have summarized what you know, decide what you want to know. Then it is simply a matter of finding the appropriate equation. It is always a good idea to write the equation you are going to use on your worksheet. Insert the known values into the equation. Then you merely complete the arithmetic to get the answer. Check to see if your answer makes sense. For example, if you just calculated the time it takes to accelerate from a stop across two lanes of traffic and your answer is 44 seconds, you clearly have made an error. Go back and recheck your work.

The remaining part of this topic has examples using the equations given in Exhibit 1. Try to follow the procedure given in the solution for these problems. Generally this approach has been found to be very successful.

4. EQUATIONS FOR ACCELERATION

Exhibit 1 lists three equations for acceleration. Any of the three can be used to calculate acceleration as long as the needed information is provided.

$$a = \frac{v_e - v_i}{t} \qquad (1)*$$

$$a = \frac{2d - 2v_i t}{t^2} \qquad (2)$$

$$a = \frac{v_e^{\,2} - v_i^{\,2}}{2d} \qquad (3)$$

Acceleration Knowing t, v_i and v_e

Problem Statement (U.S.A. Units):

If a vehicle accelerates from a stop to a velocity of 30 ft/sec in 6.5 seconds, calculate the acceleration of the vehicle.
Given:

$$v_i = 0 \text{ ft/sec}$$
$$v_e = 30 \text{ ft/sec}$$
$$t = 6.5 \text{ sec}$$

*The numbers for the equations refer to the equation numbers in Exhibit 1.

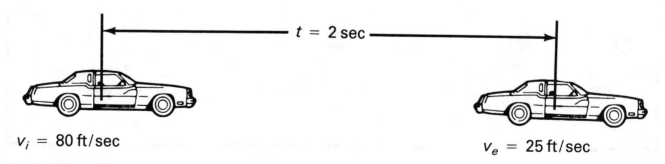

$v_i = 80 \text{ ft/sec}$ $v_e = 25 \text{ ft/sec}$

Exhibit 3. *When a car slows (decelerates) it has negative acceleration. In this case the car has lost 55 ft/sec in velocity over 2 sec in time.*

Required: a

Solution:

$$a = \frac{v_e - v_i}{t} = \frac{30 - 0}{6.5} = 4.6$$

Answer:

$$a = 4.6 \text{ ft/sec/sec}$$

Problem Statement (Metric Units):

If a vehicle accelerates from a stop to a velocity of 9 m/sec in 6.5 seconds, calculate the acceleration of the vehicle.

Given:

$$v_i = 0 \text{ m/sec}$$
$$v_e = 9 \text{ m/sec}$$
$$t = 6.5 \text{ sec}$$

Required: a

Solution:

$$a = \frac{v_e - v_i}{t} = \frac{9 - 0}{6.5} = 1.4$$

Answer:

$$a = 1.4 \text{ m/sec/sec}$$

Acceleration Knowing t, v_i, d

Problem Statement (U.S.A. Units):

If a vehicle decelerates over a distance of 75 feet from a velocity (speed) of 60 mi/hr. for 5 seconds, determine the vehicle's acceleration.

Given:

$$d = 75 \text{ ft.}$$
$$v_i = (60)(1.47) = 88 \text{ ft/sec}$$
$$t = 5 \text{ sec}$$

Required: a

Solution:

$$a = \frac{2d - 2v_i t}{t^2} = \frac{(2)(75) - 2(88)(5)}{5^2}$$

$$a = \frac{150 - 880}{25} = \frac{-730}{25} = -29.2$$

Answer:

$$a = -29.2 \text{ ft/sec/sec}$$
Note: the negative sign means
the vehicle is decelerating.

Problem Statement (Metric Units):

If a vehicle decelerates over a distance of 25 m from a velocity (speed) of 95 km/hr. for 5 sec, determine the vehicle's acceleration.

Given:

$$d = 25m$$
$$v_i = (95)(0.278) = 26.4 \text{ m/sec}$$
$$t = 5 \text{ sec}$$

Required: a

Solution:

$$a = \frac{2d - 2v_i t}{t^2} = \frac{(2)(25) - (2)(26.4)(5)}{5^2}$$

$$a = \frac{50 - 264}{25} = \frac{-214}{25} = -8.56$$

Answer:

$$a = -8.56 \text{ m/sec/sec}$$
Note: the negative sign means
the vehicle is decelerating.

Acceleration Knowing v_e, v_i and d

Problem Statement (U.S.A. Units):

A car slows from 88 ft/sec to 44 ft/sec over a distance of 130 ft. What is the vehicle's acceleration?

Given:

$$v_i = 88 \text{ ft/sec}$$
$$v_e = 44 \text{ ft/sec}$$
$$d = 130 \text{ ft.}$$

Required: a

Solution:

$$a = \frac{v_e^2 - v_i^2}{2d} = \frac{44^2 - 88^2}{(2)(130)}$$

$$a = \frac{1,936 - 7,744}{260} = \frac{-5,808}{260} = -22.3$$

Answer:

$$a = -22.3 \text{ ft/sec/sec}$$

Problem Statement (Metric Units):

A car slows from 30 m/sec to 15 m/sec over a distance of 45 m. What is the vehicle's acceleration?

Given:

$$v_i = 30 \text{ m/sec}$$
$$v_e = 15 \text{ m/sec}$$
$$d = 45 \text{ m.}$$

Required: a

Solution:

$$a = \frac{v_e^2 - v_i^2}{2d} = \frac{15^2 - 30^2}{(2)(45)}$$

$$a = \frac{225 - 900}{90} = \frac{-625}{90} = -7.5$$

Answer:

$$a = -7.5 \text{ m/sec/sec}$$

5. EQUATIONS FOR INITIAL VELOCITY

Exhibit 1 lists three equations for determining initial velocity.

$$v_i = v_e - at \qquad (4)$$

$$v_i = d/t - at/2 \qquad (5)$$

$$v_i = \sqrt{v_e^2 - 2ad} \qquad (6)$$

Note that Equations (4) and (5) have the value time, whereas Equation (6) does not. For that reason, Equation (6) is often very useful when values of time are unknown.

Initial Velocity Knowing v_e, a, and t

Problem Statement (U.S.A. Units):
A vehicle accelerates to 30 ft/sec for 5 sec at 4 ft/sec/sec. What is its initial velocity (speed) in mi/hr?
Given:

$$v_e = 30 \text{ ft/sec}$$
$$t = 5 \text{ sec}$$
$$a = 4 \text{ ft/sec/sec}$$

Required: v_i
Solution:

$$v_i = v_e - at = 30 - (4)(5) = 30 - 20$$
$$v_i = 10 \text{ ft/sec}$$

Answer:

$$v_i = 10 \text{ ft/sec} = (10)/1.47 = 6.8 \text{ mi/hr}$$

Problem Statement (Metric Units):
A vehicle accelerates to 10m/sec for 5 sec at 1.2 m/sec/sec. What is its initial velocity (speed) in km/hr?
Given:

$$v_e = 10 \text{ m/sec}$$
$$t = 5 \text{ sec}$$
$$a = 1.2 \text{ m/sec/sec}$$

Required: v_i
Solution:

$$v_i = v_e - at = 10 - (5)(1.2)$$
$$v_i = 10 - 6 = 4$$

Answer:

$$v_i = 4 \text{ m/sec} = 4/.278 = 14.4 \text{ km/hr}$$

Initial Velocity Knowing t, a, and d

Problem Statement (U.S.A. Units):
A car has slowed over a distance of 120 feet with a drag factor equal to 0.75 for 2.5 secs. What was its velocity immediately prior to slowing?
Given:

$$d = 120 \text{ ft}$$
$$a = fg = -(.75)(32.2) = -24.2 \text{ ft/sec/sec}$$
$$t = 2.5 \text{ sec}$$

Note: a must have the negative sign because you are told the vehicle is slowing.

Required: v_i
Solution:

$$v_i = d/t - at/2$$
$$= \frac{120}{2.5} - \frac{(-24.2)(2.5)}{2}$$
$$= 48 - (-30.2)$$
$$= 48 + 30.2$$
$$= 78.2$$

Answer:

$$v_i = 78.2 \text{ ft/sec}$$

Problem Statement (Metric Units):
A car has slowed over a distance of 40 m with a drag factor equal to 0.75 for 2.5 secs. What was its velocity immediately prior to slowing?
Given:

$$d = 40 \text{ m}$$
$$a = fg = -(.75)(9.8) = -7.35 \text{ m/sec}$$
$$t = 2.5 \text{ sec}$$

Note: a must have the negative sign because you are told the vehicle is slowing.

Required: v_i
Solution:

$$v_i = d/t - at/2$$
$$= \frac{40}{2.5} - \frac{(-7.35)(2.5)}{2}$$
$$= 16 - (-9.19)$$
$$= 16 + 9.19$$
$$v_i = 25.2$$

Answer:

$$v_i = 25.2 \text{ m/sec}$$

Initial Velocity Knowing a, v_e, d

Problem Statement (U.S.A. Units):
A vehicle decelerates to a stop over a distance of 150 ft with a drag factor of 0.80. What was the vehicle's initial velocity?
Given:

$$v_e = 0 \text{ ft/sec}$$
$$a = fg = -(.80)(32.2) = -25.8 \text{ ft/sec/sec}$$
$$d = 150 \text{ ft}$$

Required: v_i
Solution:

$$v_i = \sqrt{v_e^2 - 2ad}$$
$$v_i = \sqrt{0^2 - 2(-25.8)(150)}$$
$$v_i = \sqrt{7,740} = 88$$

Answer:

$$v_i = 88 \text{ ft/sec}$$

Problem Statement (Metric Units):
A vehicle decelerates to a stop over a distance of 50 m with a drag factor of 0.80. What was the vehicle's initial velocity?

Given:

$$v_e = 0$$
$$a = fg = -(.80)(9.8) = -7.84 \text{ m/sec/sec}$$
$$d = 50 \text{ m}$$

Required: v_i

Solution:

$$v_i = \sqrt{v_e^2 - 2ad}$$
$$v_i = \sqrt{0^2 - 2(-7.84)(50)}$$
$$v_i = \sqrt{784} = 28$$

Answer:

$$v_i = 28 \text{ m/sec}$$

6. EQUATIONS FOR END VELOCITY

Exhibit 1 lists two equations to calculate an end velocity.

$$v_e = v_i + at \qquad (7)$$

$$v_e = \sqrt{v_i + 2ad} \qquad (8)$$

Remember that end velocity simply means the velocity of a vehicle (or body, particle, etc.) after a time period of acceleration. This can be any time period that you specify. Examples of the two equations follow.

End Velocity Knowing t, a, v_i

Problem Statement (U.S.A. Units):
A vehicle accelerates from an initial velocity of 5 ft/sec at a rate of 4 ft/sec/sec. What is the vehicle's velocity after 2 secs of acceleration? After 3 secs of acceleration?

Given:

Part 1	Part 2
$v_i = 5$ ft/sec	$v_i = 5$ ft/sec
$a = 4$ ft/sec/sec	$a = 4$ ft/sec/sec
$t = 2$ sec	$t = 3$ sec

Required: v_e

Solution:

$$v_e = v_i + at \qquad\qquad v_e = v_i + at$$
$$= 5 + (4)(2) \qquad\qquad = 5 + (4)(3)$$
$$= 5 + 8 \qquad\qquad\qquad = 5 + 12$$
$$= 13 \qquad\qquad\qquad\quad = 17$$

Answer:

$$v_e = 13 \text{ ft/sec} \qquad v_e = 17 \text{ ft/sec}$$

Problem Statement (Metric Units):
A vehicle accelerates from an initial velocity of 3 m/sec at a rate of 2 m/sec/sec. What is the vehicle's velocity after 2 secs of acceleration? After 3 seconds of acceleration?

Given:

Part 1	Part 2
$v_i = 3$ m/sec	$v_i = 3$ m/sec
$a = 2$ m/sec/sec	$a = 2$ m/sec/sec
$t = 2$ sec	$t = 3$ sec

Required: v_e

Solution:

$$v_e = v_i + at \qquad\qquad v_e = v_i + at$$
$$= 3 + (2)(2) \qquad\qquad = 3 + (2)(3)$$
$$= 3 + 4 \qquad\qquad\qquad = 3 + 6$$
$$= 7 \qquad\qquad\qquad\quad = 9$$

Answer:

$$v_e = 7 \text{ m/sec} \qquad v_e = 9 \text{ m/sec}$$

End Velocity Knowing a, v_i and d

Problem Statement (U.S.A. Units):
A vehicle slows from an initial velocity of 90 ft/sec over a distance of 125 ft at a rate of 20 ft/sec/sec. What is its velocity at that point?

Given:

$$v_i = 90 \text{ ft/sec}$$
$$d = 125 \text{ ft}$$
$$a = -20 \text{ ft/sec/sec}$$

Required: v_e

Solution:

$$v_e = \sqrt{v_i^2 + 2ad}$$
$$v_e = \sqrt{90^2 + 2(-20)(125)}$$
$$v_e = \sqrt{8,100 - 5,000}$$
$$v_e = \sqrt{3,100}$$
$$v_e = 55.7$$

Answer:

$$v_e = 55.7 \text{ ft/sec}$$

Problem Statement (Metric Units)
A vehicle slows from an initial velocity of 30 m/sec over a distance of 40 m at a rate of 6 m/sec/sec. What is its velocity at that point?

Given:

$$v_i = 30 \text{ m/sec}$$
$$d = 40 \text{ m}$$
$$a = -6 \text{ m/sec/sec}$$

Required: v_e

Solution:

$$v_e = \sqrt{v_i^2 + 2ad}$$
$$v_e = \sqrt{30^2 + 2(-6)(40)}$$
$$v_e = \sqrt{900 - 480}$$
$$v_e = 20.5$$

Answer:

$$v_e = 20.5 \text{ m/sec}$$

7. EQUATIONS TO CALCULATE DISTANCE

Exhibit 1 gives three equations to use for calculating distance:

$$d = v_i t + 1/2 \, at^2 \qquad (9)$$

$$d = \frac{v_e^2 - v_i^2}{2a} \qquad (10)$$

$$d = \frac{t \,(v_i + v_e)}{2} \qquad (11)$$

As stated earlier in this topic, all the equations given in Exhibit 1 apply whether a vehicle accelerates to or from any velocity (not just to/from a stop). Equation (9) would also apply if you do not have acceleration. If acceleration equals zero, then constant velocity occurs. For Equation (9), the term $1/2 \, at^2$ drops out because a is zero. Thus, Equation (9) becomes

$$d = v_i t$$

In Equation (11), for *constant velocity*, $v_i = v_e$. Therefore, Equation (11) becomes

$$d = \frac{t \,(v_i + v_i)}{2} = \frac{t \,(2v_i)}{2}$$

$$d = v_i t$$

Again, this would *only* apply for constant velocity.

Distance When *t, a,* and v_i Are Known

Problem Statement (U.S.A. Units):
A vehicle decelerates from 100 ft/sec for 2.3 sec at a rate of 20 ft/sec/sec. What is the distance traveled?
Given:

$$v_i = 100 \text{ ft/sec}$$
$$t = 2.3 \text{ sec}$$
$$a = -20 \text{ ft/sec/sec}$$

Required: *d*
Solution:
$$d = v_i t + 1/2 \, at^2$$
$$= (100) \, (2.3) + 1/2 \, (-20) \, (2.3)^2$$
$$= 230 - 52.9$$

Answer:
$$d = 177 \text{ feet}$$

If the vehicle had not decelerated (i.e., had traveled at a constant velocity of 100 ft/sec), it would have traveled 230 ft. Because it decelerated, 52.9 ft. is subtracted from the 230 ft. to obtain the final answer of 177 ft.

Problem Statement (Metric Units):
A vehicle decelerates from 35 m/sec for 2.3 sec at a rate of 6 m/sec/sec. What is the distance traveled?
Given:

$$v_i = 35 \text{ m/sec}$$
$$t = 2.3 \text{ sec}$$
$$a = -6 \text{ m/sec/sec}$$

Required: *d*
Solution:
$$d = v_i t + 1/2 \, at^2$$
$$= (35) \, (2.3) + 1/2 \, (-6) \, (2.3)^2$$
$$= 80.5 - 15.9$$
$$= 64.6$$

Answer:
$$d = 64.6 \text{ m}$$

Distance When *a*, v_i and v_e Are Known

Problem Statement (U.S.A. Units):
A vehicle decelerates to a stop from a velocity (speed) of 60 mi/hr with a drag factor of 0.5. What is the distance required for it to stop?
Given:

$$v_e = 0$$
$$v_i = (1.47) \, (60) = 88 \text{ ft/sec}$$
$$a = fg = -(.5) \, (32.2) = 16.1 \text{ ft/sec/sec}$$

Required: *d*
Solution:

$$d = \frac{v_e^2 - v_i^2}{2a} = \frac{0^2 - 88^2}{2(-16.1)}$$

$$d = \frac{-7,744}{-32.2} = 240$$

Answer:
$$d = 240 \text{ ft}$$

Problem Statement (Metric Units):
A vehicle decelerates to a stop from a velocity (speed) of 90 km/hr with a drag factor of 0.5. What is the distance required for it to stop?
Given:

$$v_e = 0$$
$$v_i = (90) \, (.278) = 25 \text{ m/sec}$$
$$a = fg = -(.5) \, (9.8) = -4.9 \text{ m/sec/sec}$$

Required: *d*
Solution:

$$d = \frac{v_e^2 - v_i^2}{2a} = \frac{0^2 - 25^2}{2(-4.9)}$$

$$d = \frac{-625}{-9.8} = 63.8$$

Answer:
$$d = 63.8 \text{ m}$$

Distance When t, v_i and v_e Are Known

Problem Statement (U.S.A. Units):
A car falls off a cliff. Its initial vertical velocity equals zero. Its vertical velocity after 2 secs is 64.4 ft/sec. What vertical distance did it travel?
Given:
$$t = 2 \text{ sec}$$
$$v_e = 64.4 \text{ ft/sec}$$
$$v_i = 0$$

Required: d
Solution:
$$d = t \frac{(v_i + v_e)}{2}$$

$$d = (2) \frac{(0 + 64.4)}{2} = \frac{128.8}{2} = 64.4$$

Answer:
$$d = 64.4 \text{ ft}$$

Problem Statement (Metric Units):
A car falls off a cliff. Its initial vertical velocity equals zero. Its vertical velocity after 2 secs is 19.6 m/sec. What vertical distance did it travel?
Given:
$$t = 2 \text{ sec}$$
$$v_e = 19.6 \text{ m/sec}$$
$$v_i = 0$$

Required: d
Solution:

$$d = \frac{t(v_i + v_e)}{2}$$

$$d = \frac{2(0 + 19.6)}{2} = 19.6$$

Answer:
$$d = 19.6 \text{ m}$$

8. EQUATION TO CALCULATE TIME

One equation is given in Exhibit 1 to calculate time to accelerate from one velocity to another.

$$t = \frac{v_e - v_i}{a} \qquad (12)$$

There are other equations that can be used to calculate time, but they are usually complicated or are for the special cases of to/from a stop. Experience in teaching this subject suggests that students make fewer errors by just using the equation listed here.

If you have a case of *constant* velocity, the equation $t = d/v$ applies. Do *not* use this equation if you have acceleration, because you will obtain the wrong answer. Example problems of these two equations follow.

Time When a, v_i and v_e Are Known

Problem Statement (U.S.A. Units):
A vehicle slows from 60 mi/hr to 30 mi/hr with a drag factor of 0.70. What is the time required to do this?
Given:
$$v_i = (60)(1.47) = 88 \text{ ft/sec}$$
$$v_e = (30)(1.47) = 44 \text{ ft/sec}$$
$$a = fg = -(.70)(32.2) = -22.5 \text{ ft/sec/sec}$$

Required: t
Solution:

$$t = \frac{v_e - v_i}{a} = \frac{44 - 88}{-22.5} = \frac{-44}{-22.5} = 1.96$$

Answer:
$$t = 1.96 \text{ sec.}$$

Problem Statement (Metric Units):
A vehicle slows from 100 km/hr to 50 km/hr with a drag factor of 0.70. What is the time required to do this?
Given:
$$v_i = (100)(.278) = 27.8 \text{ m/sec}$$
$$v_e = (50)(.278) = 13.9 \text{ m/sec}$$
$$a = fg = -(.70)(9.8) = -6.86 \text{ m/sec/sec}$$

Required: t
Solution:

$$t = \frac{v_e - v_i}{a} = \frac{13.9 - 27.8}{-6.86}$$

$$t = \frac{-13.9}{-6.86} = 2.03 \text{ sec}$$

Answer:
$$t = 2.03 \text{ sec.}$$

Time When Velocity Is Constant

Problem Statement (U.S.A. Units):
A pedestrian is walking at a velocity of 4 ft/sec. He travels a distance of 20 feet. What is the time required?
Given:
$$v = 4 \text{ ft/sec (constant velocity)}$$
$$d = 20 \text{ ft}$$
Required: t
Solution:
$$t = d/v = 20/4 = 5$$

Answer:

$$t = 5 \text{ sec}$$

Problem Statement (Metric Units):

A pedestrian is walking at a velocity of 1.3 m/sec. He travels a distance of 10 m. What is the time required?

Given:

$$v = 1.3 \text{ m/sec (constant velocity)}$$
$$d = 10 \text{ m}$$

Required: t

Solution:

$$t = d/v$$
$$t = 10/1.3 = 7.7 \text{ sec}$$

Answer:

$$t = 7.7 \text{ sec}$$

9. GENERAL TRAFFIC ACCIDENT RECONSTRUCTION PROBLEMS

Relatively simple examples have been given for the 12 equations listed in Exhibit 1. More complicated example problems are now presented. When you are trying to work your own problems, you may find it useful to approach them in the way the following problems are analyzed. First, determine what you know. You must have an idea where your starting point is. Second, decide what you want to know. Third, select the appropriate equations to get you from what you know to what you want to know. Always write the equations you use. This will make it easier to check your work at a later time.

The solutions given to the problems are only *a* solution, not *the* solution. Nearly always there are several ways to work a problem in these solutions.

Problem 1 — Uniform Acceleration

A vehicle accelerates from a stop over a distance of 72 feet in 6 seconds.

Question 1 — What is the vehicle's velocity after eight seconds of acceleration from a stop if the acceleration is uniform over the whole eight seconds?

Question 2 — What is the distance traveled in the first eight seconds?

Question 3 — What is the vehicle's velocity (speed) in mi/hr after the first three seconds of acceleration?

Question 4 — How much time does it take to accelerate over the first 36 feet?

Question 1 Solution:

Given: The statement of Question 1 only gives two values $v_i = 0$ and $t = 8 \text{ sec}$. Remember, unless it is a constant velocity condition, it's always necessary to know three variables before you can work the problem. Therefore, it is necessary to look at the first part of the problem statement, where we are given

$$v_i = 0 \text{ ft/sec}$$
$$d = 72 \text{ ft}$$
$$t = 6 \text{ sec}$$

From these three values, acceleration can be calculated; this is the same acceleration up to the 8 seconds of acceleration given in Question 1.

Required: a

Solution:

$$a = \frac{2d - 2v_i t}{t^2} \tag{2}$$

$$a = \frac{(2)(72) - 2(0)(6)}{6^2} = \frac{144 - 0}{36}$$

Answer:

$$a = 4 \text{ ft/sec/sec}$$

Now Question 1 can be answered, because three values are now known:

Given:

$$a = 4 \text{ ft/sec/sec}$$
$$v_i = 0 \text{ ft/sec}$$
$$t = 8 \text{ sec}$$

Required: v_e

Solution:

$$v_e = v_i + at \tag{7}$$
$$= 0 + (4)(8)$$

Answer:

$$v_e = 32 \text{ ft/sec}$$

Question 2 Solution:

Given:

$$v_i = 0 \text{ ft/sec}$$
$$a = 4 \text{ ft/sec/sec}$$
$$t = 8 \text{ sec}$$

Required: d

Solution:

$$d = v_i t + 1/2 \, at^2 \tag{9}$$
$$d = (0)(8) + 1/2 (4)(8^2)$$
$$d = 128$$

Answer:

$$d = 128 \text{ ft}$$

Question 3 Solution:

Given:

$$v_i = 0 \text{ ft/sec}$$
$$a = 4 \text{ ft/sec/sec}$$
$$t = 3 \text{ sec}$$

Required: v_e in mi/hr

Solution:

$$v_e = v_i + at \tag{7}$$
$$= 0 + (4)(3)$$
$$= 12$$

Answer:
$$v_e = 12/1.47 = 8.2 \text{ mi/hr}$$

Question 4 Solution:

Given:
$$d = 36 \text{ ft}$$
$$v_i = 0 \text{ ft/sec}$$
$$a = 4 \text{ ft/sec/sec}$$

Required: t

Solution:

The equation given for t is

$$t = \frac{v_e - v_i}{a} \qquad (12)$$

Clearly v_e is not known. Because three variables are known v_e can be calculated.

$$v_e = \sqrt{v_i^2 + 2ad} \qquad (8)$$
$$v_e = \sqrt{0^2 + (2)(4)(36)}$$
$$v_e = 17 \text{ ft/sec}$$

Now t can be solved: for

$$t = \frac{v_e - v_i}{a}$$

$$t = \frac{17 - 0}{4} = 4.25$$

Answer:
$$t = 4.25 \text{ sec}$$

Problem 2 — Skidding Over Two Surfaces

A vehicle skids to a stop over two surfaces. The first surface has a drag factor of 0.85 and the second surface has a drag factor of 0.60. The vehicle skidded 85 ft over the first surface and 45 ft over the second surface.

Question 1. What is the vehicle's velocity (speed) in mi/hr when the skidding first occurred?

Question 2. How much time did it take the vehicle to skid over both surfaces?

Question 3. What is the vehicle's velocity after skidding 100 ft?

Question 1 Solution:

In this case it may be useful to draw a diagram to summarize what is given. This is shown in Exhibit 4. This problem must be worked "backward." That is, start from the final position of the vehicle to calculate its velocity when it first enters the second surface. Then three quantities are known.

Given:
$$v_e = 0$$
$$a = fg = -.60 (32.2) = -19.3 \text{ ft/sec/sec}$$
$$d = 45 \text{ ft}$$

Required: v_i
Solution:
$$v_i = \sqrt{v_e^2 - 2ad} \qquad (6)$$
$$v_e = \sqrt{0^2 - 2(-19.3)(45)}$$
$$v_i = \sqrt{1,737} = 41.7 \text{ ft/sec}$$

Answer:
The velocity, 41.7 ft/sec, is the velocity where the vehicle starts to skid on the second surface. It is also the end velocity after skidding on the first surface. Thus, on the first surface these quantities are now known.

Given:
$$v_e = 41.7 \text{ ft/sec}$$
$$d = 85 \text{ ft}$$
$$a = fg - .85 (32.2) = -27.4 \text{ ft/sec/sec}$$

Using the same equation as before, but now over the first surface, allows the initial velocity at first skidding to be calculated.

Required: v_i
Solution:

$$v_i = \sqrt{v_e^2 - 2ad}$$
$$v_i = \sqrt{41.7^2 - 2(-27.4)(85)}$$
$$v_i = \sqrt{1,739 + 4,658}$$
$$v_i = 80 \text{ ft/sec}$$
$$80/1.47 = 54.4 \text{ mi/hr}$$

Answer:
$$v_i = 54.4 \text{ mi/hr}$$

Question 2 Solution:

To solve this problem, Equation (12) is used. This must be used for each surface, and then the two values of time are added.

Surface 1
Given:
$$v_i = 80 \text{ ft/sec}$$
$$v_e = 41.7 \text{ ft/sec}$$
$$a = -27.4 \text{ ft/sec/sec}$$

Required: t
Solution:
$$t = \frac{v_e - v_i}{a} = \frac{41.7 - 80}{-27.4} = 1.40 \text{ sec}$$

Surface 2

Given:

$$v_i = 41.7 \text{ ft/sec}$$
$$v_e = 0$$
$$a = -19.3 \text{ ft/sec/sec}$$

Required: t
Solution:

$$t = \frac{v_e - v_i}{a} = \frac{0 - 41.7}{-19.3}$$

$$= 2.16 \text{ sec}$$
$$\text{total } t = 1.40 + 2.16 = 3.56 \text{ sec}$$

Answer:

Total skidding time = 3.56 sec

Question 3 Solution:

The question asks the vehicle's velocity after skidding the first 100 feet. Referring to Exhibit 4, this means that 30 ft are left to skid on the second surface (85 ft on the first surface plus 15 ft on the second surface leaves 30 ft on the second surface: 45 minus 15 equals 30). Thus, the easiest way to work the problem is to use the following three given variables:

Given:

$$v_e = 0 \text{ ft/sec}$$
$$d = 30 \text{ ft}$$
$$a = -19.3 \text{ ft/sec/sec}$$

Required: v_i
Solution:

$$v_i = \sqrt{v_e^2 - 2ad} \qquad (6)$$
$$v_i = \sqrt{0^2 - 2(-19.3)(30)}$$

Answer:

$$v_i = 34 \text{ ft/sec}$$

Another approach is to calculate the end velocity knowing the initial velocity at the beginning of the second surface. For this approach distance equals 15 ft, because an additional 15 ft are required to reach a total skidding distance of 100 ft. The problem would then be solved as follows:

Given:

$$v_i = 41.7 \text{ ft/sec}$$
$$a = -19.3 \text{ ft/sec}$$
$$d = 15 \text{ ft}$$

Required: v_e
Solution:

$$v_e = \sqrt{v_i^2 + 2ad}$$
$$v_e = \sqrt{41.7^2 + 2(-19.3)(15)}$$
$$v_e = \sqrt{1{,}739 - 579}$$

Answer:

$$v_e = 34 \text{ ft/sec}$$

Problem 3 — Car/Pedestrian Collision

A car skids for 130 ft and hits a pedestrian. The car continues to skid another 90 ft before coming to a stop. These distances apply to the vehicle's center of mass. The total skidding distance is 220 ft (130 + 90 = 220; see Exhibit 5). The vehicle's drag factor during skidding was 0.85. The pedestrian walked from the pavement edge northbound a distance of 14 ft and was then struck by the car. The pedestrian's walking velocity was 4 ft/sec.

Question 1. What was the initial velocity of the car?

Question 2. What was the vehicle's velocity when the pedestrian was struck?

Question 3. How far was the car from the pedestrian when the pedestrian first stepped onto the pavement?

Question 1 Solution:

Given:

$$v_e = 0$$
$$a = fg = -.85(32.2) = -27.4 \text{ ft/sec/sec}$$
$$d = 220 \text{ ft}$$

Required:
$$v_i$$
Solution:
$$v_i = \sqrt{v_e^2 + 2ad}$$
$$v_i = \sqrt{0^2 - 2(-27.4)(220)}$$

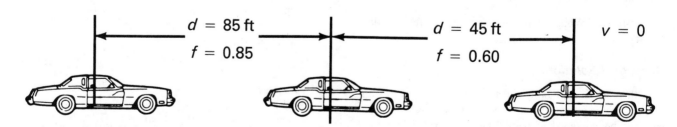

$$d = 85 \text{ ft} \qquad d = 45 \text{ ft} \qquad v = 0$$
$$f = 0.85 \qquad f = 0.60$$

Exhibit 4. *Skidding over two surfaces — a different value of acceleration (deceleration) occurs over the two surfaces. The problem must be treated as two parts starting at the end and working "backward".*

Answer:
$$v_i = 110 \text{ ft/sec or } 74.7 \text{ mi/hr}$$

For this problem it is assumed that no slowing results from the car/pedestrian collisions. Of course, this is not totally true; the collision does reduce the car's speed slightly.

Question 2 Solution:

The car has 90 ft left to skid to a stop when the pedestrian is hit. Thus the following variables apply.

Given:
$$v_e = 0 \text{ ft/sec}$$
$$a = -27.4 \text{ ft/sec/sec}$$
$$d = 90 \text{ ft}$$

Required: v_i
Solution:
$$v_i = \sqrt{v_e^2 - 2ad}$$
$$v_i = \sqrt{0^2 - 2(-27.4)(90)}$$

Answer:
$$v_i = 70.2 \text{ ft/sec or } 47.8 \text{ mi/hr}$$

Question 3 Solution:

The third question is clearly more difficult than the other two questions. Consider the following approach to this problem. What the question asks is where was the car relative to the first contact position of the pedestrian when the pedestrian stepped onto the pavement. The time the pedestrian walks to the collision point is the same time the car travels to the collision point. Therefore, first calculate the time for the pedestrian to walk to the collision point given a constant velocity of 4 ft/sec and a distance of 14 ft.
Given: $d = 14 \text{ ft}$
$v = 4 \text{ ft/sec}$

Required: t
Solution:
$$t = d/v$$
$$t = 14/4$$
Answer:
$$t = 3.5 \text{ sec}$$

All that is to be done now is to determine where the car was 3.5 sec before the collision.
First, calculate the time it took to skid the 130 ft before the collision:
Given:
$$v_i = 110 \text{ ft/sec}$$
$$v_e = 70.2 \text{ ft/sec}$$
$$a = -27.4 \text{ ft/sec/sec}$$

Required: t
Solution:
$$t = \frac{v_e - v_i}{a}$$

$$t = \frac{70.2 - 110}{-27.4} = \frac{-39.8}{-27.4}$$

Answer:
$$t = 1.45 \text{ sec}$$

Thus, of the 3.50 seconds that the pedestrian is walking toward impact, the car is skidding for 1.45 sec. During the remaining time of 2.05 sec (3.50 − 1.45 = 2.05), the car can be assumed to be traveling at the velocity calculated at the beginning of the skid (110 ft/sec). Therefore, the distance traveled for 2.05 seconds is

Given: $v = 110 \text{ ft/sec}$
$t = 2.05 \text{ sec}$

Required: d
Solution:
$$d = vt$$
$$d = (110)(2.05)$$
Answer:
$$d = 225 \text{ ft}$$

The distance the car is from its first contact position, when the pedestrian first steps onto the pavement, is therefore the sum of 225 ft plus 130 ft (distance skidded before collision).
$$total\ distance = 225 + 130$$
Answer:
$$total\ distance = 355 \text{ ft}$$

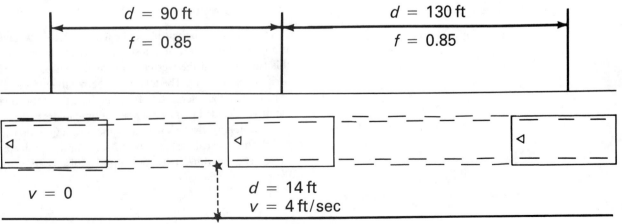

Problem 4 — Acceleration Across Street

Exhibit 6 illustrates the problem that is to be solved. A car accelerates from a stop across the intersection. An eastbound and a westbound vehicle travel at a constant speed of 55 mi/hr. The length of the northbound vehicle and the distances for it to travel are shown in Exhibit 6.

Question 1. If the northbound vehicle accelerates at 4 ft/sec/sec, how much time is required for the car to get halfway across the east-west street and completely across the street?

Question 2. How far should the stopped northbound vehicle driver be able to see the westbound vehicle from the intersection if the northbound vehicle just cleared it as it crossed the east-west street? Assume the westbound vehicle has a constant speed of 55 miles per hour.

Question 3. If the eastbound vehicle was 150 ft from the northbound vehicle when the northbound vehicle started to move, what would be the required acceleration of the northbound car if the eastbound car continued traveling at a constant speed of 55 mi/hr?

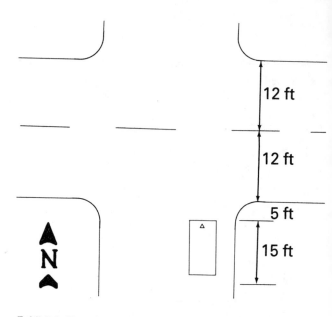

Exhibit 6. *The car starts from a stop. Remember to include the length of the accelerating car when considering the distance the car has to travel to clear the intersection.*

Question 1 Solution:

The distance the northbound car must travel to clear half the distance across the road is the sum of the length of the car plus the distance from the car front to the projected road edge plus half the width of the road.

$$d = 15 + 5 + 12 = 32 \text{ ft}$$

The other variables that are known are the initial velocity and the acceleration. The following quantities are known.

Given:
$$d = 32 \text{ ft}$$
$$v_i = 0 \text{ ft/sec}$$
$$a = 4 \text{ ft/sec/sec}$$

Required: t
Solution:

First, calculate the end velocity; then use that measurement to calculate the time.

$$v_e = \sqrt{v_i^2 + 2ad} \qquad (8)$$
$$= \sqrt{0^2 + (2)(4)(32)}$$

$$v_e = 16 \text{ ft/sec}$$

$$t = \frac{v_e - v_i}{a}$$

$$= \frac{16 - 0}{4}$$

Answer:
$t = 4$ sec to travel halfway across the street

To travel completely across the street the car must travel an additional 12 ft, or a total of 44 ft.

Given:
$$d = 44 \text{ ft}$$
$$v_i = 0 \text{ ft/sec}$$
$$a = 4 \text{ ft/sec/sec}$$

Required: t
Solution:

$$v_e = \sqrt{v_i^2 + 2ad} \qquad (8)$$
$$v_e = \sqrt{0^2 + 2(4)(44)}$$
$$v_e = 18.8 \text{ ft/sec}$$

$$t = \frac{v_e - v_i}{a} = \frac{18.8 - 0}{4}$$

Answer:
$t = 4.7$ sec to travel completely across the street

Question 2 Solution:

The driver of the northbound car must decide whether it is appropriate to start from a stop to cross the street. During this time interval the westbound vehicle continues to travel at 55 miles per hour. The total time the westbound vehicle is approaching the intersection from the time the stopped vehicle driver decided to go would be the time to cross the street plus the stopped driver's reaction time. From Question 1, the travel time was calculated to be 4.7 sec. For this problem use 1-sec reaction time. (Reaction time is discussed in other topics of the *Manual*).

$$Total\ time\ =\ 4.7\ +\ 1.0\ =\ 5.7\ sec$$

The westbound vehicle travels at a constant speed of 55 mi/hr. Thus, the distance required for the northbound vehicle to see the oncoming westbound vehicle is

Given: $t = 5.7$ sec
$\quad\quad v = 35$

Required: d
Solution:
$$d = vt$$
$$d = (1.47)\ (55)\ (5.7)$$
Answer:
$$d = 460\ ft$$

Question 3 Solution:

The time required for the eastbound vehicle to travel 150 ft. at a constant speed of 55 mi/hr can be calculated.

Given: $v = 55$ mi/hr
$\quad\quad d = 150$ ft

Required: t
Solution:
$$t = d/v$$
$$t = \frac{150}{(1.47)\ (55)}$$
Answer:
$$t = 1.86\ sec$$

Thus, the northbound car has started to move when the eastbound car is 1.86 sec from their possible collision point. The northbound car must travel 32 ft (see Question 1 Solution). The northbound car's initial velocity is zero.

Given:
$$v_i = 0\ ft/sec$$
$$d = 32\ ft$$
$$t = 1.86\ sec$$

Required: a
Solution:

$$a = \frac{2d - 2v_i t}{t^2} \quad\quad\quad (2)$$

$$a = \frac{(2)\ (32) - (2)\ (0)\ (1.86)}{1.86^2}$$

$$a = \frac{64}{3.46}$$

Answer:
$$a = 18.5\ ft/sec/sec$$

This required acceleration greatly exceeds the normal acceleration of passenger cars.

10. SOURCES

Author

Lynn B. Fricke is a traffic engineer specializing in traffic accident reconstruction. He has been with The Traffic Institute since 1975. In 1981, he became the director of the Institute's Accident Investigation Division.

Exhibits

The following are the sources of the exhibits
used in this topic:
Cooper, Gary W., Traffic Institute, Evanston, IL
  Chart: 1
Fricke, Lynn B., Traffic Institute, Evanston, IL
  Diagrams: 2, 3, 4, 5, 6

UNDERSTANDING VEHICLE BEHAVIOR IN COLLISIONS

Topic 861 of the *Traffic Accident Investigation Manual*

by
J. Stannard Baker
and
Lynn B. Fricke

NORTHWESTERN UNIVERSITY TRAFFIC INSTITUTE

UNDERSTANDING VEHICLE BEHAVIOR IN COLLISIONS

1. OBJECTIVE

The purpose of this topic is to explain what the damage done to vehicles can teach you about how vehicles are pushed around in collisions. Technically, one might think of this as the kinetics of impacts because it deals with the action of forces in producing or changing motions of masses. This topic does not involve numerical treatment, therefore, it is sometimes spoken of as *qualitative* dynamics of traffic accidents.

Importance

Understanding how vehicles behave in collisions is a very important step in most traffic-accident reconstruction, often the most important step. It can, and usually should be, done first without considering the location of the accident on the road, what drivers did, or marks on the road made by the impact. In fact, study of vehicle movements in collisions is often the key to discovering where on the road an impact took place and driver actions involved. Hence, deciding how vehicles came together and finally separated in a collision is often the first step in thinking about what happened in an accident. It is always a matter that requires very careful study.

Data Required

Information needed for this study relates mainly to vehicle damage:

1. *Personal inspection* of vehicles, including measurements of collapse, is helpful when it is possible. This inspection may be combined with vehicle examination for other purposes.
2. *Reports by others* of vehicle examination, preferably in writing, but possibly verbal.
3. *Photographs* are very useful and important, especially if properly made (see Topic 836).
4. *Dimensions* of the vehicle from actual measurements or published data.

5. *Sometimes vehicle parts* such as wheels, bumpers, lamps, and paint chips. These help in identifying contact-damage areas, especially when more than two vehicles are involved.

What informants have to say about a collision must always be considered, but judiciously. The events people see, hear, and feel during the second before collision, a fraction of a second during collision, and another second afterward give a brief and unexpected series of sensations. This is true for both occupants of vehicles and of witnesses in the vicinity. What is accurately remembered of these impressions may represent no more than a fragment of the events which actually occurred. Vivid imaginations and plausible suggestions from others soon fill in, correctly or incorrectly, many of the missing details. Moreover, how much an informant will reveal concerning what has entered his mind about the collision depends on who is asking the questions and for what purpose. Consequently, begin by forming your own opinion about how a collision occurred, by considering the physical signs of what happened rather than what informants have to say about the incident.

Especially for this part of accident reconstruction, ignore conclusions that others seem eager to obtain. Preconceived ideas almost irresistibly lead thinking along certain lines, and that is a pitfall of accident reconstruction to be earnestly avoided. It bears repeating here, however, that how far one can go in reconstructing an accident depends greatly on the quality and quantity of data which have been collected.

Systematic Approach

Topic 820 explains how systematic examination of a vehicle after a crash can lead to a simple diagram of deformation, contact damage, and impact thrust. Exhibit 1 is an example of vehicle damage observed and the resulting diagram.

The present topic, 861, carries the interpretation another important step forward. It explains how thrust forces make

Exhibit 1. *An example of damage to a vehicle and the corresponding diagram showing deformation, contact damage, thrust direction, and point of application. The diagram represents the situation at maximum engagement. Note that the whole front has been pushed a foot to the right. Contact damage extends across three quarters of the front from the left side.*

2. ELEMENTS OF A COLLISION

Three Events

An impact collision is a whole series of events in which two objects are in contact with each other. Three of these events are especially noteworthy (Exhibit 2):

1. *First contact* is the beginning of a collision. At that instant, force begins to develop between the objects.
2. *Maximum engagement.* Consider the very simple, centered-impact, fixed-object collision diagrammed in Exhibit 2. From first contact, penetration and force increase to maximum engagement. For an instant at maximum engagement with a fixed object, the vehicle, and particularly the part of it in contact with the object struck, stops. Then, for that instant, the vehicle and object are at the same speed, zero. Thereafter, due to elasticity of the material of which the vehicle is made, the vehicle moves backward. Penetration and force decrease and velocity backward increases until the last contact, when the objects in collision disengage and separate. In general terms, the greatest penetration or collapse determines the greatest force; and the amount of force determines the change in speed, in this case, deceleration. Motor-vehicle bodies have

vehicles move during impact. This understanding of vehicle behavior is a necessary foundation for many speed estimates in collisions and often also for locating collision positions on the road.

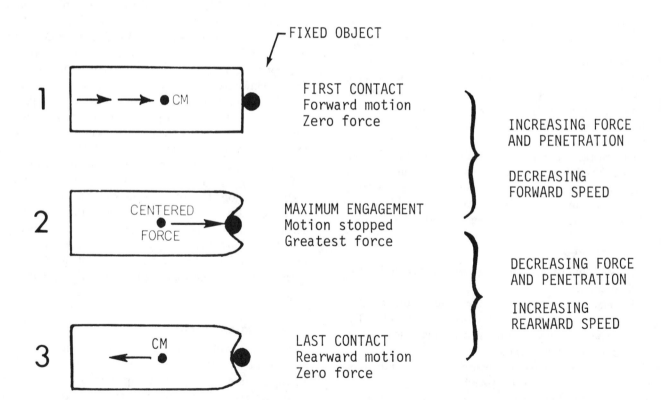

Exhibit 2. *Impact of a vehicle or other object in collision begins with first contact, progresses to maximum engagement, and ends with last contact at separation. A complete impact is illustrated here. In a complete impact, motion between the areas in contact momentarily ceases. This is a centered impact.*

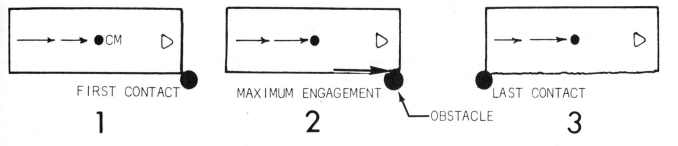

FIRST CONTACT
1

MAXIMUM ENGAGEMENT
2

OBSTACLE

LAST CONTACT
3

Exhibit 3. *When areas in contact continue to move with respect to each other during impact, the impact is incomplete. A sideswipe is an incomplete impact.*

very little elasticity so the amount of rebound (restitution) after maximum engagement is practically nil.

3. *Separation* or stopping if the vehicles or other objects remain engaged occurs when force between the colliding objects becomes zero. Virtually all of the deformation at maximum engagement remains as vehicle damage.

Two Kinds of Impact

Many people mistakenly think of impact as only the first contact or, sometimes as maximum engagement. *Impact* and *collision* mean essentially the same thing just like *speed* and *velocity* signify practically the same idea.

Impacts may be divided into two classes:

1. *Full impact* in which some part of the colliding surfaces attain the same speed during impact. (If the colliding bodies remain in contact when motion ceases, the impact is full because the parts in contact are at the same speed. Motion between parts in contact will

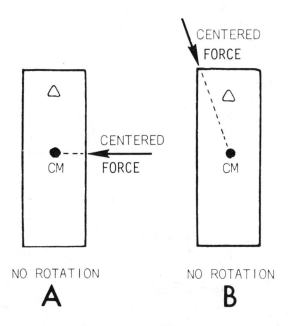

CENTERED
FORCE

CENTERED
FORCE

CM

CM

NO ROTATION
A

NO ROTATION
B

Exhibit 4. *A thrust or force directed toward the center of mass from any direction may cause an object to accelerate or decelerate, but it will not make the object rotate.*

cease momentarily. Full impact does not mean that either of the objects in collision necessarily stopped on the ground. Exhibit 2 is a diagram of a full impact.

2. *Partial impact* in which no substantial parts of colliding surfaces attain the same speed during collision. (All partial impacts involve disengagement of colliding surfaces. Exhibit 3 is a diagram of a partial impact. The parts of the vehicle engaged are not strong enough to stop any substantial part of the vehicle. It continues to move onward until disengagement.)

In opposite-direction collisions, a full impact is often loosely referred to as head-on, whereas a partial impact is spoken of as a sideswipe.

In motor-vehicle accidents, one of the colliding objects is a motor vehicle. The other may be another motor vehicle, a pedestrian, cyclist, fixed object, or the roadway surface. In some accidents the same vehicle is involved in more than one collision. Each collision can be considered more or less separately.

3. MOVEMENTS DURING IMPACT

Impacts involve forces between a vehicle and some other object. These forces modify the speed of the vehicle, its direction, its rotation, or all of these, just as friction forces change the speed or direction of a vehicle in braking and turning. But collision forces are ordinarily much more violent. Friction forces often leave signs on the road surface of what happened; collision forces also leave signs: damage to vehicles, injury to pedestrians, and scars in the road or roadside. Now, to begin with, consider the effect of collision forces on a vehicle.

In the diagrams used to illustrate the following discussions, a solid outline indicates initial and final positions of a vehicle and a dotted or dashed outline indicates intermediate or subsequent positions. A shaded or hatched area represents the position of a standing vehicle.

Right side of a vehicle means the passenger's side; left means the driver's side (except where vehicles run on the left half of a roadway).

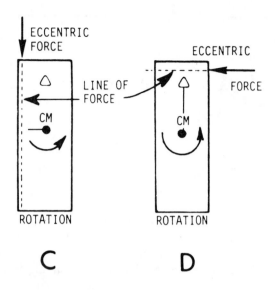

C   D

Exhibit 5. *An eccentric force may produce acceleration or deceleration but it also results in rotation. The farther the line of force is from the center of mass, the greater the rotation.*

Velocity Change

Thrust (force) between a vehicle and some other object results in collapse of vehicle parts. The extent of this collapse naturally depends on 1) the amount of force; and 2) the strength of the vehicle's structure. If the vehicle runs head-on into something, as in Exhibit 2, the vehicle is slowed (decelerated); but if another vehicle hits it from behind, the vehicle is speeded up (accelerated).

How much velocity is changed depends on the strength of the force and the mass of the object. A small thrust will give considerable velocity change to a small object; but a large object takes a big force to change its velocity much.

Rotation

In addition to changing its speed thrust may make an object rotate or spin. Rotation will depend on the strength of the thrust, its direction, and its point of application.

If the force is directly toward the center of mass of the vehicle, as in Exhibit 2, the vehicle is slowed down or speeded up in line with that force, but it does not rotate. This is a centered force. Exactly centered forces are extremely rare. Centered forces do not have to be applied at the center of the vehicle as in Exhibit 2; they may be applied anywhere on the vehicle, as at Exhibit 4, so long as they are directed toward the center of mass (center of gravity). Usually, forces produced by collision are more or less eccentric, that is, the force is not directed toward the center of mass. Then, one side of the vehicle is pushed harder than the other which results in rotation as illustrated in Exhibit 5. With the same amount of force, rotation is slight if the force is almost centered (C in Exhibit 5) and great if the force is far from centered (D in Exhibit 5).

If a centered force is produced when a vehicle strikes a fixed object, the vehicle slows and stops, but it does not rotate (Exhibit 2). Furthermore, if the vehicle is standing and is struck by another so as to produce a centered force, as Vehicle E striking Vehicle F in Exhibit 6, the struck vehicle, F, is shoved ahead of the striking force, E, without rotation. However, if the force on a standing vehicle, such as H in Exhibit 7, is eccentric, the center of mass of the struck vehicle, H, moves in the general direction of movement of the striking vehicle, G, but the side or end struck moves faster than the side or end not struck, giving the vehicle also a rotary motion. A similar result is produced if a vehicle moving sidewise, I in Exhibit 8, strikes a fixed object, J, in such a manner as to produce an eccentric force on the vehicle itself. In Exhibit 8, vehicle I is sliding exactly sidewise when it hits. The center of vehicle I keeps on going in the general direction that it was going before collision, but the struck end of the vehicle is slowed and the other is not, so the vehicle rotates.

Direction Change

In Exhibits 7 and 8, force is applied to the extreme end of the vehicle. That force produces so much rotation so quickly that the vehicle immediately disengages from the obstacle struck and the vehicle's center of mass continues

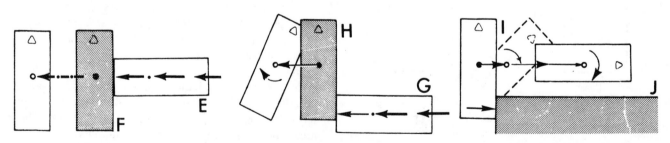

Exhibit 6. *A centered force on a standing vehicle moves the vehicle in the direction of the force but the vehicle does not rotate.*

Exhibit 7. *An eccentric force on a standing vehicle accelerates the vehicle in the direction of the force and makes it rotate rapidly.*

Exhibit 8. *A moving vehicle striking a stationary object to produce an eccentric force is slowed in the direction of movement and is rotated.*

(while the vehicle rotates) in very nearly the same direction as the force applied to it, or in the original direction of motion.

However, in many vehicle collisions, the force is produced by forward motion of the vehicle and the vehicle's front end strikes the obstacle. Except in the unusual case of an exactly centered impact while the vehicle is moving straight ahead as in Exhibit 2, the force produced is eccentric. Then, if the engagement is very slight so that only a partial impact results, the vehicle may continue on with little change in direction as in Exhibit 3, which is a sideswipe.

On the other hand, if the force is only slightly eccentric and there is a full impact, the vehicle cannot continue on in the same direction. One side of the vehicle is stopped and the other keeps on going (Exhibit 9). Then the vehicle must pivot on the part which is stopped, 2 in Exhibit 9, and the ensuing rotation forces the vehicle to take a new direction, 3 in Exhibit 9, before disengagement. In Exhibit 9, a common kind of collision, the vehicle departs from impact obliquely to the right of its approach if the rotation produced was counterclockwise, as shown, and to the left if it was clockwise (not shown). In this kind of collision, the vehicle is not moved to one side as a vehicle may be if it strikes a guardrail at a small angle; that would be a partial impact. Nor is the vehicle bounced off the obstacle; motor vehicles have too little elasticity to bounce much. It is simply a matter of pivoting about the contact area. If this pivoting were obliquely upward instead of obliquely to one side, it would be called a flip or vault. Flips and vaults are the subject of Topic 866.

Moving after collision in a new direction from that of approach to collision is an interesting and important effect of eccentric impact. In Exhibit 9, the new direction is obliquely off to the right; the vehicle continues to rotate counterclockwise after disengagement.

Thrust direction against the vehicle can change during impact as the position of the vehicle changes. The area in which thrust is applied can also change; in fact, that is another way of describing the essential characteristic of a partial impact. In a partial impact, the damaged areas in contact with each other never stop moving past each other. Motion between areas in contact only stops with full impact. Then it stops at maximum engagement.

Moving Vehicle Hits Fixed Object

If damage is great and collapse occurs straight back from front to rear at the left side of the front end, as in Exhibit 9, the force is great and eccentric. In this example, the force results in counterclockwise rotation. Then, with respect to maximum engagement, Position 2 in Exhibit 9, the vehicle was at a lesser angle at first contact, Position 1, and will be at a greater angle at separation, Postion 3. During and following engagement, the vehicle moves obliquely to the right. It is evident from the amount of collapse, that great force was involved; that force would change the speed of the vehicle greatly.

As illustrated by the foregoing examples, a number of conclusions are warranted:

- The moving vehicle struck the stationary object; there is no question of which hit which.
- The direction of force developed in the collision is in the direction of movement of the moving vehicle.
- All of the damage and all of the motion after collision is due to the energy of the moving vehicle, because no additional damage due to motion can be inflicted by a stationary object. This total energy is an indication of the speed of the striking vehicle.

Moving Vehicle Hits Stopped Vehicle

Exhibit 10 shows a moving vehicle, K, colliding at right angles with an identical stopped vehicle, L. The thrust

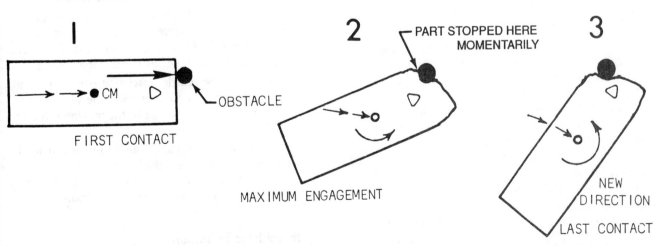

Exhibit 9. *If a vehicle strikes a fixed object to produce an eccentric force in such a way that rotation will not permit it to clear the object struck, the vehicle pivots about the contact point. Its rotation before disengagement gives it a new direction, obliquely away from the object struck.*

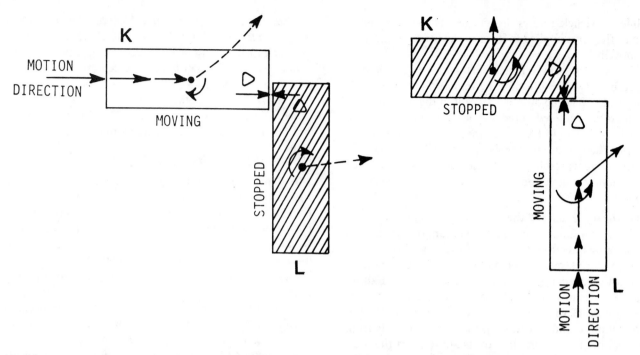

Exhibit 10. *With first contact position as shown here and with K moving while L stands, thrust against L will be in the direction of motion of K. Both will rotate in the same direction, clockwise.*

Exhibit 11. *In the same first contact positions as in Exhibit 10 but with L moving while K stands, thrust against K will be in the direction of motion of L. K and L will both rotate counterclockwise.*

against K is straight back from the right front opposite to the direction of K's motion. The force on L is across its front from left to right at the left front corner in the direction of K's motion. With respect to K, L acts something like a fixed object. During this collision, K is slowed, the force on K is eccentric so K rotates, in this case clockwise; and K moves off forward and obliquely to its left. Because L is not a fixed object, it is moved by the impact in the direction of the force against it, that is, to its right. The force against L is highly eccentric, so L rotates rapidly, in this case clockwise.

Exhibit 11 is like Exhibit 10 except that L is moving and K is stopped. The L is slowed and K is set in motion. Both vehicles have eccentric forces and rotate, in this case, counterclockwise. The thrust of L against K is in the direction of L's motion before collision.

When the stopped and moving vehicles are not at right angles, how they move and rotate during impact depends on how they are positioned when they collide. For example, in Exhibit 12, the vehicles are so positioned that the force in the direction of the moving vehicle, N, is centered on both. Then the moving vehicle, N, is slowed and the standing vehicle, M, is set in motion in this case backwards, but neither vehicle rotates. In Exhibit 13, positions of M and N at first contact are such that force in the direction of motion of N will be eccentric on both vehicles. In the positions shown, both vehicles will rotate: M clockwise and N counterclockwise. You can see from this diagram that an instant after first contact, the front of N will be

squarely against the left side of M. The resulting damage to the two vehicles is likely to suggest a simple right angle collision and so lead to a mistaken conclusion about the angle between the vehicles at first contact.

Certain conclusions are possible with respect to a collision between a moving and stopped vehicle:

- The moving vehicle strikes the stopped vehicle; there can be no question about that.
- The initial force against the standing vehicle is in the direction of motion of the moving vehicle.
- The moving vehicle will be slowed, and if the thrust is sufficient to overcome tire-road friction, the stopped vehicle will be set in motion in the general direction of movement of the moving vehicle.
- Rotation of the vehicles after first contact depends on the first contact point on each, the angle between the vehicles, and the angle of the moving vehicle to its direction of motion.
- Damage to both vehicles can be attributed to the energy of the moving vehicle, but this total damage is an indication of that vehicle's velocity only if neither vehicle moves much after collision.

Both Vehicles in Motion

If both vehicles are moving when they collide, each contributes to the change of velocity, rotation and direction of the other.

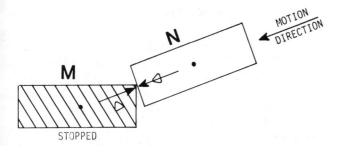

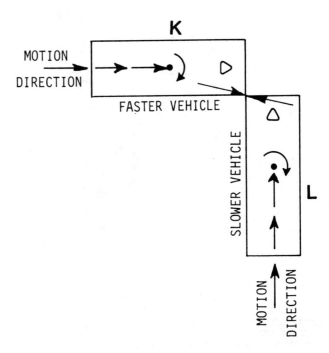

Exhibit 12. *If the moving vehicle N strikes the standing vehicle, M, in such a manner that initial impact on each is centered, neither will rotate. N will be slowed, and M accelerated in the direction of motion of the moving vehicle.*

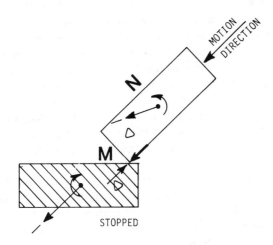

Exhibit 13. *If the moving vehicle, N, strikes the standing vehicle, M as show here with eccentric thrusts for each, both will rotate, M clockwise and N counterclockwise, but at different rates. That can make maximum engagement position at right angles.*

Exhibit 14. *With both vehicles moving as they collide, the thrust between them will not be aligned with the motion of either. Each vehicle's motion affects the behavior of the other.*

In Exhibit 14, the identical vehicles, K and L, both moving, are in the same right angle positions relative to each other as in Exhibits 10 and 11, but in Exhibit 14, K is moving faster than L. In Exhibit 10, the force was straight ahead for the moving vehicle, K; but with both vehicles moving (Exhibit 14) the initial thrust direction is closer to the direction of motion of the faster vehicle (K in Exhibit 14 and L in Exhibit 15).

If both identical vehicles are at the same speed in a corner-to-corner collision (Exhibit 16), the force direction on each is at the same angle to the vehicle and its motion, but not in the direction of movement of either.

In Exhibit 16, the impact forces on both vehicles are eccentric. The vehicles rotate in opposite directions. The thrust direction on the vehicles changes constantly during impact so that the thrust direction at maximum engagement is not the same as at first contact.

If two moving vehicles collide, you can say certain things about the collision:

- It is useless to discuss which vehicle hit which; they simply struck each other.

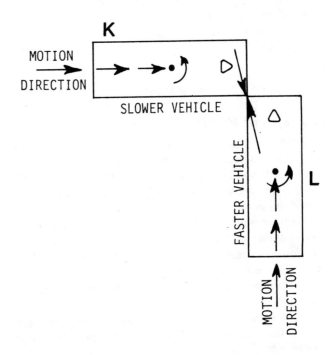

Exhibit 15. *With both identical vehicles moving in a front corner to front corner right angle impact, the thrust force is more nearly aligned with the motion of the faster vehicle.*

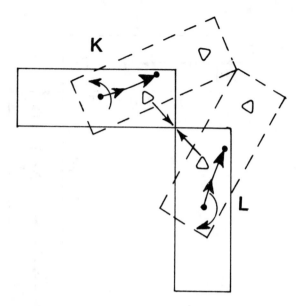

Exhibit 16. *When identical vehicles collide with identical velocities, as shown here, the thrust direction is halfway between the directions of motion of the two vehicles involved.*

- The direction of thrust on neither vehicle is the same as its direction of approach (except in exact same direction or opposite direction collisions).
- Movement of the slower and/or lighter vehicle is more affected by the collision than the other.
- Damage to the vehicles is not an indicator of the speed of either.

Many people confuse direction of motion with direction of force in a collision; it is very important to keep the differences clearly in mind.

4. DAMAGE

Damage and Movement

From damage alone, you cannot tell which of two vehicles in a collision was moving faster. Consider two vehicles, P and Q. Exactly the same damage is possible with P moving and Q stopped as with Q moving and P standing, or with both moving.

Damage is done by the forces of impact which deform the materials of the vehicles. At all times during impact, the force against P is exactly the same as the force against Q but in the opposite direction. Then whatever material in the contact area that is weakest will collapse first and most.

Three conditions are necessary to have the same damage result from different vehicle velocities in two-vehicle collisions:

1. The first contact position (FCP) of the vehicles must be the same.

2. The vehicles must be approaching each other from the same directions.

3. The closing (approaching) velocity must be the same.

Exhibits 17, 18, and 19 show how this can happen. In all three the FCP relationships of each vehicle to the other is the same. In Exhibit 17, Q is standing and P moving, let us say south at 40 ft/s. The resulting crush damage will reflect that velocity. In Exhibit 18, P is standing and Q moving north sidewise at 40 ft/s, the same closing velocity. But in Exhibit 19, P is moving south at 10 ft/s while Q moves north at 30 ft/s, giving the same 40 ft/s closing velocity. The resulting damage will be the same in all three cases.

Of course, the position and movement of the two vehicles on the *ground* will be quite different. With the situation as illustrated in Exhibit 17, both vehicles will move south during and after impact; whereas with Exhibit 18, both will move north. With both vehicles moving toward each other (Exhibit 19), if the vehicles weigh the same, both will move north during and after collision in the direction of motion of the faster vehicle.

Thus damage reflects only motion of the vehicles with respect to each other, not movement with respect to the road. The latter requires additional data of one kind or another. It is important to remember this. If someone shows you two vehicles which have collided with each other — or photos of them — and asks you, "Which one was going faster?", your answer must be "From the damage alone, I cannot tell; nobody can. Other information is needed to determine that."

Damage and Speed

Another matter, which is often misunderstood, ought to be cleared up at this time. Too many people have the idea that the faster vehicle in a two-vehicle collision suffers the most damage. There are others who argue the opposite. Both are wrong.

The fact is that in a two-vehicle collision, the stronger vehicle suffers the least damage. With the forces between the impacting vehicles equal and opposite at all times, the weaker structure of either is crushed and broken most. Thus, in an impact between the channel-iron bumper of a big truck and the ornamental grill on a compact car, the truck bumper remains virtually unscathed whereas the grill is torn and crushed.

This is true with the truck stopped and the car moving, with the car stopped and the truck moving or with both moving; the angle of impact makes no difference. It is only the strength of the parts in contact that counts.

Damage and Thrust

At first contact, the force of one vehicle against another vehicle or some other object, begins to crush parts of the vehicle in the direction of the thrust.

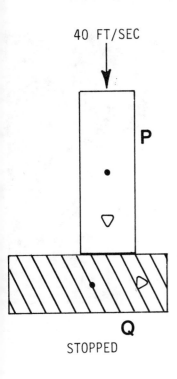

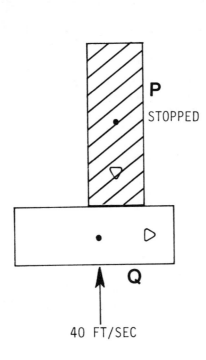

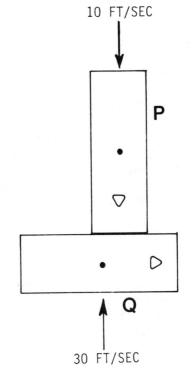

Exhibit 17. *In this situation, P and Q will experience exactly the same impact force. Total damage will reflect their closing speed and the structural strength of each.*

Exhibit 18. *In the same situation but with P standing and Q moving (in this case sidewise), the closing rate and resulting damage will be exactly the same as for Exhibit 17.*

Exhibit 19. *Here both vehicles are moving in opposite directions with a closing velocity equal to that shown in Exhibits 17 and 18. Resulting impact force and damage will be the same as for the situations in Exhibits 17, 18, and 19.*

But more often than not, as impact progresses, the vehicles rotate at different rates or in different directions (Exhibit 13). Consequently, the direction of forces between them changes. A corresponding change takes place in the direction of crush of vehicle parts. The direction of crush at maximum engagement, when forces between vehicles are greatest, gives the final direction and penetration of one vehicle into the other. After that the force lessens, deformation remains because vehicle parts are essentially inelastic; they do not return to their original shape after deformation.

Therefore, what you see after a collision is damage which indicates the direction and extent of penetration at maximum engagement, not that at first contact. There may be a slight difference between the maximum deformation in a collision (called dynamic collapse) and the final deformation (called static collapse).

Contact Damage Areas

Everybody realizes that looking at vehicle damage can reveal which areas have been in contact with some other object; but most people do not realize how much examination of contact damage areas can tell about how vehicles behaved in a collision. Obviously, contact damage (CD) areas of two vehicles were against each other during col-

lision, but deciding exactly how they were in contact may be difficult.

The easiest cases are those in which there is a definite, recognizable imprint of a part of one vehicle on the other. Such details of damage are discussed in Topic 820.

Sometimes an imprint is easily recognized, for example, that of a headlamp rim; sometimes the imprint is faint, obscured, or confused with other damage. If contact damage areas on two vehicles have the same dimensions they can often be easily matched (Exhibits 2, 6, 17, 18, 19).

If the contact damage area is smeared, scratched or abraded, there was probably movement between the surfaces during contact.

If one contact damage area is small or short and the other is extensive, there was probably movement or slippage during engagement. It is easy to perceive this in the case of fixed object collisions as in Exhibit 3 in which the CD area on the pole is a few inches wide while that on the car goes from end to end.

But if the corner of one car runs into the side of another moving vehicle, as in Exhibit 13, the corner damage may be only a foot wide whereas the damage to the other may extend for five feet or more along the side. If the damage to the side of a car is approximately as long as the width of the car that hit it, the damage may suggest a right angle collision whereas only a corner of a car at an angle was indeed involved.

A long CD area on one vehicle and short one on the other usually indicates a sideswipe or incomplete impact; but do not imagine that this is always so. One vehicle moving at an angle with a corner against the side of another can leave a long damage area. Penetration increases from first contact to maximum engagement where slippage stops. Then impact is complete. You may have to study the damage to both vehicles very carefully to discover this by noting in which way particular damaged parts were deformed. It may even be difficult to decide at which end of the CD area penetration was greatest and, therefore, which was the point of principal force or thrust.

Recording Damage Observations

Carefully made measurements and photos are desirable to substantiate your observations of damage.

In addition to the description of vehicle damage in Topic 820, a special section of that topic describes detailed measurements that are desirable and Topic 836 includes instructions for photographing damage to best advantage.

5. ANALYZING IMPACT

Now, how do we apply the foregoing principles to working out how a collision occurred?

The data you have to depend on to start with is the damage to the vehicles and their dimensions. Observation and documentation of vehicle damage is described in Topic 820. If you cannot remember how contact damage and thrust direction are determined by examining a vehicle, review parts of that topic. The following discussion of two-vehicle collisions really starts where Topic 820 left off.

For impact analysis, you will find the Traffic Template quite useful. You will also need tracing paper and a pencil as illustrated in Exhibit 20.

The first step in understanding vehicle behavior in a particular collision is to draw an outline of each vehicle approximately to scale. On each diagram, show the collapsed or deformed area, contact-damage area, and direction of principal force, as described in Topic 820 and illustrated in Exhibit 1.

In these diagrams, represent force by an arrow pointing in the direction of force at maximum engagement. Place the point of an arrow at the place of greatest penetration; where the force was greatest. Thus the force arrow in your vehicle diagram represents the "direction of principal force."[1] This is the amount and direction of force at maximum engagement. To simplify discussion, we can refer to this force simply as *thrust*.

During impact, the amount of force between the vehicles is constantly changing. In much less than a second, it in-

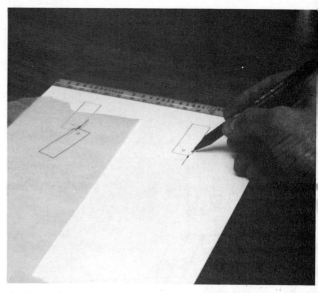

Exhibit 20. *An outline of one collapse and thrust diagram on tracing paper assists in locating its maximum engagement position with respect to the outline of the collapse and thrust diagram of the vehicle with which it collided.*

creases from zero to a very high value at maximum engagement and decreases to zero. The direction of force may also change, but not nearly so much as the amount.

Thrust is not nearly so easily determined from examination of the vehicle or pictures of it as you might think. It requires very careful observation especially to distinguish contact from induced damage and to determine the point of maximum penetration. The best way to determine thrust direction is to note the maximum engagement (greatest penetration) position of some particular part such as a headlamp, and then measure its longitudinal and transverse displacement from its normal position.

Be careful that a uniform crush stiffness is not assumed along the entire side, or end, of the vehicle. It is obvious that the area surrounding a wheel will offer much more resistance to a crushing force than the quarter-panel region. Likewise, the area at the height of the frame in a side impact will be much stronger than the area a few inches above it.

Consider a case where two vehicles approach each other at a 90° angle and collide. The entire front end of one vehicle strikes the side of another vehicle forward of the driver's area. In this manner it causes extensive penetration into the front door hinge area by the front bumper-frame area of the other vehicle and little penetration into the wheel area. This could lead to positioning the thrust arrow incorrectly because the area of "greatest penetration" was not where the greatest force was applied. Rather the greatest force was applied at the wheel and left front bumper-frame area of the respective vehicles. Here the weakness of the door panel allowed greater penetration than the much stronger wheel area.

Exhibit 21 is an example of a pair of collapse and thrust diagrams for two vehicles in an opposite-direction collision. To these have been added a curved arrow around the center of mass (CM) of the vehicle on the right to show that with the eccentric force, it rotates counterclockwise. The vehicle on the left does not have such an arrow because thrust on it is centered and there is no rotation.

Maximum engagement position of each vehicle with respect to the other can be derived from these diagrams. Two simple rules govern this operation:

1. The greatest collapse in the contact-damage area of each vehicle must be against the greatest collapse in the contact-damage area of the other.
2. Thrust directions must be in line, that is, the thrust of one must be directly opposite to the thrust of the other.

The easiest way to determine maximum engagement position is to trace the diagram of one vehicle on tracing paper, lay it over the diagram of the other and adjust it until the conditions imposed by the two rules are met, as in Exhibit 20. Another way is to make the outlines on stiff paper or light cards. Then cut them out so that they can be adjusted in position to each other.

In this manner, the two diagrams in Exhibit 21 are combined into a maximum-engagement diagram, Exhibit 22. Note that in this particular case, Vehicle N has an eccentric thrust and Vehicle M does not. Vehicle N, the one with the eccentric thrust, rotates and Vehicle M does not. Therefore, the angle between the vehicles changes during impact.

First contact position (FCP) of the two will then be as shown in Exhibit 23. Note that the angle between them is less than at maximum engagement because Vehicle N has rotation while Vehicle M has none.

Separation position of the two cars before they disengage is approximately as shown in Exhibit 24. Again, because Vehicle N rotates more than the other, its position changes more and is at a greater angle at last contact than at maximum engagement.

At this stage of analysis, much has been said about the *relative* positions of the vehicles during contact, but nothing has yet been said about movement of the vehicles immediately before impact nor after separation.

From consideration of the damage to two vehicles in collision, something can be concluded about how they behaved with respect to each other during collision, but nothing can be said about the speed of either. The amount of damage gives an indication of how fast the vehicles were approaching each other, but not about how fast either was moving. Exactly the same damage could have been done with Vehicle M standing and Vehicle N moving, with Vehicle N standing and Vehicle M moving, or with both moving.

Dissimilar vehicles. Always, during impact, the forces between the vehicles are equal and in opposite directions. If the vehicles are identical, and the forces are equally eccentric, the rotation of the two vehicles during collision is the same. This situation can be called a "symmetrical impact." However, if forces between vehicles are equally eccentric and the vehicles are not similar, the equal forces do not have the same effect on the two vehicles. For example, a lighter vehicle is more affected and rotates more than a heavier one.

The fact that the vehicles were damaged in a collision indicates that motion was involved before and during contact. Great damage to either suggests plainly that the motion was rapid; slight damage usually indicates that it was not. However, great damage to one vehicle and slight damage to the other does not mean that the vehicle with more damage was going slower or faster. It only means that the vehicle which was damaged most severely had weaker material and structure in the area damaged, and so, with the identical impact, was subject to greater collapse.

However, *if* we know how fast and in which direction one of the vehicles was moving, damage to the two vehicles enables us to judge reasonably well about how fast and in what direction the other was moving.

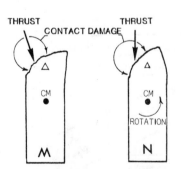

Exhibit 21. *Diagrams of vehicles show contact-damage areas, thrust directions, and resulting rotation of vehicles based on observations of damage to the vehicles. These diagrams are the first step in collision analysis.*

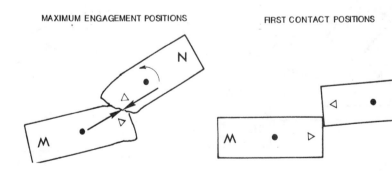

Exhibit 22. *Maximum engagement positions are derived from collapse and thrust diagrams.*

Exhibit 23. *Relative rotation of two vehicles in a collision determines the FCP based on maximum engagement force direction.*

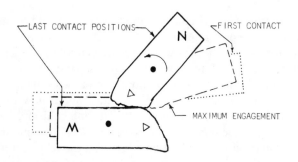

Exhibit 24. *Relative rotation of vehicles also determines separation positions. Dashed and dotted lines show stages of impact.*

Perhaps an illustration will help explain this. Exhibit 23 shows the first-contact positions of two vehicles with respect to each other, positions derived from damage to them; but this diagram does not suggest what the motion before impact might have been. If only one vehicle was moving, the force developed in impact was in the direction of motion of that vehicle. Thus, if we know or assume that Vehicle M was stopped when the vehicles collided, and the force was in the direction shown in Exhibit 21, Vehicle N would have been moving in the direction of force indicated by damage as illustrated by the right diagram in Exhibit 21. In this case, Vehicle N was moving straight ahead at maximum engagement. On the other hand, if Vehicle N was stopped, Vehicle M would have had to be moving in the direction of the force to produce the damage. In this case, Vehicle M was moving obliquely toward its left front corner. If a vehicle is not moving in the direction toward which it is headed, it is yawing. In this case, Vehicle M was turning sharply to its right to make it sideslip to the left. We can *speculate* that this turn was

made as an evasive tactic to get out of the way of Vehicle N.

If we know or assume that Vehicle M was moving straight ahead, it follows that to give force directions shown by damage, Vehicle N could not also have been moving straight ahead. Vehicle N would have been moving to the left of straight ahead.

If both vehicles are moving, it is more difficult to conclude how the collision occurred. To produce the damage observed, the direction and velocity of each depends on the direction and velocity of the other and their respective weights. In theory, if we had exact information about the weights, dimensions, and damage of both vehicles and the velocity (including direction) of one, the velocity of the other could be computed. But in practice, such refined data are unavailable.

Significance of the Analysis

Analysis of movements of vehicles in collision has meaning only when coupled with other data. For example, if a theory of how two vehicles collided is developed from marks on the road, the theory can be tested by considering how well vehicle movements, according to the theory, correspond to those developed by collision analysis. If the movements correspond closely, the theory is supported (but not necessarily proved); if the movements do not correspond well, the value of the theory must be questioned.

In this manner, alternate theories may be evaluated. A simple example will illustrate this procedure. Suppose the analysis of movements in an opposite-direction collision gives the results described in Exhibits 21 to 24. Final positions of the vehicles are known but there are no eyewitnesses and no reported marks on the road. Two theories

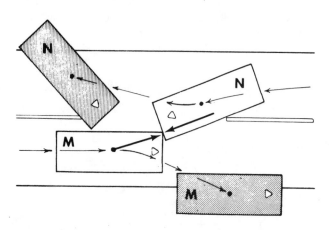

Exhibit 25. *To test alternative assumptions, vehicles can be diagrammed on a roadway according to each assumption. Their behavior in collision subsequently can then be studied to determine where they would come to rest. Often assumptions used are derived from statements of people involved.*

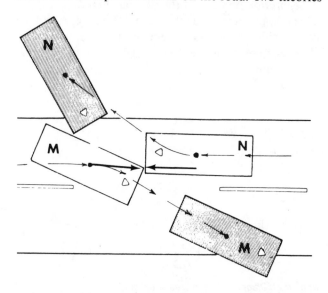

Exhibit 26. *Whichever assumption results in final positions and other results of the accident that correspond most closely to observations is supported by the analysis and contrary assumptions are denied. More than two assumptions must often be tested.*

come to mind at once: 1) Vehicle M was travelling normally in its lane, and Vehicle N was across the center line (Exhibit 25); and 2) Vehicle N was travelling normally in its lane and Vehicle M was across the center line (Exhibit 26). Obviously, one of these theories must be wrong. A diagram to illustrate each of these two theories can be drawn (Exhibits 25 and 26). These diagrams indicate about where the vehicles would have come to rest under each theory providing the vehicles behaved in collision as damage to them indicates they must have. Clearly, if observed final positions of the vehicles with respect to the roadway and to each other correspond to that in Exhibit 25, in which Vehicle M was moving in its lane, that explanation of the accident is more credible than the opposite theory.

6. SYSTEMATIC PROCEDURE

Start by recalling advice given early in this topic: ignore conclusions that others seem eager to obtain and suppress any notions you already have about what happened. Then, for the moment, put aside the after-accident situation map. Thus free your mind of preconceived ideas so that you can follow the facts in an orderly manner.

Procedure

The processes which have been explained up to this point can be summarized and reviewed as the following steps in a typical traffic-accident reconstruction.

1. Draw an outline of each vehicle approximately to scale and preferably to the same scale as the after-accident situation map. The *Traffic Template*[2] is useful for this purpose.
2. For each vehicle study the damage (or photos of the damage) and show on the vehicle outline its collapsed or deformed shape.
3. Also indicate on the outline, by a bracket with a pointer at each end, the extent of the contact damage area as in Exhibit 1 and other exhibits.
4. Locate the spot of greatest collapse, penetration, or distortion in the contact damage area, and then estimate the direction a vehicle part was moved to force it to that position. Show this on the outline as a thrust arrow. You will probably have to study the damage from several viewpoints to do this properly.
5. Consider carefully how the direction of thrust (force line) is related to the center of mass of the vehicle. (For study purposes, you can consider the center of mass to be at the center of the wheel base of the vehicle). This gives you the eccentricity of the maximum engagement force and indicates rotation, if any, of the vehicle. On the outline, show direction of rotation by a curved arrow partly encircling the center of mass as indicated in several exhibits.

6. Now you are ready to put the vehicles together at maximum engagement position. Put a tracing of one vehicle outline over the outline of the other or use cutout patterns of the two vehicles. Adjust these so that the maximum engagement deformation of each is against that of the other and the thrust arrows are aligned. You may have to reexamine vehicle damage and adjust your vehicle outlines at this point. To keep the maximum engagement positions in mind, stick the adjusted outlines together or trace them on a single sheet.
7. Compare carefully the direction of rotation and its rate for the vehicles involved. This is the basis for estimating the change in angle between the vehicles from first contact to maximum engagement. Then adjust positions of original outlines (which do not show damage) to represent first contact positions.
8. Do the same to show positions of vehicles at separation.
9. Now you can go to your after-accident situation map. Look for signs of first contact position (FCP): mainly irregularities in tire marks but sometimes scars on fixed objects. Look for signs of maximum engagement positions: collision scrubs, gouges, scrapes, spatter. Place your outline of the two vehicles on the map as well as you can. Put maximum

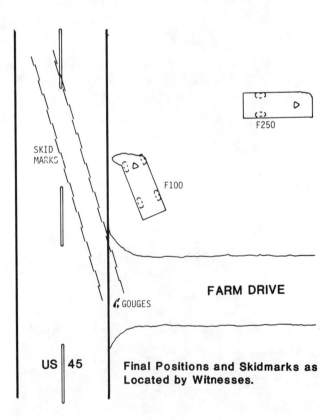

Exhibit 27. *After-accident situation map for the example of an opposite-direction collision between two pickup trucks, F100 and F250.*

Exhibit 28. *Right side of the F100 pickup. Note that the right front wheel has been forced back as far as it will go. Little contact damage shows from this side.*

Exhibit 29. *Left side of the F100. Only induced damage is visible on this side.*

Exhibit 30. *Front of the F100. Contact-damage area is outlined. The whole front end has been shoved from right to left. Greatest force and maximum displacement was at the right front wheel.*

Exhibit 31. *Outline of the F100 showing extent of contact damage, direction and point of application of thrust and corresponding counterclockwise rotation.*

Exhibit 32. F250 pickup. Practically no contact damage on the right half of the vehicle. There is contact damage to the left side of the windshield due to force from inside.

Exhibit 33. Front of F250 with contact-damage area outlined. Note the pocket at the left end of the bumper. This locates the point of maximum force application. The left front wheel back of this pocket was heavily damaged and displaced. The bumper and hood have not been displaced right or left.

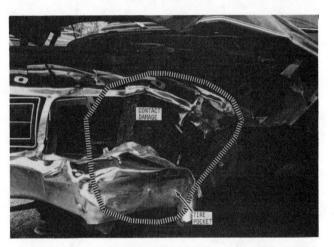

Exhibit 34. Pocket in bumper shows signs of rubber rub off. Damage shows force to have been straight back from front toward rear at extreme left front corner. Left front wheel was displaced as induced damage.

engagement outlines on signs of maximum engagement, and so on. If there are no signs on the map of first contact or maximum engagement, place the outline according to the statement of a witness, if any, or according to some theory of what happened, as in Exhibits 25 and 26.

10. Think about how each vehicle would move from its maximum engagement position to its final position. Consider how it must rotate and translate (move). You may have to change the maximum engagement position to make it conform to rotation predicated on vehicle damage, perhaps several times. You may even have to restudy your analysis of thrust direction and rotation.

Exhibit 35. Outline of F250 showing extent of contact damage, direction and point of application of thrust, and corresponding counterclockwise rotation.

11. Try to account for all signs of the accident: tire marks, gouges, debris and so on — reported or showing in photographs. If any seem not to be associated with the accident, be prepared to explain exactly what makes you think so.

Two illustrative examples follow. They will help you understand how this systematic process applies in practice. You may have to work through dozens of cases yourself to be able to imagine peculiar circumstances which are the keys to resolution of issues raised in such cases as these examples.

Opposite Direction Example

Collision between Ford *F250* pickup northbound and Ford *F100* southbound. Neither driver contemplated a turn or other maneuver at this point.

On straight, level, dry, paved, 2-lane, 30-ft. roadway with center line. Daylight.

At farm driveway which had nothing to do with the accident.

Issues:
1. *First contact position* (FCP) location
2. *Approach paths* to FCP

Data:
- After-accident situation Map (Exhibit 27)
- Photos of damage to F100 (Exhibits 28, 29, 30)
- Photos of damage to F250 (Exhibits 32, 33, 34)

Diagram each vehicle separately. In Exhibit 30, you can see that the whole front end of F100 has been pushed from its right to its left as well as from front to back. The corresponding rearward displacement of the right side shows in Exhibit 28. Note that the right front wheel is pushed back. This deformation is shown in the car outline (Exhibit 31).

Exhibits 28 and 30 also show that the maximum penetration is near the right front wheel. This is the position of the point of the thrust arrow in Exhibit 31.

To displace the front end to the rear and left, the force must have been from the opposite direction as shown by the thrust arrow in Exhibit 31.

Finally the thrust arrow direction (maximum force line) is extended past the center of mass. It passes to the left of the center of mass. That means that the vehicle rotated counterclockwise (Exhibit 31). Because damage shows that the thrust was great, the rotation would have been strong.

Next, look at the damage to the F250 (Exhibits 32, 33, 34). The contact damage area is across the left half of the front. The bumper remains centered on the undamaged top of the vehicle; therefore, there is no right or left deformation. Note this deformation and the extent of the contact damage area on the vehicle outline (Exhibit 35).

The thrust at maximum engagement is clearly in the pocket at the left end of the bumper (Exhibits 33 and 34). This is represented by the thrust arrow in the diagram. Extend the line of force past the center of mass. It passes to the left. That means rotation was counterclockwise. Show that by a rotation arrow in the diagram.

Combine the two collapse and thrust diagrams by fitting them together. Put the maximum collapse areas against each other and the thrust directions opposite as in Exhibit 36.

Note that both vehicles rotate counterclockwise. But the force against F250 is more eccentric than that against F100, which is a comparable vehicle. Therefore, F250 will rotate more than F100 and the angle between them will change during impact; at first contact it will be less than at maximum engagement. Show this lesser angle in a first-contact diagram such as Exhibit 37. The outlines in this combined diagram do not show collapse and thrust because at first contact there has not yet been any collapse, and no thrust forces have developed.

Place the first contact diagrams on the after-accident situation map (Exhibit 38). On the map, there are indications of where the collision occurred and where the vehicles came to rest. These are not as precise as one would like, but they are the best available and cannot be ignored.

Place the outline of the F100 at the end of the southbound tire marks slightly north of where maximum engagement would have produced the reported gouges in the road surface. Then the first contact position of the F250, determined by its relation to the F100, is approximately as shown in Exhibit 38.

With the addition of the first contact positions, the map ceases to represent the after accident situation. It becomes a kind of collision diagram. Actually you might make it a transparent overlay for the after-accident situation map.

Maximum engagement positions can also be shown on Exhibit 38, the collision diagram.

Now it is time to consider whether the first-contact position you have selected is consistent with available facts. In this case, could the vehicles have reached the final positions described? With both cars rotating counterclockwise, the center of mass of each could readily have followed a direct path from maximum engagement to final position. During its after-collision movement, the F100 rotated about 180° to head back generally in the direction from which it approached its final position; but the F250 rotated about 300°. That is more than the F100 which had less eccentricity and, therefore, less rapid rotation during engagement. You can account for the greater rotation of the F250 by the fact that it travelled farther after separation than the F100 did.

Because the F250 pushed the F100 backward and then itself continued farther on, it is clear that the F250 was travelling considerably faster at impact than the F100. Indeed, the F100 may actually have skidded to a stop before

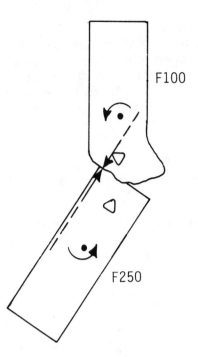

Exhibit 36. *Collapse and thrust diagrams of the two vehicles fitted together at maximum engagement. Points of maximum thrust are against each other and thrust directions are opposite. Both vehicles rotate counterclockwise.*

impact. The higher speed of the F250 is consistent with the impact force direction being close to its direction of motion before collision as explained heretofore.

Finally, you can sketch events of the accident compatible with reasonable driver tactics, strategy and possibly other human factors.

To get his northbound vehicle at the first-contact angle indicated (Exhibit 38) at anything like the speed suggested by damage and after-impact movement of both cars, the F250 driver must have steered very sharply to the right just before collision. At his speed, this turn could only have been made from the southbound lane along the path shown in Exhibit 38.

This situation explains why the driver of the F100, on straight road in broad daylight, suddenly steered left and skidded across the center line into the opposite lane. When this driver saw a car approaching on a collision course in his lane, he decided to try to get out of the way by steering left toward the unoccupied half of the road and braking. Because his hands were already on the steering wheel, the turn began before his foot moved from the accelerator to the brake. When braking locked the car's wheels, steering no longer had any effect; the car simply skidded ahead.

The driver of the F250 discovered that the cars were on a collision course at about the same time as the driver of

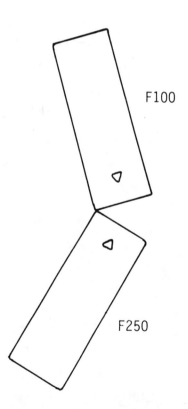

Exhibit 37. *First contact positions of F100 and F250. Angle between them is less than at maximum engagement because one vehicle rotates more rapidly than the other. At first contact, no force has yet developed and no damage has been done.*

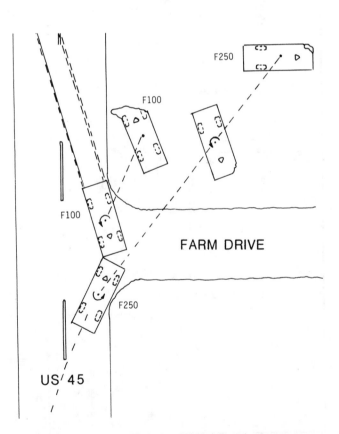

Exhibit 38. *Collision diagram superimposed on after-accident situation map. It shows first contact positions on the road and appropriate paths of approach for each vehicle.*

the F100 and decided to get back into his own lane, apparently without braking. Once starting a turn to the free side of the road, there was no time for either driver to avoid collision by again changing course.

There is no explanation of why the F250 driver was on the wrong side of the road to begin with.

Thus the issues have been resolved by a systematic impact analysis based largely on examinations of damage. In an opposite-direction collision, positions on the road and approach directions rather than speed are the critical issues.

Example of Angle Impact

Collision between full-size Pontiac, eastbound, and a full-size Buick, northbound. Neither driver planned to turn at this junction.

On north-south, straight level, dry paved pair of two lane 24-ft. roadways separated by a 4-ft. raised median

At an east-west, straight, level, dry, paved pair of 2-lane roadways separated by a 4-ft. raised median with an 11-ft. left turn lane in each direction. The two roads intersect at right angles.

Control by traffic signals with all turns permitted.
Issue: Speed of each vehicle at FCP.
Data:

- After-accident situation map (Exhibit 39)
- Photos of damage to Pontiac (Exhibits 40, 41, 42)
- Photos of damage to Buick (Exhibits 44, 45)

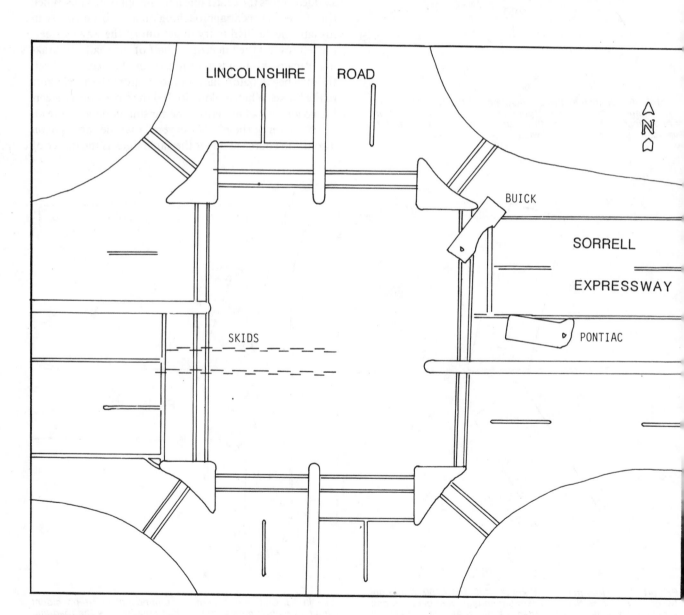

Exhibit 39. *After-accident situation map for accident described in example of angle collision analysis.*

Exhibit 40. *Front of Pontiac. Note contact damage across entire front bumper and extent to which front end has been forced to the left.*

Exhibit 41. *Right front corner of Pontiac showing rearward and leftward collapse. This is the maximum deformation area.*

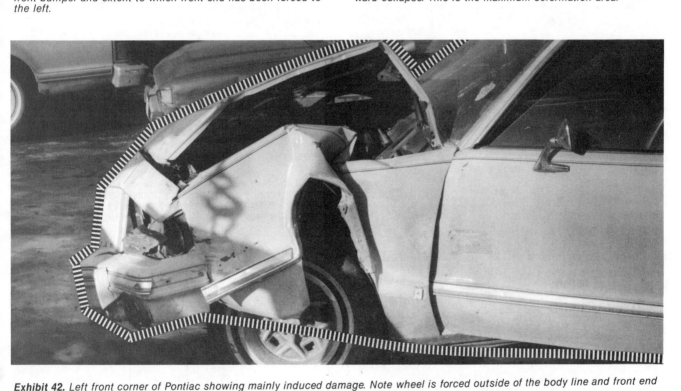

Exhibit 42. *Left front corner of Pontiac showing mainly induced damage. Note wheel is forced outside of the body line and front end is forced rearward.*

Exhibit 43, *at left, is the diagram of damage to the Pontiac. Contact damage is entirely across the front which has been displaced severely to the left. Thrust direction is from the right front toward the right front corner. Force is moderately eccentric giving counterclockwise rotation.*

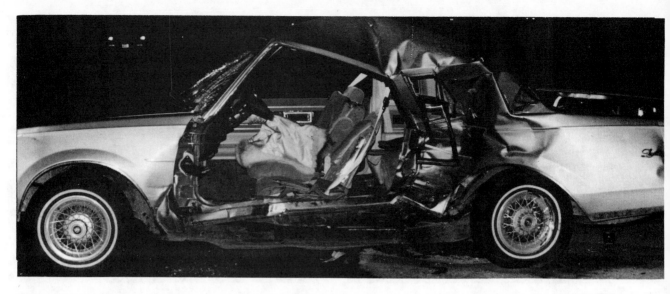

Exhibit 44. *The side of the Buick has a very long contact damage area. Examine this carefully to decide whether it is a partial or complete impact.*

Exhibit 45. *Maximum penetration and thrust is just ahead of the rear wheel.*

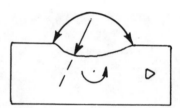

Exhibit 46 *is a diagram of damage to the Buick. It shows the contact damage area and thrust direction at maximum engagement, from the left and rearward. The force is slightly eccentric and results in moderate counterclockwise rotation.*

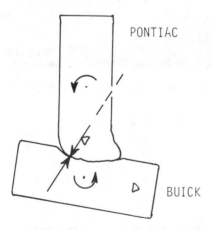

PONTIAC

BUICK

Exhibit 47. *Maximum engagement positions of the Buick and Pontiac. Thrust directions are opposite. The Pontiac rotates more rapidly than the Buick. Therefore the angle between them changes during rotation, although both are rotating in the same direction.*

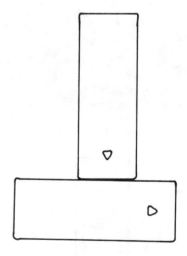

Exhibit 48. *First-contact positions of the Pontiac and Buick. The angle between them is greater than at maximum engagement because during impact they rotate at different rates. They are nearly at right angles which would be expected from other information relating to this crash.*

Diagram each vehicle separately. The Pontiac (Exhibit 40) shows contact damage across the entire front but more on the right front corner where it extends around to the right front wheel. The combination of rearward and right to left collapse gives the deformation profile shown in Exhibit 43. The striking thing about this damage is the displacement of the entire front end a foot or more toward the left. The thrust which produced this rearward and right to left collapse must have come at an angle toward the right front corner at maximum engagement as indicated by the thrust arrow in Exhibit 43.

An extension of the thrust line passes to the left of the center of mass far enough to give a brisk counterclockwise rotation during impact. All this is represented diagrammatically in Exhibit 43.

Contact-damage on the Buick is all on the left side. Side impacts are typically more difficult to figure out than end impacts. That is because easily recognizable parts, such as headlamps, bumpers, and wheels, may not be displaced.

Contact damage and penetration on the Buick (Exhibit 44) extends from the hinge on the left front door to the rear wheel on that side, a distance greater than the width of a car. That means that there was slippage along this area during impact which may make it difficult to decide exactly where the greatest thrust was applied. In this case, careful examination of Exhibit 45 shows that greatest penetration is just ahead of the rear wheel. The body panel has been pushed clear into the back seat and the rear edge of the door frame has definitely been forced backward at its midpoint. The penetration profile and extent of contact damage is shown on the vehicle outline (Exhibit 46). It follows that the thrust at this maximum engagement point is obliquely from ahead and the left. This is the basis for the position of the thrust arrow in Exhibit 46.

The thrust line extended passes to the left of and behind the center of mass; consequently, during impact, the Buick rotated counterclockwise. The rotation arrow shows this on the now completed damage analysis diagram for the Buick.

Translation of observation or photographs of vehicle damage is no simple routine like adding two and three to get five. It is as much art as science, perhaps more. Therefore, it is sensible to have another experienced person do the analysis independently. If your diagram and his are alike in all important respects, you can feel satisfied that you are both on the right track. But if his diagram and yours differ in important respects, discuss the matter with him at once to find out why your conclusions differ from his.

Now put the damage outlines of the Pontiac and Buick together as explained earlier and illustrated in Exhibit 47

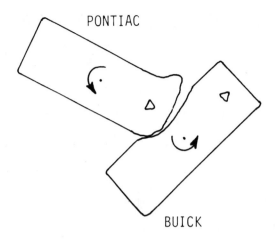

Exhibit 49. *Positions of Buick and Pontiac at separation. The angle between the cars is determined by differences in rates of rotation.*

for the maximum engagement positions. Do not make the mistake of assuming that the FCP (first contact positions) are the same as those at maximum engagement. Note that the thrust is more eccentric on the Pontiac than on the Buick. Both vehicles are essentially the same size. Therefore, during impact, the Pontiac rotated more than the Buick, although both cars rotated counterclockwise. At first contact, the right front corner of the Pontiac will not have penetrated the left side of the Buick; the cars will be at or close to right angles with each other (Exhibit 48).

As they continue to rotate at different rates, the vehicles will be related to each other approximately as shown in Exhibit 49 when they finally separate.

The combined outline of the vehicles at first contact can now be put on the after-accident situation map (Exhibit 50). This is about the position they would occupy approaching at right angles if neither vehicle had started to turn before impact. The position of the Pontiac is determined by the skidmarks it made before impact.

After impact, the Buick travelled about 45 ft. and rotated 105° whereas the Pontiac travelled 58 ft. and rotated 355°. This is consistent with the differences in rate of rotation of the two vehicles determined by examination of damage to them.

The issue of speeds of the vehicles is not resolved by the foregoing impact analysis. It is just a first step: determining the direction of approach and of departure of each vehicle and the distance each moved from first contact to final position. Two steps remain: 1) estimating the after-impact velocity of each vehicle, and 2) applying the principles of conservation of momentum to calculate the speed of each at FCP. These procedures are explained in other topics.

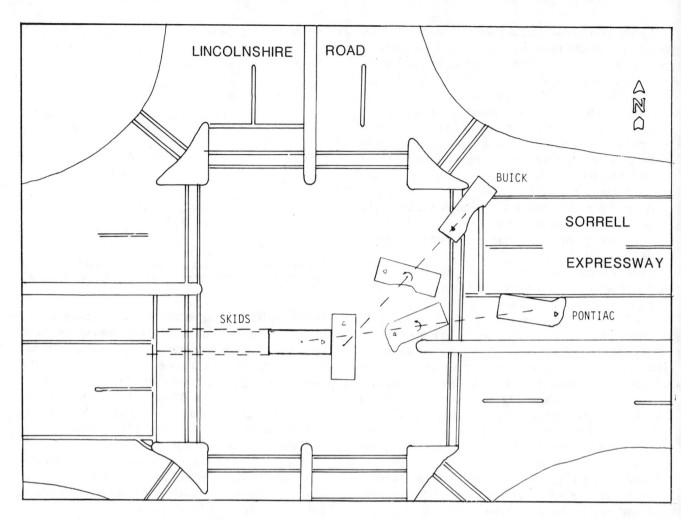

Exhibit 50. *Collision diagrams superimposed on the after-accident situation map. This is a preliminary step to speed estimates.*

7. SOURCES

Authors

J. Stannard Baker is a traffic engineer specializing in traffic accident investigation. He was Director of Research and Development at the Northwestern University Traffic Institute from 1946 to 1971. Since then he was a consultant and guest lecturer at The Traffic Institute.

Lynn B. Fricke is a traffic engineer specializing in traffic accident investigation. He joined The Traffic Institute staff in 1975. In 1981, he became the Director of the Accident Investigation Division of the Northwestern University Traffic Institute.

References

Superscript numbers in the preceding pages refer to the following publications:

1. *Collision Deformation Classification* (SAE J224a Mar80)

1983, Society of Automotive Engineers, Warrendale, PA 15096 (11 pages)
2. Baker, J. Stannard, *Traffic Template* (SN1000), 1983, The Northwestern University Traffic Institute, Evanston, IL 60604

Exhibits

The following are the sources of the exhibits used in this topic:

Baker, J. Stannard, San Diego, CA
Diagrams: 2, 3, 4, 5, 6, 7, 8, 9, 12, 13, 16, 17, 18, 19, 20, 22, 23, 24, 25, 26, 37
Photo: 21

Fricke, Lynn B., Traffic Institute, Evanston, IL
Photos: 1, 28, 29, 30, 32, 33, 34, 40, 41, 42, 44, 45
Diagrams: 10, 11, 14, 15, 31, 35, 36, 38, 43, 46, 47, 48, 49, 50
Maps: 27, 39

DRAG FACTOR AND COEFFICIENT OF FRICTION IN TRAFFIC ACCIDENT RECONSTRUCTION

Topic 862 of the *Traffic Accident Investigation Manual*

by
Lynn B. Fricke
and
J. Stannard Baker

NORTHWESTERN UNIVERSITY TRAFFIC INSTITUTE

DRAG FACTOR AND COEFFICIENT OF FRICTION IN TRAFFIC ACCIDENT RECONSTRUCTION

1. INTRODUCTION

The rate at which vehicles decelerate from braking is often of great concern in traffic accident reconstruction. If the distance the vehicle decelerated is known, along with its rate of deceleration, the vehicle's initial velocity can often be calculated using the equation

$$v_i = \sqrt{v_e^2 - 2ad} \qquad (1)$$

where v_i = initial vehicle velocity in ft/sec or m/sec

v_e = end vehicle velocity in ft/sec or m/sec

a = the vehicle's acceleration in ft/sec/sec or m/sec/sec (a is negative, $-$, when the vehicle is slowing)

d = distance the vehicle accelerated (or decelerated) in ft or m.

(This equation is discussed in some detail in Topic 860; see that topic if you are unfamiliar with its use.) The most difficult problem is usually encountered when the acceleration/deceleration of the vehicle must be determined. A vehicle's acceleration or deceleration is related to its drag factor, f, and the coefficient of friction, μ (Greek letter mu). Drag factor is related to acceleration by the following equation:

$$a = fg \qquad (2)$$

where f = drag factor (no dimensions)

and g = the acceleration of gravity (either 32.2 ft/sec/sec or 9.81 m/sec/sec).

The subject of this topic is how drag factor and the coefficient of friction are obtained. The two are related. For now, assume that coefficient of friction deals with the slowing force at the tire-road interface and drag factor relates to the slowing of the whole vehicle. (Although not entirely accurate, this will be explained in more detail later in the topic).

Drag factors and coefficients of friction are generally similar for all types of four-tired vehicles (essentially, passenger cars and pickup trucks). However, drag factors for motorcycles and heavy vehicles (large trucks, both single-unit and articulated) can often differ from those for four-tired vehicles. This topic deals primarily with the latter. For a discussion of motorcycles and heavy vehicles and their drag factors, consult Topics 874 and 878.

2. DEFINITION OF FRICTION

Friction can be thought of as the resisting force to motion between two surfaces at their interface (contact). We are accustomed to thinking of this as a bad thing. After all, considerable money is spent every year in attempting to reduce friction in engines. When it comes to stopping, however, friction from brakes is a very good thing.

A more precise definition of the coefficient of friction is the ratio of the tangential force (parallel to the surface) applied to an object sliding across a surface to the normal force (perpendicular to the surface) on the object. A typical diagram you will see in an engineering mechanics book is shown in Exhibit 1. It might be easier to visualize what is going on if the object is sliding on a level surface as shown in Exhibit 2. In this simpler diagram the coefficient of friction, μ, is simply the horizontal force divided by the vertical force which is the object's weight when the object is sliding across the surface.

$$\mu = F/w \qquad (3)$$

Generally, only three types of friction are considered in traffic accident reconstruction:

1. *Static friction* is defined using equation (3) (for a level surface) when sliding is just beginning. When an object is just beginning to slide, more force is required to start its movement than after movement has started. Thus, on a level surface the horizontal force, F, is greater at the beginning of sliding than it is after movement has started. The force required to start the sliding is used in computing static friction.

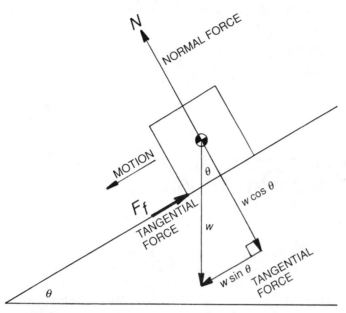

Exhibit 1. The weight component pushing perpendicular to the surface is w sin θ and the weight component parallel to the surface is w cos θ as shown in the diagram.

2. *Dynamic friction* also uses equation (3) for a level surface. In this case, however, F represents the force being applied after the object is sliding. This force is less than the horizontal force used in the static friction computation.

3. *Rolling friction* (rolling resistance) refers to the resisting forces that come into play when a vehicle is rolling with no braking. Generally these values are very low and are assumed to be insignificant in most accident reconstruction problems. Rolling friction is, however, important in tire design and other vehicle design considerations.

In hard braking (with non-antilock brakes) the time delay between the beginning of braking and full lockup of the first

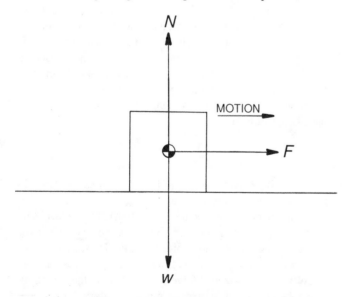

Exhibit 2. For a level surface the coefficient of friction is simply the ratio of the horizontal force required to slide an object to the weight of the object.

wheel is generally very short. Hard braking tests done using a Ford LTD at 40 mi/hr on a tar and gravel-chip pavement[1] gave a delay of 0.12 sec for the first wheel to lock from the time the brakes were first applied. Reed[2] suggests that wheel lockup could take slightly longer (in the neighborhood of 0.5 secs). Nevertheless, the amount of time that static friction could be considered is very short as compared to the total time a vehicle is normally skidding. Thus, for accident reconstruction purposes, there is little reason to be concerned with static friction. If you have a case with a vehicle equipped with air brakes, there may be a much greater delay in wheel lockup from the time brakes were first applied. For a more thorough discussion of heavy-truck braking, see Topic 878.

3. BASIC ASSUMPTIONS FOR FRICTION

For sliding friction, several conditions are generally always expected. With a rubber tire sliding on pavement, however, some of these conditions might not be present. The general properties of friction are as follows:

1. If the sliding surface is horizontal, the horizontal force required to slide the object is proportional to the object's weight. Thus, if the weight of the sliding object is increased by 20 percent, then the required horizontal force to cause it to slide is also increased by 20 percent.

2. Dynamic friction is lower than static friction. That is, after an object starts sliding, it takes less force to keep it sliding.

3. The friction force does not depend on how much area of the sliding object is in contact with the surface. That is, if you increased the area that is in contact with the surface over which an object is sliding (keeping everything else constant), the amount of force required to slide the object would stay the same.

4. The friction force does not change when velocity changes. Thus, the friction force at a higher sliding speed would be the same as that at a lower sliding speed.

5. The friction force does not change when the temperature changes. That is, the friction force is the same for an object sliding over a surface at 80° Fahrenheit as it is at 20° Fahrenheit.

Friction Force Proportional to Weight

If you are on a level surface and sliding a car with locked wheels, there is an increase in the horizontal friction force if weight is added to the car. If the weight is increased by 20 percent, you can expect the horizontal friction force to be increased by approximately 20 percent. Generally, it is expected that friction capability will decrease some with increased load[1].

If tires on a large, heavy truck are tested for friction coefficient over a given pavement and are compared to tire friction values on a much smaller passenger car, do *not* expect to see the same friction values. This is because of the *far greater* load placed on truck tires and other inherent differences between truck tires and passenger car tires[1].

For passenger cars the friction force (with locked wheels and similar tires) that can be generated over a given pavement does not differ significantly between sizes of cars. For example, if you have a compact car and an intermediate/full-size car sliding with locked wheels at 30 mi/hr over the same pavement with similar tires, expect to get essentially the same friction values.

Dynamic and Static Friction

In discussing the transition from static to dynamic friction, it is useful to consider how the drag of the road on a tire varies from onset to a locked wheel skid. This is illustrated in Exhibit 3. Before braking, the wheel has full rotation; but where the tire touches the road surface, there is, momentarily, no movement relative to the road surface. Compared to the vehicle's speed, the speed of the tire in contact with the road is then 0 percent. As soon as brakes are applied, a retarding force on the tire is developed by the road. When this force begins, elastic tire material is pressed into road surface irregularities (asperities). Thus, the drag force stretches the tread rubber for an instant while the body of the tire begins to slow down. At this point, the speed of the tire close to the road surface compared to the vehicle's speed has increased.

As the braking force is increased, the tire loses its grip on the pavement and starts to slip. As slipping increases, the amount of time for the rubber to grip the road surface becomes less and less. When the wheel reaches lockup, the tire now has 100 percent slip. At 100 percent slip, the tire is sliding with dynamic friction. As can be seen in Exhibit 3 (which is for a particular tire), the friction force reaches a maximum at 10 to 20 percent slip for the tire.

For panic braking situations, drivers generally apply their brakes very rapidly and very hard. This will lock the wheels rapidly (for non-antilock brakes), thus causing nearly all of the braking to occur at 100 percent slip.

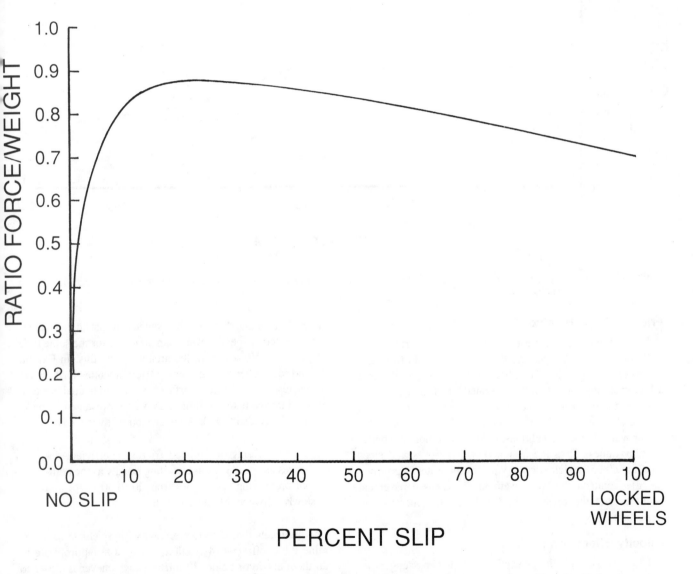

Exhibit 3. *As a tire first starts to slip on a hard surface, the friction force increases and reaches a maximum. Then the friction force decreases somewhat. There is not much difference in the friction force at high values of slip.*

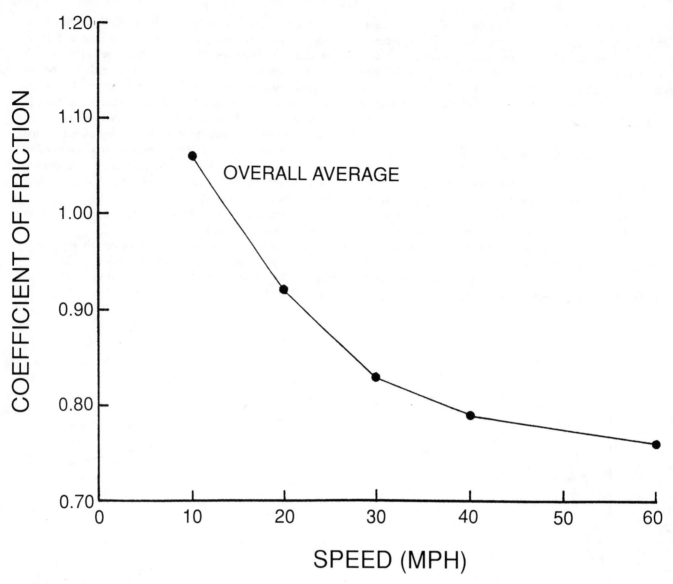

Exhibit 4. *It is generally found with normal passenger car tires that the coefficient of friction reduces with increasing speed. This exhibit shows the results of one such study.*

Friction Force Related to Sliding Area

In some instances a greater tire-pavement interface area will contribute to a higher friction force. For bald (no tread grooves) tires on a clean, dry, hard surface, it is possible that a higher sliding force will be generated[3]. Definitely, a lower value would not be expected. Also, a higher value of friction can be obtained with bald tires on ice.

For wet pavement conditions, bald tires do not give better friction values. Tires are designed with grooves and sipes (see Topic 825) which allow a place for the water to go when the tire contacts the wet pavement. Thus, as a pavement becomes wet the presence of tread becomes increasingly important.

Velocity Effects on Friction

The effects of velocity on friction on typical passenger-car tires is noticeable. For years, the table given in the *Traffic Ac-*

cident Investigation Manual has suggested that higher values are expected at speeds lower than 30 mi/hr for the same type of pavement. Research in the area supports this. In Exhibit 4 Ohio researchers[1] took average friction values for four vehicles tested over three surfaces at the indicated speeds. Small, intermediate and large cars were represented. A pickup truck was also tested. A conclusion of their study was:

> . . . the average calculated friction coefficient decreases as speed increases, falling rapidly as the nominal prebraking speed goes from 10 to 30 mi/hr and slowly between 30 and 60 mi/hr.

This indicates that if tests are done with a vehicle to determine the coefficient of friction, it would be appropriate to do them above or below 30 mi/hr — whichever is closer to the accident vehicle's speed. Collins[4] suggests reduction factors for coefficients of friction where the expected accident speed is greater than 40 mi/hr. Friction reduction factors are used in some computer programs.

Temperature Effects on Friction

The effects of temperature on the coefficient of friction are insignificant unless radical temperature differences are encountered. In general, friction will decrease slightly with an increase in air temperature. Reference 2 indicates that over a temperature range of 45° to 80° Fahrenheit on a dry asphalt surface, friction only decreased 0.10. On a wet surface the difference was even less. Compared to other factors, then, temperature effects are so minimal as to be rarely worth considering. If you have reason to be concerned about them, just be sure to do your friction test on a day with a similar temperature.

Other Considerations for Friction

Snow tires have little effect on braking with locked wheels over a snow-packed surface. Studded tires can enhance braking over icy surfaces, but can reduce friction under other conditions[5]. The effect of tire inflation pressure is sometimes raised. A higher air pressure than normal for a given tire reduces the contact area of a tire, just as lower tire pressures tend to increase the contact area. The effect of this small difference will have insignificant effects in most cases. High-performance tires may give higher friction values than normal passenger tires. This usually does not cause problems when speed estimates are done. Simply use the lower, "normal" friction coefficient to obtain a conservative estimate or do tests with similar high-performance tires. Antilock braking systems (ABS) do not operate at 100 percent slip. Thus, the performance of ABS-equipped cars could be better than that of locked-wheel-braked cars. Other advantages of ABS-equipped cars will be discussed later.

4. DEFINITION OF DRAG FACTOR

The term *drag factor* will not be found in typical engineering mechanics or physics books. It has been used for many years in traffic accident investigation/reconstruction. Drag factor is given the symbol *f*. Drag factor is defined as the force required for acceleration (or deceleration) in the direction of the acceleration (or deceleration) divided by the object's (vehicle's) weight. In equation form drag factor is defined as:

$$f = F/w \qquad (4)$$

Often some confusion is created when equations (3) and (4) are compared. The right sides of both equations are clearly the same. The difference is that equation (3) deals with coefficient of friction, μ, and equation (4) deals with drag factor, *f*. For μ, the object must be **sliding** across the surface. This is not the case for drag factor. Drag factor and coefficient of friction will be equal only in cases where all wheels are locked and sliding on a level surface.

Drag Factor Related to Vehicle Types

Consider a motorcycle on a level surface with the rear wheel locked and the front wheel rotating with no braking. There is sliding of the rear wheel on the pavement. Thus, the retarding force at the rear wheel is dependent on the coefficient of friction. However, not all wheels in contact with the road are braking. Therefore, the drag factor on the motorcycle is clearly not the same as the coefficient of friction between the rear wheel and the road surface. Actually, the drag factor of the motorcycle will be less than the coefficient of friction. A more detailed discussion of motorcycle braking is given in Topic 874.

Like motorcycles, tractor and semi-trailer vehicles can have different drag factors at each axle. The wheels on one axle may be locked, while wheels on another axle may have much less than 100 percent slip. Indeed, it is possible that the wheels on a particular axle may have different drag factors. Nevertheless, the drag factor on the *whole* vehicle is *one* value.

After a collision, the damaged vehicles usually travel some distance before they decelerate to a stop. Wheels are often jammed and will not rotate as a result of the collision. Also, the damaged vehicles are usually rotating as they move off to their rest positions. With a rotating vehicle the drag factor will most likely be changing as it rotates and moves to its rest position. In all cases there is a drag factor associated with the deceleration of the vehicle to a stop.

Drag Factor Related to Gravity

Earlier in this topic you were given the relationship between acceleration (*a*), drag factor (*f*), and the acceleration of gravity (*g*) in equation (2):

$$a = fg \qquad (2)$$

If you are using equation (1) to solve for the initial velocity when a vehicle is slowing, be sure to use a negative ($-$) value for acceleration (*a*). Drag factor (*f*) does not have a sign ($+$ or $-$) associated with it. So if you use equation (2), you will need to add the negative sign. The use of this equation is discussed with sample problems in Topic 860.

Drag factor can easily be solved from equation (2) to get:

$$f = a/g \qquad (5)$$

So it can be seen that *f* is simply a ratio of acceleration of the object to the acceleration of gravity. Thus in free-fall, where acceleration, *a*, is equal to the acceleration of gravity, *g*, drag factor, *f*, is equal to 1.0 ($a = a/g = g/g = 1.0$).

Recall the basic definition of drag factor from equation (4):

$$f = F/w$$

where F is the force in the direction of the acceleration and w is the weight of the object. The only time that drag factor could be equal to 1.0 is when the acceleration force, F, is equal to the object's weight. So clearly when drag factor equals 1.0, the force on the object is equal to its weight and the acceleration is equal to g.

Because drag factor is always a ratio of the acceleration of the object to the acceleration of gravity, drag factor may be thought of as the percentage of the acceleration of gravity expressed as a decimal. So if someone says, "That car decelerated at 0.5g," he means that the drag factor was equal to 0.5.

Drag Factor for Increasing and Decreasing Velocity

Usually, drag factor refers to conditions where a vehicle or object is slowing. Clearly, the word *drag* implies slowing. Nevertheless, drag factor or f can be used for cases where a vehicle or object has increasing velocity (positive acceleration) or decreasing velocity (negative acceleration). If you convert f to a (acceleration) to use in one of the equations given in the *Manual*, always be careful to use a positive value for a if the velocity is increasing and a negative value for a if the velocity is decreasing.

5. FRICTION CIRCLE

Essentially, all of the normally occurring forces on a car are transferred through the tires at their interface with the road surface. Other forces not considered are such things as air loads (wind resistance) and collision forces. If a car is steered, the wheels are turned and a side force is generated because of the slip angle between the plane of the tire and the direction of motion of the car. When a car is braked, the slip between tires and pavement might reach 100 percent. At that point there is no significant friction left to steer the car. For example, the skidmarks shown in Exhibit 5 were made by locked wheels due to hard braking. After the wheels were locked, the steering wheel was turned hard to the left. The car continued to travel straight ahead; the steering of the wheels had no appreciable effect. All of the available friction had been used in the 100 percent slip in braking. In Exhibit 6, which is a continuation of the tire marks shown in Exhibit 5, the brakes were released at Point A in the photograph. Then the car immediately started turning in the direction of the steering and ultimately went into a yaw.

If both of the rear wheels are locked on a passenger car while the front wheels continue to rotate, an unstable condition develops. Because the front wheels are free to rotate, they can continue to have side friction forces. However, with the rear wheels locked, they have no effective friction available to keep the rear of the car from sliding to the left or the

Exhibit 5. *This photograph shows the typical mark observed with locked wheel skids. Note that the striations in the skidmark are parallel to the mark.*

Exhibit 6. *This photograph is a continuation of the mark shown in Exhibit 5. The driver began to steer while the car was sliding with locked wheels. Then the brakes were released and the car went into a yaw. Note how different the striations are from those in Exhibit 5.*

Exhibit 7. *Only the rear wheels have been locked by the emergency brake. The rear-tire/pavement interface can no longer provide enough side friction to keep the rear wheels in line with the front. The rear has started to slide sideways.*

Exhibit 8. *This photograph shows the continued movement of the car from the point shown in Exhibit 7. Note how the car has come around a considerable amount.*

right. If the pavement has a cross slope, the rear tires will tend to slide in that direction. Once the rear has started to slide sideways with only the rear tires locked, the car will continue rotating (if there is enough speed) until the car is going backward. If the driver steers hard as the rear tires are locked, the back of the car will slide in the direction of the centrifugal force caused by the steering. An example of this phenomenon is shown in Exhibits 7 and 8. These marks were made by locking the rear wheels with the emergency brake. As in the case shown in Exhibits 5 and 6, all the friction was used in the braking (100 percent slip) and no other significant side force was available.

To describe more effectively what is happening in the two previous examples, the forces being applied to the tire will be discussed. This is often diagrammed as the *friction circle* shown in Exhibit 9. As you can see, the lateral and longitudinal directions of force are indicated on the tire. The longitudinal forces are either for braking or for driving the car forward. The lateral is, of course, for steering. If the tire could have equal friction both laterally and longitudinally, then the friction circle would indeed be a circle. Actually, the friction capability is not quite identical for every direction the force is applied to the tire, so the circle is more of an ellipse; but for this explanation a circle will be adequate. The maximum force available is the radius of the circle. The direction of the force indicates how much force is being used in the longitudinal and lateral directions.

In Exhibit 9A the force on the tire is a driving force and a steering force. The vector sum of the lateral and longitudinal force is clearly less than the maximum allowable. In Exhibit 9B there is some steering and a considerable amount of braking force. In Exhibit 9C the tire is skidding and the direction of motion is opposite the resultant friction force.

A more detailed discussion of the effects of braking and yawing together is included in the topic on yaws, Topic 872.

6. DRAG FACTOR/FRICTION COEFFICIENT FOR AN ACTUAL ACCIDENT

If you are working on an accident case in which you need to know the appropriate drag factor (friction coefficient) to use, there are several methods for determining this:

1. Test-skid the accident vehicle or an exemplar vehicle.
2. Slide a test tire (not the whole vehicle) to get a friction coefficient.
3. Use existing highway department skid numbers for the road in question.
4. Look up friction coefficients in a table and apply the appropriate adjustments to them for the case at hand.

Each method has its own merits and problems. The method you select will depend on such variables as time, cost, disruption to traffic, and safety.

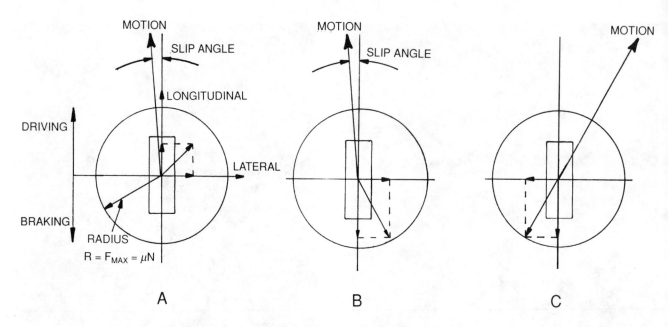

Exhibit 9. *In A a tire is rolling with a slip angle. This gives a lateral force that does not exceed the maximum available. In B there is a slip angle, along with a braking force. The resultant force approaches the maximum friction available. In C there is a locked wheel, and the tire force is along the same line as the motion vector.*

Test Skids Without Special Equipment

For the ideal test, use the same vehicle that made the accident skidmarks (if it is not too severely damaged), at the same spot, with the same load and surface conditions. Drive the test vehicle at what you believe may have been the speed of the vehicle that made the marks. You need not make the tests at an extremely high speed just to be near the accident vehicle speed. If the ideal test situation is not possible — which is usually the case — then approximate it as closely as possible. It is important to use the same pavement in the same condition; it is less important to use the same vehicle. Drive the vehicle at the estimated accident speed. Again, do not go over a reasonably safe speed. A good test speed is the speed limit (if it is 35 mi/hr or less). Then, if the accident skids are longer than the speed-limit skids, there is direct proof that the vehicle's speed was greater than the speed limit. Hold the speed constant as the vehicle reaches the right place on the road, note the speed shown on the speedometer, hold the steering wheel steady, put on the brake *very* hard and *very* quickly, and *hold* it until the vehicle stops. Now measure the the length of each mark. Repeat the test at the same speed. If there is a difference of only 10 percent or less between the two tests (compare the longest skid from the first test to the longest skid from the second), consider the test adequate. If not, repeat the test until consistent results are obtained.

Good skid tests are more difficult to make than you might think. Adjusting speed and holding the indication on the speedometer can give trouble, but the main difficulty is applying brakes quickly and strongly. It may take several trials, especially with massive tires and without power brakes. If

brakes are applied too slowly or not strongly enough, the vehicle loses considerable speed before wheels lock and tires slide. Skidmarks are then too short for the initial speed reading, and the calculated coefficient of friction too high, resulting in a high estimate of accident speed. Reed[6] suggests that 15 to 30 percent of the initial energy of a car may be dissipated before clearly (easily) visible skidmarks are produced. (This does not mean that 15 to 30 percent of the velocity has been lost before the marks are seen). This clearly illustrates

Exhibit 10. *This device fires a pigment on the road surface when braking starts. Both inertial and electrical models are used.*

the importance of detecting where the vehicle first started to slow.

Speedometer error must be reckoned with. If there is any question about it, test the speedometer as follows. With the speedometer continuously indicating the same speed as when the test skids were made, measure how many seconds it takes to drive the measured mile between two mileposts (or the measured kilometer between two kilometer markers). Then divide 3,600 by the measured number of seconds to get the actual speed. For example, if it took 75 sec to cover a measured mile, the speed would be 3,600/75 = 48 mi/hr. If the speedometer was reading 50 mi/hr throughout this trial run, it would have indicated 2 mi/hr high. If the test skid had been made with the speedometer reading 50 mi/hr, the coefficient of friction calculation would have to be made on the basis of the actual speed of 48 mi/hr. Using the correct initial speed is extremely important. Say, for example, you did a test that resulted in 40 ft of skids. The drag factors you would get if the initial speed was 29, 30 and 31 mi/hr are shown in the table below.

Speed (mi/hr)	Drag factor
29	.70
30	.75
31	.80

As you can see, there are significant differences between the 29 and 31 mi/hr tests. Clearly, it is important not to minimize the effect of speed when friction/drag factor tests are being done.

Test Skids With a Pavement Spotter and Radar

Often it is not easy to detect when a skid starts. The beginning of a skidmark is not nearly as dark as it becomes later in the skid. Topic 817 has a fairly long discussion about the difficulty of detecting skidmarks; if you have questions regarding their physical appearance, consult that topic. A pavement spotter can be used to determine the beginning of the deceleration of a vehicle doing a test skid. The spotter is sometimes referred to as a *bumper gun* (see Exhibit 10). A pigment is shot onto the pavement when the brakes are first pushed. This can be actuated by the brake light or some other electrical or inertial device. In this case, you may be adding deceleration distance to that caused by the full lock-up condition of the wheels. The effect of this is to calculate a lower drag factor, which will give a lower speed estimate of the accident vehicle.

Another way to increase your accuracy when doing test skids is to use radar to get the speed when the brakes are first applied. Most police agencies have ready access to such equipment. Both on-board and external radar units are very useful in making skid tests.

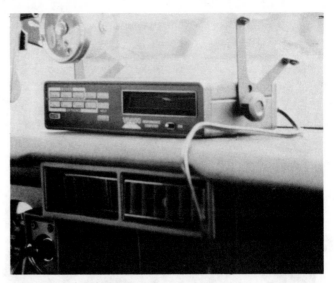

Exhibit 11. *Accelerometers like the one shown in the photograph will probably be used more as their price comes down. This model is very easy to install and gives reliable results.*

Test Skids With Accelerometers

Several accelerometers are available at a price that is affordable (less than $400) to many agencies that do test skids. Two such accelerometers are shown installed in cars in Exhibits 11 and 12. The model in Exhibit 11 is easy to install and gives peak and average g's in the longitudinal direction. It also gives the total time of deceleration and distance. Exhibit 12 shows a unit that can record up to eight minutes of data. It measures both longitudinal and lateral acceleration. Data from the accelerometer memory unit can then be transferred to a microcomputer.

Accelerometers are particularly helpful when a test must be made on a road with considerable traffic. Excepting the police, most people cannot close the road to traffic to do test skids. The accelerometer allows you to wait until there is a break in traffic, accelerate the car to the appropriate speed, check again for traffic, and slam on the brakes. When the vehicle stops, immediately move it off the roadway; the accelerometer will hold the data in its memory. After getting off the road, look at your data. This is certainly safer than trying to do the test when traffic is using the road. It is not necessary, of course, to measure the length of skids when you use the accelerometer. The deceleration is recorded in the unit. If there is simply too much traffic to do the test, use common sense and do *not* attempt it.

Sliding Test Tire

There are different methods that can be used to devise a test by dragging a test tire. A whole tire and wheel can be used as shown in Exhibit 13. Another method is to use part of a tire and fill it with concrete as shown in Exhibit 14. Both methods are often criticized because the load on the tire is considerably less than what a normal passenger car tire will

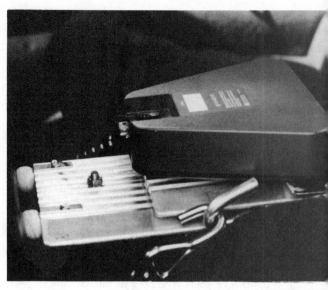

Exhibit 12. *This model of accelerometer allows several minutes of data to be stored. Later it can be transferred to a personal computer for printing or storage.*

be carrying. It is generally accepted that the friction capability of a rubber tire on pavement tends to deteriorate as the load is increased. It is also argued that at typical skidding speeds, the tire is heated due to friction. However, it is not expected that the heating of the pulled tire (or part of a tire) will have the same effect as the heating of a tire on a car that is being skidded. Thus, it is generally expected that friction data collected in this manner should be reduced to reflect

this. Indeed, one commercial drag sled manufacturer[7] gives suggested reduction factors.

If you are in a location where skidding a car is inherently dangerous, using a test tire could be appropriate. Sliding a test tire might *not* be appropriate, however, on soft turf, loose gravel, or other soft surfaces. A car skidding on such surfaces will normally have material build up in front of the sliding tires; whereas the sliding test tire may not weigh enough to

Exhibit 13. *Coefficient of friction can be measured by dragging a tire of known weight along the pavement and measuring the pull required. You must make corrections of the angle of pull.*

Exhibit 14. *Coefficient of friction can be measured by dragging part of a tire filled with concrete, as shown here. The angle of pull should be parallel to the surface.*

cause such build-up, resulting in lower friction coefficient values. On the other hand, it has been reported that a test tire sliding on grass can give a higher reading than a car sliding on grass. The reason for this is not clear. Perhaps there is some interaction of the tire and grass at a light load that does not occur with typical wheel loads.

Highway Department Skid Numbers

State highway departments (departments of transportation) regularly test their roads for friction coefficients. The tests are to determine *skid numbers*. A skid number is obtained by using an ASTM (American Society for Testing and Materials) tire in a specially designed drag trailer. The skid number is simply the friction coefficient obtained with these standard tests, multiplied by 100. Often the highway department will have done a test in the area of an accident. The question that sometimes comes up is whether the skid number represents the friction coefficient that a normal passenger car could be expected to get. In the Ohio tests (Reference 1), ASTM skid numbers were compared to calculated friction coefficients. At lower speeds it was concluded that the calculated friction coefficients were well above the ASTM skid numbers. However, there was generally good agreement at the higher speeds. This was partially attributed to the ASTM skid number test speed being at 40 mi/hr.

Several arguments against using highway department ASTM skid numbers in actual accident cases have been made. One is that the standard test tire does not have the same characteristics as typical passenger cars. It is generally argued that the ASTM tire will give lower friction values. Another argument is that the highway department tests may be dated and the surface condition has somehow changed. Also, the load on the tire may not approximate the load a nor-

mal passenger car would have. Thus, it may be just as well to do your own tests with an exemplar vehicle to eliminate these criticisms. However, if you get the case three years after the accident date and the road has since been repaved, a highway department skid number obtained near the accident date can be a useful place to start.

Table of Coefficients of Friction

Exhibit 15[8] gives a range of friction coefficients for several surface descriptions. The values given in Exhibit 15 are for passenger cars and pickup trucks equipped with typical tires. They are *not* typical values seen for heavy trucks. (See Topic 878 for typical deceleration values for heavy trucks). If tests cannot be made at an accident site, it may be necessary to use a range of typical values that have been seen for your surface description. Pavements described in the same words may have a considerable range of friction characteristics, depending on the exact material used and the detailed characteristics of the surface. The figures given are average coefficients of friction throughout the skid.

It can be seen in Exhibit 15 that higher friction coefficients are suggested for the lower speed range. This is consistent, of course, with the findings shown in Exhibit 4. For conservative speed estimates, use the lower coefficients given in the table. Also, you can see there is considerable difference between wet and dry surfaces. In nearly all cases, friction coefficients decrease considerably with wet surfaces. One exception is loose gravel. It is not uncommon to get higher friction coefficients with wet, loose gravel. The single most important factor affecting tire friction force in practice is the presence of water (in its various forms)[9]. The effect of water, snow, and ice is clearly evident by inspecting Exhibit 15.

Generally, it is very rare to see a friction coefficient much over 0.90. Exhibit 15 does list friction coefficients over 0.90 and even as high as 1.2. The value of 1.2 or even 1.0 is *rarely* experienced. If you have this high friction coefficient when you run a skid test, expect to see a great deal of abrasion to the tires on your test vehicle — and make sure that you are getting the full length of the test vehicle deceleration. If you are not using a pavement spotter (bumper gun), put a chalk mark or a piece of white tape on the sidewalls of your tires and have someone watch the marked wheels to see when they lock. Compare this location to the skidmarks left on the road. If they are different, make the appropriate corrections.

7. VELOCITY EQUATIONS FOR SKIDDING

At the beginning of this topic, equation (1) was given to calculate initial braking velocity when the distance the vehicle decelerated (d), the deceleration of the vehicle (a, negative for slowing), and the end velocity (v_e) are known. Equation (1) is repeated here:

$$v_i = \sqrt{v_e^2 - 2ad} \qquad (1)$$

COEFFICIENTS OF FRICTION OF VARIOUS ROADWAY SURFACES

DESCRIPTION OF ROAD SURFACE	DRY				WET			
	Less than 30 mph		More than 30 mph		Less than 30 mph		More than 30 mph	
	From	To	From	To	From	To	From	To
PORTLAND CEMENT								
New, Sharp	.80	1.20	.70	1.00	.50	.80	.40	.75
Traveled	.60	.80	.60	.75	.45	.70	.45	.65
Traffic Polished	.55	.75	.50	.65	.45	.65	.45	.60
ASPHALT or TAR								
New, Sharp	.80	1.20	.65	1.00	.50	.80	.45	.75
Travelled	.60	.80	.55	.70	.45	.70	.40	.65
Traffic Polished	.55	.75	.45	.65	.45	.65	.40	.60
Excess Tar	.50	.60	.35	.60	.30	.60	.25	.55
GRAVEL								
Packed, Oiled	.55	.85	.50	.80	.40	.80	.40	.60
Loose	.40	.70	.40	.70	.45	.75	.45	.75
CINDERS								
Packed	.50	.70	.50	.70	.65	.75	.65	.75
ROCK								
Crushed	.55	.75	.55	.75	.55	.75	.55	.75
ICE								
Smooth	.10	.25	.07	.20	.05	.10	.05	.10
SNOW								
Packed	.30	.55	.35	.55	.30	.60	.30	.60
Loose	.10	.25	.10	.20	.30	.60	.30	.60

Exhibit 15. *This table lists coefficients of friction of various roadway surfaces. This table is not intended for large, heavy trucks.*

Of course, acceleration is related to drag factor by equation (2):

$$a = fg \qquad (2)$$

Again, remember that if a vehicle is slowing, you must insert a negative sign, $-$, in front of the value for acceleration.

A simple example problem follows. Assume a car skidded to a stop ($v_e = 0$) with a drag factor (f) of 0.75 over a distance (d) of 95 ft. The acceleration, a, is calculated from equation (2):

$$
\begin{aligned}
a &= fg \qquad (2)\\
&= -(.75)(32.2 \text{ ft/sec/sec})\\
&= -24.2 \text{ ft/sec/sec}
\end{aligned}
$$

The initial velocity is calculated from equation (1):

$$
\begin{aligned}
v_i &= \sqrt{v_e^2 - 2ad} \qquad (1)\\
&= \sqrt{0^2 - 2(-24.2)(95)}\\
&= 67.8 \text{ ft/sec}
\end{aligned}
$$

Validation of Equation (1)

At times the application of equation (1) to accident reconstruction has been questioned. One of the objectives of the study listed as Reference 1 was to look at equation (1) coupled with equation (2) to determine whether other equations could be more accurate. The NHTSA researchers concluded that the use of the theoretical equations, (1) and (2), is valid; they were the most accurate of the equations tried. The researchers further concluded that the assumptions used in the theoretical equations are valid. Concerns such as constant deceleration throughout the skid were shown to be essentially correct. The difference in deceleration throughout the skid was found to be too small to affect the results. They did point out the concern to do your test skids at a similar speed. Once wheels lock, they stay locked, leaving marks. Not always would a wheel lock. This was found not to cause problems during hard (panic) braking. The effect of other forces, such as aerodynamic drag, was found to be insignificant when compared to the braking force. Finally, the slide friction coefficient of a wheel was found to depend only on the vehicle's overall weight, tire type, and pavement composition (as long as the speed effect was taken care of as stated before). Variations in at-rest loads on the tires, weight shift, and temperature were found to be insignificant.

Tables and Nomographs to Determine Skidding Vehicle Speeds

For those not used to using equations, tables have been developed to determine the initial speed of vehicles that skid to a stop. Typical tables are shown as Exhibits 16 and 17. Exhibit 16 has been worked in the units of mi/hr. To use the table you must first determine the drag factor and length of the slide to stop in feet. You need to know the same variables to use Exhibit 17. However, Exhibit 17 requires that the length of the slide to stop be measured in meters, with the resulting speed in km/hr.

Another method that can be used to determine the initial speed of a vehicle that skids to a stop is to use a nomograph. Two such nomographs are Exhibits 18 (for U.S.A. units) and 19 (for metric units). Put a straight edge on the appropriate drag factor and distance at which the vehicle slid to a stop. Where the straight edge intersects the speed line, read the initial speed in either mi/hr or km/hr.

Unequal Drag Factors on Axles

Passenger cars do not have the same load on each axle when they are not being accelerated (i.e., when at rest or moving at constant velocity). During hard braking, load is shifted to the front axle. Because of this load shift, no correction needs to be made when all wheels are locked. If, however, one axle has a drag factor different from that of the other axle, you cannot assume the car was braked with a drag factor equal to locked wheel conditions (that is, drag factor for the whole vehicle equal to the sliding coefficient of friction). Equation (6) addresses this (see Topic 890 for the derivation):

$$f_R = \frac{f_f - x_f(f_f - f_r)}{1 - z(f_f - f_r)} \qquad (6)$$

where f_R = drag factor on the vehicle,
f_f = drag factor on the front axle,
f_r = drag factor on the rear axle,
x_f = horizontal distance of the center of mass from the front axle as a decimal fraction of the wheelbase, and
z = height of the center of mass as a decimal fraction of the wheelbase.

Consider the following example. Assume the height of the vehicle's center of mass is 2.08 ft and is located 4.22 ft behind the front axle. The wheelbase of the car is 9.39 ft. Therefore, z is equal to .222 (2.08/9.39 = .222) and x_f is equal to .449 (4.22/9.39 = .449). Assume there is no braking on the front axle, resulting in a drag factor determined only by the rolling resistance, 0.01. Assume the rear wheels are locked by brakes and slide on a pavement with a coefficient of friction averaging 0.65. Then summarizing, the values for the required quantities are:

$$z = 0.222$$
$$x_f = 0.449$$
$$f_f = 0.01$$
$$f_r = 0.65$$

Substitute these values for the symbols in the equation:

$$f_R = \frac{0.01 - 0.449(0.01 - 0.65)}{1 - 0.222(0.01 - 0.65)}$$
$$f_R = 0.297/1.14$$
$$f_R = 0.26$$

Therefore, the drag factor for the *whole* vehicle is 0.26.

Drag Factors for Other Vehicles

This topic does not discuss how to determine drag factors for motorcycles and articulated vehicles. These vehicle types are discussed in Topics 874 and 878. Unlike passenger cars and pickup trucks, the operators of motorcycles and articulated vehicles generally have the option of applying brakes on only some of the axles. Therefore, do not assume that the drag factors for motorcycles and large trucks are the same as the values that can be obtained for four-tired vehicles.

Drag Factor on a Grade

For the case where a vehicle is skidding with all wheels locked on a non-level surface (that is, up or down a grade), the drag factor is not equal to the coefficient of friction. In Topic 890 it was shown that the drag factor on a grade is given by the following formula:

$$f_G = (\mu + G)/\sqrt{1 + G^2} \qquad (7)$$

Exhibit 16
U.S.A. Units
SPEED IN MILES PER HOUR REQUIRED TO SLOW TO A STOP

FOR VARIOUS DISTANCES AND SURFACES

Average drag factor during slide to stop

Surface groupings: Ice → · Clean, wet paving · Snow · Gravel · Clean, dry paving

Brake groupings: Illegal brakes · Fair brakes · Good brakes · Excellent brakes

Length of slide to stop in meters	0.05	0.10	0.20	0.30	0.35	0.40	0.45	0.50	0.55	0.60	0.65	0.70	0.75	0.80	0.85	0.90	0.95	1.00	1.10	1.20
2	2	2	3	4	5	5	5	5	6	6	6	6	7	7	7	7	8	8	8	8
4	2	3	5	6	6	7	7	8	8	8	9	9	9	10	10	10	11	11	11	12
6	3	4	6	7	8	8	9	9	10	10	11	11	12	12	12	13	13	13	14	15
8	3	5	7	8	9	10	10	11	11	12	12	13	13	14	14	15	15	15	16	17
10	4	5	8	9	10	11	12	12	13	13	14	14	15	15	16	16	17	17	18	19
12	4	6	8	10	11	12	13	13	14	15	15	16	16	17	17	18	18	19	20	21
14	5	6	9	11	12	13	14	14	15	16	17	17	18	18	19	19	20	20	21	22
16	5	7	10	12	13	14	15	15	16	17	18	18	19	20	20	21	21	22	23	24
18	5	7	10	13	14	15	16	16	17	18	19	19	20	21	21	22	23	23	24	25
20	5	8	11	13	14	15	16	17	18	19	20	20	21	22	23	23	24	24	26	27
25	6	9	12	15	16	17	18	19	20	21	22	23	24	24	25	26	17	17	29	30
30	7	9	13	16	18	19	20	21	22	23	24	25	26	27	28	28	29	30	31	33
35	7	10	14	18	19	20	22	23	24	25	26	27	28	29	30	31	32	32	34	35
40	8	11	15	19	20	22	23	24	26	27	28	29	30	31	32	33	34	35	36	38
45	8	12	16	20	22	23	25	26	27	28	30	31	32	33	34	35	36	37	38	40
50	9	12	17	21	23	24	26	27	29	30	31	32	34	35	36	37	38	39	41	42
55	9	13	18	22	24	26	27	29	30	31	33	34	35	36	37	39	40	41	43	44
60	9	13	19	23	25	27	28	30	31	33	34	35	37	38	39	40	41	42	44	46
65	10	14	20	24	26	28	30	31	33	34	36	37	38	39	41	42	43	44	46	48
70	10	14	20	25	27	29	31	32	34	35	37	38	40	41	42	43	45	46	48	50
75	11	15	21	26	28	30	32	34	35	37	38	40	41	42	44	45	46	47	50	52
80	11	15	22	27	29	31	33	35	36	38	39	41	42	44	45	46	48	49	51	54
85	11	16	23	28	30	32	34	36	37	39	41	42	44	45	47	48	49	50	53	55
90	12	16	23	28	31	33	35	37	39	40	42	43	45	46	48	49	51	52	54	57
95	12	17	24	29	32	34	36	38	40	41	43	45	46	48	49	51	53	53	56	58
100	12	17	24	30	32	35	37	39	41	42	44	46	47	49	50	52	53	55	57	60
105	13	18	25	31	33	35	38	40	42	43	45	47	49	50	52	53	55	56	59	61
110	13	18	26	31	34	36	39	41	43	44	46	48	50	51	53	54	56	57	60	63
115	13	19	26	32	35	37	39	42	44	45	47	49	51	53	54	56	57	59	62	64
120	13	19	27	33	35	38	40	42	44	46	48	50	52	54	55	57	58	60	63	66
125	14	19	27	34	36	39	41	43	45	47	49	51	53	55	56	58	60	61	64	67
130	14	20	28	34	37	39	42	44	46	48	50	52	54	56	58	59	61	62	65	68
135	14	20	28	35	38	40	43	45	47	49	51	53	55	57	59	60	62	64	67	70
140	14	20	29	35	38	41	43	46	48	50	52	54	56	58	60	61	63	65	68	71
145	15	21	29	36	39	42	44	47	49	51	53	55	57	59	61	63	64	66	69	72
150	15	21	30	37	40	42	45	47	50	52	54	56	58	60	62	64	65	67	70	73
155	15	22	30	37	40	43	46	48	51	53	55	57	59	61	63	65	66	68	72	75
160	15	22	31	38	41	44	46	49	51	54	56	58	60	62	64	66	68	69	73	76
165	16	22	31	39	42	44	47	50	51	54	57	59	61	63	65	67	69	70	74	77
170	16	23	32	39	42	45	48	50	53	55	58	60	62	64	66	68	70	71	75	78
175	16	23	32	40	43	46	49	51	54	56	58	61	63	65	67	69	71	72	76	79
180	16	23	33	40	43	46	49	52	54	57	59	61	64	66	68	70	72	73	77	80
185	17	24	33	41	44	47	50	53	55	58	60	62	65	67	69	71	73	74	78	82
190	17	24	34	41	45	48	51	53	56	58	61	63	65	68	70	72	74	75	79	83
195	17	24	34	42	45	48	51	54	57	59	62	64	66	68	70	72	74	76	80	84
200	17	24	35	42	46	49	52	55	57	60	62	65	67	69	71	73	75	77	81	85
220	18	26	36	44	48	51	54	57	60	63	65	68	70	73	75	77	79	81	85	89
240	19	27	38	46	50	54	57	60	63	66	68	71	73	76	78	80	83	85	89	93
260	20	28	39	48	52	56	59	62	65	68	71	74	76	79	81	84	86	88	93	97
280	20	29	41	50	54	58	61	65	68	71	74	77	79	82	84	87	89	92	96	100
300	21	30	42	52	56	60	64	67	70	73	76	79	82	85	87	90	92	95	99	104
325	22	31	44	54	58	62	66	70	73	76	80	83	86	88	91	94	96	99	104	108
350	23	32	46	56	61	65	69	72	76	79	83	86	89	92	94	97	100	102	107	112
375	24	34	47	58	63	67	71	75	79	82	85	89	92	95	98	101	103	106	111	116
400	24	35	49	60	65	69	73	77	81	85	88	92	95	98	101	104	107	109	115	120

Exhibit 17
Metric Units
SPEED IN KILOMETERS PER HOUR REQUIRED TO SLOW TO A STOP

FOR VARIOUS DISTANCES AND SURFACES

Length of slide to stop in meters	Average drag factor during slide to stop																			
	Ice →		Snow →			← Clean, wet paving →				← Clean, dry paving →									
	← Illegal brakes →					► ◄ Fair brakes →			► ◄		← Good brakes →			► ◄ Excellent brakes →				
	0.05	0.10	0.20	0.30	0.35	0.40	0.45	0.50	0.55	0.60	0.65	0.70	0.75	0.80	0.85	0.90	0.95	1.00	1.10	1.20
1	4	5	7	9	9	10	11	11	11	12	13	13	14	14	15	15	15	16	17	17
2	5	7	10	12	13	14	15	16	17	17	18	19	19	20	20	21	22	22	24	25
3	6	9	12	15	16	17	18	19	20	21	22	23	24	25	25	26	27	28	29	30
4	7	10	14	17	19	20	21	22	24	25	26	27	28	28	29	30	31	32	33	35
5	8	11	16	20	21	22	24	25	26	28	29	30	31	32	33	34	35	36	37	42
6	9	12	17	21	23	24	26	26	29	30	31	33	34	35	36	37	38	39	41	44
7	9	13	19	23	25	27	28	28	31	33	34	35	36	37	39	40	41	42	44	46
8	10	14	20	25	27	28	30	32	33	35	36	38	39	40	41	43	44	45	47	49
9	11	15	21	26	28	30	32	34	35	37	38	40	41	43	44	45	46	48	50	52
10	11	16	22	28	30	32	34	36	37	39	41	42	44	45	46	48	49	50	53	55
11	12	17	24	29	31	33	35	37	39	41	43	44	46	47	49	50	51	53	55	58
12	12	17	25	30	33	35	37	39	41	43	44	46	48	49	51	52	54	55	58	60
13	13	18	26	31	34	36	38	41	43	44	46	48	50	51	53	54	56	57	60	63
14	13	19	27	33	35	37	40	42	44	46	48	50	51	53	55	56	58	59	62	65
15	14	19	28	34	36	39	41	43	46	48	50	51	53	55	57	58	60	62	65	67
16	14	20	28	35	38	40	43	45	47	49	51	53	55	57	59	60	62	64	67	70
17	15	20	29	36	39	41	44	46	49	51	53	55	57	58	60	62	64	66	69	72
18	15	21	30	37	40	42	45	48	50	52	54	56	58	60	62	64	66	67	71	74
19	16	22	31	38	41	44	47	49	51	54	56	58	60	62	64	66	67	69	73	76
20	16	22	32	39	42	45	48	50	53	55	57	59	62	64	66	67	69	71	75	78
22	17	24	33	41	44	47	50	53	55	58	60	62	65	67	69	71	73	75	78	82
24	17	25	35	43	46	49	52	55	58	60	63	65	67	70	72	74	76	78	82	85
26	18	26	36	44	48	51	54	57	60	63	65	68	70	73	75	77	79	81	85	89
28	19	27	38	46	50	53	56	59	62	65	68	70	73	75	78	80	81	84	88	92
30	19	28	39	48	52	55	58	62	65	67	70	73	75	78	80	83	85	87	91	95
32	20	28	40	49	53	57	60	64	67	70	73	75	78	80	83	85	88	90	94	99
34	21	29	41	51	55	58	62	66	69	72	75	78	80	83	85	88	90	93	97	102
36	21	30	43	52	56	60	64	67	71	74	77	80	83	85	88	90	93	95	100	105
38	22	31	44	54	58	62	66	69	73	76	79	82	85	88	90	93	95	98	103	107
40	23	32	45	55	59	63	68	71	75	78	81	84	87	90	93	95	98	101	106	110
42	23	33	46	56	61	65	69	72	76	80	83	86	89	92	95	98	100	103	108	113
44	24	33	47	58	62	66	71	75	78	82	85	88	91	94	97	100	103	105	111	115
46	24	34	48	59	64	68	72	76	80	84	87	90	93	96	99	102	105	108	113	118
48	25	35	49	60	65	69	74	78	82	85	89	92	95	98	102	105	107	110	116	121
50	25	36	50	62	67	70	75	79	83	87	91	94	97	101	104	107	110	112	119	123
52	26	36	51	63	68	72	77	81	85	89	92	96	99	103	106	109	112	115	120	126
54	26	37	52	64	69	74	78	83	87	91	94	98	101	105	108	111	114	117	123	128
56	27	38	53	65	70	75	80	84	88	92	96	100	103	106	110	113	116	118	125	130
58	27	38	54	66	72	76	81	86	90	94	98	101	105	108	112	115	118	121	127	133
60	28	39	55	68	73	78	83	87	91	95	99	103	107	110	114	117	120	123	129	135
62	28	40	56	69	74	79	84	88	93	97	101	105	108	112	115	119	122	125	131	137
64	28	40	57	70	75	80	85	90	94	99	103	106	110	113	117	121	124	127	133	139
66	29	41	58	71	76	81	87	91	96	100	104	108	112	115	119	122	126	129	135	141
68	29	41	59	72	78	83	88	93	97	102	106	110	114	117	121	124	128	131	138	144
70	30	42	60	73	79	84	89	94	99	103	107	111	115	119	123	126	130	133	140	146
75	31	44	62	75	81	87	92	97	102	107	111	115	119	123	127	131	134	138	144	151
80	32	45	64	78	84	89	95	100	105	110	115	119	123	127	131	135	139	142	149	156
85	33	46	66	80	87	92	98	104	109	114	118	123	127	131	135	139	143	147	154	161
90	34	48	67	83	89	95	101	107	112	117	123	126	131	135	139	143	147	151	158	165
95	35	49	69	85	92	98	104	110	115	120	125	130	134	139	143	147	151	155	163	170
100	36	50	71	87	94	100	107	112	118	123	128	133	138	142	147	151	155	159	167	174
110	37	53	75	91	99	105	112	118	124	129	134	140	144	149	154	158	163	167	175	183
120	39	55	78	95	103	110	117	123	129	135	140	146	151	156	161	165	170	174	183	191
130	41	57	81	99	107	114	123	128	134	140	146	152	157	162	167	172	177	181	190	199
140	42	59	84	103	111	118	126	133	139	147	152	157	163	168	173	178	183	188	197	206

Exhibit 18.

U.S.A. Units
NOMOGRAPH RELATING STOPPING DISTANCE AND TIME, INITIAL SPEED, AND AVERAGE DRAG FACTOR

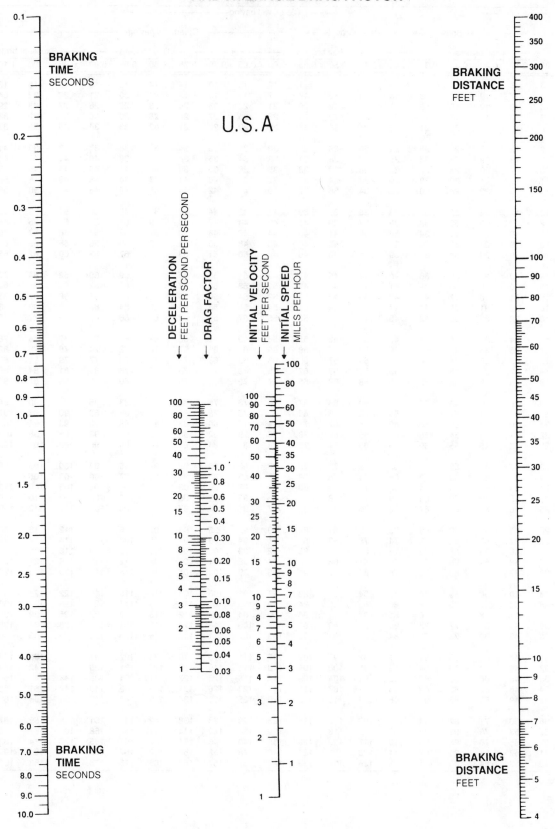

Exhibit 19.

Metric Units

NOMOGRAPH RELATING STOPPING DISTANCE AND TIME, INITIAL SPEED, AND AVERAGE DRAG FACTOR

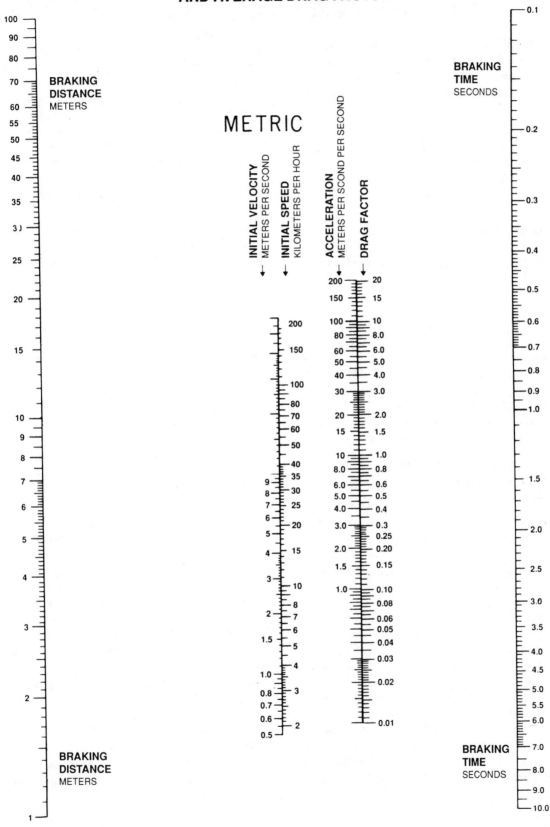

where
f_G = drag factor on a grade,

μ = coefficient of friction between the tires and pavement, and

G = the percent grade expressed as a decimal [positive ($+$) for an upgrade and negative ($-$) for a downgrade].

Consider the following example. Assume the coefficient of friction, μ, is equal to 0.80 and the vehicle in question is sliding down a 4 percent grade ($G = -.04$). Substituting into equation (7), the effective drag factor on a grade is calculated as follows:

$$
\begin{aligned}
f_G &= (\mu + G)/\sqrt{1 + G^2} \qquad (7) \\
&= (0.80 - 0.04)/\sqrt{1 + (-.04)^2} \\
&= 0.76/1.0016 \\
&= 0.76
\end{aligned}
$$

As you can see in this example, the denominator is so close to 1.0 that there is little reason to include it in the calculation. Because of this, equation (7) is normally shortened to the following:

$$ f_G = \mu + G \qquad (8) $$

For the example that was just worked, there is no significant difference whether equation (7) or (8) is used. With a downgrade or upgrade as high as 12 percent ($G = -0.12$ or 0.12), there is no significant difference between the answers obtained by using either equation. A grade of 12 percent is hardly ever seen on a typical roadway. Thus, for nearly all cases, the use of equation (8) is very acceptable.

8. SPEED ESTIMATES FROM IRREGULAR SKIDMARKS

Four different patterns of skidmarks are encountered in examining the roadway after an accident:

1. No sign of skidmarks is found, although there may be other kinds of tire marks. In this case, there is no indication on the road of any braking whatsoever. This does not mean there was no braking, only that braking was insufficient to lock wheels or that skidmarks disappeared before they were observed. There may be other indications of braking, such as the reports of witnesses. The car might have been equipped with an anti-lock braking system (ABS). With ABS-equipped cars, skidmarks may or may not be seen.

2. Skidmarks of nearly the same length are made by all wheels. No mark is more than 5 percent longer than the shortest mark. Such marks indicate that all wheels were locked suddenly and that the whole vehicle slid. This is a common circumstance. Unless there is reason to believe otherwise, one may conclude that the wheels were locked by braking. Use the longest skidmark and a drag factor

based on coefficient of friction to estimate speed as it has already been described.

3. There are definite skidmarks from all wheels, but they vary considerably in length.

4. Some, but not all, wheels make skidmarks.

The last two of these cases are irregular skidmarks.

To estimate speeds from skidmarks, you need to know values for drag factor (deceleration) and the distance through which it operated. In Case 1, there were no skidmarks, so no estimate of speed from skidmarks is possible. In Case 2, the length of the longest skidmark indicates the distance and the fact of sliding determines the drag factor, so estimating the speed the vehicle had to be going when it started to slide to a stop is a simple matter. For Cases 3 and 4 (irregular skidmarks), adjustments have to be made to get the equivalent complete skid or an equivalent reduced drag factor.

Two different assumptions are commonly made in speed estimates based on irregular skidmarks:

1. Average skidmark length is assumed to be the equivalent all-wheel sliding distance.

2. The longest skidmark is assumed to be the equivalent all-wheel sliding distance.

In both cases, pavement coefficient of friction is the basis for drag factor estimates and calculations.

Implications of whatever assumptions are made must be understood to be able to appraise the significance of the estimate based on them. These implications will be discussed and illustrated by applying each assumption to the same example of a set of irregular skidmarks.

Skidmarks from All Wheels

If all wheels do eventually leave genuine skidmarks, two conclusions are immediately warranted:

1. Brakes were capable of locking all wheels.

2. The driver was able to apply sufficient pedal pressure to cause them to do so.

As brake pedal pressure increases for one or more of several reasons, some wheels lock before the others.

Differences in pavement are sometimes responsible. Other things being equal, the wheel with the least pavement coefficient of friction will lock first as brake pedal pressure increases. A pavement may have greater coefficient of friction in some places than in others because of wear; because of foreign material such as loose dirt, oil spatter, or moisture; or because of different surface material, for example in patched paving.

Differences in weight on wheels may also account for some wheels skidding and others not. Other things being equal, the wheel with the least load on it will lock first as brake pedal pressure is increased. Differences in static load are produced in two ways:

1. Uneven loading of passengers or freight;

2. Crossways tilt of the road, which shifts weight from the uphill to the downhill side.

Unequal load, front and rear, due to weight shift (dynamic load) in braking may be compensated for in vehicle brake design. As brake pedal pressure is increased, the wheel with least weight in proportion to its braking strength will lock first. Cars equipped with ABS brakes compensate automatically for differences in wheel loads.

Differences in tire radius may affect which wheel locks first. Other things being equal, the wheel with the least radius will lock first as brake pedal pressure is increased. The maximum torque (rotational moment) of a wheel on a vehicle in motion is the coefficient of friction of the tire on the road times the weight on the tire times the leverage (moment arm). The moment arm is the distance from the axle to the road — that is, the tire radius. With equal road friction, weight, and brake resistance to rotation, the wheel with the greatest moment arm can overcome brake resistance, while the wheel with the least moment arm cannot. Thus, with increasing but equal brake effort, the wheel with the least radius (moment arm) will be the first to start sliding. The rolling radius of a tire may be decreased by two things:

1. Tread wear;
2. Overdeflection due to overloading or underinflation or both.

If brakes are applied very quickly and very hard, brake force will almost instantly lock all wheels; but if braking is applied gradually, the wheel with the least resistance to locking locks first, followed in turn by the others. Such gradual brake application often produces skidmarks varying considerably in length.

In ordinary vehicle operation, brakes are usually applied gradually and rarely to the full extent of the capabilities of brakes and driver. In emergency braking, brakes may also be applied gradually because the driver does not, at first, perceive the need for maximum braking or because the driver is reluctant to do as much braking as he can.

During partial skidding, tires which are sliding are producing all the drag of which the pavement at that point is capable. The other tires, which have not yet started to slide, are also being braked and so are also producing a slowing drag on the vehicle. Indeed, a wheel which leaves no skidmark may produce more road drag but with less drag factor than one which is skidding. This may be due to greater weight on it or because the pavement under it has greater friction or both. These conditions give the tire a better grip on the roadway so it can use more of the brake system capability. Furthermore, the friction drag of the tire on the road is greatest just before the tire begins to slide (static friction compared to dynamic friction).

Assumption 1 — Average Skidmark Length

Using average skidmark length as the basis for estimating a slide-to-stop speed assumes that there is the equivalent of complete locked-wheel skidding for a distance equal to the average skidmark length, but no other braking. However, if all wheels eventually lock, all will be doing some braking — often much braking — from the instant brakes are applied. Thus, average skidmark length gives a low speed estimate.

Such a "conservative" speed estimate favors the defendant who is being tried for speeding. In civil cases, however, what benefits the defendant is disadvantageous to the plaintiff, and the "conservative" skidmark assumption may do as much harm as good.

Example. Exhibit 20 shows a set of four skidmarks varying considerably in length. To begin with, the investigator must be sure that these are really skidmarks, especially toward the end where the vehicle swerves. That they are indeed skidmarks is indicated by the fact that striations throughout the marks are parallel to the marks. (See Topic 817 for a detailed description of skidmarks).

The speed limit at this point was 55 mi/hr. The pavement was dry, clean, well-traveled Portland cement concrete and had a three percent downgrade ($G = -0.03$) in the direction of travel.

The vehicle turned almost end for end during the last part of its approach to the collision point. This is because the rear wheels locked first. Having used all available traction by skidding, the rear wheels offered no more resistance to side-slipping downhill to the right on the cross slope of the pavement surface. The front wheels, not locked, had surplus friction which kept them from sliding downslope toward the right, resulting in the vehicle's assuming an angle to the roadway. The angle continued to increase rapidly until the vehicle was moving almost backward.

The vehicle was nearly stopped when it reached the tracks, where it was snagged by the passing train and carried off the roadway.

The four skidmarks measured

Right rear	407 ft
Left rear	201
Left front	115
Right front	96
Total	819
Average	205 ft

Lacking test skids, the coefficient of friction range given in Exhibit 15 can be used. For high speed on the pavement described, this would be 0.60 to 0.75. With a grade of -0.03, the drag factor would be between 0.57 and 0.72 for all wheels locked.

For an equivalent sliding distance of 205 ft and a drag factor of 0.57 to 0.72, Exhibit 16 gives slide-to-stop speeds of 59 to 66 mi/hr. Because this method gives an inherently low estimate, the best conclusion might be that the speed at the beginning of the slide was definitely more than 59 mi/hr.

Some people who use average skidmark length in estimating speed justify this method by pointing out that the average

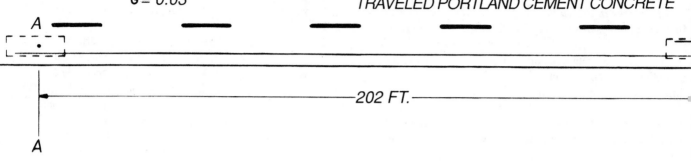

Exhibit 20. *This diagram is used for an irregular skidmark case to illustrate a method of dividing braking distance into sections to estimate the initial speed more accurately.*

of several measurements is more reliable than any of the individual measurements. This is a spurious explanation, because measuring the lengths of four skidmarks is not the same as four measurements of the same skidmark.

Assumption 2 — Longest Skidmark

Using the longest skidmark as a basis for estimating speed assumes that there was braking on all wheels throughout the length of the longest skidmark, and that braking on wheels that did not make marks was as much as it would have been if the tire had been sliding. The fact that wheels eventually locked indicates that all wheels had braking. As explained earlier, it is possible that a wheel that left no skidmark was actually developing more pavement drag — and so contributing more to slowing the vehicle — than another wheel on the same vehicle which was sliding and making a mark.

Example. Apply the longest-skidmark assumption to the skidmarks illustrated in Exhibit 20. Using the appropriate equations ($v_i = \sqrt{v_e^2 - 2ad}$ and $a = fg$), the longest mark, 407 ft, gives a brake - to-stop speed of 83 to 94 mi/hr. Because the longest-skidmark method gives an inherently high estimate, the best conclusion might be that the speed at the beginning of the slide was definitely less than 94 mi/hr.

Comparison of the two assumptions is as follows:

1. Average skidmark — more than 59 mi/hr
2. Longest skidmark — less than 94 mi/hr

Using both assumptions, you would conclude that the brake-to-stop speed was between 59 and 94 mi/hr.

Part of this combined estimate range is due to using a range of values for coefficient of friction. If careful examination of the road surface or skillfully made test skids provide a lesser range of values for coefficient of friction, the estimate could be somewhat more precise.

Of course, if the vehicle did not slide to a stop but was stopped by a collision, minimum and maximum estimated speeds would both be greater.

Such a wide range of estimated values for brake-to-stop speed could make the estimate almost useless. But if the low value obtained from average skidmark length or the high value obtained from the longest skidmark serve the purpose for which the estimate was made, the estimate is satisfactory.

More Precise Estimate

If the simple assumptions just described are inadequate, more precise estimates with a lower range of values can be made. A more accurate estimate can be illustrated by applying the procedure to the same example, Exhibit 20. For this purpose, the same range of values for coefficient of friction will be continued, with the understanding that the estimate range might be further narrowed by achieving a lesser range of values for coefficient of friction.

Center of mass movement. If the vehicle rotates while skidding, as in Exhibit 20, the longest skidmark exaggerates the distance the vehicle as a whole slid while rotating. Then it is better to consider the length of skid as the distance moved by the vehicle's center of mass. In the example, the longest skidmark is 407 ft, but the center of mass movement measures 395 ft — that is, the vehicle moved 395 ft while skidding. Using this distance, the brake-to-stop speed estimate becomes 82 to 92 mi/hr. The reduction from the 83-to - 94 mi/hr range is not much for such a long skid, but it is more accurate. The difference would be greater for a shorter total skidding distance.

Dividing the skidding distance into sections and applying equation (1) below (working backward from the vehicle's final position) will give a better final estimate than either of the assumptions heretofore described.

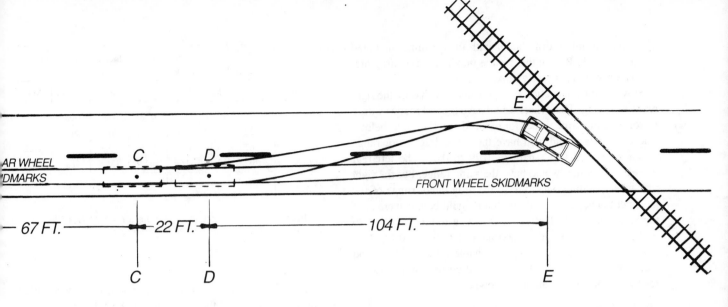

$$v_i = \sqrt{v_e^2 - 2ad} \qquad (1)$$

More careful analysis of the rate of slowing as determined by the coefficient of friction during movement in each section will also contribute to the reliability of the estimate. Refer again to the example, Exhibit 20. There are four sections, as follows:

1. A to B 202 ft — one skidmark
2. B to C 67 ft — two skidmarks
3. C to D 22 ft — three skidmarks
4. D to E 104 ft — complete skidmarks

These are center-of-mass distances. Their sum is 395 ft.

Begin with the simplest section, D to E. During these 104 ft, the vehicle was completely sliding with all four wheels. Calculating the slide-to-stop speed for this distance, therefore, is not difficult. The usual equation, with the previously used drag factor range of 0.57 to 0.72, gives a slide-to-stop speed estimate of 42 to 47 mi/hr.

The remaining incomplete skids are more complicated. Consider the movement from B to C, 67 ft. It is clear that both rear wheels are sliding. Therefore, the rear axle develops the full drag factor provided by roadway friction. But the rolling front wheels are not developing that much drag factor, despite their being on the same surface. Front wheel drag factor is therefore less than pavement coefficient of friction, but certainly much more than rolling friction, because beyond Point C the front wheels begin to skid. Now a drag factor or range of drag factors between rolling plus air resistance and maximum roadway drag factor must be chosen. A reasonable assumption would be that the non-sliding front wheels developed at least half of the minimum roadway drag factor — that is, 0.57/2 = 0.29 — and as much as nine tenths of the maximum roadway drag factor — that is, (0.9)(0.72) = 0.65. The half and nine tenths suggested here are simply matters of judgment on the part of the investigator. On the basis of

what you know about the situation, you must choose values or limits which can reasonably be expected to embrace the range of possibilities. This gives the following reasonable values for front and rear axle drag factors:

Section B to C		
Axle	Minimum	Maximum
Front, f_f	0.29	0.65
Rear, f_r	0.57	0.72

These values can now be applied as described for irregular braking. Assume, for example, that the vehicle involved has a wheelbase $l = 10$ ft, that its center of mass is $x_f l = 4.3$ ft behind the front axle, and that the center of mass is $zl = 2.0$ ft above the road surface. Then $x_f = 0.43$ and $z = 0.20$.

The equation for resultant total drag factor when axles have different drag factors is

$$f_R = \frac{f_f - x_f \, (f_f - f_r)}{1 - z(f_f - f_r)} \qquad (6)$$

Substitute the vehicle constants in this equation for repeated use:

$$f_R = \frac{f_f - 0.43(f_f - f_r)}{1 - 0.20(f_f - f_r)}$$

Substitute the minimum axle drag factors for this particular section of the skid, noting that $f_f - f_r = 0.29 - 0.57 = -0.28$:

$$f_R = \frac{0.29 - 0.43(-0.28)}{1 - 0.20(-0.28)}$$

$$f_R = 0.4104/1.056$$

$$f_R = 0.39$$

62-23

Thus, the minimum drag factor with the assumptions noted is equal to 0.39. Repeat this for the maximum axle drag factor. The result is $f = 0.67$, maximum.

Movement from section A to B is made with only the right rear tire sliding. That wheel would have the full roadway drag factor. Use the same values for reduced drag factor as before. The front *axle* would then have the same drag factor range as for section B to C, namely, 0.29 to 0.65. The left rear wheel, not sliding, would have the same range, but the right rear wheel, sliding, would have the drag factor range of the pavement. The rear *axle* drag factor would be the average of the rear *wheel* drag factors — that is, a minimum of $(0.29 + 0.57)/2 = 0.43$ and a maximum of $(0.65 + 0.72)/2 = 0.69$. This gives the following reasonable values for front and rear axle drag factors. The calculated corresponding values for the whole vehicle are also shown.

Section A to B

Axle	Minimum	Maximum
Front, f_f	0.29	0.65
Rear, f_r	0.43	0.69
Vehicle	0.34	0.66

The remaining section, C to D, can be calculated in the same way:

Section C to D

Axle	Minimum	Maximum
Front, f_f	0.43	0.69
Rear, f_r	0.57	0.72
Vehicle	0.48	0.70

The initial velocity of the vehicle can now be calculated, because the drag factor (or acceleration value) is now known for each section. Use the equation

$$v_i = \sqrt{v_e^2 - 2ad} \qquad (1)$$

to calculate the end velocity of the preceding section. Remember that $a = fg$. For these calculations, a will always be negative. For example, use the distance and drag factors to calculate the initial speed at D, using the distance and acceleration values from D to E. The initial velocity calculated at D is the end velocity for the C to D section. Then use that end velocity for the C to D section to calculate the initial velocity at C. Continue this procedure until the initial velocity is finally calculated at A. This procedure is summarized in Exhibit 21.

Section	Distance (ft)	Drag factor Min	Drag factor Max	Initial velocity (ft/sec) Min	Initial velocity (ft/sec) Max	End velocity (ft/sec) Min	End velocity (ft/sec) Max
D to E	104	0.57	0.72	61.8	69.4	00.0	00.0
C to D	22	0.48	0.70	67.1	76.2	61.8	69.4
B to C	67	0.39	0.67	78.6	93.3	67.1	76.2
A to B	202	0.34	0.66	102.9	131.5	78.6	93.3
Overall	395	0.41	0.68				

Exhibit 21. *Summary of example of velocity estimate of incomplete skidmarks illustrated in Exhibit 20.*

The table shows the initial velocity at A to be between 102.9 and 131.5. Round off these velocities to be between 103 ft/sec and 132 ft/sec. The average drag factor for the entire 395 ft ranges between 0.41 and 0.68. The velocity in ft/sec changed to the units of mi/hr gives a range of 70 to 89 mi/hr.

Although an estimate of 70 to 89 mi/hr may seem like a large range, it is certainly much better than the minimum of 59 mi/hr obtained by averaging skidmarks and the maximum of 94 mi/hr from the longest single tire mark. From the more precise estimate of a minimum of 70 mi/hr, you can conclude with confidence that the vehicle was exceeding the speed limit of 55 mi/hr.

Further adjustment might be made in the precise estimate. The method outlined assumes that the drag factor is constant throughout each section of the slide. This means that at the end of each section of skidding, the drag factor would have to increase instantly to a greater value as another wheel begins to skid. This is, of course, impossible, especially because the pattern of the skidmarks strongly suggests that the driver steadily increased brake pressure during the approximately 8 sec of skidding. It would be more accurate to assume that the estimated drag factor for, say, section A to B was at A and that the drag factor increased steadily to B. The effective drag factor for the A to B section would be the average of the drag factors at A and B. For example, Exhibit 21 shows that the minimum drag factor assigned to the A to B section is 0.34, and that for the B to C section is 0.39. If these are the values at the beginning of each section, the more precise drag factor for A to B would be $(0.34 + 0.39)/2 = 0.365$.

Furthermore, if brakes are applied gradually, there would undoubtedly have been brake application before any tires started to slide. This braking would have had an average drag factor between zero and the beginning of skidding at A, where it is assigned a value of 0.34. That makes an initial non-skid distance with an average minimum drag factor of $(0 + 0.34)/2 = 0.17$. The distance is indeterminate.

Both of these adjustments increase drag factor estimates in all but the last section and so increase the total brake-to-stop speed estimate. This increase would be small, and in view of the broad range of possible values assigned to pavement coefficients of friction, would add little to the speed estimates. Omitting such an adjustment makes the speed estimate, both minimum and maximum, slightly on the low side.

Another refinement might also be considered. In estimating axle drag factors for the example, no distinction was made between right and left wheels. That is the same as assuming that right and left wheels were equally loaded. The fact of cross slope in the vehicle's lane because of road crown means that, even if the vehicle has equal weight on right and left sides, the right wheel will carry a little more load than the left. This can produce two effects on skidmarks which can only be distinguished by close observation:

1. Both right and left tires on the axle slide, but the one with less load heats so little that the mark it makes is faint and may go unnoticed.
2. The wheel with more load, usually on the downhill side, grips the roadway a little better and so does not lock, whereas the opposite wheel on the axle, with less load, does slide and leave a mark.

In the example discussed, Exhibit 20, the uphill left tire at first makes no mark that was reported. Perhaps that tire was also sliding but making a mark too light to be observed, or perhaps it carried enough weight because of lopsided loading to grip the pavement better than the right downhill tire. It is also possible that the road surface had different characteristics for right and left tires, that the brakes were somewhat different in their rate of application, or that right and left tires had a somewhat different rolling radius. These are imponderables which must be considered even if they cannot be evaluated. In the example, the cross slope of the traffic lane is small and the conclusion is warranted that the effect of these circumstances would be small and surely within the broad range of the speed estimate produced by the range of values chosen for pavement coefficient of friction.

Judgment is required in choosing limits of values to make speed estimates, as it is in many other kinds of engineering. It is important that the ultimate estimate have sufficient range reasonably to embrace conceivable variables. In the illustrative example and in most similar problems, the judgments involve consideration of such matters as:

• Selection of a range of roadway coefficients of friction
• Selection of values of drag factor for wheels that are braking but make no tire marks
• Consideration of possible rates of brake application
• Evaluation of reliability of reported observations and measurements of tire marks on the road
• Interpretation of possible effect of distribution of load and cross slope on roadway.

A lesser range of speeds in the final estimate is most easily achieved by more careful evaluation of coefficient of friction. Well made test skids or skillful examination of the road surface may yield a lesser range of values than those suggested by Exhibit 15.

It is also possible that skidmarks from some wheels may be so faint or obscure as to escape notice and so go unreported. Occasionally those matters can be cleared up by careful examination of photos.

Some Wheels Making No Skidmarks

If some but not all wheels make skidmarks, other considerations are involved. Two circumstances are possible:

1. All wheels were braking, but some not sufficiently to lock the wheel.
2. Some wheels were doing no braking at all.

If some wheels make no skidmarks when others do, it is important to discover whether these wheels were without brakes. There are three possibilities:

1. A wheel has no brake — for example, a wheel on a small trailer or a wheel on the front axle of a tractor and semi-trailer.
2. A wheel has a brake, but it was not used — for example, the front wheel on a motorcycle or a wheel on a tractor-trailer combination with independently controlled trailer brakes.
3. A brake fails to function.

Which wheels have no brakes can be ascertained ordinarily by vehicle inspection or by statements from the vehicle operator or owner. Whether independently operated brakes were used can sometimes be discovered by questioning the driver. Sometimes careful mechanical examination will reveal that a brake could not have functioned. Driver statements are not to be trusted with respect to whether brakes failed to function.

If it is clear that a wheel was without braking, its drag factor is only that of rolling resistance, which may be taken as 0.01 or simply omitted altogether. Therefore, it is possible to ascribe a very small but definite drag factor to wheels without brakes. Then the matter can be handled as described for irregular braking, in which wheels and axles have different drag factors and weight shift can be taken into consideration. This is essentially what was done for the skid from A to D in Exhibit 20 where some wheels made no skidmarks.

If wheels with optional braking make skidmarks, the skidmarks are proof that brakes were applied; the skidmarks establish a drag factor for the wheel based on the roadway coefficient of friction. If the skidmarks made by such wheels are approximately as long as skidmarks from other wheels, treat the case as one of complete braking with all wheels locked and tires sliding. If the mark made by a wheel with optional braking is shorter than the others, the brake on that wheel was apparently applied later or sooner than the others. Consider as a complete skid the distance the vehicle moved while all wheels made skidmarks. The remaining distance is complicated, because there is no way to know how much the optional brake was applied. The drag factor for the nonskidding wheel must then be handled as a range of values, possibly as little as rolling resistance drag factor and as much as full skidding. The exact values may be governed by what has been learned from any source about the possible application of brakes. Thus, the partial braking may be treated as two sections: one distance in which skidding is complete, with a drag factor based on the coefficient of friction; and the other distance an estimated possible range of drag factors. The calculated brake-to-stop speeds for the two sections are then combined in the usual manner. This usually gives a wide range of estimated speed, but there is no help for that.

Finally, if all brakes are applied by the same control and there is nothing to suggest brake malfunction, you can infer, if skidmarks are irregular, that all brakes were contributing to slowing. Then the matter can be handled like the first three sections of the skid described in Exhibit 20, perhaps with a greater range of drag factor for wheels which do not make skidmarks.

Clues from skidmarks may indicate to some extent what braking took place and so aid in assigning upper and lower limits for drag factors. If a skidmark is made from only one side of a vehicle and this mark is quite straight for 50 ft (15 m) or more, you can infer that there was about the same braking, more or less, on both sides of the vehicle. With significantly unequal braking, the vehicle would be expected to swerve. Without such a swerve, the drag factor of the wheels on the side where there was no mark can be considered about the same as the drag factor on the side which did make marks. The possibilities of difference are reflected in the range of drag factors selected. Conversely, if there is a swerve with skidmarks from only one side of the vehicle, you can infer that braking was unequal. Then a range of possible drag factors can be assigned to reflect this difference with regard to the direction of the swerve. In this connection, you must be very careful to distinguish between braking skidmarks and steering yawmarks. (See Topic 817 for a discussion of the difference between the two).

Sometimes there are definite skidmarks from the right and left sides of the vehicle but it is not clear whether these are from front wheels, rear wheels, or both. If rear wheels track closely in the path of front wheels, it may not be clear where the marks from front or rear wheels begin. Careful examination of the marks or even detailed examination of photographs can settle questions of this kind.

If there is no way to find out how far individual wheels slid, you must assume a minimum and a maximum possibility which will give a greater range of speed in the final estimate. The most common circumstance of this kind is a report that there were, for example, "50 feet of skidmarks." From this information alone, you have no way of knowing whether

1. The measurements were made from the beginning of the rear tire marks to the end of the front tire marks, in which case the actual sliding was 50 feet minus the wheelbase of the vehicle.

2. The measurements were made from the beginning to the end of a rear or front tire mark, in which case 50 feet represents the length of a complete skid.

Both distances must be used as a basis for estimating, and this may add greatly to the range of the final brake-to-stop speed estimate.

If tire marks continue straight for 50 ft (15 m) or more, the front wheels can be assumed to have locked first because, if the rear wheels had locked while the front ones were rolling, the vehicle would probably have turned around during the last part of the skid as illustrated in Exhibit 20.

Braking Distance

If braking distance from a specified speed is wanted, estimates are less complicated because brake capabilities are stated. If sliding is involved, maximum and minimum drag factors need to be assigned only to pavement coefficient of friction. One of several levels of brake performance may be specified, such as:

- Brakes meet but do not exceed legal requirements. Drag factor is then determined by the law and by the roadway grade.
- Brakes lock all wheels. Drag factor is then determined by the roadway coefficient of friction and grade.
- Brakes lock certain specified wheels but not others. Resultant drag factor is then calculated as described for irregular braking. This requires special data on the vehicle as loaded.

Once the applicable drag factor has been determined, the brake-to-stop distance for the specified speed is found from the appropriate equation, table or nomograph.

Skidmarks Leaving One Surface and Entering Another

To determine the speed required to skid to a stop when skidmarks show that the vehicle slid from one surface to another, you need to know the coefficients of friction of the surface and, to be precise, the location of the vehicle's center of mass. Calculations are accomplished by dividing the total skidding distance into a number of sections, depending on how many wheels are on each surface. Start at the vehicle's rest position and work backward to its initial braking point using equation (1):

$$v_i = \sqrt{v_e^2 - 2ad} \qquad (1)$$

You will recall that $a = fg$ and a is negative for a skidding condition.

An example, Exhibit 22, illustrates how such an estimate is made. All wheels make skidmarks, and rear-wheel skidmarks follow front-wheel skidmarks closely. The pavement's coefficient of friction is taken as 0.75 to 0.90, that of the shoulder as 0.45 to 0.65. There is no grade.

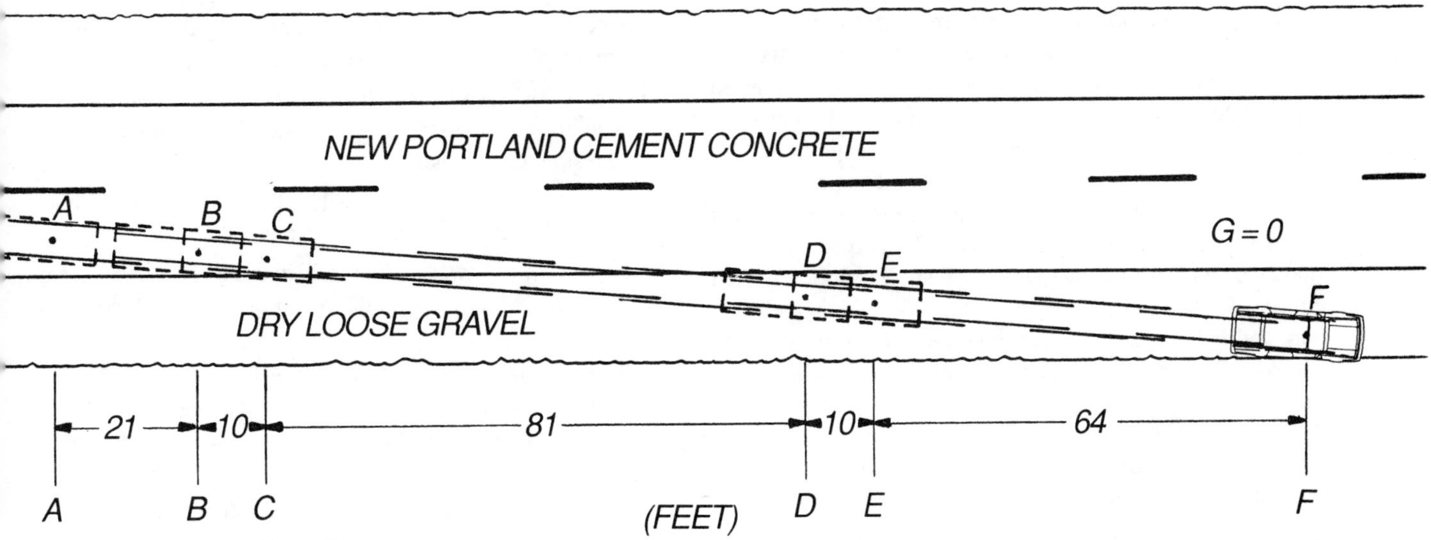

Exhibit 22. *This diagram of skidmarks on two surfaces is used to illustrate a method of dividing the total distance into sections to estimate the initial speed more accurately.*

The center-of-mass movement is divided into five sections as follows:

1. A to B 21 ft — entirely on roadway
2. B to C 10 ft — one wheel on shoulder
3. C to D 81 ft — two wheels on shoulder
4. D to E 10 ft — three wheels on shoulder
5. E to F 64 ft — entirely on shoulder

Section A to B, with all wheels sliding on the roadway, is calculated as a complete skid for 21 ft center-of-mass movement at $f = 0.75$ to 0.90, a somewhat narrower range than indicated in Exhibit 15.

In section E to F the vehicle slides entirely on loose gravel of the shoulder. The section drag factor is assumed to range between 0.45 to 0.65.

In section C to D both front and rear axles have one wheel sliding on the roadway and one on the shoulder; therefore, front and rear braking drag factors are the same. The effective drag factor for both axles and the whole vehicle is then the average drag factor for the two sides, which is $f = (0.75 + 0.45)/2 = 0.60$ minimum and $f = (0.65 + 0.90)/2 = 0.78$ maximum.

In section B to C both rear wheels are on the roadway, but one front wheel is on the roadway and the other is on the shoulder. Therefore, the rear-axle drag factor is the coefficient of friction of the roadway, $f_r = 0.75$ to 0.90; but the front-axle drag factor is the average of the roadway and shoulder as calculated for section C to D, $f_f = 0.60$ to 0.78. Different front and rear drag factors call for computation of the resultant drag factor. For minimum braking, $f_f = 0.60$ and $f_r = 0.75$. Use the same vehicle data as in the example for skidmarks of different lengths, $x_f = 0.43$ and $z = 0.20$:

$$f_R = \frac{f_f - x_f (f_f - f_r)}{1 - z (f_f - f_r)}$$

$$f_R = \frac{0.60 - 0.43 (0.60 - 0.75)}{1 - 0.20 (0.60 - 0.75)}$$

$$f_R = \frac{0.60 - 0.43 (- 0.15)}{1 - 0.20 (- 0.15)}$$

$$f_R = 1 - 0.20 (- 0.15)$$

$$f_R = 0.664/1.03$$

$$f_R = 0.64$$

Calculate the maximum drag factor the same way. With $f_f = 0.78$ and $f_r = 0.90$, the resultant maximum drag factor is $f = 0.81$.

Section D to E is similar to section B to C. Both front wheels are on the shoulder, left rear wheel is on the roadway, and right rear wheel is on the shoulder. Therefore, the front axle drag factor is that of the shoulder, $f_f = 0.45$ to 0.65, and the rear axle drag factor is the average of the roadway and shoulder, $f_r = 0.60$ to 0.78. This difference requires computation for the resultant drag factor using equation (6). The resulting drag factor range is $f = 0.50$ to 0.69.

		Drag factor		Initial velocity (ft/sec)		End velocity (ft/sec)	
Section	Distance (ft)	Min	Max	Min	Max	Min	Max
E to F	64	0.45	0.65	43.1	51.8	00.0	00.0
D to E	10	0.50	0.69	46.6	55.9	43.1	51.8
C to D	81	0.60	0.78	72.8	84.8	46.6	55.9
B to C	10	0.64	0.81	75.6	87.8	72.8	84.8
A to B	21	0.75	0.90	82.0	94.5	75.6	87.8
Overall	186	0.56	0.74				

Exhibit 23. *Summary of example of vehicle skidding over different surfaces.*

Finally, the section drag factors are entered into Exhibit 23. Minimum and maximum values for the initial and end velocities for each section are then calculated and inserted into Exhibit 23 to come up with the initial velocity when skidding started. The resulting initial velocity range is 82.0 to 94.5 ft/sec. Converted to mi/hr, the range is 56 to 64 mi/hr.

For this example, the estimate can be simplified without much loss of accuracy by neglecting the two short transitional sections B to C and D to E. The first section is then entirely on the roadway, the second section half on the roadway and half on the shoulder, and the third entirely on the shoulder. The vehicle drag factor for the second section is the average of those provided by the shoulder and the roadway. The lengths of these sections are determined by the point at which the center of mass crosses the edge of the roadway, making the data as follows:

		Drag Factor	
Section	Length	Max	Min
DE to F	69	0.45	0.65
BC to DE	91	0.60	0.78
A to BC	26 ft	0.75	0.90
All	186 ft		

Using these data and the same equations as before, the resulting initial speed range for the entire 186 ft is 56 to 65 mi/hr, compared to 56 to 64 mi/hr for the more accurate calculations. Therefore, no significant difference is found between the two methods.

9. DRAG FACTORS AFTER A COLLISION

Perhaps the most difficult situation for estimating an appropriate drag factor is after a collision. This is complicated by several conditions:

- One or more wheels may be jammed in the damage and are unable to rotate or have their rotation restricted.
- The vehicle will most likely have rotated, causing the weight to shift from one set of axles to the other and from one side to the other.
- After the collision, it is possible that the vehicle will have traveled over more than one surface.
- In the case of a two-vehicle collision, the vehicles may stay together, which can produce complicated after-collision motion.
- The vehicles' shapes are often considerably altered (even to the extent of a vehicle being in two pieces), which may cause tires and other parts of the vehicle to be in contact with the surface.

It is often necessary to know deceleration rates (drag factors) after a collision, because this is needed to do a momentum analysis (see Topic 868 for a discussion of momentum considerations).

Two Vehicles Engaged After Collision

After a two-vehicle collision, the vehicles sometimes move off as one unit. This may occur as shown in Exhibit 24. The bullet car front has struck the target car's side. Because the target car had little forward movement at the time of the collision and the principal direction of force (thrust) was directed through each vehicle's center of mass, the two cars stayed engaged and moved together, essentially in a straight line, to their rest position. The question to be answered is the velocity of the two vehicles as they moved off after the collision.

The data given for this example are as follows:

- Target car weight equals 2,200 lbs.
- Bullet car weight equals 3,100 lbs.
- After-collision travel distance equals 135 ft.

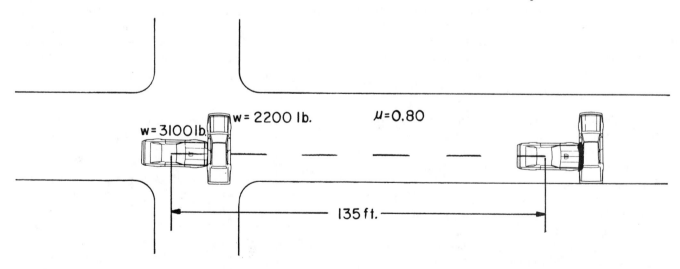

Exhibit 24. *Because the 2,200-lb. car has essentially zero velocity and the direction of force in the collision is through both vehicles' centers of mass, the vehicles move down the road together in the same direction in which the striking car was traveling before the collision.*

- Pavement coefficient of friction (μ) equals 0.80.
- The road is level.

For an actual case like this, you should inspect the bullet car to see whether the front wheels are jammed in as a result of the collision. It is also possible that as a result of the collision, the front wheels of the bullet car are partially supported by the target car. This, of course, adds more weight to the target car. For this case, assume that the front wheels of the bullet car were jammed due to damage and would not rotate.

If *equal weight* is assumed for each car's wheels as they moved to their final position, a simple estimate of the drag factor of the unit (the two cars together) can be easily calculated. Recall that drag factor is simply the *total* force in the direction of the acceleration divided by the vehicle's weight ($f = F/w$). The weight on each wheel of the target car would be 550 lbs (2,200/4 = 550). The weight on each wheel of the bullet car would be 775 lbs (3,100/4 = 775). All four wheels on the target car would have been sliding because the car was traveling completely sideways. Thus, the drag factor on *each* wheel of the target car would be equal to the coefficient of friction. The bullet car would have drag factors of the front wheel equal to the coefficient of friction. However, there is no reason to believe that the rear wheels would be locked due to damage. For this case, assume that the bullet car is a front−engine, front-wheel-drive car. Thus, the drag factor on the rear wheels of the bullet car is equal to the rolling resistance ($f = 0.01$).

The drag force (F) in pounds on each wheel can be calculated by multiplying the drag factor (f) of each wheel times the weight (w) in pounds on the wheel ($F = fw$). The total drag force on the unit (both cars together) is the sum of the drag forces on each wheel. Then the drag factor for the total unit is equal to the total drag force divided by the total weight of the unit. The drag factors and forces for each wheel are now entered in Exhibit 25.

	Bullet Car			Target Car			
Wheel	w	f	F	w	f	F	Total F
RF	775	0.80	620	550	0.80	440	1,060
LF	775	0.80	620	550	0.80	440	1,060
RR	775	0.01	8	550	0.80	440	448
LR	775	0.01	8	550	0.80	440	448
					Total Drag Force		3,016 lb

Exhibit 25. *Calculations to determine the drag factor for the after-collision movement of the combined vehicles shown in Exhibit 24.*

Thus, the drag factor on the two combined vehicles equals the total drag force, 3,016 lbs, divided by the total weight (3,100 + 2,200), 5,300 lbs. So the drag factor equals 0.57 (3,016/5,300).

In virtually all cases, the weight on each wheel of a car will be different, even in a static condition. In a dynamic condition as the vehicles decelerate to a stop, it is even more likely that the weights will be different. For the case depicted in Exhibit 24, it is more important to evaluate the effect of the increased load on the front axle (and of course the reduced load on the rear axle) of the bullet car. This can be done as before by developing another table like Exhibit 25.

Assume that *70 percent of the bullet car's weight is on the front axle*. Then the weight on the front axle will be 2,170 lbs and the rear axle will be 930 lbs. Assume the weight is equal on each of the two front wheels (1,085 lbs) and on the rear wheels (465 lbs). As long as the four wheels on the target car are sliding, the distribution of the target car's weight over the four wheels will not affect the final drag factor for the unit (two cars together). Insert these values into Exhibit 26.

	Bullet Car			Target Car			
Wheel	w	f	F	w	f	F	Total F
RF	1,085	0.80	870	550	0.80	440	1,310
LF	1,085	0.80	870	550	0.80	440	1,310
RR	465	0.01	5	550	0.80	440	445
LR	465	0.01	5	550	0.80	440	445
					Total Drag Force		3,510 lb

Exhibit 26. *Calculations to determine the drag factor for the after-collision movement of the combined vehicles shown in Exhibit 24 with 70 percent of the bullet car's weight on the front axle.*

As before, the total drag force is divided by the total weight of the unit to calculate the unit's drag factor. A drag factor of 0.66 is obtained (3,510/5,300). When equal weight on all wheels was assumed for the bullet car, the drag factor was 0.57; this time it is 0.66. When the initial speed after the collision is calculated, there is not as much difference as you might think. The calculations are shown below.

For drag factor of 0.57:

$$v_i = \sqrt{v_e^2 - 2ad} \qquad (1)$$
$$= \sqrt{-2(-0.57)(32.2)(135)}$$
$$= 70.4 \text{ ft/sec}$$
$$= 47.9 \text{ mi/hr}$$

For drag factor of 0.66:

$$v_i = \sqrt{v_e^2 - 2ad} \qquad (1)$$
$$= \sqrt{-2(-0.66)(32.2)(135)}$$
$$= 75.7 \text{ ft/sec}$$
$$= 51.5 \text{ mi/hr}$$

Clearly, there is not a lot of difference in mi/hr for the two sets of calculations. This example could be worked another time with even more weight shifted to the front axle of the bullet car. The equation for weight shift could be used as before for braking. However, the car is obviously modified somewhat because of damage, which may make the assumptions for horizontal and vertical locations of the center of mass incorrect if you have assumed the characteristics of an undamaged car.

Single Vehicle Translating and Rotating After Collision

Consider the following situation. A car has significant front-end damage. The damage is completely across the front of the car, and the front wheels are jammed-in due to the damage. Neither front wheel will rotate because of the damage. The car rotates counterclockwise 180 degrees, while at the same time it translates a distance, d, until it comes to rest. This situation is shown in Exhibit 27.

At position A the car is essentially moving sideways; not only are the front wheels not rotating (they are locked because of damage) but also the rear wheels are not rotating because of the sideways movement. Therefore, at position A the drag factor on the vehicle would be equal to the coefficient of friction. At position B the rear wheels are free to roll, while the front wheels provide a drag factor of more than 50 percent of the friction coefficient (if more than 50 percent of the vehicle's weight is on the front wheels). At position C the vehicle is again moving sideways, so the drag factor is equal to the coefficient of friction. Thus, it can be seen that the drag factor at position A decreases to something near one-half the coefficient of friction at position B and then increases to the maximum again at position C. This is plotted in Exhibit 28 as a function of distance.

If the vehicle in Exhibit 27 decelerated to a stop at position C, the initial velocity at position A could be calculated. Most likely, you would want to use the following equation:

$$v_i = \sqrt{v_e^2 - 2ad} \qquad (1)$$

However, acceleration (a) or drag factor (f) constantly changes from positions A to B to C. Thus, to use the above equation, an average value of drag factor would have to be assumed for the entire distance. An option that should yield more accurate results is to divide the total distance into smaller distances and apply the equation for each of the smaller distances. For each distance increment a different drag factor would be used. For example, note how the distances are divided into equal increments in Exhibit 29. Each increment has a drag factor associated with it. (That is, for d_1 use f_1, for d_2 use f_2, etc.). You would then start at the rest position, C, and "back up", using the above equation until you get to position A.

Another option to determine the initial velocity at position A is to calculate the work done in each increment of distance shown in Exhibit 29. The work done is simply the drag factor times the distance times the weight. The total work is simply the sum of the work done in each distance increment. Equate this to the initial kinetic energy at position A and solve for the initial velocity. In equation form this becomes:

$$Work_{total} = f_1wd_1 + f_2wd_2 + f_3wd_3 + f_4wd_4 + \ldots \qquad (7)$$

$$v = \sqrt{(2g\,work_{total})/w} \qquad (8)$$

The number of terms for the right side of equation (7) depends on the number of surfaces. You could have more than four terms, as indicated in equation (7).

Often a vehicle does not travel over the same surface after a collision. If, for example, the car that rotated 180 degrees in Exhibit 27 traveled over three surfaces, the coefficient of friction would most likely be different over each surface. Thus, the resulting drag factors on the car as it travels to a stop would also be different. If it is known how the vehicle moves over the surface (that is, how it translates and rotates), the same approach can be used. Say, for example, that the car in Exhibit 27 first traveled over a hard surface for the first third of its total after-collision distance, then traveled for the next third over gravel, and for the final third over grass. Test values for the coefficients of friction were found to be 0.80 for pavement, 0.50 for gravel, and 0.40 for grass. Exhibit 30 shows how the drag factor could be re-plotted to show how drag factor varied on the vehicle from position A to B to C.

Case Study: Front Half of Car

Exhibit 31 shows the front part of a car. The car hit a large utility pole broadside and broke into two pieces. One question that needs to be answered is the speed of the front part of the car after it hit the pole. So the problem is to determine the drag factor of the "vehicle" (that is, the front of the car) as it traveled approximately 80 ft after the collision.

There were no marks in the grass to indicate that the vehicle was digging into the turf as it moved to its final position. There is no reason to believe that the vehicle was moving through the air. No apparent vertical component of force was acting on the vehicle to make it travel through the air. Thus, the vehicle must have been in contact with the ground. An eccentric force was applied to the vehicle that would have caused it to rotate at least 180 degrees. Inspection of the vehicle showed that the two wheels were free to rotate. Actually, the two wheels looked to be essentially normal. This is a rear-wheel-drive car, so there was no transaxle to act as a decelerating force on the two wheels. Therefore, it would appear that a two-wheeled vehicle (almost like an ox cart) rotated at least 180 degrees and translated with free-rolling wheels approximately 80 ft without digging into the turf. This does not suggest a very high drag factor. Clearly, it would be more than rolling resistance on a hard surface. The grass would be more difficult to roll over than would a hard, smooth surface. The vehicle did rotate. However, consider the effort required to

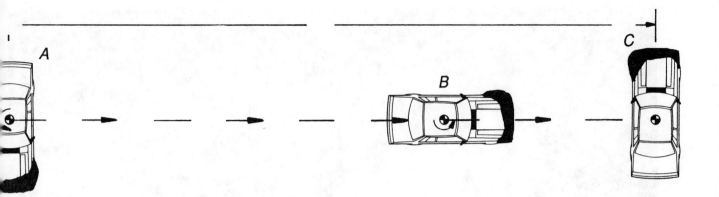

Exhibit 27. The car shown in the drawing has its front wheels locked due to damage. At A it is sliding essentially sideways while it continues rotating counter-clockwise. The deceleration on the car decreases as it moves to A. At B the rear wheels are free to roll. Then, as the car moves to C, the deceleration on the car continues to increase until the drag factor is equal to the coefficient of friction.

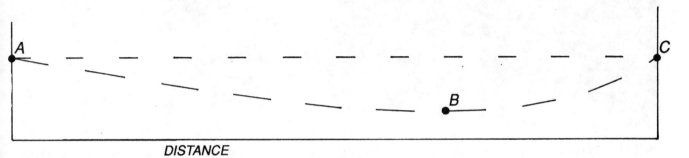

Exhibit 28. The drag factor has been plotted against distance for the movement of the car shown in Exhibit 27. Notice how the drag factor decreases from A to B and increases from B to C.

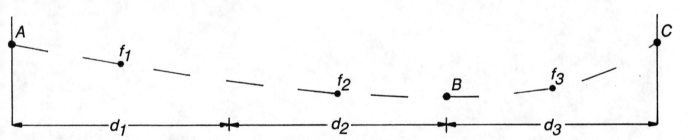

Exhibit 29. To calculate the velocity of the center of mass of the vehicle at A shown in Exhibit 27, you can divide the total distance into smaller increments and use an average drag factor for each distance.

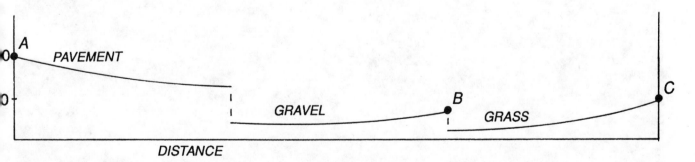

Exhibit 30. If the vehicle shown in Exhibit 27 traveled over several surfaces from A to C, you must take into account the difference in the drag factor caused by this. One way is to determine how the drag factor varied over each surface, as illustrated here.

Exhibit 31. *The front part of this car was separated from the rest by a side impact with a pole. The wheels were free to roll as it moved to its final position after separating from the pole. If no part of the car front dug into the ground, it would be difficult to support a high after-collision drag factor.*

Exhibit 32. *This photograph shows two cars still engaged in their rest positions. In this case, the cars clearly attain a common velocity.*

rotate a two-wheeled trailer. If the weight is balanced fairly evenly over the two wheels, one person can push the tongue sideways and cause it to rotate without any great effort. If rolling resistance (drag factor) is 0.01 on a hard, level surface, then it would be very difficult to support any drag factor in excess of 0.10 for this case.

A velocity estimate of the vehicle as it left the pole can be done by using the equation $a = fg$ and equation (1):

$$v_i = \sqrt{v_e^2 - 2ad} \tag{1}$$

$$= \sqrt{0^2 - (2)(-0.10)(32.2)(80)}$$

$$= 22.7 \text{ ft/sec} = 15 \text{ mi/hr}$$

An argument could be made that the drag factor is too high. However, if this speed estimate is combined with the speed require to break the car into two pieces, it can be clearly seen that this is a fairly insignificant value. With the data given, it would be very difficult to support a larger drag factor. For example, if someone suggests a value approaching 0.50, there would be nothing in the data to support such a conclusion.

Case Study: Two Vehicles Together from Maximum Engagement to Rest Positions

Exhibit 32 shows two vehicles (Plymouth and Pontiac) still together at their rest positions. Exhibit 33 shows the after-accident situation map. Exhibit 34 shows maximum-engagement positions of the two vehicles and intermediate positions as the vehicles travel together to their rest positions. Test skids on the Portland cement concrete gave a coefficient of friction of 0.75. Test skids on the grass gave a coefficient of friction of 0.45. The data clearly supports that the Pontiac slid sideways the entire distance after the collision. Thus, all four of its wheels were sliding without rotation. As a result of the collision, the Plymouth's driveshaft came off the car (note its final position). Thus, the rear wheels were free to rotate. This case is similar to the scenario described in Exhibit 24.

As a first-cut analysis, assume that the weights on all the wheels were equal when the two vehicles moved as one unit to their rest positions. If that was the case, then six of the eight wheels were not rotating, while the other two were free to rotate. If the weight was equal on all eight wheels, then the drag factor acting on the combined unit would be six-eighths, or 75 percent of the drag factor over the two surfaces.

Thus, the drag factors were:

Grass: $f = 0.75\mu$
$\quad\quad = (0.75)(0.45)$
$\quad\quad = 0.34$
Concrete: $f = 0.75\mu$
$\quad\quad\quad = (0.75)(0.75)$
$\quad\quad\quad = 0.56$

The cars moved as a unit for 40 ft over grass and 80 ft over the concrete. Then the velocity after maximum engagement can be calculated using equation (1) twice, as follows:

$$v_i = \sqrt{v_e^2 - 2ad} \tag{1}$$

$$= \sqrt{0^2 - 2(-0.34)(32.2)(40)}$$

$$= 29.6 \text{ ft/sec}$$

Thus, as the cars start to slide on the grass, they are traveling 29.6 ft/sec. Use this value as the end velocity, v_e, in equation (1):

$$v_i = \sqrt{v_e^2 - 2ad} \tag{1}$$

$$= \sqrt{29.6^2 - 2(-0.56)(32.2)(80)}$$

$$= 61.3 \text{ ft/sec}$$

The approach used above assumes that the weight on each wheel is equal. Clearly, this is not going to be the usual situation. If the rear axle of the bullet car (Plymouth) had less than the assumed weight, then the assumed drag factor for the two vehicles together after the collision would be less than what the two vehicles would experience. To check the sensitivity of this analysis, assume that the rear axle has 20 percent of the Plymouth's weight. The gross weight of the Plymouth is 3,700 lbs, that of the Pontiac 3,600 lbs. The easiest way to understand the effects of the assumptions is to create a table similar to Exhibit 26. This has been done in Exhibit 35 for the sliding across the pavement. The target car (Pontiac) has been assumed to have equal weight on all four wheels. This clearly is not the case. However, because all four wheels were sliding sideways, there will be no difference in the total resisting force. If you had a case where the weight distribution was not equal *and* all the wheels were not sliding, this should be considered. The total resisting force is 4,930 lbs and the total weight is 7,300 lbs (3,600 + 3,700). Thus, the drag factor across the pavement is 4,930/7,300 ($f = F/w$)

Wheel	Plymouth			Pontiac			Total F
	w	f	F	w	f	F	
RF	1,480	0.75	1,110	900	0.75	675	1,785
LF	1,480	0.75	1,110	900	0.75	675	1,785
RR	370	0.01	5	900	0.75	675	680
LR	370	0.01	5	900	0.75	675	680
					Total Drag Force		4,930 lb

Exhibit 35. *Calculations to determine the drag factor on thePlymouth/Pontiac vehicle as it moves across the pavement, with 20 percent of the Plymouth weight on the rear axle and an equal weight distribution on the Pontiac wheels.*

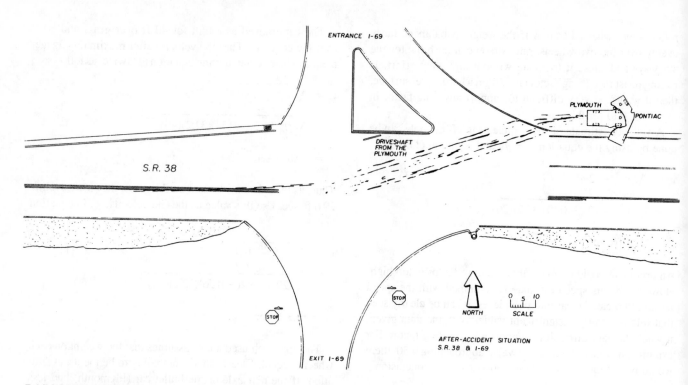

Exhibit 33. *This diagram shows the after-accident situation map for the cars in Exhibit 32.*

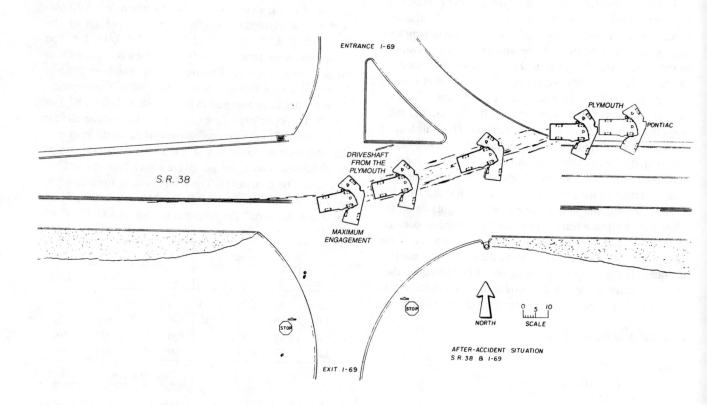

Exhibit 34. *The movement of the two vehicles from engagement to final positions is depicted here.*

or 0.68. The first estimate of the pavement drag factor (assuming equal weight on all eight wheels) was 0.56.

Another table can be developed for the sliding across the grass. This is done in Exhibit 36. Again, an equal weight distribution is assumed for the wheels of the Pontiac. The total sliding force is 2,960 lbs. This gives a drag factor of 2,960/7,300, or 0.41. The previous drag calculation for equal weight on all wheels was 0.34.

Wheel	Plymouth			Pontiac			Total F
	w	f	F	w	f	F	
RF	1,480	0.45	665	900	0.45	405	1,070
LF	1,480	0.45	665	900	0.45	405	1,070
RR	370	0.01	5	900	0.45	405	410
LR	370	0.01	5	900	0.45	405	410
					Total Drag Force		2,960 lb

Exhibit 36. *Calculations to determine the drag factor on the Pontiac/Plymouth vehicle as it moves across the grass, assuming 20 percent of the Plymouth's weight is on the rear wheels.*

Using the drag factor of 0.41 for the grass and 0.68 for the pavement, let's see what difference it makes. Again using Equation (1):

$$v_i = \sqrt{v_e^2 - 2ad} \tag{1}$$

$$= \sqrt{0^2 - 2(-0.41)(32.2)(40)}$$

$$= 32.5 \text{ ft/sec}$$

Thus, as the cars start to slide on the grass, they are traveling 32.5 ft/sec. Use this value as the end velocity, v_e, in Equation (1):

$$v_i = \sqrt{v_e^2 - 2ad} \tag{1}$$

$$= \sqrt{32.5^2 - 2(-0.68)(32.2)(80)}$$

$$= 67.5 \text{ ft/sec}$$

The previous estimate was 61.3 ft/sec. Thus, the difference is 6.2 ft/sec or 4.2 mi/hr. In this case, very little change resulted from using the "rough cut" method — mainly because the vehicle weights were very similar, which helped to minimize the difference.

The after-collision speeds calculated for the Pontiac and Plymouth are *not* the speeds of either car at first contact. To calculate those speeds, a momentum analysis must be done. This is discussed in Topic 868.

10. VEHICLE CENTER OF MASS LOCATION

Earlier in this topic the height and horizontal location of a vehicle's center of mass were used in a calculation to deter-

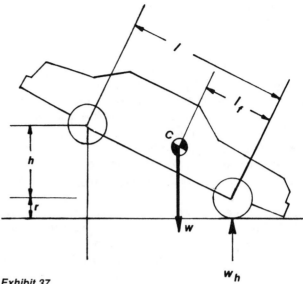

Exhibit 37.

mine the resultant drag factor. Published data on vehicle dimensions rarely include location of center of mass. However, manufacturers publish information giving the amount of weight on front and rear axles separately or the fraction (percent) of weight on one axle, which amounts to the same thing. From this available information, the longitudinal (fore and aft) position of the center of mass can be calculated, but not its height.

Data needed to calculate the location of the center of mass are as follows:
1. Static weight on the front (w_f) and rear (w_r) axles or the fraction (percent) of weight on either front or rear axle;
2. Wheelbase of vehicle (l) — that is, the distance from the front to the rear axle;
3. Radius of wheels with tires (r);
4. Weight on one axle (w_h) when the other axle is lifted to a height (h);
5. Height (h) to which the axle is lifted for weighing to locate the center of mass.

Symbols for these quantities are given in Exhibit 37. Measurements can be made to obtain values for these quantities with a particular vehicle.

Center of Mass Longitudinal Position

The longitudinal (fore and aft) position of the center of mass requires knowledge of the static (standing) weight on the front and rear axles and wheelbase length (the first two items in the list above).

The most useful way to describe the longitudinal position of the center of mass is as a decimal fraction of the wheelbase behind the front axle, x_f. The quantity x_f is equal to l_f/l (see Exhibit 37 for l_f). Therefore, the actual distance of the center of mass to the rear of the front axle is calculated as follows:

$$l_f = x_f l \tag{9}$$

In terms of static weight on the front axle,

$$x_f = w_r/w \qquad (10)$$

where w is equal to the total weight of the vehicle. Similar equations can be developed to obtain a horizontal center-of-mass measurement from the rear axle. The *wheelbase length* (expressed as a decimal fraction) between the center of mass and one axle is proportional to the *vehicle weight* on the other axle. If a vehicle's weight distribution is given as a percentage of total weight on one axle, the vehicle's center of mass is the same percentage of wheelbase length away from the other axle.

To obtain the static weight on front and rear axles, drive only the front wheels of the vehicle on a commercial platform scale and weigh it. Then place only the rear wheels on the scale and weigh again. The entire vehicle may be weighed to verify the measurements. Therefore, $w_f + w_r = w$.

Example. On a given car, the front wheels (axle) carry a weight, w_f, of 1,750 lbs, and the rear a weight, w_r, of 1,425 lbs. The total weight of the vehicle is therefore $1,750 + 1,425 = 3,175$ lb. The position of the center of mass behind the front axle is

$$x_f = w_r/w = 1,425/3,175 = 0.449$$

The wheelbase of this car measures 9.39 ft. The actual distance of the center of mass behind the front axles is therefore

$$l_f = x_f l = (0.449)(9.39) = 4.22 \text{ ft}$$

Center of Mass Height

Additional data for the height of the center of mass above the ground are obtained by weighing the front or rear axle and wheels on a platform scale when the other axle (not just the body) is lifted several feet off the ground.

A tow truck is usually necessary to lift the axle high enough, about a third of the wheelbase of the vehicle. For a full-size car, this is 3 ft (1m) or more. If the hoist is less, the change in weight will be too small to be recorded adequately on a commercial platform scale, which usually weighs only in increments of 25 lbs (10kg). Note that the amount of hoist, h, is the distance the axle is lifted, not its height above the ground (that would be $h + r$). The quantity r is the radius of the wheel with tire. The distance of the tire from the ground is the same as the axle lift and can often be more easily measured. With the required data at hand, the equation of the height of the center of mass is, **with rear end lifted** as in Exhibit 37,

$$l_z = \frac{l\sqrt{l^2 - h^2}\,(w_h - w_f)}{hw} + r \qquad (11)$$

where l = wheelbase in ft or m,
l_z = height of the center of mass in ft or m,

h = the height the rear wheels were hoisted in ft or m,
r = radius of tire and wheel together in ft or m,
w_f = level weight on front axle in lbs or N, and
w_h = weight on front axle after hoisting in lbs or N.

If the front of the car is lifted, the term $(w_h - w_f)$ is replaced by $(w_h - w_r)$. Of course, w_h would be the weight on the rear after it was lifted, and w_r would be the level static weight on the rear wheels.

The height of the center of mass, expressed as a decimal fraction of the wheelbase, is

$$z = l_z/l \qquad (12)$$

Example. The vehicle is the same as in the previous example (see Exhibit 38 for the following dimensions). The wheelbase, $l = 9.39$ ft; weight on the rear axle with the car level, $w_r = 1,425$ lbs; weight on rear axle with front axle hoisted h ft, $w_h = 1,525$ lbs; total weight, $w = 3,175$ lbs; distance from ground to wheel center with wheel hoisted, 3.43 ft; radius of wheel with tire, $r = 0.99$ ft. Then the distance the axle was hoisted is $h = 3.43 - 0.99 = 2.44$ ft. Substitute these values in the equation for l_z *with the front* lifted:

$$l_z = \frac{l\sqrt{l^2 - h^2}\,(w_h - w_r)}{hw} + r \qquad (11)$$

$$l_z = \frac{9.39\sqrt{9.39^2 - 2.44^2}\,(1,525 - 1,425)}{(2.44)(3,175)} + 0.99$$

$$l_z = 8514/7747 + 0.99$$

$$l_z = 1.10 + 0.99$$

$$l_z = 2.09 \text{ ft}$$

Expressing this as a decimal fraction of the wheelbase, you obtain

$$z = l_z/l = 2.09/9.39 = 0.226$$

Accuracy. The greatest source of error is in weighing the vehicle. In the example, the weight of the rear wheel with vehicle level is 1,425 lbs. But the scales weigh only to the nearest 25 lbs. Therefore, the actual weight might be as much as 1437.5 or as little as 1412.5 lbs. The weight on the rear wheel with the front wheel hoisted might be as much as 1537.5 and as little as 1512.5 lbs. The difference of these weights, $w_h - w_r$, might be as little as 75 or as much as 125 lbs. Using this range of values in the equation with the measured amount of hoist gives a possible range of values for z of 0.198 to 0.252, and a possible range of 1.81 to 2.45 ft for the actual height of the exemplar car's center of mass. That would be a spread of 0.65 ft, or about 7.8 in. (20.6 cm).

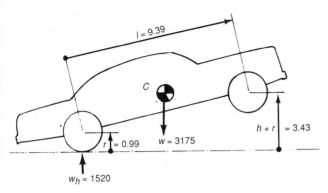

Exhibit 38. *Dimensions for hoisted car.*

The height of the center of mass can also be found by weighing the right and left sides of the vehicle and then weighing one side with the other side hoisted. The same equation is used, except that the track width of the vehicle is used instead of the wheelbase. Hoisting one side of the vehicle, however, is less convenient than hoisting one end, especially given the layout of most available platform scales.

If data are not available to calculate the height of the center of mass, a useful estimate can be made of its position. The center of mass is generally near where the most weight is concentrated. Hence, except in unusual vehicles, it would not be below the center of the wheels or much above the top of the wheels. By noting whether the engine and other heavy parts are set high or low, a reasonable judgment can usually be reached as to a range of levels between which the height of the center of mass would be located. The limit of this range can be used in preliminary calculations, which will indicate whether more refined methods of locating the height of the center of are needed. If calculations made using the estimated high and low figures do not differ significantly, some estimated figure between them can be used with reasonable confidence that calculated results are not greatly in error.

Crossway Location of Center of Mass

Crossway position of center of mass can also be found by weighing right and left wheels separately and using track width instead of wheelbase length. In most vehicles, the center of mass is very close to the longitudinal (lengthwise) centerline of the vehicle. Therefore, unless there is reason to believe that there is a significant difference between load on left and right wheels, one can assume that the center of mass is on the longitudinal centerline. The right and left positions of the center of mass have little significance in most problems relating to slowing to a stop.

Load Effects

Load must be included in center-of-mass calculations. If the vehicle is available as loaded, it is not difficult to determine the longitudinal position of the center of mass by weighing the front and rear wheels separately. If the load has been removed fron the vehicle or if the vehicle and load are no longer available, it is often possible to obtain a similar vehicle and load it, for purposes of testing, approximately as the actual vehicle was loaded. However, it is usually impractical to tilt a loaded vehicle to obtain the height of the center of mass. Then the vehicle's center of mass and the load's center of mass may be estimated separately and combined by calculations. Sample calculations illustrating this methodology are shown in the topic on heavy trucks (Topic 878).

11. OTHER ACCELERATION VALUES

As stated earlier in this topic, the quantity f is simply the number of g's of acceleration a vehicle has. Normally, f is used in the context of slowing (that is, decreasing velocity). The quantity f can also be used for positive acceleration (increasing velocity). If a car pulls away after stopping at a stop sign, the car is clearly accelerated. It may be useful to calculate the maximum velocity a car could have accelerated by using an appropriate acceleration rate. Typical f values (and the resulting acceleration values in ft/sec^2 and m/sec^2) are shown in Exhibit 39[8]. Also shown in Exhibit 39 are typical deceleration values for vehicles that do not have locked wheel skids. Note that positive (+) and negative (−) signs are used to indicate positive acceleration (increasing velocity) and negative acceleration (decreasing velocity) conditions.

Exhibit 39 gives typical values for normal and rapid acceleration rates of passenger cars. As would be expected, a car cannot maintain the same acceleration rate as its speed increases. Representative values are suggested in Exhibit 39 to reflect this. Some cars may have better performance values than the values listed. Nevertheless, the driver has the ultimate decision on how much acceleration is selected.

Typical slowing drag factors are included in Exhibit 39. As noted, these are not skidding values. They have been included to give you an idea of typical deceleration values encountered under several situations that do not involve locked wheel skids or very hard braking.

12. SUMMARY

This topic has explained the difference between drag factor and coefficient of friction. Clearly, they are not the same quantities. Perhaps the most often observed misconception regarding drag factor occurs when after-collision drag factors are estimated. A drag factor is often assumed to be equal to the coefficient of friction for a vehicle after a collision. Usually this is not the case. Such an assumption can result in mistakenly high values for first-contact speeds.

Other errors in estimating drag factors stem from assuming that large trucks and motorcycles have the same values cars have. Rarely is this appropriate. Large-truck and motorcycle drag factors are addressed in Topics 874 and 878. Consult these for more information.

Determining drag factors for automobiles and pickup trucks is not always such an easy task. Test skids of exemplar vehicles can help considerably. If tests are not done, tables

Condition	Speed range	Acceleration, a		
		Drag factor $f = a/g$	Meters per sec^2	Feet per sec^2
Free fall		+ 1.00	+ 9.81	+ 32.2
Normal acceleration of passenger car	Less than 20 mph (30kph)	+ 0.15	+ 1.47	+ 4.8
	20 to 40 mph (30 − 60 kph)	+ 0.10	+ 0.98	+ 3.2
	More than 40 mph (60kph)	+ 0.05	+ 0.48	+ 1.6
Rapid acceleration of passenger car	Less than 20 mph (30kph)	+ 0.30	+ 2.94	+ 9.7
	20 to 40 mph (30 − 60 kph)	+ 0.15	+ 1.47	+ 4.8
	More than 40 mph (60kph)	+ 0.10	+ 0.98	+ 3.2
Passenger car coasting out of gear	Less than 20 mph (30kph)	− 0.01	− 0.10	− 0.3
	20 to 40 mph (30 − 60 kph)	− 0.02	− 0.20	− 0.6
	More than 40 mph (60kph)	− 0.04	− 0.39	− 1.3
Passenger car engine braking in high gear	Less than 20 mph (30kph)	− 0.04	− 0.39	− 1.3
	20 to 40 mph (30 − 60 kph)	− 0.05	− 0.48	− 1.6
	More than 40 mph (60kph)	− 0.08	− 0.78	− 2.6
Gradual slowing, light braking		− 0.10	− 0.98	− 3.2
Normal braking, no skidding		− 0.20	− 1.96	− 6.4

Exhibit 39. *Typical values of acceleration and deceleration for motor vehicles on level surfaces.*

such as Exhibit 15 can provide a usable range of values.

If you are using an equation to calculate speed from braking skids, be certain that you indeed have braking skids and not some other type of tire mark. Failure to identify the correct type of tire mark will lead you to use inappropriate equations for speed estimates, even if you have done test skids. Review the topic on tire marks (Topic 817) if you are not sure what you have.

13. SOURCES

Authors

Lynn B. Fricke is a traffic engineer specializing in accident reconstruction. He has been with The Traffic Institute since 1975. In 1981 he became the director of the Institute's Accident Investigation Division.

J. Stannard Baker is a traffic engineer specializing in accident reconstruction. He was director of research and development at The Traffic Institute from 1946 to 1971 and is a guest lecturer for the Institute.

References

Superscript numbers in the preceding pages refer to the following publications:

1. Garrott, W.R., D. Guenther, et al, *Improvement of Methods for Determining Pre-Crash Parameters from Skid Marks*. National Highway Traffic Safety Administration Technical Report DOT HS − 806 − 063, May 1981.

2. Reed, Walter and Keskin, A. Taner, *Vehicular Response to Emergency Braking*, Society of Automotive Engineers Paper 870501, 1987.

3. Barzelay, Martin E., and George W. Lacy, *Scientific Automobile Accident Reconstruction*. Matthew Bender and Co., New York, 1988.

4. Collins, James C., *Accident Reconstruction*, Charles C. Thomas Publisher, Springfield, IL, 1979.

5. Kummer, H.W., and W. E. Meyer, *Tentative Skid-Resistance Requirements for Main Rural Highways*. National Cooperative Highway Research Program Report 37, 1967.

6. Reed, Walter and Keskin, A. Taner, *Vehicular Deceleration and its Relationship to Friction*, Society of Automotive Engineers Paper 890736.

7. Smith, Richard A., *Drag Sled Measurement Systems Manual*. Olympia, Washington.

8. Baker, J. Stannard, *Traffic Accident Investigation Manual*, Northwestern University Traffic Institute, 1975.

9. Warner, Charles Y., Gregory C. Smith, et al, *Friction Application in Accident Reconstruction*. Society of Automotive Engineers Paper 830612, 1983.

Exhibits

The following are the sources of the exhibits used in this topic.

Baker, J. Stannard, San Diego, CA
Photos: 13
Diagrams: 18 − 20, 37 − 38
Tables: 15 − 17, 22, 39
Graphs: 3

Baker, Kenneth S., Evanston, IL
Photos: 7 − 8

Beck, Michael, Indiana Law Enforcement Training Academy, Plainfield, IN
Photo: 14

Cooper, Gary W., Wauconda, IL
Photos: 32
Diagrams: 33 − 34

Fricke, Lynn B., Lincolnshire, IL
Photos: 5 − 6, 10 − 12
Diagrams: 1 − 2, 24, 27
Tables: 21, 23, 25 − 26, 35 − 36
Graphs: 28 − 30

Garrott, W.R., Ohio State University, Columbus, OH
Graph: 4

Warner, Charles W., Orem, UT
Diagrams: 9

Unknown
Photo: 31

PERCEPTION AND REACTION IN TRAFFIC ACCIDENTS

Topic 864 of the *Traffic Accident Investigation Manual*

by
J. Stannard Baker

NORTHWESTERN UNIVERSITY TRAFFIC INSTITUTE

PERCEPTION AND REACTION
IN TRAFFIC ACCIDENTS

1. PURPOSE

The intent of this topic is to summarize information on certain human factors, such as reaction time, as they relate to motor vehicle operation and traffic accident reconstruction.

In traffic accident reconstruction, perception and reaction values are mainly used to

1. *Estimate* possible stopping distances of motor vehicles, usually to determine whether a hazard could have been avoided under specified circumstances.
2. *Compare* actual points of perception with possible points of perception to estimate perception delay as an indication of attentiveness.
3. *Determine* whether a highway user's response to a situation hazard was the best possible under existing circumstances.

It is hoped that this topic will help those unfamiliar with psychological testing to understand better how a particular accident happened.

To begin with, consider three facts:

1. The line between perception and reaction is not clear. They overlap.
2. Although you might only think of visual (seeing) stimuli in connection with highway use, audible (hearing) and tactile (feeling) often play a significant role as well.
3. Perception and reaction are important in automotive engineering, traffic engineering and highway design, as well as in traffic accident reconstruction.

2. THE DRIVING PROCESS

A brief review of the driving process is a good beginning for this topic.

The driver or pedestrian (highway user) is the *thinking* part of the highway transportation system. The decisions in this thinking serve three main purposes:

1. *To follow a route*: the observations, decisions and operations required to go from a trip's origin to its destination.

2. *To plan driving strategy*: adjusting speed, position, and direction of motion on the road; giving signals of intent to turn or slow down; making any maneuvers that increase the chance of success in avoiding a hazard.

3. *To devise driving tactics*: actions taken by a traffic unit to avoid a hazardous situation – steering, braking, accelerating, etc. to avoid collision or other accident.

To a large extent, how well a person performs these three tasks, especially the last two, determines the risks he runs in traveling on highways. Failure in precautionary strategy predisposes a highway user to situations in which no evasive tactic can be completely successful in avoiding a mishap.

Situation Hazards

Certain very common circumstances which, to some degree, regularly endanger traffic units must be avoided to prevent accidents.

Static situation hazards involve no moving object other than the traffic unit. The most common static situation hazard is the edge of the roadway. To avoid running off the road, the driver must repeatedly correct the heading of his vehicle – unless it runs on rails. On straight roads, only slight corrections are needed now and then; but on curves and at turns, greater and more frequent adjustments are required. In ordinary driving, steering to correct vehicle heading is usually required every 2 or 3 secs. A driver can rarely go more than 15 secs without a tactical reaction to avoid some situation hazard. That means that if a driver loses consciousness, he will surely be in trouble in less than half a minute.

Dynamic situation hazards involve other things in motion, generally vehicles or pedestrians on collision courses. Such hazards require not only considering the position and motion of other traffic units, but also anticipating what these other traffic units may do. For example, you discover another car approaching you in *your* lane at a rapid rate. It is easily perceived. Now you must try to guess what it will do. Will it return to its side of the roadway before reaching you? Will it try to stop in your lane? Will it leave the roadway on your right? In this situation, you are confronted with perhaps the most difficult decision about what to do, and with the shortest time in which to make that decision.

Often, one situation hazard is confronted so quickly after another that the driver or pedestrian must start to cope with the second before he has finished tactics dealing with the first. There may be a continual flow of problems to be handled.

Thus, when a traffic unit confronts a dynamic situation hazard, some evasive tactic is required to avoid the danger or to ameliorate its effects. All three elements of the highway transportation system – road, vehicle, and driver – are in some way involved in most evasive tactics. So far as the driver is concerned, every evasive tactic requires a sequence of three acts (see Exhibit 1):

1. *Perception* of the situation as a hazard (A, B, and C);

2. *Decision* about how to avoid the hazard (D);

3. *Performance* of the acts decided on (E).

Thus, the tactic is a series of events in which the first ones generally involve only the driver and the final ones depend on the vehicle's response to control. For now, we are interested only in the first, or human, elements.

Alternate Terminology

Not all writers use the same names that appear in this topic for steps in the driving process. This can lead to misunderstanding and confusion.

Road users' responses to external stimuli (situational hazards) have been described by some people[7] in four steps rather than in the three listed above. These four are usually designated by the acronym PIEV:

P. *Perception* – seeing, hearing or feeling the stimulus (hazard);

I. *Identification* or intellection – understanding what is seen as a hazard;

E. *Emotion* or judgment – the decision-making process;

V. *Volition* or reaction – executing the decision.

Perception and *Identification* are combined into step 1 of the more common classification; *Emotion* and *Volition* are essentially the same as steps 2 and 3. If a driver fails to comprehend how his safety is affected by what he sees, feels and hears, he is unlikely to respond to the sensory stimulus – at least not promptly and sensibly.

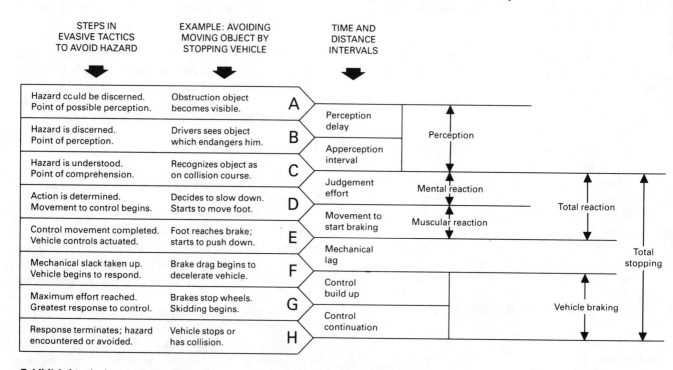

Exhibit 1. *A typical emergency stop involves a series of operations. Beginning with the appearance of the hazard, the first operations are performed by the driver without effect on the vehicle's speed. When brakes are locked, slowing depends on the vehicle and the road; the driver can do no more.*

Another writer [8] breaks down the sequence of response to hazard as follows:

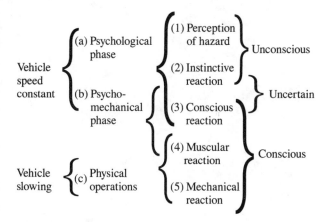

The special feature of this scheme is the distinction between *unconscious* and *conscious* reactions (with *uncertain* falling somewhere between the two). Instinctive, habitual or automatic actions are contrasted with conscious tactical maneuvers.

The foregoing simplified explanation of perception-reaction operations is couched in terms of automobile driving; with minor adaptations, it could apply just as easily to pedestrians and cyclists.

3. PERCEPTION AND REACTION

Definition of Perception

In this topic, *perception* means "the general process of detecting some object or situation and comprehending its significance." Therefore, perception is a human factor in highway transportation; it involves comprehending the risk of starting or continuing a movement in driving. It corresponds to points B and C in Exhibit 1.

Discerning

A *visual* stimulus occurs when light from objects in the field of view passes through the lens of the eye and forms an image of the scene on the retina at the back of the eyeball. From there, the optic nerve conducts the image to the brain.

The brain has stored millions of images of things seen in the past and connects these with things learned and experiences remembered.

Upon receiving a visual stimulus, the brain tries to relate the incoming image to stored images and decide what the combination might mean. If the stimulus image is only seen briefly as it flashes across the field of view, or if an important part of the image is unclear because it is at the edge of the field of view, the brain may turn the eyes or even the head to get a better look. This pause is *fixation*. Scanning and fixation go on continually. If some object is visualized clearly enough and long enough to be matched with previously stored knowledge, we say that it has been *discerned*. This is the beginning of perception (Exhibit 1, point B).

Apperception

Discernment leads to considering whether what is seen is a situational hazard. This is understanding, or *apperception* (Exhibit 1, point C). Perception is now complete.

The foregoing description uses a visual stimulus as an illustration. Other stimuli are also possible. For example, the sound of an automobile horn would be an audible stimulus; a jolt of the vehicle would be a tactual stimulus that tells the driver a wheel has left the pavement.

An object might be very clearly discerned but not at all apperceived. An example of this, rare today, but which occasionally occurred before drivers were licensed, will illustrate this phenomenon. Imagine a rancher who drove his car into the city for the first time since traffic signals had been installed. He had never heard of traffic signals or what they are for. He clearly discerned the first one he came to but had no experience or learning to give it meaning for him. Without apperception, there was no perception and no evasive tactic.

Obstacles to Perception

Nearly everybody realizes that reduced visibility hinders visual perception. Rain, snow, smoke, and darkness all make seeing more difficult.

The size of the object viewed also affects its visibility. Large sign letters are easier to distinguish than small ones; a foot of the front end of a vehicle emerging from behind a view obstruction is much more difficult to recognize than half or more of the vehicle's length (see Exhibits 2 and 3). However, good experimental data sufficient to estimate how much difficult visibility prolongs apperception are unavailable.

Speed also affects discernment. Lower speeds give more time for an obstacle or sign to become more recognizable in the field of vision.

Perhaps the most important factor in perception time is the alertness or expectancy of the individual. One whose focus of attention is wandering here and there and who has no reason to believe any hazard exists for him will have more delay and difficulty in perceiving an object than one who has been warned to look for the hazard or who expects a hazard to appear.

Obstacles to Apperception

Ignorance and lack of skill or experience hinder comprehension of the significance of certain hazards.

In driving, vehicle speed limits time for both perception and apperception. Time limitation can result in incomplete and often incorrect apperception. This is demonstrated by a laboratory experiment. A subject is allowed only half a second to decide how many circles are displayed before him. He instantly perceives the circles, but when he tries to count them, they have disappeared. When he tries to remember exactly what he saw, this leads to guesswork and mistakes.

Drivers commonly compensate for difficulties of perception and apperception by driving strategy: they reduce speed

Exhibit 2. When a vehicle just begins to appear from behind a view obstruction it cannot be perceived instantly.

Exhibit 3. If half or more of the vehicle is visible, no perception delay has to be allowed for, provided of course, the driver's attention is directed toward the vehicle.

and increase alertness. This gives more time to decide whether what was seen was indeed a hazard to be avoided.

Definition of Reaction

In this topic, *reaction* will mean "a person's voluntary or involuntary response to a hazard or other situation that has been perceived; the response to a sensory stimulus."[3]

Mental Reaction

The first phase of reaction is deciding on a suitable evasive tactic for the perceived situation hazard. This is purely a thinking or mental process.

In perception, the mind tries to match a visual image with images stored in memory to comprehend the nature of the hazardous situation that has been discerned. Then the mind tries to match the hazardous situation with the memory of tactics that were successful in similar situations in the past. Most driving involves choosing a response to a visual stimulus. For example, a curve in the road ahead requires turning the steering wheel an appropriate amount. This becomes so habitual that it is done without conscious thought. Stored in the mind are thousands of little instructions for muscles to control the vehicle so as to avoid a hazard. When a hazard is perceived, the mind immediately dispatches the proper prepared message to arms and legs or other parts of the body. When one first learns to drive, each such procedure has to be thought out. For example, how much must the vehicle be slowed to negotiate a particular curve comfortably, and exactly how much must the steering wheel be turned to follow the proper path? Experience develops skill so that the

proper messages can be dispatched by way of nerves, without conscious consideration.

This brings us to point D in Exhibit 1. The required action has been determined, but perception and mental reaction have not yet had any effect on the movement of the vehicle; it is still on a collision course.

Muscular Reaction

When the mind gives the message to the hands and feet, muscular reaction starts. In the case of slowing the vehicle, this is when pressure on the accelerator begins to be released and other controls are put in motion.

Muscular reaction continues until the behavior of the vehicle is affected (point E in Exhibit 1).

Perception-reaction operations are very quick. They are carried out continuously in driving. The driver may watch to see whether his reaction produced the desired result. If not, a correcting response may be started.

When ordinary vehicle control efforts are made, resulting in successful evasive tactics, the vehicle transporation system is operating without fault. But there may be mistakes at any step in the driving process, often with disastrous results; then it may be up to the traffic accident investigator to discover and describe just how the highway transportation system failed at that point.

4. SIMPLE REACTION TIME

Definition

Reaction time is the "time required from perception to start of vehicle control for tactical or strategic operations."[3]

Uses

In traffic accident reconstruction, perception and reaction time are considered mainly for two significant purposes:

1. To compare the best possible reaction under the circumstances with evasive tactics actually undertaken; this helps to evaluate the knowledge and skill of a driver or pedestrian.

2. To establish the possible slowing or stopping distance of a vehicle at a stipulated speed.

For the latter purpose, part of the stopping distance is that traveled by the vehicle during the driver's reaction time at the vehicle's estimated speed before the vehicle began to slow. This is the time and distance from D to E in Exhibit 1. The other part is the distance traveled in slowing, F to H in Exhibit 1.

Measuring

Reliable information on driver response time is difficult to find. Many experiments and demonstrations were made years ago when driver reaction time was being considered as one of the tests for licensing drivers. The publications reporting these experiments are generally out of print.

Many traffic accident investigators have made test skids and other experiments to determine the coefficient of friction of roadways; but few have tested drivers for reaction time, and still fewer have made tests for other than simple reaction.

Laboratory Method

In a laboratory, a chronometer is used to measure the brief interval between perception of a stimulus and the start of a muscular response. Because the end of perception and the start of reaction occurs in the mind and may overlap, it is impossible to determine the exact instant when perception ends and reaction starts. As a practical matter, therefore, the experimenter makes the stimulus strong and clear and its meaning unmistakable so that perception will be virtually instantaneous. For example, the object to be perceived – the stimulus – is the appearance of a bright light directly in front of the person being tested. The attention of the subject is fixed on this expected signal and he understands exactly what he is to do when the light comes on: press a little button as quickly as he can. The timer starts when the light appears, and stops when the button is touched.

This time measurement includes perception time: discerning the light and recognizing what it means (apperception). But these two phases of perception are made so strong and simple, and the person being tested is so prepared, that the time for perception is negligible. Then the time recorded is, for practical purposes, reaction time. This is "simple reaction, a preplanned reaction to an expected stimulus."[3]

Exhibit 4 shows equipment for laboratory timing of simple reaction – lifting the foot from the accelerator or pressing on the brake pedal – to the expected appearance of a bright light. The total reaction (mental plus muscular) will be timed if the

Exhibit 4. *Laboratory equipment for measuring simple reaction time with a light for a visual signal and an accelerator release as a response. This equipment can also time the application of the brake.*

clock is started when the light appears and stopped when the shoe touches the brake pedal.

Field Measurement

To relate reaction time measurements more realistically to driving, a test vehicle can be equipped with a pair of "guns" for firing pigment pellets on the roadway. With the vehicle at a known velocity, the experimenter fires one of the guns as an audible stimulus or signal to apply brakes as quickly as possible, shooting pigment on the pavement at that instant. Pressure on the brake pedal fires the other gun and leaves a second spot on the roadway. The distance in ft (or m) between the two spots, divided by the velocity in ft per sec (or m per sec) gives the driver's total (mental plus muscular) simple reaction time in seconds.

The distance from the spot made by the second gun to the position of that gun on the vehicle when it stops is the vehicle's *stopping distance*. That distance combined with the initial velocity of the vehicle will give the average deceleration of the vehicle and the drag factor during stopping.

Exhibit 5 shows a pair of guns mounted on the front bumper to spot the pavement for measuring reaction time.

Accident reconstruction commonly involves estimating values for various factors. Perhaps the most common is the friction coefficient (or drag factor) of the road surface. Another common factor is the reaction time of a driver or pedestrian. There are several ways of measuring road friction at the scene of an accident with reasonable reliability; but no practical way of measuring driver reaction time at the scene of an accident has been developed or recommended. Certainly that would be impossible if the driver were killed

Exhibit 5. *A driver's reaction time can be measured by "guns" which shoot pigment pellets on the pavement. The sound of the first gun, when it marks the car's position on the roadway, is the signal to apply brakes. When the driver's foot touches the brake pedal, the second gun marks the pavememt. The distance between the two marks divided by the vehicle's velocity gives the driver's response time to an audible stimulus, including foot movement.*

or even seriously injured. Yet it is as important to use an appropriate value for reaction time as it is for drag factor; both are used in estimating stopping distances.

Simple Demonstration

There are several ways to demonstrate simple reaction time. In one, the experimenter holds a yardstick vertically with its lower end level with and at the edge of a table top. The person being tested holds his thumb and forefinger at the edge of the table ready to grasp the yardstick when it begins to fall. The subject is instructed to grab and hold the yardstick as soon as the experimenter lets it drop. The number of inches the stick falls before the subject stops it is noted (see Exhibits 6 and 7).

In this experiment, the stimulus is visual (seeing the stick begin to fall), the signal is anticipated, and the response is preplanned; so perception time is negligible. Simple reaction time is the number of seconds the stick falls before the subject stops it. The time can be computed by this equation:

$$\text{seconds} = \sqrt{\text{inches}/193.2}$$

Exhibit 8 shows this relationship without calculation.

Remember that measurements made as just described are for *simple* reactions which involve

1. A strong and unmistakable stimulus that can be perceived instantly, such as a traffic signal;

2. An *anticipated* signal or stimulus;

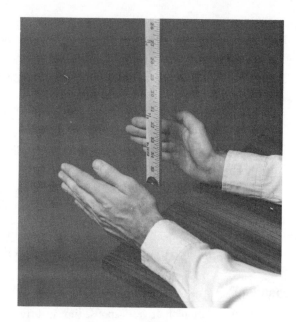

Exhibit 6. *Position of the yardstick ready to be dropped to measure reaction. The hand is ready to grab it as soon as it begins to fall.*

3. A response that requires minimum muscular movement and effort;

4. A test subject who knows exactly what to do when the stimulus appears and has practiced doing it; all decisions have been made in advance.

Estimating Response Time

Such a simple basic reaction to a visual stimulus by normal adults will take about 0.2 sec.[4] You can use this figure as a

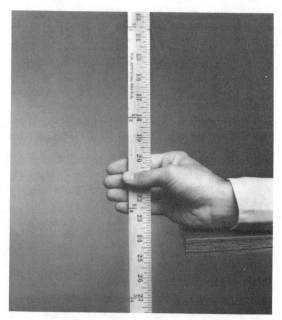

Exhibit 7. *The yardstick has been grasped by the subject and stopped in its fall. The time taken for the fall is the subject's simple reaction time.*

Inches Dropped	Corresponding Time, secs
2	0.10
4	0.14
6	0.18
8	0.20
10	0.23
12	0.25
14	0.27
17	0.30
20	0.32
24	0.35
30	0.39
36	0.43

Exhibit 8

reasonable starting point. Double it to 0.4 sec for a complex reaction requiring decisions about what to do; add more for very complex situations. Quadruple it to 0.8 sec if the person was surprised by a completely unfamiliar situation. Add about 0.2 sec more if the driver had to move his or her foot from accelerator to brake or otherwise prepare to operate vehicle controls. Additional small increments of time can be added for other special situations such as low visibility, confusing signs, or intoxication.

Such estimating is very crude by engineering standards, but is the best available. Do not add a "safety factor" when dealing with a specific situation; try to approximate reality as closely as you can. For this purpose, it may be useful to make and use two estimates: one for maximum time and one for minimum time.

Which sense receives the stimulus makes a difference. Seeing is slower than hearing or feeling.[4] (Exhibit 9).

Which part of the body responds makes a difference in the time required for response. The heel-ankle pivot required in taking the foot off the accelerator takes longer than the index finger movement commonly used in testing.[4] (Exhibit 10).

Age affects reaction time. Older drivers take longer to respond to stimuli, especially the very old (Exhibit 11).

Sex has no significant effect on mental reaction time.

Fatigue is supposed to lengthen reaction time, but because evaluating degrees of fatigue is so difficult, trustworthy data are not available.

Ingested alcohol increases thinking reaction time as might be expected[5] (Exhibit 12). A Swiss physician has reported that after drinking alcoholic beverages, reaction time of soldiers was more affected high in the mountains than at much lower altitudes. The amount of this effect was not reported.

Impaired faculties, usually mental, may interfere with calling to mind quickly the proper response to a perceived hazard.

Muscular Reaction

Response to a stimulus is incomplete until vehicle behavior is affected. If the foot is already on the brake pedal in anticipation of possible slowing, then of course foot movement time is negligible. But if the foot has to be moved from the accelerator to the brake pedal, which is usually the case, measurable additional reaction time is required[9] (see Exhibit 13). How much time depends on the horizontal and vertical distance moved, the weight of foot and shoe, and the vigor with which the movement is executed. Exhibit 13 gives you some idea of how much time might be required for a surprise stimulus.

Truly simple reactions in driving are probably rare. Common situational hazards, such as roadway edges and traffic signals, are naturally quite simple, and are usually anticipated and understood without delay. For experienced drivers, habit makes most responses so familiar that appropriate decisions have been made in advance, even to selecting the appropriate *degree* of response. In the case of a curve, the degree of response is how much to turn the steering wheel for the particular situation.

Yet, numerous traffic situations do require essentially simple reactions. For example, a driver following another car closely, especially in heavy traffic, decides in advance to brake if the slow signal of the car ahead flashes on. The signal is expected, it is unmistakable, what to do has been decided, and the right foot is already on the brake pedal in anticipation of need. In this case, allow 0.2 sec minimum time for response if the signal does appear.

Most reported experiments of stopping a vehicle while it is being driven give the total mental and muscular reaction time, from appearance of the stimulus to application of brakes. This makes the results directly useful in calculating yellow-interval traffic signal distances and vehicle-sight stopping distances in highway design. Some of these experiments were done in laboratories, others in specially equipped vehicles; some drivers were alerted to expect the stimulus (signal), others were not.

Exhibit 14 summarizes the results of driving tests to determine total mental and muscular reaction or response time. The considerable variation in these times – from 0.50 to 1.23 sec – is doubtless due to differences in the circumstances under which the tests were made.

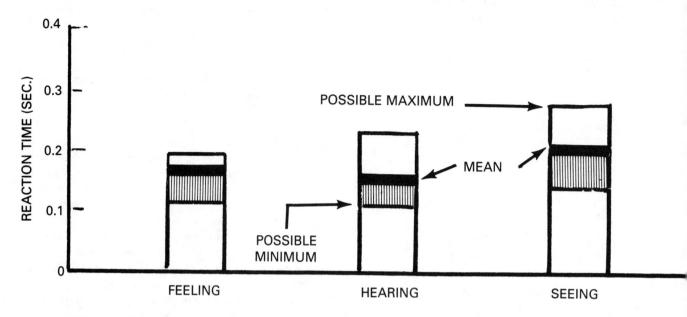

Exhibit 9. More time is required to see than to hear. Each bar represents the mean of test made on a number of subjects. Each subject was tested for simple reaction to a tactual, an audible, and a visual stimulus.

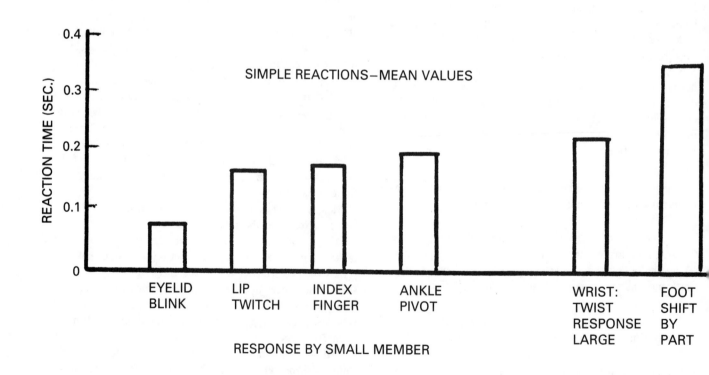

Exhibit 10. Response by heavier body parts takes more time. Longer movements also take more time. These data are from a number of different experimenters. The "foot shift" means movement of the foot from the accelerator to the brake pedal.

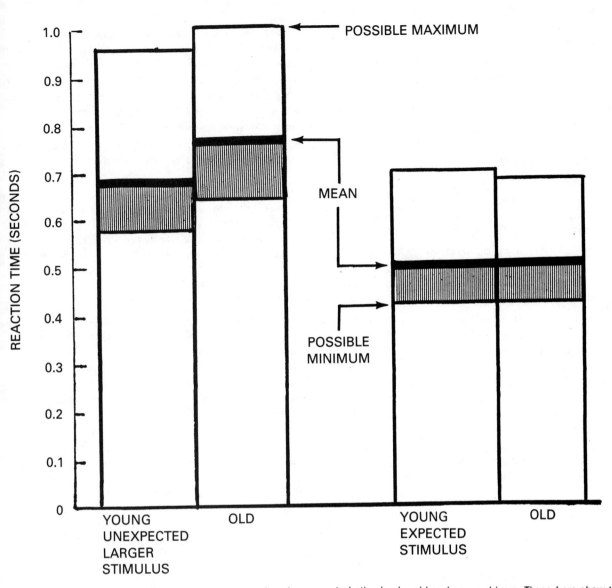

Exhibit 11. Example of reaction times for expected and unexpected stimulus by old and young drivers. These bars show the mean and possible maximum and minimum values.

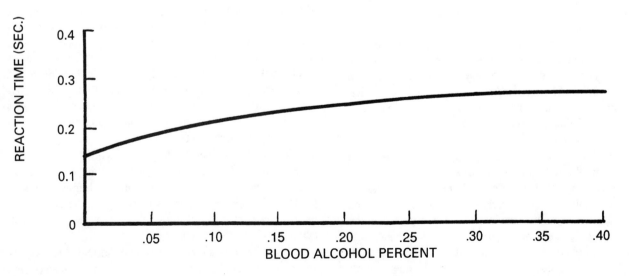

Exhibit 12. Increase in reaction time with increase in blood alcohol content of body fluids.

Accelerator to Brake Foot Movement Time, secs		
	Younger	Older
Minimum	0.31	0.25
Median	0.39	0.33
Maximum	0.67	0.44

Subjects surprised by stimulus.

Exhibit 13

5. COMPLEX REACTION

In driving or walking, one may encounter unexpected and unfamiliar hazardous situations where habitual and practiced tactics are of no help, and more than simple remembering is called for. The time required for this complex reaction procedure is naturally longer than that needed for a simple reaction.

Laboratory measurements of complex reaction time usually confront the person being tested with one of several possible stimuli, for which he must choose the appropriate response. For example, a green light might require pressing a button and a red light would mean apply the brake. The subject knows what he is supposed to do for each signal, but has to decide after the stimulus appears which reaction it requires.

Simple Demonstration

The effect of complexity on the average reaction time of a group of 10 or more persons is easily demonstrated. All you need is a stopwatch or other timer. For comparison purposes, start by determining the average simple reaction time of the group. Ask the group to form a chain by grasping hands. Instruct them to press the hand of the next person in line as soon as they feel one of their hands being squeezed, and to close their eyes to prevent someone from jumping the gun. Start the timer the moment you press the free hand of the first person in the chain. When the signal reaches the last person in line, he raises his free hand to tell you to stop the timer. The total time measured divided by the number of people in the chain, including yourself, is the average *simple* reaction time of the group – usually about 0.25 sec.

To measure the *complex* reaction time, the experiment must be complicated a bit. Form the chain by having each person place both his hands on the shoulders of the next in line. Then explain that the signal will be transmitted along the line by squeezing the shoulder of the next person in the chain, but on the *opposite* side from the shoulder which was pressed. This requires a little thinking by each subject to determine which shoulder of the next subject in line he must

press. Start the timer the instant you press one shoulder of the first subject in line. The last subject in line waves his hand to signal you to stop the timer. The total time divided by the number of persons in the chain will give the average *complex* reaction time. Remember to have the subjects close their eyes so that the response will be from a tactual, rather than visual, stimulus. You must also watch carefully to see that the proper shoulder is pressed by each subject. This small complication will usually about double the simple reaction time.

Multiple Stimuli

Exhibit 15[4] shows the results of complex reaction tests with different numbers of stimuli. In Exhibit 15, the time for a single stimulus is essentially that of a simple reaction. Additional stimuli to be sorted out definitely increased reaction times.

Unexpected Stimuli

When a person does not expect a hazardous situation, it takes more complex reaction time to sort out the proper response. Experimentally, the subject is set to a task which keeps him occupied, such as reading a story, assembling a picture puzzle, or writing a letter. Then, at irregular intervals, a timer is started at the instant a recognizable signal is given. The subject responds according to his instructions, for example by uttering the word "stop." Experiments like this simulate the unexpected appearance of a hazard when one is engaged in a simple repetitive task such as routine motor vehicle driving.

It may take a person being tested quite a while to memorize the response required for each stimulus. Until he has had sufficient practice, his response may be delayed while he tries to remember what he should do for each situation. This is like a person learning to drive a motor vehicle.

Errors

With simple reaction, there is little chance for error because only one response is required and that is anticipated. But with complex reactions, there is a possibility of making a wrong response. As the complexity of the reaction increases, not only is more time required, but more mistakes are made (see Exhibit 15)[4]. Hence, if subjects try to respond more quickly, they do so at the risk of making more mistakes; conversely, if they must be absolutely sure not to make a mistake, they do well to allow a little more time to think about each decision – much more if they have had little practice in making the required reactions.

A learner drives very slowly to begin with. That gives him time to consider what to do in each situation he confronts. The habits he forms while learning provide him with sets of predecided responses so that perceiving familiar situational hazards requires only selecting the appropriate program of action for a given situation.

Driving involves a continual flow of stimuli, each requiring an appropriate response. Usually these are perceived suf-

Exhibit 14

Summary of Studies of Total Reaction Time

Investigators	Year	Sample	Mean time, .Seconds	Stimulus Comments
Laboratory and Similar Studies				
Greenshields	1936	1461	0.50	Laboratory
"	1936	13	0.86	Automobile
"	1936	27	0.74	
Forbes and Katz	1936			
DeSilva and Forbes	1937	907	0.64	
Jones and others	1936	889	0.70	Truck Drivers
Konz and Daccarett	1967	12	0.59	
"	1967	40	0.47	

On the Road Studies

Investigators	Year	Sample	Mean time, .Seconds	Stimulus Comments
Moss and Allen	1925	46	0.54	Auditory
Mass. Inst. of	1934	144	0.66	Men Brake
Technology	1934	36		Women light
Drew	1968	1000	0.57	Men Alerted
"			0.62	Women Alerted
Norman	1953	53	0.73	Alerted
Johansson and Rumar	1971	321	0.75	Expected Audible
"	1971	5	0.89	Surprise Audible
Mortimer	1970	80	1.30	Brake light
Sivak and others	1981	311	1.23	Brake light

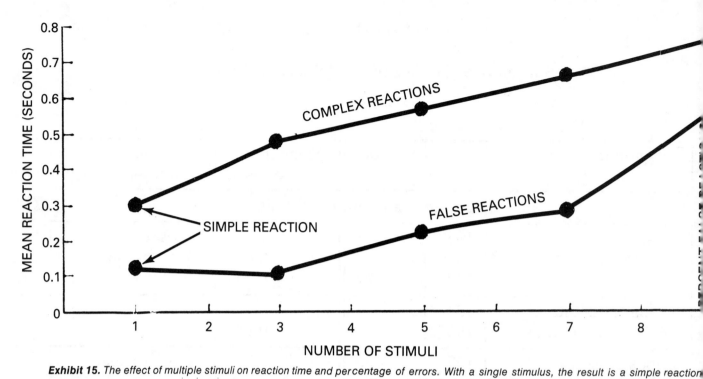

Exhibit 15. *The effect of multiple stimuli on reaction time and percentage of errors. With a single stimulus, the result is a simple reaction*

ficiently in advance and are familiar enough so that there is time to consider and execute a suitable reaction. Often, there is time to make a corrective reaction if the first response is perceived to be inadequate. For example, when a car is steered for a curve, the driver may find, when he enters the curve, that he is drifting toward one edge of his lane. Then he usually has time to adjust his steering a bit to follow the proper path.

Most of the factors mentioned as affecting simple reaction time, like age and alcohol, also affect complex reaction time; but these factors have an additional important effect on complex reaction: they increase, often greatly, the chance of wrong responses.

The effect of increasing the number of stimuli has already been noted. In driving, there are many kinds of possible stimuli. Some are very common, others rare. Often, two or more hazards appear at the same time, competing for the driver's attention. Then the driver has another decision to make; he must decide which hazard to handle first.

Anticipation of a hazard can reduce complex reaction time. Anticipation gives time to bring to mind a number of possible responses. Then the selection process is simplified when the hazard does appear. Anticipation, like slowing, is part of driving strategy. It is associated with the level of attention.

6. REFLEX AND DISCRIMINATIVE REACTIONS

In trying to determine which driver reactions were involved in a motor vehicle accident, an investigator will usually conclude that the reaction was simple or complex and estimate the time required accordingly. But sometimes there are peculiar circumstances that do not fit well with these two major categories. It may be that one of the two uncommon kinds of reaction was involved: *reflex* or *discriminative*.

Reflex Reaction

Definition: Reflex reaction is an involuntary response to a stimulus, an instinctive act resulting from perception of an imminently hazardous situation. Time: 0.2 sec, more or less.[2]

The perception of the hazard is complete, but the consequences are so overwhelming that the driver or pedestrian skips the usual thinking process of selecting the appropriate reaction and responds with whatever action comes first to mind. Afterwards, as a rule, the driver cannot recall exactly what happened, or has some implausible explanation. Often, the statement of observers or an examination of scars on the roadway will be a clue to exactly what happened.

Examples: At a grade crossing, a locomotive on a freight train struck the right rear wheel of a stationary automobile and spun it around clockwise. Afterwards, the automobile driver claimed that his engine stalled. Skid marks on the roadway clearly indicated that car brakes had been applied and that the car was moving when hit. A speed analysis showed that if brakes had not been applied, the car would have cleared the tracks before the locomotive reached it. Clearly, if the driver had accelerated rather than braked, there would have been no collision. Instead of a thoughtful complex reaction, there had been an impulsive response, skipping the thoughtful part of what to do.

A small truck and a car approached each other from opposite directions. The truck swerved across the center line and hit the car in the car's half of the roadway. The truck driver claimed that when he tried to keep his vehicle in the right half of the roadway, the steering wheel spun freely in his hands and he could not help crossing the center line. But tire marks and witnesses clearly indicated that the truck had been steered sharply to the left just before collision, probably to avoid running off the road to the right, a reflex overreaction.

A pedestrian crossing a street was surprised by squealing tires on an approaching car. The pedestrian froze instantly and was struck a couple of seconds later by the car's left front corner. Witnesses agreed that had the pedestrian kept on, she would have escaped being struck.

At a street junction, right-turning and left-turning vehicles moving in opposite directions came into collision alignment, both at moderate speeds. Both drivers perceived instantly that there would be a head-on collision. One driver did the best he could simply by applying brakes to minimize damage. The other screamed, "My God," and put her hands over her eyes with no attempt at evasive tactics. The perception of both drivers was proper and prompt. One had a thoughtful complex reaction; the other had a worthless panic response.

A reflex reaction may be a form of unplanned response like the unconscious leg twitch or muscular jerk that doctors look for when they bump your patella (knee cap) with a small rubber hammer to test for reflexes. Such unconscious muscular jerks can occur when one hears a big bang close by, or finds oneself slipping or falling.

Time for a reflex reaction is not easily measured, but is probably something like 0.10 sec.

Discriminative Reaction

Definition: Discriminative reaction is a response to perception of an unfamiliar hazard or other situation which requires more information than is immediately available to make a decision or which presents several choices of possible evasive tactics.[2] Time required is 1.5 sec or possibly much more.

The driver realizes that something must be done quickly but has no clear idea of what. Several steps may be required, but delay in considering these may add new hazardous situations to deal with. There is a temptation to do indiscriminately whatever first comes to mind. Often this is stopping, which is the most generally useful reaction because it reduces speed and therefore limits damage in case of collision or rollover. But stopping may sprout new and nasty hazards to cope with.

For example, a driver comes to a fork in the road. He is traveling fast and is not sure which branch to take to his destination. He postpones decision until he has to slam on brakes or swerve sharply into the path of his choice. Either action may involve other traffic units, loss of control, or dangerous overcorrections. The best way is to resolutely choose and follow one branch, right or wrong, until there is a time and place safely to resolve the situation and proceed accordingly.

Another discriminative reaction occurs when something in the vehicle or on the road makes a sudden loud noise or jerk, resulting in an inappropriate reaction which produces a more serious situation.

One difference between a reflex and a discriminative reaction in driving is that in the latter, the driver takes too much time to decide what to do and in the former, he takes too little time.

7. PERCEPTION DELAY

The general role of perception in driving and walking was discussed earlier in this topic; explanation of the time involved was left until now.

Perception takes place in three steps: A, B, and C in Exhibit 1.

A. *Possible perception.* Sometimes an object may appear before a driver without his being aware of it. This is usually because something attracts his attention elsewhere, but it may be due to some lapse of attention, perhaps drowsiness or even sleep. The time from possible perception to actual discernment cannot be given an average value for use in accident reconstruction; the circumstances differ too widely from one accident to the next. But delay is a very important consideration in an investigation.

B. *Actual perception* or discernment is a mental activity. It can be thought of as eye fixation which requires too little time to be reckoned with in practical accident investigation.

C. *Apperception*, the time for considering what the object perceived signifies, is virtually impossible to evaluate, and may simply be treated as part of reaction time.

Variations in Responses

Not all drivers respond the same way to identical perceptions. Imagine three drivers waiting for the same red traffic light to turn green. When the green light appears, their responses differ.

Driver 1, who is probably in a hurry, starts off very quickly when he perceives the green signal. He perceives the signal instantly and loses no time in reacting to it.

Driver 2, a normal driver, also perceives the green light instantly, but when he reacts, he chooses a more leisurely and less energetic acceleration, possibly because he feels that less hurry is better driving strategy. His more gradual response is not delayed perception or slower perception; it is less hurried reaction.

Driver 3 remains motionless when the green light appears. He does not start until he sees one of the other cars move or hears the horn of the car behind. This driver does not see the green signal appear. His attention is elsewhere. We call him absent-minded. His is a delay in perception, and should be treated as such.

In traffic accident investigation, it is usually preferable to think in terms of perception delay after the first stimulus the person could and should have perceived regardless of whether he actually did. The longest delay, then, occurs when the stimulus or signal is never perceived – as when a driver falls asleep, in which case he may never have perceived the edge of the road as a hazard. His first awareness of the hazardous situation is noise or the sensation of leaving the roadway. Or he may never be aware of leaving the road, especially if he is killed in so doing.

Accident Investigation Techniques

In connection with perception, there are two very useful techniques which should be routinely considered in traffic accident investigation.

The first is to ask each driver or informant this question: "How did you first know an accident was happening, where were you, and what were you doing?" The answer will usually reveal how, when, and where he perceived the situation. For example, if his answer is, "The first I knew was when he clobbered me," you know that there was no pre-collision perception on his part. This suggests important follow-up questions.

The second technique is to locate the place where the driver or pedestrian could first have perceived the hazard confronting him. Compare this with the spot where he says he was when he first realized he was in trouble, or with the point where skidmarks or other signs indicate his first reaction to the hazard. The distance between these points is how far the person traveled before he actually perceived what endangered him. Determining this distance may be difficult or impossible, but is well worth trying. In this connection, consider visibility of vehicles and pedestrians, amount of light, positions of light sources, and eye and vehicle heights.

Gradual Appearance

Often, the object perceived becomes more visible as time passes. There are three kinds of such increases in visibility: 1) fog, haze and brightness; 2) increase in amount of object visible; and 3) increase in size of visible details.

Haze, dust, smoke, fog, rain, and snow all make perception of size, shape, and color difficult. At a distance, an object may be invisible; but as it becomes nearer, it looms up until it is quite easy to perceive. Headlight illumination has a somewhat similar effect. At a distance, a car's headlights may illuminate an object too little to make it recognizable; but up close, where the illumination is many times as intense, the object may be clearly seen. Simple experiments at the scene of an accident may be very useful in establishing visibility distances. Using a car with headlamps like those on the car in question, drive it slowly toward the object to be perceived –

another vehicle, railroad car, pedestrian, road marking, or whatever. Stop the car when its occupants can perceive the object in question. Record measurement of maximum visibility distance between observer and object. You may find that observers perceive from different distances. Then record the range of sight distances. Remember that this experiment involves sight distances with *alerted* observers. The surprise visibility distance will be less, often much less. It is possible but more difficult to make tests of surprise sight distance. In such an experiment, you do not tell the observer, who is driving, that he is to encounter a hazard. This test is risky because the surprised subject may react unpredictably. As a precaution, arrange to have the object encountered easily pushed aside or run over – for example, a cardboard box colored to represent the real object to be visualized. The perception point is where the driver-observer applies brakes or steers to one side.

Amount of object visible. If a view obstruction obscures part of an object, the object will be less visible. Exhibits 2 and 3 show a car beginning to poke its front bumper out from behind a view obstruction. Will an observer recognize this as a hazard when only one inch is showing, or must a foot be showing? How fast the object is moving will also affect the perception distance. So will the speed at which the observer is approaching. Experiments may help in estimating the distance at which the part of a car may be recognized.

Perception of an object observed approaching the crest of a hill will also depend on how much of it has come into view. In this case, the eye height of the observer above the road surface is very important.

Size of details makes a difference in perceptibility. For example, how large the letters on a street sign appear to a viewer determines the distance from which the sign is legible (apperceived). Visual acuity of the observer is also important in this connection. A person with 20/20 vision can recognize street signs from twice as far away as an observer with only 20/40 vision. Lighting is also very important. A sign against the sun may not be legible from any distance, regardless of the observor's visual acuity. Direction and intensity of illumination at night will affect legibility, as will brightness contrast between background and lettering.

Vehicle Lights

A traffic accident investigator is often asked to estimate from how far vehicle lights can be seen (perceived). Brief observations on a main highway demonstrate that approaching headlamps can be seen easily on a clear night from several miles away. Fog, rain, dust and snow may reduce that distance to a hundred feet or less. Darkness increases the distance from which vehicle lights are visible because it heightens the contrast between lamps and background. Reflectors and reflectorized number plates are visible from hundreds of feet away when headlight beams shine on them after dark, depending on how close and in what direction the headlights are located.

8. USAGE

Perception and reaction are used in traffic accident reconstruction to describe certain steps in the driving process, especially with respect to the time they take and the distance traveled during that time.

Numerical Values

After an accident, certain values for specific factors, like roadway width or vehicle weight, can usually be measured quite accurately or found in published information. But precise measurements for reaction time or perception delay of individuals involved are almost never available. Therefore, values used for perception and reaction must be based on figures for typical population groups. Such figures are *stochastic data*, or information involving conjecture or guesswork. This does not mean that such data are useless. It merely means that reaction time and perception delay must often be expressed with less certainty, and with a greater range of numerical values, than would more easily verifiable factors like roadway width or vehicle weight.

In the preceding pages, we have tried to give some idea of the normal or mean values for perception and reaction time and the probable effect of several possible circumstances. From this you can try to allow suitable times for specific circumstances, such as age of the individual or moving the foot from accelerator to brake.

In this connection, one must guard against "ready-made" estimates found in various publications. For example:

0.0 sec. "If a driver is intently watching the stop light of the car ahead and it comes on bright red, he will perceive it almost instantly; for practical purposes his perception time is zero."[11] This corresponds to the minimum value of perception time described in Section 7 of this topic.

3/4 sec. "A typical reaction for most drivers under most traffic conditions after driver has perceived the hazard requiring a stop."[11] If this value were used for the simple reaction of an alert driver who already had his foot on the brake pedal, the time estimate would be about three times what it should be.

0.75 sec. "It is usually safe to assume driver perception time at this value. The time may vary from 0.38 seconds for middle-aged experienced drivers . . . to one second for the young, inexperienced driver and the elderly driver."[14] "Unless proof exists to the contrary, a reaction time of three fourths of a second is a good value to use for most drivers."[14]

1.0 sec. "Perception-reaction time for the driver in seconds"[12] used for timing traffic signals. This figure is taken to accommodate the slowest drivers, not just the average driver, and presumably includes time for moving the foot from accelerator to brake pedal.

1.0 sec. "Although a driver response time of 1.0 second for driver reaction and control input is assumed in many reconstructions, observations of drivers in post-accident interviews may reveal larger values, particularly in older or handicapped people."[13] This leaves the way open for exaggerated estimates of reaction time.

2.50 sec. is the brake reaction time given in some official publications.[9,10] This has been used in traffic accident reconstruction for simple reaction, whereas in ordinary stopping distance calculations, the average, simple, expected reaction time, 0.25 sec, is used as most representative. In stopping-sight distance calculations for proposed highway designs, the reaction time of the slowest possible driver is allowed for; hence the 2.5 sec figure is used, for the benefit of one driver in perhaps 100,000. Investigators have grabbed this figure, *2.5 sec*, without pausing to consider what it was for and what it represented. This is like assuming that because an architect uses a standard 80-inch door height, the average person is that tall.

Another difficulty may arise in using published data: different names may be used for the same time interval. For example, one investigator defines "perception time only as that time from first sighting of the obstacle until the subject began to respond by lifting his/her foot from the accelerator."[9] This would have perception time represented by intervals B, C, and D in Exhibit l, whereas in this topic, perception time is defined only by intervals B and C in the same exhibit.

Improving Credibility

Unfortunately, examples of traffic accident reconstruction often exhibit serious deficiencies which undermine their credibility and trustworthiness. For example, there might be no clue whether values used for perception and reaction are reasonable estimates or simply guesswork and speculation. So here are some suggestions for improving credibility.

If you estimate a value for reaction time, state whether it represents simple, complex, discriminatory, or reflex reaction, and whether it includes muscular reaction to move the foot from accelerator to brake. Give your reasons for making your estimate as you did.

Explain where your data came from: personal experiments or measurements, reference to publications, etc. Do not express the results of calculations with more significant figures than are warranted by the data on which the calculation is based.[16] Be sure you try to explain what the value you estimate means.

The Investigator's Task

By reconstructing the accident, the investigator tries to resolve more or less specific issues relating to it. What went

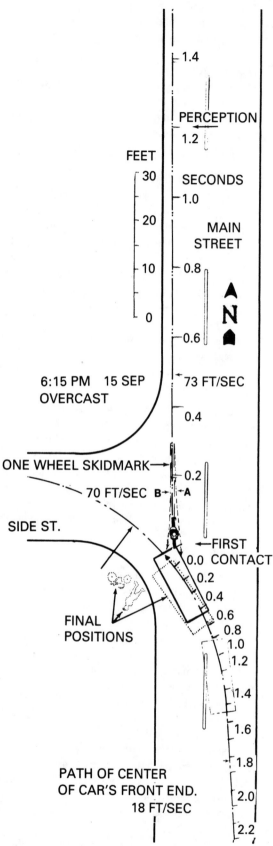

FEET

30

20

10

0

1.4

PERCEPTION

1.2

SECONDS

1.0

MAIN
STREET

0.8

N

0.6

73 FT/SEC

0.4

6:15 PM   15 SEP
OVERCAST

ONE WHEEL SKIDMARK

70 FT/SEC   B → | ← A

0.2

SIDE ST.

FIRST
CONTACT

0.0

0.2

0.4

0.6

0.8

1.0

1.2

1.4

1.6

1.8

2.0

2.2

FINAL
POSITIONS

PATH OF CENTER
OF CAR'S FRONT END.
18 FT/SEC

Exhibit 16. *This is an after-accident situation map on which are also shown the results of reconstruction efforts to establish the first contact positions of the two vehicles involved, their approach paths, and their positions along these paths at intervals of 0.2 sec. Each vehicle had a single occupant. There was no reason to believe that either vehicle or the roadway was deficient in any way.*

wrong? Which driver or pedestrian could have avoided the accident? Were there significant defects in the roadway or in the vehicle?

Exhibit 16 describes an accident up to the point of resolving issues relating to driver behavior. It is an after-accident situation map to which have been added some of the results of accident reconstruction: position of vehicles at first contact, approach path of each vehicle, and time intervals along each vehicle's path. With this data we can estimate accurately the velocity of approach of each vehicle, which prepares us to think about driver behavior.

Consider the cyclist first. His replies to the key questions were as follows: "I saw the car beginning to cross the center line; I slammed on my brake and skidded into the car; I was going about 45 mi/hr; the car driver did not give a left turn signal; I do not believe I had my headlight on; it was still daylight."

Could the cyclist have avoided the accident?

Reconstruction analysis shows that the car had begun to cross the center line about 1.2 sec and 21 ft before first contact at 18 ft/sec. It also shows that the cyclist applied his rear wheel brake only when his front wheel was 16 ft from first contact and his velocity was about 73 ft/sec.

When the cyclist saw the car beginning to cross the center line, he recieved a signal (stimulus) that the vehicles might be on a collision course. He was then the same time from first contact, 1.2 sec, as the car but at a greater distance, approximately 87 ft.

The cyclist had no reason to anticipate the car's turn and was taken completely by surprise. His perception time, including apperception, probably took 0.1 sec or less. His reaction would be complex, because a choice had to be made between braking and steering; this choice was not anticipated, so we allow 0.7 sec of thinking reaction time. Then a little time would be required to apply the brake of the motorcycle, say about 0.2 sec. This gives a total of about 1.0 sec for response time and puts the motorcyclist's perception about a second before the beginning of the skidmark. Hence, perception appears to be prompt and reaction reasonable. With braking by the rear wheel only (drag factor f = 0.3) and an initial velocity of 73 ft/sec, the stopping distance from the point of perception would be 73 ft for the 1 sec perception time, plus braking distance of 276 ft, for a total of 349 ft.

But suppose the cyclist had applied both front and rear brakes. The response time and distance would be the same as before, 1 sec and 73 ft. Brakes would still have been applied 22 ft before collision. The stopping distance from 73 ft/sec (with a drag factor equal to 0.70) would then have been not 349 ft but 73 ft, plus 118 ft for braking, for a total of 191 ft. The crash would still have taken place, but it would have been a little less severe.

Now suppose the motorcycle operator had chosen to steer left to escape collision. His steering input would have been a fraction of a second sooner because, with hands already on the handlebars, he would require no time to move into control position (as was the case in braking). Brakes would have been applied about 16 ft before collision. Starting to steer at a fraction of a foot further from the collision point, with a velocity of 73 ft/sec and f = 0.7 instead of 0.3, the critical turn radius would be about 240 ft, as at point A in Exhibit 16. (Actually motorcycles steer differently that a passenger car. For a more in-depth discussion of the steering maneuverablity of motorcycles, see Topic 874). This turn would swerve the cycle a maximum of about 1 ft to the left. There would be no advantage in that. Collision would then be with the right front fender and wheel.

Could a swerve to the right have avoided collision? The maximum swerve to the right would give the same displacement as the swerve to the left (see point B in Exhibit 16). A right swerve of one foot would result in the cycle striking the middle of the car's front end. There would be no advantage in that.

There might be a question of whether the motorcycle was traveling at an "excessive speed." At 73 ft/sec, the initial speed is very close to 50 mi/hr. Whether this is considered excessive would depend on the speed limit or the eighty-fifth percentile vehicle speed at that point.

Examination of the motorcycle headlamp showed that it was not on when smashed by the collision. Even if it had been on, it is debatable whether the car driver would have perceived the motorcycle soon enough to avoid the collision. The fact that it was off would be grounds for convicting the motorcycle operator of that offense, but would not prove that such negligence contributed to the accident.

Now consider the car. The driver said: "I first saw the motorcycle in a flash just as it hit my car. I was going about 10 mi/hr and did not have time to brake or sound my horn at all. I gave the left turn signal about 100 feet before I began my turn. I always put my left turn signal on. The motorcycle did not have its headlight on. He was going at least 60 mi/hr."

With or without the headlight on, the car driver could and probably did see the motorcycle when it was several hundred feet away, but failed to recognize it as a hazard. He could have perceived it as a hazard at least 5 sec before collision – plenty of time to slow or stop before completing his turn. The car driver was confronted with two hazards: the left turn and the approaching motorcycle. This increases the possibility of error in reaction. There was a long delay, 5 sec or more, in perceiving the motorcycle. It is possible that the car driver caught sight of the motorcycle and concluded carelessly that it was no immediate hazard. Then he fixed his attention on the turn into the narrow side street. It is possible that some distraction interfered with his observation of oncoming traffic.

Under these circumstances, there is no purpose in computing possible stopping distances or corrections in the car's path when the delay in the car driver's perception was so great. Nor is there any reason to believe that there was anything wrong with the roadway or either vehicle.

Whether the car driver gave a left turn signal is indeterminate. The car driver said it was on, but his statement was not very convincing. The motorcycle operator said it was off. The left turn signal lamps were undamaged after collision, so no determination could be made by examining them. Examination of the damaged motorcycle headlamp showed that it was off when broken. This corresponds to the motorcycle operator's statement.

The foregoing description of a simple collision illustrates the need for considering perception and reaction in connection with traffic accidents. Perhaps more than half of all traffic accidents involve circumstances calling for careful consideration of these two factors in connection with traffic accident reconstruction.

9. SOURCES

Author

J. Stannard Baker is a traffic engineer specializing in traffic accident reconstruction. He was director of research and development at the Northwestern University Traffic Institute from 1947 to 1971. Thereafter, he became a consultant and guest lecturer at The Traffic Institute.

References

Superscript numbers in the preceeding pages refer to the following publications:

1. Baker, J. Stannard, "Traffic Accident Information from and about People," *The Traffic Accident Investigation Manual* (1986 Ed.), Northwestern University Traffic Institute, Evanston, IL (pages 15-27).

2. Baker, J. Stannard, *The Traffic Accident Investigation Manual* (1975 Ed.), Northwestern University Traffic Institute, Evanston, IL.

3. Baker, J. Stannard, and Lynn B. Fricke, *The Traffic Accident Investigation Manual* (1986 Ed.), Northwestern University Traffic Institute, Evanston, IL (Index and Glossary).

4. Forbes, T.W., and M.S. Katz, *Summary of Human Engineering Research Data and Principles Related to Highway Design and Traffic Engineering Problems*, American Institute for Research, Pittsburgh, PA, 1957 (page 12).

5. Laves, Wolfgang, "Medizinische Probleme bei Strassenverkehrsenfallen," *Der Strassenverkehrsunfall*, Ferdinand Enke Verlag, Stuttgart, 1956 (page 207).

6. DeSilva, Harry R., and Theodore W. Forbes, *Driver Testing Results*, Works Progress Administration of Massachusetts, 1937 (page 69).

7. Pignataro, Louis J., *Traffic Engineering, Theory and Practice*, Prentice-Hall, Inc., Englewood Cliffs, NJ, 1973.

8. Beux, Armindo, *La Visibilite' et L'accident Imprevisible*, La Commission de l'Eclairage et du Conseil International d'Ophtalmologie, Paris, France, 1980.

9. Olson, P.L., D.E. Cleveland, P.S. Fancher, L.P. Costynuik and L.W. Schneider, "Parameters Affecting Stopping Sight Distance," *National Cooperative Highway Research Program Report 270*, Washington, DC.

10. *A Policy on Geometric Design of Highways and Streets*, American Association of State Highway and Transportation Officials, Washington, DC, 1984. 20001.

11. *Charts and Tables for Stopping Distances of Motor Vehicles*, Northwestern University Traffic Institute, Evanston, IL, 1973.

12. Cass, Samuel, "Traffic Signals," *Transportation and Traffic Engineering Handbook* (Institute of Transportation Engineers), Prentice-Hall, Inc., Englewood Cliffs, NJ, 1976.

13. Limpert, Rudolf, *Motor Vehicle Accident Reconstruction and Cause Analysis*, The Michie Company, Charlottesville, VA, 1978.

14. Collins, James, *Accident Reconstruction*, Charles C. Thomas Publisher, Springfield, IL, 1979.

15. Hooper, Kevin G., and Hugh W. McGee, "Driver Perception-Reaction Time: Are Revisions to Current Specification Values in Order?," *Transportation Research Record 904*, Transportation Research Board, National Research Council, Washington, DC, 1983.

16. Baker, J. Stannard, and Lynn B. Fricke, *The Traffic Accident Investigation Manual* (1986 Edition), Northwestern University Traffic Institute, Evanston, IL (pages 832-27).

17. Henderson, Robert L., *NHTSA Driver Performance Data Book*, Rept. No. DOT HS 807 121, 1987.

Exhibits

The following are the sources of the exhibits used in this topic:

Baker, J. Stannard, San Diego, CA
    Photos: 6, 7
    Diagrams: 1, 16
    Graphs: 9-12, 15
    Tables: 8, 13, 14

Fricke, Lynn B., Lincolnshire, IL
    Photos: 2-5

SPEED ESTIMATES FOR VEHICLES THAT FALL, FLIP, OR VAULT

Topic 866 of the *Traffic Accident Investigation Manual*

by
J. Stannard Baker
and
Lynn B. Fricke

NORTHWESTERN UNIVERSITY TRAFFIC INSTITUTE

SPEED ESTIMATES FOR VEHICLES
THAT FALL, FLIP, OR VAULT

1. INTRODUCTION

In traffic accidents, vehicles often travel through the air. This motion can usually be considered as a fall, flip or vault. If certain information is known, such as the point where the vehicle left the ground and the point where it first came back into contact with the ground, you might be able to determine the speed of the vehicle when it first left the ground.

the wheels hitting a curb or furrowing in loose material. That is, a "tripping" of the vehicle occurs with a fairly large horizontal movement through the air. Nearly always, you must assume an angle of departure with the ground that will give the minimum speed. The term *rollover* is sometimes used to describe a flip. However, in this text, flip and rollover do not describe the same thing. A rollover may occur without the wheels striking a curb or furrowing in loose material. Roll-

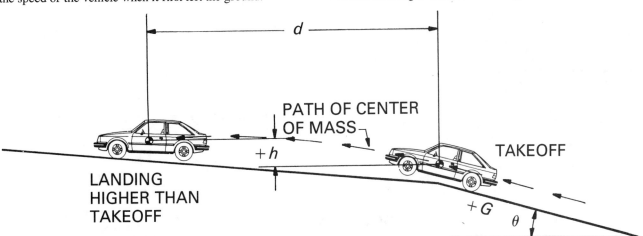

Exhibit 1. *It is possible for a vehicle to fall through the air and land at a higher point than takeoff. This requires a steep slope up at the takeoff point.*

A *fall* occurs when a vehicle is traveling forward and is no longer supported by the surface it is moving over. When the fall starts, the vehicle can be traveling on an upgrade, a downgrade, or a level surface. Or it could be sideslipping. If the vehicle is going up a grade at the beginning of the fall, the landing point could be higher than the takeoff point, although this is not common; a condition where it might take place is shown in Exhibit 1.

Flips occur when vehicles are moving sideways and the resistance at the tires is sufficient to cause the vehicle to rise and move through the air. This motion is typically caused by

overs are discussed in another topic.

Vaults are similar to flips, except they are "end-for-end" flips: the vehicle is moving forward instead of sideways (as with a flip). The term *vault* is often interchanged with the term *fall*. Clearly, these are not the same thing.

2. SPEED INDICATED BY A FALL

The most accurate estimates of speed in accident reconstruction are those made from reliable observations and measurements in a situation where the vehicle left the ground and fell through the air before it landed. This situation is indicated by lack of any marks on the road, as explained in Topic 817.

In a fall, the vehicle nearly always lands right side up, although it may roll or flip after it lands.

Principles

When a car is moving through the air and is no longer supported by the ground, it tends to keep going in a straight line in the direction it was headed when it left the ground. But the car's weight (force of gravity) makes it fall toward the ground with increasing vertical velocity until it lands. If the car at its takeoff point is traveling on a grade, the car will have a vertical component of velocity (either up or down). The only force acting in the vertical direction is gravity, which will cause the car to be accelerated downward at a rate of 32.2 ft/sec/sec (9.81 m/sec/sec). An equation to calculate the time it took a vehicle to fall the vertical distance, from where it left the ground to where it landed, can be easily developed according to natural laws relating to falling objects.

A car's horizontal component of velocity will remain essentially the same at landing as it was at takeoff. The only

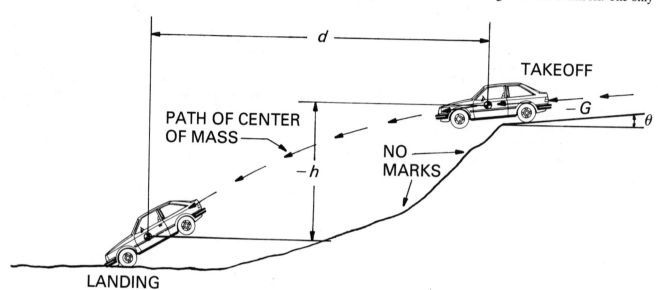

Exhibit 2. *When a vehicle leaves the ground, the measurements required for speed estimates are the horizontal distance that the center of mass moved from takeoff to landing, d, the vertical distance the center of mass fell, h, and the slope, up or down of the takeoff, G. The takeoff slope must be very carefully measured.*

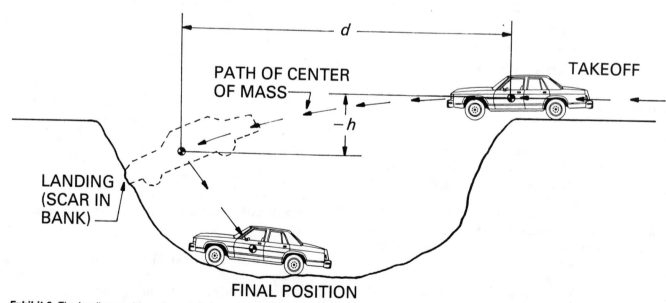

Exhibit 3. *The landing position after a fall may not be the point where the vehicle finally comes to rest. Then the landing position has to be located from marks on the ground and dimensions of the vehicle. Surveying instruments may be required to measure the distances in a fall and the slope of takeoff.*

force acting on the car as it travels through the air is air resistance. This can be calculated, but the change in velocity typically seen for the distance traveled is insignificant. An equation to calculate the time it takes a car to travel a known horizontal distance can easily be developed.

If we can develop equations to determine the time it takes a car to travel both the vertical and horizontal distances in a fall, then we can also calculate the velocity of the car at the beginning of the fall. That procedure is followed in the derivation of the fall equation in Topic 890.

Data Needed

To make the necessary calculations, three items of information are needed:

1. The horizontal distance from the point where the vehicle left the ground to where it landed (see Exhibits 1 through 5);

2. The vertical distance the vehicle dropped, from where it left the ground to where it landed (see Exhibits 1 through 5);

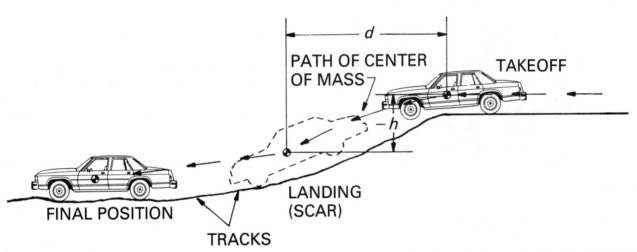

Exhibit 4. *Usually the vertical distance of a fall is well enough represented by the vertical distance between takeoff and landing surfaces, but if the vehicle lands on a slope, a correction must be made on the basis of marks made where the vehicle first struck the ground after a fall.*

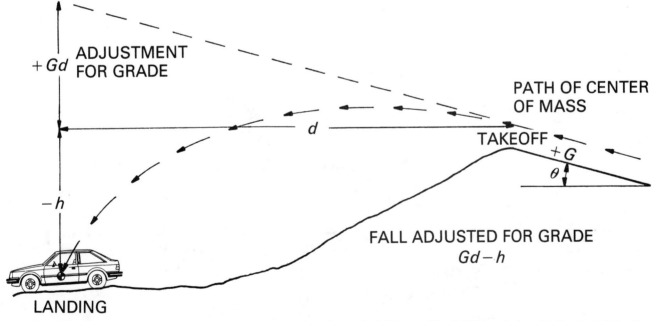

Exhibit 5. *When the takeoff slopes, an adjustment must be made to the vertical distance of the fall. This adjustment is the slope times the horizontal distance, that is, the amount the vehicle would have gone up or down had it continued on in a straight line from the takeoff slope. The adjustment is added to the vertical fall for a slope up and subtracted for a slope down.*

3. The grade, up or down, of the path the car was traveling before it left the ground.

For a detailed look at how the horizontal distance, *d*, and the vertical distance, *h*, is measured, be sure to study carefully the diagrams in Exhibits 1 through 5.

Usually, a vehicle does not come to a rest where it strikes the ground. It rolls or slides on the surface until it stops. It is very important to make measurements from the point where the vehicle left the ground to its position when it first landed. These may have to be figured out from scars in banks or slopes, as in Exhibits 2 and 3. Improperly made, these measurements can introduce serious error into calculations.

The takeoff grade (slope) must be measured along the path the vehicle actually traveled before it left the ground. This path is often shown by tiremarks of one kind or another. The takeoff grade is neither the grade along the roadway where the vehicle left the road, nor is it the slope of the shoulder away from the road (see Exhibit 6). You usually need special measurements to determine the takeoff grade. It can rarely be obtained from conventional engineering drawings. Methods to measure the grade are explained in Topic 834.

Equations

The 1975 edition of *The Traffic Accident Investigation Man-*

ual[2] only gave one equation for calculating a vehicle's speed at the beginning of a fall, omitting trigonometric functions (sine and cosine). Because many students find these helpful, this topic provides equations with and without trigonometric functions. For the derivation of these equations, consult Topic 890.

The equation to calculate the velocity of a vehicle at the point of takeoff is

$$v = d \sqrt{\frac{g}{2 \cos \Theta (d \sin \Theta - h \cos \Theta)}} \qquad (1)$$

where

v = velocity of the vehicle at takeoff in either ft/sec or m/sec.

d = distance traveled horizontally by the vehicle's center of mass from takeoff to landing, measured in either ft or m.

g = acceleration of gravity – either 32.2 ft/sec/sec or 9.81 m/sec/sec.

h = distance traveled vertically by the vehicle's center of mass from takeoff to landing, measured in either ft or m. The

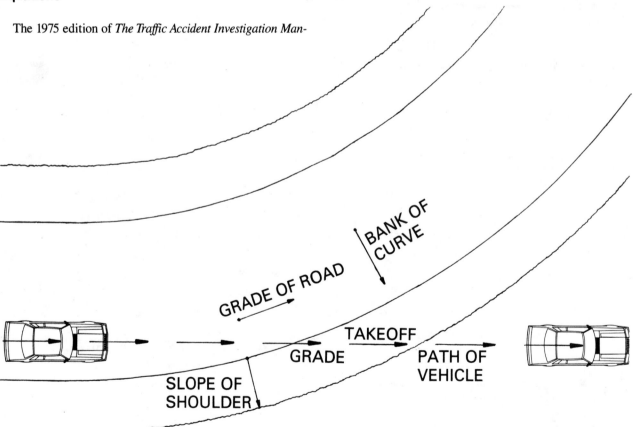

Exhibit 6. *The slope of the take-off for a fall is important. Usually this is neither the longitudinal slope of the roadway nor the transverse slope of the shoulder. It is the slope of the exact path that the vehicle followed. A slope down is negative, – and a slope up is positive, +.*

Exhibit 7
SPEED (MILES PER HOUR) REQUIRED TO FALL

Level distance in feet	Vertical distance of fall in feet																			
	1	2	3	4	5	6	7	8	9	10	12	14	16	18	20	25	30	35	40	50
10	27	19	16	14	12	11	10	10	9	9	8	7	7	6	6	5	5	5	4	4
12	33	23	19	16	15	13	12	12	11	10	9	9	8	8	7	7	6	6	5	5
14	38	27	22	19	17	16	14	14	13	12	11	10	10	9	9	8	7	6	6	5
16	44	31	25	22	20	18	17	15	15	14	13	12	11	10	10	9	8	7	7	6
18	49	35	28	25	22	20	19	17	16	16	14	13	12	12	11	10	9	8	8	7
20	55	39	32	27	24	22	21	19	18	17	16	15	14	13	12	11	10	9	9	8
22	60	43	35	30	27	25	23	21	20	19	17	16	15	14	13	12	11	10	10	9
24	66	46	38	33	29	27	25	23	22	21	19	18	16	15	15	13	12	11	11	9
26	71	50	41	36	32	29	27	25	24	22	21	19	18	17	16	14	13	12	11	10
28	77	54	44	38	34	31	29	27	26	24	22	20	19	18	17	15	14	13	12	11
30	82	58	47	41	37	34	31	29	27	26	24	22	21	19	18	16	15	14	13	12
32	88	62	51	44	39	36	33	31	29	28	25	23	22	21	20	18	16	15	14	12
34	93	66	54	47	42	38	35	33	31	29	27	25	23	22	21	19	17	16	15	13
36	98	70	57	49	44	40	37	35	33	31	28	26	25	23	22	20	18	17	16	14
38	104	74	60	52	46	42	39	37	35	33	30	28	26	25	23	21	19	18	16	15
40	109	77	63	55	49	45	41	39	36	35	32	29	27	26	24	22	20	18	17	15
42	115	81	66	57	51	47	43	41	38	36	33	31	29	27	26	23	21	19	18	16
44	120	85	69	60	54	49	45	43	40	38	35	32	30	28	27	24	22	20	19	17
46	126	89	73	63	56	51	48	44	42	40	36	34	31	30	28	25	23	21	20	18
48	131	93	76	66	59	54	50	46	44	42	38	35	33	31	29	26	24	22	21	19
50	137	97	79	68	61	56	52	48	46	43	39	37	34	32	31	27	25	23	22	19
52	142	101	82	71	64	58	54	50	47	45	41	38	36	34	32	28	26	24	22	20
54	148	104	85	74	66	60	56	52	49	47	43	39	37	35	33	30	27	25	23	21
56	153	108	88	77	69	63	58	54	51	48	44	41	38	36	34	31	28	26	24	22
58	159	112	92	79	71	65	60	56	53	50	46	42	40	37	35	32	29	27	25	22
60	164	116	95	82	73	67	62	58	55	52	47	44	41	39	37	33	30	28	26	23
62	170	120	98	85	76	69	64	60	57	54	49	45	42	40	38	34	31	29	27	24
64	175	124	101	88	78	71	66	62	58	55	51	47	44	41	39	35	32	30	28	25
66	181	128	104	90	81	74	68	64	60	57	52	48	45	43	40	36	33	31	29	26
68	186	132	107	93	83	76	70	66	62	59	54	50	47	44	42	37	34	31	29	26
70	192	135	111	96	86	78	72	68	64	61	55	51	48	45	43	38	35	32	30	27
72	197	139	114	98	88	80	74	70	66	62	57	53	49	46	44	39	36	33	31	28
74	202	143	117	101	91	83	77	72	67	64	58	54	51	48	45	40	37	34	32	29
76	208	147	120	104	93	85	79	74	69	66	60	56	52	49	46	42	38	35	33	29
78	213	151	123	107	95	87	81	75	71	67	62	57	53	50	48	43	39	36	34	30
80	219	155	126	109	98	89	83	77	73	69	63	58	55	52	49	44	40	37	35	31
82	224	159	130	112	100	92	85	79	75	71	65	60	56	53	50	45	41	38	35	32
84	230	162	133	115	103	94	87	81	77	73	66	61	57	54	51	46	42	39	36	32
86	235	166	136	118	105	96	89	83	78	74	68	63	59	55	53	47	43	40	37	33
88	241	170	139	120	108	98	91	85	80	76	69	64	60	57	54	48	44	41	38	34
90	246	174	142	123	110	101	93	87	82	78	71	66	62	58	55	49	45	42	39	35
92	252	178	145	126	113	103	95	89	84	80	73	67	63	59	56	50	46	43	40	36
94	257	182	148	129	115	105	97	91	86	81	74	69	64	61	58	51	47	43	41	36
96	263	186	152	131	117	107	99	93	88	83	76	70	66	62	59	53	48	44	42	37
98	268	190	155	134	120	109	101	95	89	85	77	72	67	63	60	54	49	45	42	38
100	274	193	158	137	122	112	103	97	91	87	79	73	68	64	61	55	50	46	43	39
105	287	203	166	144	128	117	109	102	96	91	83	77	72	68	64	57	52	49	45	41
110	301	213	174	150	135	123	114	106	100	95	87	80	75	71	67	60	55	51	48	43
115	315	222	182	157	141	128	119	111	105	99	91	84	79	74	70	63	57	53	50	44
120	328	232	190	164	147	134	124	116	109	104	95	88	82	77	73	66	60	55	52	46
130	356	251	205	178	159	145	134	126	119	112	103	95	89	84	80	71	65	60	56	50
140	383	271	221	192	171	156	145	135	128	121	111	102	96	90	86	77	70	65	61	54
150	410	290	237	205	184	168	155	145	137	130	118	110	103	97	92	82	75	69	65	58
160	438	310	253	219	196	179	165	155	146	138	126	117	109	103	98	88	80	74	69	62
170	465	329	269	233	208	190	176	164	155	147	134	124	116	110	104	93	85	79	74	66

Exhibit 8

SPEED (KILOMETERS PER HOUR) REQUIRED TO FALL

Level distance in meters	Vertical distance of fall in meters																			
	0.5	1.0	1.5	2.0	2.5	3.0	3.5	4.0	4.5	5.0	6.0	7.0	8.0	9.0	10.0	11.0	12.0	14.0	16.0	18.0
2	23	16	13	11	10	9	9	8	8	7	7	6	6	5	5	5	5	4	4	4
3	34	24	20	17	15	14	13	12	11	11	10	9	8	8	8	7	7	6	6	6
4	45	32	26	23	20	18	17	16	15	14	13	12	11	11	10	10	9	9	8	8
5	56	40	33	28	25	23	21	20	19	18	16	15	14	13	13	12	12	11	10	9
6	68	48	39	34	30	28	26	24	23	21	20	18	17	16	15	14	14	13	12	11
7	79	56	46	39	35	32	30	28	26	25	23	21	20	19	18	17	16	15	14	13
8	90	64	52	45	40	37	34	32	30	29	26	24	23	21	20	19	18	17	16	15
9	101	72	59	51	45	41	38	36	34	32	29	27	25	24	23	22	21	19	18	17
10	113	80	65	56	50	46	43	40	38	36	33	30	28	27	25	24	23	21	20	19
11	124	88	72	62	55	51	47	44	41	39	36	33	31	29	28	26	25	23	22	21
12	135	96	78	68	61	55	51	48	45	43	39	36	34	32	30	29	28	26	24	23
13	147	104	85	73	66	60	55	52	49	46	42	39	37	35	33	31	30	28	26	24
14	158	112	91	79	71	64	60	56	53	50	46	42	39	37	35	34	32	30	28	26
15	169	120	98	85	76	69	64	60	56	53	49	45	42	40	38	36	35	32	30	28
16	180	128	104	90	81	74	68	64	60	57	52	48	45	43	40	38	37	34	32	30
17	192	136	111	96	86	78	72	68	64	61	55	51	48	45	43	41	39	36	34	32
18	203	144	117	101	91	83	77	72	68	64	59	54	51	48	45	43	41	38	36	34
19	214	151	124	107	96	87	81	76	71	68	62	57	54	50	48	46	44	40	38	36
20	225	159	130	113	101	92	85	80	75	71	65	60	56	53	50	48	46	43	40	38
21	237	167	137	118	106	97	89	84	79	75	68	63	59	56	53	50	48	45	42	39
22	248	175	143	124	111	101	94	88	83	78	72	66	62	58	55	53	51	47	44	41
23	259	183	150	130	116	106	98	92	86	82	75	69	65	61	58	55	53	49	46	43
24	271	191	156	135	121	110	102	96	90	86	78	72	68	64	61	58	55	51	48	45
25	282	199	163	141	126	115	107	100	94	89	81	75	70	66	63	60	58	53	50	47
26	293	207	169	147	131	120	111	104	98	93	85	78	73	69	66	62	60	55	52	49
27	304	215	176	152	136	124	115	108	101	96	88	81	76	72	68	65	62	58	54	51
28	316	223	182	158	141	129	119	112	105	100	91	84	79	74	71	67	64	60	56	53
29	327	231	189	163	146	133	124	116	109	103	94	87	82	77	73	70	67	62	58	54
30	338	239	195	169	151	138	128	120	113	107	98	90	85	80	76	72	69	64	60	56
31	350	247	202	175	156	143	132	124	117	111	101	93	87	82	78	75	71	66	62	58
32	361	255	208	180	161	147	136	128	120	114	104	96	90	85	81	77	74	68	64	60
33	372	263	215	186	166	152	141	132	124	118	107	99	93	88	83	79	76	70	66	62
34	383	271	221	192	171	156	145	136	128	121	111	102	96	90	86	82	78	72	68	64
35	395	279	228	197	176	161	149	140	132	125	114	105	99	93	88	84	81	75	70	66
36	406	287	234	203	182	166	153	144	135	128	117	108	101	96	91	87	83	77	72	68
37	417	295	241	209	184	170	158	147	139	132	120	111	104	98	93	89	85	78	74	70
38	428	303	247	214	192	175	162	151	143	135	124	115	107	101	96	91	87	81	76	71
39	440	311	254	220	197	180	166	155	147	139	127	118	110	104	98	94	90	83	78	73
40	451	319	260	225	202	184	170	159	150	143	130	121	113	106	101	96	92	85	80	75
41	462	327	267	231	207	189	175	163	154	146	133	124	116	109	103	99	94	87	82	77
42	474	335	273	237	212	193	179	167	158	150	137	127	118	112	106	101	97	89	84	79
43	485	343	280	242	217	198	183	171	162	153	140	130	121	114	108	103	99	93	86	81
44	496	351	286	248	222	203	188	175	165	147	143	133	124	117	111	106	101	94	88	83
45	507	359	293	254	227	207	192	179	169	160	146	136	127	120	113	108	104	96	90	85
46	519	367	299	259	232	212	196	183	173	164	150	139	130	122	116	111	106	98	92	86
47	530	375	306	265	237	216	200	187	177	168	153	142	132	125	118	113	108	100	94	88
48	541	383	312	271	242	221	205	191	180	171	156	145	135	128	121	115	110	102	96	90
49	552	391	319	276	247	226	209	195	184	175	159	148	138	130	124	118	113	104	98	92
50	564	399	325	282	252	230	213	199	188	178	163	151	141	133	126	120	115	107	100	94
51	575	407	332	288	257	235	217	203	192	182	166	154	144	136	129	123	117	109	102	96
52	586	415	338	293	262	239	222	207	195	185	169	157	147	138	131	125	120	111	104	98
53	598	423	345	299	267	244	226	211	199	189	172	160	149	141	134	127	122	113	106	100
54	609	431	352	304	272	249	230	215	203	193	176	163	152	144	136	130	124	115	108	101
55	620	438	358	310	277	253	234	219	207	196	179	166	155	146	139	132	127	117	110	103
56	631	446	365	316	282	258	239	223	210	200	182	169	158	149	141	135	129	119	112	105

value of h is positive if the landing point is above the takeoff point, negative if the landing point is below the takeoff point.

G = the percent grade expressed as a decimal. If there is a downgrade, G is negative.

Θ = the angle of takeoff as measured relative to a horizontal plane.

Usually, the angle at takeoff is fairly small. Only rarely is the grade at takeoff greater than 12 percent. This translates to an angle Θ of 6.84 degrees. The values of sin, cos and tan (tangent) of 6.84 degrees are as follows:

$$\sin 6.84° = 0.119$$
$$\cos 6.84° = 0.993$$
$$\tan 6.84° = 0.120$$

At small angles, $\sin \Theta$ and $\tan \Theta$ are approximately the same. This is quite obvious for the above values of sin and tan of 6.84 degrees. The $\tan \Theta$ is equal to the percent of grade expressed as a decimal by definition. At small angles the $\cos \Theta$ is approximately equal to one. Thus, if G replaces $\sin \Theta$ and $\cos \Theta$ is assumed to be equal to one, equation (1) becomes

$$v = d\sqrt{\frac{g}{2(dG - h)}} \qquad (2)$$

The difference between the answers obtained by using equation (1) versus equation (2) is very small. Normally, other assumptions have to be made that are more significant than the effect of including the $\sin \Theta$ and $\cos \Theta$ functions. For example, the greatest slope typically seen on a road is 8 percent. This gives an angle Θ of 4.57 degrees. This clearly would give less difference than the values given earlier for a 12 percent grade.

The effect of grade, which can be significant, is clearly included in equations (1) and (2). Percent grade expressed as a decimal is the same as the $\tan \Theta$.

Calculations

With today's calculators and microcomputers, the calculations required to obtain a car's initial velocity when it falls can be done fairly easily[1]. Consider an example with the following givens:

$$d = 42 \text{ ft}$$
$$h = -9.6 \text{ ft}$$
$$G = 0.08$$
$$\Theta = 4.57 \text{ degrees}$$

Using equation 1:

$$v = d\sqrt{\frac{g}{2 \cos \Theta (d \sin \Theta - h \cos \Theta)}} \qquad (1)$$

$$v = 42\sqrt{\frac{32.2}{2[\cos 4.57°][42(\sin 4.57°) - (-9.6)(\cos 4.57°)]}}$$

$$= 46.9 \text{ ft/sec}$$

Using equation 2:

$$v = d\sqrt{\frac{g}{2(dG - h)}}$$

$$= 42\sqrt{\frac{32.2}{2[(42)(0.08) - (-9.6)]}}$$

$$= 46.8 \text{ ft/sec}$$

As can be seen from the above example, including the $\sin \Theta$ and $\cos \Theta$ functions [equation (1)] has little effect.

There are no examples in this topic using metric units, but working with them is not difficult. Just remember that h and d are measured in meters and that g is equal to 9.81 m/sec/sec. The values for Θ and G will be the same. Also, do not forget that h is positive if the vehicle lands at a higher elevation than when it left the ground. (Usually, h will be negative because the vehicle will, in most cases, land at a lower elevation).

Those who have difficulty with the mathematics (arithmetic) involved in equation (1) or (2) should consider using a computer program such as A-I-CALC[1] or the table in Exhibit 7 or (for metric units) Exhibit 8. The velocity values in Exhibit 7 are expressed in units of mi/h, *not* ft/sec, and are for *level takeoff*. The speeds corresponding to various horizontal and vertical distances can be obtained from the table in Exhibit 7. The velocity (mi/hr) is given where the column for vertical distance intersects the line for horizontal distance. For example, suppose a car traveled horizontally in the air 60 ft while dropping 10 ft. In the column headed 10 ft, find the line for 60 ft. There the speed of the vehicle is shown as 52 mi/hr.

When the takeoff is not level, adjust the measured vertical falling distance from the takeoff point to the landing point. The calculation then involves the following three steps, using Exhibit 7 (or Exhibit 8 for metric units):

1. Multiply the grade of the takeoff by the horizontal distance the vehicle traveled forward. Remember that the grade is + (positive) if the vehicle is moving upgrade and − (negative) if it is moving downhill.

For example, with an upward grade of +0.10 (up 10 percent) and a horizontal distance of 60 ft, then +0.10 × 60 = 6 ft is the adjusting amount.

2. Add the adjusting amount to the vertical falling distance. Suppose that the vertical fall in the example was 10 ft. Then the adjusted falling distance is 10 + 6 = 16 ft.

3. Use the table, Exhibit 7, to find the corresponding speed. In this example, a horizontal distance of 60 ft and an adjusted vertical fall of 16 ft has a speed of 41 mi/hr – 11 mi/hr less than if the takeoff had been level.

But suppose the slope had been downward instead of upward – –.10 instead of +0.10. The calculation would be as follows:

1. Slope multiplied by horizontal distance is –.10 × 60 = –6 ft.

2. Adding the adjusting amount, which is negative and must therefore be subtracted, gives 10 – 6 = 4 ft for the adjusted falling distance.

3. The table, Exhibit 7, gives a speed of 82 mi/hr, which is 30 mi/hr more than it would have been with a level takeoff.

These examples show how important correction for grade is in estimating speed with data from a falling vehicle. Correction for grade amounts to considering that the vertical fall began where the vehicle would have been had it continued straight ahead on the same grade until it was directly above the landing spot before it started to fall, as illustrated in Exhibit 5.

If the adjusting figure for down grade (horizontal distance multiplied by the slope) is greater than that for vertical fall, there is some mistake in measurements or calculations. With an up grade, it is possible for the landing to be at the same level as the takeoff, or even higher (Exhibit 1).

Significance of Estimate

You can say that the speed calculated is how fast a vehicle would have had to be going to take off on the slope where it left the ground and traveled the distance horizontally while dropping the vertical distance to its landing spot.

This is neither a maximum nor a minimum speed. That is, if the measurements are accurate, you could *not* say that the vehicle would have had to be going faster or slower than the speed calculated. Hence, the calculated speed is a very good estimate.

Special Problems

There may be difficulties in determining the vehicle's position when it first landed, especially if the landing place is a steep slope, a water surface, or is covered with rocks or trees. Finding the landing position may involve considering three circumstances:

1. Dimensions of the vehicle, to determine the location of its center of mass;
2. Scars on the ground showing where the vehicle first landed;
3. Damage to the vehicle showing which part of it struck the ground first.

Damaged parts of the vehicle must then be matched to the scars to determine the position of the center of mass when the vehicle landed. Measuring distances and grades may require the help of a surveyor with the appropriate instruments.

Recall which dimensions you are trying to determine when using equation (1) or (2). You need to know how far, in terms of vertical and horizontal distances (h and d), the center of mass traveled as the vehicle fell. Remember, you are concerned with the distance traveled by the center of mass, *not* with the distance traveled by the front or rear wheels. If, for example, you have a fall with the vehicle traveling forward, the front wheels will be unsupported before the rear wheels leave the supporting surface. This will induce a pitch rotation about the vehicle's center of mass. At fairly high speeds, a vehicle takes very little time to travel the length of its wheelbase. Thus, if the vehicle does not have a long fall, little pitch will take place before the vehicle touches the ground. Only in rare cases does the rotation of the vehicle need to be considered; it is difficult enough just to determine where some part of the vehicle first made contact. If the pitch is not considered, the net effect is to overestimate the vertical drop, h, which results in a lower estimate of speed at takeoff.

Be aware of what you are assuming when you use the fall equations. If the fall takes place as shown in Exhibit 1, do the tires touch the ground earlier than they would if the car were considered to be a rigid body? When the front wheels are no longer supported by the ground, the wheels will fall. However, because the wheels are spring-loaded, they initially will fall at a rate faster than just the acceleration of gravity. Consider what happens in a very short fall. The wheels will touch down faster than in a simple free-fall situation. If the driver applied brakes soon enough to leave skids, and the skids are used to indicate first contact with the ground, the horizontal distance, d, would be less than if normal, free-fall conditions had prevailed. This lower value of d would then yield a slightly lower speed estimate than was actually the case. For a fall with fairly long horizontal and vertical distances, the spring effect is of no importance.

It is impossible to consider all the possible situations that might occur. Simply be aware of the assumptions you are making. People often try to use a fall equation to calculate the speed of a motorcycle operator who becomes separated from his motorcycle. Generally, neither the angle of takeoff nor the first contact position with the ground is clearly known. Thus, many assumptions are made that simply cannot be supported. For motorcycle cases, other methods for estimating speed are usually more appropriate.

The speed of the vehicle increases during a fall; if the landing is below the takeoff point, the landing speed is greater than the takeoff speed. While the vehicle is in the air, its *horizontal* velocity remains constant or nearly so; but while in the air, the vehicle starts to fall, gaining speed because of the force of gravity. For example, if a vehicle runs off a high bridge just fast enough to get it over the edge, it will pick up speed as it falls, moving many times faster by the time it finally lands. In this case, damage to the vehicle would represent the speed gained in the fall rather than the speed of the vehicle at takeoff. The total velocity of the vehicle when it lands is the vector sum of its horizontal and vertical components.

3. SPEED INDICATED BY A FLIP

Motor vehicles may move through the air not only by falling and landing right side up, but also by leaving the ground in a *flip*, in which the vehicle usually lands on its top. Falls and flips are quite different. Mistaking one for the other can result in serious errors for speed estimates.

Principles

If a vehicle moving on a road surface strikes an object that stops forward movement of part of the vehicle at or near the ground, the rest of the vehicle tends to keep going. It can only do this by pivoting on the part that is stopped, usually a wheel, as illustrated in Exhibit 9. This pivoting requires that the vehicle's center of mass rise or lift. The vehicle may be going so fast that, while its center of mass continues forward in this pivoting, it is also accelerated upward at a rate higher than that due to gravity; if so, then this upward velocity can lift the entire vehicle off the ground and into the air. The pivoting also causes rapid rotation or roll of the vehicle. Consequently, when the vehicle comes to earth again, it will have turned more or less bottom up. When it lands, it usually leaves a scar in the road or roadside, which marks the landing spot. The vehicle rarely stops where it first lands, but flips or rolls further until coming to a rest, sometimes on its side. If you know from marks on the road how far the vehicle went through the air on its first movement to the ground, the minimum speed required to accomplish that passage can be estimated.

Data Needed

To make a speed estimate from a flip, the following data are needed:

1. The horizontal distance the vehicle moved in the air from *first* takeoff to landing. (This is determined from marks on the road where the vehicle left the road and on the roadside where it landed. The distance required is that traveled by the vehicle's center of mass.)

2. Vertical difference in elevation of the vehicle's center of mass between takeoff and landing (if any).

3. The angle of takeoff. (Rarely can this be determined accurately). An equation can be used to calculate the angle at which the minimum speed can be determined. An angle of approximately 45 degrees results, which will give the greatest distance for the lowest speed.

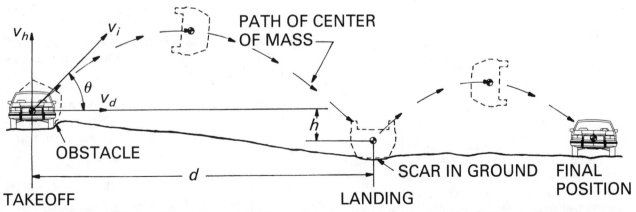

Exhibit 9. *A flip occurs when a vehicle sliding nearly sideways strikes an obstacle, such as a curb, or furrows in which stops further movement at the ground level. The vehicle usually lands upside down and may roll or flip again after that. Speed estimate is based on the horizontal distance the center of mass moves through the air to the first landing and the difference in elevation between landing and takeoff, if any. Rarely can the angle of takeoff be determined. Subsequent roll, flip, slide, or collision are of no consequence in speed estimates.*

4. Assurance that the case being analyzed is indeed a flip and not a fall or rollover. (In a flip, the obstacle that stopped the forward motion is clear, such as a curb or a pile-up of dirt at the end of a furrow. See Exhibit 10.)

Exhibit 10. *In photograph A a car was sideslipping and was "tripped" by striking the guardrail. In B the car was sliding nearly sideways and furrowed in. Note the accumulation of material at the end of the furrow which "tripped" the vehicle.*

Calculations

First, an estimate has to be made of how far horizontally the *center of mass* traveled from takeoff to landing. This may require some knowledge of the vehicle's dimensions, and perhaps a drawing of the vehicle in takeoff and landing positions. In general, however, the distance can be obtained by taking the shortest distance between any sign of where the vehicle took off (a curb or dig-in at the end of a furrow) and any sign of where it first landed, and adding the width of the vehicle (see Exhibit 9). In many investigations, data collected are not adequate to indicate this distance, and so assumptions about it may have to be made, thereby diminishing the accuracy of the estimate.

The general equation for a flip is as follows:

$$v = d\sqrt{\frac{g}{2\cos\Theta(d\sin\Theta - h\cos\Theta)}} \qquad (3)$$

where

v = velocity of the vehicle at takeoff in either ft/sec or m/sec.

d = distance traveled horizontally by the vehicle's center of mass from takeoff to landing, measured in either ft or m.

g = acceleration of gravity – either 32.2 ft/sec/sec or 9.81 m/sec/sec.

h = distance traveled vertically by the vehicle's center of mass from takeoff to landing, measured in either ft or m. The value of h is positive if the landing point is above the takeoff point and is negative if the landing point is below the takeoff point.

Θ = the angle of takeoff as measured, relative to a horizontal plane.

It is, of course, a rare event when you will be able to tell the angle of takeoff of a vehicle that does a flip. For example, if you know its takeoff point and you know that it just touched a fence as it continued through the air, it may be possible to estimate an angle of takeoff. Do not expect to look at the dirt pile-up at the end of a furrow and be able to tell the angle of takeoff. This might indicate the takeoff angle of the part that made the furrow, but certainly not the center of mass. The minimum speed estimate using equation (3) is obtained when the angle of takeoff, Θ, is assumed to be approximately 45 degrees. The equation for the angle, Θ, that allows the minimum speed estimate to be calculated is

$$\Theta = \tfrac{1}{2}\cos^{-1}[-h/\sqrt{(d^2+h^2)}] \qquad (4)$$

For those less familiar with trigonometry, the term $\cos^{-1}$ (arc cos) simply means the angle that has the cos value for the quantity $[-h/\sqrt{(d^2+h^2)}]$.

An example will help to explain the equation. Assume that a vehicle flipped moving horizontally 50 ft ($d = 50$ ft) and dropping vertically 10 ft ($h = -10$). Substituting into equation (4):

$$\Theta = \tfrac{1}{2}\cos^{-1}[-h/\sqrt{(d^2+h^2)}]. \qquad (4)$$

$$\Theta = \tfrac{1}{2}\cos^{-1}[-(-10)/\sqrt{50^2+(-10)^2}]$$

$$\Theta = \tfrac{1}{2}\cos^{-1}[.196]$$

$\Theta = \frac{1}{2}(78.7°)$

$\Theta = 39.3°$

For nearly all cases encountered with a fall, a value of Θ equal to 45 degrees will give a reasonable estimate of speed at takeoff. If a 45 degree takeoff is used and substituted into equation (3), the following simplified equation results:

$$v = d\sqrt{\frac{g}{d-h}} \qquad (5)$$

Note that for either equation (3) or (5), the difference in elevation, h, is positive, $+$, if the landing is higher and is negative, $-$, if the landing is lower. So if a vehicle goes downhill in a flip, the difference of elevation is minus and the denominator under the square root becomes

$$d-(-h) = d+h$$

Remember, you cannot take the square root of a negative number.

Consider the following simple problem. A car flips and travels 55 ft horizontally while dropping 6 ft vertically (landing lower than takeoff). It is impossible to make any reasonable estimate of the angle of takeoff. Thus, you must either use the value that will give the minimum speed estimate [equations (3) and (4) together] or calculate the speed using the 45 degree takeoff [equation (5)]. This problem will be worked by using both methods.

First, the angle that will give the minimum speed is calculated by using equation (4):

$$\Theta = \frac{1}{2}\cos^{-1}[-h/\sqrt{(d^2+h^2)}] \qquad (4)$$

$$\Theta = \frac{1}{2}\cos^{-1}[-(-6)/\sqrt{55^2+(-6)^2}]$$

$$\Theta = 41.9°$$

$$v = d\sqrt{\frac{g}{2\cos\Theta(d\sin\Theta - h\cos\Theta)}} \qquad (3)$$

$$v = 55\sqrt{\frac{32.2}{2\cos 41.9°[55\sin 41.9° - (-6)\cos 41.9°]}}$$

$$v = 39.9 \text{ ft/sec} = 27.1 \text{ mi/hr}$$

Using equation (5), the minimum speed at takeoff can be determined:

$$v = d\sqrt{\frac{g}{d-h}} \qquad (5)$$

$$v = 55\sqrt{\frac{32.2}{55-(-6)}}$$

$$v = 40 \text{ ft/sec} = 27.2 \text{ mi/hr}$$

An example using metric units is not included here. However, there is no significant difference in the manipulation of the numbers to arrive at the final answer. Equations (3), (4) and (5) apply. Just use the values for horizontal distance, d, and vertical distance, h, in meters instead of feet. The value for acceleration of gravity, g, is 9.81 m/sec/sec instead of 32.2 ft/sec/sec. The final answer, v, will have the units of m/sec.

For those unaccustomed to using equations, tables can be used to determine the speed at takeoff for a flip. Exhibit 11 is one such table. After you have determined the vertical and horizontal distances for the flip, it is relatively easy to use Exhibit 11. For the difference in elevation between takeoff and landing, speed is shown in the column; the difference in horizontal distance is shown in the row. Suppose, for instance, a vehicle flipped on the shoulder of the road and landed bottom up in a ditch with the center of mass 55 ft away from and 6 ft below its takeoff point. Where the column for 6 ft (landing lower than takeoff) crosses the line for 55 ft, the flip speed is given as 27 mi/hr. Exhibit 12 gives metric values for flips. Exhibits 11 and 12 assume a 45 degree take-off.

What Can Be Said

Speed of the vehicle was actually greater than that estimated, possibly much greater, so the calculated speed is minimum.

What the vehicle does after landing, whether it rolls or slides, has no effect on the estimated speed. Nor should such movement be considered as speed to be combined with that obtained from the equation for flips.

Special Problems

Speeds from flips calculated in this manner are subject to the usual, generally minor errors mainly reflecting inaccuracies of original measurements. Such errors can be evaluated by calculating maximum and minimum values of speed, using maximum and minimum values for each measurement. Following this approach when you are not absolutely sure of the exact values is an effective method to fully evaluate your conclusions.

However, the speed estimate is inherently minimal for two reasons:

1. The calculation assumes that the angle of takeoff is that at which the vehicle would go farthest for its speed. (This angle can be calculated, but it is gener-

Exhibit 11

SPEED (MILES PER HOUR) REQUIRED TO FLIP OR VAULT

Level distance in feet	Landing Higher than Takeoff (+h)								None	Landing Lower than Takeoff (−h)										
	10	8	6	4	3	2	1	0.5	h = 0	0.5	1.0	1.5	2	3	4	6	8	10	12	15
8	—	—	22	15	14	13	12	11	11	11	10	10	10	9	9	8	8	7	7	6
9	—	35	20	16	14	13	12	12	12	11	11	11	10	10	10	9	8	8	8	7
10	—	27	19	16	15	14	13	13	12	12	12	11	11	11	10	10	9	9	8	8
11	43	25	19	16	15	14	13	13	13	13	12	12	12	11	11	10	10	9	9	8
12	33	23	19	16	15	15	14	14	13	13	13	13	12	12	12	11	10	10	9	9
14	27	22	19	17	16	16	15	15	14	14	14	14	14	13	13	12	12	11	11	10
16	25	22	20	18	17	17	16	16	15	15	15	15	15	14	14	13	13	12	12	11
18	25	22	20	19	18	17	17	17	16	16	16	16	16	15	15	14	14	13	13	12
20	24	22	21	19	19	18	18	18	17	17	17	17	16	16	16	15	15	14	14	13
22	25	23	21	20	20	19	19	18	18	18	18	18	17	17	17	16	16	15	15	14
24	25	23	22	21	20	20	19	19	19	19	19	18	18	18	18	17	16	16	15	15
26	25	24	22	21	21	21	20	20	20	20	19	19	19	19	18	18	17	17	16	16
28	26	24	23	22	22	21	21	21	20	20	20	20	20	19	19	19	18	18	17	17
30	26	25	24	23	22	22	22	21	21	21	21	21	21	20	20	19	19	18	18	17
32	26	25	24	23	23	23	22	22	22	22	22	21	21	21	21	20	20	19	19	18
34	27	26	25	24	24	23	23	23	23	22	22	22	22	22	21	21	20	20	19	19
36	27	26	25	25	24	24	24	23	23	23	23	23	23	22	22	21	21	21	20	20
38	28	27	26	25	25	25	24	24	24	24	24	23	23	23	23	22	22	21	21	20
40	28	27	27	26	25	25	25	25	24	24	24	24	24	24	23	23	22	22	21	21
45	29	29	28	27	27	27	26	26	26	26	26	26	25	25	25	24	24	23	23	22
50	31	30	29	29	28	28	28	27	27	27	27	27	27	27	26	26	25	25	25	24
55	32	31	30	30	30	29	29	29	29	29	28	28	28	28	28	27	27	26	26	25
60	33	32	32	31	31	30	30	30	30	30	30	30	29	29	29	29	28	28	27	27
65	34	33	33	32	32	32	31	31	31	31	31	31	31	30	30	30	29	29	29	28
70	35	34	34	34	33	33	33	32	32	32	32	32	32	32	31	31	31	30	30	29
75	36	35	35	34	34	34	34	34	34	33	33	33	33	33	33	32	32	31	31	31
80	37	36	36	36	35	35	35	35	35	34	34	34	34	34	34	33	33	33	32	32
85	38	37	37	37	36	36	36	36	36	36	35	35	35	35	35	34	34	34	33	33
90	39	38	38	38	37	37	37	37	37	37	37	36	36	36	36	36	35	35	34	34
100	41	40	40	39	39	39	39	39	39	39	38	38	38	38	38	38	37	37	37	36

ally reasonable to use a 45 degree takeoff.) If the vehicle takes off at a greater or lesser angle, it needs more speed to flip the distance.

2. Speed is lost in tearing up the ground or possibly damaging wheels (for example, when curbs are struck).

In general, the higher the vehicle's center of mass with respect to its track width, the more likely the vehicle will roll over. That is to say, a vehicle that is "top heavy" because of its design, its load or both, rolls over more easily than a vehicle that is low on the road. But the vehicle with a low center of mass and a wide track is likely to go higher if it flips. Most vehicles do not flip when sliding sideways on good paving. Some, especially motorcycles and trucks, may roll over. If a truck or car hits a steep curb while sliding sideways, or digs into dirt so as to stop its sideslip, it may flip. More refined calculations of flips can take into consideration the dimensions of the wheelbase and the height of the center of mass. Rarely will the required data inputs be sufficiently accurate

to justify these more complex equations.

There can be combinations of flips and vaults, with the vehicle turning over in the air in complicated ways. These are brought about by peculiarities in the road which stop one side or end of the vehicle more suddenly than the other side or end. Normally, you would treat these just as you would a simple fall. However, be very clear on how the vehicle moved in the air so that the correct *d* and *h* values are used.

4. SPEED INDICATED BY A VAULT

Fall and flip are not the only ways in which motor vehicles move through the air. A *vault* is essentially an "end-for-end" flip. If a vault is mistakenly interpreted as a fall, a serious error can result – one that happens more often than it should. Falls and vaults are very different. A fall occurs when the wheels are no longer supported and the vehicle leaves the ground. There are no extraordinary forces on the front of the vehicle or its tires. A vault occurs under different circumstances.

Exhibit 12
SPEED (KILOMETERS PER HOUR) REQUIRED TO FLIP OR VAULT

Level distance in meters	Difference in Elevation between Takeoff and Landing (Meters)																				
	Landing Higher than Takeoff (+h)								None	Landing Lower than Takeoff (−h)										
	4.0	3.5	3.0	2.5	2.0	1.5	1.0	0.5	0	0.5	1.0	1.5	2.0	2.5	3.0	3.5	4.0	4.5	5.0	6.0
3	—	—	—	48	34	28	24	21	20	18	17	16	15	14	14	13	13	12	12	11
4	—	64	45	37	32	29	26	24	23	21	20	19	18	18	17	16	16	15	15	14
5	56	46	40	36	33	30	28	27	25	24	23	22	21	21	20	19	19	18	18	17
6	48	43	39	36	34	32	30	29	28	26	26	25	24	23	22	22	21	21	20	19
7	46	42	39	37	35	34	32	31	30	29	28	27	26	26	25	24	24	23	23	22
8	45	43	40	38	37	35	34	33	32	31	30	29	29	28	27	27	26	26	25	24
9	45	43	41	40	38	37	36	35	34	33	32	31	31	30	29	29	28	28	27	26
10	46	44	43	41	40	39	38	37	36	35	34	33	33	32	31	31	30	30	29	28
11	47	45	44	43	41	40	39	38	37	37	36	35	34	34	33	33	32	32	31	30
12	48	46	45	44	43	42	41	40	39	38	38	37	36	36	35	34	34	33	33	32
13	49	48	46	45	44	43	42	41	41	40	39	38	38	37	37	36	36	35	35	34
14	50	49	48	47	46	45	44	43	42	41	41	40	39	39	38	38	37	37	36	35
15	51	50	49	48	47	46	45	44	44	43	42	42	41	40	40	39	39	38	38	37
16	52	51	50	49	48	47	47	46	45	44	44	43	43	42	41	41	40	40	39	38
17	53	52	51	50	49	49	48	47	46	46	45	45	44	43	43	42	42	41	41	40
18	54	53	52	52	51	50	49	48	47	47	46	45	45	44	44	44	43	43	42	41
19	55	54	54	53	52	51	50	50	49	49	48	47	47	46	46	45	45	44	44	43
20	56	56	55	54	53	52	52	51	50	50	49	49	48	48	47	47	46	46	45	44
21	57	57	56	55	54	54	53	52	52	51	50	50	49	49	48	48	47	47	46	46
22	58	58	57	56	55	55	54	53	53	52	52	51	51	50	50	49	49	48	48	47
23	59	59	58	57	57	56	55	55	54	53	53	52	52	51	51	50	50	49	49	48
24	61	60	59	58	58	57	56	56	55	55	54	54	53	53	52	52	51	51	50	49
25	62	61	60	59	59	58	58	57	56	56	55	55	54	54	53	53	52	52	51	51
26	62	62	61	60	60	59	59	58	57	57	56	56	55	55	54	54	54	53	53	52
27	63	63	62	62	61	60	60	59	59	58	58	57	57	56	56	55	55	54	54	53
28	64	64	63	63	62	61	61	60	60	59	59	58	58	57	57	56	56	55	55	54
29	65	65	64	64	63	62	62	61	61	60	60	59	59	58	58	57	57	56	56	55
30	66	66	65	64	64	63	63	62	62	61	61	60	60	59	59	58	58	58	57	56
31	67	67	66	65	65	64	64	63	63	62	62	61	61	60	60	60	59	59	58	57
32	68	68	67	66	66	65	65	64	64	63	63	62	62	61	61	61	60	60	59	59

Principles

For a vault to occur, the forward movement of part of the vehicle must stop. The line of force must be fairly low on the vehicle (below its center of mass) for the vehicle to vault. Then the front part of the vehicle momentarily stops relative to the ground while the rest of the vehicle continues forward. If the speed is great enough, the center of mass will lift and the vehicle will travel through the air. Exhibit 13 illustrates the vault of a car. The marks left by a vaulting car are shown in Exhibit 14.

For a vehicle to vault, the center of mass must have more acceleration on it than the acceleration of gravity. The center of mass essentially pivots about the front of the vehicle at the beginning of the vault. Because these requirements are not often met, vaults are rare. Usually if a car collides with a fixed object, a vault does not occur, because the car either runs over the object, hits it and rotates around it, or strikes it and simply comes to a stop. Obviously, if the front of a car came into contact with a curb while moving forward, it would simply tend to run over the curb, with some bouncing. Some investigators have tried to use the vault equation for a car running over a curb. They assume an arbitrary landing point and use it in their calculations. The results obtained do not relate at all to the assumptions made in the derivation of the vault equation. (See Topic 890 for this derivation).

As with falls and flips, a vehicle that vaults will most likely continue moving after it lands. It may slide or roll to its final position. The data needed are the vertical and horizontal distance the center of mass traveled from takeoff to landing. Thus, its final position is of little interest as far as speed estimates are concerned.

Data Needed

The data needed for a vault are the same as those for a fall. They are repeated for your reference:

1. The horizontal distance the vehicle moved in the air from *first* takeoff to landing. (This is determined

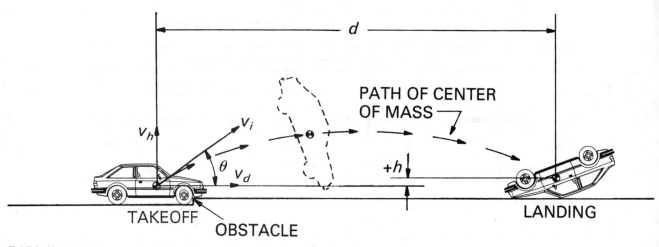

Exhibit 13. *A vault occurs when the front of a vehicle strikes an object in which further movement at the ground level stops. By knowing the horizontal and vertical distance that the vehicle's center of mass traveled a speed estimate can be measured. Similar to the flip situation, the angle of takeoff (Θ) can rarely be measured. Nevertheless, a minimum speed estimate can be made.*

from marks on the road where the vehicle left the road and on the roadside where it landed. The distance required is that traveled by the vehicle's center of mass.)

2. Vertical difference in elevation, if any, between takeoff and landing of the vehicle's center of mass.

3. The angle of takeoff. (Rarely can this be determined accurately. The angle that will give the minimum speed can be calculated. Normally, a 45 degree angle is assumed, which will give more than adequate results.)

Calculations

Just as in the case of a flip, an estimate must be made for the horizontal and vertical distances the vehicle's center of

Exhibit 14. *For the situation shown here, a car went off the road at a fairly high speed and struck the culvert/driveway resulting in a vault. The height of the obstacle was not high enough to stop the vehicle and was also not low enough for the vehicle to simply travel over it.*

mass traveled from takeoff to *first* landing. In general, the horizontal distance can be obtained by taking the shortest distance between any sign of where the vehicle took off and any sign of where it first landed, and adding the length of the vehicle. In many cases the collected data may not be as good as you would like. Make the necessary assumptions and be aware of the possible diminishing of your estimate's accuracy.

The three equations that can be used for a vault are identical to the equations for a flip:

$$v = d\sqrt{\frac{g}{2 \cos \Theta(d \sin \Theta - h \cos \Theta)}} \qquad (3)$$

$$\Theta = \frac{1}{2} \cos^{-1} \left[-h/\sqrt{(d^2 + h^2)} \right] \qquad (4)$$

$$v = d\sqrt{\frac{g}{d - h}} \qquad (5)$$

The variables, v, d, g, Θ, and h are the same variables used for a flip. Because the equations are identical for flips and vaults, the tables given in Exhibits 11 and 12 can also be used for vaults.

Special Problems

Errors in speed estimates from a vault are related mainly to the poor quality of the measurement data. If you have concern over this, do a sensitivity analysis. That is, use the minimum and maximum values that are practical and see how much the speed estimate changes. If little change results, then clearly you have a sound speed estimate.

Using the vault equation results in the minimum values for at least two reasons:

1. Using either equation (3) and (4) together or equation (5), the calculation assumes the angle of takeoff is such that the vehicle would go the farthest with its initial speed (if it takes off at a different angle, it needs more speed to travel the same distance).

2. Considerable speed would be lost in damaging the front of the vehicle before the vehicle actually began its vault (the vault equation gives the speed at the beginning of the vault and does not give the speed of the vehicle when it first contacted the fixed object that prompted the vault).

Other, more complex equations for vaults could be developed. However, it is unlikely that the data required from the accident scene will ever be accurate enough to justify using them.

What the vehicle does after it lands has no influence on the speed estimate using the vault equation. Any speed estimate made for the vehicle after it lands must not be combined or added to the speed estimate made from the vault.

5. SUMMARY

Good estimates of vehicle speeds can be made when vehicles travel through the air. As with any speed estimate technique, good measurement data are essential when estimates of speed from falls, flips or vaults are made. It is absolutely essential to recognize the difference between falls, flips and vaults. Often the wrong equation is used, resulting in wrong answers. Be aware of the assumptions you are making when you use these equations. Are they consistent with the assumptions made in their derivation? If not, then do not assume that it will be acceptable to use them for your case.

Rollovers (when a vehicle is not tripped by a curb or furrow), pedestrian accidents, motorcycle accidents, and large truck accidents are covered in other Accident Investigation topics in this series. For many of those accidents it is *not* appropriate to use the equations that have been discussed in this topic. You should consult those topics to determine whether you have a case where the equations for falls, flips or vaults apply.

6. SOURCES

Authors

J. Stannard Baker is a traffic engineer specializing in accident investigation. He was Director of Research and Development at the Northwestern University Traffic Institute from 1946 to 1971 and was a guest lecturer for The Traffic Institute.

Lynn B. Fricke is an engineer specializing in traffic accident reconstruction. He has been with The Northwestern University Traffic Institute since 1975. In 1981 he became the Director of the Institute's Accident Investigation Division.

References

Superscript numbers in the preceding pages refer to the following publications:

1. *AICALC Microcomputer Manual*, Northwestern University Traffic Institute, 1987.

2. Baker, J. Stannard, *Traffic Accident Investigation Manual*, Northwestern University Traffic Institute, 1975.

3. Collins, James, *Accident Reconstruction*, Charles C. Thomas-Publisher, Springfield, IL, 1979.

4. LeFevre, William, "Vehicle Motions in Free Fall," unpublished paper, William LeFevre Company, Beachwood, OH.

5. McHenry, Raymond R., "Speed Estimates in Vehicle Rollovers," Calspan Report No. ZQ-5639-V-1, January 1976.

Exhibits

The following are the sources of the exhibits used in this topic:

Baker, J. Stannard, San Diego, CA
Diagrams: 1-6, 9, 13
Tables: 7-8, 11-12

Cooper, Gary W., Traffic Institute, Evanston, IL
Photos: 10B, 14
Fricke, Lynn B., Traffic Institute, Evanston, IL
Photo: 10A

MOMENTUM APPLICATIONS IN RAFFIC ACCIDENT RECONSTRUCTION

Topic 868 of the *Traffic Accident Investigation Manual*

by
Lynn B. Fricke

NORTHWESTERN UNIVERSITY TRAFFIC INSTITUTE

MOMENTUM APPLICATIONS IN TRAFFIC ACCIDENT RECONSTRUCTION

This topic applies conservation of linear momentum to traffic accidents. The main reason for using momentum is to determine the velocities of vehicles when they first come into contact with each other. To do this it is necessary to understand how the vehicles moved from first contact to maximum engagement to separation and finally to their rest positions. If you do not know how to do this, consult Topics 817, 820 and 861. To understand the present topic, you should at least have an understanding of algebra; a grasp of trigonometry will make it much easier. You may also want to refer to Topic 856, *Mathematics and Physics Review for Traffic Accident Reconstruction*.

1. DEFINITION

Newton first expressed the notion of a body's *quantity of motion* by multiplying the body's mass by its velocity. This quantity of motion is called *momentum*. Momentum is a vector quantity. That is, it not only has a magnitude, but it also has a direction. The international standard symbol for momentum is P (see Topic 856). Thus, the momentum of an object (or vehicle) is expressed as:

$$P = m\vec{v} \qquad (1)$$

where P = momentum in lb-sec or N-sec,
   m = mass in slugs or kg, and
   v = velocity in ft/sec or m/sec.

The arrow (→) above v indicates that momentum is a *vector quantity*. Recall that mass is equal to the weight (w, in pounds or Newtons) divided by the acceleration of gravity (g, 32.2 ft/sec/sec or 9.81 m/sec/sec). Thus, equation (1) could be rewritten as:

$$P = (w/g)\vec{v} \qquad (2)$$

Because the acceleration of gravity is a constant, it can be seen in equation (2) that momentum is directly proportional to an object's weight and velocity. That is, if you double the

weight of an object and keep the velocity the same, the momentum is twice as much. Or if you double the velocity with the weight held constant, the momemtum is doubled. Therefore, if you had a 2,000 lb car traveling eastbound at 30 ft/sec, it would have the same momentum as a 4,000 lb car traveling eastbound at 15 ft/sec.

Units of Momentum and Impulse

The units of momentum (lb-sec or N-sec) may at first seem confusing. Using the right side of equation (2) and U.S.A. units, you can see that the units become, after canceling:

$$\frac{wv}{g} : \frac{(\text{lb})(\text{ft})}{\dfrac{(\text{ft})(\text{sec})}{(\text{sec})^2}} = \frac{(\text{lb})}{\dfrac{1}{(\text{sec})}} = \text{lb sec}$$

In a collision between two bodies, momentum is transferred between them. This transfer of momentum is called *impulse*. Impulse is the product of force times time, or in U.S.A. units, lb-sec. Thus, in a collision for a finite period of time, each body pushes on the other with a force. This force times the time is the *impulse*, which also works out to be the transfer of momentum from one body to another. Later in this topic it is explained how the direction of the force (principal direction of force, PDOF, or direction of thrust) is important in doing a proper momentum analysis.

Often in a momentum analysis the weights of the vehicles are used in place of the vehicles' mass. That is, the weight is not divided by the acceleration of gravity when the calculations are made. This does not introduce any error into the vehicles' initial speed estimate. Nevertheless, you should be aware that the correct definition of momentum is that given in equation (1).

2. CONSERVATION OF MOMENTUM

The law of conservation of momentum can be stated as follows: **In any group of objects that act upon each other,**

the total momentum before the action equals the total momentum after the action. Applied to traffic accident reconstruction, the action is the collision between two vehicles and the objects are the two vehicles. Using Newton's Second and Third Laws of Motion, an equation for conservation of momentum can be developed. In Topic 890 it is shown that conservation of momentum can be expressed as the following equation:

$$m_1\vec{v}_1 + m_2\vec{v}_2 = m_1\vec{v}_1{}' + m_2\vec{v}_2{}' \qquad (3)$$

The subscripts refer to vehicles one and two. As you learned from equation (1), the arrows above velocity indicate that each term is a vector quantity. The symbol ′ above the velocity is read "velocity prime" and refers to the after-collision velocity. Thus, the left side of the equation is the momentum before and the right side is the momentum after.

Working Equation

Because equation (3) has mass in each term and mass is equal to weight divided by the acceleration of gravity ($m = w/g$), w/g can replace the value for m in each term of equation (3). Because each term would then have g in it, the g's can be canceled to get equation (4). (If you have questions about this, see Topic 890).

$$\vec{v}_1 w_1 + \vec{v}_2 w_2 = \vec{v}_1{}' w_1 + \vec{v}_2{}' w_2 \qquad (4)$$

Equation (4) is the "working" equation you will use to make momentum calculations. Be sure to notice that the arrows over each term in equation (4) clearly indicate that this is a vector equation and not a simple algebraic equation. (If you have questions about this distinction, refer to Topic 856). Essentially, all that equation (4) says is that the momentum before the collision is equal to the momentum after.

Simple Example

Beginning students in accident reconstruction usually have a hard time visualizing how the momentum of two vehicles before a collision is the same as the momentum of the two vehicles after the collision. An example may help to clarify this problem.

Consider the two cars heading toward each other in Exhibit 1. Both cars have equal weight. They have the same velocity, but in *opposite* directions. Assume the cars are lined up headlight to headlight (that is, they have collinear directions of travel but are going in opposite directions). Most people would agree that after the vehicles collide, they will immediately slow to a stop because of the collision. This indeed is what they would do, as shown in Exhibit 1A. After the collision there is no momemtum, because neither vehicle has any velocity. Thus, if there is no *after*-collision momentum, there is no *before*-collision momentum. This is where people begin to have problems. The reason there is no be-

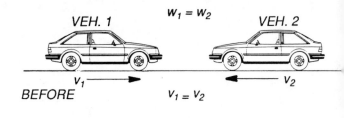

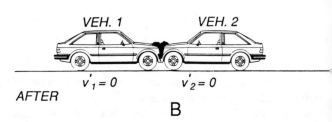

Exhibit 1. *In part A two cars with exactly the same weight are headed toward each other with the same velocity but in opposite directions. In B the two vehicles have collided and, as you would expect, both vehicle velocities have gone to zero.*

fore-collision momentum is because you must think of the momentum of the system — that is, the two cars *together* before the collision. You can think of the momentum before the collision in terms of positive and negative quantities, because the collision takes place along the same line of travel. If the direction of travel of vehicle 1 is considered positive, then the *before*-collision momentum can be expressed as:

$$v_1 w_1 + v_2 w_2 = vw + (-vw) = 0$$

The quantity v replaced both v_1 and v_2 because both vehicle 1 and vehicle 2 have the same velocity. The v for vehicle 2 is negative because it is in the opposite direction of vehicle 1. The quantity w replaced both w_1 and w_2 because the weights were identical for both vehicles.

That the after-collision velocity of both vehicles is zero does not go against your intuition. The cars have some coefficient of restitution; that is, they try to go back to their original shape. But car-to-car collisions are generally considered to be inelastic collisions, because cars do not bounce. Once they are deformed, they essentially stay deformed. You might need to consider restitution as a factor in very low-speed car collisions.[1] But for typical collision speeds encountered in traffic accident reconstruction cases, the coefficient of restitution can be considered to be zero.

The equation for coefficient of restitution is given below.

$$\epsilon = -\frac{v_1{}' - v_2{}'}{v_1 - v_2} \qquad (5)$$

where
ϵ = the coefficient of restitution
v_1' = the after-collision velocity of vehicle 1
v_2' = the after-collision velocity of vehicle 2
v_1 = the before-collision velocity of vehicle 1
v_2 = the before-collision velocity of vehicle 2

The equation deals with the ability of two colliding objects to bounce. It might be easier to consider this equation by applying it to a vehicle colliding into an immovable barrier. Because the barrier has no velocity before or after the collision, equation (5) reduces to

$$\epsilon = -v_1'/v_1$$

If a car hits the barrier at 44 ft/sec and rebounds off the barrier at 2 ft/sec, the coefficient of restitution would be

$$\epsilon = -(-2)/44$$
$$= 0.045$$

The value for v_1' is negative because the direction of the velocity is opposite the velocity direction before the collision.

Collinear Collision

Consider the example shown in Exhibit 2. Vehicle 1, a large vehicle ($w_1 = 5,000$ lbs) traveling 20 ft/sec eastbound, is about to have an opposite-direction collision with vehicle 2 ($w_2 = 2,500$ lbs) traveling westbound at 20 ft/sec. Assume the impact is centered so that the vehicles have no significant lateral movement after the collision. (Generally, in opposite-direction collisions between two vehicles, there is

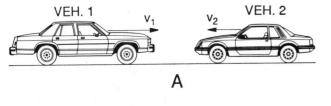

A

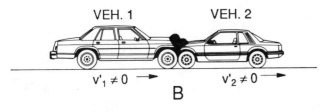

B

Exhibit 2. Vehicles 1 and 2 are moving toward each other with their longitudinal axes on the same line. Vehicle 1 has twice the weight of vehicle 2. The two vehicles are traveling the same velocity. Clearly in B, just after the collision, the vehicles will not have zero velocity.

not enough overlap across the vehicle fronts to result in the two vehicles moving away after the collision along the same line of travel). The sum of the momentum before the collision can be calculated from these data. In this case, the two vehicles were not moving in the same direction before the collision. Because momentum is a *vector* quantity, the direction of travel must be considered. To do so, you must assume one direction as positive and the other as negative. For this example, assume that the direction of travel of vehicle 1 (eastbound) is the positive direction. Thus, the momentum sum before the collision can be determined.

$$v_1 w_1 + v_2 w_2 = (20)(5,000) + (-20)(2,500)$$
$$= 100,000 - 50,000$$
$$= 50,000$$

Therefore, the momentum before the collision is 50,000 units in the direction of vehicle 1 (eastbound). This is also the momentum after the collision. Therefore, both vehicles after the collision would move in vehicle 1's before-collision travel direction.

The after-collision velocity can be calculated for the example. For the type of collision that has been described, the after-collision velocities of both vehicles are the same ($v_1' = v_2'$). Therefore, the right side of equation (4) can be rewritten for this case with one after-collision velocity.

$$v_1' w_1 + v_2' w_2 = v'(w_1 + w_2)$$

Because the after-collision momentum is equal to the before-collision momentum, then

$$v'(w_1 + w_2) = 50,000$$

Substitute the weights for vehicle 1 and vehicle 2 and solve for v'.

$$v'(5,000 + 2,500) = 50,000$$
$$7,500v' = 50,000$$
$$v' = 50,000/7,500$$
$$v' = 6.7 \text{ ft/sec eastbound}$$

Let's now consider what has been calculated along with the given conditions. Vehicle 1, traveling eastbound at 20 ft/sec, collided with vehicle 2. As a result of the collision, vehicle 1 slowed to 6.7 ft/sec. The change in velocity for vehicle 1 was 13.3 ft/sec ($20 - 6.7 = 13.3$). Vehicle 2 was traveling 20 ft/sec westbound before it collided with vehicle 1. As a result of the collision, vehicle 2 was stopped and accelerated backward at a velocity of 6.7 ft/sec. Therefore, vehicle 2 experienced a change in velocity of 26.7 ft/sec. (That is, it was going 20 ft/sec forward and then was redirected to 6.7 ft/sec backward). In this case, each car was traveling the same speed but in opposite directions. Vehicle 2 had one half the weight of vehicle 1. As a result of the collision, vehicle 2 received a change in velocity twice that of vehicle 1. Clearly, the occupants of vehicle 2 could expect to have a higher potential for injury than those of vehicle 1.

Someone not familiar with the technical aspects of momentum might be tempted to say that momentum was "lost" in the collision just described. Clearly, *each* vehicle's velocity changed as a result of the collision. However, the momentum of the *system* was the same before and after the collision. Indeed, it was the application of the conservation of momentum that allowed these calculations to be done.

3. SAME-DIRECTION COLLISION

Normally, you do not know the before-collision velocities of two vehicles involved in a collision. Applying the principles of conservation of momentum, you will usually start by determining how the vehicles first came together relative to each other, based on a vehicle damage analysis (covered in Topic 861). Then you must decide where the vehicles came together on the road itself. This can be done by examining the road surface for tire friction marks, gouges, debris, etc. (Techniques for this type of analysis are discussed in Topic 817.)

If you have a same-direction collision case like the example in Exhibit 3, and neither vehicle's before-collision velocity is known, you cannot reach a specific speed estimate for each vehicle by using equation (4). From equation (4) you can see that you should be able to determine the after-collision velocity of each vehicle (v_1' and v_2') by knowing how the vehicles decelerated to a stop after the collision.

$$v_1 w_1 + v_2 w_2 = v_1' w_1 + v_2' w_2 \qquad (4)$$

(Techniques to do this are discussed in Topic 862.) You should be able to determine the weights of each vehicle. Then the only variables you do not have values for are the before-collision velocities, v_1 and v_2. Unfortunately, you have only one equation with two unknowns, which would give you an infinite number of solutions. To handle this type of problem, you need to use an energy equation along with equation (4).

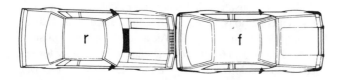

Exhibit 3. *The collision depicted in this exhibit involves two vehicles moving in the same direction before the collision. The longitudinal axes of the cars are more or less on the same line before and after the collision. Vehicle r is designated as the rear vehicle and vehicle f is designated as the front vehicle.*

Work and energy is covered in Topic 870. You should consult that topic if the following discussion is unclear.

Before the collision, both vehicles had a given amount of kinetic energy. After the collision, both vehicles would have some kinetic energy (less than before the collision). Some of the striking vehicle's initial (before-collision) kinetic energy would be used in damaging both vehicles. If the symbol E_D is used to represent the *total* work done in damaging the two vehicles, an energy equation can be written. The total kinetic energy before the collision has to be equal to the sum of the energy due to damage and the after-collision kinetic energy of the two vehicles. This is shown below in equation (6) for two vehicles (vehicles 1 and 2).

$$1/2 m_1 v_1^2 + 1/2 m_2^2 = E_D + 1/2 m_1 (v_1')^2 + 1/2 m_2 (v_2')^2 \qquad (6)$$

In Exhibit 3 the striking vehicle is labeled as vehicle r (rear) and the struck vehicle is labeled as vehicle f (front). The closing velocity (v_c) of vehicle r on vehicle f is given by equation (7) below.

$$v_c = v_r - v_f \qquad (7)$$

If equations 4, 6 and 7 are used along with the relationship of $m = w/g$, an equation can be developed to calculate the closing velocity based on the work done in damaging the two vehicles. The details of this algebra problem are given in Topic 890. The final equation is

$$v_c = \sqrt{\frac{2g E_D (w_r + w_f)}{w_r w_f}} \qquad (8)$$

Because the overlap across the front of the striking car and the struck car is wide enough to cause the cars to continue traveling along the same line of travel after the collision as they were before the collision, the after-collision velocities of both vehicles are equal. Using this property and substituting r and f for the subscripts in equation (6), you obtain the following equation:

$$v_r w_r + v_f w_f = v' w_r + v' w_f \qquad (9)$$

From the definition of v_c [equation (7)], v_f can be solved for:

$$v_f = v_r - v_c \qquad (10)$$

Combining equation (9) and (10) and solving for v_r, the following equation can be determined:

$$v_r = \frac{v_c w_f}{w_r + w_f} + v' \qquad (11)$$

Analysis Procedure

Based on what has been presented thus far, it may not be obvious how you can solve for the velocities of two vehicles involved in a same-direction collision. The first step you must take before using any equation is to determine how the vehicles came together at first contact. If the directions of travel of *both* vehicles are along the same line (collinear) before and after the collision, then you have a candidate for this form of analysis. If not, then you will have to do something different. Assuming you have met this first criterion, follow the steps listed below.

1. Determine the after-collision velocities. Because both vehicles will be traveling essentially the same velocity after the collision, you will find it useful to get an after-collision velocity estimate of both vehicles to check the accuracy and consistency of your analysis. To do this analysis you will need to estimate after-collision drag factors. (The methodology for doing this is discussed in Topic 862.)

2. Calculate the work done (E_D) in damaging *both* vehicles. The number of ft-lbs of work done in damaging the vehicles can usually be determined from the methodology discussed in Topic 870.

3. Using the quantity (E_D) obtained in step 2, calculate the closing velocity from equation (8).

$$v_c = \sqrt{\frac{2gE_D(w_r + w_f)}{w_r w_f}} \qquad (8)$$

4. Because you now know the closing velocity (v_c) and the after-collision velocities (v'), you can calculate the velocity of the striking car (v_r) if you know the vehicle weights. Use equation (11) to do this.

$$v_r = \frac{v_c w_f}{w_r + w_f} + v' \qquad (11)$$

5. The last calculation you need to make is that for the struck vehicle's velocity (v_f). This is done by using equation (10).

$$v_f = v_r - v_c \qquad (10)$$

Speed Estimate Accuracy

After completing these five steps, be sure to consider how accurate your estimate may be. There are several points worth considering.

1. *Vehicle damage.* One of the most important parts of this analysis is to determine the work done in damaging the vehicles. This may be the weakest part of your analysis. If your analysis of vehicle damage is based on tests of like vehicles, then your conclusions may have higher relia-

bility than those based on tests of vehicles that are merely in the same class.

2. *After-collision velocities.* After the collision, the vehicles move off to their final positions. After-collision drag factor estimates are often complicated by travel over more than one surface and the lack of friction test data for the specific surfaces traveled over. Also, not all wheels are likely to be braking equally. Therefore, it may be appropriate to use a *range* of after-collision drag factors. After-collision velocity estimates are often more difficult for vehicles that go off the road or strike other vehicles.

3. *Large difference in weights.* In general, the smaller the weight difference between the two colliding vehicles, the more accurate the momentum solution will be. If, for example, a large truck of 40,000 lbs struck a small car of 2,000 lbs, most likely the methodology presented here would not yield useable results. If there is a high closing velocity, the difference between this and the after-collision velocity of the truck would be very little compared to the truck's before-collision velocity. It might be possible to determine a reasonable minimum speed estimate for the truck, but it would be difficult to obtain a reliable speed estimate for the car's before-collision speed.

One last word of caution. If you do not have a collinear collision, do not consider using this methodology. Your speed estimates will not be meaningful.

4. ANGLE COLLISIONS SOLVED GRAPHICALLY

Collisions between two vehicles occur more often at an oblique angle than collinearly. Many of these collisions are at or near a 90 degree collision. If the vehicles have about the same weight and they travel some distance (50 ft or 15 m), a momentum analysis to determine first-contact speeds may work very well. To do this analysis, you must first know the following information:

1. The approach path of each vehicle to its first-contact position;
2. The departure path of each vehicle from the collision;
3. The total weight of each vehicle (including its load);
4. The after-collision velocity of each vehicle.

The ***approach and departure paths*** of the vehicles should be based on the marks on the road and a vehicle damage analysis. Great care should be taken in this part of the analysis. If significant errors are made here, your first-contact speed estimates will be considerably off the mark. Consult Topic 861 for the general procedure for this part of the analysis.

The ***weights*** used in the momentum calculations are the gross weights of the vehicles. The best data for vehicle weights are determined by weighing the vehicles on a platform scale. If you use published curb weights or actual scale weights for the vehicles involved in the collision, be sure to add the weights of the occupants (and other loads, if any) to arrive at an accurate gross weight for each vehicle. You should have little trouble obtaining published curb weights of passenger cars. However, weights for vans and trucks can vary considerably, depending on how they are equipped.

The *after-collision velocity* of each vehicle depends on the distance each vehicle traveled after the collision and the after-collision drag factor. If good measurement data are available, then the distance traveled by each vehicle's center of mass should be easy to determine. The after-collision drag factor may not be so easy to determine. See Topic 862 for a discussion of how to do this.

Vector Addition

As noted earlier in this topic, momentum is a vector quantity. For collinear collisions, only the direction in terms of a positive or negative quantity has to be accounted for. For angle collisions, however, vectors cannot just be added algebraically, but must be added graphically by using parallelograms (or use trigonometry). The general procedure for this is covered in Topic 856. For this topic, the following brief discussion will suffice.

Consider the two vectors in Exhibit 4A. Each has a different direction and magnitude. Both vectors originate at the same point, as shown in Exhibit 4A. The arrow end of the vector is referred to as the *head,* and the other end is referred to as the *tail.* Thus, you could say the two tails of P and Q are at the same origin. To add the vectors P and Q using the parallelogram method, follow the steps below.

1. Draw a line parallel to Q through the head of P. The length of the line is not important, although you will

find it is better to make it too long than too short. Techniques for drawing parallel lines are discussed in Topic 834.
2. Draw a line parallel to P through the head of Q. Extend the line until it intersects with the line drawn in step 1.
3. Draw the diagonal line connecting the origin to the intersection of the two lines done in step 2. This diagonal line, or *resultant*, is the sum of the two vectors, P and Q.

Example Problem

As noted earlier in this section, several factors must be known before a momentum analysis can be done. For now, assume the following information is known:

$$
\begin{aligned}
w_1 &= 3{,}000 \text{ lbs} \\
w_2 &= 3{,}500 \text{ lbs} \\
v_1' &= 40 \text{ ft/sec} \\
v_2' &= 40 \text{ ft/sec} \\
\theta_1' &= 20° \\
\theta_2' &= 30°
\end{aligned}
$$

Until now the angles, θ_1' and θ_2', have not been mentioned. They are measured in the usual mathematical way, counterclockwise from the positive x-axis. Because each angle is designated with a prime ('), they are after-collision departure angles. The angles of these vectors are shown in Exhibit 5.

The direction of the vectors is known, but the magnitude (length) is not. The magnitude of the vectors is simply weight times the after-collision velocity.

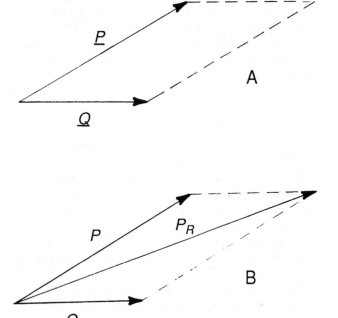

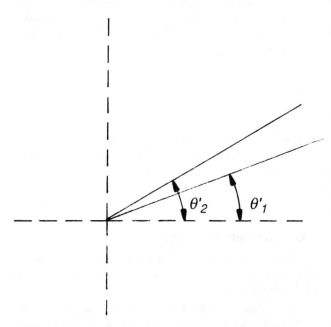

Exhibit 4. *To add the two vectors P and Q, a parallelogram is constructed. The diagonal of the parallelogram is the resultant (vector sum) of vectors P and Q.*

Exhibit 5. *The after-collision angles of departure for each vehicle's center of mass is shown in this exhibit. The angles are shown here measured counterclockwise from the positive x-axis.*

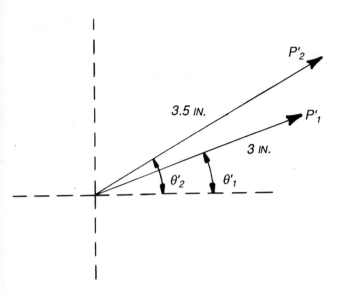

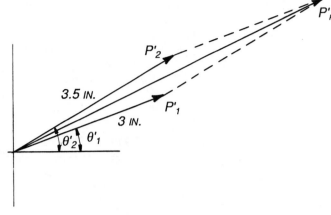

Exhibit 7. *This exhibit shows the after-collision momentum vectors added together. The diagonal of the parallelogram is the resultant (sum) after-collision momentum.*

Exhibit 6. *The lengths of the after-collision momentum vectors represent their magnitude. Choose a scale small enough so that the vectors fit on the paper, but not so small that inaccuracies result.*

$$P_1' = v_1'w_1 = (40)(3,000) = 120,000$$
$$P_2' = v_2'w_2 = (40)(3,500) = 140,000$$

Thus, the magnitude of P_1' is 120,000 and that of P_2' is 140,000. However, a vector of 120,000 or 140,000 inches is too long to put on paper. A scale must be chosen, one that allows the drawing to fit on normal-size paper and each vector to be at least one inch (2.5 cm). Generally, the larger your drawing is, the greater your accuracy will be. For this case, use a scale of 1 inch = 40,000. The lengths of P_1' and P_2'

become

$$P_1' = 120,000/40,000 = 3.0 \text{ inches}$$
$$P_2' = 140,000/40,000 = 3.5 \text{ inches}$$

These lengths are now drawn on Exhibit 6.

The vectors, P_1' and P_2', are summed by completing the parallelogram and drawing the resultant (diagonal). The resultant vector, P_R', is shown in Exhibit 7 to be 6.5 inches long. P_R' is the after-collision momentum. Then P_R' is also equal to the before-collision momentum sum, P_R.

For this example, assume that the before-collision travel direction of vehicle 1's center of mass was at right angles to vehicle 2's center-of-mass direction of travel. These angles relative to the departure angles are shown in Exhibit 8.

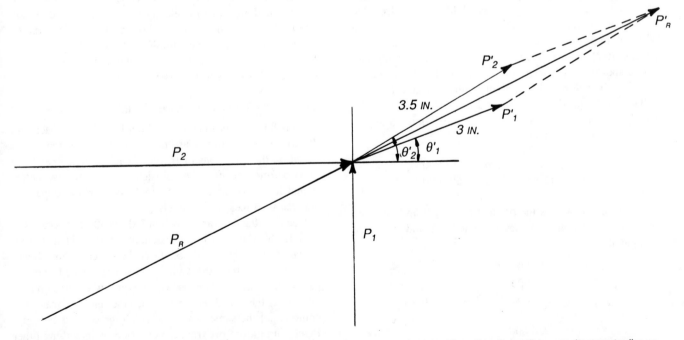

Exhibit 8. *The after-collision momentum sum is equal to the before-collision momentum sum. Thus, the after-collision resultant vector lies on the same line as the resultant before-collision momentum. Also, the before-collision resultant is the same length as the after-collision resultant.*

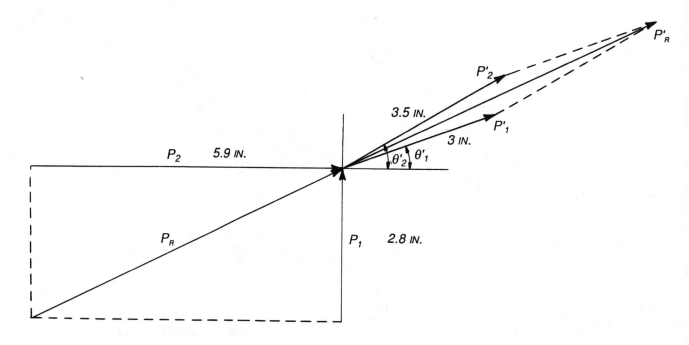

Exhibit 9. The before-collision momentum parallelogram is constructed. These parallel lines are drawn through the tail of the before-collision resultant vector.

The before-collision momentum is equal to the after-collision momentum. Now extend P_R' along its line so it lies between the P_1 and P_2 vectors. P_R' extended between P_1 and P_2 is P_R, the before-collision momentum sum. Make the length of P_R equal to P_R'. This has been done in Exhibit 9.

Now the before-collision momentum of vehicle 1 and vehicle 2 can be determined. Through the tail of P_R draw a line parallel to vehicle 1's momentum line until it intersects vehicle 2's momentum line. Then the length of this line (from the intersection point to the origin) is P_2, the before-collision momentum of vehicle 2. Through the tail of P_R draw a line parallel to P_2 until it intersects vehicle 1's momentum line. The distance of this intersection point to the origin represents P_1, the before-collison momentum of vehicle 1.

The length of P_1 is 2.8 in and P_2 is 5.9 in. Now the lengths need to be converted to their original units. Multiply by the scale to achieve this.

$$P_1 = (2.8)(40,000) = 112,000$$
$$P_2 = (5.9)(40,000) = 236,000$$

Because momentum is the product of weight and velocity, the before-collision velocities of vehicles 1 and 2 can be computed.

$$v_1 w_1 = 112,000$$
$$v_1 = 112,000/w_1$$
$$v_1 = 112,000/3,000 = 37.3 \text{ ft/sec}$$

$$v_2 w_2 = 236,000$$
$$v_2 = 236,000/w_2$$
$$v_2 = 236,000/3,500 = 67.4 \text{ ft/sec}$$

Let's consider what these calculations mean. Vehicle 1 was northbound at 37.3 ft/sec when it hit vehicle 2. After the collision, vehicle 1's travel path was changed 70 degrees clockwise ($90° - 20° = 70°$) and its velocity was increased to 40 ft/sec. Vehicle 2 was westbound at 67.4 ft/sec when first contact was made with vehicle 1. As a result of the collision, its travel path was changed 30 degrees counterclockwise and its velocity was reduced to 40 ft/sec. Both vehicles had a change in velocity and a change in direction due to the collision. So obviously, each vehicle *individually* had a change in its momentum. Nevertheless, the momentum of the *system* (both vehicles taken together) was the same before the collision as it was after the collision.

Center-of-Mass Travel Directions

Thus far, little has been said about how the approach and departure vector angles are determined. These angles are based on the directions of travel of each vehicle's *center of mass* before and after the collision. After you have determined how the vehicles first came together and departed, you can then measure the angles.

Consider the diagram shown in Exhibit 10. In this case the vehicles have moved off in essentially a straight line from contact to rest. This will not always be the case. You should get very clear how the vehicles first approached and departed the collision. If a car was in a yaw when first contact was made, then the direction in which the center of mass was going is not the same as that in which the car was heading. If the cars moved off from the collision in something other than a more or less straight line to their final position, then you should take this into account. If the cars approached and

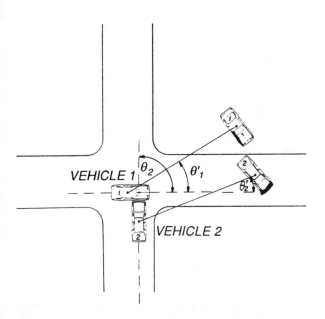

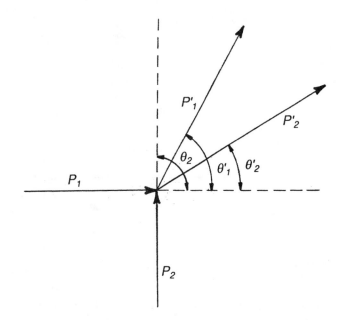

Exhibit 10. *The after-collision travel path of each vehicle's center of mass is shown moving off in a straight line. (This will not always be the case.) If the vehicles move off this way, the resulting angles for the momentum diagram will be those shown in Exhibit 11.*

Exhibit 11. *These are after-collision momentum angles for the vehicles shown in Exhibit 10.*

departed the collision as shown in Exhibit 10, then the vector angles would be as shown in Exhibit 11. To determine these angles, assume the direction of travel of one vehicle before the collision to be your base line to measure from. In Exhibit 10 the direction of travel of vehicle 1's center of mass is assumed for the base line. Note how the angles shown in Exhibit 10 match those in Exhibit 11.

A word of caution is in order here. The vector diagram shown in Exhibit 11 represents the directions of travel of each vehicle's center of mass immediately before and after the collision. Do not assume that vehicles always move off from a collision along a straight line. You can check this by drawing a straight line from each vehicle's center of mass at contact to its rest position. Then, using car cutouts or model cars scaled to the after-accident situation map, move the vehicles from first contact to maximum engagement to separation and finally to their rest positions. While moving the cars, account for all the marks on and off the road. If the center of mass follows the same line of travel as the lines you have drawn from contact to rest, you have a good candidate for the assumption that the vehicles moved off along that line.

Non-Right-Angle Collisions

When vehicles come together in a collision, they often do not approach each other at right angles as in the example just worked. If the angle of approach relative to each other is greater or less than 90 degrees, the problem can still be worked. If the angle between the two vehicles is approaching 180 degrees or 0 degrees, then significant problems can result. Consider the example shown in Exhibit 12. The angle between the two vehicles as they approach each other is 165 degrees. The parallelograms are constructed as in the previ-

ous example. The only difference between this example and Exhibit 11 is the parallelogram for the "before" conditions. Exhibit 13 shows how the parallelogram for the "before" conditions changed between the two vehicles from 165 degrees relative to each other to 170 degrees. When you compare the before-collision vectors in Exhibit 12 to those of Exhibit 13, you can see that for angles approaching 180 degrees, the before-collision velocities are very sensitive to the before-collision angles. This same problem occurs when the angle between the before-collision vectors approaches 0 degrees.

Sensitivity Analysis

When a momentum analysis is used, you should be very careful to use a range of before- and after-collision angles. Rarely can you be absolutely certain of these angles. Choose a representative range of angles. Use this range to determine how sensitive your before-collision velocities are. If the difference is only 5 mi/hr, then you do not have much concern. However, if the range is on the order of 20 or 30 mi/hr, then the use of a momentum analysis may not be appropriate. Generally, you will find that a momentum analysis is less sensitive when 1) the before-collision angles are close to 90 degrees, 2) the vehicles are nearly the same weight, and 3) the vehicles move at least 50 to 60 ft (15 to 20 m) after the collision.

Graphic Procedure

A sample problem was worked in Exhibit 11 that illustrated the graphic solution of a typical momentum analysis. The procedure is fairly simple. A step-by-step discussion of the procedure follows. First, consider the situation that occurs when **two vehicles move off together** after a collision.

68-11

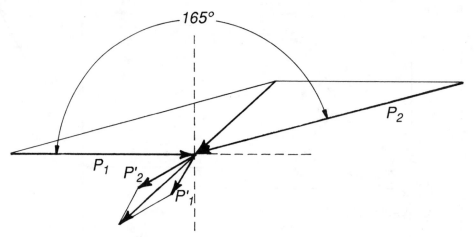

Exhibit 12. *This exhibit shows the vector diagram that is close to a 180 degree collision. The before-collision vectors can change a great deal with a small angle change.*

For this situation, a common after-collision angle can be assumed.

1. Draw an *x*- and *y*-axis as shown in Exhibit 14. It is not important whether the positive *x*-axis points to the east or some other direction.

2. Draw the approach path for vehicle 1 at the appropriate approach angle. Generally, you will find it easier (at least at the beginning) to have the vehicle 1 approach path be on the *x*-axis as shown in Exhibit 15.

3. Place the approach path vector for vehicle 2 relative to the approach path for vehicle 1. This represents the direction of the momemtum for vehicle 2 before the collision. An example of this is shown in Exhibit 16.

4. Put the tail of the departure (after-collision) vector at the origin. This represents the direction of travel of the two vehicles moving off together after the collision. An example is shown in Exhibit 17.

5. Calculate the after-collision velocity (*v′*) of vehicles 1 and 2. Of course, you must know the after-collision drag factor of both vehicles and the distances they traveled.

6. Calculate the after-collision momentum of the two vehicles. Use the equation $P_R' = v'(w_1 + w_2)$.

7. Select a scale for the after-collision momentum (P_R'). Divide the momentum calculated in step 6 by the scale factor to get a momentum "distance" in inches. Choose a scale that will allow for momentum vectors of at least one inch (2.5 cm).

8. Mark off the momentum "distance" for the after-collision momentum as shown in Exhibit 18.

9. Extend the after-collision momentum line through the origin so that it lies between the before-collision momentum directions. (If it does not lie between the before-collision travel directions, either you have made a mistake or one of the vehicles was going backward at the time of the collision). Make this line (the total before-collision momentum, P_R) the same length as the after-collision momentum. See the example in Exhibit 19.

10. Through the tail of P_R draw a line parallel to vehicle 1's momentum line until it intersects vehicle 2's momentum line. See Exhibit 20.

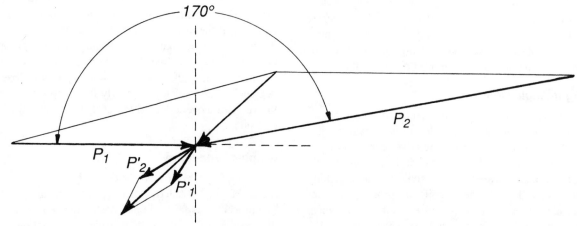

Exhibit 13. *This is the Exhibit 12 diagram, but with the angle of approach of the two vehicles changed by 5 degrees. The resulting before-collision vectors change significantly.*

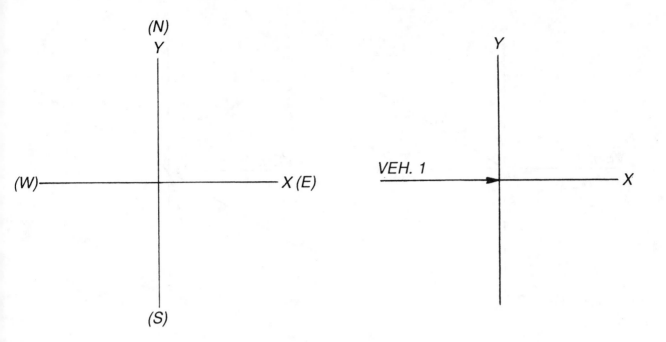

Exhibit 14. *The first step in the graphic procedure for momentum is to establish a coordinate system.*

Exhibit 15. *After establishing a coordinate system, place the before-collision travel path of the vehicle's center of mass at the appropriate angle. Generally, it is easiest if one of the vehicle's before-collision travel paths is on the x-axis.*

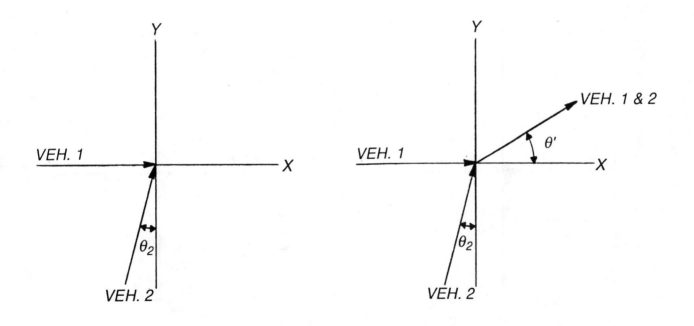

Exhibit 16. *Place the before-collision approach path for the second vehicle relative to the coordinate system.*

Exhibit 17. *In this case, the two vehicles moved off together. Place the departure angle relative to the coordinate system as shown here.*

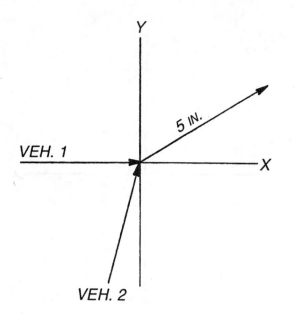

Exhibit 18. *Scale the appropriate length for the after-collision vector to represent the after-collision momentum.*

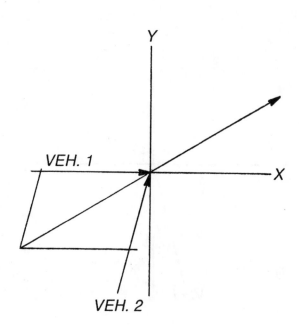

Exhibit 19. *Extend the after-collision momentum line between the two before-collision travel paths. The length of this before-collision vector is the same as the after-collision vector sum.*

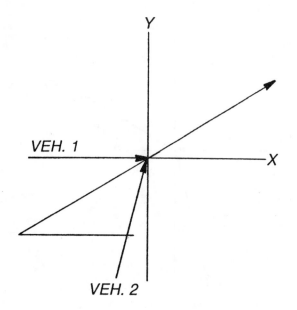

Exhibit 20. *Through the tail of the before-collision momentum resultant (sum) vector, draw a line parallel to vehicle 1's travel path until it intersects vehicle 2's travel path.*

Exhibit 21. *Through the tail of the before-collision momentum resultant (sum) vector, draw a line parallel to vehicle 2's travel path until it intersects vehicle 1's travel path.*

11. Through the tail of P_R draw a line parallel to vehicle 2's momentum line until it intersects vehicle 1's momentum line. As you can now see in Exhibit 21, you have completed the before-collision parallelogram.

12. Measure the before-collision vectors for vehicles 1 and 2 in inches (or cm). See these distances in Exhibit 22.

13. Multiply the measured length in inches (cm) for the before-collision momentum for both vehicles 1 and 2 by the scale factor. This will give the before-collision momentum.

$$P_1 = (d_1)(\text{scale factor})$$
$$P_2 = (d_2)(\text{scale factor})$$

14. The final step is to calculate the velocities of both vehicles at first contact. Because $P = wv$, the velocity of each vehicle can be obtained by dividing the momentum values obtained for each vehicle in step 13 by the appropriate vehicle's weight.

$$v_1 = P_1/w_1$$
$$v_2 = P_2/w_2$$

If the two vehicles *did not move off as one unit*, then the procedure illustrated above will need additional steps. There is little complication when this occurs. The following procedure is listed for such cases. (The first three steps are the same as those listed earlier for vehicles moving off together after a collision.)

1. Draw an x- and y-axis as shown in Exhibit 23. It is not important whether the positive x-axis points to the east or some other direction.

2. Draw the approach path for vehicle 1 at the appropriate approach angle. Generally, you will find it easier (at least at the beginning) to have the vehicle 1 approach path be on the x-axis as shown in Exhibit 24.

3. Place the approach path vector for vehicle 2 relative to the approach path for vehicle 1. This represents the direction of momentum for vehicle 2 before the collision. An example of this is shown in Exhibit 25.

4. Place the after-collision path angle for vehicle 1 as shown in Exhibit 26. The angle measured counterclockwise from the positive x-axis is Θ_1'.

5. Draw the after-collision path angle for vehicle 2 as shown in Exhibit 27. The angle measured from the positive x-axis is Θ_2'.

6. Calculate the after-collision momentum for both vehicles 1 and 2. ($P_1' = v_1'w_1$ and $P_2' = v_2'w_2$)

7. Divide the after-collision momentum for vehicles 1 and 2 by the scale factor to obtain a length in inches (cm). Try to have the length of each be at least one inch (2.5 cm).

8. Measure the length calculated for the after-collison momentum for vehicle 1 on its after-collision path as shown in Exhibit 28.

9. Measure the length calculated for the after-collision momentum for vehicle 2 on its after-collision path as shown in Exhibit 29.

10. Draw a line parallel to the vehicle 1 after-collision vector through the head of the vehicle 2 after-collision vector as shown in Exhibit 30.

11. Draw a line parallel to the vehicle 2 after-collision vector through the head of the vehicle 1 after-collision vector until it intersects the line drawn in step 10 as shown in Exhibit 31.

12. Draw the diagonal of the parallelogram shown in Exhibit 31. The diagonal of the parallelogram as shown in Exhibit 32 is the vector sum of the after-collision momentum of vehicles 1 and 2.

13. Extend the diagonal between the before-collision travel paths of vehicles 1 and 2. If the extended diagonal does not fall between the before-collision travel paths, then one of the vehicles was traveling backward when first contact occurred or you have made a serious mistake.

14. Follow steps 10 through 14 of the preceding example that was given for common after-collision travel paths.

Accuracy

We have discussed the general procedure for solving the momentum problems of two-vehicle collisions graphically. This can also be done mathematically. You should get the same answer whether you use a graphic or a mathematical procedure, so long as your analysis inputs are the same and you use reasonable care in making your diagrams. One advantage of a graphic technique is that you can see what you are drawing, making it more obvious if you have done something wrong. This is particularly advantageous for those not mathematically inclined.

5. IMPULSE

During impact between two vehicles, the velocity of each vehicle changes. Hence the momentum of each vehicle *individually* changes. Each vehicle has the same change in momentum, but in opposite directions. The change in momentum is the impulse. Impulse has the units of force times time or lb-sec (N-sec). The impulse takes place along the principal direction of force (thrust) during the collision. The force of the collision is often thought of as one force for a very short time period. Actually, the direction of force on the vehicle will vary from first contact to maximum engagement to separation. The principal direction of force or thrust is taken to be the line of force that represents the sum of the forces from first contact to separation. That is, the principal direction of force takes the place of the impact forces applied to the vehicle from first contact to separation. Because the force is greatest at maximum engagement, the principal direction of force essentially represents the direction of force applied to the vehicle at maximum engagement.

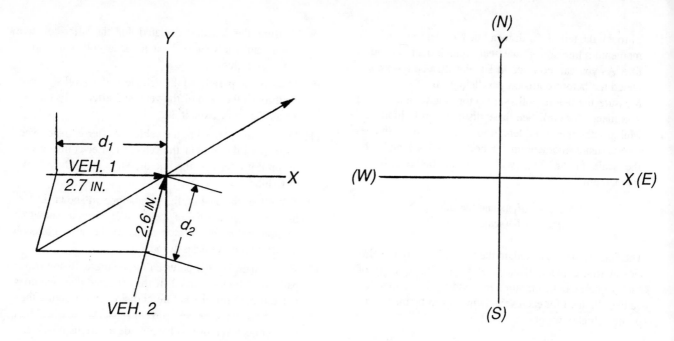

Exhibit 22. *Measure the distance for vehicles 1 and 2's momentum as shown. From this you multiply the length by the appropriate scale factor and solve for each vehicle's before-collision velocity.*

Exhibit 23. *If you have a case where the vehicles moved off separately, the initial steps are the same as in the case where the vehicles moved off together after the collision. The first step is to establish a coordinate system.*

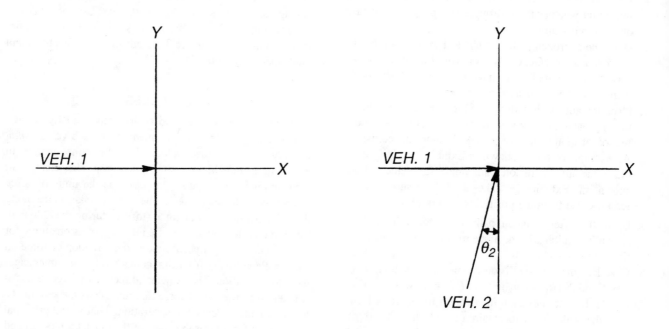

Exhibit 24. *Place the approach path of vehicle 1 on the coordinate system. It is usually easier to have vehicle 1 on the x-axis.*

Exhibit 25. *Draw the before-collision travel path direction for vehicle 2. The angle is normally measured as shown here.*

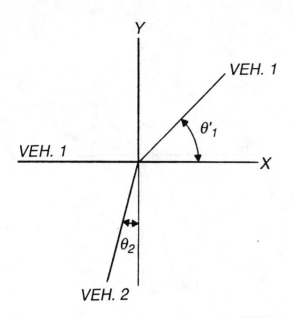

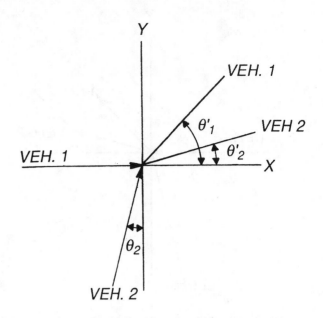

Exhibit 26. *Draw the after-collision travel path direction for vehicle 2.*

Exhibit 27. *Draw the after-collision travel direction for vehicle 2.*

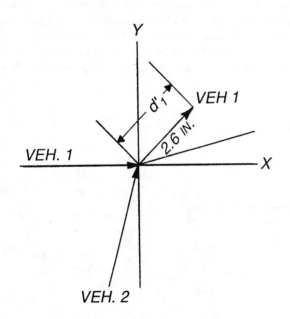

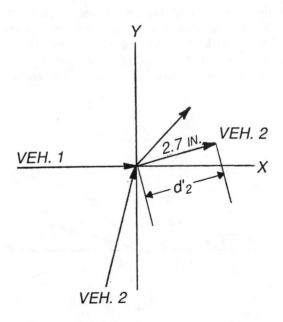

Exhibit 28. *After calculating the after-collision momentum for vehicle 1 and dividing by the scale factor, draw the appropriate length of P$_1$'.*

Exhibit 29. *After calculating the after-collision momentum for vehicle 2 and dividing by the scale factor, draw the appropriate length of P$_2$'.*

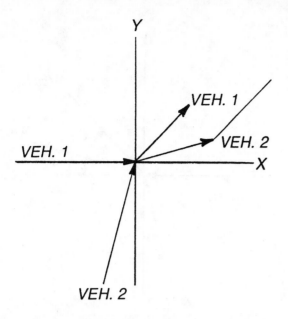

Exhibit 30. *Through the head of the after-collision momentum of vehicle 2, P$_2$', draw a line parallel to the after-collision momentum of vehicle 1, P$_1$'.*

Principal Direction of Force

The principal direction of force is used to determine how two vehicles are positioned relative to each other at maximum engagement. This analysis is based on the damage to each vehicle. From the vehicles' maximum engagement positions, judgments can be made of their relative positions at first contact. Using these conclusions, coupled with data collected at the accident scene, you can position the vehicles relative to each other on the road at first contact. This, of course, is an essential input to the momentum analysis procedure, discussed in Topic 861. If you are not familiar with

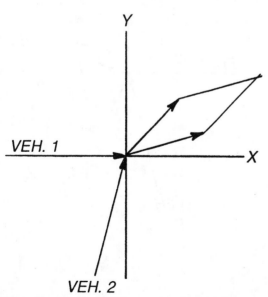

Exhibit 31. *Through the head of the vehicle 2 after-collision momentum, draw a line parallel to the vehicle 1 after-collision momentum line.*

Exhibit 32. *Draw the diagonal of the parallelogram. This represents the total after-collision momentum, P$_R$'.*

these techniques, you should spend some time reviewing that topic. Without a clear understanding of these techniques, you will have difficulty doing momentum analyses.

Impulse Line from the Graphic Momentum Solution

Earlier in this topic you learned about the parallelogram method of solving a momentum problem. Using a similar graphic technique, the impulse line (or principal direction of force) can be determined graphically. This can then be compared to the conclusions made earlier in analyzing the principal directions of force based on the damage to the two

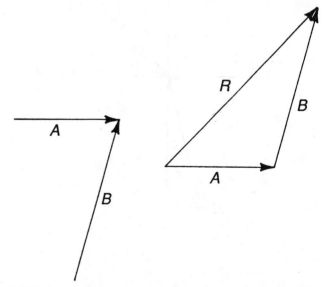

Exhibit 33. *Two vectors in a plane can be added graphically by placing the tail of one vector on the head of another. The vector sum is the line from the tail of the first vector to the head of the second vector.*

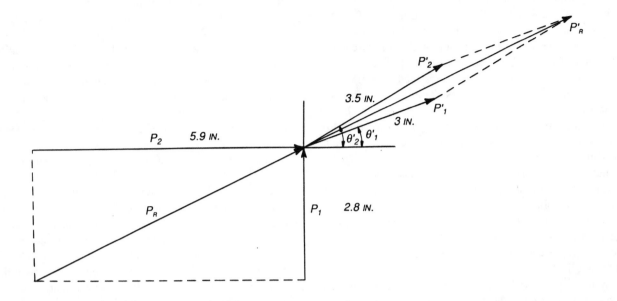

Exhibit 34. *This exhibit is a duplicate of Exhibit 9. It is placed here so that you can easily compare it to the analysis given in Exhibits 35, 36, and 37.*

vehicles.

Two vectors in a plane can be added by moving one vector's tail onto the head of the other. By drawing a line from the first vector's tail to the head of the other vector, you have the vector sum. This procedure is shown in Exhibit 33. Note how the direction (angle) of the vector that was moved does not change. A more detailed discussion of this technique is given in Topic 856.

To illustrate how the impulse line can be determined graphically, an example worked earlier is discussed. Exhibit 34 is a duplicate of Exhibit 9; it is repeated here so you can see how it is used on the same page with Exhibits 35 and 36, which will be used to explain this procedure. Exhibit 34

shows the after-collision momentum parallelogram that was drawn so the before-collision momentum vectors could be determined. This procedure could have been done by adding vectors "head to tail". Exhibit 35 shows these vectors added head to tail. The first part of this procedure is to start at the origin, O. Draw the length of P_1' in the correct direction from O. Place the tail of P_2' on the head of P_1'. Then the vector drawn from O to the head of P_2' is the after-collision resultant vector, P_R'. Of course, P_R' is equal to P_R. The next step is to draw the before-collision travel direction of vehicle 1 starting at O. Then through the head of P_2' draw a line in the before-collision travel direction of vehicle 2 until it intersects the before-collision travel direction of vehicle 1. The

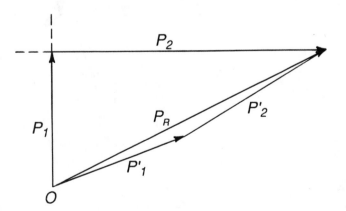

Exhibit 35. *The momentum problem shown in Exhibit 34 has been solved in this exhibit by adding the vectors "head to tail". Note how the sum of the before-collision momentum, P_R, and the after-collision momentum, P_R' are the same line.*

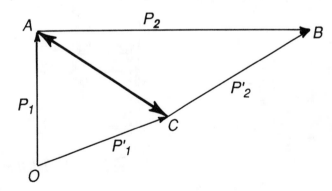

Exhibit 36. *The vector AC represents the change in momentum and impulse to vehicle 1. The vector CA represents the change in momentum and impulse to vehicle 2.*

resulting lengths of P_1 and P_2 can now be clearly seen in Exhibit 35. As you will note, the resulting lengths of P_1', P_2', P_1, and P_2 are the same in both Exhibits 34 and 35.

Consider what is shown in Exhibit 36. This is essentially the same as Exhibit 35 with some changes. The before-collision momentum for vehicle 1 is represented by P_1. Vehicle 1's before-collision momentum was changed to its after-collision momentum, P_1'. If you start at the origin, O, and move in the direction of the P_1 vector, you get to point A in Exhibit 36. If you now start at A and go to C, you will be at the same point you would have been at if you had started at O and traveled along the vector P_1'. Thus, the vector P_1 added to the vector AC is equal to the vector P_1'. Because P_1 is the before-collision momentum of vehicle 1 and P_1' is the after-collision momentum of vehicle 1, the vector AC represents the change in momentum to vehicle 1. Therefore, the vector AC represents the line of impulse that has been placed on vehicle 1.

By inspecting Exhibit 36, you can see that the vector CA (the opposite direction of AC but on the same line) represents the change in momentum for vehicle 2. Of course, this represents the impulse that has been placed on vehicle 2, as can be seen by starting at point C and moving along vector P_2' to point B. P_2' was added to P_1' to get the after-collision resultant vector. If you start at point C and try to get to point B by following the direction of P_2, you first have to move along vector CA. Thus, vector CA plus vector P_2 is equal to

vehicle 2's after-collision momentum, P_2'. So vector CA represents the change in momentum that was received by vehicle 2 in the collision.

When the momentum diagram for Exhibit 36 was initially drawn in Exhibit 8, weight in lbs was used in lieu of mass in slugs. If you wanted to know the actual impulse in the correct units (lb sec), you would first have to determine the length of AC and convert it to lb ft/sec. If you then divide this by the acceleration of gravity (32.2 ft/sec^2), you will then have the correct units for impulse in lb-sec.

The most useful part of Exhibit 36 is to know the *direction* of the impulse and not necessarily its *magnitude*. This can be used to check the assumptions underlying your conclusion as to how the vehicles came together at first contact. If there is a significant difference between the calculated impulse direction and your earlier principal direction of force analysis, re-examine the latter. Exhibit 37 shows the two vehicles coming together at first contact, based on the travel directions implied in Exhibit 36. It is assumed that the center of mass is moving in the same direction in which the vehicles are headed. Of course, the P_1 and P_2 vectors are the travel directions of vehicles 1 and 2's centers of mass. (The vehicles could be in a yaw and not be heading in the same direction in which their centers of mass were moving). The impulse lines from Exhibit 36 have been transferred to Exhibit 37. Of course, the *point of application* of the impulse is not implied from Exhibit 36. You should place the vehicles

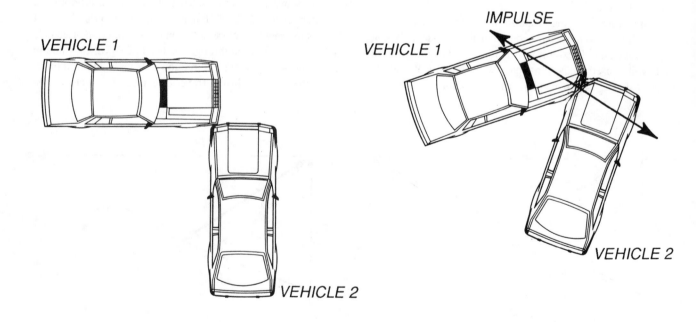

Exhibit 37. *The impulse or principal direction of force vectors are shown here. These are based on the momentum analysis. The momentum analysis does not tell you the point of application of the force. You must relate that to the damage. The momentum results should be the same as your first principal-direction-of-force analysis.*

at their assumed first-contact positions and move them to their maximum-engagement positions. Most of the impulse (that is, the maximum force) is applied when the vehicles are at maximum engagement. In an actual case, you can now compare your principal direction of force analysis to the impulse line (such as that shown in Exhibit 37). If they do not match, resolve the differences.

6. ANGLE COLLISIONS SOLVED MATHEMATICALLY

Momentum problems, which clearly involve vectors, can be solved graphically or mathematically. We have already discussed two graphic techniques in this topic. The mathematical solution to a momentum problem can be done fairly easily. However, the same information that must be known to solve the problem graphically must also be known for a mathematical solution. The correct input data is generally more difficult to come by than the solution, whether the latter is arrived at graphically or mathematically.

Components of Momentum

If the momentum of a system consisting of two vehicles just before and after impact is conserved (that is, if the momentum before the collision is equal to the momentum after the collision), then momentum resolved into rectangular components has to have the same rectangular components before and after impact. Any vector quantity (force, velocity, momentum) can be resolved into rectangular components. (If you are unfamiliar with this principle, refer to Topic 856). In Exhibit 38, vector P has been resolved into x- and y-components. For the vector P shown in Exhibit 38, the x- and y-components are as follows:

$$P_x = P \cos \Theta$$
$$P_y = P \sin \Theta$$

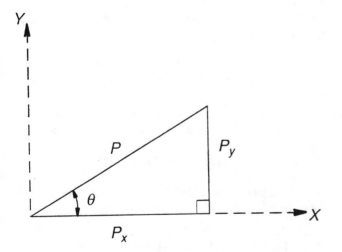

Exhibit 38. *The vector P can be resolved into x- and y-components, P_x and P_y, if the angle Θ is known.*

The angle Θ is measured counterclockwise from the positive x-axis. Sin and cos are the trigonometric functions sine and cosine.

Essentially, conservation-of-momentum problems are solved mathematically by resolving the after-collision momentum into x- and y-components and setting these components equal to the before-collision x- and y-components.

Example Using Rectangular Components

Perhaps the easiest way to explain the use of rectangular-momentum components is by example. Consider the two after-collision momentum vectors, P_1' and P_2', shown in Exhibit 39. The following information also is known:

$$
\begin{aligned}
w_1 &= 3,000 \text{ lbs} \\
w_2 &= 3,500 \text{ lbs} \\
\Theta_1' &= 20° \\
\Theta_2' &= 30° \\
v_1' &= 40 \text{ ft/sec} \\
v_2' &= 40 \text{ ft/sec}
\end{aligned}
$$

Using these data, you can determine the after-collision momentum x- and y-components. First, calculate the after-collision momentum for vehicles 1 and 2:

$$P_1' = v_1'w_1 = (40)(3,000) = 120,000$$
$$P_2' = v_2'w_2 = (40)(3,500) = 140,000$$

Now P_1' and P_2' can be resolved into x-components, P_{1x}' and P_{2x}':

$$P_{1x}' = P_1' \cos \Theta_1' = (120,000)(\cos 20°) = 113,000$$
$$P_{2x}' = P_2' \cos \Theta_2' = (140,000)(\cos 30°) = 121,000$$

Because P_{1x}' and P_{2x}' are in the same direction, they can be added to obtain the total after-collision momentum in the x-direction.

$$P_x' = P_{1x}' + P_{2x}' = 113,000 + 121,000 = 234,000$$

The y-components are determined in a similar way. The only significant difference is sin Θ is used in lieu of cos Θ.

$$P_{1y}' = P_1' \sin \Theta_1' = (120,000)(\sin 20°) = 41,000$$
$$P_{2y}' = P_2' \sin \Theta_2' = (140,000)(\sin 30°) = 70,000$$

$$P_y' = P_{1y}' + P_{2y}' = 41,000 + 70,000 = 111,000$$

The before-collision momentum directions for vehicles 1 and 2 are shown in Exhibit 40. The angle Θ_2 is *not* measured in the usual direction (that is, counterclockwise from the positive x-axis). As shown in Exhibit 40, P_1 does not have any y-component of momentum, because it is lying on the x-axis. Thus, P_1 has only momentum in the x-direction. However, P_2 will have both an x- and y-component, because

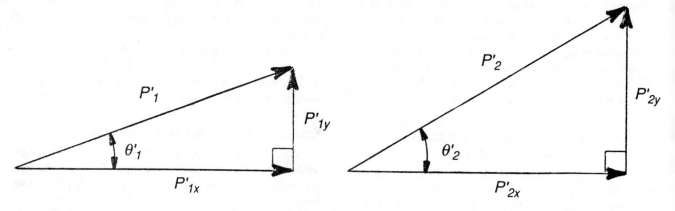

Exhibit 39. The two vectors, P_1' and P_2', are shown here resolved into their x- and y-components. Now the x- and y-components can be added.

it does not lie on only the x- or y-axis. Therefore, the x- and y-components of momentum for vehicles 1 and 2 are the following:

$$P_{1x} = P_1$$
$$P_{2x} = P_2 \sin \Theta_2 = P_2 \sin 25°$$

Then the total before-collision momentum in the x-direction, P_x, is as follows:

$$P_x = P_1 + P_2 \sin 25°$$

The before-collision momentum in the x-direction, P_x, is equal to the after-collision momentum in the x-direction,

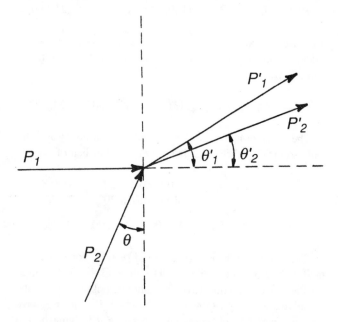

Exhibit 40. The before-collision travel direction of vehicle 2 is shown here. Note that the angle Θ is not measured from the standard position.

P_x'. Therefore, the following equation applies:

$$P_1 + P_2 \sin 25° = 234,000$$

The P_2 vector has a y-component of momentum which is equal to

$$P_{2y} = P_2 \cos \Theta_2 = P_2 \cos 25°$$

Because P_1 has no y-component, the total before-collision momentum in the y-direction P_y is calculated as follows:

$$P_y = P_2 \cos 25°$$

The y-component of momentum before the collision is equal to the y-component of momentum after the collision. Therefore, the following equation applies:

$$P_2 \cos 25° = 111,000$$

The process thus far has been to set the x- and y-components of momentum for the before- and after-collision vectors equal to each other. The final step is to solve the two equations for the two unknowns, P_1 and P_2. The two equations are repeated below.

$$P_1 + P_2 \sin 25° = 234,000$$
$$P_2 \cos 25° = 111,000$$

P_2 can be solved in the second equation because there is only one unknown. Divide each side by cos 25° to solve for P_2.

$$P_2 = 111,000/\cos 25° = 122,000$$

Now substitute $P_2 = 122,000$ into the other equation and solve for P_1.

$$P_1 + (122,000)(\sin 25°) = 234,000$$
$$P_1 = 234,000 - (122,000)(\sin 25°)$$
$$P_1 = 182,000$$

To obtain the before-collision velocities of vehicles 1 and 2, you simply need to solve for velocity by dividing the before-collision momentum values by the appropriate vehicle's weight.

$$v_1 = P_1/w_1 = 182,000/3,000 = 60.7 \text{ ft/sec}$$
$$v_2 = P_2/w_2 = 122,000/3,500 = 34.9 \text{ ft/sec}$$

The procedure presented here can be confusing to those not familiar with trigonometry. You must keep track of positive and negative components. For the case worked here, all of the components were in the positive direction. If P_2 had been 25 degrees from the negative y-axis (on the other side of the y-axis in the fourth quadrant), then the x-component would have been negative. This is just one more thing you have to be aware of. It is also somewhat time-consuming to go back and rework the problem using different approach and departure angles. Nevertheless, if you have trouble drawing parallel lines using the graphic method, this provides an alternative.

Standard Angle Definitions

General equations can be developed to replace the rectangular component procedure outlined in the previous section. But to do this you must use a standard definition of the angles. Otherwise, problems will result because the equation only recognizes the angles in a certain way. This section presents the standard that will be followed for developing the momentum equations in the next section.

Exhibit 41 shows the direction of before- and after-collision momentum vectors. None of the vectors is on the x-axis. Generally, it is easier to calculate the first-contact velocities

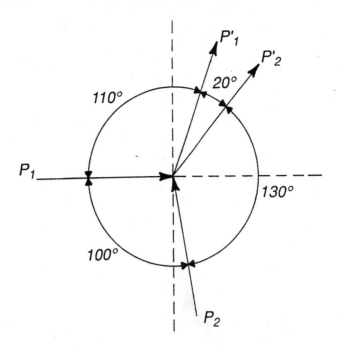

Exhibit 42. *This exhibit shows the vectors in Exhibit 41 rotated so that P_1 is on the x-axis.*

if the before-collision vector for vehicle 1 is on the x-axis. There is little effort involved in simply rotating the vectors shown in Exhibit 41 until the before-collision vector for vehicle 1 is on the x-axis. This has been done in Exhibit 42.

Earlier in this topic you learned how vectors can be moved in a plane and not change their value as long as their direction and magnitude do not change. For the vectors in Exhibit 42, the magnitudes are not known at this point. But the vectors can still be moved if their directions are kept the same.

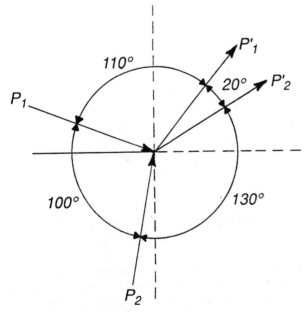

Exhibit 41. *None of these vectors is on the x-axis. You will find that generally it is easier if one of the before-collision vectors is on the x-axis.*

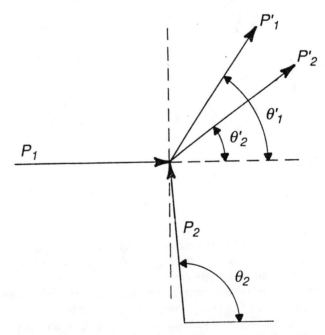

Exhibit 43. *This exhibit shows the vectors in Exhibit 42 moved in such a way that they all have their tails at the origin. The only vectors affected are P_1 and P_2.*

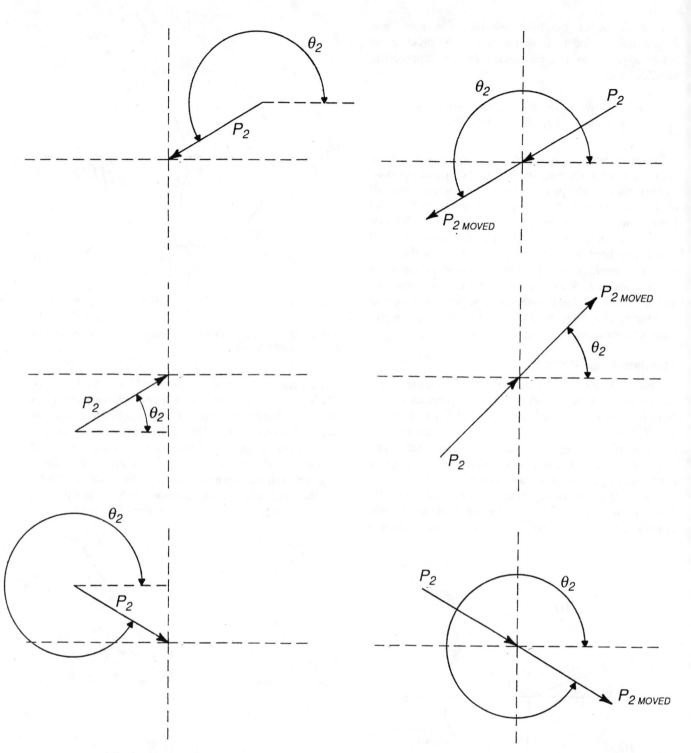

To measure the angles correctly, move to the origin any vector whose tail is not at the origin. This has been done in Exhibit 43 for the vectors shown in Exhibit 42. The vectors are now in the standard position. The angles are measured counterclockwise from the positive *x*-axis as shown in Exhibit 43. If the vectors have their heads at the origin, an alternative method to measure the standard angle is to draw a parallel line through the tail and measure counterclockwise from this line to the vector as shown in Exhibit 43. If you have diffi-

culty understanding how to measure the angles for the standard position, refer to Exhibit 44 where six angles are illustrated.

The angles are designated following the previous convention set forth in this topic. Angles θ_1' and θ_2' are the before-collision angles for vehicles 1 and 2, respectively. Angles θ_1' and θ_2' are the after-collision angles for vehicles 1 and 2, respectively.

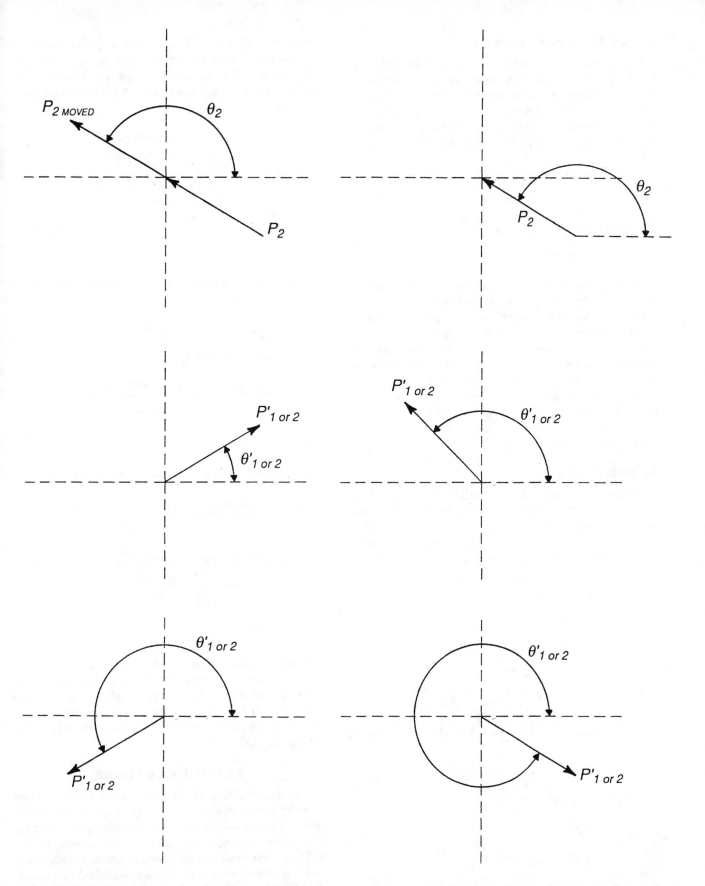

Exhibit 44. *This exhibit shows the many possible ways vectors can be moved to their standard positions. All that is necessary is to have each vector's tail at the origin.*

General Momentum Equations

The derivation of these equations is given in Topic 890. Essentially, what is done is to resolve the before- and after-collision momentum vectors into their x- and y-components. Then the x- and y-components for the before and after conditions are set equal to each other and the before-collision velocities are solved for. The resulting equations are:

$$v_1 = \frac{v_1'w_1 \cos \Theta_1' + v_2'w_2 \cos \Theta_2' - v_2w_2 \cos \Theta_2}{w_1 \cos \Theta_1} \quad (12)$$

$$v_2 = \frac{v_1'w_1 \sin \Theta_1' + v_2'w_2 \sin \Theta_2'}{w_2 \sin \Theta_2} \quad (13)$$

By inspecting equation (12) you can see that all of the variables on the right side can be determined except for v_2, the before-collision velocity of vehicle 2. For equation (13) all the variables can be solved for on the right side of the equation. This is because of the coordinate system that was selected when the equations were developed. Because vehicle 1 has its before-collision momentum on the x-axis, there is no y-component for vehicle 1's momentum before the collision. Therefore, the only y-component of before-collision momentum is from vehicle 2. Equation (13) results from the y-components of momentum.

Example Problem

Consider the example shown in Exhibit 45. The travel direction of vehicle 1's center of mass before the collision (shown as P_1) is on the x-axis in the negative direction. This, of course, means that the angle Θ_1 is equal to 180 degrees. The vector, P_2, is shown in the third quadrant of the coordi-

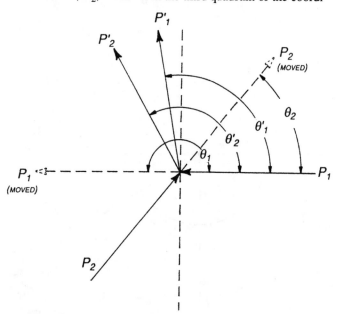

Exhibit 45. *The vectors shown in this exhibit are used in a sample problem. Obviously, Θ_1 is equal to 180 degrees.*

nate system. The head of P_2 is at the origin. Of course, the standard position of the vectors is with the tail at the origin. Thus, moving P_2 to the standard position gives an angle, Θ_2, of 50 degrees. So the given values for this example are as follows:

$$
\begin{aligned}
w_1 &= 2{,}500 \text{ lbs} \\
w_2 &= 3{,}500 \text{ lbs} \\
v_1' &= 44 \text{ ft/sec} \\
v_2' &= 44 \text{ ft/sec} \\
\Theta_1 &= 180° \\
\Theta_2 &= 50° \\
\Theta_1' &= 100° \\
\Theta_2' &= 120°
\end{aligned}
$$

To solve this problem, start with equation (2) and insert the known quantities.

$$v_2 = \frac{v_1'w_1 \sin \Theta_1' + v_2'w_2 \sin \Theta_2'}{w_2 \sin \Theta_2} \quad (13)$$

$$v_2 = \frac{(44)(2{,}500)(\sin 100°) + (44)(3{,}500)(\sin 120°)}{(3{,}500)(\sin 50°)}$$

$$v_2 = 90.2 \text{ ft/sec}$$

Now use the calculated value for v_2 in equation (12).

$$v_1 = \frac{v_1'w_1 \cos \Theta_1' + v_2'w_2 \cos \Theta_2' - v_2w_2 \cos \Theta_2}{w_1 \cos \Theta_1} \quad (12)$$

$$v_1 = \frac{\begin{array}{c} 44(2{,}500)\cos 100° + 44(3{,}500)\cos 120° \\ - 90.2(3{,}500)\cos 50° \end{array}}{(2{,}500)\cos 180°}$$

$$v_1 = 120 \text{ ft/sec}$$

Thus, for this example, vehicle 1 was traveling 120 ft/sec at first contact with vehicle 2. Its travel direction during the collision was changed by 80 degrees ($180° - 100°$). Vehicle 2 was traveling 90.2 ft/sec when the vehicles first had contact. Its travel direction was changed during the collision by 70 degrees ($120° - 50°$).

7. COMPUTER METHODS

Calculations that result in a momentum analysis can be done by hand with a calculator or by using a personal computer (or even a mainframe computer). Writing the computer code to do the calculations required when equations (12) and (13) are used would not be difficult. Several commercially available programs that do this are available, such as AI-CALC[2]. More sophisticated programs for momentum analysis are also available, including CRASH3[3], EDCRASH[4],

CRASHEX[5], and IMPAC[6]. For a more detailed discussion of these programs see Topic 892.

Simple Computer Programs

Simple computer programs like AI-CALC are useful in doing momentum problems. They are relatively simple to use, but require you to input specific data relating to after-collision velocities and departure angles. A trajectory analysis is not done. Therefore, you must clearly understand how the vehicles moved after the collision. In any case, you should try a range of input variables to assess the sensitivity of the outputs. Simple computer programs make this relatively easy to do. They also require you to make specific decisions regarding the input values in an organized manner. A printout of the inputs and outputs in an organized manner is easily done and will serve as a record of the analysis. Like any analysis, however, if the assumptions made for the inputs are not realistic, then the solutions (outputs) will be no more accurate.

Sophisticated Computer Programs

The more sophisticated programs such as CRASH3, CRASHEX and EDCRASH allow you to have inputs such as coefficient of friction (over more than one surface), percentage of wheel lockup, first-contact headings, and other data. Then the program calculates after-collision velocities. A trajectory analysis is done. A recent paper[7] suggests this might not be as useful as you might think for certain accident cases. The IMPAC program is a useful tool. It considers both linear and angular momentum. These sophisticated programs are fairly easy to use, and both hardware and software are less expensive than they were as recently as five years ago. However, these programs generally require very specific inputs. Because these values are often not known and must be estimated within a broad range of values, there may be little advantage in using these programs as compared with the less sophisticated programs. You might start to believe your answers are more accurate than they actually are, forgetting that many of the inputs are only slightly better than guesses. Clearly, this is a time to exercise caution and understand the limitations of your analysis.

8. CASE STUDY

A relatively simple case study is included in this topic to apply conservation of linear momentum to a real-world problem. An after-accident situation map is shown in Exhibit 46. As you can see, both vehicles traveled together after the collision and are still engaged at their rest positions. Before the collision, the Plymouth left a braking skidmark. The end of this mark is an excellent indication of the Plymouth's first-contact position.

Vehicle Damage Analysis

The damage to the Pontiac is shown in Exhibits 47 and 48. The resulting direction of thrust to obtain the damage shown in these photographs is indicated in Exhibit 49. Note that the thrust direction indicates that little, if any, rotation would be expected as a result of the collision.

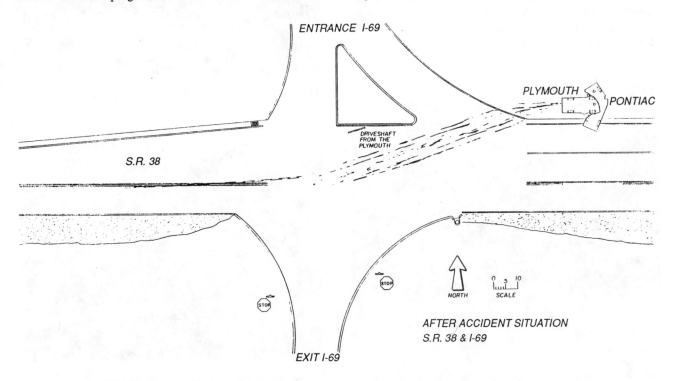

Exhibit 46. *The after-accident situation map is shown here for an intersection accident between a Plymouth and Pontiac.*

Exhibit 47. *A considerable amount of intrusion has taken place on the Pontiac, which is shown clearly in the photograph.*

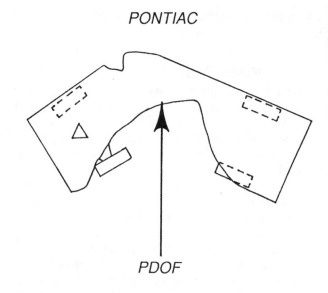

PONTIAC

PDOF

Exhibit 49. *The damage to the Pontiac is diagrammed in this exhibit along with the principal direction of force that resulted from the collision.*

The damage to the Plymouth is shown in Exhibits 50 and 51. Notice in these photographs that the crush on the front of the Plymouth is mainly to the rear. There is a small amount of displacement of the front to its left. The resulting direction of thrust is shown in Exhibit 52. Note that for this car also, there is little expected rotation because of the thrust direction.

For this case there would be little rotation of one vehicle relative to the other from first contact to maximum engagement. That is, relative to each other, the longitudinal axes of each car stay in approximately the same position. (This is not entirely true, because the Pontiac experiences a fair amount of bowing as a result of the collision. Nevertheless, their relative positions at first contact — based solely on the damage analysis — would be as shown in Exhibit 53.)

Exhibit 50. *Contact damage is completely across the front on the Plymouth.*

Exhibit 48. *In this photo you can see the width of the contact damage on the Pontiac.*

Exhibit 51. *There has been considerable rearward movement of the front of the Plymouth as a result of the collision.*

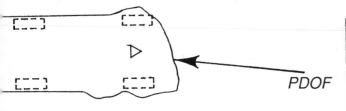

PLYMOUTH

Exhibit 52. *The crush that resulted to the Plymouth is shown here along with the principal direction of force.*

Approach and Departure Angles

The marks on the road are shown in Exhibits 54, 55 and 56. The after-accident situation map (Exhibit 46) has the significant marks located. Thus, based on the marks on the road and the vehicle damage analysis, the first-contact positions of the two vehicles were determined as shown in Exhibit 57. After the collision, the vehicles moved off approximately along a straight line. Their after-collision travel direction was altered when they left the paved road. Exhibit 57 shows how the angles (Θ_1, Θ_2, and Θ') are measured. Exhibit 58 shows these angles transferred to a coordinate system. Only one after-collision angle, Θ', is shown because the vehicles moved off together.

The vectors shown in Exhibit 58 are not in the standard position, so you cannot use equations (12) and (13) without making adjustments. Perhaps the easiest way to put vehicle 1 on the x-axis is to rotate the Exhibit 58 diagram 90 degrees clockwise as shown in Exhibit 59. Then simply "move" P_2 so the tail is on the origin. The vectors are now in the standard position.

After-Collision Velocities

The after-collision velocity for this case study was calculated in Topic 862. First, the after-collision drag factors on

Exhibit 54. *The before-collision position of the Plymouth can be established from the location of the braking skidmark shown in this exhibit. By determining, from the vehicle damage analysis, how the vehicles were positioned relative to each other at first contact, you can also establish the first contact position of the Pontiac.*

Exhibit 55. *The metal marks and liquid debris left on the pavement from the vehicles indicate the direction of movement of the vehicles after the collision.*

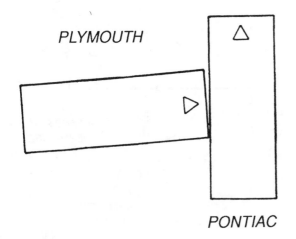

PLYMOUTH

PONTIAC

Exhibit 53. *The first contact positions of the two vehicles are shown in this exhibit. They were obtained from the damage analysis only.*

Exhibit 56. *When the vehicles hit the curb, their travel direction obviously was altered.*

68-29

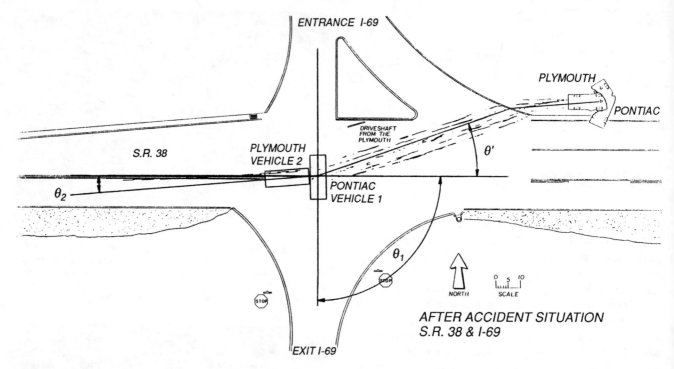

Exhibit 57. *Based on the vehicle damage analysis and marks on the road, this after-accident situation map shows how the two vehicles were positioned at first contact.*

and off the pavement were calculated. Two after-collision velocities were then calculated: 61.3 ft/sec and 67.5 ft/sec. For this analysis the lower value, 61.3 ft/sec, is used. You might find it very useful to review the procedure discussed in Topic 862 for calculating after-collision drag factors.

Mathematical Solution

The before-collision velocities can be calculated by using the standard angle positions shown in Exhibit 59, the after-collision velocity, and the vehicle weights shown below.

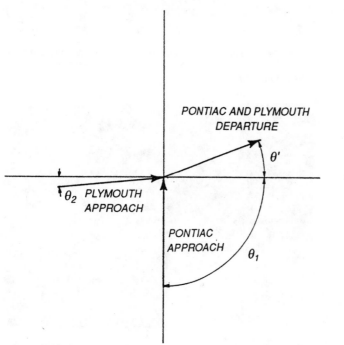

Exhibit 58. *The angles of approach and departure are shown for the Pontiac and Plymouth. They are not in the standard position.*

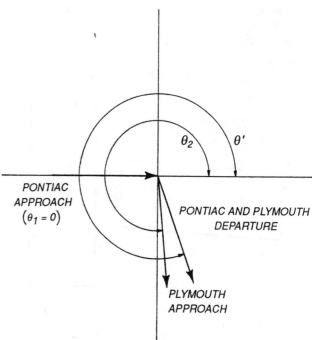

Exhibit 59. *The vectors shown in Exhibit 58 have been moved to their standard position.*

Because the vehicles moved off together after the collision, $v_1' = v_2' = v'$ and $\Theta_1' = \Theta_2' = \Theta'$ in equations (12) and (13).

$$
\begin{aligned}
w_1 &= 3{,}600 \text{ lbs} \\
w_2 &= 3{,}700 \text{ lbs} \\
\Theta_1 &= 0° \\
\Theta_2 &= 275° \\
v' &= 61.3 \text{ ft/sec} \\
\Theta' &= 290°
\end{aligned}
$$

First solve for v_2 using equation (13).

$$
v_2 = \frac{v_1'w_1 \sin \Theta_1' + v_2'w_2 \sin \Theta_2'}{w_2 \sin \Theta_2} \qquad (13)
$$

$$
v_2 = \frac{(61.3)(3{,}600)\sin 290° + (61.3)(3{,}700)\sin 290°}{(3{,}700)\sin 275°}
$$

$$
v_2 = 114 \text{ ft/sec}
$$

Now use equation (12) to solve for v_1.

$$
v_1 = \frac{v_1'w_1 \cos \Theta_1' + v_2'w_2 \cos \Theta_2' - v_2 w_2 \cos \Theta_2}{w_1 \cos \Theta_1} \qquad (12)
$$

$$
v_1 = \frac{\begin{array}{c}61.3(3{,}600)\cos 290° + 61.3(3{,}700)\cos 290° \\ - 114(3{,}700)\cos 275°\end{array}}{(3{,}600)\cos 0°}
$$

$$
v_1 = 32.3 \text{ ft/sec}
$$

Graphic Solution

This problem can be worked graphically with the same accuracy as it was done mathematically. You need not have the vectors in the standard position given in Exhibit 59. The angles shown in Exhibit 58 are used for this method; the positions shown there will work without modification. The first step is to calculate the after-collision momentum. Because both vehicles moved off together, the resultant after-collision momentum is simply P'.

$$
\begin{aligned}
P' &= v'(w_1 + w_2) \\
&= 61.3(3{,}600 + 3{,}700) \\
&= 447{,}000
\end{aligned}
$$

Now select a scale that will allow the diagram to fit on your paper. For this example use 1 inch = 100,000 units. Divide P' by 100,000 to get a length of 4.47 inches. Draw the after-collision momentum as shown in Exhibit 60. Complete the parallelogram for the before-collision conditions. Measure the length of P_1 as 1.16 inches. The length of P_2 is 4.22 inches. Convert these back to the correct units by multiplying by the scale.

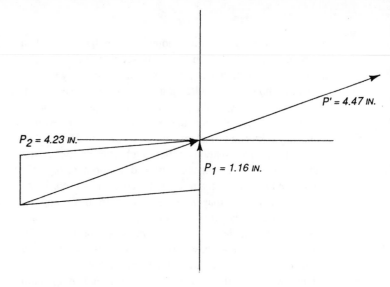

Exhibit 60. *The graphic solution to the Pontiac-Plymouth collision is shown in this exhibit.*

$$
\begin{aligned}
P_1 &= 1.16(100{,}000) \\
P_1 &= 116{,}000
\end{aligned}
$$

$$
\begin{aligned}
P_2 &= 4.23(100{,}000) \\
P_2 &= 423{,}000
\end{aligned}
$$

Now solve for the first-contact velocities by dividing by the appropriate weight for vehicles 1 and 2.

$$
\begin{aligned}
v_1 &= 116{,}000/3{,}600 \\
v_1 &= 32.2 \text{ ft/sec}
\end{aligned}
$$

$$
\begin{aligned}
v_2 &= 423{,}000/3{,}700 \\
v_2 &= 114 \text{ ft/sec}
\end{aligned}
$$

Analysis Summary

The velocity analysis using momentum for this case is relatively simple. The after-collision departure angles are fairly easy to determine, and the vehicles moved off together. Because the collected data allows an accurate estimate of the departure angle, a small range of angles can be used to determine the sensitivity of the final speed estimate. Also, a range of the after-collision drag factors can be used to get a range of after-collision velocities. Again, the data allows a very good estimate of how the vehicles decelerated to their final positions, enabling an accurate estimate of the after-collision velocities. Perhaps the greatest variability in the input data would be the before-collision angles. The braking skidmark left by the Plymouth helps in this part of the analysis. A range in the approach angles can be used. Again, you see very little change in the final speed estimate at first contact.

9. SUMMARY

This topic has illustrated how linear conservation of momentum can be applied in traffic accident reconstruction problems. To do an accurate momentum analysis good data are required, from both the accident scene and the vehicles themselves. Before starting a momentum analysis, you must determine how the vehicles first came together, separated, and moved to their final positions. If this is not done accurately, the results of your analysis will be unreliable. It is extremely important to understand how the vehicles decelerated to their final positions. Often, high after-collision drag factors are used that cannot be justified. Computer programs can prove helpful when a momentum analysis is used. However, the mere fact that the results came from a computer does not make the answers accurate. You should always make a careful review of the input variables and how sensitive the outputs are to these inputs. This applies whether you are using a computer or a hand-held calculator.

Clearly, good results can be expected from a momentum analysis if the analysis process is thorough. Momentum will generally work best if 1) the weights of the two vehicles are fairly close, 2) the angles of approach are in the neighborhood of 90 degrees, and 3) the vehicles moved some distance after the collision. If these criteria are not met, try changing your input variables to see how sensitive the outputs are. If the before-collision velocity of one vehicle changes from 50 mi/hr to 80 mi/hr with a 5 degree change in approach angles, you had better consider using a different method of analysis.

10. SOURCES

Author

Lynn B. Fricke, principal author, is an engineer specializing in traffic accident reconstruction. He has been with the Northwestern University Traffic Institute since 1975. In 1981 he became the director of the Institute's Accident Investigation Division.

References

Subscript numbers in the preceding pages refer to the following publications:

1. Collins, James C., *Accident Reconstruction*, 1979, Charles C. Thomas Publisher, Springfield, IL.

2. *AI-CALC Reference Manual*, 1987, Northwestern University Traffic Institute, Evanston, IL.

3. *CRASH3 User's Guide and Technical Manual*, National Highway Traffic Safety Administration, Washington, DC.

4. *EDVAP Vehicle Analysis Package*, 1988, Engineering Dynamics Corp., Lake Oswego, OR.

5. Fonda, Albert G., *CRASH Extended for Desk and Hand-held Computers*, Society of Automotive Engineers paper 870044, Warrendale, PA.

6. Woolley, Ronald L., *The IMPAC Program for Collision Analysis*, Society of Automotive Engineers paper 870046, Warrendale, PA.

7. Day, Terry D., and Randall L. Hargens, *Further Validation of EDCRASH Using the RICSAC Staged Collisions*, Society of Automotive Engineers paper 890740, Warrendale, PA.

Exhibits

The following are the sources of the exhibits used in this topic:

Cooper, Gary W., Wauconda, IL

Diagrams: 4 – 9, 14 – 32, 34, 38 – 46, 49, 52 – 53, 57 – 60
Photos: 47 – 48, 50 – 51, 54 – 56

Fricke, Lynn B.

Diagrams: 1 – 3, 10 – 13, 33, 35 – 37

WORK, ENERGY, AND SPEED FROM DAMAGE IN TRAFFIC ACCIDENTS

Topic 870 of the *Traffic Accident Investigation Manual*

by
Gary W. Cooper

NORTHWESTERN UNIVERSITY TRAFFIC INSTITUTE

WORK, ENERGY, AND SPEED FROM DAMAGE IN TRAFFIC ACCIDENTS

In traffic accident reconstruction, many concepts associated with physics are used, especially those dealing with work and energy. These concepts can be used to answer questions concerning speed estimates from skidmarks and vehicle damage, the effect of grade on drag factor, and many other issues. This topic explains the basic concepts and then applies them to traffic accident reconstruction problems.

1. WORK

The word *work* has different meanings, depending upon the context in which it is used. It usually means some mental or physical exertion – "I worked the problem," or "I worked the accident." In physics, however, work means something very specific. Technically, work is done when a force acts on an object through a distance. Work is also a measure of what effect the force has on changing the object. The amount of change produced, i.e., the amount of work done, is reflected in changes in the object's velocity, position, size, shape, and so forth.

A more quantitative description of the term *work* can be established from the above definition. Work (W) is equal to the product of the force (F) and the distance (d) through which the force acts, provided the force and distance covered are in the same direction. This may be written in equation form:

$$W = Fd \qquad (1)$$

In the U.S.A. system, the unit for force is pound (lb) and the unit for distance is foot (ft). The unit for work in the U.S.A. system therefore is foot-pound (ft-lb). In the metric system, the unit for work is Newton meter (N-m). Therefore, in the equation

$$W = Fd \qquad (1)$$
$$F = \text{force (lb, N)}$$
$$d = \text{distance (ft, m)}$$
$$W = \text{work (ft-lb, N-m)}$$

For example, suppose a force of 300 lbs is required to push a crate 25 ft as shown in Exhibit 1. The amount of work done can be found by substituting these values into the equation for work:

$$W = Fd \qquad (1)$$
$$W = (300 \text{ lbs})(25 \text{ ft})$$
$$W = 7500 \text{ ft-lbs}$$

If the force and distance are not in the same direction (collinear), then the equation is rewritten to become

$$W = Fd \cos \Theta \qquad (2)$$

where

$$W = \text{work (ft-lbs, N-m)}$$
$$F = \text{force (lbs, N)}$$
$$d = \text{distance (ft, m)}$$
$$\Theta = \text{angle between the force vector and the direction of travel}$$

This situation is illustrated in Exhibit 2.

Suppose the force (F) is equal to 300 lbs, the angle (Θ) is equal to 60 degrees, and the distance (d) is 25 ft. The work done is

$$W = Fd \cos \Theta \qquad (2)$$
$$W = (300)(25)(\cos 60°)$$
$$W = 3750 \text{ ft-lbs}$$

Work is a *scalar* quantity, or the product of the *magnitudes* of force and distance. Being a scalar quantity, work has only magnitude and sign (positive or negative), but has no direction associated with it. Work is positive if Θ is greater than or equal to 0 degrees but less than 90 degrees. Work is negative if Θ is greater than 90 degrees but less than or equal to 180 degrees. An example of positive work is a vehicle that is accelerating. The force accelerating the vehicle is in the direction of travel (that is, Θ is equal to 0 degrees). This example is shown in Exhibit 3.

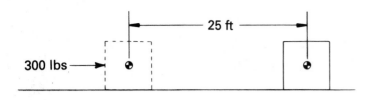

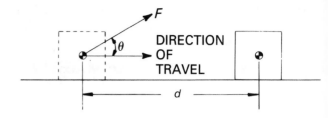

Exhibit 1 *The work (W) done moving an object is equal to the force (F) required to move it, times the distance (d) it is moved: W = Fd.*

Exhibit 2 *The work (W) done moving an object when the force required to move it is not collinear with the direction of travel is equal to the force (F) times the distance (d) it is moved times the cosine of the angle (Θ) between the force and direction of travel: W = Fd cos Θ.*

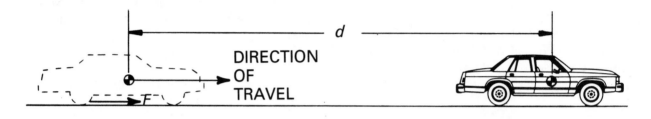

Exhibit 3 *Work is positive when the applied force is in the direction of travel, such as when a vehicle is accelerating.*

If in Exhibit 3 the net force (F) acting on the vehicle is 1000 lbs, the distance (d) the force acts through is 50 ft, and the angle (Θ) is 0 degrees, then the work done is

$$W = Fd \cos \Theta \qquad (2)$$
$$W = (1000)(50)(\cos 0°)$$
$$W = 50,000 \text{ ft-lbs}$$

On the other hand, if the vehicle is decelerating, the work is negative because the force is opposite to the direction of travel (that is, Θ is equal to 180 degrees). In Exhibit 4, if the angle (Θ) is 180 degrees, the force (F) is equal to 2,100 lbs, and the distance (d) is 25 ft, then the work done is

$$W = Fd \cos \Theta \qquad (2)$$
$$W = (2100)(25)(\cos 180°)$$
$$W = -52,500 \text{ ft-lbs}$$

2. ENERGY

Relationship Between Work and Energy

By doing work, energy is transferred between different objects. The energy an object possesses is a measure of its ability to do work. The more energy an object has, the more work it can perform. Equations can be derived to calculate the amount of energy transferred between objects when work is done under a variety of conditions. The derivations use the sign convention of positive if the object's energy is increased, and negative if it is decreased when work is done. This coin-

cides with the earlier examples of positive work being done on an accelerating vehicle and negative work being done on a decelerating vehicle. The accelerating vehicle is gaining energy and the decelerating vehicle is losing energy.

Types of Energy

Energy can be grouped into three general categories:

1. Rest energy
2. Kinetic energy
3. Potential energy

Rest energy is energy an object possesses due to its mass. This form of energy is related to Einstein's theory of relativity and will not be discussed.

Kinetic energy (KE) is energy an object possesses due to its motion. A vehicle in motion has more kinetic energy than a vehicle at rest. An equation for calculating the kinetic energy of an object can be found by considering the equation for work, Newton's second law of motion and kinematics (see Topic 856).

When a vehicle accelerates, it gains velocity and also increases its energy. In Topic 890 it was shown that the kinetic energy of a moving body is equal to

$$KE = \tfrac{1}{2}mv^2 \qquad (3)$$

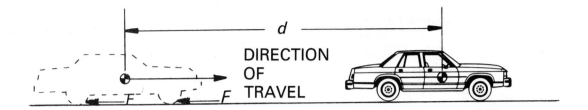

Exhibit 4 *Work is negative when the applied force is in the opposite direction of travel, such as when a vehicle is decelerating.*

where

> m = mass of the body (weight divided by acceleration of gravity), and
> v = velocity (ft/sec or m/sec)

This equation calculates the amount of work required to accelerate the vehicle from rest to a given velocity. It is also the amount of energy gained by the vehicle. Specifically, the energy gained is kinetic energy.

Mass and weight are related by the acceleration due to gravity. Using this relationship in the equation yields another equation for kinetic energy:

$$KE = wv^2/2g \qquad (4)$$

where

> KE = kinetic energy (ft-lbs, N-m)
> w = weight (lbs, N)
> v = velocity (ft/sec, m/sec)
> g = 32.2 ft/sec², 9.81 m/sec²

Suppose, for example, a 3,000-lb vehicle is accelerated from rest to a velocity of 40 ft/sec. The amount of work done and energy gained can be calculated as follows:

$$KE = wv^2/2g \qquad (4)$$
$$KE = (3,000)(40)^2/(2)(32.2)$$
$$KE = 74,500 \text{ ft-lbs}$$

To bring the vehicle to rest requires the same amount of work to be done, and dissipation of the same amount of energy that originally was gained.

The energy is dissipated by converting it into mainly thermal (heat) energy. This is accomplished through friction between the tires and road surface, tires and brake system, or simply through rolling resistance in coasting to a stop.

In Topic 890, an equation was found which calculates the amount of kinetic energy that must be converted to another form in order to bring the vehicle to a stop:

$$W = wfd \qquad (5)$$

where

> W = work (ft-lbs, N-m)
> w = weight (lbs, N)
> f = drag factor, and
> d = distance (ft, m)

If the 3,000 lb vehicle from the earlier example skidded to a stop with a drag factor of 0.71 from 40 ft/sec, it would slide approximately 35 ft. Use this information in the following equation:

$$W = wfd \qquad (5)$$
$$W = (3,000)(0.71)(35)$$
$$W = 74,500 \text{ ft-lbs}$$

The two equations

$$W = wfd \qquad (5)$$

and

$$KE = wv^2/2g \qquad (4)$$

can be used together to calculate speed estimates from skidmarks. The first equation is used to find the amount of kinetic energy the vehicle dissipated while skidding. The second equation, solved for velocity, uses the energy calculated to find the velocity of the vehicle. This equation is

$$v = \sqrt{(2g)(KE)/w} \qquad (6)$$

Because the quantity of one form of energy is the same as the quantity of any other form of energy, this equation can be written

$$v = \sqrt{(2g)(E)/w} \qquad (7)$$

From the earlier example, the amount of kinetic energy that was dissipated while skidding was approximately 74,500 ft-lbs and the vehicle weighed 3,000 lbs. Substitute these values into the equation:

$$v = \sqrt{(2g)(E)/w} \qquad (7)$$
$$v = \sqrt{(2)(32.2)(74,500)/3000}$$
$$v = 40 \text{ ft/sec}$$

In summary, kinetic energy, like all energies, is a scalar quantity. The kinetic energy of a given mass depends on the magnitude of its velocity and not on the direction of travel. Any change in kinetic energy depends on the sign of the work done. If the work is positive, the kinetic energy increases. If it is negative, the kinetic energy will decrease. Acceleration rate is not a factor in kinetic energy. The kinetic energy of a body depends on its mass and its velocity. It is not affected by how quickly the body reaches that velocity.

Potential energy (PE) is energy an object possesses due to its position. Two forms of potential energy will be addressed in this topic:
1. Gravitational potential energy (PE_h)
2. Elastic potential energy (PE_k)

Gravitational potential energy is the energy an object possesses due to its position above some reference plane. The reference plane is usually the surface of the earth.

Suppose a vehicle is hoisted by a hydraulic lift at a service station as shown in Exhibit 5. The downward gravitational force is the vehicle's weight (w) and the distance moved is the height (h) of the vehicle's center of mass above its original position. Substitute these two variables into the equation for work:

$$W = Fd \qquad (1)$$
$$W = wh \qquad (8)$$

This is the equation for gravitational potential energy:

$$PE_h = wh \qquad (9)$$

where

$$PE_h = \text{gravitation potential energy (ft-lbs, N-m)}$$
$$w = \text{weight (lbs, N)}$$
$$h = \text{vertical distance (ft, m)}$$

If the vehicle in Exhibit 5 weighs 3,000 lbs and its center of mass is 10 ft above the position where it would be if the vehicle were on the floor, then the vehicle's gravitational potential energy is

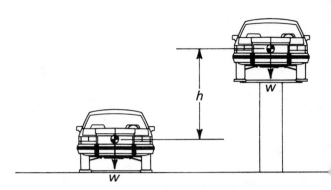

Exhibit 5 *A vehicle hoisted by a hydraulic lift has gravitational potential energy (PE$_h$) due to its weight (w) and its height (h) above the ground.*

$$PE_h = wh \qquad (9)$$
$$PE_h = (3000)(10) \qquad (10)$$
$$PE_h = 30,000 \text{ ft-lbs}$$

This is the same amount of energy the vehicle would have if it were traveling approximately 25 ft/sec.

In summary, gravitational potential energy depends only on the vertical distance (height) the object is above some reference plane, not on any horizontal change in position. Shown in Exhibit 6 is a box originally at position 1 and h_1 above the reference plane. When the box is moved to position 2 the vertical distance, h_2, is the same. Therefore:

$$PE_{h1} = PE_{h2}$$

The change in gravitational potential energy depends only on the difference between the initial and final heights of the object, not on the path taken to reach the final height. In Exhibit 7 the vehicle moves up and down while going from position 1 to position 2. However, the change in gravitational potential energy is only dependent upon the difference between h_1 and h_2:

$$PE_h = w(h_2 - h_1)$$

Elastic potential energy (PE_k) is energy an object possesses because of its shape.

A compressed or stretched spring has elastic potential energy because of its shape. The amount of elastic potential energy a spring possesses depends on the amount of work done to compress or stretch it. Assume a spring is compressed. A force is required to compress the spring from its free length or equilibrium position (length with no force applied). The force required to compress the spring is not constant. The force increases as the spring is compressed more and more. Experiments by Robert Hooke several hundred years ago indicated the force is directly proportional to the amount the spring is compressed. This relationship is known as Hooke's Law. The proportionality constant for Hooke's Law depends on the stiffness of the spring and is called the force constant (k). A stiff spring is not easily stretched or compressed and will have a larger force constant than a spring that can be easily stretched or compressed.

In Exhibit 8 the spring is compressed a certain distance, x, from its free length. The force required is given by the equation

$$F = kx \qquad (10)$$

where

F = force (lbs, N)
k = force constant (lbs/ft, N/m)
x = distance compressed (ft, m)

In Exhibit 8 the distance, x, is zero when the spring is at its free length; therefore, the force is also zero. When the spring is compressed a certain distance, x, the force is

$$F = kx \qquad (10)$$

The average force would be calculated as follows:

$$F_{avg} = (0 + kx)/2$$

or

$$F_{avg} = \tfrac{1}{2}kx$$

The work equation is

$$W = Fd \qquad (1)$$

Therefore, the work done to compress the spring is

$$W = F_{avg}x$$

or

$$W = (\tfrac{1}{2}kx)(x)$$

or

$$W = \tfrac{1}{2}kx^2 \qquad (11)$$

where

W = work (ft-lbs, N-m)
k = force constant (lb/ft, N/m)
x = distance compressed/stretched (ft, m)

In Exhibit 9 the force is plotted on the vertical axis, and the distance the spring is compressed is plotted on the horizontal axis. The further the spring is compressed, the greater the force required. The graph formed is a straight line. If you drop a perpendicular line from the maximum force, a triangle is formed with the x-axis. The base of the triangle is the distance the spring is compressed. The height of the triangle is

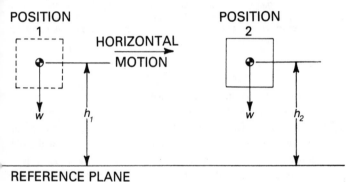

Exhibit 6 *Gravitational potential energy (PE_h) depends only on the vertical height (h) above the reference level, not on any change in horizontal position.*

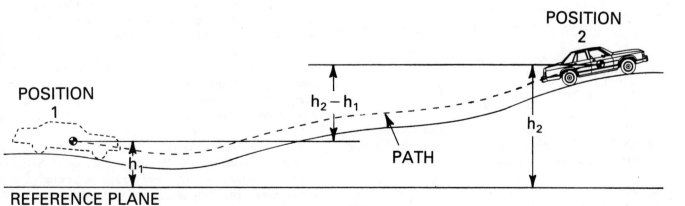

Exhibit 7 *The change in gravitational potential energy (PE_h) depends only on the difference between the initial height (h_1) and the final height (h_2), not on the path taken.*

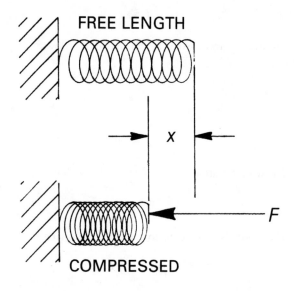

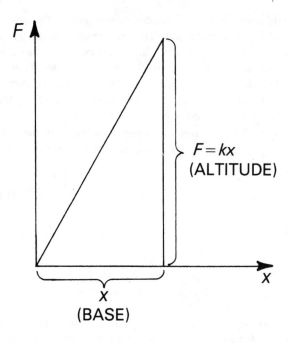

Exhibit 8 Hooke's law states that the force (F) required to compress or stretch a spring is directly proportional to the distance (x) the spring is compressed or stretched.

the force. The slope of the plotted line is the force constant. The area of the triangle is the work done to compress the spring. The area of a triangle is calculated as follows:

$$Area = \tfrac{1}{2}(base)(height)$$

or

$$Area = \tfrac{1}{2}(x)(kx)$$

The work is therefore equal to the area:

$$Area = W = \tfrac{1}{2}kx^2 \qquad (11)$$

where

$W =$ work (ft-lbs, N-m)
$k =$ force constant (lb/ft, N/m)
$x =$ distance compressed/stretched (ft, m)

This, of course, is also equal to the amount of elastic potential energy possessed by the spring:

$$PE_k = \tfrac{1}{2}kx^2 \qquad (12)$$

Suppose, for example, a spring with a force constant of 10,000 lbs/ft is compressed 2 ft from its free length. The elastic potential energy is given by

$$PE_k = \tfrac{1}{2}kx^2 \qquad (12)$$
$$PE_k = \tfrac{1}{2}(10,000)(2)^2$$
$$PE_k = 20,000 \text{ ft-lbs}$$

Exhibit 9 Plotting the force (F) required to compress or stretch a spring against the distance (x) the spring is compressed or stretched forms a straight line from which a triangle can be constructed with an altitude equal to the force (F) and a base equal to the distance (x).

In summary, the equation for elastic potential energy applies equally to a spring that is stretched and to one that is compressed. The elastic potential energy is equal to one-half the product of the force constant times the *square* of the distance compressed/stretched from its free length. Therefore, if the distance is doubled, the energy increases by a factor of 4.

3. CONSERVATION OF ENERGY

One of the most useful aspects of energy is that it is a conserved quantity. This means that the *total amount* of energy remains the same, but may be in *differing forms*. When work is done, energy is converted from one form into another. The *law of conservation of energy* states that when work is done and energy is converted from one form into another, no energy is created and no energy is destroyed. The total amount remains constant.

The law of conservation of energy can be used to develop an energy balance equation. First, a small section of the universe is chosen as the part, called the *system*, in which special interest exists. This system is considered to be an isolated system in which nothing can cross its boundary. Within this isolated system, the total amount of energy remains the same, but may change form.

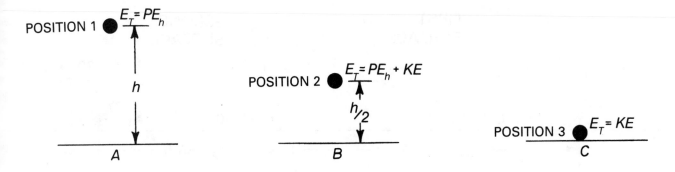

Exhibit 10 *At position 1 the ball is stationary above the earth and possesses only gravitational potential energy (PE$_h$). If the ball is dropped, it is accelerated due to gravity. When it reaches a point half-way between its initial position (h) and the earth, some of the original gravitational potential energy (PE$_h$) is now kinetic energy (KE) due to the velocity of the ball. Just as the ball reaches the earth, all the original gravitational potential energy (PE$_h$) possessed by the ball is now in the form of kinetic energy (KE).*

Assume that the system consists of a ball and the earth as shown in Exhibit 10A. The ball is stationary several feet above the surface of the earth at position 1. This means the total initial energy possessed by the ball is in the form of gravitational potential energy. If the ball is allowed to fall, some of the gravitational potential energy is transformed into kinetic energy. At a point half way between the ball's initial height and the earth, shown as position 2 in Exhibit 10B, half the gravitational potential energy has been converted into kinetic energy. Finally, as the ball first reaches the earth, all the gravitational potential energy is now in the form of kinetic energy, shown as position 3 in Exhibit 10C.

An energy balance equation can be written for this situation:

$$E_T = E_1 + E_2 + E_3 + E_4 \qquad (13)$$

where

E_T = total initial energy of the ball
E_1 = kinetic energy of the ball
E_2 = gravitational potential energy of the ball
E_3 = elastic potential energy of the ball
E_4 = thermal energy of the ball

As an example, let the initial height be equal to 30 ft and the weight of the ball be equal to 2 lbs. The energy possessed initially by the ball is in the form of gravitational potential energy. The kinetic energy is zero because the ball has no velocity, the elastic potential energy is zero because the ball is neither stretched nor compressed, and the thermal energy is assumed to be zero. This can be written in the following equation form:

$$E_T = E_1 + E_2 + E_3 + E_4 \qquad (13)$$
$$E_T = 0 + wh + 0 + 0$$
$$E_T = (2)(30)$$
$$E_T = 60 \text{ ft-lbs}$$

After the ball has fallen to the second position (Exhibit 10B), the ball possesses gravitational potential energy and kinetic energy. The velocity of the ball at the second position is found as follows:

$$v_2 = \sqrt{v_1^2 + 2ad} \ (d = h/2 \text{ and } a = g)$$
$$v_2 = \sqrt{0^2 + (2)(32.2)(15)}$$
$$v_2 = 31.1 \text{ ft/sec}$$

Therefore:

$$E_T = E_1 + E_2 + E_3 + E_4 \qquad (13)$$
$$E_T = wv_2^2/2g + wh_2 + 0 + 0$$
$$E_T = (2)(31.1)^2/(2)(32.2) + (2)(15)$$
$$E_T = 60 \text{ ft-lbs}$$

Just as the ball reaches the ground (Exhibit 10C), all the gravitational potential energy is transformed into kinetic energy. The final velocity of the ball is calculated as follows:

$$v_e = \sqrt{v_1^2 + 2ad} \ (d = h \text{ and } a = g)$$
$$v_e = \sqrt{(0)^2 + (2)(32.2)(30)}$$
$$v_e = 44 \text{ ft/sec}$$

Therefore:

$$E_T = E_1 + E_2 + E_3 + E_4 \qquad (13)$$
$$E_T = wv_e^2/2g + 0 + 0 + 0$$
$$E_T = (2)(44)^2/(2)(32.2)$$
$$E_T = 60 \text{ ft-lbs}$$

This same principle can be applied to a system consisting of a vehicle and road. Assume the vehicle was traveling at some initial velocity on a level road. The energy was initially in the form of kinetic energy. Now assume the driver applied the brakes and slowed to a new velocity by skidding. Some of the initial kinetic energy was dissipated (transformed) into thermal energy because of the frictional force between the

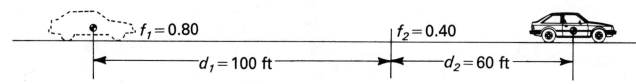

FIRST
SURFACE

SECOND
SURFACE

$v = 30$ FPS

$f_1 = 0.80$ $f_2 = 0.40$

$d_1 = 100$ ft $d_2 = 60$ ft

Exhibit 11 *The law of conservation of energy can be used to find the initial kinetic energy (KE) possessed by a vehicle that slides across two different surfaces and is still moving at the end of the second surface.*

vehicle's tires and the road surface. The vehicle still had some kinetic energy left at the end of the skidding because it still had motion. An energy balance equation for this situation would be

$$E_T = E_1 + E_2 \qquad (13)$$

where

> E_T = total initial energy (kinetic energy)
> E_1 = amount of energy dissipated while skidding (thermal energy), and
> E_2 = amount of energy remaining after skidding (kinetic energy)

Suppose the vehicle weighs 3,000 lbs, was initially traveling at 40 ft/sec, skidded 30 ft with a drag factor of 0.50, and its velocity after skidding was 25 ft/sec. Use these values in the energy balance equation:

$$E_T = E_1 + E_2 \qquad (13)$$
$$E_T = wv_1^2/2g \qquad (4)$$
$$E_T = wv_s^2/2g + wfd \qquad (4 \& 5)$$

Therefore:

$$wv_1^2/2g = wv_e^2/2g + wfd \qquad (4 \& 5)$$

$$(3,000)(40^2)/(2)(32.2) = (3,000)(25^2)/(2)(32.2) + (3,000)(0.50)(30)$$
$$74,500 \text{ ft-lbs} = 29,500 \text{ ft-lbs} + 45,000 \text{ ft-lbs}$$

Clearly, then:

$$E_T = 74,500 \text{ ft-lbs} = 74,500 \text{ ft-lbs}$$

A more universal energy balance equation can be written:

$$E_T = E_1 + E_2 + E_3 + \ldots E_i \qquad (13)$$

where

> E_T = total initial kinetic energy
> E_1 = first amount of energy dissipated
> E_2 = second amount of energy dissipated
> E_3 = third amount of energy dissipated
> E_i = ith (last) amount of energy dissipated or the amount of initial energy left unchanged

Suppose that the vehicle in Exhibit 11 weighs 4,000 lbs and skidded with a drag factor of 0.80 for 100 ft on one surface, then continued to slide an additional 60 ft on the second surface that produced a drag factor of 0.40. At the end of the 60 ft on the second surface, the vehicle's brakes were released and it was still going 30 ft/sec. The total amount of energy possessed by the vehicle can be found by using the energy balance equation:

$$E_T = E_1 + E_2 + E_3 \qquad (13)$$

where

> E_T = initial energy possessed by the vehicle
> E_1 = the amount of energy dissipated while sliding on the first surface
> E_2 = the amount of energy dissipated while skidding on the second surface
> E_3 = the amount of initial energy not yet dissipated

The proper equations are now substituted into the energy balance equation with their appropriate values:

$$E_1 = wf_1d_1 + wf_2d_2 + wv_e^2/2g \qquad (4 \& 5)$$
$$E_T = (4,000)(0.80)(100) + (4,000)(0.40)(60) + (4,000)(30^2)/(2)(32.2)$$
$$E_T = 320,000 + 96,000 + 55,900$$
$$E_T = 471,900 \text{ ft-lbs}$$

This represents the initial amount of energy the vehicle possessed when it first began to slide. Because this energy was in the form of kinetic energy, the velocity of the vehicle can be found as follows:

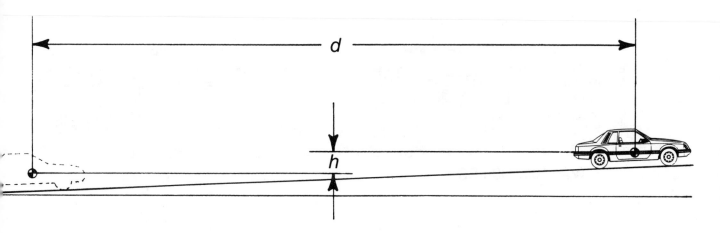

Exhibit 12 *The law of conservation of energy can be used to calculate the initial kinetic energy (KE) possessed by a vehicle that slides to a stop on a surface with a grade.*

$$v = \sqrt{2gE/w} \qquad (7)$$
$$v = \sqrt{(2)(32.2)(471,900)/(4000)}$$
$$v = 87 \text{ ft/sec}$$

Consider the vehicle in Exhibit 12. If you know that the vehicle weighs 3,500 lbs and skidded to a stop in 100 ft up a 4 percent grade, then you can find the vehicle's initial kinetic energy. This is done by taking into account the amount of kinetic energy transformed into thermal energy by skidding and the amount transformed into gravitational potential energy due to the change in height. Suppose the drag factor for this surface, if level, is 0.60. The amount of energy dissipated by the vehicle due to skidding can be found by the following equation:

$$W = E_1 = wfd \qquad (5)$$
$$E_1 = (3,500)(0.60)(100)$$
$$E_1 = 210,000 \text{ ft-lbs}$$

A vehicle traveling 100 ft up a 4 percent grade will rise approximately 4 ft. The gravitational potential energy gained by the vehicle due to this height change can be found by this equation:

$$PE_h = E_2 = wh \qquad (8)$$
$$E_2 = (3,500)(4)$$
$$E_2 = 14,000 \text{ ft-lbs}$$

An energy balance equation can be written to determine the amount of kinetic energy the vehicle initially possessed:

$$KE = E_T = E_1 + E_2 \qquad (13)$$
$$E_T = (210,000) + (14,000)$$
$$E_T = 224,000 \text{ ft-lbs}$$

The velocity of the vehicle when it first began to slide can be found by the equation

$$v = \sqrt{2gE_T/w} \qquad (7)$$
$$v = \sqrt{(2)(32.2)(224,000)/(3500)}$$
$$v = 64.2 \text{ ft/sec}$$

If the vehicle was sliding down the grade instead of up, the initial energy would be the sum of the initial kinetic energy and gravitational potential energy. If the vehicle still stopped in 100 ft, the energy dissipated would have to equal the sum of the initial kinetic energy and gravitational potential energy:

$$KE_i + PE_h = E_1$$

or

$$KE_i = E_1 - PE_h$$
$$KE_i = (210,000) - (14,000)$$
$$KE_i = 196,000 \text{ ft-lbs}$$

The velocity of the vehicle when it first began to slide would be calculated as follows:

$$v = \sqrt{2gE_T/w} \qquad (7)$$
$$v = \sqrt{(2)(32.2)(196,000)/(3500)}$$
$$v = 60 \text{ ft/sec}$$

The above illustrates that a vehicle will require less initial velocity (kinetic energy) to slide down a grade than to slide the same distance up the grade.

It is sometimes difficult to account for all the different ways energy is dissipated. For instance, suppose there are two railroad box cars, each weighing 100,000 lbs and on the same track as shown in Exhibit 13A. One box car is stationary and the other is traveling at 10 ft/sec toward the stationary one. The two collide and couple together with no apparent damage (Exhibit 13B). The equation for momentum (Topic 868) can be used to find their after-collision velocity.

A

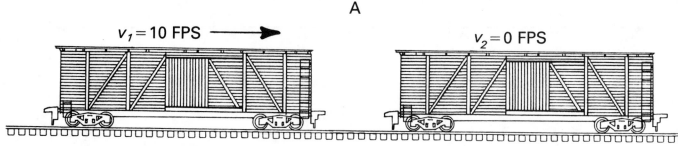

$v_1 = 10$ FPS

$v_2 = 0$ FPS

$w_1 = 100,000$ LBS

$w_2 = 100,000$ LBS

B

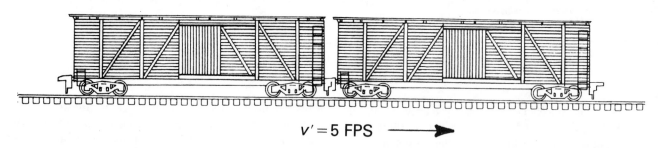

$v' = 5$ FPS

Exhibit 13 *Two railroad boxcars colliding demonstrates that energy may be dissipated in many subtle ways, making it difficult to account for all of the initial energy.*

$$v_1' = v_1 w_1 / (w_1 + w_2)$$
$$v_1' = (10)(100,000)/(100,000) + 100,000)$$
$$v_1' = 5 \text{ ft/sec}$$

Using the kinetic energy equation, the energy before and after can now be calculated:

Before $E_B = w_1 v_1^2 / 2g$ (4)
$$E_B = (100,000)(10)^2/(2)(32.2)$$
$$E_B = 155,300 \text{ ft-lbs}$$
After $E_A = (w_1 + w_2)(v^2)/2g$
$$E_A = (100,000 + 100,000)(5^2)/(2)(32.2)$$
$$E_A = 77,650 \text{ ft-lbs}$$

The energy does not seem to balance, because some of the initial energy was dissipated in subtle ways – due to vibration, the heat from friction between the two coupling devices, etc. These and other subtle ways energy might be dissipated may make it difficult to account for all the energy in an energy balance equation.

4. SPEED ESTIMATES FROM VEHICLE DAMAGE

Energy is dissipated in ways other than by sliding. In a previous example, the vehicle was still traveling at 30 ft/sec when the brakes were released. If the vehicle had struck a solid (non-deforming) immovable barrier at this point and come to a rest, the remaining 55,900 ft-bs of energy would have to be dissipated. The result of the energy dissipation would be damage to the vehicle. It can be assumed that negligible damage to the barrier also resulted. The quantity of energy used to do damage to a vehicle must be determined in order to obtain a speed estimate based on that damage.

Permanent damage (plastic deformation) remains after the force of the collision is removed. The crush measurements taken on a damaged vehicle show the resulting static damage to the vehicle. In a collision, the vehicle will have slightly more damage. This damage is generally referred to as *dynamic collapse*. In a collision the vehicle, like all bodies, has some *restitution* – that is, it tries to go back to its original shape. In nearly all severe collisions, the effect of restitution is insignificant. In very low-velocity impacts, however, restitution may have to be considered.

The definition of work indicates that the amount of energy dissipated is related to the force and the distance through which the force acts. The distance can be determined by making crush measurements. Then, if information is known about the amount of force required to produce the damage, the quantity of energy dissipated can be estimated. This quantity of force is related to the *dynamic force deflection characteristics*, or crush resistance (stiffness), of the vehicle structure being crushed.

The dynamic force-deflection characteristics of a vehicle are determined by tests, primarily barrier impact tests. In a barrier impact test, all the energy is assumed to be used in doing damage to the vehicle. The velocity at which the vehicle strikes the barrier indicates the amount of kinetic energy (crush energy) available to damage the vehicle. The assumed relationship between a barrier test vehicle and a similar-accident vehicle is that an equal quantity of energy must be used to damage the latter the same as the barrier test vehicle. The barrier impact speeds are known as the *equivalent barrier speed (EBS)* or *barrier equivalent velocity (BEV)*. Once the *EBS* for the accident vehicle has been determined, the amount of energy dissipated in doing damage can be found. This energy, along with energy dissipated in other ways, can be used in an energy balance equation as described by the law of conservation of energy to determine the vehicle's initial velocity.

For example, suppose a 2,500 lb vehicle (1) skids with a drag factor of 0.65 for 80 ft, then strikes a parked vehicle (2) weighing 3,000 lbs in the front. Barrier impact tests run at 55 ft/sec using the same type of vehicle as the striking vehicle (1) and tests run at 40 ft/sec using the same type of vehicle as the struck vehicle (2) resulted in similar damage patterns as existed on the two respective accident vehicles. After impact, the two vehicles remained locked together and slid as a unit for 60 ft, with a drag factor of 0.50. In this two-vehicle system, the striking vehicle has all the initial energy. Determining the amount of energy initially possessed by the striking vehicle is done by calculating the amount of work done in sliding and doing damage.

Energy (work) dissipated (transformed) by vehicle 1 while skidding, before impact:

$$E_1 = wfd \qquad (5)$$
$$E_1 = (2,500)(0.65)(80)$$
$$E_1 = 130,000 \text{ ft-lbs}$$

Energy (work) dissipated in doing damage to vehicle 1:

$$E_2 = w_1 v_1^2/2g \qquad (4)$$
$$E_2 = (2500)(55^2)/(2)(32.2)$$
$$E_2 = 117,400 \text{ ft-lbs}$$

Energy (work) dissipated in doing damage to vehicle 2:

$$E_3 = w_2 v_2^2/2g \qquad (4)$$
$$E_3 = (3,000)(40^2)/(2)(32.2)$$
$$E_3 = 74,500 \text{ ft-lbs}$$

Energy (work) dissipated by vehicles 1 and 2 while sliding after impact:

$$E_4 = (w_1 + w_2)f'd' \qquad (5)$$
$$E_4 = (2,500 + 3,000)(0.50)(60)$$
$$E_4 = 165,000 \text{ ft-lbs}$$

Total amount of energy possessed by the striking vehicle (1) when it first began to skid:

$$E_T = E_1 + E_2 + E_3 + E_4 \qquad (13)$$
$$E_T = 130,000 + 117,400 + 74,500 + 165,000$$
$$E_T = 486,900 \text{ ft-lbs}$$

This amount of energy can be used to determine the velocity of the striking vehicle when it first began to skid:

$$v = \sqrt{2gE_T/w_1} \qquad (7)$$
$$v = \sqrt{(2)(32.2)(486,900)/(2500)}$$
$$v = 112 \text{ ft/sec}$$

From the above example, it is obvious that the key to this method of estimating speed is assigning an appropriate *EBS* value for the amount of energy required for damage. One method to estimate the EBS in an accident, though impractical in all but a few accidents, is to conduct as many crash tests as necessary until the actual accident scenario is reproduced. Another way is to compare the accident damage to crash tests that have already been performed. But because the number of different damage profile configurations is virtually infinite, it is desirable to have a general mathematical model. This model would relate energy to damage (crush) for as many damage profile configurations as possible[1].

Historical Background

Early tests by Emori[2] were undertaken to examine the dynamics of automobile collisions. The results of this study indicated that the deceleration force on an automobile in a head-on collision was directly proportional to the deformation. Emori further concluded that the front ends of the 1956 vehicles used in the study behaved like linear plastic springs-- in other words, like springs that dissipate energy rather than storing it. Exhibit 14A shows a vehicle traveling at some velocity with a linear plastic spring at its free length attached to the front. As the vehicle makes contact with the barrier as shown in Exhibit 14B, the spring begins to compress, dissipating energy, and the vehicle begins to slow. Finally, Exhibit 14C shows the vehicle stopped and the spring compressed. The kinetic energy originally possessed by the vehicle due to its motion was dissipated by compressing the spring.

The elastic potential energy of a compressed spring can be determined from the following equation developed earlier in this Topic:

$$PE_k = \tfrac{1}{2} kx^2 \qquad (12)$$

BARRIER

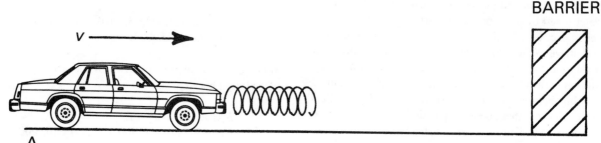

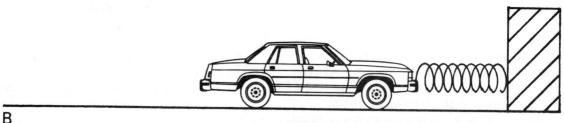

Exhibit 14A *Vehicles behave like linear plastic springs when they are crushed, dissipating energy. This is modeled by a spring at its free length attached to the vehicle.*

Exhibit 14B *The vehicle makes contact with a barrier and the spring begins to compress, dissipating kinetic energy (KE) and slowing the vehicle.*

Exhibit 14C *The vehicle stops when all the kinetic energy (KE) it originally possessed has been dissipated by compressing the spring.*

This equation also applies to a linear plastic spring, i.e., one that does not return to its original shape. For example, if the vehicle in Exhibit 14 was going 30 ft/sec initially and weighed 3,000 lbs, it would initially possess approximately 41,900 ft-lbs of kinetic energy. To bring the vehicle to a stop, the spring would have to deform enough to dissipate this amount of kinetic energy. In equation form this is written:

$$\tfrac{1}{2}\,mv^2 = \tfrac{1}{2}kx^2 \qquad (3 \& 12)$$

The actual amount of deformation would depend on the spring's stiffness.

The linear plastic spring analogy can therefore be used to estimate the amount of energy dissipated by damage if the permanent deformation to the vehicle and the vehicle's stiffness are known. Using this analogy, Emori indicated that permanent deformation of a vehicle involved in a frontal impact with a barrier is directly proportional to the impact velocity. He arrived at an equation to show this:

$$C = 0.9v \text{ or } v = 1.1C \qquad (14)$$

where

$C = $ maximum permanent crush (in.)
$v = $ impact velocity (mi/hr)

Mason and Whitcomb[3] performed a study in 1972 from which they established approximate equations for estimating impact speeds for various accident vehicles and conditions. The study verified the conclusion reached originally by Emori, i.e., the linear relationship between impact velocity and crush:

$$C = a + bv \qquad (15)$$

where

$C = $ crush (in.)
$a = $ constant
$b = $ constant
$v = $ impact speed (mi/hr)

Campbell[4], in 1974, reported that vehicle damage and the dynamic force deflection characteristics (stiffness) of the vehicle structure could be used to estimate the energy absorbed in permanent (plastic) deformation of a vehicle. He further stated that the force deflection characteristics of the vehicle structure could be estimated from frontal barrier impact tests by plotting permanent crush against the impact speed. This confirmed the linear relationships found in the two earlier studies. Exhibit 15 shows a typical plot of barrier tests.

The results of the tests were expressed by the linear equation

$$V = b_0 + b_1 C \qquad (16)$$

where

$V = $ impact speed (mph)
$C = $ permanent crush (in.)
$b_0 = $ intercept (mi/hr)
$b_1 = $ slope (mi/hr/in.)

Slope b_1 in Exhibit 16 (the change in impact speed to the change in crush) was chosen to represent the test data as accurately as possible. The intercept, b_0, is the maximum impact speed at which no permanent damage occurs.

Campbell concluded that the equation could be refined to consider the force per unit width as a function of the crush. McHenry[5] used this in the CRASH (Calspan Reconstruction of Accident Speeds on the Highway) computer program to estimate impact speeds. The equation took the form

$$F/W = A + BC \qquad (17)$$

where

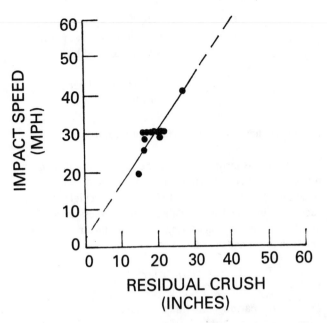

Exhibit 15 *A typical plot of speed vs. residual crush for several barrier tests results in a straight line graph.*

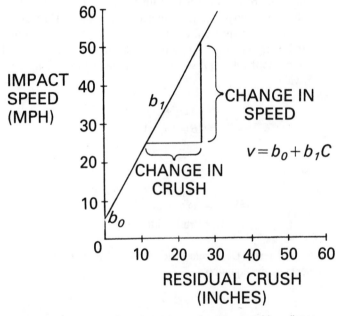

Exhibit 16 *The graph of barrier tests can be expressed by a linear equation: $v = b_0 + bC$.*

$F/W = $ The force per inch of damage width required to produce the resulting crush deformation (lb/in.)

$A = $ The maximum force per inch of damage width which will not cause permanent damage (lb/in.)

B = The linear spring stiffness (crush resistance) per inch of damage width (lb/in.²)

C = The measured permanent crush depth (in.)

Exhibit 17 shows this equation in graphical form.

The A and B terms are called the *stiffness coefficients* and reflect the force defection characteristics of the vehicle structure. The front, rear and sides of the vehicle structure each have unique A and B values. The stiffness coefficients are determined by considering the initial linear relationship between crush and speed:

$$v = b_0 + b_1 C \qquad (16)$$

This can be rearranged to find the value of b_1:

$$b_1 = (v - b_0)/C \qquad (18)$$

The value of b_o is the maximum barrier impact speed that will produce no permanent damage to the vehicle. The values for the impact speed, v, and the crush, C, are obtained from barrier impact tests. Campbell used this to write equations to determine the A and B stiffness coefficients from the b_o and b_1 values:

$$A = wb_0b_1/gW$$
$$B = wb_1/gW \qquad (20)$$

where

w = vehicle weight (lbs)
g = 32.2 ft/sec²
W = crush width (in.)

A third term, G, is related to the A and B stiffness coefficients by the equation

$$G = A^2/2B \qquad (21)$$

The G term can be thought of as the energy dissipated without permanent damage. The relationship between A, B, F/W and C was shown graphically in Exhibit 17. Exhibit 18 shows the same relationship now with G added.[7] Exhibit 19[6] contains some generally applicable A, B, and G values for front, side and rear impacts.

Further refinement to the equation was suggested by Campbell. He concluded that the energy dissipated by permanent damage could be estimated by considering the volume of the damage. McHenry used this in the CRASH computer program and modeled the vehicle's energy-dis-

sipating characteristics by surrounding it with linear springs (Exhibit 20).

In Exhibit 20, the springs extend beyond the vehicle's surface. This is to account for energy dissipated without permanent damage. The distance the spring extends out beyond the vehicle's surface can be found by considering Exhibit 21, which is derived from Exhibit 18. Here the C is the "crush" associated with the dissipated energy – crush that does not result in permanent damage. A is the preload force per inch of damage width and B is the slope of the line, which is determined from

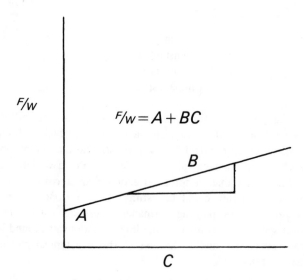

Exhibit 17 *The linear equation from the graph of barrier tests can be refined to consider the force per unit of width of crush resistance and stiffness constants: $F/W = A + BC$.*

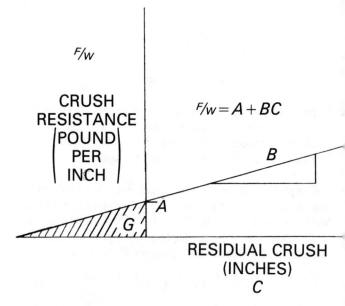

Exhibit 18 *The G term can be thought of as the energy dissipated without permanent damage resulting, and can be shown graphically as the area to the left of the original graph.*

STIFFNESS CATEGORY	1	2	3	4	5(6)	7	8	9	10	11
VEHICLE** MODELS	Pinto (FRONT) Accord Honda CVCC Prelude Corolla Chevette Fiesta Bobcat Datsun 210 Datsun 310 Arrow Champ Colt Porsche 924 Mazda GLC Fiat 124 Spider Fiat X/19 Datsun 280ZX Opel MG Midget Tri. Spitfire VW Rabbit VW Sirocco	Pinto (REAR) Chev. Monza Celica ST Celica GT Corona Spirit Pacer Gremlin VW Dasher Vega Skyhawk Omni Sunbird Starfire Mustang (74-) Horizon Fiat 128 Sedan Capri 280ZX 2 + 2 Challenger BMW 320i Audi Fox Mazda Cosmo Mazda RX-7 Renault LeCar Saab 900 Saab 99 Subaru	Celica Supra Mustang (-73) AMC Concord Malibu (78-) Monarch Zephyr Fairmont Granada Firebird Cressida Datsun 810 Monte Carlo (78-) Grand Prix (78-) Cutlass (78-) LeMans (78-) Regal Aspen Peugot 604L BMW 528i Volvo (all) Audi 5000	Chevelle (-76) Monte Carlo (-77) Grand Prix (-77) Cutlass (-77) LeMans (-77) Phoenix Chev V-8 (-77) LaSabre (77-) Volare Monaco (77-) Magnum Century LeBaron Riviera (77-) Marquis (77-) LTD (77-) Cordoba Nova Eldorado (79-) Delta 88 (77-) Diplomat T-Bird (77-) Seville Ventura Cougar	LeSabre (-76) Chev. V-8 (-76) Monaco (-76) Riviera (-76) Marquis (-76) LTD (-76) Eldorado (-78) Delta 88 (-76) T-Bird (-76) Olds 98 St. Regis Newport Brghm. DeVille Electra Fleetwood Continental Checker Cab	VANS*** Econo. E150 Dodge B-200 Chev G-20 Ford P-500 GMC G-35 GMC G-1500 VW Vanagon OTHER*** Datsun P/U Honcho 4 × 4 P/U Wagoneer Scout II Chev. Blazer	PICKUPS*** Courier El Camino Ford 1450 Chev Luv Ford F250 Dodge D-100 Ranchero F10 Ford F100 ½ Ton GC 1500 Toyota SR5 lg. bd.	FRONT DRIVE**** Citation Phoenix Skylark Omega Reliant Aries Escort Lynx	MOVABLE BARRIER	IMMOVABLE BARRIER
FRONT A	302 lb/ip	259	317	356	325	383	480	373	–	–
B	47 lb/in²	43	56	34	37	126	50	38	–	–
G	967 lb	778	901	1874	1429	580	2315	1849	–	–
REAR A	366	391	410	357	297	300	346	**	–	–
B	38	41	44	13	70	55	25	**	–	–
G	1755	1874	1931	4986	628	818	2373	**	–	–
SIDE A	77	140	173	143	177	**	**	**	–	–
B	37	67	57	50	47	**	**	**	–	–
G	81	148	263	203	331	**	**	**	–	–

* For test modes or vehicle models not listed, use a structurally similar category or choose a category by wheelbase dimension.

** Includes all model years unless otherwise specified.

*** Front and rear crash modes only; for side damage, pick a category (1-6) by wheelbase.

**** Front crash mode only; for side and rear, pick a category (1-6) by wheelbase.

Exhibit 19 Vehicles possessing similar stiffness characteristics can be grouped with general applicable A, B, and G values for front, side, and rear impacts.

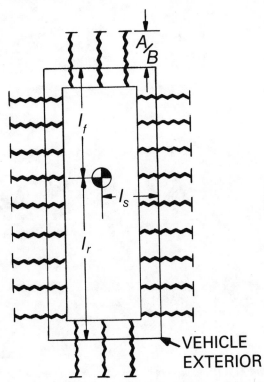

Exhibit 20 The energy-dissipating characteristics of a vehicle can be modeled by surrounding it with linear springs. The springs extend beyond the vehicle's surface to account for energy dissipated without permanent damage resulting.

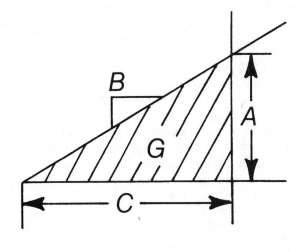

Exhibit 21 The distance the springs should extend out beyond the vehicle's surface is found by considering the energy associated with no permanent damage. This is represented by the area G on the graph.

$$B = A/C \qquad (22)$$

This is solved for C:

$$C = A/B \qquad (23)$$

Therefore, the spring should extend a distance A/B out from the surface of the vehicle to account for energy dissipated without permanent damage.

The front of the vehicle is l_f forward of the center of mass and the rear of the vehicle is l_r rearward. The sides of the vehicle are l_s left or right of the center of mass (Exhibit 20). The linear spring is ($l_f + (A/B)$ front) forward of the center of mass, ($l_r + (A/B)$ rear) rearward of the center of mass, and ($l_{s+} (A/B)$ side) to either side of the center of mass. The amount of energy dissipated is found by how much the spring is deflected. The amount of deflection is determined from damage profile measurements (Exhibit 22A-D). The damage profile indicates the depth of crush to the vehicle by C measurements. The total spring deflection is therefore $C + A/B$.

The amount of energy dissipated by a spring in the model is given by the equation

$$E = \tfrac{1}{2} kx^2 \qquad (12)$$

where

$E =$ energy
$k =$ spring force constant
$x =$ deflection

This equation can be refined to include the A, B and C value:

$$E = B/2 \, (C + A/B)^2$$

Rearranged, the equation is

$$E = A^2/2B + AC + C^2B/2 \qquad (24)$$

This equation can be further refined by considering the width (W) and volume of damage as suggested by Campbell. When this is done the equation becomes

$$E = (A^2/2B)W + ACW + (BC^2/2)W$$

or

$$E = (A^2/2B)W + (A + BC/2)WC \qquad (25)$$

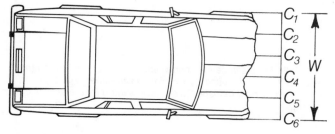

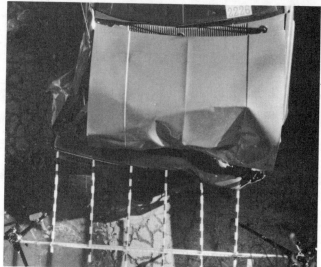

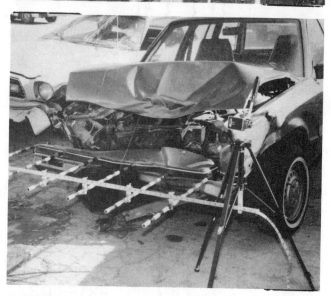

Exhibit 22 A-D *The amount of deflection is determined from damage profile measurements made in specific ways.*

The term $C/2$ represents the distance the centroid (center) of the crush region is from the vehicle's surface. This distance is given the symbol $\bar{x}$. The area of the crush region is WC. The term $A^2/2B$ is G. These values can be substituted into the following equation:

$$E = GW + (A + B\bar{x})\ \text{Area} \qquad (26)$$

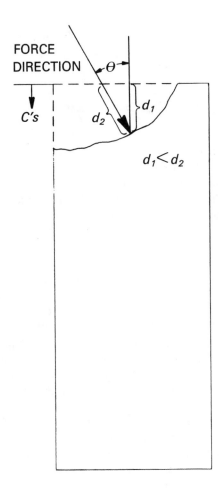

FORCE DIRECTION

$C's$

Exhibit 23 An additional factor must be included if the force of the collision is at an angle to the vehicle's surface $(1 + \tan^2\theta)$.

where

$E =$ energy dissipated (in.-lbs)
$G = A^2/2B$ (lbs)
$W =$ width of crush region (in.)
$A =$ the maximum force per inch of damage width which will not cause permanent damage (lb/in.)
$B =$ the spring stiffness per inch of damage width (lb/in.²)
Area $=$ Area of crush (in.²)
$\bar{x} =$ the distance the centroid (center) of the damage area area is from the exterior surface of the vehicle (in.)

The crush of the vehicle is measured perpendicular to the vehicle's surface. If the direction of the force which caused the damage is not perpendicular to the vehicle's surface, an additional factor must be included. In Exhibit 23 the force is at an angle to the vehicle's surface. The force therefore acts through a greater distance. The angle between a line perpendicular to the vehicle's surface and the force is θ. From trigonometry:

$$d_2 = d_1\cos\theta$$
$$\text{or}$$
$$d_1/d_2 = 1/\cos\theta \qquad (27)$$

This increase in distance is part of the spring deflection, which is used in the energy equation; therefore it must be squared:

$$1/\cos^2\theta$$

From trigonometric identities:

$$1/\cos^2\theta = 1 + \tan^2\theta \qquad (30)$$

This factor has a significant influence on the energy calculations[8]. It is recommended that this factor not exceed 2.0 ($\theta = 45°$). This factor can now be placed into the equation:

$$E = [GW + (A + B\bar{x})\ \text{Area}](1 + \tan^2\theta) \qquad (31)$$

The variables, $\bar{x}$ and Area, depend on the number of crush (C) measurements taken (Exhibit 22A-D and Topic 820). This, in turn, changes the equation for calculating the energy dissipated. The equations for two, four and six crush measurements are shown in Exhibit 24–equations 32, 33 and 34, respectively.

For example, suppose the following information in known:

$A = 235$ lb/in.	$C_3 = 30$ in.
$B = 58.8$ lb/in.2	$C_4 = 25$ in.
$W = 60.8$ in.	$C_5 = 12$ in.
$C_1 = 41$ in.	$C_6 = 4$ in.
$C_2 = 37$ in.	$\theta = 0°$

First the value for G must be found:

$$G = A^2/2B \qquad (21)$$
$$G = (235)^2/(2)(58.8)$$
$$G = 470\ \text{lbs}$$

This and the other values can now be used in equation 34 to find the energy dissipated in doing damage.

$$E = W/5[5G + A/2(C_1 + 2C_2 + 2C_3 + 2C_4 + 2C_5 + C_6) + B/6(C_1^2 + 2C_2^2 + 2C_3^2 + 2C_4^2 + 2C_5^2 + C_6^2 + C_1C_2 + C_2C_3 + C_3C_4 + C_4C_5 + C_5C_6)]\ (1 + \tan^2\theta) \qquad (34)$$

$$E = W\left[G + \frac{A}{2}(C_1 + C_2) + \frac{B}{6}(C_1^2 + C_2^2 + C_1 C_2)\right](1 + TAN^2\theta) \qquad (32)$$

$$E = \frac{W}{6}\left[6G + A(C_1 + 2C_2 + 2C_3 + C_4) + \frac{B}{3}(C_1^2 + 2C_2^2 + 2C_3^2 + C_4^2 + C_1 C_2 + C_2 C_3 + C_3 C_4)\right](1 + TAN^2\theta) \qquad (33)$$

$$E = \frac{W}{5}\left[5G + \frac{A}{2}(C_1 + 2C_2 + 2C_3 + 2C_4 + 2C_5 + C_6) + \frac{B}{6}(C_1^2 + 2C_2^2 + 2C_3^2 + 2C_4^2 + 2C_5^2 + C_6^2 + C_1 C_2 + C_2 C_3 + C_3 C_4 + C_4 C_5 + C_5 C_6)\right](1 + TAN^2\theta) \qquad (34)$$

Exhibit 24 A-C *The equation used for determining the amount of energy dissipated by damage depends on the number of "C" measurements made.*

$$E = (60.8)/(5)\{ (5)(470) + (235)/(2)[41 + (2)(37) + (2)(30)$$
$$+ (2)(25) + (2)(12) + 4] + (58.8/6)[(41)^2 + (2)(37)^2$$
$$+ (2)(30)^2 + (2)(25)^2 + (2)(12)^2 + (4)^2 + (41)(37)$$
$$+ (37)(30) + (30)(25) + (25)(12) + (12)(4)]\}\{1 + 0\}$$

$$E = (12.2)[(2350) + (117.5)(253) + (9.8)]$$

$$E = 1,766,046 \text{ in-lbs or } 147,170 \text{ ft-lbs}$$

Campbell equated this energy to the kinetic energy a vehicle would have to possess in a barrier impact test. He called this velocity the *equivalent barrier speed (EBS)*.

In the previous example, if the vehicle weighed 3,000 lbs, the *EBS* would have to be calculated as follows:

$$EBS = v = \sqrt{2gE/w} \qquad (7)$$

$$v = \sqrt{(2)(32.2)(147,200)/(3000)}$$

$$v = 56 \text{ ft/sec or } 38 \text{ mi/hr}$$

Limitations of the Model

Certain limitations exist in this, as in *all* models. The most obvious limitation exists with the crush stiffness coefficients.

The A and B stiffness coefficients are established from barrier tests of many vehicles. The vehicles are grouped into categories based on similar vehicle characteristics. If the accident vehicle was not one of the vehicles tested, then it must be assigned to a group, and that group's A and B stiffness coefficients must be used. This may or may not be appropriate.

A different uniform stiffness is assumed for the entire front and rear widths and the entire lengths of the sides.

Frame or unibody structure involvement is an important factor in front and rear collisions. If one or both of the frame rails or the unibody structure is involved, the stiffness coefficients may be correct. However, if only fender sheet metal is involved, the stiffness values may be too high. This is also true with the sides. There are "hard" spots at the wheel areas and "soft" spots between the wheels in the passenger area.

This model does not make allowances for vertical variations in crush. In underride or override damage conditions, the damage is not uniform vertically (Exhibit 25). Averaging the vertical crush wrongly assumes that the stiffness was uniform from top to bottom. The frame and frame-type structures provide the major stiffness to the vehicle. It is likely to be more accurate to weight the crush measurement in favor of the deformation in the frame or unibody structure area.

Damage in general is difficult to measure. The difficulty arises with shifting body parts, bowing of the vehicle, deep and shallow damage areas, mushrooming, and many other difficult-to-assess irregularities like those shown in Exhibit 26 A-D. Measuring protocols have been suggested for properly measuring difficult or irregular damage profiles.[10]

The stiffness characteristics of the vehicle may change somewhat as the speed and crush increase. As the larger, stronger components dissipate as much energy as possible, weaker components also begin to dissipate energy. This results in a stiff vehicle changing into a softer one. The reverse could occur also. As components "bottom out," they stiffen, making the overall vehicle structure stiffer at that point.[11]

In some areas of the U.S. during winter, salt is used to help melt ice and snow on the roads. This tends to accelerate rusting, which weakens the vehicle structure. In the cases where the stronger support structures are *severely* rusted, the available stiffness coefficients may not apply.

The empirical database limits what type of accident this model can be used on. Therefore, stiffness coefficient analysis is inappropriate for investigating certain types of accidents. The rollover type of accident shown in Exhibit 27A is not suited for this model, nor is a sideswipe accident like the one shown in Exhibit 27B. No data exists on stiffness coefficients for large trucks. Therefore, truck accidents like the one shown in Exhibit 27C should not be analyzed using this model. Motorcycles have been crash-tested, but these tests are not the same as non-deformable barrier tests. Motorcycles damaged like the one shown in Exhibit 27D can be analyzed as described in Topic 874, but not using the model described here. If a vehicle is disintegrated like the one in Exhibit 27E, the components have completely failed and this model should not be used. Clearly, you should not use the model's empirical data to analyze any collision that diverges from that data.

Exhibit 25 *The damage is not uniform vertically in an underride/override collision.*

Exhibit 26 A-D *Shifting body parts, bowing of vehicle, deep and shallow areas, mushrooming, and other irregular damage make measurements difficult.*

Exhibit 27 A-E Speed estimates based on damage cannot be done using the method developed here for (A) rollover damage, (B) sideswipe damage, (C) large-truck damage, (D) motorcycle damage, and (E) vehicle disintegrating damage.

5. SUMMARY

Many traffic accident reconstruction cases require estimating the speed of the vehicle(s) involved. The speed estimate issue can be answered in several ways. In recent years, more and more attention has focussed on using the damage received by the vehicle(s) to estimate speed.

This involves determining the amount of energy required to do the damage. A general model must be used to estimate the crush energy. This model uses the force deflection characteristic (stiffness) of the vehicle and the permanent deformation (damage) to the vehicle to estimate the energy dissipated. Once the amount of energy dissipated doing damage is known, it is used in an energy balance equation to estimate the initial velocity of the vehicle.

The use of this model is limited to the empirical data upon which the model is based. Estimating speed from damage is only one tool to be used with other tools for reconstructing a traffic accident. As in the use of any tool, it should be used only in accident cases where the model adequately represents the manner in which damage occurred to the vehicle.

6. SOURCES

Author

Gary W. Cooper is senior consultant and lecturer at The Traffic Institute's Accident Investigation Division, and has an A.A.S. degree in Mechanical Engineering Technology. Before joining the Institute in 1984, he was with the Indiana State Police.

References

Superscript numbers in the preceding pages refer to the following publications:
1. Strother, D., R. Wooley, M. James, and C. Warner, "Crush Energy in Accident Reconstruction," SAE 860371, 1986.
2. Emori, R.I., "Analytical Approach to Automobile Collisions," SAE 680016, 1968.
3. Mason, R., and D. Whitcomb, "The Estimation of Accident Impact Speed," Cornell Aeronautical Laboratory Inc., Report No. YB = 3109 = v = 1, 1972.
4. Campbell, K., "Energy Basis for Collision Severity," SAE 740565, 1974.
5. McHenry, R.R., "Mathematical Reconstruction of Highway Accidents," DOT HS 801 = 405; Calspan Document No. ZQ = 5341 = v = 2, Washington, DC, 1975.
6. Noga, T., and T. Oppenheim, "Crash 3 User's Guide and Technical Manual," U.S. Dept. of Transportation, 1981.
7. Hargens, R., and T. Day, "Vehicle Crush Stiffness Coefficients for Model Year 1970 = 1984 with Damage Profile Supplement," Engineering Dynamics Corporation, Lake Oswego, OR, 1987.
8. Day, T.D., *EDCRASH* Training Manual, Engineering Dynamics Corporation, Lake Oswego, OR 1986.
9. Monk, M., and D. Guenther, "Update of CRASH 2 Computer Model Damage Tables, Vol. I," Vehicle Research and Test Center, National Highway Traffic Safety Administration, East Liberty, OH, 1983.
10. Tumbas, N., and R. Smith, "Measuring Protocol for Quantifying Vehicle Damage from an Energy Basis Point of View," SAE 880072, 1988.
11. Navin, F., M. Macnabb, and N. Navin, "CRASH III and Canadian Test Data," SAE 870499, 1987.

Exhibits

The following are the sources of the exhibits used in this topic:
Campbell, K., Society of Automotive Engineers
  Diagram: 15
Cooper, G.W., Northwestern University Traffic Institute
  Diagrams: 1-14
  Photos: 24, 25, 26A, 26C, 27A-C, 27E
Fricke, L.B., Northwestern University Traffic Institute
  Photo: 26B
Hargens, R., and T. Day, Engineering Dynamics Corporation
  Diagrams: 16-18
Noga, T., and T. Oppenheim, U.S. Department of Transportation
  Table: 19
Smith, J., Kansas Department of Transportation
  Photo: 26D
Unknown
  Photo: 27D

STEERING OVERCORRECTION IN TRAFFIC ACCIDENT RECONSTRUCTION

Topic 872 of the *Traffic Accident Investigation Manual*

by
Gary W. Cooper
and
Lynn B. Fricke

NORTHWESTERN UNIVERSITY TRAFFIC INSTITUTE

STEERING OVERCORRECTION IN
TRAFFIC ACCIDENT RECONSTRUCTION

1. INTRODUCTION

The intent of this topic is to give you a basic understanding of the dynamics of a vehicle in a steering overcorrection maneuver as they relate to traffic accident reconstruction. Our discussion will focus on estimating the vehicle's velocity in such a maneuver.

All of the driving, braking, and cornering forces a vehicle is subjected to must be generated through the four tire contact patches and the road (tire-road interface). The forces acting on the tires have an important effect on the vehicle's cornering. Understanding these forces will allow us to discuss the forces generated during cornering as they apply to the whole vehicle.

The information about the forces a vehicle is subjected to during cornering is used to develop equations for estimating the vehicle's velocity. Estimating the velocity of a vehicle can take two forms. The first is a simplification of the principles used in the second, more rigorous and mathematical treatment. We will use both methods in an example and compare the results.

Empirical studies using various vehicles to estimate velocity from yawmarks are also discussed in this topic. We will use a vehicle simulation computer program to predict vehicle behavior in various maneuvers, and the last section of the topic will cover methods for estimating the distance required for a basic avoidance maneuver.

The effects of four wheel steer (4WS) are not covered in this topic. It is possible the 4WS-equipped cars may become more prevalent in the future.

2. FORCES ON A TIRE

How braking and driving forces are developed by a tire is fairly straightforward and is covered in Topic 862. The manner in which a tire develops cornering force, however, and what affects it is complicated. To address this process, we must first describe the vehicle coordinate system and standard tire terminology.

The fixed directional control coordinate system for a standard vehicle is shown in Exhibit 1[1]. This coordinate system establishes longitudinal, lateral, and vertical axes of reference for the vehicle that will be used in this topic. The x-axis is for longitudinal (lengthwise) reference, the y-axis is for lateral (crosswise) reference, and the z-axis is for vertical (up and down) reference. The vehicle's center of mass serves as the origin for the coordinate system. The distances between the center of mass to the front and rear axles are l_f and l_r, respectively, the height of the center of mass is l_z, and the distance the center of mass is from the side of the vehicle is l_y (Exhibit 2).

The standardized terminology and the tire axis system recommended by the Society of Automotive Engineers (SAE) for references made to a tire are indicated in Exhibit 3[1]. This terminology will be used in this topic to explain cornering forces.

Several of the geometric and kinematic variables, of which the motion and orientation of a tire relative to the road are a function, are shown in Exhibit 3 and are given in the following functional equation form[2,3]:

$$(F_x, F_y, F_z, M_x, M_y, M_z) = f(r_r, \Omega, \gamma, r, v) \quad (1)$$

where

$$F_x, F_y, F_z = \text{the forces in the } x, y, \text{ and } z \text{ direction, respectively}$$

$$M_x, M_y, M_z = \text{the moments about the x, y, and z axis, respectively}$$

$$r_r = \text{rolling radius of loaded tire}$$

$$\Omega = \text{angular velocity of the tire about the spin axis (Greek letter Omega)}$$

$$\gamma = \text{inclination of the center plane of the tire with respect to the z-axis (Greek letter gamma)}$$

$$r = \text{radius of the curved path of the tire}$$

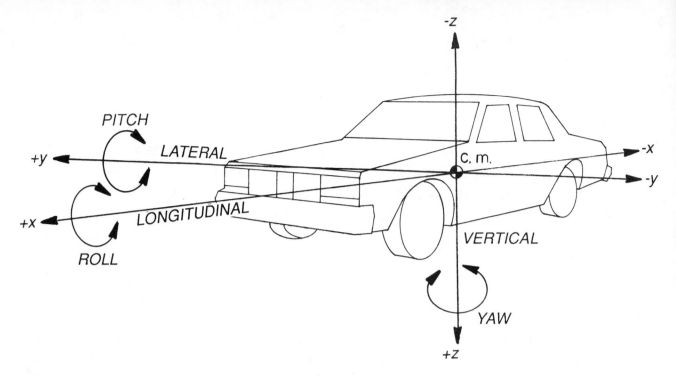

Exhibit 1. The fixed directional control coordinate system for a standard vehicle establishes longitudinal, lateral, and vertical axes of reference for the vehicle.

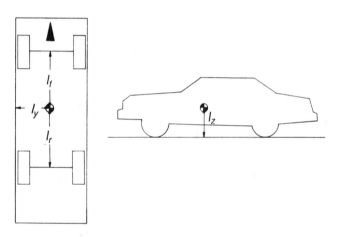

Exhibit 2. The center of mass of the vehicle serves as the origin for the vehicle coordinate system. The distance between the center of mass and the front axle is l_f, between the center of mass and the rear axle l_r, between the center of mass and the ground l_z, and between the center of mass and the side of the vehicle l_y.

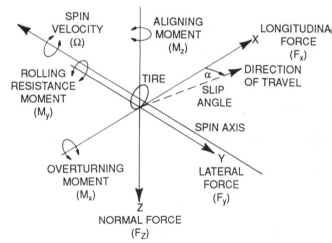

Exhibit 3. The Society of Automotive Engineers (SAE) has recommended standardized terminology and a tire axis system.

v = the velocity vector of the center of the tire contact in the x-y plane

This equation indicates that all the forces and moments the tire is subjected to are a function of (dependent upon or influenced by) the rolling radius, r_r, angular velocity, Ω, inclination angle, γ, radius of the curved path, r, and the velocity vector, v. Equation (1) can be simplified by only considering the tire traction which consists of the forces in the x and y

direction, F_x, and F_y, and the moment, M_z[2,3]. By doing this, equation (1) becomes:

$$(F_x, F_y, M_z) = f(F_z, \alpha, \gamma, r, S_x, v_x, \mu) \quad (2)$$

where

F_x, F_y = the forces in the x and y direction, respectively

M_z = the moments about the z-axis

F_z = the forces in the z direction

α = the slip angle (Greek letter alpha)

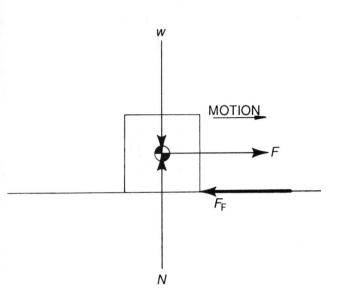

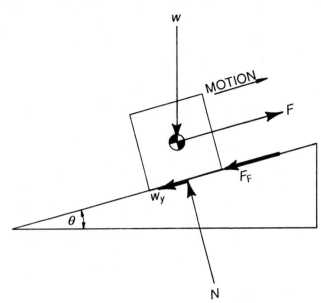

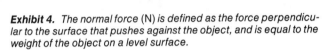

Exhibit 4. *The normal force (N) is defined as the force perpendicular to the surface that pushes against the object, and is equal to the weight of the object on a level surface.*

Exhibit 5. *The normal force is the force perpendicular to the surface, even on an incline.*

γ = the inclination of the tire center with respect to the z-axis

r = the radius of the curved path of the tire

S_x = the longitudinal slip of the tire

v_x = the longitudinal component of the velocity vector of the center of the tire contact

μ = the coefficient of friction (Greek letter mu)

Tire Cornering Force

The variables in equation (2) that influence the cornering force, F_y, the most are F_z, μ, S_x, and α[2,3,4]. The force in the z direction, F_z, is the weight on the tire. The weight or load on the tire in combination with the coefficient of friction, μ (Greek letter mu), produces the frictional force, F_F (see Topic 862). The longitudinal slip, S_x, is directly related to the driving and braking forces, F_{xd} and F_{xb}. The longitudinal slip will be shown to influence the amount of frictional force, F_F, that is available for cornering force, F_y. The slip angle, α (Greek letter alpha), is the angle between the direction the tire is traveling in and the direction in which it is pointing. A tire generates cornering force, F_y, by running at a slip angle.

If a tire is free-rolling, then all the frictional force, F_F, is available for producing cornering force, F_y. The value of the maximum frictional force, F_F, is found by the equation

$$F_F = N \mu$$

The normal force, N, is shown in Exhibit 4 for a level surface and in Exhibit 5 for an incline. The *normal* force is defined as the force perpendicular to the surface that pushes against

the tire. If the surface is level with no outside forces (Exhibit 4), the normal force is equal to the weight of the object and the equation becomes:

$$F_F = w \mu \qquad (3)$$

where

F_F = frictional force (lbs, N)

w = weight (lbs, N)

μ = coefficient of friction

If the tire is subjected to a driving force (F_{xd}) or braking force (F_{xb}), the amount of cornering force (F_y) available is reduced. In Exhibit 6, the radius of the circle surrounding the tire is a vector representing the maximum frictional force (F_F) available as determined by equation (3). The tire can be subjected to a driving force (F_{xd}), a braking force (F_{xb}), a cornering force (F_y), or a combination of cornering and braking forces (F_y and F_{xb}) or cornering and driving forces (F_y and F_{xd}). All of these forces are vector quantities, so their vector sum (Topic 856) cannot exceed the maximum frictional force (F_F) available. This can be shown by the equation[5]

$$F_F = \sqrt{F_x^2 + F_y^2} \qquad (4)$$

where

F_F = frictional force (lbs, N)

F_x = longitudinal force (lbs, N)

F_y = lateral force (lbs, N)

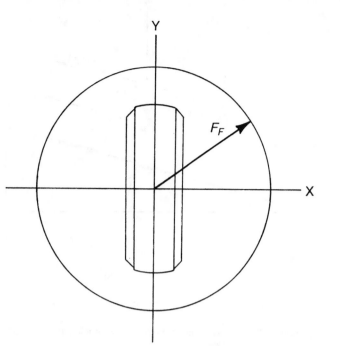

Exhibit 6. *The radius of the friction circle surrounding the tire is a vector representing the maximum frictional force (F_F) available.*

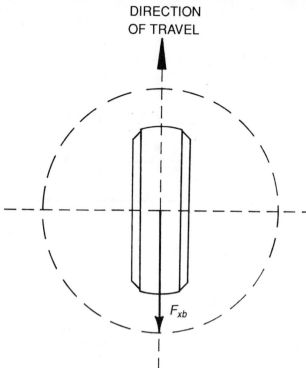

Exhibit 7. *A tire that is sliding due to braking force (F_{xb}) will use all the available frictional force (F_F) longitudinally to slow the vehicle. The vector is pointed straight down (backward).*

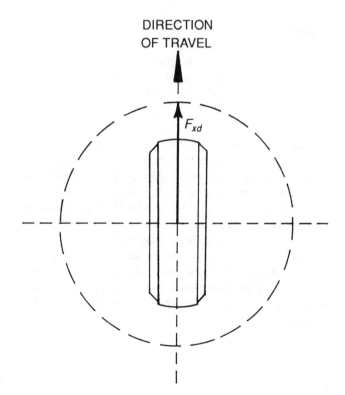

Exhibit 8. *A tire that is spinning due to driving force (F_{xd}) will use all the available frictional force longitudinally to propel the vehicle. The vector is pointed straight up (forward).*

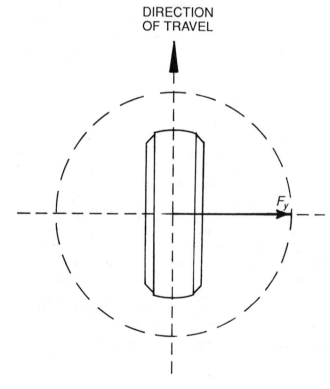

Exhibit 9. *A free-rolling tire developing maximum cornering force (F_y) will use the available frictional force laterally to steer the vehicle. The vector is pointed toward the inside of the turn, perpendicular to the tire.*

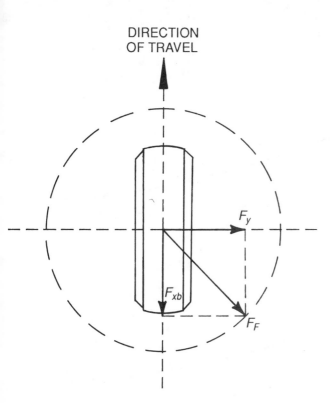

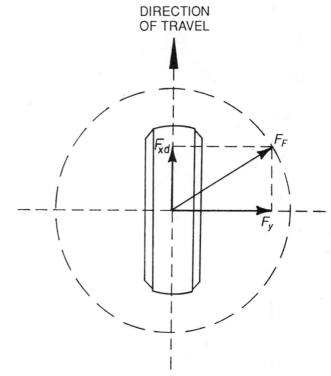

Exhibit 10. *If a tire is subjected to both a cornering force* (F_y) *and a braking force* (F_{xb}), *the vector sum of the forces cannot exceed the available frictional force* (F_F). *The values of the individual forces are lower than the maximum that would have been possible were the available friction force used purely for braking or cornering.*

Exhibit 11. *If a tire is subjected to both a cornering force* (F_y) *and a driving force* (F_{xd}), *the vector sum of the forces cannot exceed the available frictional force* (F_F). *The values of the individual forces are lower than the maximum that would have been possible were the available friction force purely for driving or cornering.*

The frictional force can be used purely in the form of braking force (F_{xb}), driving force (F_{xd}), or cornering force (F_y). Exhibit 7 shows a tire that is sliding due to a braking force. The tire in Exhibit 7 will use all the available frictional force longitudinally to slow the vehicle; therefore, the vector is pointed straight down (backward). A sliding tire can only generate resisting force in a direction opposite to the motion of the tire. Exhibit 8 shows a tire that is spinning due to a driving force; because all the frictional force is being used longitudinally to propel the vehicle, the vector is pointed straight up (forward). Exhibit 9 shows a free-rolling tire developing maximum cornering force and the vector pointing toward the inside of the turn, perpendicular to the tire.

The frictional force can also be used in combinations of cornering force and braking or driving force. In Exhibits 10 and 11, the tire is subjected to a cornering force (F_y) and a braking force (F_{xb}), and a cornering force and driving force (F_{xd}), respectively. In these two cases of a combination of two forces, the vector sum of the forces (required force) cannot exceed the available frictional force (F_F), as dictated by equations (3) and (4). Therefore, the values of the individual forces are lower than the maximum that would have been possible were the available friction force used purely for braking or driving or cornering (indicated by the length of the vector arrows). The various combinations cause the resultant, F_R, to swing around in different directions, depending on how

much of the available friction force was used for each component.

A continuous plot of the resultant maximum force vector (F_R) in a horizontal plane results in a circular figure (approximately an ellipse) that is called a *g-g diagram,* or a friction circle. This concept is based on the theory that the maximum resultant force that can be developed is equal to the available frictional force ($F_R = F_F$). This is not strictly true, because of nonlinear relationships affecting the tire forces and other related differences; the result is that generally a tire is capable of developing slightly more lateral force than longitudinal force for a given coefficient of friction. However, the friction circle still serves as an excellent way to describe conceptually the actions of forces on a tire and hence the entire vehicle[4,5,6].

The friction circle concept demonstrates why a vehicle cannot be steered after the tires begin to slide. All the available frictional force (F_F) is used for braking, leaving none for cornering. Exhibit 12 is a graph plotting braking force (F_{xb}) and cornering force (F_y) against percentage of wheel slip (amount of sliding between tire and road surface). At 100 percent wheel slip, the tire is sliding and the available cornering force goes virtually to zero. This phenomenon is one reason why antilock brakes have been designed so that the average driver can develop high braking forces while retaining the ability to steer. This is also why a vehicle tends to swing around and slide backwards if only the rear tires are

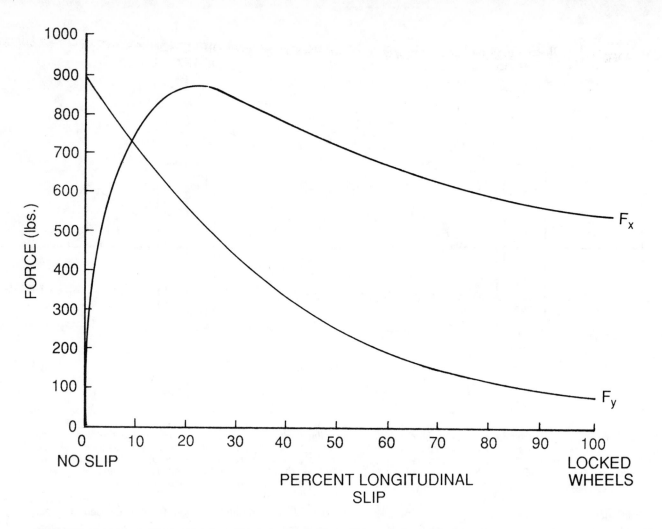

Exhibit 12. *A graph plotting braking force (*F_x*) and cornering force (*F_y*) against percent wheel slip indicates that, at 100 percent wheel slip, the available frictional force is used to slow the vehicle and the cornering force goes virtually to zero.*

sliding. The inability to have side force with 100 percent longitudinal slip is shown clearly in Exhibit 12. With the previous scenario of locked wheels on only the rear wheels, it is clear that no significant side force (F_y) can be generated at the rear tires to keep the rear from sliding sideways if a significant force is applied to the car (such as sideslope or the centrifugal force resulting from steering).

Slip Angle

The *slip angle*, $\propto$, is defined as the angle between the heading of a tire (direction the tire is pointing) and its velocity vector (direction the tire is traveling)[7]. When a tire is steered, it is turned at an angle called the *steer angle*, δ (Greek letter delta). A slip angle (α) results when the tire is turned and cornering force (F_y) is produced by deformation of the tire at its contact patch as the tire is forced to follow its direction of travel rather than its circumference[5]. The greater the slip angle, the greater the side force (up to a point). The front and rear tires will each travel at a slip angle as the vehicle is cornering, but these slip angles are seldom the same. Exhibit 13 is an overhead view of a front tire showing the steer angle (δ) and the slip angle (α).

The amount of lateral or cornering force (F_y) developed by a particular tire per degree of slip angle (α) is called the *cornering stiffness, C_α,* of the tire. Cornering stiffness can be defined as the rate of change of side force with respect to zero slip angle for a free-rolling tire at a zero inclination angle[7]. A tire with a higher cornering stiffness value can generate more cornering force for a given slip angle. The cornering stiffness varies from tire to tire, can become highly nonlinear, and is mainly a function of the tire's construction, inflation pressure, tread compound, size, and the load carried[8]. The cornering stiffness (linear range) and slip angle can be used to find the cornering force by the equation

$$F_y = C_\alpha \propto \qquad (5)$$

where

F_y = cornering force (lbs, N)
C = cornering stiffness (lbs/degree, lbs/radian, N/degree, N/radian)
α = slip angle (degrees, radian)

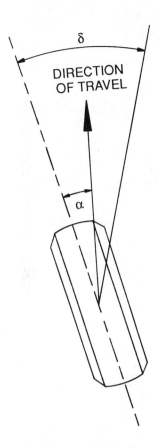

δ

DIRECTION
OF TRAVEL

α

Exhibit 13. *The slip angle (∝) is defined as the angle between the heading of a tire and the direction the tire is traveling. The steer angle (δ) is defined as the angle between the vehicle heading and tire heading.*

The amount of cornering force a tire can generate as a function of slip angle is limited. Exhibit 14 shows the relationship between slip angle (α) and side force (F_y) for a particular tire; the graph indicates that for a given load, F_z, and coefficient of friction, μ, as the slip angle increases, the cornering force also increases at a constant rate. At some point, the cornering force begins to increase at a lesser rate and will ultimately reach a point where more slip angle produces no more cornering force. This point is generally called the *critical slip angle*[5], or saturation point. The cornering force decreases somewhat as the slip angle increases beyond this point until reaching 90 degrees. A tire with a 90 degree slip angle equates to a tire with 100 percent longitudinal slip, that is, a locked tire. Typical slip angles for normal maneuvers are 3 to 5 degrees and, for turning maneuvers near peak traction, 10 to 15 degrees[9].

3. FORCES ON THE VEHICLE

According to Newton's first law of motion, a vehicle (like any other object), once set into motion, tends to keep going in a straight line unless acted upon by a force. It can be seen from this law that for a vehicle to make a turn, there must be a force on the vehicle. The force that makes a vehicle turn is a sideways force toward the center of the curve in which the

vehicle is turning. This force is called *centripetal* force (toward the center), which refers to the effect of the force produced by friction between the tires and road and, in cases where the vehicle is on a positive cross grade, the weight of the vehicle. The term *centrifugal* force (from the center) is often used to make motion in a circular path easier to understand, though technically it does not exist. Centrifugal force will be used in this topic to explain the motion of a vehicle in a turn.

Centrifugal force is considered to be the opposite force (Newton's third law of motion) to centripetal force. Centrifugal force is an inertial force tending to make the vehicle follow a straight path, and is produced by the vehicle's velocity, weight, and the radius of its curved path. The amount of centripetal force and the amount of centrifugal force can be calculated. The equation developed in Topic 890 for calculating these two forces when they are in balance is

$$F_{cent} = w \, v^2 / g \, r \qquad (6)$$

where

F_{cent} = centripetal (centrifugal) force (lbs, N)
w = weight (lbs, N)
v = velocity (ft/sec, m/sec)
g = acceleration due to gravity (32.2 ft/sec^2, 9.81 m/sec^2)
r = radius of the curved path (ft, m)

If the inertial force (with no braking) is less than the *available* frictional force between the tires and road (centrifugal < available centripetal), the vehicle will make the turn. However, if the opposite is true (centrifugal > available centripetal), the vehicle will start to sideslip and will not follow the intended curved path.

The frictional force needed to steer the vehicle through a curved path is produced by the tires as they are subjected to a slip angle. The steering mechanism of the vehicle turns the front tires in such a way as to achieve the desired slip angle, which in turn creates the required cornering force (centripetal force). Exhibit 15 shows a vehicle in a turn to the right. The center of the turn, with no slip, can be found by drawing a line perpendicular to each tire toward the center of the turn. If the vehicle is to turn with none of the tires slipping, the perpendicular lines must all intersect at one location. The common intersection is accomplished by allowing the outer front wheel to turn in a larger radius (r_2) than the inner wheel (r_1). The outer wheel turns in a larger radius than the inner wheel because the inner wheel is turned at a sharper steer angle (δ_1). The difference between the steer angle of the outer wheel (δ_2) and inner wheel (δ_1) is known as the *turning angle*[10] ($\delta_1 - \delta_2$).

The principle used by most vehicle manufacturers to accomplish the required turning angle is known as the *Acker-*

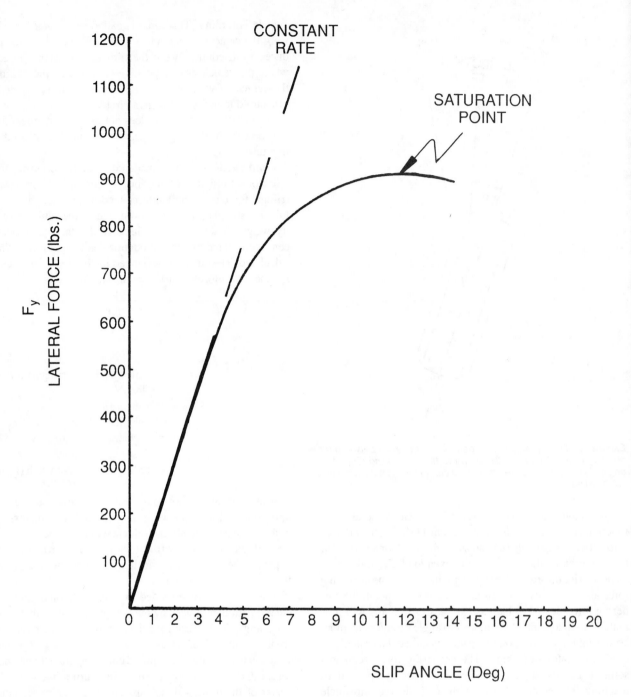

Exhibit 14. *The amount of cornering force a tire can generate as a function of slip angle is limited.*

mann principle[10]. Exhibits 16 and 17 illustrate a typical application of the Ackermann principle. In Exhibit 16 the wheels are each attached to a steering spindle assembly that is free to rotate about a spindle bolt (kingpin). Both of the steering spindle assemblies have steering arms which are connected to each other by a tie rod. The steering arms are not parallel to each other and are closer together where the tie rod connects them. When the steering wheel is turned – to the right, for example (Exhibit 17) – the tie rod is shifted to the left (unless forward of the steering spindle assembly), and the

wheels begin to turn to the right from a straight-ahead position. The angles between the two steering arms and tie rod, both initially obtuse (greater than 90 degrees), begin to change. The angle between the right steering arm and tie rod becomes more obtuse, while the angle between the left steering arm and tie rod closes to 90 degrees and then to an acute angle (less than 90 degrees). This motion results in a greater change on the right inner wheel than on the left outer wheel and thereby achieves a larger turning radius for the outer wheel. The same motion is also accomplished for a left turn.

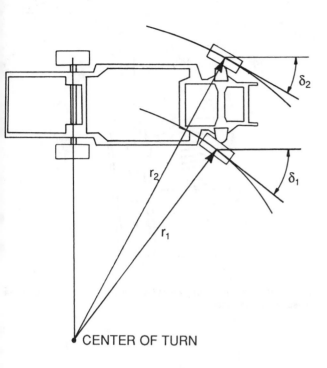

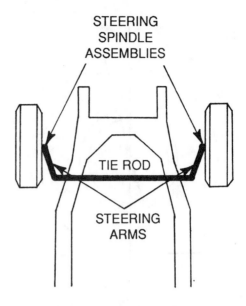

Exhibit 16. *The front wheels of a vehicle are each attached to a steering spindle assembly that is free to rotate about a spindle bolt. Both steering spindle assemblies have steering arms which are not parallel to each other and are closer together where a tie rod connects them.*

Exhibit 15. *The center of a turn, with no slip, can be found by drawing a line perpendicular to each tire toward the center of the turn.*

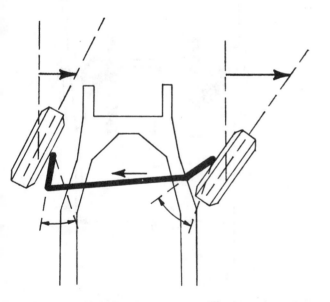

Exhibit 17. *When the steering wheel is turned, the tie rod is shifted and the wheels begin to turn from a straight-ahead position. The angles between the two steering arms and tie rod, both initially obtuse, begin to change. The angle between one steering arm and tie rod becomes more obtuse, while the angle for the other one closes to 90 degrees and then to an acute angle. This motion results in a greater change on the inner wheel than on the outer wheel and thereby achieves a larger turning radius for the outer wheel.*

The Ackermann principle achieves truly slip-free steering in only three positions, the straight-ahead position and in a specifically designed angle to the left and right. Even when the vehicle is steered at the specific left or right angle, its speed must be low to achieve nearly slip-free steering. However, the Ackermann principle is satisfactory in practical use[10].

The steering system geometry consists of several angles built into the steering and suspension system[11]. The five basic angles are as follows:

1. Caster
2. Camber
3. Spindle bolt inclination
4. Toe-in and toe-out
5. Turning angle

Caster is defined as the forward or backward tilt of the top of the spindle bolt from true vertical (Exhibit 18). *Positive caster* is the top of the spindle bolt tilted rearward (shown in Exhibit 18) and *negative caster* is the amount tilted forward. Caster helps provide directional control for a vehicle.

Camber is the inward or outward tilt of the top of the wheel from true vertical (Exhibit 19). *Positive camber* is the top of the tire tilted outward (shown in Exhibit 19) and *negative camber* is the top of the tire tilted inward. *Zero camber* is a tire at true vertical. The main purpose of camber is to provide even tire wear, although camber can produce lateral force on a tire.

Spindle bolt inclination is the tilt of the top of the spindle bolt toward the center of the vehicle (Exhibit 20). The spindle bolt inclination reduces the need for excessive camber and

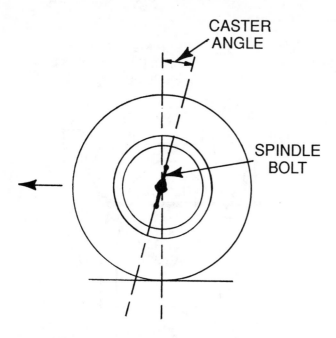

Exhibit 18. *Caster is defined as the forward or backward tilt of the top of the spindle bolt from true vertical.*

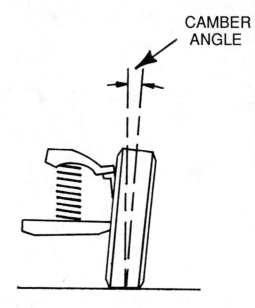

Exhibit 19. *Camber is the inward or outward tilt of the top of the wheel from true vertical.*

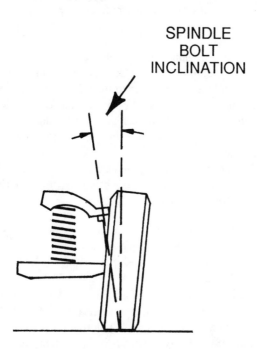

Exhibit 20. *Spindle bolt inclination is the tilt of the spindle bolt top toward the center of the vehicle.*

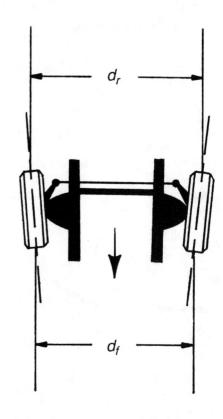

Exhibit 21. *Toe-in and toe-out are the difference between the measurement at the front of the wheels* (d$_f$) *and the rear of the wheels* (d$_r$) *at a specific height.*

caster, and tends to cause the wheel to return to a straight-ahead position after a turn.

Toe-in and *toe-out* is the difference between the measurement at the front of the wheels (d_f) and the rear of the wheels (d_r) at a specific height (Exhibit 21). Toe-in helps correct the wheels' tendency to toe-out as a result of road friction and steering system play. It is the cause of most tire wear from the steering system.

Turning angle is the difference between the steer angle of the inner wheel (δ_1) and outer wheel (δ_2) in a turn to the right or left (Exhibit 22). This angle has already been discussed, and is usually measured with the outside wheel turned 20 degrees[10].

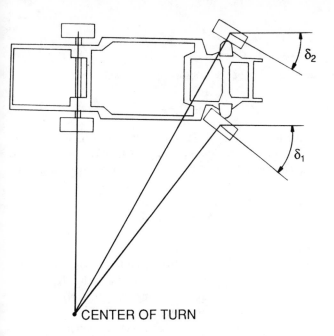

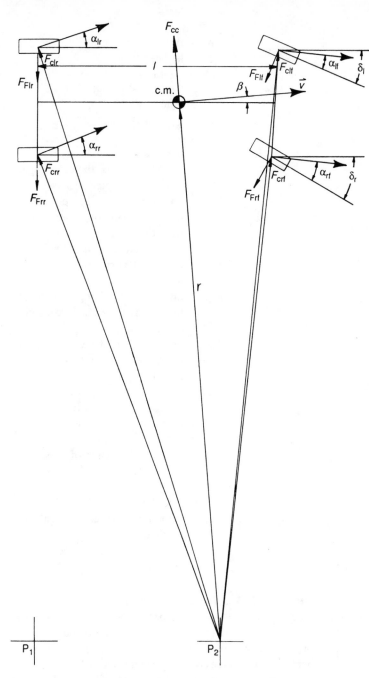

Exhibit 22. *Turning radius is the difference between the steer angle of the inner wheel (δ_1) and outer wheel (δ_2) in a turn to the right or left.*

DIRECTION
OF TRAVEL

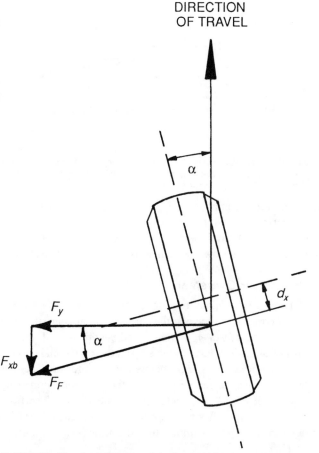

Exhibit 24. *The line of action of the force of friction acts perpendicular to the tire. The slip angle (α) of the tire causes the line of action of the cornering force (F_y) to be perpendicular to the direction of travel of the center of the tire.*

Exhibit 23. *Forces acting on the vehicle cause all the tires to slip some at virtually any velocity, which results in the actual turning center (P_2) being ahead of the theoretical turning center (P_1).*

Theoretically, a vehicle should turn in a circle whose center is the point where lines drawn perpendicular to the tires intersect, as shown in Exhibit 22. This is the actual turning center only if no tires are slipping. Forces acting on the vehicle cause all the tires to slip somewhat at virtually any velocity. The result of this slipping is that the actual turning center is ahead of the theoretical turning center. Exhibit 23 is a diagram of a vehicle turning to the right (with no braking nor driving force) and showing the forces on the vehicle and various associated angles:

$$\delta_r = \text{right steer angle}$$
$$\delta_l = \text{left steer angle}$$
$$\alpha_{rf} = \text{right front slip angle}$$
$$\alpha_{lf} = \text{left front slip angle}$$
$$\alpha_{rr} = \text{right rear slip angle}$$
$$\alpha_{lr} = \text{left rear slip angle}$$
v = direction of travel of the center of mass
F_{cc} = line of action of the centrifugal force at the center of mass
F_{crf} = line of action of the centrifugal force and cornering force, right front tire
F_{clf} = line of action of the centrifugal force and cornering force, left front tire
F_{crr} = line of action of the centrifugal force and cornering force, right rear tire
F_{clr} = line of action of the centrifugal force and cornering force, left rear tire
F_{Frf} = frictional force, right front
F_{Flf} = frictional force, left front
F_{Frr} = frictional force, right rear
F_{Flr} = frictional force, left rear
r = radius of the center of mass
l = wheelbase
$c.m.$ = center of mass
β = side slip angle
P_1 = theoretical turn center (with no slipping)
P_2 = actual turn center

Exhibits 23 and 24 indicate that the line of action of the force of friction (F_F) acts perpendicular to the tire. The slip angle ($\propto$) of the tire causes the line of action of the cornering force (F_y) to be perpendicular to the direction of travel (velocity vector v) of the center of the tire contact. The cornering force acts at the center of the deformed tread, which is behind the center of the contact patch (Exhibit 24). This distance (d_x) is called the *pneumatic trail* and causes a self-aligning moment (M_z), which tends to reduce the slip angle; the pneumatic trail is determined by the slip angle[5]. The slip angles of the tires combine to cause the vehicle in Exhibit 23 to have a side slip angle, β (Greek letter beta), which in this case (as in most) causes the vehicle to head toward the inside of the curve.

The differing lines of action between the frictional force (F_F) and cornering force (F_y) causes the available frictional force to be split into two components (see Topic 856). One component is the cornering force, F_y, and the other is a drag force, F_{xb} (Exhibit 24). If the front tire in Exhibit 24 is at its frictional limit, the value of the cornering force (F_y) is

$$F_y = F_F \cos \propto_f \qquad (7)$$

and the value of the drag force (F_{xb}) is

$$F_{xb} = F_F \sin \propto_f \qquad (8)$$

If the tire (front or rear) is at its frictional limit, the value for the force of friction, F_F, in equation (3) can be substituted into equations (7) and (8) to form two new equations:

$$F_y = w\,\mu \cos \propto \qquad (9)$$
$$F_{xb} = w\,\mu \sin \propto \qquad (10)$$

where

F_F = frictional force (lbs, N)
F_y = cornering force (lbs, N)
F_{xb} = braking force (lbs, N)
w = weight on tire (lbs, N)
μ = coefficient of friction
$\propto$ = slip angle of tire (degrees)
$\sin$ = the trigonometric function *sine*
$\cos$ = the trigonometric function *cosine*

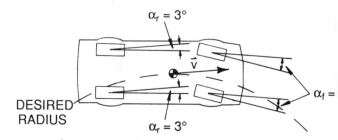

Exhibit 25. *A vehicle with understeer tendencies will require a greater slip angle at the front tires than at the rear tires ($\propto_f > \propto_r$).*

The force component, F_{xb}, is known as *cornering drag*. Cornering drag limits the amount of frictional force available to be used for developing cornering force to counteract centrifugal force; it slows the vehicle as it goes through the turn.

Understeer/Oversteer

Three terms widely used to describe the relationship between cornering force and the cornering characteristics of a vehicle are *understeer, oversteer,* and *neutral steer*. The front tires of an understeered vehicle reach their frictional cornering force limit ($F_{yf} \geq F_{Ff}$) before the rear tires do. The rear tires of an oversteered vehicle reach their frictional cornering force limit ($F_{yr} \geq F_{Fr}$) before the front tires do. The front and rear tires of a vehicle with neutral steer reach their frictional cornering force limit at the same time ($F_{yf} = F_{yr} \geq F_{Ff} = F_{Fr}$).

A vehicle's tendency toward understeer, oversteer, or neutral steer can also be described in terms of the slip angle at the front and rear tires. The tires produce the necessary force

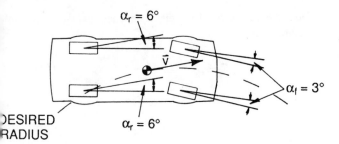

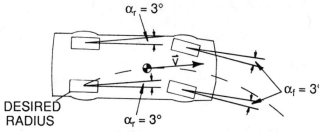

Exhibit 26. *A vehicle with oversteer tendencies will require a greater slip angle at the rear tires than at the front tires ($\alpha_r > \alpha_f$).*

Exhibit 27. *A vehicle with neutral steer has equal slip angles for front and rear tires ($\alpha_f = \alpha_r$).*

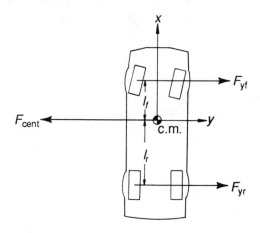

Exhibit 28. *The frictional force (F_F) developed by the tires must equal the centrifugal force (F_{cent}) for the vehicle to turn at the desired radius. The frictional force is the cornering force (F_y) that must be produced by the front tires (F_{yf}) and rear tires (F_{yr}): ($F_y = F_{yf} + F_{yr}$).*

through a slip angle (α), discussed earlier in this topic. If the front tires are at a greater slip angle than the rear tires ($\alpha_f > \alpha_r$), the vehicle assumes understeer characteristics as it goes through a curve. Exhibit 25 shows a vehicle with understeer characteristics. A vehicle that has oversteer tendencies has a greater slip angle at the rear tires than at the front tires ($\alpha_r > \alpha_f$). Exhibit 26 shows a vehicle with oversteer characteristics. A vehicle with neutral steer characteristics (Exhibit 27) has equal slip angles for the front and rear tires ($\alpha_f = \alpha_r$).

Cornering Force Front and Rear Tires

Exhibit 28 shows the forces on a vehicle that is turning to the right. If the frictional force (F_F) developed by the tires is equal to the centrifugal force (F_{cent}), the vehicle will turn at the desired radius. The frictional force is the cornering force (F_y) that must be produced by the front tires (F_{yf}) and rear tires (F_{yr}): $F_y = F_{yf} + F_{yr}$. These forces can be found by considering the location of the center of mass of the vehicle, where the centrifugal force acts. Sum the forces acting along the y-axis:

$$\vec{\rightarrow} \Sigma F_y = 0 = F_{yf} + F_{yr} - F_{cent}$$

or

$$F_{cent} = F_{yf} + F_{yr} \qquad (11)$$

where

ΣF_y = the sum of the forces along the y-axis (lbs, N)
F_{cent} = centrifugal force (lbs, N)
F_{yf} = frictional cornering force front axle (lbs, N)
F_{yr} = frictional cornering force rear axle (lbs, N)

Sum the moments about the center of mass:

$$\oplus \Sigma M_{cm} = 0 = F_{yr} l_r - F_{yf} l_f$$

or

$$F_{yf} l_f = F_{yr} l_r \qquad (12)$$

where

ΣM_{cm} = the sum of the moments about the center of mass (ft lbs, N m)
F_{yf} = frictional cornering force front axle (lbs, N)
F_{yr} = frictional cornering force rear axle (lbs, N)
l_f = the distance the center of mass is behind the front axle (ft, m)
l_r = the distance the center of mass is in front of the rear axle (ft, m)

Solve equation (12) for F_{yr}:

$$F_{yr} = F_{yf} l_f / l_r$$

Substitute the value for F_{yr} in this equation into equation (11) and solve for F_{yf}:

$$F_{yf} = (F_{cent} l_r)/(l_f + l_r)$$

Because the wheelbase (l) is equal to $l_f + l_r$, this equation becomes

$$F_{yf} = F_{cent} l_r / l \qquad (13)$$

72-15

In Topic 890, it was shown that

$$l_r/l = x_r$$

and

$$l_f/l = x_f$$

Substitute the value for l_r/l into equation (13):

$$F_{yf} = F_{cent}\, x_r \qquad (14)$$

The equation for the force at the rear axle can be found in the same manner and is

$$F_{yr} = F_{cent}\, x_f \qquad (15)$$

Newton's second law of motion, written in equation form (Topic 856), is

$$F = ma$$

This equation, rewritten in terms of centrifugal force, weight and lateral acceleration, is

$$F_{cent} = (w/g)a_y \qquad (16)$$

The equation from Topic 890 for finding the lateral acceleration (a_y) experienced by an object following a circular path is

$$a_y = v^2/r$$

where

a_y = lateral acceleration (ft/sec^2, m/sec^2)
v = velocity (ft/sec, m/sec)
r = radius of circular path (ft, m)

Substitute the above value for a_y into equation (16):

$$F_{cent} = (wv^2)/(gr)$$

Substitute this into equations (14) and (15) for F_{cent}:

$$F_{yf} = (wv^2 x_r)/(gr) \qquad (17)$$
$$F_{yr} = (wv^2 x_f)/(gr) \qquad (18)$$

Changing the Cornering Characteristics

Equations (17) and (18) calculate the cornering force at the front and rear axles. Both equations use as factors the relationship between the wheelbase and the distance of the vehicle's center of mass from the front or rear axle. These two distances are a function of the amount of weight on the front axle (w_f) and rear axle (w_r) and the total weight (w). There-

fore, the ratios of the weight on each axle to the total weight are:

$$w_f/w = x_r \qquad (19)$$

and

$$w_r/w = x_f \qquad (20)$$

An equation was developed in Topic 890 to determine the amount of weight shifted (w_{sx}) between the front and rear axles during longitudinal acceleration (a_x, negative when slowing). This equation can be written as follows:

$$w_{sx} = wa_x z/g$$

Assuming there is no lateral weight transfer due to steering, the amount of weight on each front tire during longitudinal acceleration is calculated as follows:

$$w_{xf} = (w_f - w_{sx})/2$$

or

$$w_{xf} = (w_f - wa_x z/g)/2 \qquad (21)$$

and for each rear tire:

$$w_{xr} = (w_r + wa_x z/g)/2 \qquad (22)$$

where

w_{xf} = weight on each of the front tires during longitudinal acceleration (lbs, N)
w_{xr} = weight on each of the rear tires during longitudinal acceleration (lbs, N)
w_f = static weight on the front axle (lbs, N)
w_r = static weight on the rear axle (lbs, N)
w = total weight (lbs, N)
a_x = longitudinal acceleration – negative for deceleration, positive for acceleration (ft/sec^2, m/sec^2)
z = height of center of mass (l_z) divided by the wheelbase (l)
g = acceleration due to gravity (32.2 ft/sec^2 or 9.81 m/sec^2)

Equations (21) and (22) indicate that through longitudinal acceleration, the weight on the front and rear axles can be changed; therefore, so can the vehicle's tendency toward oversteer, understeer, or neutral steer. Earlier in this topic it was shown that added load could increase the cornering force generated by a tire (up to a point). This "weight management" is one way race car drivers change the characteristics of a race car to fit the driving situation. This sounds much easier

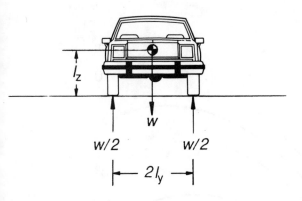

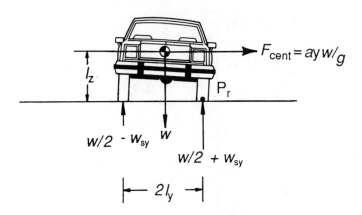

Exhibit 29. A vehicle will generally have equal weight on the left and right tires when its motion is straight ahead.

Exhibit 30. A vehicle making a turn has an inertia force acting at its center of mass. This inertia force causes the weight carried on the right outer tires to increase and the weight on the left inner tires to decrease.

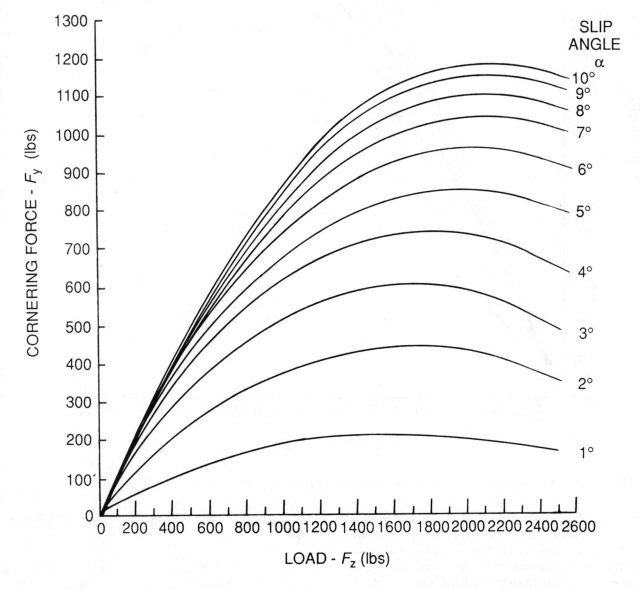

Exhibit 31. A graph that has load (F_z) plotted against cornering force (F_y) for various slip angles (α) for a specific tire indicates that cornering force increases rapidly, then declines to a lower level with an increasing load and constant slip angle.

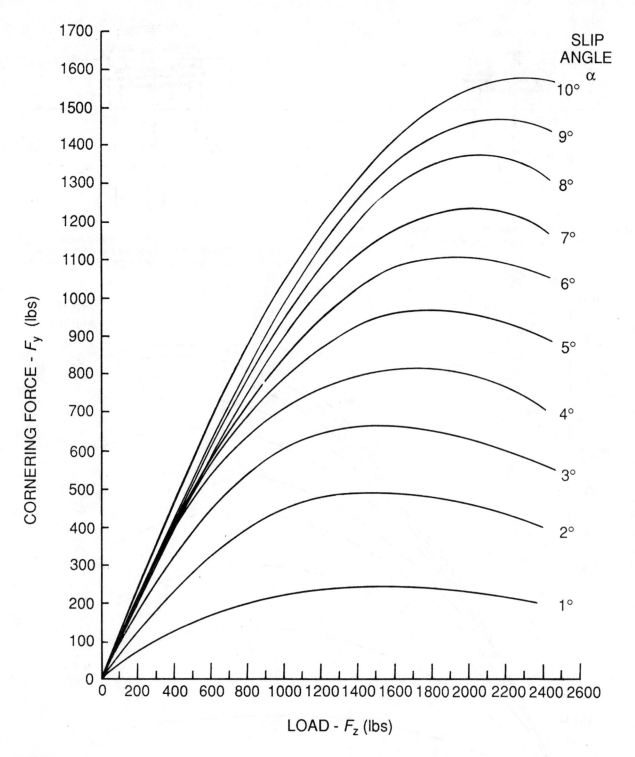

Exhibit 32. *Each tire has a unique graph of load (F$_z$) versus cornering force (F$_y$) for various slip angles ($\propto$).*

than it actually is. Remember, braking force, driving force, and too much loading diminishes the cornering force a tire can produce; therefore, the exact amount of longitudinal acceleration is difficult to achieve. With too much braking, for example, virtually all the cornering force is lost.

Equations (17) and (18) can be used with equation (5) to find the required slip angle (α) to produce the required cor-

nering force (F_y), given the cornering stiffness (C_∞) (linear range):

$$
\begin{aligned}
F_y &= C_\alpha \alpha \\
F_{yf} &= C_{\alpha f} \alpha_f \\
F_{yr} &= C_{\alpha r} \alpha_r \\
C_{\alpha f} \alpha_f &= (wv^2 x_r)/(gr)
\end{aligned}
\tag{5}
$$

$$C_{\alpha r}\alpha_r = (wv^2x_f)/(gr)$$
$$\alpha_f = (wv^2x_r)/(grC_{\alpha f}) \qquad (23)$$
$$\alpha_r = (wv^2x_f)/(grC_{\alpha r}) \qquad (24)$$

Cornering Force: Right and Left Tires

A vehicle generally has equal weight on the left and right tires when its motion is straight ahead as shown in Exhibit 29. However, if this same vehicle is making a turn to the left as shown in Exhibit 30, an inertia force acts at the vehicle's center of mass to the right. This inertia force causes the weight carried on the right outer tires (w_o) to increase and the weight on the left inner tires (w_i) to decrease.

The added weight on the outer tires causes them to produce more cornering force than the cornering force produced by the inner tires in a turn. The increase in cornering force produced by the outer tires does not completely compensate for the decrease experienced by the inner tires[8]. Exhibits 31 and 32 are graphs that have load (F_z) plotted against cornering force (F_y) for various slip angles (α) for two different tires. From the graphs in Exhibits 31 and 32, it can be seen that cornering force increases rapidly, then declines to a lower level with an increasing load and constant slip angle[5,9,12]. Therefore, as load is added to a tire, the generated cornering force for a given slip angle will also increase. The cornering force initially increases linearly with the load; however, eventually it begins to increase at a decreasing rate until finally it begins to decrease with additional load. This indicates that there is a limit to the side force a tire can produce as a function of load (F_z). Therefore, the average cornering force produced (in the non-linear range) can be somewhat less for an actual turn than if the load remained equally distributed between the right and left tires.

The effect of weight shift on the cornering characteristics of a vehicle is one reason why sports cars and race cars are built with a center of mass as close to the ground as possible, with a wide track width, and with suspensions stiffer than those of other vehicles[13]. The lower center of mass and wider track width limits the amount of weight shift. The stiffer suspension does not allow the weight shift to change the cornering characteristics of the vehicle as much.

The amount of weight shifted from one side of a vehicle to the other (w_{sy}) (ignoring the effects of suspension) can be found by summing the moments about the outside tires (P_r). From Exhibit 30:

$$\oplus\Sigma M_{Pr} = 0 = (wl_y) - (w/2 - w_{sy})2l_y - (a_ywl_z)/g$$

Solve this equation for w_{sy}:

$$w_{sy} = (wa_yl_z)/(g2l_y) \qquad (25)$$

Equation (25) can be used to find the weight on the front inside and outside tires, w_{fi} and w_{fo}, and the rear inside and outside tires, w_{ri} and w_{ro}, of a vehicle subjected to lateral

acceleration (assumed always to be positive for these equations):

$$w_{fi} = w_f/2 - (wa_yl_z)/(4gl_y) \qquad (26)$$
$$w_{fo} = w_f/2 + (wa_yl_z)/(4gl_y) \qquad (27)$$
$$w_{ri} = w_r/2 - (wa_yl_z)/(4gl_y) \qquad (28)$$
$$w_{ro} = w_r/2 + (wa_yl_z)/(4gl_y) \qquad (29)$$

where

w_{fi} = weight on front inside tire (lbs, N)
w_{fo} = weight on front outside tire (lbs, N)
w_{ri} = weight on rear inside tire (lbs, N)
w_{ro} = weight on rear outside tire (lbs, N)
w_f = weight on front axle (lbs, N)
w_r = weight on rear axle (lbs, N)
w = weight of vehicle (lbs, N)
a_y = lateral acceleration (ft/sec^2, m/sec^2)
l_z = height of the center of mass (ft, m)
l_y = lateral location of the center of mass from left or right side (ft, m)
g = 32.2 ft/sec^2, 9.81 m/sec^2

Exhibits 33 and 34 graphically demonstrate the concept of weight shift[14]. They represent two different views of the four tire contact patches (tire-road interface) of a vehicle looking up through the road surface. Exhibit 33 represents the tire contact patches of the vehicle while at rest. Exhibit 34 shows the tire contact patches of the vehicle while it is in a cornering maneuver. Notice that in Exhibit 33 the tire contact patches are approximately equal. In Exhibit 34, the outside tires are more loaded than at rest due to the lateral weight transfer. Similarly, the inside tires shown in Exhibit 34 are less loaded than at rest.

Equations (26), (27), (28) and (29), in conjunction with the tire data illustrated in Exhibits 31 and 32, can be used to estimate the cornering performance of a vehicle. The following example will be used to illustrate how this is done. Assume for this example that the following information is given:

w = 3,500 lbs = vehicle weight
l = 9 ft = wheelbase
r_h = 1 ft = distance from rear axle to ground with vehicle level
w_f = 2,100 lbs = weight on front axle with vehicle level
w_r = 1,400 lbs = weight on rear axle with vehicle level
h = 4 ft = rear axle hoisted height
w_h = 2,250 lbs = weight on front axle with rear axle hoisted
T = 6 ft = track width
r = 220 ft = radius of turn

Find: l_y, the lateral location of the center of mass.

Exhibit 33. *The four tire contact patches of a vehicle while at rest (looking up through the road surface) are approximately equal.*

The static weight is approximately equally distributed left and right; therefore, the track width can be used:

$$a.\ l_y = T/2$$
$$b.\ l_y = (6)/(2)$$
$$c.\ l_y = 3\ \text{ft}$$

Find: l_z, the height of the center of mass.

An equation was developed in Topic 890 to determine the height of the center of mass, and can be used here with the information provided:

$$a.\ l_z = \{[l\sqrt{(l^2 - h^2)}\,(w_h - w_f)]/(h)(w)\} + r_h$$
$$b.\ l_z = \{[(9)(\sqrt{9^2 - 4^2})(2{,}250 - 2{,}100)]/(4)(3{,}500)\} + (1)$$
$$c.\ l_z = 1.8\ \text{ft}$$

Find: z, the ratio of the height of center of mass to the wheelbase.

This ratio is the height of the center of mass as a decimal fraction of the wheelbase:

$$z = l_z/l$$
$$z = (1.8)/(9)$$
$$z = 0.2$$

Find: l_f, the longitudinal distance the center of mass is from the front axle.

Find: l_r, the longitudinal distance the center of mass is from the rear axle.

Exhibit 34. *The tire contact patches of a vehicle while it is in a cornering maneuver are different from when it is at rest. The outside tires are more loaded than at rest due to the lateral weight transfer, and the inside tires are less loaded.*

Two equations were developed in Topic 890 for finding the longitudinal location of the center of mass with respect to the front and rear axles:

$$l_f = w_r l/w$$
$$l_f = (1{,}400)(9)/(3{,}500)$$
$$l_f = 3.6\ \text{ft}$$

$$l_r = l - l_f$$
$$l_r = (9) - (3.6)$$
$$l_r = 5.4\ \text{ft}$$

Find: x_f, the ratio of the distance the center of mass is from the front axle to the wheelbase.
Find: x_r, the ratio of the distance the center of mass is from the rear axle to the wheelbase.

These ratios are the longitudinal distances of the center of mass from the front and rear axles expressed as a decimal fraction of the wheelbase:

$$x_f = l_f/l$$
$$x_f = (3.6)/(9)$$
$$x_f = 0.4$$

$$x_r = l_r/l$$
$$x_r = (5.4)/(9)$$
$$x_r = 0.6$$

Find: F_{cent}, the centrifugal force.

Equation (6) can be used to find the centrifugal force:

$$F_{cent} = wv^2/gr \qquad (6)$$

Assume an initial velocity of 66 ft/sec.

$$F_{cent} = (3,500)(66^2)/(32.2)(220)$$
$$F_{cent} = 2,150 \text{ lbs}$$

Find: F_{yf}, the required side force at the front axle.
Find: F_{yr}, the required side force at the rear axle.

The side forces at each axle can be found by using equations (14) and (15):

$$F_{yf} = F_{cent}x_r \qquad (14)$$
$$F_{yf} = (2,150)(0.6)$$
$$F_{yf} = 1,290 \text{ lbs}$$

$$F_{yr} = F_{cent}x_f \qquad (15)$$
$$F_{yr} = (2,150)(0.4)$$
$$F_{yr} = 860 \text{ lbs}$$

Find: a_y, the lateral acceleration.

The equation from Topic 890 can be used to find the lateral acceleration:

$$a_y = v^2/r$$
$$a_y = (66^2)/(220)$$
$$a_y = 20 \text{ ft/sec}^2$$

Find: w_{fi}, the weight on the front inside tire.
Find: w_{fo}, the weight on the front outside tire.
Find: w_{ri}, the weight on the rear inside tire.
Find: w_{ro}, the weight on the rear outside tire.

Equations (26), (27), (28) and (29) can be used to find the loading on each tire:

$$w_{fi} = w_f/2 - (wa_yl_z)/(4gl_y) \qquad (26)$$
$$w_{fi} = (2,100)/(2)$$
$$\quad - (3,500)(20)(1.8)/(4)(32.2)(3)$$
$$w_{fi} = 725 \text{ lbs}$$

$$w_{fo} = w_f/2 + (wa_yl_z)/(4gl_y) \qquad (27)$$
$$w_{fo} = (2,100)/(2)$$
$$\quad + (3,500)(20)(1.8)/(4)(32.2)(3)$$
$$w_{fo} = 1,375 \text{ lbs}$$

$$w_{ri} = w_r/2 - (wa_yl_z)/(4gl_y) \qquad (28)$$
$$w_{ri} = (1,400)/(2)$$
$$\quad - (3,500)(20)(1.8)/(4)(32.2)(3)$$
$$w_{ri} = 375 \text{ lbs}$$

$$w_{ro} = w_r/2 + (wa_yl_z)/(4gl_y) \qquad (29)$$

$$w_{ro} = (1,400)/(2)$$
$$\quad + (3,500)(20)(1.8)/(4)(32.2)(3)$$
$$w_{ro} = 1,025 \text{ lbs}$$

Find: α_f, the required slip angle for the front tires.
Find: α_r, the required slip angle for the rear tires.

Locate the load on the tire in Exhibit 31 on the x-axis and draw a line vertically until intersecting with the desired slip angle curve. From the intersection of the first line and slip angle curve, draw a horizontal line over to the y-axis and read the side force generated. Repeat this process for both of the front and rear tires until the sum of all the generated forces equals the total required side force.

1. Weight distribution:
   $w_{fi} = 725$ lbs
   $w_{fo} = 1,375$ lbs
   $w_{ri} = 375$ lbs
   $w_{ro} = 1,025$ lbs
2. Side force required:
   $F_{yf} = 1,290$ lbs
   $F_{yr} = 860$ lbs
3. Front tires, from Exhibit 31 at $\alpha = 4°$:
   $w_{fi} = 725$ lbs $F_{yfi} = 510$ lbs
   $w_{fo} = 1,375$ lbs $F_{yfo} = 710$ lbs
   Total side force: $F_{yf} = 1,220$ lbs
4. Front tires, from Exhibit 31 at $\alpha = 5°$:
   $w_{fi} = 725$ lbs $F_{yfi} = 560$ lbs
   $w_{fo} = 1,375$ lbs $F_{yfo} = 790$ lbs
   Total side force: $F_{yf} = 1,350$ lbs
5. Slip angle front tires: $\alpha_f = 4°$ to $5°$
6. Rear tires, from Exhibit 31 at $\alpha = 4°$:
   $w_{ri} = 375$ lbs $F_{yri} = 320$ lbs
   $w_{ro} = 1,025$ lbs $F_{yro} = 620$ lbs
   Total side force: $F_{yr} = 940$ lbs
7. Rear tires, from Exhibit 31 at $\alpha = 3°$:
   $w_{ri} = 375$ lbs $F_{yri} = 260$ lbs
   $w_{ro} = 1,025$ lbs $F_{yro} = 510$ lbs
   Total side force: $F_{yr} = 770$ lbs
8. Slip angle rear tires: $\alpha = 3°$ to $4°$

An iterative process of increasing the velocity and hence the lateral acceleration can be used until the tires at either the front axle (as would be the case in this example) or rear axle reach a point where they can no longer generate the required lateral force (saturation point). The tire *saturation point* is the peak of the slip angle curve at the largest slip angle in Exhibit 31. The saturation point indicates the maximum lateral acceleration that can be generated by the vehicle and is an indication of the cornering performance of the vehicle and tire combination for the given velocity and radius, provided the pavement coefficient of friction is sufficient.

The same process can be performed using Exhibit 32:

1. Weight distribution:

$w_{fi} = 725$ lbs
$w_{fo} = 1,375$ lbs
$w_{ri} = 375$ lbs
$w_{ro} = 1,025$ lbs

2. Side force required:
$F_{yf} = 1,290$ lbs
$F_{yr} = 860$ lbs

3. Front tires, from Exhibit 32 at $\alpha = 3°$:
$w_{fi} = 725$ lbs $F_{yfi} = 510$ lbs
$w_{fo} = 1,375$ lbs $F_{yfo} = 660$ lbs
Total side force: $F_{yf} = 1170$ lbs

4. Front tires, from Exhibit 32 at $\alpha = 4°$:
$w_{fi} = 725$ lbs $F_{yfi} = 610$ lbs
$w_{fo} = 1,375$ lbs $F_{yfo} = 790$ lbs
Total side force: $F_{yf} = 1,400$ lbs

5. Slip angle front tires: $\alpha_f = 3°$ to $4°$

6. Rear tires, from Exhibit 32 at $\alpha = 3°$:
$w_{ri} = 375$ lbs $F_{yri} = 300$ lbs
$w_{ro} = 1,025$ lbs $F_{yro} = 610$ lbs
Total side force: $F_{yr} = 910$ lbs

7. Rear tires, from Exhibit 32 at $\alpha = 2°$:
$w_{ri} = 375$ lbs $F_{yri} = 210$ lbs
$w_{ro} = 1,025$ lbs $F_{yro} = 440$ lbs
Total side force: $F_{yr} = 650$ lbs

8. Slip angle rear tires: $\alpha_r = 2°$ to $3°$

The tire with the characteristics shown in Exhibit 32 is able to develop the required cornering force ($F_{yf} = 1,290$ lbs and $F_{yr} = 860$) at a smaller slip angle than the tire with the characteristics shown in Exhibit 31. As with the first tire, an iterative process of increasing the velocity and hence the lateral acceleration can be used until the tires at either the front axle or rear axle reach a point where they can no longer generate the required lateral force. This is an indication of the cornering performance of the vehicle and tire combination.

Weight shift can occur not only due to lateral acceleration but also due to longitudinal acceleration. Equations (21), (22), (26), (27), (28) and (29) are combined for determining the weight on each tire of a vehicle (ignoring suspension) during simultaneous cornering and acceleration (negative or positive):

$$w_{fi} = (4w_f g l_y - 2l_y w a_x z - w a_y l_z)/(4g l_y) \quad (30)$$

$$w_{fo} = (4w_f g l_y - 2l_y w a_x z + w a_y g l_y)/(4g l_y) \quad (31)$$

$$w_{ri} = (4w_r g l_y + 2l_y w a_x z - w a_y l_z)/(4g l_y) \quad (32)$$

$$w_{ro} = (4w_r g l_y + 2l_y w a_x z + w a_y l_z)/(4g l_y) \quad (33)$$

where

w_{fi} = weight on front inside tire (lbs, N)
w_{fo} = weight on front outside tire (lbs, N)
w_{ri} = weight on rear inside tire (lbs, N)
w_{ro} = weight on rear outside tire (lbs, N)
w_f = weight on front axle (lbs, N)
w_r = weight on rear axle (lbs, N)
w = weight of vehicle (lbs, N)
a_x = longitudinal acceleration (ft/sec^2, m/sec^2)
z = height of center of mass (l_z) divided by the wheelbase (l)
a_y = lateral acceleration (ft/sec^2, m/sec^2)
l_z = height of the center of mass (ft, m)
l_y = lateral location of the center of mass (ft, m)
g = 32.2 ft/sec^2, 9.81 m/sec^2

4. BASIC ESTIMATES OF VELOCITY TO SIDESLIP

When a wheel is free-rolling straight down the road, where the tire touches the road surface (tire-road interface), there is basically no movement relative to the road surface. The velocity of the tire contact patch is zero relative to the road. The tracks on a bulldozer or military tank provide the best way to visualize this. When the track is in contact with the ground, the track does not move relative to the ground (straight motion). Conversely, the top of the track must move at twice the velocity of the vehicle relative to the ground. A tire is similar to this, only on a different scale.

A retarding force on the tire is generated by the road when braking is applied. The velocity of the tire contact patch is now no longer zero but is increasing. The tire begins to slide completely, usually leaving skidmarks, once the tire is locked by the brakes. Braking skidmarks, along with information about the surface friction, can be used for estimating a vehicle's velocity (Topic 862).

Slipping of a tire relative to the road occurs not only when braking but also when steering. With braking, the slippage occurs longitudinally because the tire is rotating slower than the angular velocity required for it to roll on the surface with no slippage. The slippage that occurs during steering is lateral and, for most steering inputs, imperceptible. However, during extreme cornering maneuvers at higher velocities, the tires may exceed friction limits and slip excessively, causing the vehicle to go into a yaw and begin to leave tire marks. For this situation, the required force at the tires exceeds the available force. Refer to Exhibit 9, which shows the friction circle. Actually, the friction circle is more of an ellipse than a circle. That is, many vehicles show a higher lateral limit than longitudinal limit. The marks left by a vehicle in a yaw (Topic 817) can be used to estimate the velocity of the vehicle similarly to the way braking skidmarks are used.

A *yaw* friction mark (Exhibit 35) on the road surface is a sign that the tire was sideslipping and, therefore, exceeded its frictional limit. The yawmark also shows the curved path taken by the vehicle. The velocity at which a vehicle will begin to sideslip on a given surface and along the radius indicated by the yawmark can be calculated if certain data are known.

Exhibit 35. *A yaw friction mark on the road surface is a sign that the tire was sideslipping and, therefore, had reached its frictional limit.*

Data Needed

To make the necessary calculations, the following items of information are needed:

1. Confirmation that the marks observed on the road were indeed yawmarks.
2. The grade in the direction of slippage.
3. The coefficient of friction of the road surface.
4. The radius of the curve followed by the vehicle.

A *yawmark* is a scuffmark made on a surface by a rotating tire which is slipping more or less parallel to its axis. Yawmarks have characteristics that distinguish them from other tire marks, and are discussed in Topic 817. Sometimes yawmarks are called critical speed scuffmarks, centrifugal skidmarks, or sideslip marks.

The *grade* in the direction of slippage is the combination of any cross-grade (superelevation) and grade (slope) that is present. The percent grade is measured parallel to the direction the vehicle is slipping. Grade is positive (+) if the surface rises in the direction of slippage and negative (−) if it falls in that direction. Methods for measuring grade are explained in Topic 832.

Coefficient of friction can be thought of as the ratio of the force resisting motion between two objects in contact, to the force pushing them together, called the normal force. The normal force is perpendicular to the surface and has the symbol *N*. Coefficient of friction and how it is measured are discussed in Topic 862.

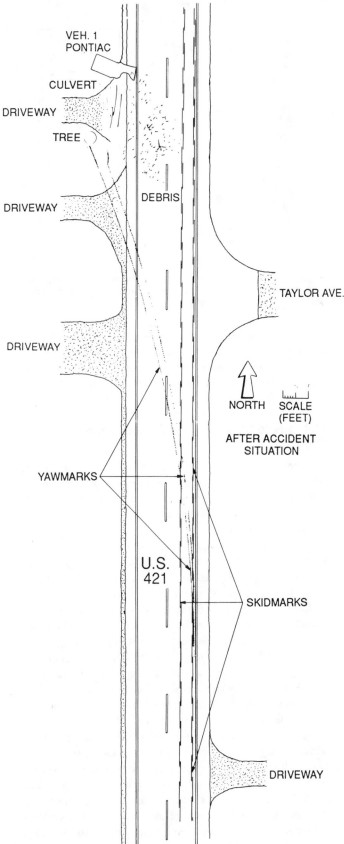

Exhibit 36. *Draw a diagram of the location to a scale of 1 in. = 10 ft or larger with the observed yawmarks plotted as accurately as possible from available measurements.*

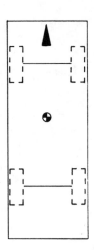

Exhibit 37. *A diagram of the vehicle can be made on tracing paper showing wheel positions and center of mass to use for establishing the vehicle's path on the diagram.*

The *radius of the curved path* taken by the center of mass of the vehicle must be determined. The required radius is determined from measurements of the yawmarks left by the vehicle which can be made at the scene or from a diagram of the accident scene.

Methods to Determine the Radius of the Curved Path

There are essentially two methods for determining the radius taken by the vehicle's center of mass. The first method requires drawing a scale diagram from which measurements are made. The second method involves making the measurements at the site of the accident.

For the first method, draw a diagram of the location to a scale of 1 in = 10 ft or larger, with the observed yawmarks plotted as accurately as possible from available measurements (Topic 828) as shown in Exhibit 36.

To the same scale as the diagram, make a pattern of the wheelbase and track width of the vehicle. This can be either a diagram of the vehicle on tracing paper, showing wheel positions and center of mass (Exhibit 37); or a rectangular template cutout of a card, with its length corresponding to the wheelbase, its width corresponding to the track width of the vehicle, and a small hole through the card at the location of the vehicle's center of mass (Exhibit 38).

Place wheel locations of the vehicle pattern on the corresponding tire marks on the diagram or on another, similar diagram with only the yawmarks drawn in (Exhibit 39) at a succession of positions along the marks. At each position, mark the location of the center of mass of the vehicle on the diagram (Exhibit 39). Connect these center-of-mass points with a smooth curve representing the path of the vehicle's center of mass (Exhibit 39).

The radius of the curved path of the center of mass drawn on the diagram can be determined by measuring a chord and middle ordinate as described in Topic 832. These measure-

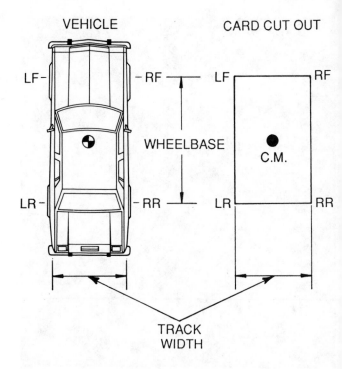

Exhibit 38. *To establish the vehicle's path, you can cut a rectangular template out of a card, with its length corresponding to the wheelbase, its width corresponding to the track width of the vehicle, and a small hole through the card at the location of the vehicle's center of mass.*

ments are shown in Exhibit 39. The radius is found by substituting the values for the chord and middle ordinate into the following equation:

$$r = l^2/(8h) + h/2 \qquad (34)$$

where

r = radius (ft, m)
l = chord (ft, m)
h = middle ordinate (ft, m)

You can also find the radius by referring to the nomograph shown in Exhibit 40 (both U.S. and metric units). The use of the nomograph is discussed in Topic 832.

The second method requires using surveying equipment or a simple device called a vehicle jig to make the required measurements at the accident scene. (The method using surveying equipment can be found in surveying texts[15] and will not be discussed in this topic.)

Using the vehicle jig to obtain the required measurements is much the same as the first method described above, only to actual scale. The vehicle jig can be made in a variety of ways, and is used to duplicate the wheelbase and track width of the vehicle that left the yawmarks. Exhibit 41 shows a vehicle jig made from plastic water pipe available at most hardware stores. Some of the pipe sections are smaller in diameter so as to slip easily into the larger ones. This allows you to adjust the jig for both track width and wheelbase. Tee-

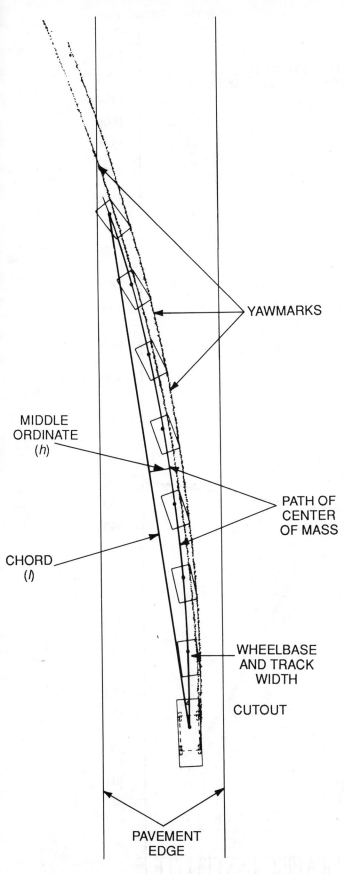

YAWMARKS

MIDDLE
ORDINATE
(h)

PATH OF
CENTER
OF MASS

CHORD
(l)

WHEELBASE
AND TRACK
WIDTH

CUTOUT

PAVEMENT
EDGE

Exhibit 39. *To establish the path of the vehicle's center of mass, place the wheel locations of the vehicle pattern on the corresponding tire marks on the diagram, or on a similar diagram showing the yawmarks only, in a succession of positions along the marks.*

nuts and thumb screws in the larger pipe sections hold the smaller ones in position once they have been properly adjusted.

Once you have adjusted the vehicle jig to the track width and wheelbase dimensions of the vehicle in question, use a marker on the jig to represent the location of the vehicle's center of mass. In Exhibit 42 the width of the jig is equal to the front and rear track widths (A and B), the length of the jig corresponds to the wheelbase (C), and the location of the center of mass (D) is shown by a marker held onto the jig by u-bolts.

The ends of the jig that represent the vehicle tires are placed on the corresponding tire marks at the accident site near the beginning of the yawmarks, and the position of the center of mass is marked on the road. This position is shown in Exhibit 43. The jig is repositioned 50 to 100 feet from its original location, placed on the yawmarks, and the center-of-mass position is marked on the road. This position is shown in Exhibit 44. A measuring tape is placed between these two marks to serve as the chord. The jig is repositioned on the yawmarks so that the center-of-mass marker is located above the midpoint of the chord. This is shown in Exhibits 45 and 46. The perpendicular distance from the midpoint of the chord to the location of the center of mass in this last position is the middle ordinate. The values for the chord and middle ordinate are then used in equation (34) to find the radius of the curved path followed by the vehicle's center of mass.

You can use a variation of this method for a rough first approximation of the radius of the curved path followed by the vehicle's center of mass. This method involves making the chord and middle ordinate measurements, using one of the tire marks to establish its radius. In most cases, this will be a fair estimate of the radius of the curved path followed by the vehicle's center of mass (see Empirical Studies section of this topic). The measurements should be taken as near to the beginning of the yawmark as possible.

Exercise caution when measuring the radius (as with all measurements), no matter which method you use. The measurements should be taken as close to the beginning of the yaw as possible, because that is were the radius is greatest. You should not take the measurements past a point where the yawmarks begin to change radius rapidly. The offset between the front and rear tires should not be more than half the track width over the length of the chord.

The chord and middle ordinate are used to determine the radius, which is used to calculate the velocity. Any error in the chord or middle ordinate will result in an error in the velocity estimate calculated. For example, consider a case with a chord of 100 ft and a middle ordinate of 2.0 ft. Using equation (34) results in a radius of 626 ft. If the middle ordinate was actually 2.25 ft and not 2.0 ft, the radius calculated would be 556 ft. The sensitivity of the measurements is even more evident when the chord and middle ordinate are small. Suppose the chord is 30 ft and the middle ordinate is measured to be 0.5 ft; the calculated radius is 225 ft. If the middle

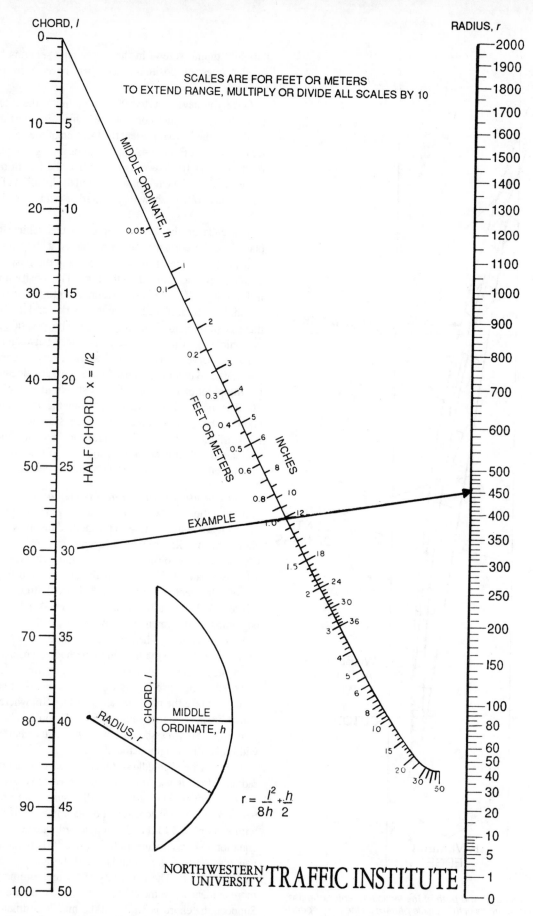

Exhibit 40. *The radius can be found by referring to a nomograph when the chord and middle ordinate are known.*

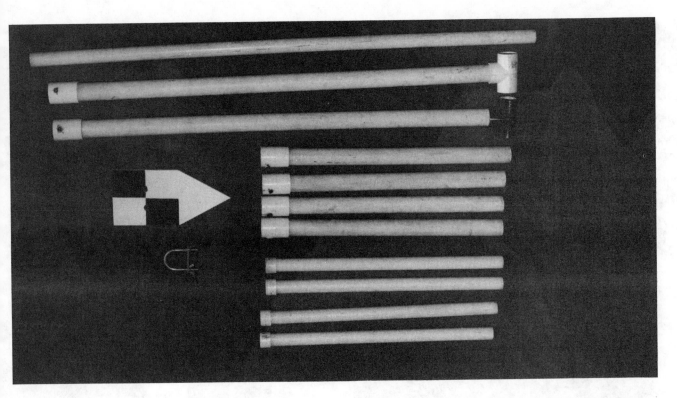

Exhibit 41. *A vehicle jig can be made in a variety of ways and is used to duplicate the wheelbase and track width of the vehicle that left the yawmarks.*

ordinate were 0.25 ft instead of 0.5 ft, the radius would be 450 ft—twice as large as the first calculated radius. Clearly, it can be seen that a fairly large chord is desireable. This will give a larger middle ordinate which will cause the radius calculation to be somewhat less sensitive to the middle ordinate dimension.

Equations for Estimating Velocity

The velocity at which the vehicle will *just* begin to sideslip is called the *critical velocity*. It occurs when centrifugal force equals the *maximum* attainable traction (centripetal) force. This can be shown mathematically by placing equations (6) and (3) equal to each other:

$$w\mu = wv^2/gr$$

This equation solved for velocity (v) yields an equation for calculating the velocity at which the vehicle will begin to sideslip:

$$v = \sqrt{gr\mu} \qquad (35)$$

where

> v = velocity (ft/sec, m/sec)
> g = 32.2 ft/sec^2, 9.81 m/sec^2
> r = radius (ft, m)
> μ = coefficient of friction

Equation (35) does not take into account any grade (slope or superelevation) that might exist in the road in the direction of slippage where the yawing occurs. In Topic 890, an equation was derived that does take this into consideration:

$$v = \sqrt{gr(\mu + G)/(1 - \mu G)} \qquad (36)$$

where

> v = velocity (ft/sec, m/sec)
> g = acceleration due to gravity (32.2 ft/sec^2, 9.81 m/sec^2)
> r = radius (ft, m)
> μ = coefficient of friction
> G = grade (expressed as a decimal)

If the grade (G) is small, as it is on nearly all curves, the factor $(1 - \mu G)$ is insignificant and equation (36) becomes:

$$v = \sqrt{gr(\mu + G)} \qquad (37)$$

If the effect of grade is completely ignored – that is, G is assumed to equal zero – equations (36) and (37) become equation (35).

Note that grade is positive (+) if the surface rises in the direction of slippage, negative (−) if it falls in that direction, and you always measure it parallel to the direction of slippage.

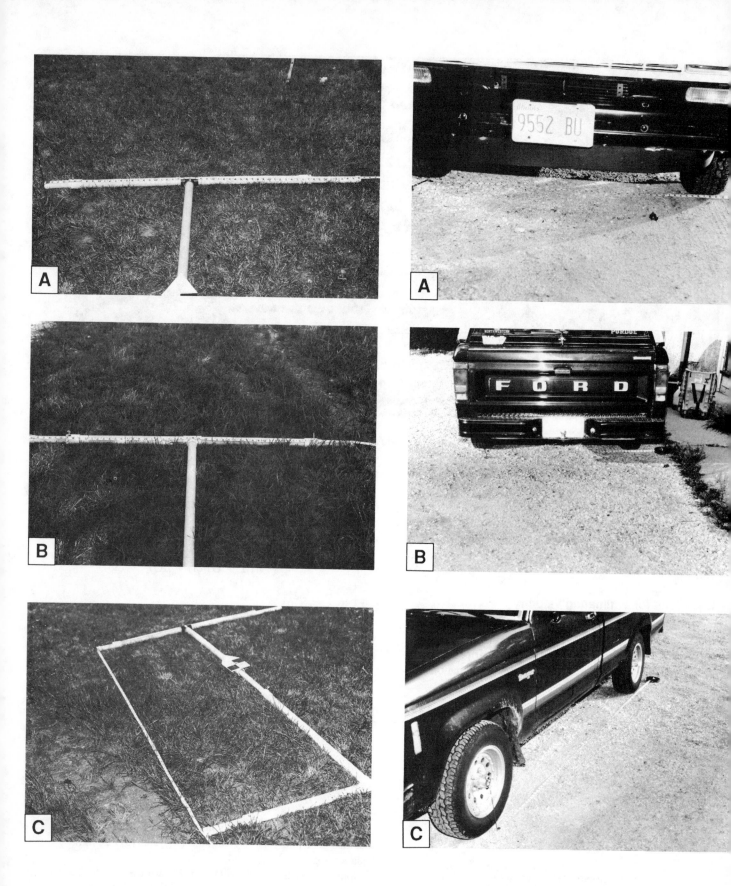

Exhibit 42.

The calculations required to obtain a vehicle's velocity using equations (34), (35), (36) and (37) are fairly straightforward. Suppose, for example, that the following information is known:

$$l = 100 \text{ ft}$$
$$h = 2 \text{ ft}$$
$$\mu = 0.70$$
$$G = 0.03 \ (3\%)$$

Equation (34) is used first to calculate the radius:

$$r = l^2/(8h) + h/2 \qquad (34)$$
$$r = (100)^2/(8)(2) + (2)/(2)$$
$$r = 626 \text{ ft}$$

This value and the other given information is used in equation (36) to calculate the velocity:

$$v = \sqrt{gr(\mu + G)/(1 - \mu G)} \qquad (36)$$

$$v = \sqrt{(32.2)(626)(0.70 + 0.03)/[(1-(0.70)(0.03)]}$$

$$v = 122.6 \text{ ft/sec} = 83.5 \text{ mi/hr}$$

If the factor $(1 - \mu G)$ is dropped, equation (37) is used:

$$v = \sqrt{gr(\mu + G)} \qquad (37)$$

$$v = \sqrt{(32.2)(626)(0.70 + 0.03)}$$

$$v = 121.3 \text{ ft/sec} = 82.7 \text{ mi/hr}$$

Exhibit 42. The width of the jig is equal to the front and rear track width (A and B), the length of the jig corresponds to the wheelbase (C), and the center-of-mass location (D) is shown by a marker held onto the jig by u-bolts.

Exhibit 43. The ends of the jig that represent the tires of the vehicle are placed on the corresponding tire marks near the beginning of the yawmarks, and the position of the center of mass is marked on the road.

Exhibit 44. *The jig is repositioned 50 to 100 feet from its original location, placed on the yawmarks, and the position of the center of mass is marked on the road.*

Exhibit 45. *The jig is repositioned on the yawmarks so that the center-of-mass marker is located above the midpoint of the chord. The perpendicular distance from the midpoint of the chord to the location of the center of mass in this last position is the middle ordinate.*

Exhibit 46. *The values for the chord and middle ordinate are then used to find the radius of the curved path followed by the vehicle's center of mass.*

If the grade is completely ignored, equation (35) is used:

$$v = \sqrt{gr\mu} \qquad (35)$$

$$v = \sqrt{(32.2)(626)(0.70)}$$

$$v = 118.8 \text{ ft/sec} = 81 \text{ mi/hr}$$

As can be seen from the above examples, including small values of grade has no significant effect on the calculated velocity. If the grade in the direction of slippage is less than 10 percent (6 degrees), which it almost always is, it will not have a major effect on the velocity estimate.

No example using metric units is included in this topic, because there should be little difficulty in using those units in the equation. The equations are the same; only the values for the variables change. For g use 9.81 m/sec/sec; l, h, and r are measured in meters.

If you have difficulty with the calculations involved in equations (35) and (37), Exhibit 47 (Exhibit 48 for metric) can be used. The velocity (mi/hr or km/hr) is given where the column for the coefficient of friction (or coefficient friction plus the grade) intersects the line representing the radius of the curved path, followed by the center of mass. For example, suppose a vehicle begins to sideslip while making a turn on a level curve and the path of the center of mass has a radius of 200 ft on a pavement with a coefficient of friction of 0.65. Follow down the drag factor column headed 0.65 to the line for 200 ft. The sideslip speed is 44 mi/hr.

Side Slip Case

Exhibit 49 shows an accident involving side slip. Exhibit 36 is the after-accident situation diagram of the same accident. The stolen Pontiac, traveling northbound, was being pursued by a police officer. The Pontiac left the pavement on the east side, was steered back across the roadway off the west side of the pavement, and struck a tree. The pursuing police officer locked his brakes and began to slide to a stop just as the Pontiac went across the roadway. The police officer indicated in his statement that he was traveling at the same velocity as the Pontiac when it left the pavement.

One of the issues in this case was the velocities of the Pontiac and the police car. The radius of the Pontiac's center-of-mass path was calculated from a chord and middle ordinate measured in the manner described earlier in this topic (Exhibit 39). The chord and middle ordinate measurements were used in equation (34) to calculate the radius, and yielded a value of 626 feet. Tests were conducted to establish the coefficient of friction (Topic 862). The tests resulted in a value of between 0.80 and 0.85. No grade was present, and therefore equation (35) was used to calculate the velocity of the Pontiac using the above values. The estimated velocity for the Pontiac was between 85 and 90 mi/hr.

The police car's center of mass traveled 305 feet while the vehicle was sliding to a stop. This value, along with the value of the coefficient of friction, yielded a velocity estimate (Topic 862) for the police car of between 85 and 90 mi/hr.

The police officer stated that the velocities of both vehicles were the same when the Pontiac left the road. The two estimates were determined using two different methods. Both estimates support the velocity estimate of the Pontiac and police car as being 85 to 90 mi/hr.

Critical Velocity of a Curve

You can calculate the critical velocity of a curve on a roadway by using equations (35), (36), or (37). The radius of the center of the travel lane in question is used for this calculation. To find the lane radius, first determine the radius of one edge or center line of the road as described in Topic 834. Then add or subtract the distance from the center of the lane to the edge or center line measured.

Critical velocity of a curve can be used to indicate vehicle velocity when there are no yawmarks or when yawmarks have been inadequately reported. There must be reliable information that the vehicle sideslipped off the curve, as opposed to being driven off the curve. For example, a tired individual driving at an appropriate speed might fall asleep and drive off the curve, with no initial attempt to steer the vehicle around it. The driver is awakened by running off the road and attempts to steer back onto the road, but is unsuccessful. The use of the critical velocity of the curve to estimate the velocity of the vehicle would be *completely inappropriate* in this case.

For the purposes of estimating sideslip velocity, be very careful not to assume, without justification, that the vehicle was moving normally or attempting to move normally in its lane when it slid off the curve. A vehicle is often turned more or less sharply than the road because of lane changing, steering overcorrection or other maneuvers, such as attempting to "straighten out" the curve. If the vehicle is moving from one lane to another as it rounds the curve (Exhibit 50A), then the radius of the curved path the vehicle followed will not be the same as that of the lane (Exhibit 50B). On the other hand, if the vehicle is moving toward the outside of the curve, its path will not be as sharp as the lane it started from and the radius will be greater than that of the lane in which the vehicle had been traveling (Exhibit 50C).

Design velocity of a curve, which highway and traffic engineers speak of, is not the same as critical velocity; it is much lower. The design velocity, or advisory velocity, is based on a much lower coefficient of friction (lateral acceleration) than is actually present on a dry, clear road to provide a reasonable factor of safety, to help inattentive drivers, and to provide for unusually slippery conditions.

Significance of Estimate

Velocity estimates obtained using equations (35), (36) or (37) should *never* be used to estimate after-collision velocities. The equations are based on balancing centrifugal

Exhibit 47
SPEED (MILES PER HOUR) REQUIRED TO SIDESLIP

Drag Factor categories: Ice (0.05–0.20), Snow (0.30–0.35), Gravel (0.40–0.55), Clean, wet paving (0.40–0.70), Clean, dry paving (0.75–1.20)

Radius of curve in feet	0.05	0.10	0.20	0.30	0.35	0.40	0.45	0.50	0.55	0.60	0.65	0.70	0.75	0.80	0.85	0.90	0.95	1.00	1.10	1.20
25	4	6	9	11	11	12	13	14	14	15	16	16	17	17	18	18	19	19	20	21
30	5	7	9	12	13	13	14	15	16	16	17	18	18	19	20	20	21	21	22	23
35	5	7	10	13	14	14	15	16	17	18	18	19	20	20	21	22	22	23	24	25
40	5	8	11	13	14	15	16	17	18	19	20	20	21	22	23	23	24	24	26	27
45	6	8	12	14	15	16	17	18	19	20	21	22	22	23	24	25	25	26	27	28
50	6	9	12	15	16	17	18	19	20	21	22	23	24	24	25	26	27	27	29	30
60	7	9	13	16	18	19	20	21	22	23	24	25	26	27	28	28	29	30	31	33
70	7	10	14	18	19	20	22	23	24	25	26	27	28	29	30	31	32	32	34	35
80	8	11	15	19	20	22	23	24	26	27	28	29	30	31	32	33	34	35	36	38
90	8	12	16	20	22	23	25	26	27	28	30	31	32	33	34	35	36	37	38	40
100	9	12	17	21	23	24	26	27	29	30	31	32	34	35	36	37	38	39	41	42
110	9	13	18	22	24	26	27	29	30	31	33	34	35	36	37	39	40	41	43	44
120	9	13	19	23	25	27	28	30	31	33	34	35	37	38	39	40	41	42	44	46
130	10	14	20	24	26	28	30	31	33	34	36	37	38	39	41	42	43	44	46	48
140	10	14	20	25	27	29	31	32	34	35	37	38	40	41	42	43	45	46	48	50
150	11	15	21	26	28	30	32	34	35	37	38	40	41	42	44	45	46	47	50	52
160	11	15	22	27	29	31	33	35	36	38	39	41	42	44	45	46	48	49	51	54
170	11	16	23	28	30	32	34	36	37	39	41	42	44	45	47	48	49	50	53	55
180	12	16	23	28	31	33	35	37	39	40	42	43	45	46	48	49	51	52	54	57
190	12	17	24	29	32	34	36	38	40	41	43	45	46	48	49	51	52	53	56	58
200	12	17	24	30	32	35	37	39	41	42	44	46	47	49	50	52	53	55	57	60
220	13	18	26	31	34	36	39	41	43	44	46	48	50	51	53	54	56	57	60	63
240	13	19	27	33	35	38	40	42	44	46	48	50	52	54	55	57	58	60	63	66
260	14	20	28	34	37	40	42	44	46	48	50	52	54	56	58	59	61	62	65	68
280	14	20	29	35	38	41	43	46	48	50	52	54	56	58	60	61	63	65	68	71
300	15	21	30	37	40	42	45	47	50	52	54	56	58	60	62	64	65	67	70	73
325	16	22	31	38	41	44	47	49	52	54	56	58	60	62	64	66	68	70	73	78
350	16	23	32	40	43	46	49	51	54	56	58	61	63	65	67	69	71	72	76	79
375	17	24	34	41	44	47	50	53	56	58	60	63	65	67	69	71	73	75	79	82
400	17	24	35	42	46	49	52	55	57	60	62	65	67	69	71	73	75	77	81	85
450	18	26	37	45	49	52	55	58	61	64	66	69	71	73	76	78	80	82	86	90
500	19	27	39	47	51	55	58	61	64	67	70	72	75	77	80	82	84	87	91	95
550	20	29	41	50	54	57	61	64	67	70	73	76	79	81	84	86	89	91	95	99
600	21	30	42	52	56	60	64	67	70	73	76	79	82	85	87	90	92	95	99	104
650	22	31	44	54	58	62	66	70	73	76	80	83	85	88	91	94	96	99	103	108
700	23	32	46	56	61	65	69	72	76	79	83	86	89	92	94	97	100	102	107	112
750	24	34	47	58	63	67	71	75	79	82	86	89	92	95	98	101	103	106	111	116
800	24	35	49	60	65	69	73	77	81	85	88	92	95	98	101	104	107	110	115	120
850	25	36	50	62	67	71	76	80	84	87	91	94	98	101	104	107	110	113	118	124
900	26	37	52	64	69	73	78	82	86	90	94	97	101	104	107	110	113	116	122	127
1000	27	39	55	67	72	77	82	87	91	95	99	102	106	110	113	116	119	122	128	134
1100	29	41	57	70	76	81	86	91	95	100	104	107	111	115	118	122	125	128	135	141
1200	30	42	60	73	79	85	90	95	99	104	108	112	116	120	124	127	131	134	141	147
1300	31	44	62	76	83	88	94	99	104	108	113	117	121	125	129	132	136	140	146	153
1400	32	46	65	79	86	92	97	102	107	112	117	121	125	129	133	137	141	145	152	159
1500	34	47	67	82	89	95	101	106	111	116	121	125	130	134	138	142	146	150	157	164
1600	35	49	69	85	92	98	104	110	115	120	125	130	134	139	143	147	151	155	157	164
1700	36	50	71	87	94	101	107	113	118	124	129	134	138	143	147	151	156	160	167	175
1800	37	52	73	90	97	104	110	116	122	127	132	137	142	147	152	156	160	164	172	180
1900	38	53	75	92	100	107	113	119	125	131	136	141	146	151	155	160	164	169	177	185
2000	39	55	77	95	102	109	116	122	128	134	139	145	150	155	160	164	169	173	181	190
2100	40	56	79	97	105	112	119	125	132	137	143	148	154	159	164	168	173	177	186	194
2200	41	57	81	99	107	115	122	128	135	141	146	152	157	162	167	172	177	182	191	199
2300	42	59	83	102	110	117	125	131	138	144	150	155	161	166	171	176	181	186	195	203
2500	43	61	87	106	114	122	130	137	143	150	156	162	168	173	179	184	189	193	203	212

Exhibit 48
SPEED (KILOMETERS PER HOUR) REQUIRED TO SIDESLIP

Radius of curve in meters	Drag Factor																				
	← Ice →																				
			← Snow →			← Gravel →			← Clean, wet paving →				← Clean, dry paving →								
	0.05	0.10	0.20	0.30	0.35	0.40	0.45	0.50	0.55	0.60	0.65	0.70	0.75	0.80	0.85	0.90	0.95	1.00	1.10	1.20
8	7	10	14	17	19	20	21	23	24	25	26	27	28	29	29	30	31	32	33	35
10	8	11	16	20	21	23	24	25	26	28	29	30	31	32	33	34	35	36	37	39
12	9	12	17	21	23	25	26	28	29	30	31	33	34	35	36	37	38	39	41	43
14	9	13	19	23	25	27	28	30	31	33	34	35	37	38	39	40	41	42	44	46
16	10	14	20	25	27	29	30	32	33	35	36	38	39	40	42	43	44	45	47	49
18	11	15	21	26	28	30	32	34	35	37	39	40	41	43	44	45	47	48	50	52
20	11	16	23	28	30	32	34	36	37	39	41	42	44	45	46	48	49	50	53	55
22	12	17	24	29	31	33	35	37	39	41	43	44	46	47	49	50	52	53	55	58
24	12	17	25	30	33	35	37	39	41	43	45	46	48	49	51	52	54	55	58	61
26	13	18	26	31	34	36	39	41	43	45	46	48	50	51	53	55	56	57	60	63
30	14	20	28	34	37	39	41	44	46	48	50	52	53	55	57	59	60	62	65	68
35	15	21	30	37	39	42	45	47	49	52	54	56	58	60	61	63	65	67	70	73
40	16	23	32	39	42	45	48	50	53	55	57	60	62	64	66	68	70	71	75	78
45	17	24	34	41	45	48	51	53	56	59	61	63	65	68	70	72	74	76	79	83
50	18	25	36	44	47	50	53	56	59	62	64	67	69	71	74	76	78	80	84	87
55	19	26	37	46	49	53	56	59	62	65	67	70	72	75	77	79	81	84	88	92
60	20	28	39	48	52	55	59	62	65	68	70	73	76	78	81	83	85	87	92	96
65	20	29	41	50	54	57	61	64	67	70	73	76	79	81	84	86	89	91	95	100
70	21	30	42	52	56	60	63	67	70	73	76	79	82	84	87	89	92	94	99	103
75	22	31	44	53	58	62	65	69	72	76	79	82	85	87	90	93	95	98	102	107
80	23	32	45	55	60	64	68	71	74	78	81	84	87	90	93	96	98	101	106	110
85	23	33	46	57	61	66	70	74	77	81	84	87	90	93	96	99	101	104	109	114
90	24	34	48	59	63	68	72	76	79	83	86	89	93	96	99	101	104	107	112	117
95	25	35	49	60	65	70	74	78	81	85	89	92	95	98	101	104	107	110	115	120
100	25	36	50	62	67	71	76	80	84	87	91	94	98	101	104	107	110	113	118	124
110	26	37	53	65	70	75	79	84	88	92	95	99	102	106	109	112	115	118	124	130
120	28	39	55	68	73	78	83	87	92	96	100	103	107	110	114	117	120	124	130	135
130	29	41	57	70	76	81	86	91	95	100	104	108	111	115	119	122	125	129	135	141
140	30	42	60	73	79	84	89	94	99	103	108	112	116	119	123	127	130	133	140	146
150	31	44	62	76	82	87	93	98	102	107	111	116	120	124	127	131	135	138	145	151
160	32	45	64	78	84	90	96	101	106	110	115	119	124	128	131	135	139	143	150	156
170	33	46	66	81	87	93	99	104	109	114	119	123	127	131	136	139	143	147	154	161
180	34	48	68	83	89	96	101	107	112	117	122	127	131	135	139	144	147	151	159	166
190	35	49	70	85	92	98	104	110	115	120	125	130	135	139	143	147	151	155	163	170
200	36	50	71	87	94	101	107	113	118	124	129	133	138	143	147	151	155	159	167	175
220	37	53	75	92	99	106	112	118	124	130	135	140	145	150	154	159	163	167	175	183
240	39	55	78	96	103	110	117	124	130	135	141	146	151	156	161	166	170	175	183	191
260	41	57	81	100	108	115	122	129	135	141	147	152	157	163	168	172	177	182	191	199
280	42	60	84	103	112	119	127	133	140	146	152	158	163	174	184	189	198	207		
300	44	62	87	107	116	124	131	138	145	151	157	163	169	175	180	185	190	195	205	214
330	46	65	92	112	121	130	137	145	152	159	165	171	177	183	189	194	200	205	215	224
360	48	68	96	117	127	135	144	151	159	166	172	179	185	191	197	203	209	214	224	234
390	50	70	100	122	132	141	149	157	165	172	180	186	193	199	205	211	217	223	234	244
420	52	73	103	127	137	146	155	163	171	179	186	193	200	207	213	219	225	231	242	253
450	53	76	107	131	141	151	160	169	177	185	193	200	207	214	221	227	233	239	251	262
480	55	78	110	135	146	156	166	175	183	191	199	207	214	221	228	234	241	247	259	271
510	57	81	114	139	151	161	171	180	189	197	205	213	221	228	235	242	248	255	267	279
540	59	83	117	144	155	166	176	185	194	203	211	219	227	234	242	249	255	262	275	287
570	60	85	120	147	159	170	181	190	200	209	217	225	233	241	248	255	262	269	282	295
600	62	87	124	151	163	175	185	195	205	214	223	231	239	247	255	262	269	276	290	303
650	64	91	129	157	170	182	193	203	213	223	232	240	249	257	265	273	280	287	301	315
700	67	94	133	163	176	189	200	211	221	231	240	250	258	267	275	283	291	298	313	327
750	69	98	138	169	183	195	207	218	229	239	249	258	267	276	285	293	301	309	324	338
800	71	101	143	175	189	202	214	225	236	247	257	267	276	285	294	303	311	319	334	349
850	74	104	147	180	194	208	221	232	244	255	265	275	285	294	303	312	320	329	345	360

Exhibit 49. In this accident, the vehicle began to side slip, went cross the roadway and off the pavement, and struck a tree.

and centripetal forces and ***not*** collision forces. Therefore, using these equations after a collision to establish velocity is totally inappropriate.

Nor is the use of equations (35), (36) or (37) for estimating the velocity of an articulated vehicle (Topic 878) recommended. Although the theory on which these equations are based still applies for articulated vehicles, applying it practically is difficult at best. An articulated vehicle consists of a towing and a towed vehicle joined together at a pivot connection. In a high-velocity turn, offtracking (trailer swingout) occurs due to a change in the articulation angle between the towing and towed vehicles. The towed vehicle tends to rotate about the pivot connection and, if allowed to continue, the combination will end up in a jackknife position. This causes the two to travel in different paths, which might result in the towed vehicle side sliding while the towing vehicle does not. Therefore, an attempt to calculate velocity from yawmarks left by the towing or towed vehicle would be suspect.

A motorcycle will begin to slide if the velocity and radius of the curved path followed by its center of mass create a centrifugal force greater than the frictional force between the tires and road. Equations (35), (36) and (37) can be used with caution for estimating the velocity of a motorcycle in a yaw. In cases involving motorcycles in a yaw, the yawmarks typically are very short, because the rider is leaning at such an angle that he falls off as the motorcycle slides out from beneath him. The vehicle begins to slide on its side, so a different approach must be taken (Topic 874).

Exhibit 50. *Be very careful not to assume that a vehicle was moving normally or attempting to move normally in its lane when it slid off a curve.*

Measuring the radius of the curved path followed by the vehicle's center of mass from a chord and middle ordinate cannot be done at the very beginning of the sideslip where the radius is greatest and, therefore, velocity estimates highest. Such a radius is further along the curve and therefore shorter than it would be at the beginning. Because the vehicle loses velocity as it begins to sideslip, the velocity calculated is somewhat lower than it would have been at the very beginning. You can infer that in order to sideslip on a path indicated by yawmarks, a vehicle has to be going faster than the estimated sideslip velocity at the beginning of the yaw.

Estimating the velocity of a vehicle from the radius of the center of the travel lane would yield the lowest possible figure, because in order to slide off the curve, the vehicle would have to have been going faster than the critical velocity of the curve. It may have been going much faster, because a higher velocity would more certainly have made it sideslip off the curve. The estimate is only valid if the information at the accident site supports the conclusion that the driver attempted to follow the travel lane.

Estimates of velocity based on yawmarks are likely to be less accurate than those based on braking skidmarks. The inaccuracies result mainly from not having made properly the more detailed measurements and observations required for the analysis. Yawmarks are often mistaken for braking skidmarks and only their length, not their curvature, is measured, which is virtually useless for estimating velocity. Conversely, braking skidmarks are all too often mistaken for yawmarks.

5. DETAILED VELOCITY ESTIMATES CONSIDERING SPECIAL CONDITIONS

Several conditions affect the sideslip velocity to some degree: vehicle characteristics, tire properties, the vehicle slip angle, and whether brakes or power were applied can all affect the velocity estimate[16].

Certain characteristics of the vehicle will affect the sideslip velocity and make one vehicle able to corner a little faster than another, without producing yawmarks. This generally is not significant, but can be taken into consideration by using a range of pavement coefficients of friction. A highly technical consideration of these properties is usually not justified and requires using specialized computer programs that are

beyond the scope of this topic. The only vehicle characteristic considered in this topic is the location of center of mass and its relationship to lateral (sideways) and longitudinal (lengthwise) weight transfer.

The force necessary for a vehicle to turn a corner is developed by the tires. The properties of tires obviously affect the generation of force. Tire properties and their relationship to cornering force have already been addressed. Their relationship to velocity estimates was demonstrated with the weight shift and vehicle performance calculations performed earlier in this topic.

When a vehicle begins to sideslip, the slippage is parallel to the axle if the wheel is free to rotate. However, the axle is not exactly parallel to the radius of the curve. Consequently, for very careful estimates, a correction for sideslip angle (β) can be made. At the beginning of the yaw, the sideslip angle (β) is small and the correction is insignificant. The procedures for considering sideslip angle (β) by itself and with longitudinal acceleration are discussed in this topic.

The equations presented thus far for velocity estimates from sideslip are derived with the assumption that no longitudinal acceleration (a_x) was present during the yaw. This means that neither braking nor power was applied to the vehicle during the yaw, which is usually the case. The vehicle will sideslip more easily if brakes or engine power are being applied. You can sometimes determine whether the driver applied brakes or power by noting the angle of the striations in the yawmark. The effects of braking and acceleration on sideslip velocity estimates, and how to determine whether either was present, are discussed later in this topic

Velocity Estimate Considering Side Slip Angle

The side slip angle (β) is defined as the angle between the heading of the vehicle (x-axis) and the vehicle's direction of travel (velocity vector, v)[1] (Exhibit 51). As the vehicle begins to yaw, the side slip angle is small. However, the angle increases as the yaw progresses (Exhibit 39). This increase in side slip angle results in the tires sliding more and rolling less, which slows the vehicle much the same as braking would, only to a lesser degree. The tires sliding more and rolling less reduces the amount of friction force available for cornering force (friction circle). An equation can be derived to take side

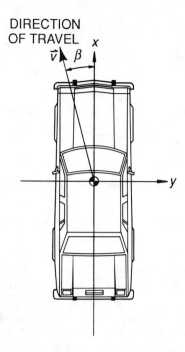

DIRECTION
OF TRAVEL x

$\vec{v}$ β

y

Exhibit 51. *The side slip angle (β) is defined as the angle between the heading of the vehicle (x-axis) and the vehicle's direction of travel.*

slip angle into consideration in velocity estimates. Grade will be included in developing this equation, even though it generally has a minimal effect on velocity estimates from yaws.

Consider Exhibit 52, consisting of a cross-sectional view of a vehicle on an elevation (exaggerated for clarity) at an angle of θ (Greek letter theta). The weight (w) and centrifugal force (F_{cent}) are divided into their vertical (w_z and F_{centz}) and horizontal (w_y and F_{centy}) components (relative to the inclined surface). The normal force (N) represents the resultant of all forces perpendicular to the surface (Topic 860) and F_y represents all the forces parallel to the surface. The values for the component forces are as follows:

Vertical: $F_{centz} = F_{cent} \sin \theta$
$w_z = w \cos \theta$
Horizontal: $F_{centy} = F_{cent} \cos \theta$
$w_y = w \sin \theta$

Sum the forces in the vertical (z) direction:

$$\downarrow + \Sigma F_z = 0 = F_{centz} + w_z - N$$

Substitute into this equation the values for F_{centz} and w_z found above:

$$\downarrow + \Sigma F_z = 0 = F_{cent} \sin \theta + w \cos \theta - N$$

Solve this equation for the normal force (perpendicular to the surface) (N):

$$N = F_{cent} \sin \theta + w \cos \theta \qquad (38)$$

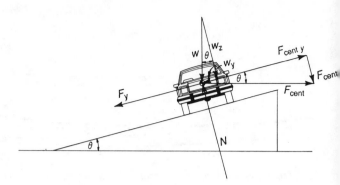

Exhibit 52. *A cross-sectional view of a vehicle on an elevation angle of Θ, showing the weight (w) and centrifugal force (F$_{cent}$) divided into their vertical (w$_z$ and F$_{centz}$) and horizontal (w$_y$ and F$_{centy}$) components and the normal force (N).*

Sum the forces in the horizontal (y) direction:

$$\rightarrow + \Sigma F_y = 0 = F_{centy} - w_y - F_y$$

Solve this equation for F_{centy}:

$$F_{centy} = w_y + F_y \qquad (39)$$

Exhibit 53 is an overhead or plan view of the same vehicle that was shown in Exhibit 52 at an exaggerated side slip angle (β). The lateral force (F_{centy}), the side force (F_y), and the frictional force (F_F) are indicated.

The value for F_y is:

$$F_y = F_F \cos \beta$$

Recall from before:

$$F_{centy} = F_{cent} \cos \theta$$
$$w_y = w \sin \theta$$

Substitute these values into equation (39):

$$F_{cent} \cos \theta = w \sin \theta + F_F \cos \beta$$

The definition of friction can be written (Topic 862):

$$F_F = N\mu$$

Substitute this value into the previous equation:

$$F_{cent} \cos \theta = N\mu \cos \beta + w \sin \theta$$

Substitute into this equation the value for N from equation (38):

$$F_{cent} \cos \theta = (F_{cent} \sin \theta + w\cos \theta)\mu \cos \beta + w \sin \theta$$

Expand the equation:

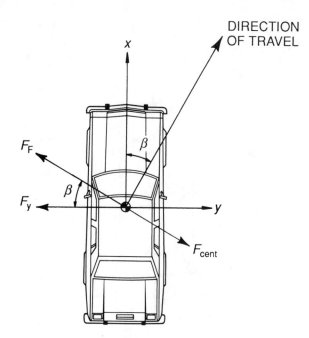

DIRECTION OF TRAVEL

Exhibit 53. *A plan view of a vehicle at a side slip angle (β), showing the lateral force (F_{centy}), the side force (F_y), and the frictional force (F_F).*

$$F_{cent} \cos \theta = \mu F_{cent} \sin \theta \cos \beta + \mu w \cos \theta \cos \beta + w \sin \theta$$

Subtract from both sides of the equation $\mu F_{cent} \sin \theta \cos \beta$ and simplify:

$$F_{cent} (\cos \theta - \mu \sin \theta \cos \beta) = \mu w \cos \theta \cos \beta + w \sin \theta$$

Divide both sides of the equation by $\cos \theta - \mu \sin \theta \cos \beta$ and cancel:

$$F_{cent} = (\mu w \cos \theta \cos \beta + w \sin \theta)/ (\cos \theta - \mu \sin \theta \cos \beta)$$

The value for F_{cent} was given by equation (6):

$$F_{cent} = wv^2/gr \qquad (6)$$

Substitute this value into the previous equation:

$$wv^2/gr = (\mu w \cos \theta \cos \beta + w \sin \theta)/ (\cos \theta - \mu \sin \theta \cos \beta)$$

Solve the equation for v:

$$v = \sqrt{[gr(\mu \cos \theta \cos \beta + \sin \theta)/(\cos \theta - \mu \sin \theta \cos \beta)]} \qquad (40)$$

where

v = velocity (ft/sec, m/sec)
g = 32.2 ft/sec^2, 9.81 m/sec^2
r = radius (ft, m)
μ = coefficient of friction
θ = angle of grade (degrees) (negative if grade is negative)
β = side slip angle (degrees)

It is not necessary to use equation (40) if the required measurements for establishing the radius are taken as close to the start of the yaw as possible. At the beginning of the yaw the sideslip angle is very small, making its effect negligible. If the radius measurements are obtained at the start of the yaw:

$$\beta \approx 0°$$
$$\cos 0° = 1$$

Substitute this value for $\cos \beta$ into equation (40):

$$v = \sqrt{[gr(\mu \cos \theta \cos \beta + \sin \theta)/(\cos \theta - \mu \sin \theta \cos \beta)]} \qquad (40)$$

$$v = \sqrt{[gr(\mu \cos \theta \cos 0 + \sin\theta)/(\cos \theta - \mu \sin \theta \cos 0)]}$$

$$v = \sqrt{[gr(\mu \cos \theta (1) + \sin \theta)/(\cos \theta - \mu \sin \theta (1)]}$$

$$v = \sqrt{[gr(\mu \cos \theta + \sin \theta)/(\cos \theta - \mu \sin \theta]}$$

Most grades are very small, which results in:

$$\theta \approx 0°$$
$$\cos 0° = 1$$
$$\sin \theta \approx \tan \theta$$

Substitute these values into the previous equation:

$$v = \sqrt{[gr(\mu \cos \theta + \sin \theta)/(\cos \theta - \mu \sin \theta]}$$

$$v = \sqrt{[gr(\mu \cos 0° + \tan \theta)/(\cos 0° - \mu \tan \theta]}$$

$$v = \sqrt{[gr(\mu + \tan \theta)/(1 - \mu \tan \theta]}$$

The grade (G) is the tangent of the angle θ. Substitute into the equation G for $\tan \theta$:

$$v = \sqrt{[gr(\mu + G)/(1 - \mu G]} \qquad (36)$$

This is, of course, the same equation that was discussed earlier in this topic.

Velocity Estimates Considering Sideslip Angle and Braking

Consider Exhibits 54 and 55, consisting of two overhead or plan views of a vehicle at an exaggerated sideslip angle

72-37

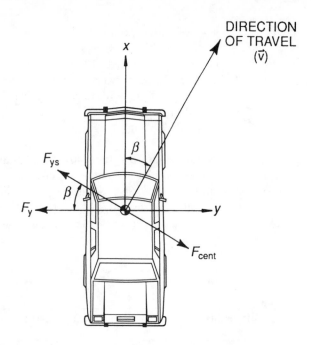

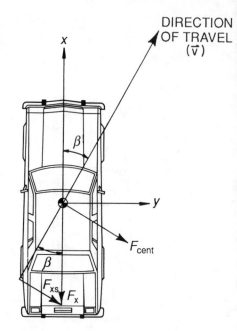

Exhibit 54. *A plan view of a vehicle at a side slip angle (ß), showing the maximum side force (F$_y$) and the component of the maximum side force (F$_{ys}$) used to balance the centrifugal force (F$_{cent}$).*

Exhibit 55. *A plan view of a vehicle at a side slip angle (ß), showing the maximum braking force (F$_x$) and the component of the maximum side force (F$_{xs}$) in the same direction as the centrifugal force (F$_{cent}$).*

$$F_{xs} = F_x \sin \beta \qquad (42)$$

Grade, even though it generally has a minimal effect on velocity estimates from yaws, will be included in developing this equation. In Exhibit 56, the vehicle in Exhibits 54 and 55 is now shown in a cross-sectional view on an elevation (exaggerated for clarity) at an angle, θ. Shown in Exhibit 56 are the forces, F_{ys} and F_{xs}, and their vertical (F_{ysz} and F_{xsz}) and horizontal (F_{ysy} and F_{xsy}) components (relative to vertical). The normal force (force perpendicular to the surface) (N), its vertical component (N_z), its horizontal component (N_y), and the vehicle weight are also shown in Exhibit 56. The values for the component forces in Exhibit 56 are as follows:

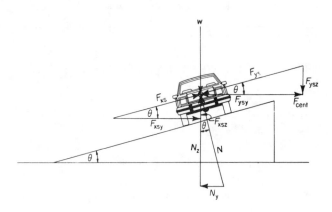

Exhibit 56. *A cross-sectional view of a vehicle on an elevation at an angle (ө). Shown are the forces (F$_{y\,s}$ and F$_{x\,s}$) and their vertical (F$_{y\,s\,z}$ and F$_{x\,s\,z}$) and horizontal (F$_{y\,s\,y}$ and F$_{x\,s\,y}$) components; the normal force (N) and its vertical (N$_z$) and horizontal (N$_y$) components; and the vehicle weight (w).*

Vertical:

$$F_{ysz} = F_{ys} \sin \theta$$
$$F_{xsz} = F_{xs} \sin \theta$$
$$N_z = N \cos \theta$$

Substitute into the above equations the values for F_{ys} and F_{xs} from equations (41) and (42), respectively:

$$F_{ysz} = F_y \cos \beta \sin \theta$$
$$F_{xsz} = F_x \sin \beta \sin \theta$$

Horizontal:

$$F_{ysy} = F_{ys} \cos \theta$$
$$F_{xsy} = F_{xs} \cos \theta$$
$$N_y = N \sin \theta$$

(β). The maximum side force (F_y) is shown in Exhibit 54. The component of the maximum side force used to balance the centrifugal force (F_{cent}) is shown as F_{ys}. The value for F_{ys} is:

$$F_{ys} = F_y \cos \beta \qquad (41)$$

Exhibit 55 shows the maximum braking friction force, F_x. The component of the maximum braking friction force that acts in the same direction as the centrifugal force is shown as F_{xs}. The value for F_{xs} is:

Substitute into the above equations the values for F_{ys} and F_{xs} from equations (41) and (42), respectively:

$$F_{ysy} = F_y \cos \beta \cos \theta$$
$$F_{xsy} = F_x \sin \beta \cos \theta$$

Sum the forces in the vertical (z) direction:

$$\downarrow + \Sigma F_z = 0 = w + F_{ysz} - F_{xsz} - N_z$$
$$\downarrow + \Sigma F_z = 0 = w + F_y \cos \beta \sin \theta - F_x \sin \beta \sin \theta - N \cos \theta$$

Solve this equation for N:

$$N = (w + F_y \cos \beta \sin \theta - F_x \sin \beta \sin \theta)/\cos \theta \quad (43)$$

Sum the forces in the horizontal (y) direction:

$$+ \Sigma F_y = 0 = F_{cent} + F_{xsy} - F_{ysy} - N_y$$
$$\rightarrow + \Sigma F_y = 0 = F_{cent} + F_x \sin \beta \cos \theta - F_y \cos \beta \cos \theta - N \sin \theta$$

Solve this equation for F_{cent}:

$$F_{cent} = F_y \cos \beta \cos \theta + N \sin \theta - F_x \sin \beta \cos \theta$$

Substitute the value for F_{cent} in equation (6) into this equation:

$$F_{cent} = wv^2/gr \quad (6)$$
$$wv^2/gr = F_y \cos \beta \cos \theta + N \sin \theta - F_x \sin \beta \cos \theta$$

Substitute into this equation the value for N in equation (43):

$$wv^2/gr = F_y \cos \beta \cos \theta + [(w + F_y \cos \beta \sin \theta - F_x \sin \beta \sin \theta)/\cos \theta] \sin \theta - F_x \sin \beta \cos \theta$$

Simplify the equation:

$$wv^2/gr = F_y \cos \beta \cos \theta + [(w + F_y \cos \beta \sin \theta - F_x \sin \beta \sin \theta)\tan \theta] - F_x \sin \beta \cos \theta$$

Divide both sides of the equation by w:

$$v^2/gr = (F_y/w)(\cos \beta \cos \theta) + [1 + (F_y/w)(\cos \beta \sin \theta) - (F_x/w)(\sin \beta \sin \theta)] \tan \theta - (F_x/w)(\sin \beta \cos \theta)$$

Expand the equation:

$$v^2/gr = (F_y/w)(\cos \beta \cos \theta) + \tan \theta + (F_y/w)(\cos \beta \sin \theta \tan \theta) - (F_x/w)(\sin \beta \sin \theta \tan \theta) - (F_x/w)(\sin \beta \cos \theta)$$

Group like terms and simplify the equation:

$$v^2/gr = (F_y/w) \cos \beta (\cos \theta + \sin \theta \tan \theta) - (F_x/w) \sin \beta (\cos \theta + \sin \theta \tan \theta) + \tan \theta$$

Simplify the equation further and rearrange:

$$v^2/gr = [(F_y/w) \cos \beta - (F_x/w) \sin \beta] (\sin \theta \tan \theta + \cos \theta) + \tan \theta$$

Solve the equation for v:

$$v = \sqrt{\{gr[(F_y/w) \cos \beta - (F_x/w) \sin \beta)(\sin \theta \tan \theta + \cos \theta) + \tan \theta]\}} \quad (44)$$

Newton's second law of motion is used to determine the force for a given amount of acceleration and can be written:

$$F = ma$$

An equation was derived in Topic 890 that showed the relationship between mass and weight:

$$m = w/g$$

Substitute the value for mass in this equation into the equation for Newton's second law of motion:

$$F = (w/g)a$$

The resulting equation, rewritten for longitudinal force in terms of longitudinal acceleration, is:

$$F_x = wa_x/g \quad (45)$$

Drag factor (Topic 862) is defined as a number representing the acceleration or deceleration of a vehicle or other body as a decimal fraction of the acceleration of gravity. This is sometimes referred to as the number of "g's" of acceleration. Drag factor, like acceleration, can be broken down into lateral and longitudinal components. An equation was derived in Topic 890 that showed the relationship between drag factor and acceleration:

$$f = a/g$$

This equation can be rewritten in terms of longitudinal drag factor and acceleration:

$$f_x = a_x/g$$

Substitute this into equation (45):

$$F_x = wf_x$$

Similarly, the same relationships can be applied laterally:

$$F_y = wf_y$$

Substitute the new values for F_x and F_y into equation (44) and simplify:

$$v = \sqrt{\{gr[(f_y \cos \beta - f_x \sin \beta)(\sin \theta \tan \theta + \cos \theta) + \tan \theta]\}} \quad (46)$$

where

v = velocity (ft/sec, m/sec)
g = 32.2 ft/sec^2, 9.81 m/sec^2
r = radius (ft, m)
f_y = lateral drag factor
f_x = longitudinal drag factor
θ = angle of grade (degrees)
β = side slip angle (degrees)

If the grade is negative – that is, if the road surface falls in the direction of slippage – the angle becomes negative and equation (46) becomes

$$v = \sqrt{\{gr[(f_y \cos \beta - f_x \sin \beta)(\cos \theta - \sin \theta \tan \theta) + \tan \theta]\}} \quad (47)$$

Recall from Exhibits 6 through 11 that the radius of the circle surrounding the tire is a vector representing the maximum frictional force, F_F. The tire can be subjected to longitudinal force (F_x), to a cornering force (F_y), or to any combination of the two. The vector sum of the forces (Topic 856) cannot exceed the available frictional force (F_F). This was shown by equation (4):

$$F_F = \sqrt{F_x{}^2 + F_y{}^2} \quad (4)$$

The limiting frictional force available for any tire was given by equation (3):

$$F_F = w\mu \quad (3)$$

This is similar to the equations found earlier:

$$F_x = wf_x$$
$$F_y = wf_y$$

Substitute the values for F_x and F_y above, and the value for F_F in equation (3), into equation (4):

$$w\mu = \sqrt{(wf_x)^2 + (wf_y)^2}$$

Simplify the equation:

$$\mu = \sqrt{f_x{}^2 + f_y{}^2}$$

Solve this equation for f_y:

$$f_y = \sqrt{\mu^2 - f_x{}^2} \quad (48)$$

Equation (48) indicates how the available frictional force is distributed under lateral and longitudinal acceleration in terms of drag factor for level pavement. It is a good approximation for grade on most curves.

The required measurements for establishing the radius should be taken as close as possible to the start of the yaw, where the side slip angle (β) is small. If the measurements are taken at the start of the yaw and no substantial braking occurs, equation (46) is the same as equation (37).

With no substantial braking:

$$f_x = 0$$

and

$$f_y = \mu$$

Substitute these values into equation (46):

$$v = \sqrt{\{gr[(f_y \cos \beta - f_x \sin \beta)(\sin \theta \tan \theta + \cos \theta) + \tan \theta]\}} \quad (46)$$

$$v = \sqrt{\{gr[(\mu \cos \beta - 0 \sin \beta)(\sin \theta \tan \theta + \cos \theta) + \tan \theta]\}}$$

$$v = \sqrt{\{gr[(\mu \cos \beta)(\sin \theta \tan \theta + \cos \theta) + \tan \theta]\}}$$

Expand the equation:

$$v = \sqrt{\{gr[(\mu \cos \beta \sin \theta \tan \theta + \mu \cos \beta \cos \theta + \tan \theta]\}}$$

Square both sides of the equation and rearrange:

$$v^2/gr = \mu \cos \beta \sin \theta \tan \theta + \mu \cos \beta \cos \theta + \tan \theta$$

Combine like terms and simplify:

$$v^2/gr = \tan \theta(\mu \cos \beta \sin \theta + 1) + \mu \cos \beta \cos \theta$$

Substitute sin θ/cos θ for tan θ:

$$v^2/gr = \sin \theta/\cos \theta(\mu \cos \beta \sin \theta + 1) + \mu \cos \beta \cos \theta$$

Expand the equation:

$$v^2/gr = (\mu \cos \beta \sin^2 \theta + \sin \theta + \mu \cos \beta \cos^2 \theta)/\cos \theta$$

Combine like terms and simplify:

$$v^2/gr = [\mu \cos \beta (\sin^2 \theta + \cos^2 \theta) + \sin \theta]/\cos \theta$$

From trigonometry, $\sin^2\theta + \cos^2\theta = 1$. Substitute this into the equation:

$$v^2/gr = [\mu \cos \beta + \sin \theta]/\cos \theta$$

Expand the equation:

$$v^2/gr = \mu \cos \beta/\cos \theta + \sin \theta /\cos \theta$$

Substitute $\tan \theta$ for $\sin \theta/\cos \theta$:

$$v^2/gr = \mu \cos \beta/\cos \theta + \tan \theta$$

Substitute G for $\tan \theta$ in the equation:

$$v^2/gr = \mu \cos \beta/\cos \theta + G$$

If the radius measurements are taken at the start of the yaw:

$$\beta \approx 0°$$
$$\cos 0° = 1$$

Substitute this value for $\cos \beta$ into the previous equation:

$$v^2/gr = \mu/\cos \theta + G$$

If the grade is small:

$$\theta \approx 0°$$
$$\cos 0° = 1$$

Substitute this value for the $\cos \theta$ into the previous equation:

$$v^2/gr = \mu + G$$

Solve the equation for v:

$$v = \sqrt{gr(\mu + G)} \qquad (37)$$

This is the same equation that was discussed earlier.

Equations (40) and (46) are based on the balancing of the centrifugal and centripetal forces and should **not** be used for after-collision velocity estimates.

6. VELOCITY ESTIMATE COMPARISON

Perhaps one example using the equations presented up to now will best illustrate how they are used to estimate vehicle velocity and how the estimates from each compare. First, the basic equations will be used to estimate the velocity. Next, the more detailed equations developed to consider side slip angle and braking will be used.

Assume for this example that the following information is given about a vehicle attempting to negotiate a turn:

$w = 3,500$ lbs = vehicle weight
$f_x = 0.10$ = longitudinal drag factor
$l = 100$ ft = chord
$h = 5.0$ ft = middle ordinate
$\mu = 0.55$ = coefficient of friction
$G = 0.02$ = grade, therefore $\theta = 1.2°$
$\beta = 5°$ = side slip angle

Radius

Find: r, the radius of the path of the vehicle's center of mass as indicated by the yawmarks.

Equation (34) can be used to find the radius.

$$r = l^2/8h + h/2 \qquad (34)$$
$$r = (100^2)/(8)(5.0) + (5.0)/(2)$$
$$r = 250 \text{ ft (rounded to the nearest 10 ft)}$$

Basic Equations for Estimating Sideslip Velocity

Find: v, the velocity of the vehicle considering the radius and the coefficient of friction.

If grade is ignored, equation (35) can be used to estimate the velocity:

$$v = \sqrt{gr\mu} \qquad (35)$$
$$v = \sqrt{(32.2)(250)(0.55)}$$
$$v = 66.5 \text{ ft/sec}$$

Equation (36) takes grade into account and can be used to estimate the velocity:

$$v = \sqrt{gr(\mu + G)/(1 - \mu G)} \qquad (36)$$
$$v = \sqrt{[(32.2)(250)(0.55 + 0.02)]/[(1) - (0.55)(0.02)]}$$
$$v = 68.1 \text{ ft/sec}$$

Simplifying the grade allows equation (37) to be used to estimate the velocity:

$$v = \sqrt{gr(\mu + G)} \qquad (37)$$
$$v = \sqrt{[(32.2)(250)(0.55 + 0.02)]}$$
$$v = 67.7 \text{ ft/sec}$$

Velocity Estimates Considering Special Conditions

Find: v, the velocity of the vehicle considering the radius, coefficient of friction, grade, and side slip angle.

Equation (40) can be used to estimate the velocity:

$$v = \sqrt{[gr(\mu \cos \theta \cos \beta + \sin \theta)/(\cos \theta - \mu \sin \theta \cos \beta)]} \quad (40)$$

$$v = \sqrt{\{\{(32.2)(250)[(0.55)(\cos 1.2°)(\cos 5°) + (\sin 1.2°)]\}/[(\cos 1.2°) - (0.55)(\sin 1.2°)(\cos 5°)]\}}$$

$$v = 68.0 \text{ ft/sec}$$

Find: v, the velocity of the vehicle considering the radius, coefficient of friction, grade, side slip angle, and longitudinal acceleration.

Equations (46) and (48) can be used to estimate the velocity:

$$f_y = \sqrt{\mu^2 - f_x^2} \quad (48)$$

$$f_y = \sqrt{[(0.55)^2 - (0.10)^2]}$$

$$f_y = 0.54$$

$$v = \sqrt{\{gr[(f_y \cos \beta - f_x \sin \beta)(\sin \theta \tan \theta + \cos \theta) + \tan \theta]\}} \quad (46)$$

$$v = \sqrt{\{(32.2)(250)\{[(0.54)(\cos 5°) - (0.10)(\sin 5°)][(\sin 1.2°)(\tan 1.2°) + (\cos 1.2)] + (\tan 1.2°)\}\}}$$

$$v = 66.6 \text{ ft/sec}$$

The results from equations (35), (36), (37), (40) and (46) are summarized below:

$$v = \sqrt{gr\mu} \quad (35)$$

$$v = 66.5 \text{ ft/sec}$$

$$v = \sqrt{gr(\mu + G)/(1 - \mu G)} \quad (36)$$

$$v = 68.1 \text{ ft/sec}$$

$$v = \sqrt{gr(\mu + G)} \quad (37)$$

$$v = 67.7 \text{ ft/sec}$$

$$v = \sqrt{[gr(\mu \cos \theta \cos \beta + \sin \theta)/(\cos \theta - \mu \sin \theta \cos \beta)]} \quad (40)$$

$$v = 68.0 \text{ ft/sec}$$

$$v = \sqrt{\{gr[(f_y \cos \beta - f_x \sin \beta)(\sin \theta \tan \theta + \cos \theta) + \tan \theta]\}} \quad (46)$$

$$v = 66.6 \text{ ft/sec}$$

Summary

The difference between the estimate using the simplified equation (36) and the one using the more detailed equation (46) is 1.5 ft/sec (1.0 mi/hr). This demonstrates that even with light braking and a small side slip angle, the difference between the two methods is not large.

If the measurements to calculate the radius of the path of the center of mass are not taken near the beginning of the yawmarks, where the side slip angle is small, the difference between the two methods will increase. One factor that tends to counterbalance the effect of side slip angle is that the velocity of the vehicle and its radius decrease as the vehicle progresses though the yaw. The end result is that the velocity estimate is also reduced.

In most situations there is no substantial longitudinal acceleration present, and the estimate from equation (36) is only slightly higher than the estimate using equation (40) which takes only side slip angle into consideration. The main drawback to using equations (40) and (46) lies in determining the appropriate side slip angle and longitudinal acceleration values. The side slip angle and longitudinal acceleration values are impossible to determine in most cases.

The amount of off-tracking between the right or left yawmarks suggests the amount of side slip angle. Exhibit 57 shows a vehicle (wheelbase and track width) at various locations throughout a yaw. As the vehicle progresses through the yaw, the side slip angle (β) becomes larger. Similarly, the yawmarks from the right front and rear tires off-track more and suggest the amount of slip angle.

Investigations of actual cases indicate that a vehicle in a sideslip maneuver rarely has any braking or power added. The tests referred to in this topic suggest that, in most cases, adding power has very little effect on velocity estimates for moderate-to-high-velocity situations. The tests also indicate that substantial braking, short of locking the tires, does not affect the velocity estimates significantly.

The most likely choice of a driver whose vehicle is in a yaw is to apply the brakes. Applying the brakes can result in locking the tires and skidding, which is usually very obvious when it occurs. Exhibit 58 shows a tire mark that is a combination of a yawmark and skidmark. The beginning of the tire mark is a yawmark (A) and toward the end it becomes a skidmark (B) when the brakes are applied hard enough to lock the tires. Notice that the change from a yawmark (rolling and sliding tire) to a skidmark (sliding tire) is indicated by the abrupt change in the angle of the striations (indicated by the chalk marks).

The yawmarks themselves can usually suggest whether any substantial longitudinal acceleration was present. A tire that is side slipping usually leaves a tire mark with striations in it (Topic 817). The configuration of these striations is different for a free-rolling tire than for a tire being accelerated (brakes or power applied).

Exhibit 59 shows the tire and axle superimposed over the striations in three different yawmarks (marks A, B, and C). Mark A was left by a tire that was free to rotate, B by a tire subjected to brakes being applied, and C by a tire subjected to power being applied. If the tire is free-rolling and side-slipping, the striations will be more or less parallel to the axle the tire is on. When a tire is being decelerated (brakes ap-

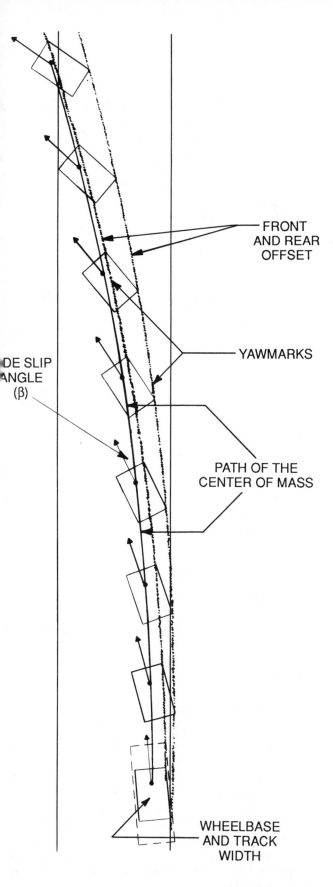

Exhibit 58. *The beginning of the tire mark is a yawmark (A), and toward the end it becomes a skidmark (B) when the brakes are applied hard enough to lock the tires.*

plied) and is side slipping, the striations will not be parallel to the axle the tire is on. The striations will angle more toward being parallel to the tire mark. If the tire becomes locked, any striations will be parallel to the tire mark, and it will be a skidmark (Topic 817). If the tire is being accelerated (power applied) and is side slipping, the striations will not be parallel to the axle the tire is on. The striations will angle behind the axle and tend to be more perpendicular to the tire mark.

Exhibit 60 is similar to Exhibit 59, except the tires leaving the yawmarks are now steered. The configuration of the striations will still tend to be the same in all three situations, even if the tire is at a steer angle.

One method to determine whether the yawmark striations are more or less parallel to the axle the tire is on is to use the vehicle jig discussed earlier in this topic for determining the radius of the vehicle's center-of-mass path. The method consists simply of laying the properly adjusted jig on the yawmark and noting how the striations align with the "axles." Exhibit 61 is a photograph of a jig being used to determine whether any acceleration was present during side slipping. The direction of the striations (denoted by the pen) is parallel to the "axle" of the jig, indicating that no substantial longitudinal acceleration was present. The jig can also be used to estimate the side slip angle, β

Typical Case

A typical case where yawmarks are left on the road occurs when a car goes off the the roadway onto the shoulder. The driver probably perceives this condition as much by the sound change that occurs as by the visual stimulus. The typical reaction is to put in too much steer (overcorrect). This causes the car to go into a yaw. It takes some time before the driver is fully aware of the car's yaw condition. (Perception and reac-

Exhibit 57. *As a vehicle progresses through a yaw, the side slip angle (ß) becomes larger and the yawmarks from the right front and rear tires off-track more and more.*

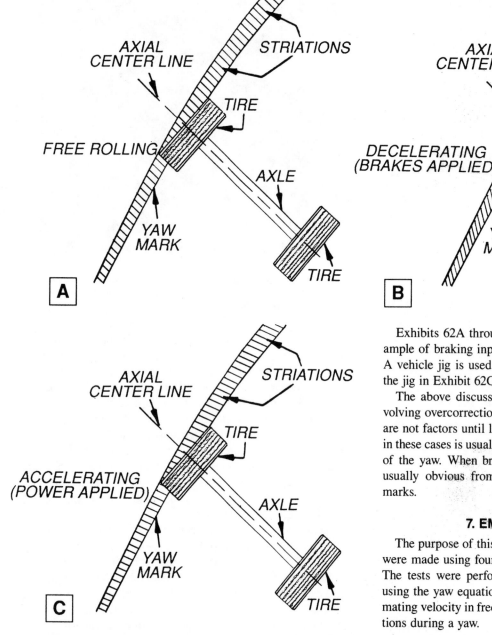

Exhibit 59. *The configuration of the striations in a yawmark is different for a free-rolling tire than for a tire that is being accelerated (brakes or power applied). Mark A was left by a tire that was free to rotate, B by a tire subjected to brakes being applied, and C by a tire subjected to power being applied.*

tion are more fully discussed in Topic 864.) After putting in steer, it can take the driver one second or longer to become fully aware of the condition. If the driver then decides to brake, the car could have been in a yaw in excess of 1.5 seconds. If the car has a fairly high speed of around 60 mi/hr (88 ft/sec), it could have been in a yaw for more than 130 ft. The radius of travel of the vehicle's center of mass could be determined in the initial 130 ft. So there would be no reason to be concerned that any significant braking input was involved.

Exhibits 62A through G are photographs showing an example of braking input some time after the yaw has begun. A vehicle jig is used in these photographs. The position of the jig in Exhibit 62G is where the vehicle began to skid.

The above discussion indicates that for typical cases involving overcorrection yaws, the side slip angle and braking are not factors until later in the incident. The side slip angle in these cases is usually small, especially during the first part of the yaw. When braking effort becomes significant, it is usually obvious from the change in striations of the tire marks.

7. EMPIRICAL STUDIES

The purpose of this section is to summarize yaw tests that were made using four different types of passenger vehicles. The tests were performed to evaluate the effectiveness of using the yaw equation [specifically, equation (35)] for estimating velocity in free-rolling, braking, and power-on conditions during a yaw.

Background Information

The three days during which the tests were conducted were very hot. On the first two days the high temperature approached 100 degrees Fahrenheit, and the third day was only slightly cooler with a high of 95 degrees F.

Four 1988-model test vehicles were used: Chevrolet Camaro, Chevrolet Caprice Classic station wagon, Buick Century, and Pontiac Firebird. The front and rear axle curb weights were obtained from General Motors. The only load in each vehicle was the driver and a small amount of test equipment. Vehicle center of mass was calculated using the axle curb weights.

Drag factors were determined from longitudinal test skids using a Vericom accelerometer. The Vericom shows the dis-

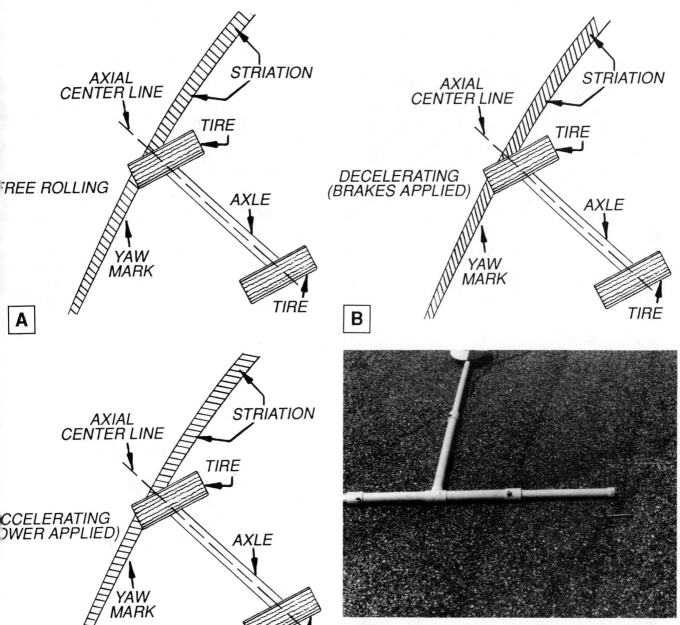

A FREE ROLLING
AXIAL CENTER LINE
STRIATION
TIRE
AXLE
YAW MARK
TIRE

B DECELERATING (BRAKES APPLIED)
AXIAL CENTER LINE
STRIATION
TIRE
AXLE
YAW MARK
TIRE

C ACCELERATING (POWER APPLIED)
AXIAL CENTER LINE
STRIATION
TIRE
AXLE
YAW MARK
TIRE

Exhibit 60. *The striation configuration in a yawmark is different for a free-rolling tire than for a tire that is being accelerated (brakes or power applied), even when the tire is steered. Mark A was left by a tire that was free to rotate, B by a tire subjected to brakes being applied, and C by a tire subjected to power being applied.*

Exhibit 61. *Using a vehicle jig is one method to determine whether yawmark striations are more or less parallel to the axle the tire is on.*

tance, initial speed, time to stop, and peak and average *g* (decimal fraction of the acceleration due to gravity).

During the yaw tests, each vehicle was fitted with a g-Analyst. The g-Analyst records lateral and longitudinal *g*'s of acceleration [lateral (f_y) and longitudinal (f_x) drag factors]. One useful feature of the g-Analyst is that the data can be stored and entered into an IBM PC compatible computer; a printed copy of the results can then be made. This was done for all of the yaw tests. Radar was used to determine initial velocities.

Test Procedure

Before each vehicle was tested in a yaw, a longitudinal skid test was made to determine the longitudinal drag factor (f_x). This was accomplished by using the Vericom accelerometer. The first longitudinal skid test was made with the Camaro, which was also equipped with a bumper gun. Using radar in a different vehicle allowed the Camaro's velocity to be determined as well. Because the Vericom accelerometer reading matched so well with the calculated drag factor using skid distance and radar velocity, only the Vericom was used on the other three vehicles.

When time allowed, the yaw tests were performed under three conditions for the four vehicles: free-rolling, braking, and power-on. For safety reasons (since vehicles would leave

Exhibit 62.

Exhibit 62. *A typical case involving side slip occurs when an inattentive driver runs off of the roadway and onto the shoulder and then attempts to steer the vehicle back onto the roadway.*

the paved area), the maximum practical velocity was limited to approximately 50 mi/hr.

The radius of the curved path followed by the center of mass of the tested vehicles was determined by using equation (34). The chord and middle ordinate were determined by employing the vehicle jig method described earlier in this topic, only three jigs were used instead of one.

Initially, there was some concern that the tires might roll off the rim and dig into the pavement, which would clearly cause some problems. To address this concern, the tires of the Camaro were inflated to 50 pounds per square inch (psi). The other three vehicles were tested with the tire pressure at 35 psi.

Chevrolet Camaro

The Chevrolet Camaro represents one of the "sports car" type of vehicles seen on the road today. It is a rear-wheel-drive, front-engine car with a stiffer suspension than that found on most other cars.

Two skid tests were done with the Camaro. One test had an initial velocity of 42 mi/hr and the other had an initial velocity of 43 mi/hr. The two average drag factors were 0.767 and 0.756, respectively.

The Camaro was the first car tested, and there were some of the usual glitches that come with first attempts. Because of the limited amount of data obtained from the Camaro tests, it was decided that additional tests would be appropriate for this type of vehicle. Thus, the Firebird tests were done on the third day.

Two Camaro tests were done with the following results:

Radius (ft)	Calculated Velocity (mi/hr)	Radar Velocity (mi/hr)	Comments
141	40.0	47	Rolling
226	50.7	57	Rolling

The value used for drag factor was the one obtained in the longitudinal skid tests. The second test value for radius was obtained by drawing to scale the tire marks that were measured at the test site with 10 ft stations (Topic 834). The chord and middle ordinate were then measured from the drawing as described earlier in this topic (Exhibit 39). The first test radius was based on the measured chord and middle ordinate taken at the test site, using the vehicle jigs.

The peak lateral g (drag factor, f_y) the Camaro experienced was 0.87. This, of course, is more than the maximum longitudinal value obtained in the skid tests. At the onset of the yaw, the lateral g hit the peak in about 0.5 sec. The lateral value stayed near the peak for at least 1 second. After 4 seconds, the lateral g was still slightly greater than 0.60. Thus, it would appear appropriate to use the drag factors obtained from the longitudinal skid tests.

Due to time constraints and the problems encountered for the first vehicle in the series of tests, only two tests with data were done using the Camaro.

Chevrolet Caprice Station Wagon

The Chevrolet station wagon represents one of the largest passenger cars seen on the road today. It is a rear-wheel-drive, front-engine car with a long wheelbase and wide track width. Tire pressure used in this vehicle for all of the tests was 35 psi.

The skid tests were done at 42 and 46 mi/hr. The resulting average drag factors were 0.731 and 0.744, respectively. These values are slightly different from those obtained with the Camaro.

Five tests were performed using the station wagon where data was collected. The results of the tests are given below:

Radius (ft)	Calculated Velocity (mi/hr)	Radar Velocity (mi/hr)	Comments
152	40.8	44	Rolling
189	45.5	49	Rolling
156	41.4	42	Braking
112	35.0	42	Braking
141	39.3	41	Power

The braking that was applied was not enough to lock any of the tires. There was a noticeable change in the angle of the striations in the yawmarks relative to the axle. The angle of the striations was determined using the vehicle jig as described earlier and shown in Exhibit 61.

The peak lateral g value obtained for the rolling tests was 0.74. This is, of course, less than that obtained for the Camaro. For the tests with braking, the peak lateral values were 0.68 and 0.69. The calculated velocities were obtained using a drag factor of 0.731. By inspecting the previous table, you can see that this had no adverse effect. The method used to determine the radius gives a value lower than what the vehicle actually experiences at the beginning of the yaw. The radius is the average radius, which is less than the radius at the immediate beginning of the yaw where the radar speed is obtained. So these two differences tend to compensate each other and still yield a value lower than the actual initial velocity.

The last test with power on reduced the lateral maximum g value to 0.64. Again, no significant problem appears to have been encountered when the calculated velocity is compared to the radar velocity.

Buick Century

The Buick is a front-engine, front-wheel-drive car. This type of vehicle is becoming increasingly popular in the U.S. The center of mass is a little more forward of the midpoint of the wheelbase as compared to the other, rear-wheel-drive vehicles.

Three test skids were done with the Buick. The test velocities were 38, 41, and 42 mi/hr. The resulting drag factors were 0.720, 0.694, and 0.688, respectively. The middle value, 0.694, was used when the velocities were calculated for the yaw tests. These values differ from those obtained with the Camaro and station wagon. We were told to expect different drag factors in different areas of the test facility.

Six tests were done using the Buick. The results of these tests are shown below:

Radius (ft)	Calculated Velocity (mi/hr)	Radar Velocity (mi/hr)	Comments
117	34.8	39	Rolling
96	31.7	37	Rolling
157	40.5	47	Braking
170	42.1	49	Braking
163	41.1	44	Power
163	41.1	48	Power

As before, the calculated values are lower than the radar values in all cases. This is true for rolling, braking, and power-on conditions.

For the rolling tests, the peak lateral g values were 0.80 and 0.79. The peak lateral values for braking were 0.76 and 0.72. As with the station wagon tires, none of the tires on the Buick locked, due to the brake application, and a change in the striation pattern could be distinguished. The peak lateral g values obtained in the power-on tests were 0.81 and 0.82. A change in the striation pattern was mainly noticeable in the marks left by the less-loaded inside tires.

Pontiac Firebird

The Firebird was tested to add to the data obtained from the Camaro tests. The Firebird represents the same "sports car" class of vehicle as the Camaro. It is a rear-wheel-drive, front-engine car with a stiffer suspension than that found on most other cars.

Four test skids were performed with the Firebird at velocities of 45, 40, 41, and 42 mi/hr. The resulting drag factors

were 0.730, 0.754, 0.772, and 0.799, respectively. A drag factor of 0.764 was used when the velocities from the yaw tests were calculated.

Eight tests were performed using the Firebird. For six of the tests the chord and middle ordinate measurements of the outside tire marks resulting from the tests were also taken and used to calculate the velocities. The results from the tests are shown below:

Radius (ft)	Calculated Velocity (mi/hr)	Radar Velocity (mi/hr)	Comments
123	37.5	44	Rolling – jig
134	39.2	44	Rolling – tire
131	38.7	46	Rolling – jig
144	40.5	46	Rolling – tire
121	37.3	45	Rolling – jig
135	39.4	45	Braking – jig
134	39.2	45	Braking – tire
133	39.0	44	Braking – jig
116	36.5	40	Power – jig
112	35.8	40	Power – tire
114	36.1	40	Power – jig
112	35.8	40	Power – tire
243	52.7	58	Rolling – jig
223	50.6	58	Rolling – tire

As before, the calculated values are lower than the radar values in all cases. This is true for rolling, braking, and power-on conditions.

The peak lateral g value obtained during the rolling tests was 0.94. The value for peak lateral g was the highest obtained from any of the four vehicles.

The peak lateral g value for the tests with braking was 0.76. In the latter tests the two inside tires were locked and sliding.

The peak lateral g value obtained with power-on was 0.92.

Conclusions

Several conclusions have already been mentioned. Other observations were prominent and are now discussed.

The radar operator commented that after the velocity was locked on, the next velocity that would show on the monitor was typically 5 to 6 mi/hr less than the initial velocity. When the g-Analyst data was inspected, it was clear that fairly high longitudinal deceleration values resulted. This indicates that a car may slow more rapidly when it is in a yaw than many people might think.

The road surface showed all four tire marks, with the outside marks more visible than the inside ones. Striations in the marks could be easily detected. Under free-rolling conditions, you would expect the striations in the tire marks to be parallel to the axle. Some of the results obtained did not show this to be exactly true. The striations were approximately 15 to 20 degrees more forward of what would be expected. The striation angles were more indicative of what would have been expected if some braking had been applied. The best explanation at this time is that the unexpected striation angles were due to the deformation of the tire and then its subsequent movement back to its original shape, along with the cornering drag present during the yaw. With power on, the mark striations approximated the expected angle for a free-rolling condition. The braking with yaw tests gave the expected results for striations, more or less. The inside tires left marks that more closely matched what was expected; that is, the striations for free rolling were more or less parallel to the axle. The striations for yaw with braking were more nearly parallel to the mark, and the striations for yaw with power on were more nearly perpendicular to the mark.

The effect of power on was minimal in the yaw tests. You would expect this at higher velocities, since the vehicle would have even less effective acceleration capability under such conditions.

It became increasingly clear during the tests that using a vehicle jig for traffic accidents when a yaw occurs is a valuable tool. Not only can you get measurements for the vehicle's center of mass, but you can also see how the tire mark striations compare to the axle position. It then is an easy procedure to photograph this, looking down on the mark and the jig. By laying a pencil/pen or by drawing a chalk mark at the same angle as the striation, it will be easier to tell the angle in the photograph (Exhibit 61).

A major concern in yaw cases is data collection. If a very high velocity is involved, a minor error in locating the yaw-marks could be significant. Using the jig on the traveled surface will help to minimize these problems. Essentially, this provides you with a "full scale drawing" of the marks.

The tests that were performed represent the typical situation encountered in traffic accidents when a yaw is present. That is, the driver for some reason has *overcorrected,* or put in too much steer for the available friction between the tires and pavement. This onset of steering is rapid. In nearly all cases, it will take the driver more than a second to realize that the choice of hard steering was not a good one. Before braking or (less likely) acceleration (power-on) is re-selected by the driver, the vehicle has traveled too far to be corrected. If the curvature of the vehicle's travel path is determined early in the yaw, there is little reason to believe that any braking or power-on conditions exist. Use of the vehicle jig described earlier will help further establish this.

The tests have done nothing to detract from the use of the yaw equation when a true yaw exists. Limited braking (that is, not enough to lock any tires) appears to have no significant effect. For that matter, no significant problem was introduced when the two inside tires were locked. The same applies to conditions of power-on. Similar tests performed by others also support this conclusion[17].

The present tests have clearly supported using the yaw equation. Similar tests also support its use[18]. However, the

obvious caveats apply when using the equation. Make sure the yaw was caused by the friction force between the tire and road surface being exceeded by the centrifugal force on the vehicle. Clearly, the yaw equation is *never* to be used after a collision has caused the vehicle to yaw.

8. COMPUTER ANALYSIS

Computer simulations can be used to test different theories people have regarding how an accident occurred. If, for example, there is concern that a driver put in some braking when a vehicle was in a yaw, a computer simulation could be done. Other "what if" conditions can also be simulated. If the actual vehicle travel path is known, then different simulation alternatives can be tested to see which "what if" situations match that path. To thoroughly test these alternatives, a scaled map of the accident vehicle's tire marks should be made. A major purpose of these programs is to determine the changes in trajectory made by steering and braking input. These inputs can be adjusted until the trajectory predicted by the simulation matches the vehicle trajectory indicated by the accident site data. A useful feature of most of these types of programs is their ability to display the vehicle travel path in a graphics display. This pictorial representation (to scale) can then be printed or plotted.

One useful simulation program is the Single Vehicle Simulator (SVS)[19] developed at the University of Michigan Transportation Research Institute. A microcomputer version with excellent graphics output is available from Engineering Dynamics Corporation (see Topic 892 for more discussion). The user of SVS must input a considerable amount of data relating to the vehicle. The following list gives an indication of the data needed to run the program:

1. Vehicle class category. This describes the general vehicle configuration. The user may use the "autoload" feature which will load default values for vehicle parameters.
2. Initial position. The *x, y,* and heading coordinates must be given.
3. Initial velocity. The *x, y,* and rotational velocities for the vehicle must be specified.
4. General brake and wheel configurations—whether the vehicle has antilock brakes or dual wheels, for example—must be specified.
5. Suspension characteristics. The lateral load transfer coefficient is specified. A three-degree freedom analysis of suspension and chassis effects is not included.
6. Dimensional and inertial data. Basic geometric values, such as center-of-mass positions of the vehicle and payload (if present), are specified. Inertial data such as the yaw moment of inertia are needed.
7. Tire data. Tire cornering stiffness data, peak friction coefficient, and sliding friction coefficient are needed.
8. Wheel force and steer tables. The user must input the driver's input to the car. That is, how much steer and braking and how fast the steering and braking take place

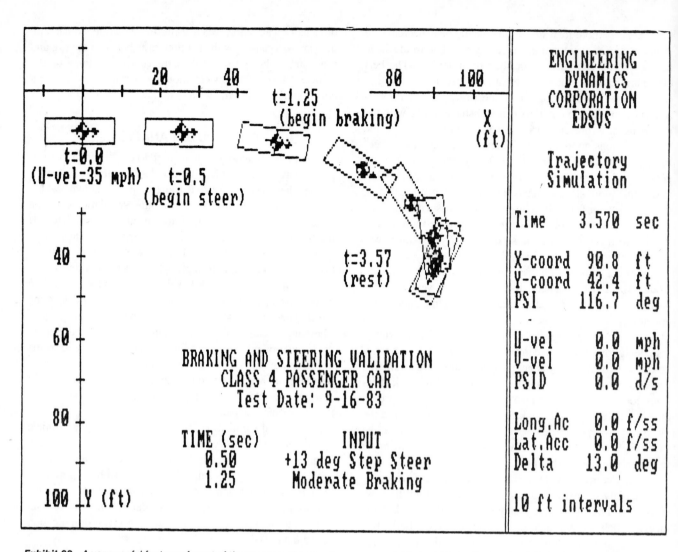

Exhibit 63. *A very useful feature of most of these types of computer programs is their ability to display the vehicle's trajectory instantly in a pictorial representation.*

must also be put into the simulation.

The output of SVS includes such information as:

1. Time. The output is displayed as a function of time.
2. Center-of-mass position. The x, y, and heading angle of the vehicle are displayed.
3. Center-of-mass velocity. The x and y components of velocity, along the with angular velocity of the vehicle, are given. Sideslip (β) is determined from the heading and total velocity vector.
4. Center-of-mass acceleration. The components of acceleration and the angular acceleration are provided.
5. Tire/wheel forces. The steering and braking table inputted by the user is displayed. Also, the computed longitudinal, lateral, and vertical loads on each wheel are displayed. If the user-inputted attempted force was greater than the allowable force, the program only uses the available force.
6. Tire slip angles (α). These angles are provided for every tire and are responsible for the cornering force.

These output data can be used to generate graphic output showing the vehicle position as a function of time. This can be very useful in the comparison against the marks generated by the accident vehicle.

As can be seen, a fairly significant effort has to be made when SVS is used. However, the results can be very helpful. Exhibit 63 is a trajectory simulation obtained from the Engiering Dynamics Single Vehicle Simulator (EDSVS) program.

Other programs can be used to simulate vehicle response to braking and steering inputs. The SMAC (Simulation of Accidents) program can also be used. However, SMAC does not consider lateral and longitudinal load shifts which may be important. A detailed discussion of vehicle simulation programs can be found elsewhere (see Topic 892).

9. EVASIVE MANEUVER

A vehicle moving forward can slow, speed up, turn left, or turn right to avoid a collision. If the vehicle slows with locked brakes, it will continue more or less straight ahead and cannot be turned. However, if the brakes are not applied hard enough to lock the tires, the vehicle can turn; but turning is

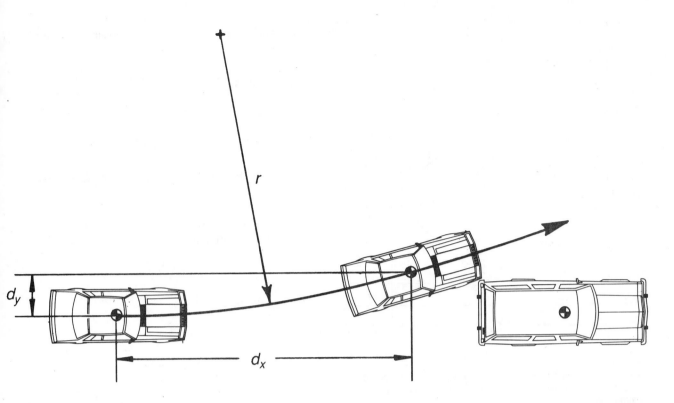

Exhibit 64. *The longitudinal distance required for a vehicle to make a turn to the left to avoid a stopped vehicle with the radius (r) is* d_x*, and the lateral distance the vehicle must move to avoid the other vehicle is* d_y.

limited. To calculate the vehicle's exact path would require a vast amount of data about the vehicle, the amount of braking, steer angle, tire data, etc. Some of these are impossible to know after an accident has occurred. Useful approximations are possible, although the calculations are very complex. These approximations can then be used to estimate the distance required to avoid an obstacle.

Exhibit 64 shows a vehicle making a turn to the left to avoid a stopped vehicle. The longitudinal distance required to complete the maneuver with the radius (r) is d_x, and the lateral distance the vehicle must move to avoid the other vehicle is d_y. Examining the turning maneuver indicates that the middle ordinate is equal to d_y and half the chord is equal to d_x; therefore, the chord is equal to $2d_x$. Substitute these values into equation (34) for the chord (l) and middle ordinate (h):

$$r = l^2/8h + h/2 \qquad (34)$$
$$r = (2d_x)^2/8d_y + d_y/2$$

Solve for d_x:

$$d_x = \sqrt{(2d_y r - d_y^2)} \qquad (49)$$

where

d_x = longitudinal distance (ft, m)
d_y = lateral distance (ft, m)
r = radius (ft, m)

Equation (49) indicates that the longitudinal distance (d_x) in Exhibit 64 required to swerve over a lateral distance (d_y) depends on the radius (r) of the curved path that the vehicle follows. This radius depends on the vehicle's velocity, the roadway's coefficient of friction, and the amount of lateral acceleration the vehicle is subjected to. Most drivers seldom use more than half of the vehicle's available lateral acceleration capabilities. General Motors performed tests with different drivers executing several maneuvers in vehicles equipped to measure lateral acceleration[20]. Ninety-five percent of the drivers did not exceed 0.38g (12.24 ft/sec^2) of lateral acceleration at 20 mi/hr, or 0.24g (7.73 ft/sec^2) at 55 mi/hr. Other investigations indicate that drivers rarely exceed a lateral acceleration value of 0.25 to 0.30g (8.05 to 9.66 ft/sec^2)[6].

The radius is found by solving equation (35) for the radius, then using the appropriate velocity and lateral acceleration:

$$v = \sqrt{gr\mu} \qquad (35)$$

$$r = v^2/g\mu$$

The relationship between coefficient of friction (μ) and lateral acceleration is

$$\mu = a_y/g$$

Substitute this value for μ into the previous equation:

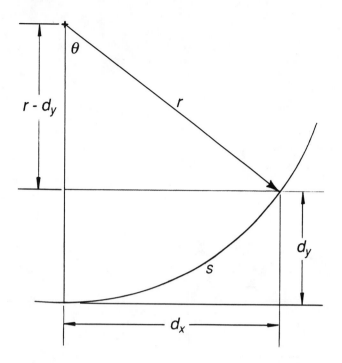

Exhibit 65. *Estimating the required longitudinal distance (d_x) to avoid an obstacle with a single turn involves several geometric relationships.*

$$r = v^2/a_y \qquad (50)$$

The value for the radius (r) found in equation (50) is used in equation (49) to find the distance (d_x) required for the maneuver. For example, the driver of a vehicle traveling 60 mi/hr (88 ft/sec) steers to avoid another vehicle and does so with a lateral acceleration (a_y) of 0.30g (9.66 ft/sec^2). The radius of the turn is calculated as follows:

$$r = v^2/a_y \qquad (50)$$
$$r = (88^2)/(9.66)$$
$$r = 800 \text{ ft}$$

If the lateral distance (d_y) the vehicle must move is 10 ft, the longitudinal distance (d_x) is calculated as follows:

$$d_x = \sqrt{(2d_yr - d_y^2)} \qquad (49)$$
$$d_x = \sqrt{[(2)(10)(800) - (10^2)]}$$
$$d_x = 125 \text{ ft}$$

Another method of estimating the required longitudinal distance (d_x) to avoid an obstacle with a single turn can be found from Exhibit 65:

$$\cos \theta = (r - d_y)/r$$

or:

$$\cos \theta = 1 - d_y/r$$

The cosine of an angle (radian measure) expressed as a series is:

$$\cos \theta = 1 - \theta^2/2! + \theta^4/4! - \ldots$$

or simply:

$$\cos \theta = 1 - \theta^2/2$$

Substitute this cosine value into the previous equation:

$$1 - \theta^2/2 = 1 - d_y/r$$

Solve this equation for θ:

$$\theta = \sqrt{2\,d_y/r}$$

For small angles:

$$d_x \approx r\theta$$

or:

$$\theta = d_x/r$$

Substitute this value for θ into the equation above and solve for d_x:

$$d_x = r\sqrt{2d_y/r}$$

or:

$$d_x = \sqrt{2d_yr}$$

Lateral acceleration is found by solving equation (50) for a_y:

$$a_y = v^2/r$$

Solve this equation for r and substitute it into the previous equation:

$$d_x = v\sqrt{2d_y/a_y} \qquad (51)$$

where

v = velocity (ft/sec, m/sec)
d_x = longitudinal distance (ft, m)
d_y = lateral distance (ft, m)
a_y = lateral acceleration (ft/sec^2, m/sec^2)

The information given in the previous example can be used in equation (51) to estimate the required distance:

$$d_x = v\sqrt{2\,d_y/a_y} \qquad (51)$$

$$d_x = (88)\sqrt{(2)(10)/(9.66)}$$

$$d_x = 125 \text{ ft}$$

Caution should be used in applying equations (49) or (51) to an actual case. Some of the assumptions in the derivation of these equations are that the steering input was instantaneous (i.e., there was no transition period), no vehicle variables (such as suspension) exist, no slowing was taking place, and the lateral acceleration was constant and at a known value. The actual path followed by the vehicle is curved and is longer than the longitudinal distance calculated. This does not mean the equations cannot serve to estimate the required distance for a maneuver as described, but rather, that the results should be interpreted as a first estimate only.

Neither equation (49) nor (51) considers what happens to the vehicle after it avoids a hazard. That is, you may calculate the longitudinal distance it takes to avoid a hazard, but then fail to consider what the vehicle might have to do to avoid another hazard. For example, let's consider a car traveling on a freeway. The driver was confronted with a large wheel lying on the road surface but may not have been able to see it because a large van was in front of him. The van swerved suddenly (at the last instant) and avoided the wheel. The driver of the car was suddenly confronted with an obstacle in front of him. If he swerved to the left hard enough to avoid the wheel, he would then be confronted with an almost sure collision with a median barrier. In using equations (49) and (51), be aware that you may need to consider where the vehicle must have traveled after missing the hazard.

A computer simulation using SVS or SMAC could be used for evasive maneuvers. You could use non-instantaneous steering inputs, which would generally be more realistic than using equations (49) and (51). However, it is still important to use realistic lateral accelerations and steering inputs. You could simulate what the driver may have done to avoid a second hazard that resulted from trying to avoid the first. In the example noted in the previous paragraph, the travel path of the car avoiding the wheel in the road could be simulated, along with the resulting travel path after the first hazard avoidance.

10. SOURCES

Authors

Gary W. Cooper is senior consultant and lecturer in The Traffic Institute's Accident Investigation Division, and has an engineering degree from Purdue University. Before joining the Institute in 1984, he was with the Indiana State Police.

Lynn B. Fricke is an engineer specializing in accident investigation. He has been with The Traffic Institute since 1975. In 1981, he became director of the Institute's Accident Investigation Division. He has B.S. and M.S. degrees in engineering.

The authors wish to thank the following individuals: *Wilton D. Nelson,* of Crash Analysis and Reconstruction (Howell, Michigan) for his assistance in performing the empirical studies and for his review of and comment on the topic; *Colonel Arthur R. Raney, Jr.,* executive director of the Indiana Law Enforcement Academy, and his staff in Plainfield, Indiana, for the use of their Emergency Vehicle Operation Course (EVOC) in performing the empirical studies.

References

Superscript numbers in the preceding pages refer to the following publications:

1. Society of Automotive Engineers, *Vehicle Dynamics Terminology,* SAE J670e, 1984.
2. Segel, L., *Tire Traction on Dry, Uncontaminated Surfaces,* University of Michigan, 1973.
3. Brewer, H. K., and R. S. Rice, *Tires—Stability and Control,* SAE 830561, 1983.
4. Bergman, W., *Skid Resistance Properties of Tires and Their Influence on Vehicle Control,* TRB 621, 1977.
5. Bernard, J. E., L. Segel, and R. E. Wild, *Tire Shear Force Generation During Combined Steering and Braking Maneuvers,* SAE 770852, 1977.
6. Rice, R. S., *Measuring Car-Driver Interaction with the g-g Diagram,* SAE 730018, 1973.
7. Goodsell, D., *Dictionary of Automotive Engineering,* Society of Automotive Engineers, Warrendale, PA, 1989.
8. Bernard, J., P. Fancer, R. Gupta, H. Moncarz, and L. Segel, *Vehicle-In-Use Limit Performance and Tire Factor,* U.S. Dept. of Transportation, 1975.
9. Limpert, R., *Motor Vehicle Accident Reconstruction and Cause Analysis,* The Michie Company, Charlottesville, VA, 1984.
10. Ford Motor Co., *Quick Reference,* Training Handbook 3000, Vol. 67 S10 L2, 1967.
11. Abbott, S., and I. Hinerman, *Suspension and Steering,* Glencoe Publishing Company, Encino, CA, 1982.
12. Bernard, J., P. Fancer, R. Gupta, H. Moncarz, and L. Segel, *Vehicle-In-Use Limit Performance and Tire Factor,* Appendices D through G, U.S. Dept. of Transportation, 1975.
13. Daniels, J., *Handling and Roadholding Car Suspension at Work,* Motor Racing Publications, Great Britain, 1988.
14. Bondurant, B., and J. Blakemore, *Bob Bondurant on High Performance Driving,* Motorbooks International, Osceola, WI, 1987.
15. Schmidt, M., and W. Rayner, *Fundamentals of Surveying,* D. Van Nostrand Company, New York, NY, 1978.
16. Manning, L., and L. Bentson, *Highway Speed vs. Sideslip,* NAFE 064M, 1984.
17. Hink, C., *Critical Speed Tests,* Washington Association of Technical Accident Investigators, 1983.
18. Lambourn, R. F., *The Calculation of Vehicle Cornering*

Speeds from Curved Tyre Marks, Metropolitan Police Forensic Science Laboratory, 1987.

19. Day, T., *EDSVS Training Manual*, Engineering Dynamics Corporation, Lake Oswego, OR, 1984.

20. Milliken, W., and R. Rice, *Vehicle Handling Test (VHT) Program of the American Motors 1981 Jeep CJ-5*, Calspan, 1981.

Exhibits

The following are the sources of the exhibits used in this topic:

Blakemore, J., and B. Bondurant, Sonoma, CA
Diagrams: 33, 34

Cooper, G. W., Northwestern University Traffic Institute
Diagrams: 2, 4-11, 13, 15-30, 36-39, 50-57, 59A-C, 60A-C, 64, 65
Photos: 35, 41, 42A-D, 49A-C, 62A-G

Day, T., Engineering Dynamics Corporation
Diagram: 63

Fricke, L. B., Northwestern University Traffic Institute
Photos: 43, 44, 45, 46, 58, 61

Limpert, R., Salt Lake City, UT
Diagrams: 31, 32

Society of Automotive Engineers, Warrendale, PA
Diagrams: 1, 3, 12, 14

RECONSTRUCTION OF MOTORCYCLE TRAFFIC ACCIDENTS

Topic 874 of the *Traffic Accident Investigation Manual*

by
Lynn B. Fricke
and
Warner W. Riley

NORTHWESTERN UNIVERSITY TRAFFIC INSTITUTE

RECONSTRUCTION OF MOTORCYCLE TRAFFIC ACCIDENTS

1. INTRODUCTION

Motorcycle accident reconstruction is enhanced by detailed data collection at the accident scene. Preferably, this data collection takes place at a time when the colliding vehicle or vehicles are still available and in-place after collision. It is understood, however, that many times this data collection must take place in light of either slight or major movement of the vehicle(s) involved in the accident. In any instance, the meticulous data collection at the scene of the accident will assist in reconstructing both motorcycle and automobile accidents. Reconstruction is always made easier following good data collection and investigative techniques. It therefore becomes important to look for and document tire marks, vehicle parts, gouges in the pavement, abrasions on the pavement, marks caused by the motorcycle leaving the paved surface, and the location and pattern of both liquid and solid debris. Measurements documenting the location of these items are of great assistance to the reconstructionist. Photographic documentation, with points of reference, are also very helpful later in determining vehicle damage, roadway marks, and vehicle/people points of rest.

The following information on motorcycle accident reconstruction and investigation considers that there are significant differences between the motorcycle vehicle and an automobile as vehicles. Motorcycle accident reconstruction must take into account that motorcycles and motorcycle riders are different from automobiles and automobile occupants. Motorcycles can and do roll, pitch, and yaw before, during, and after collision and/or fall-down. Automobiles usually enter and leave the accident sequence (when it involves a motorcycle) with all four wheels on the ground. A motorcycle may be leaning left or right (rolling), braking or accelerating to cause pitch in the form of a modest or extreme weight change between the front and rear tire, while the motorcycle by virtue of rider activity and/or brake input may be in the process of yawing to the left or right prior to impact. The motorcycle operator and passenger (if present) are not occupants constrained by the restraints and/or interior of an automobile, but are loosely attached to the motorcycle; they may be on or off the motorcycle prior to, during, or after the collision or fall-down. The change in velocity for the motorcycle may or may not correspond with the change in velocity for the loosely coupled operator and/or passenger. Fall-down is mentioned because single-vehicle loss-of-control accidents involving motorcycles are not uncommon and may present difficult accident reconstruction problems.

The braking capability of most modern motorcycles far exceeds the braking capability of most automobiles. Motorcycle acceleration, especially on the more powerful sport motorcycles, also greatly exceeds the acceleration capabilities of most automobiles. Some of the more unusual motorcycle riding practices should also be taken into account. A motorcyclist may actually be executing something like a "wheelie" (a high-acceleration maneuver where the front wheel is lifted) prior to the accident. Certainly this would have to be taken into account as part of the collision sequence during reconstruction. In short, familiarity with motorcycles and motorcycling is very important to the complete investigation and ultimate reconstruction of a motorcycle accident.

One caution that should be passed on from experience is that eyewitness accounts of speed in motorcycle accident cases, just as in other vehicle accident cases, tend to be somewhat questionable although they should be taken into account. Eyewitness testimony may suggest that a motorcycle was traveling "at a high rate of speed." Such a statement may or may not be true. The eyewitness may be influenced by the lack of experience in observation and knowledge of motorcycles. Eyewitnesses may also be influenced by the existence of a modified motorcycle exhaust system (louder than original equipment). Thus, such information must be judged against the available physical evidence.

A typical motorcycle/automobile collision scenario is at an intersection. It is not unusual for automobile operators making a left turn across oncoming traffic and crashing into a motorcycle to claim that they did not see the motorcycle and even go so far as to say that "the motorcycle headlight was off." Typically, what the automobile operator really means is that he didn't see whether the light was on. In fact, he may have seen the motorcycle but didn't properly identify its speed, its position, or both. Therefore, in motorcycle/automobile collision investigations, motorcycle headlight examination can be important, and preservation of the headlight in its immediate post-accident condition is very helpful in resolving this issue.

Current motorcycles sold in the United States have the headlight hard-wired to the ignition system. That means the headlight automatically comes on when the motorcycle is started. There is no separate switch to then turn the headlight off. (This may not be true for "enforcement" motorcycles.) Many motorcycles also have additional running lights in the form of illuminated front turn signals. A motorcycle's headlight being on or off may become less of an issue as time goes on. Most post-1979 motorcycles have the headlight hard-wired as described.

The Motorcycle Accident Scene

The subject of inspecting an accident scene for possible clues as to how the accident occurred is covered in Topic 817, *Traffic Accident Information from Roads*. All significant marks should be located by measurements and photographs. (These subjects are covered in Topics 828 and 836.) The present topic reviews briefly the marks often seen at accident scenes.

Motorcycle tire marks on the pavement from braking are usually different from the marks created by automobiles. There are at least four types of pre-collision skidmarks for motorcycles:

1. *Rear tire hooked skid*. Through a combination of steer/lean inputs, the motorcycle operator has failed to keep the motorcycle going straight. The rear of the motorcycle has started to come around after the rear wheel was locked due to an over-application of the rear brake. When the rear wheel stops rotating, the tire has 100 percent slip relative to the road surface. At that point the rear tire of the motorcycle loses lateral stability (this phenomenon is discussed in greater detail in Topic 862). The motorcycle does not necessarily fall over, depending on the operator's skill, the roadway geometry, and the roadway surface condition. If the rear of the motorcycle comes around substantially and the operator releases the rear brake (and the motorcycle is still moving), the motorcycle may straighten up so rapidly that the operator will be thrown off the motorcycle. This is sometimes called "going over the high side".

2. *Rear tire weaved skid*. Through a combination of steer/lean inputs, the operator has kept the motorcycle going relatively straight. The tires track in more or less the same line, even though only the rear tire is locked and marking the pavement.

3. *Straight skid*. The motorcycle may have braking on both front and rear brakes. If the skid is fairly long, only the rear brake will be locked. The motorcycle is very unstable if the front wheel is locked. However, the front wheel may have brake(s) applied the whole time. The use of the front brake (but not locking the wheel) provides greater braking stability, so a straight skid is more likely to have been produced by using both the front and rear brakes, while a weaved/hooked skid is an indication of the rear brake being used alone.

4. *Front tire skid*. A front tire skid (locked wheel) will be darker than a rear tire skid because the motorcycle's forward weight transfer during braking puts more load on the front tire. It will also be straight and limited in length because the motorcycle will usually end up falling down. The mark may also get wider near the end as the handlebars turn to one side and the cycle is about to fall.

Marks made by motorcycle tires in collisions are similar to other vehicle tire marks with respect to changes in direction due to impact. However, a motorcycle tire usually does not have a flat tread; it is rounded, because motorcycle cornering is accomplished by steering/leaning. Also, motorcycle tires are usually not nearly as wide at the contact patch (tire/roadway interface) as those of an automobile, so tire marks are often much narrower. If hard braking is applied to the front wheel (but not enough to lock it) when the rear wheel is locked, considerable load is shifted to the front wheel. This unloading of the rear wheel may also contribute to a narrower skid mark. Examining the tire tread surface for flat spots in the middle of the tread or for side scuffs on the side tread blocks can often confirm which tire, front or rear, left the skidmark. Some typical motorcycle tire marks are shown in Exhibits 1-3.

Exhibit 1. Note the motorcycle skidmark between the four skidmarks from a passenger car. The motorcycle skid is not perfectly straight.

Exhibit 2. *The beginning of this rear-wheel motorcycle skid is somewhat irregular. This is most likely caused by the pavement irregularities. The end of the skid is shown in Exhibit 3.*

Motorcycles often make marks in and on the road as they fall to the pavement and move off to their final positions. In nearly all motorcycle/auto collisions, gouges in the roadway and abrasions on the roadway are likely to have been caused by the motorcycle. Gouges made as a motorcycle first contacted the pavement are shown in Exhibit 4. Typical gouges/scrapes made by a motorcycle as it moved to its final position are shown in Exhibits 5 and 6. Distinctive abrasion marks from steel, aluminum, rubber, plastic, and fiberglass parts can result from a motorcycle falling onto the pavement and sliding to its final position.

A metal abrasion mark can be made by a motorcycle's sidestand if the operator forgets to retract it and leans hard to the side where the stand is located.[1] The sidestand is often self-stowing or will retract automatically if it touches the road as the motorcycle is moving forward. Some motorcycles have an interlock to ensure that the operator stows the sidestand. If you have reason to believe that loss of control was precipitated by the failure of the operator to retract the sidestand, look at the bottom of the sidestand to see if there are any significant fresh abrasions from contact with pavement. The abrasions from failing to stow the sidestand properly should be approximately parallel to the motorcycle's longitudinal axis. You may see abrasions on the stand that are not parallel. These are more nearly perpendicular to the motorcycle's longitudinal axis and can occur during normal use as the sidestand is used to hold the motorcycle upright when it is parked. Also, look on the road surface for any sign of an abrasion/scratch that would have come from the sidestand. One situation in which the sidestand might have caused a problem would be a single-vehicle accident that left a pavement abrasion/scratch with a radius greater than that of the curve being negotiated. This situation is depicted in Exhibit 7. The motorcycle operator

Exhibit 3. *The final part of the skid shown in Exhibit 2 is shown here. The rear-wheel motorcycle skid starts to curve toward its end near the railroad tracks.*

Exhibit 4. *The gouges and scrapes shown here occurred when a motorcycle first fell to the pavement as a result of a collision.*

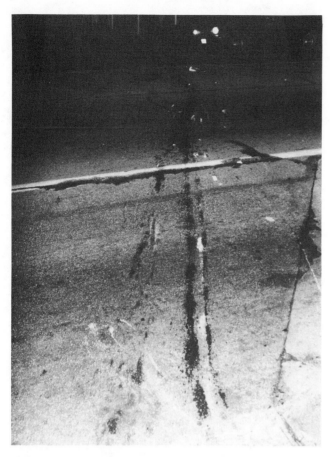

Exhibit 5. *The gouges, scrapes, and liquid debris shown here were made as the motorcycle moved to its final position after falling to the pavement.*

Exhibit 6. *The arrows show abrasion marks made by a motorcycle sliding on its side after it fell to the pavement. These marks are not as deep as gouges and will disappear more quickly.*

tried to lean in order to negotiate the curve. The unretracted sidestand prevented this, and the operator could not lean into the motorcycle far enough to stay on the curve without reducing speed. It should be noted that a sidestand can come down from the retracted or stowed position during a collision and the fact that a sidestand was found in the down position does not mean it was involved in the cause of the accident.

Motorcycle collisions often leave debris. This can be in the form of vehicle parts, liquids, dirt, broken glass, and other items. As in other types of collisions, debris is not generally a good indication of first contact positions. By the time a vehicle part comes to rest, for example, it could have traveled many feet from the first contact position. For first contact position of a motorcycle, look for a collision scrub mark from the front tire. If the rear wheel was locked as the motorcycle struck another vehicle, note the end of the rear wheel skid. Normally the impact with another vehicle will cause the rear wheel to lift off the pavement or to make an abrupt change in direction. Therefore, this will be a good indication of the location of the rear wheel when the collision first occurred. It will then be necessary to account for where the front wheel of the motorcycle was when the impact occurred. This can be done through using an owner's/shop

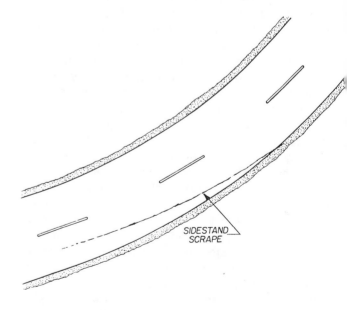

Exhibit 7. *The radius of the scratch made by the sidestand is greater than the radius of the curve. The motorcycle operator was not able to negotiate the turn because the sidestand was left down.*

manual and calculations concerning wheel/tire size and wheelbase or by measuring an undamaged exemplar motorcycle. It may also be necessary to account for the amount of front wheel collapse if extreme accuracy is desired.

As in any accident, final vehicle positions should be located and photographed. In motorcycle accidents the final positions of the motorcycle operator and passenger (if any) should be located by measurements as well. In many cases this can be of considerable help in determining how the accident occurred and in making speed estimates.

If time allows, all vehicles should be inspected at the scene of an accident to avoid introducing any additional damage due to transport. In many cases it is relatively easy to determine if motorcycle brakes are operable. If there is little damage to the motorcycle, put it on its center stand and spin the wheel in question. Then actuate the appropriate brake and see if the wheel stops. You can also roll the motorcycle and apply the appropriate brake. If the brake is working, the increased drag on the motorcycle will be easily noticed. The front brake will usually be controlled by the right-side handlebar lever, while the rear brake will usually be controlled by the right-side foot pedal. Refer to the section on motorcycle braking for more specific information.

Take special care if there is an issue regarding motorcycle headlight operation. If the headlight glass is broken, appropriate precautions should be taken to preserve the evidence. These procedures for packaging and storing lamps are discussed in Topic 823, *Lamp Examination for "On" or "Off" in Traffic Accidents*. If the "on" or "off" condition of the motorcycle headlamp is an issue, be sure to note the make, model, and year of the motorcycle. You may want to check to see whether that particular model has the headlamp hardwired to the ignition. This can be accomplished through examining the applicable owner's/shop manuals or an exemplar motorcycle. Owner's manuals are often found stowed in the damaged motorcycle or owner's/shop manuals can be purchased from a motorcycle shop that handles the brand in question. Preserving the brake/taillight lamp(s) may also be important in determining lights on/off and brake application issues.

Motorcycle Types

For those unfamiliar with motorcycles, the following is a brief discussion of the typical types. (This is not intended to be in-depth coverage of all types and their available options.)

Motorcycles, like cars, come in a variety of types. Each type of motorcycle is designed for a particular function. A nine-passenger maxi-van and a two-seat sports car, for instance, are designed for different functions and have different handling characteristics.

General-purpose motorcycle. In the U.S., motorcycles are not ordinarily used as a primary source of transportation. Most people who ride a motorcycle to work, for example, also have a car available. General-purpose motorcycles are designed for transportation only and have few fancy accessories. Engine size ranges from very small on up. Virtually all age groups ride this type of motorcycle. Exhibit 8 shows a typical general-purpose motorcycle.

Sport motorcycle. This is a production type with dropped handlebars, a very short fairing (windshield) with an aerodynamic look, higher foot pegs, additional lean angle capability, triple disc brakes, and a flashy paint job. A typical sport motorcycle is shown in Exhibit 9.

Touring motorcycle. This type has become increasingly popular over the last several years. Many have shaft drive (in lieu of chain drive) or belt drive and require little (if any) maintenance. The cost of a touring motorcycle is close to or exceeds that of some sub-compact cars. Their engine size typically ranges between 1200 cc and 1500 cc. Exhibit 10 shows a well-equipped touring motorcycle.

Dual-purpose motorcycles. These motorcycles are designed for on/off road use. Engine sizes range from 50 cc to 1000 cc. Because these motorcycles are intended to be used off-road, they have higher ground clearance, with the muffler mounted high on the side. Dual-purpose motorcycles are equipped with lights, horn, battery, and semi-knobby tires (DOT-approved). If the motorcycle is used only off-road, the owner may remove some of the required street-legal equipment (turn signals, mirrors). Exhibit 11 shows a typical dual-purpose motorcycle.

Enduro-legal motorcycle. This type may look like a dual-purpose motorcycle, but they are different. Enduro-legal motorcycles are not street-legal. They are equipped with lights, but the headlight does not have high and low beams. They are equipped with mufflers and are relatively quiet. These motorcycles are legal on public lands (where applicable). The tires are fullknobs (not street-legal) with large lugs that can grip under off-road conditions.

Motocross (dirt) motorcycles. A motocross motorcycle looks much like an enduro-legal motorcycle, except it is not equipped with lights. Full knobby tires (not street-legal) are

Exhibit 8. *General-purpose motorcycle. This type usually has few fancy accessories and is designed for street use.*

Exhibit 9. Typical sport motorcycle. Note the aerodynamic look, sport fairing, low handlebars and raised footpegs.

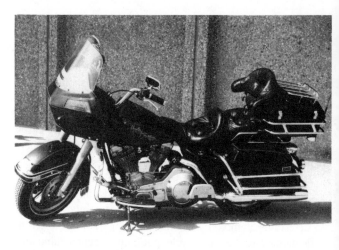

Exhibit 10. Large touring motorcycle. It has considerable storage capacity and is designed for long trips.

Exhibit 11. Dual-purpose motorcycle. It is designed for both on and off-road use. An enduro-legal motorcycle looks similar, but is not street-legal.

Exhibit 12. Motocross motorcycle. Note the absence of lights and the knobby tires.

standard. These motorcycles are usually prohibited on public lands without modification (that is, a spark arrester). Usually, the motorcycle is transported by trailer to its intended use area. A typical motocross motorcycle is shown in Exhibit 12.

Trials motorcycle. These motorcycles are not common in the U.S. They are designed for off-road competition-riding on very difficult terrain. They are geared very low and are highly stable at very low speeds. They may be equipped with lights. Exhibit 13 shows a typical trials motorcycle.

Chopper/custom motorcycle. This is an altered production motorcycle. It may have extended front forks. With greatly extended front forks, a chopper is very stable at high speeds and very difficult to control at low speeds. Sometimes a chopper may have a very small tire on the front. It may or

may not have a front brake. If it does not, the braking capability of the motorcycle is greatly reduced. Extreme examples of this type of motorcycle are not produced by manufacturers, but are owner-modified using home-built and/or after-market components. Braking, handling, and riding position are often so compromised as to make the motorcycle unsafe in certain roadway situations. A typical custom motorcycle is shown in Exhibit 14.

2. MOTORCYCLE BRAKING

Motorcycle speed estimates from braking skidmarks can be done easily if the distance the motorcycle skidded and the drag factor are known. Unfortunately, these figures may not be so easy to come by. The length of the skid may be known,

Exhibit 13. Trials motorcycle. This type is designed for off-road use over rugged terrain.

Exhibit 14. Custom motorcycle. Note the extended forks. This one is equipped with a front disk brake.

but the appropriate drag factor to use might not be so easy to determine. Motorcycle operators typically have the option of using only the rear brake, only the front brake, or both. The right hand lever usually operates the front brake. The right foot pedal usually operates the rear brake. On some motorcycles, the foot brake pedal may activate one of the front brakes and the rear brake. This is generally referred to as an integrated or unified brake system. When using this type of brake system, the operator can usually apply enough force to the foot brake pedal to lock the rear wheel. However, in normal dry conditions, using the foot brake does not apply enough force to lock the front wheel. All new motorcycles sold in the U.S. must now have the right foot pedal operate the rear brake and the left foot pedal operate the gearshift. Pre-1975 motorcycles may have the brake operated by the left foot pedal.

If you are trying to determine an appropriate drag factor and are not sure how the motorcycle operator was using the brakes, you will have a difficult time trying to make an accurate estimate of the motorcycle's drag factor. If you have only one skidmark, you will have to use a range of drag factors. Possibly only the rear brake was used. In the case of one skidmark, this would give the lowest drag factor. However, the operator might also have used the front brake without locking it, which would give a higher drag factor. If the motorcycle is of the type where the front brake is actuated along with the rear brake when the foot pedal is used, you can then make an appropriate drag factor estimate by including the effect of the front-wheel braking in the estimate. It may not be obvious whether the foot pedal also actuates the front brake. This can be determined in at least three ways:

1. If the front of the motorcycle is not severely damaged, raise the front wheel off the ground. Then spin the wheel and push on the foot brake pedal. If the front wheel stops immediately, then obviously the foot brake pedal also controls the front wheel.

2. Get a copy of the owner's/service manual for the motorcycle in question. It should have information that will answer your question. Owner's manuals are often located within the motorcycle under-seat storage areas.
3. Check with a reputable motorcycle dealer for that make of motorcycle. They should be able to tell you what type of braking system the motorcycle had when it was sold.

Equations to Determine Drag Factor

An equation that can be used to calculate drag factor on a two-axle vehicle is:

$$f_R = \frac{f_f - x_f(f_f - f_r)}{1 - z(f_f - f_r)} \quad (1)$$

where f_R = drag factor on the vehicle,
f_f = drag factor on the front axle,
f_r = drag factor on the rear axle,
x_f = horizontal distance of the center of mass from the front axle as a decimal fraction of the wheelbase, and
z = height of the center of mass as a decimal fraction of the wheelbase.

The horizontal location of the center of mass from the front axle, as a fraction of the wheelbase, is given by the equation

$$x_f = w_r/w$$

where w_r = weight on the rear axle when the vehicle is level, and $\quad (2)$
w = total weight of the vehicle.

The vertical location of the center of mass as a decimal fraction of the wheelbase is given by the following equation.

Exhibit 15. The motorcycle is shown being weighed with only the rear wheel on the scales and the front wheel raised. This will give the values needed for the equation with the front wheel lifted.

Exhibit 16. The rear-wheel weight is being measured with the motorcycle level. This will give the static weight for the rear wheel.

(The front of the motorcycle must be lifted in order to get the information needed.)

$$z = \frac{\sqrt{l^2 - h^2}\,(w_h - w_r)}{hw} + r/l \quad (3)$$

where
r = radius of the wheel,
l = wheelbase,
h = the distance the axle is lifted,
w_r = weight on the rear axle on a level surface,
w_h = weight on the rear axle when the front axle is lifted, and
w = total weight of the vehicle.

These three equations are derived in Topic 890; if you have further questions regarding them, consult that topic.

Sample Calculations for Drag Factor

A Kawasaki 1000 was weighed both level and with the front axle lifted. Exhibits 15 and 16 show the motorcycle being weighed and measured for these sample calculations, given here with the rider on the motorcycle. For this example, assume the coefficient of friction between a rubber tire and the pavement to be 0.85. The front brakes are assumed to be unused. Thus, for the front axle, only rolling resistance will be used. For this a value of 0.01 is assumed.

Horizontal location of center of mass

where
w_r = 460 lbs
w = 840 lbs
x_f = w_r/w (2)
    = 460/840
    = 0.55

Vertical location of center of mass

where
r = 1.10 ft
l = 4.88 ft
w_h = 520 lbs
w_r = 460 lbs
w = 840 lbs
h = 1.65 ft

$$z = \frac{\sqrt{l^2 - h^2}\,(w_h - w_r)}{hw} + r/l \quad (3)$$

$$z = \frac{\sqrt{(4.88^2 - 1.65^2)}\,(520 - 460)}{(1.65)(840)} + \frac{1.10}{4.88}$$

$$= .20 + .23$$
$$= .43$$

Motorcycle Drag Factor

where
f_f = .01
f_r = .85
$$f_R = \frac{f_f - x_f(f_f + f_r)}{1 - z(f_f - f_r)} \quad (1)$$

$$f_R = \frac{.01 - .55(.01 - .85)}{1 - .43(.01 - .85)}$$

$$= .34$$

Speeds from Motorcycle Skids

Speed estimates from any vehicle can be obtained from the following equation:

$$v_i = \sqrt{v_e^2 - 2ad} \qquad (4)$$

where v_i = the initial velocity in ft/sec or m/sec,
$\quad\quad\quad v_e$ = the end velocity in ft/sec or m/sec,
$\quad\quad\quad a$ = acceleration in ft/sec/sec or m/sec/sec,
and
$\quad\quad\quad d$ = acceleration distance in ft or m.

For a motorcycle skidding problem, acceleration, a, will always be negative, because the motorcycle is slowing. The value for acceleration, a, is always equal to drag factor times the acceleration of gravity ($a = fg$). The value of g, acceleration of gravity, is equal to 32.2 ft/sec/sec and 9.81 m/sec/sec.

Consider a simple problem where a motorcycle skids 95 ft with the rear brake only. Assume the drag factor is the same as the example problem just worked, where only the rear wheel brake was used to get a drag factor of 0.34. Also assume that the motorcycle skidded to a stop. The values then inserted into Equation (4) are as follows:

$$v_i = \sqrt{v_e^2 - 2ad} \qquad (4)$$

$$= \sqrt{0^2 - 2(-.34)(32.2)(95)}$$

$$= 45.6 \text{ ft/sec} = 31 \text{ mi/hr}$$

If you did not account for only the rear brake being used and assumed that the motorcycle's drag factor was equal to the coefficient of friction, 0.85, you would have obtained a considerably higher value for the speed. Using the same given values, except now using a drag factor of 0.85, you obtain the following values:

$$v_i = \sqrt{v_e^2 - 2ad} \qquad (4)$$

$$= \sqrt{0^2 - 2(-.85)(32.2)(95)}$$

$$= 72.1 \text{ ft/sec} = 49 \text{ mi/hr}$$

As you can clearly see, this can make a significant difference. If you are trying to make speed estimates from a motorcycle braking skid, be careful to get a good understanding of how the braking system operates for the particular motorcycle you are considering.

Motorcycle Braking Tests

Many individuals and organizations, including The Traffic Institute (TI), have conducted tests on the braking capability of motorcycles. Generally, it has been found that an *experienced* motorcycle operator can obtain higher drag factors than a passenger car driver can with all four wheels locked. This was the case for tests done at TI. It is also supported by Collins[2]. In the TI tests, experienced riders were asked to lock the rear brake of the test motorcycle while braking hard on the front brake, but not enough to lock the front wheel. On a road surface where a locked four-wheel passenger car was getting consistent drag factors of 0.85, the motorcycles often exceeded this value. There are several possible explanations for this. One, motorcycle tires may have different material composition from normal passenger car tires, and thus may be able to attain a higher friction value. Two, because motorcycles are shorter and higher while also having more front suspension travel than automobiles, they can experience significant forward weight transfer during braking. Three, the operators were braking the front tire very close to lockup; the friction is slightly greater right before lockup than when the brake is fully locked. It is very unlikely, however, that less experienced operators would be able to attain these high values. In particular, if an unexpected panic stop was required by a rider with little or no practice in enhancing driving skills, it is unlikely that such high values could be attained. In the tests conducted, even the experienced riders did not do as well at first as they did after some practice.

In the tests conducted with only the rear brakes being used in fully locked braking, the typical values were about 50 percent lower than those obtained in tests using a passenger car with four wheels locked (drag factor, f, equal to 0.85). Varying the types of motorcycles yielded no significant differences. That is, a small dual-purpose motorcycle had about the same drag factor as a large police motorcycle. Also tested was a large touring motorcycle with an integrated/unified braking system. This system was designed so that the front and rear brakes are applied by the foot brake, but the front wheel cannot be locked by using the foot brake on a dry surface. The rider was asked to lock the rear brake, and did so without difficulty; but he was never able to lock the front brake, even with vigorous braking. The drag factors obtained in these tests were always higher than the 0.85 figure obtained with four wheels locked on a full-size passenger car.

Typical Motorcycle Drag Factors

If you have a case where there is one skidmark from a motorcycle and you don't know whether any front wheel braking was used, you must assume, for a minimum speed estimate, that only the rear wheel was being braked. The best way to determine the appropriate drag factor would be to test the actual motorcycle that was involved in the collision. In many cases this is not possible because of motorcycle damage. An exemplar motorcycle should give very acceptable results. Yet this is often not a practical alternative due to motorcycle availability problems. If the horizontal and vertical location of the center of mass is known, then Equation (1) could be used. Unfortunately, this data is not easy to come by. Tests done at TI suggest using a value equal to about one half of the drag factor you would get from a passenger car with only rear wheel braking. Thus, using a drag factor between 0.35 and 0.40 for a clean, dry, and not traffic-polished hard surface would generally be appropriate. This should give relatively conservative speed estimates.

If both brakes were used on the motorcycle in question, you can obtain higher drag factors with a motorcycle than with a typical passenger car. For an actual accident case it is usually difficult to *prove* that the motorcycle had a very high drag factor. The reason for this is obvious. Usually you will see no skidmark from the front tire. If the motorcycle operator is unavailable or unable to describe his braking actions, then it will be difficult to show that the high drag factor was obtained. Note, however, that even experienced motorcycle operators may have trouble attaining higher drag factors than can be obtained in a typical passenger car. To expect a high drag factor from a motorcycle operator who is relatively inexperienced may be erroneous.

Anti-Lock Braking Systems

The integrated/unified braking system described earlier is not an anti-lock braking system (ABS). An ABS-equipped vehicle has sensors that determine whether a wheel is about to be locked due to braking. The system then releases the brake pressure enough so that the wheel does not lock. These systems are available on some passenger cars in the U.S. The ABS is now starting to become available on some motorcycles. If you have a case with an ABS-equipped motorcycle, do not assume that hard braking was not applied if you do not have braking skidmarks. For cars equipped with ABS, *sometimes* a skidmark can be seen with hard braking. This may or may not be the case with ABS-equipped motorcycles.

3. DRAG FACTORS FOR MOTORCYCLES SLIDING ON THEIR SIDES

After a collision with another vehicle, a motorcycle will usually be knocked to the pavement or fall over quickly. Depending on the type of collision and the motorcycle speed, it might then slide a considerable distance or hardly at all. If the motorcycle does travel some distance, its speed after it begins to slide can be calculated from Equation (4) listed earlier:

$$v_i = \sqrt{v_e^2 - 2ad} \qquad (4)$$

Of course the end velocity, v_e, will always be equal to zero (assuming the motorcycle does not hit something else after the initial collision). As before, the value for acceleration, a, is equal to drag factor times the acceleration of gravity, g, and is negative. Therefore, as in the previous skidding problem, the two unknowns that must be determined are drag factor and the distance the motorcycle slid. The distance is usually fairly easy to determine so long as the right measurements were taken. Drag factor may be a little more difficult.

Several organizations and individuals have done drag factor tests for motorcycles sliding on their sides, TI among

them. The tests have generally been done in one of two ways. One method is to drag the motorcycle along the surface and measure the horizontal force required to slide it. Of course, care is taken to measure only the horizontal force or to correct for any vertical component that may have been introduced. Then the horizontal force is divided by the weight of the sliding motorcycle to get the drag factor. Unless care is exercised, there is always the danger of getting something close to the static friction value instead of the dynamic value.

The second method is to drop a motorcycle on the road from a truck moving at a known speed. The motorcycle wheels' distance from the pavement when the drop takes place is only two or three inches. A typical arrangement is shown in Exhibit 17. If the motorcycle's velocity at the moment it strikes the pavement is known (it should be the same as the truck speed) and the distance the motorcycle slides is known, the drag factor can then be calculated. It can be argued that the drop test is more realistic than the towing test because the motorcycle can rotate and otherwise move about, whereas this is not the case if the motorcycle is being pulled along the surface. Another argument in favor of the drop test is that the motorcycle hits the road surface with a dynamic load and not just a static one as in the case of dragging the motorcycle.

Drop tests done at TI did not show much rotational movement of the motorcycle after it struck the pavement. It essentially slid along the surface without rotation. However, this might not be the case for an actual accident. Exhibit 18 shows several positions of a motorcycle as it slid to its final position. In a similar test done in Arizona[3], one test motorcycle's tires had enough contact with the pavement to make it flip. This resulted in a significantly higher drag factor.

Exhibit 17. *The lift shown here was used for "drop" tests for motorcycles sliding on their sides. The lift is set as low as possible to allow for clearance.*

Exhibit 18. *Several views of motorcycles sliding on their sides are shown in these photographs. In A the motorcycle is just starting to contact the pavement. Note how the motorcycle does not drop from a height much greater than its normal position. In B and C, the motorcycle is shown sliding to rest. In D the motorcycle is shown sliding from the truck.*

Along with the tests done at TI, several other tests[3,4,5,6] were reviewed in preparing this topic to get an idea of typical values people were getting in their drag factor tests. A summary of the ranges found for two surfaces, gravel and hard pavement, is shown in Exhibit 19. There was no apparent difference in the ranges of drag factors between Portland cement concrete and asphalt, so they are grouped together. To some extent, this would be expected. For rubber tires sliding on different types of hard surfaces, a difference in friction is expected and often seen. For a motorcycle sliding on

its side, where foot rests may be digging in, where handlebar grips may also be part of the sliding surface, and where a great deal of the sliding surface is metal itself, a considerable difference in the resulting friction data could be expected when comparing one set of road surface data to another. So there seems little to be gained by separating the data between Portland cement and asphalt concrete.

The tests done at TI on a hard surface all tended to be on the low end of the range listed for hard surfaces in Exhibit 19. The lower values were more often obtained by Day[4] and

Surface	Low	High
Asphalt or Portland Cement Concrete	0.40	0.75
Gravel	0.65	1.05

Exhibit 19. *Drag factor ranges for motorcycles sliding on their sides – dry conditions.*

SATAI[3]. Both high and low values were obtained by the Iowa study[5]. The RCMP study[6] consistently showed higher values. These comments are not meant to be critical. There are several reasons why the results may differ:

1. *Different surfaces.* Drag factor tests for rubber tires on pavement vary somewhat. So why shouldn't there be some difference between a motorcycle sliding on its side in Arizona, for example, and one in British Columbia? Also, some motorcycles may have fairings that will result in more fiberglass sliding on the surface than do other parts of the motorcycle.

2. *Different testing methods.* Two of the tests were done by dragging a motorcycle. The SATAI, TI, and Iowa tests were done by letting a motorcycle slide to a stop from a known speed and then calculating the drag factor. As stated earlier, it could be argued that this more closely duplicates an actual accident.

3. *Speeds were different.* The tests were conducted at different speeds. At very low speeds (this would be more of a factor for a drag test) you would expect the drag factor to be slightly higher than at higher speeds. In other words, a value approaching static friction would more likely be obtained in tests done at very low speeds.

4. *Inherent empirical inaccuracies.* In any empirical study, measurement errors are possible.

For an actual accident case, which drag factor values do you use for a motorcycle that is sliding on its side? Unless you have done drag factor tests on the specific motorcycle involved in the collision, you would have to use representative drag factor values such as those seen in Exhibit 19. In most cases you would be constrained to use the lower values found there. Whenever possible, do your own drag factor tests for the accident under study. If the motorcycle slid on dirt or gravel for some distance, tests done at the accident site would be the best way to get reliable drag factor data. In many cases, of course, this may be highly impractical.

4. MOTORCYCLE MANEUVERABILITY

Many people incorrectly assume that a motorcycle is much more maneuverable than a typical passenger car. True, a motorcycle is not as wide as a typical car. Thus, the lateral distance it needs to move to avoid contact with an obstacle

is likely to be less than would be the case for a car. But the assumption that a motorcycle can move to the left or right in a shorter longitudinal distance to avoid an obstacle is generally not true.

Watanabe and Yoshida[7] conducted emergency evasive maneuvering tests at various speeds, using motorcycles of different sizes and operators at different skill levels. Exhibit 20 shows the travel paths of the vehicle centerlines in an evasive maneuver to avoid an obstacle two meters (six feet) wide. The operators were not told which way to steer (left or right) until they reached the signal point. Note how the centerline of the motorcycle path goes to the left before traveling fairly sharply to the right. This is because a motorcycle is not "steered" like an automobile. To move quickly in a lateral direction, the operator must turn the handlebars in the opposite direction from where he wants the motorcycle to go. This causes the vehicle to lean in the direction toward which the operator wants to maneuver it. The motorcycle is "steered" by leaning in the direction the operator wants to go. This set of operations obviously will not work for steering a car; as the wheels are turned in the direction the driver wants to go, the car moves in that direction. Thus, steering in the desired direction of travel starts faster for a car than it does for a motorcycle. Later in the maneuver, the motorcycle is turning fairly sharply. Both vehicle types take about the same longitudinal distance to move laterally to avoid the obstacle.

Several other interesting results have come from Watanabe's and Yoshida's work. They used the test setup shown in Exhibit 21[7]. When a motorcycle moving along a straight path reached a point at a certain distance, *d,* from the two-meter (six-foot) obstacle, the direction in which the operator had to go to avoid the obstacle was indicated by a signal lamp. The operator was then to turn as quickly as possible in that direction. The distance, *d,* was set for each test velocity so that the average rider would successfully avoid the obstacle in half of his attempts. The tests were conducted on dry asphalt pavement. Other test conditions used were as follows:

Velocities: 50 km/hr (31 mi/hr), 80 km/hr (50 mi/hr), 100km/hr (62 mi/hr)
Models: CB 750, CB 350 Four, SL 125 (all Hondas)
Values of *d*: 17 m (55.8 ft) at 50 km/hr, 30 m (98.4 ft) at 80 km/hr, 40 m (131.2 ft) at 100 km/hr
Operators: High skills to low skills

The median values obtained in the tests at 50 km/hr (31 mi/hr), 80 km/hr (50 mi/hr) and 100 km/hr (62 mi/hr) were 18.5 m (60.7 ft), 28.5 m (93.6 ft) and 41.7 m (137 ft), respectively. The researchers concluded that the most significant factor affecting the data is rider skill. Low-skilled riders required 15 to 20 percent more distance to avoid the test obstacle than did highly skilled riders. The effect of motorcycle size was considered to be quite small. The tests indicated that the smallest motorcycle was actually the lowest in performance.

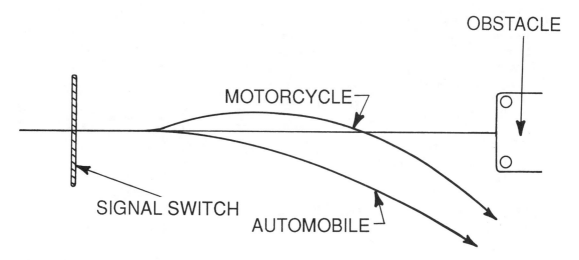

Exhibit 20. *Evasive paths of an automobile and a motorcycle are not the same.*

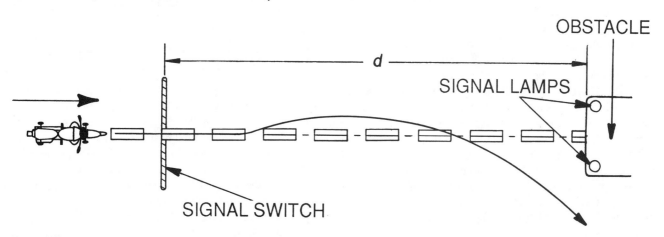

Exhibit 21. *This is the test method diagram for maneuverability used by Watanabe and Yoshida.*

When motorcycle operator tactics are considered in accident cases, the ability of the operator to "steer" around an obstacle is sometimes questioned. As noted earlier, this is a different type of operation than steering a four-tired vehicle. In most cases, the maneuverability of a motorcycle is not going to be a factor. As with all motor vehicles, there are times when it is more likely that an accident can be avoided by moving the vehicle laterally than by braking. This consideration must, however, be evaluated in the particular context of the accident case you are working on.

5. MOTORCYCLE CORNERING

Unlike an automobile, a motorcycle must be leaned while cornering to prevent it from falling outward due to the generation of centrifugal force. The balance (vector sum) of centrifugal force, due to cornering, and the motorcycle's downward force, due to its weight, act through the motorcycle/operator/passenger combined center of mass (gravity)

and must intersect a line that connects the front and rear tire contact patches. This is shown in Exhibit 22 along with the lean angle. Assuming an operator/passenger who sits straight in his seat (not hanging off like a road racer), there is a simple equation to define lean angle.

$$\tan \Theta = v^2/rg \qquad (5)$$

where v = the motorcycle velocity in ft/sec (or m/sec)

r = radius of curve of the motorcycle path in ft (or m)

g = the acceleration of gravity (32.2 ft sec/sec or 9.81 m/sec/sec)

Θ = the lean angle in degrees from the vertical

$\tan$ = the trigonometric function *tangent*

For a particular motorcycle curved path of travel, there is a unique lean angle associated with it for a specific velocity. The required lean angle for a specific velocity and radius can be calculated using Equation (5). First, calculate tan Θ using the appropriate velocity and radius values. In U.S.A. units, velocity is in ft/sec and radius is in ft. Use $g = 32.2$ ft/sec/sec. In metric units, velocity is in m/sec and the radius is in m. The acceleration of gravity, g, is equal to 9.81 m/sec/sec.

Consider the following example problem. The motorcycle speed is 60 mi/hr (88 ft/sec). The motorcycle travel path radius is 500 ft. Using Equation (5):

$$\tan \Theta = v^2/rg \qquad (5)$$
$$\tan \Theta = 88^2/(500)(32.2)$$
$$\tan \Theta = 0.481$$

The angle that has a tan equal to 0.481 is 25.7 degrees. Therefore, Θ is equal to 25.7 degrees.

6. MOTORCYCLE OPERATOR/ PASSENGER KINEMATICS

Estimating the speeds of motorcycles involved in collisions is often a difficult task. If you have been able to correctly determine how the motorcycle operator and/or passenger traveled after the collision, then you might be able to estimate the motorcycle's speed. Rarely, however, is this an easy task. Occasionally it is assumed that the operator left the motorcycle at an angle of 45 degrees relative to the plane of the ground. This may be a significant error. Using a 45 degree takeoff angle is the same as using the vault equation. (See Topic 866 for a discussion of vaults, falls and flips.) Usually there is considerable interaction between the operator and the vehicle struck by the motorcycle before his body separates from the other vehicle. In some cases the body may be redirected considerably. Normally, the use of the vault equation is not an appropriate method to calculate the motorcycle's speed.

A common error found when the vault or fall equation is used is to assume that the motorcycle operator's final position is where his body first contacted the ground. Occasionally some unbelievable speed estimates are obtained when this is assumed. Using the fall equation, for example, you could calculate a speed of 50 mi/hr (80 km/hr). If you used the final position of the body to determine the horizontal distance it traveled, this would mean the body stopped the instant it contacted the pavement. If the body had a level takeoff, then its horizontal velocity when it hit the pavement would be approximately the same as the takeoff speed. The only slowing force as the body traveled through the air was air resistance. So clearly, it would be incorrect to assume that the body hit the pavement with a horizontal velocity of 50 mi/hr and stopped immediately.

The study of how a motorcycle operator or passenger moves in a collision with another vehicle is often referred to as *operator/passenger kinematics*. Just how a body that was on a motorcycle moves after a collision is not always easy to predict. In Exhibit 23 a series of photographs shows a

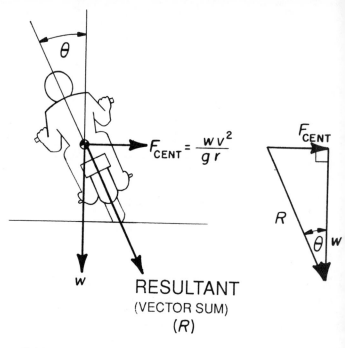

Exhibit 22. *The lean angle, centrifugal force and the weight are diagrammed here for a motorcycle.*

motorcycle with operator and passenger dummies contacting another vehicle. Note how the passenger tends to "ramp up" the operator. The bodies do not attain the same maximum height. Note how the final positions of the operator and passenger are not together. Obviously, both were traveling at the same speed when the other vehicle was struck. Without re-enacting the accident with exemplar vehicles and dummies, it can be very difficult to predict how far bodies will move as a result of a collision. There are several reasons for this. In many cases, the motorcycle comes almost immediately to a stop as a result of colliding with another vehicle. The motorcycle operator and passenger may hit the other vehicle and stop, just as the motorcycle did, or they may be deflected by the other vehicle. There may not be enough damage to the other vehicle to tell how hard the body struck it. As was shown in Exhibit 23, when a passenger is present, there may be some interaction between him and the operator. If the motorcycle is essentially stopped in a collision, its front wheel usually decelerates to a stop first, while its rear end tends to lift. The operator and passenger (if present) tend to be lofted. This is not a simple fall from a given height; a considerable vertical component was added to the operator and passenger as they separated from the motorcycle.

7. SPEED FROM MOTORCYCLE DAMAGE

The most common motorcycle/car accident occurs when a car makes a left turn in front of an oncoming motorcycle. In many cases the vehicles and the motorcycle operator (and motorcycle passenger, if present) travel very little after the collision. Occasionally a momentum analysis is attempted. Rarely does this work well. The momentum analysis is quite

Exhibit 23. The four photographs show the motorcycle with operator and passenger approaching the car prior to collision and their movement after the collision. Note in C how the passenger "ramps" up the operator. In D note that the passenger and operator have moved away from each other.

sensitive to heading and departure angles when the angles of approach are nearly collinear and the weight difference between the colliding vehicles is fairly large. In most motorcycle/car collisions, this weight difference causes great difficulty in attempting a momentum analysis. For this type of case, where little after-collision movement occurs, a speed-from-damage analysis can be attempted. For obvious reasons, in nearly all cases the motorcycle is more severely damaged than the other vehicle. Thus, the motorcycle is often the only vehicle whose damage is seriously evaluated.

There are generally accepted methods for determining speed from damage to automobiles, vans, and pickups. Topic 870 discusses this methodology. Much more data is available for crash tests of cars into barriers than for controlled crash tests of motorcycles. The most quoted document on controlled crash tests of motorcycles is by Severy and others[8]. These tests represent an important piece of research. The obvious problem when these tests are used to estimate speed from motorcycle damage is the type of motorcycles tested. In this study, three types of Honda motorcycles were tested: CL 90, CB 350, and CB 750. The front wheel on each type was the spoke-style wheel commonly found on older motorcycles. That is, they did not have the cast wheel usually used today. In addition, front forks and frames of motorcycles are designed differently today and are stiffer than those of the motorcycles used in Severy's tests.

Exhibit 24 summarizes some of the data that was collected in the Severy study. Seven tests were conducted. The motorcycles were guided into parked cars at speeds from 20 mi/hr (32 km/hr) to 40 mi/hr (65 km/hr). They were not at-

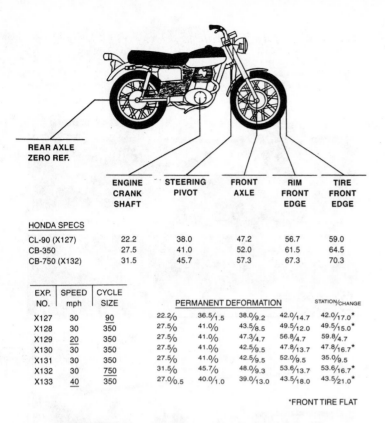

	ENGINE CRANK SHAFT	STEERING PIVOT	FRONT AXLE	RIM FRONT EDGE	TIRE FRONT EDGE
REAR AXLE ZERO REF.					
HONDA SPECS					
CL-90 (X127)	22.2	38.0	47.2	56.7	59.0
CB-350	27.5	41.0	52.0	61.5	64.5
CB-750 (X132)	31.5	45.7	57.3	67.3	70.3

EXP. NO.	SPEED mph	CYCLE SIZE	PERMANENT DEFORMATION				STATION/CHANGE
X127	30	90	22.2/0	36.5/1.5	38.0/9.2	42.0/14.7	42.0/17.0*
X128	30	350	27.5/0	41.0/0	43.5/8.5	49.5/12.0	49.5/15.0*
X129	20	350	27.5/0	41.0/0	47.3/4.7	56.8/4.7	59.8/4.7
X130	30	350	27.5/0	41.0/0	42.5/9.5	47.8/13.7	47.8/16.7*
X131	30	350	27.5/0	41.0/0	42.5/9.5	52.0/9.5	35.0/9.5
X132	30	750	31.5/0	45.7/0	48.0/9.3	53.6/13.7	53.6/16.7*
X133	40	350	27.0/0.5	40.0/1.0	39.0/13.0	43.5/18.0	43.5/21.0*

*FRONT TIRE FLAT

Exhibit 24. *This is a summary of permanent deformation values from the Severy study. All values are in inches measured from the rear axle.*

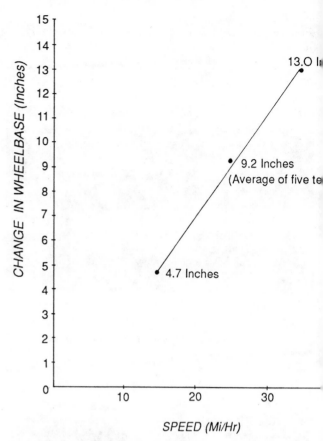

Exhibit 25. *The graph shows the relationship between wheelbase change of motorcycles and speed from the Severy study. Use this graph with care, making sure that your motorcycle has the same general characteristics as the models tested.*

tached to anything as they struck the cars. As can be seen from Exhibit 24, the cars were struck at different locations. One significant conclusion by Severy was:

> . . . it was found that the permanent shortening of the motorcycle wheelbase as a result of collision varied linearly with the speed of collision and did not appear to be significantly affected by variations in size of the motorcycle or in location of impact.

Exhibit 25 shows the relationship of the wheelbase change to the speeds of the motorcycles that were crashed into the parked cars. This suggests that the increased kinetic energy the larger motorcycles would have (when compared to a smaller motorcycle traveling at the same speed) is compensated for by their stronger front forks.

Now, what is the significance of all this information summarized in Exhibits 24 and 25? It suggests that in reconstructing a motorcycle accident having the same general attributes found in the tests, this data should be useful in estimating the motorcycle's speed. For example, if you have a case where a very slow-moving passenger car turns left in front of an oncoming motorcycle, is struck on its side, and both vehicles stop at or near the location where they collided, the data given in Exhibits 24 and 25 may apply. But if the motorcycle in question is equipped with a cast wheel instead of a spoke wheel, then the test data would be inappropriate. Nor would it be appropriate for reconstructing an accident

where the car had considerable velocity when struck.

A motorcycle/car collision is shown in Exhibit 26. Both vehicles are going 28 mi/hr and approach each other at a right angle. Note how the front wheel of the motorcycle is *not* forced straight back like those of the motorcycles tested by Severy. The forward velocity of the car gives a sideways force component to the motorcycle's front wheel. It can also cause the motorcycle to rotate, which may result in more of the side of the motorcycle striking the car than the front wheel. Consequently, there is much less rearward movement of the car's front axle than might have been anticipated.

Severy[8] describes the collapse process of his tests in the following manner:

> As front tire contact is made with the opposing car sheet metal, initial flattening of the tire occurs, accompanied by some yielding of the car body panel and cycle forks; this is followed by complete deceleration of the front wheel assembly, generally without significant distortion of the wheel. Additional car sheet metal intrusion and bending of the forks above and rearward of the suspension system occurs as the front wheel crushes further into the car side panel. Simultaneously, the principal mass of the motorcycle (all portions to the rear of the front wheel and suspension) continues forward while un-

Exhibit 26. *The motorcycle and car are both moving at 28 mi/hr at the time of the collision. Note how the front wheel of the motorcycle does not deform straight back but is turned because of the forward motion of the car. As can be seen in C, the motorcycle has almost been turned parallel to the travel path of the car. As can be seen in D, the motorcycle has continued to rotate counterclockwise.*

dergoing moderate deceleration. Contact is finally made by the forward surfaces of the engine with the trailing surfaces of the front wheel. For lower speed impacts, this constitutes the final motorcycle collapse phase; however, for 30 mi/hr (48 km/hr) and higher impact speeds with the sides of passenger vehicles, the motorcycle front wheel generally deforms permanently and even completely collapses in some cases. . .

For a cast wheel, the deformation described above will not be the same. The wheel might simply break instead of de-

Exhibit 27. *The motorcycle and the damage pattern shown in this photograph almost match the tests done by Severy and would be a good candidate for applying that damage data.*

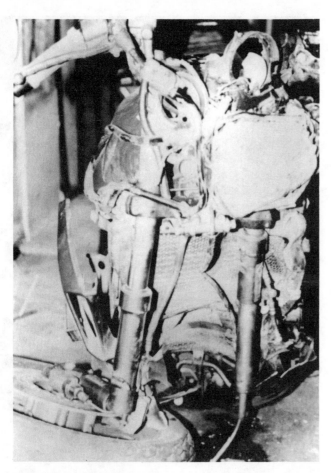

Exhibit 28. This damaged motorcycle would not be a good candidate on which to apply the Severy data shown in Exhibit 25. The front wheel is a cast wheel and the front forks are different.

forming. The whole wheel structure (relatively undamaged) would probably be forced back into the engine. This might cause more damage to the car than occurred in the Severy tests. The cast wheel pushing against the engine of the motorcycle would represent a fairly rigid structure — unlike the spoke wheel used in the tests. Thus, to use the latter in reconstructing such an accident could lead to serious errors. Also, as stated earlier, the Severy tests involved stationary cars. Had the cars been moving, the front motorcycle wheel would not have deformed the same way. The trailing part of the wheel might never have contacted the engine.

Consider the accident motorcycle shown in Exhibit 27. This Honda 750 is similar to the motorcycles used in the Severy tests. The Honda 750 and the other vehicle essentially came to a stop after the collision. Because the pickup had very little forward velocity at the time of the collision, the rearward movement of the motorcycle's front wheel was generally straight back. Obviously, this would be a good candidate on which to use the collision data collected by Severy. Now consider the motorcycle shown in Exhibit 28. It has a front wheel considerably different from the one shown in Exhibit 27. Consequently, the deformation characteristics would also be different.

8. CASE STUDY

A case study is included in this topic to illustrate some of the methodology that can be applied to reconstructing motorcycle traffic accidents.

A motorcycle and car were both going southbound on a residential street. The car was making a left turn when the collision occurred (see after-accident situation map shown in Exhibit 29). A single pre-collision motorcycle skid was observed, measured, and photographed. The mark is labeled B in Exhibit 29. The after-accident situation map also identifies scratches on the road surface at C, a scuff mark believed to be from the front motorcycle tire at D, a rear motorcycle brake lens at E, an area covered with small pieces of rusted metal debris at F, gouge marks in roadway at G, gouge marks made from two distinct metal surfaces at H, a rear motorcycle taillight/license plate assembly at I, bloodstains at K, motorcycle operator's head at L, and final position of helmet (blood inside) at M. These marks and debris are shown in Exhibits 30-34.

Photographs of the motorcycle taken at the scene are shown in Exhibits 35 and 36. The relative position of the car to the motorcycle is shown in Exhibit 36.

The damage to the car is shown in Exhibits 37-38. Note how the damaged area in front of the car's rear wheel has been moved forward. This indicates a forward component of force on the car from the motorcycle.

Vehicle and Operator Movement

The damage to the car and motorcycle indicates that the vehicles came together as shown in Exhibit 39. The motorcycle and body traveled as shown in Exhibit 40 from first contact to their final positions. The motorcycle operator went over the rear part of the car and struck the rear window as the body moved to its final position. The motorcycle took a slightly different path because it had more of a collision with the lower part of the car than did the operator. This caused the motorcycle to be re-directed more than the operator.

Motorcycle Speed Estimate

An issue in this case is the speed of the motorcycle when the braking skidmark was first made. In particular, there is a question whether the speed limit of 30 mi/hr (48 km/hr) was exceeded by the motorcycle. For this analysis, speed was lost by the motorcycle in sliding on its side to its final position, by damage to the car and motorcycle, and by pre-collision braking. For a preliminary analysis, only the motorcycle sliding on its side after the collision and its pre-collision braking will be considered. Compared to many motorcycle/car collisions, the damage to both vehicles is in the nature of a glancing hit and does not suggest much speed was lost in the collision.

The motorcycle slid approximately 80 ft from the time it first hit the pavement until reaching its final position. Most

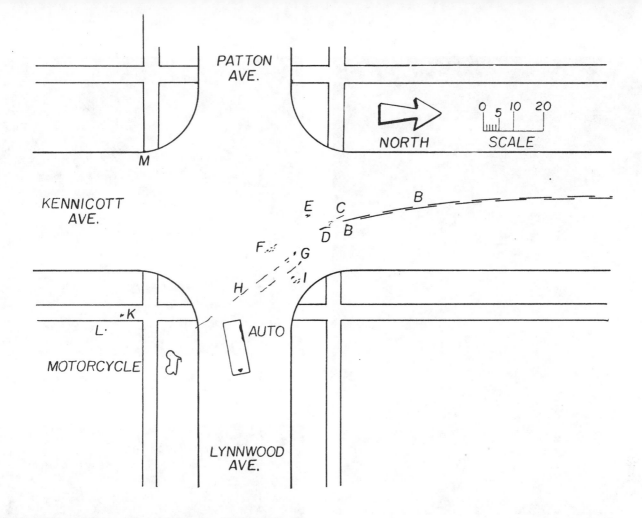

Exhibit 29. After-accident situation map of a car-motorcycle collision.

Exhibit 30. This view faces in the direction the motorcycle was coming from. Note the single braking skidmark.

Exhibit 31. This photograph shows a tire mark and gouges from the motorcycle looking in the general direction the motorcycle was traveling.

Exhibit 32. *Abrasion marks from the motorcycle and debris are shown here looking toward the final rest position of the car.*

Exhibit 34. *The final position of the car and the helmet are shown in this view.*

Exhibit 33. *A considerable amount of glass is shown on the pavement. This comes mainly from the car's broken back-window.*

Exhibit 35. *Damage to the motorcycle is shown here. Note that the front wheel has not been pushed back as much as one might have thought for an intersection collision.*

of the sliding was on the pavement. Exhibit 19 suggests a low value for drag factor to be around 0.45. Using that value and Equation (4), the velocity of the motorcycle as it first came into contact with the pavement can be calculated.

$$v_{\mathrm{i}} = \sqrt{v_{\mathrm{e}}^2 - 2ad} \tag{4}$$

$$= \sqrt{0^2 - 2(\text{-}0.45)(32.2)(80)}$$
$$= 48.1 \text{ ft/sec}$$

The motorcycle was braking before the collision for a distance of approximately 70 ft. The motorcycle operator died as a result of the collision and never made a statement regarding the accident. If only the rear brake was used, a very low value for drag factor would be appropriate. The type of road surface the motorcycle skidded on would have a coefficient of friction for a locked four-tired passenger car of at least 0.70. To be conservative for this preliminary evaluation, assume a drag factor of one-half of that, or 0.35. Using Equation (4) where the ending velocity, v_e, is equal to 48.1 ft/sec gives the following results:

$$v_i = \sqrt{v_e^2 - 2ad} \qquad (4)$$

$$= \sqrt{48.1^2 - 2(-0.35)(32.2)(70)}$$

$$= 62.4 \text{ ft/sec} = 42 \text{ mi/hr}$$

Clearly, the motorcycle was traveling at a speed greater than the 30 mi/hr speed limit. This analysis could be further

Exhibit 37. *The damage to the car is on the left rear quarter. This includes the rear door and fender area.*

Exhibit 36. *Relative rest positions of the motorcycle and the car are shown here. The car position is where the car was found when the police arrived at the scene.*

Exhibit 38. *The deformation of the car is shown here. Note also how the back window has been broken.*

refined. For example, you could check to see whether the motorcycle has a braking system that applies brakes to the front wheel when the rear foot brake is used. This would indicate that the assumed precollision drag factor of 0.35 is probably too low. Tests could be done with the accident motorcycle to determine a better estimate of the motorcycle's after-collision drag factor. In either case, the values used are lower than would ever be obtained by further study.

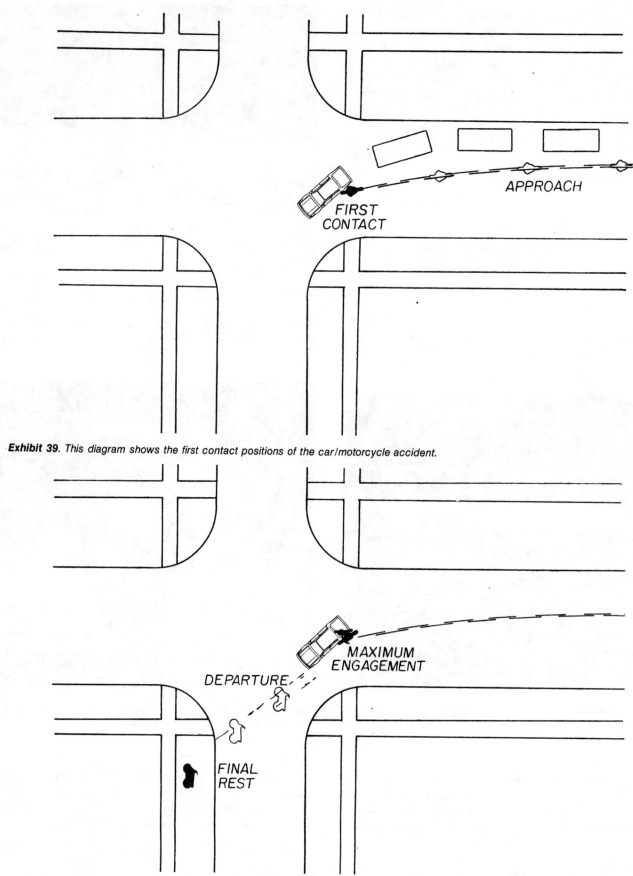

Exhibit 39. *This diagram shows the first contact positions of the car/motorcycle accident.*

Exhibit 40. *The body and motorcycle moved to their final positions as shown here. The motorcycle was re-directed more than the operator because the operator was "loosely attached" to the motorcycle.*

9. SOURCES

Authors

Lynn B. Fricke, the primary author of this topic, is an engineer specializing in traffic accident reconstruction. He has been with the Northwestern University Traffic Institute since 1975 and has been director of the Accident Investigation Division since 1981.

Warner W. Riley provided technical consultation on this topic. Mr. Riley is a consulting engineer specializing in motorcycle accident investigation, reconstruction, and design alternatives. He has had his own consulting firm since 1973 and has been a guest instructor at the Northwestern University Traffic Institute.

References

1. Korpernik, Dror, *On the Safety of Motorcycle Side Stands*, SAE paper 840905, Society of Automotive Engineers, Warrendale, PA.
2. Collins, James, *Accident Reconstruction*, Charles C. Thomas Publisher, Springfield, IL, 1979.
3. Southwestern Association of Technical Accident Investigators, *Motorcycle Drag Factor Tests*, Phoenix, AZ, 1984.
4. Day, Terry D., and Jay R. Smith, *Friction Factor for Motorcycles Sliding on Various Surfaces*, SAE paper 840250, Society of Automotive Engineers, Warrendale, PA.
5. Iowa State Patrol, *Motorcycle Test Skidding on Its Side*, Traffic Investigation Spring Seminar, Johnston, IA, 1985.
6. Royal Canadian Mounted Police, *Motorcycle Testing*, Coquitlam, BC, Canada, 1984.
7. Watanabe, Yoshinori, and Keigo Yoshida, *Motorcycle Handling Performance for Obstacle Avoidance*, Paper No. 73033, Second International Congress on Automotive Safety, San Francisco, CA, 1973.
8. Severy, Derwyn M., Harrison M. Brink, and David Blaisdell, *Motorcycle Collision Experiments*, SAE paper 700897, Society of Automotive Engineers, Warrendale, PA.
9. Ouellet, James V., "Motorcycles," Chapter 35 of *Scientific Automobile Accident Reconstruction*, Matthew Bender, NY, 1988.

Exhibits

The following are the sources of the exhibits used in this topic:

Arlington Heights Police Dept, Arlington Heights, IL
Photos:30-38
Diagrams: 29

Aycock, Thad, Northbrook, IL
Photos: 8-12, 14

Evans, John, Highland Park, IL
Photos: 18A- 18D

Fricke, Wayne, Colorado Springs, CO
Photos: 13

Fricke, Lynn B., Lincolnshire, IL
Photos: 1, 15-17
Diagrams: 40
Table: 19

Krapf, Emerson, Waukegan, IL
Photos: 2,3

Maculitus, Jerry, Elk Grove Village, IL
Photos: 6

Riley, Warner W., Lake Forest, IL
Photos: 23A-23D, 25A-25D
Diagrams: 7, 22
Graph: 25

Severy, Derwyn M.
Table: 24
Graph: 25

Watanabe, Yoshinori
Diagrams: 20-21

Unknown
Photos: 4, 5, 27, 28

UNDERSTANDING OCCUPANT BEHAVIOR IN VEHICLE COLLISIONS

Topic 876 of the *Traffic Accident Investigation Manual*

by
Lynn B. Fricke
and
Kenneth S. Baker

NORTHWESTERN UNIVERSITY TRAFFIC INSTITUTE

UNDERSTANDING OCCUPANT BEHAVIOR IN VEHICLE COLLISIONS

1. INTRODUCTION

Occupant motion is often referred to in the literature as *occupant kinematics*. Kinematics is that branch of mechanics which deals with motion of bodies without consideration of the forces required to produce or maintain the motion. It has been argued by some that force is considered in occupant motion studies and thus the term kinematics should not be used. Instead, they claim, the term *kinetics* should be used: kinetics is the study of unbalanced forces and the motion they produce. In this topic, however, the term *occupant motion* will be used.

The study of occupant motion in vehicle collisions is often done to answer such issues as
- Who was driving
- Positions of occupants before collision
- The effect of safety belts

The "who was driving" issue is of considerable interest in both civil and criminal cases. Clearly, a good defense of an accused driver would be to argue that someone else was driving (particularly if the other occupant is dead, which would eliminate any possibility of getting his or her side of the story). Occasionally there may be interest in how someone other than a driver was positioned in a vehicle – for example, how a person could be injured in a particular position in a car. Another issue that may be relevant is the effect of safety belts and whether they could have eliminated or mitigated injuries.

The general methodology involved in answering these issues involves several steps. (In not every case will sufficient data be available so that these steps can be fully examined.) They are as follows:

Step 1 – Inspect the vehicle interior for signs of contact between bodies and the interior.

Step 2 – Get a thorough understanding of how the vehicles moved from first contact to maximum engagement to separation and finally to their rest positions. (Techniques to do this are explained in detail in Topic 861.)

Step 3 – From the vehicle movements ascertained in Step 2, determine how the bodies should have moved relative to the vehicle, and which parts of the vehicle they could have struck with parts of their bodies. This step should also consider how possible it was for the occupants to have come out of the vehicle.

Step 4 – Review the injury data and determine how injuries and interior vehicle contact points match.

Step 5 – Compare the conclusions in Step 3 (how the occupants moved) with the results of matching injuries to interior contact points. If there are no significant differences, then two approaches have yielded the same conclusion. If the conclusions are in conflict, resolve the conflict.

Optional Step 6 – If the issue is whether safety belts would have reduced the injury, then a sixth step is added. This step examines the question of whether a safety belt (three-point, lap-only, or shoulder-only) would have reduced the injuries.

2. VEHICLE INSPECTION

Vehicles should be inspected as soon as possible after the accident. This is done for a variety of reasons, not the least of which is to get a good understanding of how the vehicle moved as a result of the collision. How significant parts of the vehicle have been displaced will indicate the direction of thrust (principal direction of force) that was applied to the vehicle. From this it is possible to determine whether the vehicle rotated as a result of the collision, and how much. How two vehicles came together in a collision can be evaluated from exterior vehicle damage inspection. (This whole procedure is explained in detail in Topic 861.)

A second reason for a vehicle inspection is to determine how occupants moved relative to the car: contact areas between bodies and the interior of the vehicle can provide valuable clues to how bodies moved as a result of the collision. Unrestrained bodies in a vehicle involved in a collision continue moving in the same direction they were going in when the vehicle first collided with something. The car may rotate

Exhibit 1. *Damage to the steering wheel is clearly shown here. The car slowed considerably and the driver of the car continued moving forward, striking the steering wheel.*

Exhibit 2. *In this case the principal direction of force on the vehicle caused the vehicle front to move violently to its right. This, in turn, caused the passenger to move left relative to the vehicle, striking the steering wheel very hard.*

from its original heading before the bodies strike some part of the vehicle's interior. Examining vehicle parts damaged by occupants striking them can also provide useful clues in determining occupant motion. Parts of the interior which may yield valuable information include

- Steering wheel
- Seat backs
- Interior door panels
- Windshield and other glass
- Rearview mirror
- Dash and knee bolster
- Gearshift
- Headliner (fabric lining roof inside car)
- Pillars

Steering wheels often are damaged in frontal impacts by drivers hitting them. It is also possible for a passenger to hit the steering wheel. In a side impact, or in a frontal impact where the vehicle has rotated considerably, a passenger may strike the wheel. Also, look for displacement of the steering column. This can occur in frontal impacts when the driver's body continues moving forward and strikes the steering wheel. A typical damaged steering wheel struck in this way is shown in Exhibit 1. Exhibit 2 shows a steering wheel that was struck by a passenger.

Seats can be damaged in several ways. Unrestrained passengers in the back seat of a car can move forward and strike the seat backs. A rear impact can cause an occupant to move rearward and may cause the seat back to be bent backward. Damage can also result to the seat where it is attached to the floor. Exhibit 3A shows typical seat back damage resulting from a severe rear impact; 3B shows a frontal impact where a rear occupant hit the front seat back.

The interior of a door can be hit by occupants in a vehicle. Often, the interior door liner will be bowed out. This indicates a relative movement of the occupant to the vehicle. Be careful, however, to distinguish between occupant contact

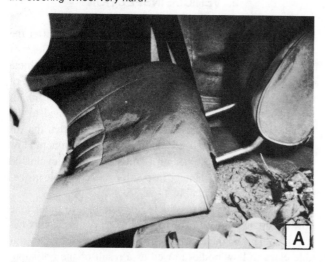

Exhibit 3. *Rearward movement of a seatback is shown in 3A. In the sequence of this collision, only the right front passenger was in his seat at the time the car was struck in its rear. This caused the right front seat back to be bent backward as the occupant moved rearward relative to the car. Forward movement on the seatback is shown in 3B. A frontal impact occurred with the resulting forward movement of the unrestrained rear passenger.*

Exhibit 4. *The outward bowing of the car's door was caused by induced damage to the car. In this case the occupants moved forward in the car and did not strike the door interior. In this photograph the investigators have positioned the vehicles together at their relative locations at maximum engagement.*

damage and damage induced by the collision itself. Exhibit 4 shows damage to a door caused by induced damage in a collision with another vehicle. In Exhibit 5, however, the interior damage shown in both photographs resulted from an occupant's striking the door. In one case the occupant struck the door very hard; the other case resulted from a lesser force.

Contact with the windshield by unrestrained occupants in vehicle collisions is fairly common. Usually this involves head contact. In some instances, hair and body fluids can be found on the windshield. If it is known how the occupants moved relative to the car as a result of the collision, it may be fairly easy to match hair and tissue samples with a particular occupant. Contact of occupants with other glass in the vehicle can also occur. For example, a head may contact the door glass. In some cases, bodies may move rearward relative to the car, and a body may hit the back window. A severe impact with side glass or the rear window may cause the glass to shatter. Unlike the laminated glass in the windshield, the other glass in the vehicle nearly always is tempered glass which will shatter. If an occupant impact with glass causes it

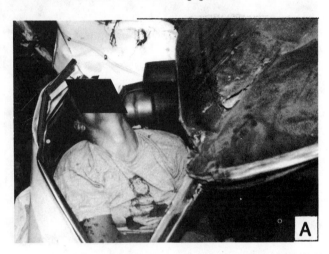

Exhibit 5. *In photograph 5A the occupant of the car has struck the door interior very hard. Outward bowing of the door is essentially a result of the body contact with the door interior. The occupant impact damage in photograph 5B is quite minor when compared to the damage seen in 5A. The force shown in 5B was clearly much less than that shown in 5A.*

Exhibit 6. *Head impact into the interior of the windshield is very common for unrestrained occupants. Note the characteristic spider-web pattern that results in the laminated windshield.*

to shatter, the person hitting the glass probably will have cuts caused by glass. A typical head impact into a windshield is shown in Exhibit 6. Note the characteristic spider web pattern that occurs. Limbs can also cause this spider web pattern.

The interior rearview mirror can be hit by either a passenger or the driver after the initial vehicle collision. Consider a case of two people in a car with both the driver and passenger in the front seat. If both are unrestrained, the factor determining who would hit the rearview mirror is *how the vehicle moves* as a result of the collision. Injuries to the face or scalp could be expected if someone hit the mirror. In Exhibit 7 the driver moved to the right of the steering wheel as a result of a collision with another vehicle. Note how the steering wheel is bent in the direction of the body's motion. The driver's face then struck the rearview mirror and windshield. The mirror

Exhibit 7. *Photograph 7A shows evidence of a body striking the inside of the windshield. Photograph 7B shows a bent steering wheel which indicates that the driver moved to her right as a result of the collision. In this case the inside rear-view mirror was struck by the driver's face resulting in a severe eye injury.*

was hit hard enough to dislodge it from its normal position, resulting in a severe eye injury to the driver.

The dash and knee bolster can often show evidence of occupant impact. Clearly, the use of restraints can reduce this. A padded knee bolster used with a restraint system can help distribute the impact forces on the body.

The femur (the bone between the knee and pelvis) is a very strong bone. Dash damage by unrestrained adult occupants in a frontal impact is to be expected. This typical damage is shown in Exhibit 8.

In cases where there is a strong sideways movement of either the driver or front-seat passenger, a floor-mounted gearshift can be moved sideways from its original position. If this condition is observed, be sure to record and photograph this information. It may be an important clue to how the occupants moved as a result of the collision.

Damage to the head liner and pillars may result from occupant contact in a collision. Look for deposits of body tissue and fluids in these areas. Sometimes damage may have occurred to the roof or pillars that is covered up by plastic or other material. In some cases it may prove worthwhile to remove coverings and inspect metal surfaces under these coverings. Be sure to document what you are doing with photographs in case someone wants to know about the condition of these parts before the coverings were removed.

3. UNDERSTANDING VEHICLE AND OCCUPANT BEHAVIOR IN COLLISIONS

How a vehicle moves after a collision depends on its pre-collision velocity and direction, and the force that was applied to it during the collision. If the force was centered (through the vehicle's center of mass), the vehicle would not have rotated as a result of the collision. If, however, the force

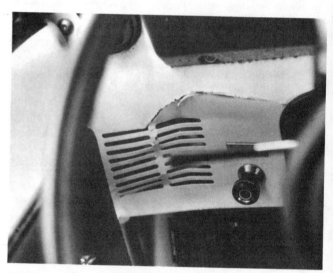

Exhibit 8. *Fairly minor dash damage is shown in this photograph. The driver's knee made contact, causing this damage.*

was eccentric (off-center), the vehicle did rotate as a result of the collision.

Understanding occupant behavior in vehicle collisions requires an understanding of Newton's first law of motion. (See Topic 856 for a discussion of Newton's laws). For its application in this topic consider the simplified explanation that follows. If a body is at rest it stays at rest, and if a body is in motion it continues moving in the same direction with the same speed until it is acted upon by an outside force. In a collision, a vehicle is either decelerated or accelerated due to the collision force. The vehicle may also rotate about its center of mass. However, if the occupants are not secured to the vehicle by safety belts, they are free to continue moving in the same direction they were moving toward before the collision. The bodies continue moving unencumbered until they strike the interior of the car. In this case, an outside force has clearly come into play.

CENTERED FORCE NO ROTATION

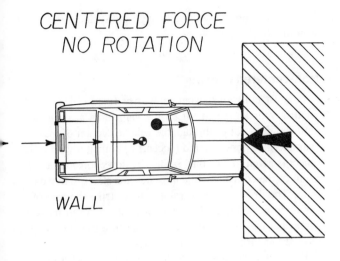

WALL

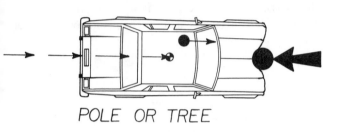

POLE OR TREE

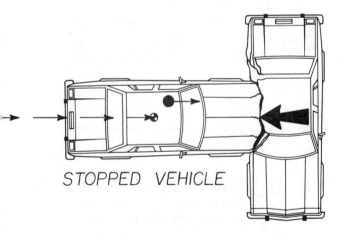

STOPPED VEHICLE

Exhibit 9. The three cases shown here have two things in common: (1) each vehicle is traveling straight ahead before the collision, and (2) the resulting direction of thrust (principal direction of force) is directed through the vehicle's center of mass, resulting in no vehicle rotation.

Centered Frontal Collision

Consider the three cases illustrated in Exhibit 9. Each case shows the vehicle's center of mass moving forward in a straight line before the collision. Consequently, the vehicle occupants are also moving in a straight line. The collision is centered, so there is no rotation after the collision. Clearly, then, the occupants continue moving forward as the vehicle strikes the object (Exhibit 10). As the vehicle slows to a stop, the bodies move forward (if unrestrained) inside the vehicle. In general, the occupants move in a direction opposite from and parallel to the principal direction of force. The final body positions are essentially the same as they were before the collision. The typical type of interior damage that would be expected was shown before in Exhibits 6 and 8.

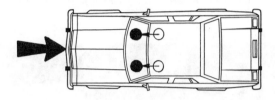

Exhibit 10. For the case depicted in Exhibit 9, the car slows to a stop and the unrestrained occupants move forward, striking the interior of the car, as shown here.

Sideways Collision

If a vehicle is moving sideways and strikes a fixed object, the force on the vehicle may be perpendicular to the vehicle's longitudinal axis. If a vehicle is standing (its velocity is zero) and is hit on its side between the front and rear wheels, the force on the vehicle may also be perpendicular to its longitudinal axis. Exhibit 11 shows a centered thrust through the vehicle's center of mass. The car in Exhibit 11 is hit on its right side. The occupants tend to keep going in the same direction they were moving before the collision, or just want to stay in the same place if the vehicle was stopped. In either case, the occupants move to the right side of the car.

In a severe collision of the type shown in Exhibit 11, the occupants on the right side of the car would be expected to have more severe injuries than those on the left side of the car. The distance which the occupants on the right side have available to increase their velocity to the same velocity of the car is very short as compared to the left-side occupants. The additional distance for the left-side occupants allows them more time to accelerate to the car's velocity. This causes them to have a lower value of acceleration. Expect the right-side occupants to have more severe injuries on the right side of their bodies than on their left. The left-side occupants would be expected to have less severe injuries, partly because the right-side occupants can serve to "pad" their impact with the interior of the car if they are unrestrained. Unfortunately, of course, this tends to load up the right-side occupants.

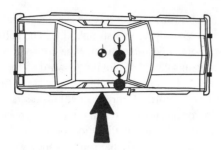

Exhibit 11. *The collision force on the car will cause the car to move suddenly to its left. Because the occupants are not attached to the car, they move to their right relative to the car. Another way of thinking, which is more accurate, is that the car moves to its left while the occupants do not move. This would cause the right inside of the car to hit the right-side occupant.*

Exhibit 12. *A severe rear impact, such as this one, can cause the occupants to move rearward in the car as a result of the collision.*

Look for signs of interior body contact with doors, center consoles, and floor-mounted gearshifts to show sideways movement of occupants.

Rear Collisions

A car could be standing or moving when hit in the rear, with the same effect on the vehicle's occupants. Exhibit 12 shows a centered rear impact. The bodies "want" to keep moving at the same velocity (relative to the car) as they were before the collision. However, the car is being accelerated forward, causing the occupants to move rearward (relative to the vehicle). In severe impacts the seat backs can be forced back as in Exhibit 3A. Safety-belt restraints in such cases are generally less helpful than in frontal impacts. However, seat belts have been found to be advantageous in rear-impact cases of higher severity.[5] The seat belts create a more positive link between the occupant and the vehicle, which can

lessen head impacts with relatively rigid surfaces such as the roof and back window.

Non-centered Impacts

In most collisions, whether with a fixed object or with another vehicle, the thrust on the vehicle as a result of the collision does not go through the vehicle's center of mass. An example of a non-centered (eccentric) collision with a fixed object is given in Exhibit 13. The car slows considerably as a result of the collision while it rotates and starts to move to its right. The driver, if unrestrained, may strike the part of the car in front of him. The driver will also tend to move left somewhat (relative to the vehicle) because the car moves to the right and rotates counterclockwise.

If a vehicle has a very eccentric thrust on it resulting from a collision with another vehicle and is forced backward as in Exhibit 14B, the driver will move forward relative to the car. The driver would also tend to move to the right if unrestrained. This, of course, is a different situation from that

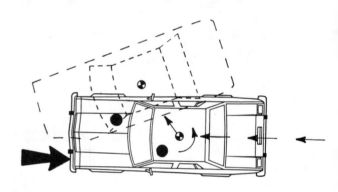

Exhibit 13. *As a result of the collision, the car slows considerably and rotates counterclockwise. The driver of the car would tend to move to his left into the driver's door hinge area as shown.*

shown in Exhibit 14A In Exhibit 14A the collision force causes the car to move backward and to its right. In this case, the driver would tend to move to his left.

Exhibit 15 shows a symmetrical collision of similar cars at identical velocities. The collision force causes both cars to rotate. If the drivers of both cars are unrestrained, they will both move forward relative to the car because the car's forward velocity has been reduced. Also, each driver will tend to move to his right or left because both cars rotate. Car A's driver will move to the right, while car B's driver will move to the left. Thus, the movement of each driver is a combination (the vector sum) of forward and sideways movement relative to the car, or opposite the direction of thrust on each vehicle.

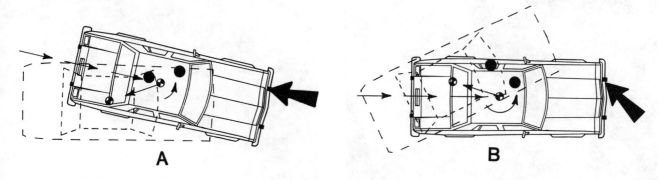

Exhibit 14. *In 14A the car would move off to its right while being accelerated backward as a result of the collision. Therefore, the driver would tend to move to his left, similarly to the case shown in Exhibit 13. The case shown in 14B is a highly eccentric force that would cause rapid counterclockwise rotation. An unrestrained driver would tend to move into the dash while also moving to the right of the steering wheel.*

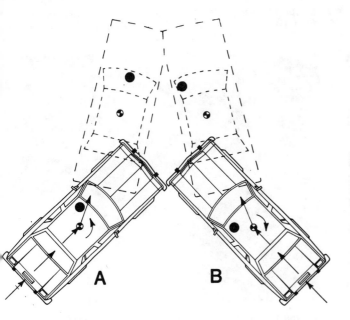

Exhibit 15. *Identical vehicles striking each other at identical speeds can cause different unrestrained occupant motions, as shown here. How the vehicles rotate and slow down as a result of the collision are the controlling factors.*

4. CASE STUDY OF A NON-CENTERED COLLISION

Many of the principles in the previous discussion can be illustrated by a simple case study. Recall from the Introduction the five suggested steps:

1. Inspect the vehicle for signs of occupant contact with the interior.
2. Understand how the vehicles moved from first contact to maximum engagement to their final positions.
3. From the vehicle motion analysis, determine how the bodies moved relative to the vehicle.
4. Review the injury data and determine how injuries and interior contact points match.
5. Compare the conclusions in Step 3 (how the occupants

moved) with the results of matching injuries to interior contact points. Resolve differences, if any.

The case in question involves a collision between a full-size Ford and a full-size Buick. The issue is who is the driver of the Ford. Two people are found in the Ford's two front bucket seats. Occupant A is found in the driver's seat and occupant B is found in the passenger's seat. The Buick was going southbound on County Line Road and the Ford was going northbound. County Line Road is a two-direction, two-lane road.

Step 1 — Interior Vehicle Inspection

After the occupants were removed, photographs of the interior were taken. The vehicle was not available for inspection. This is often the case. By the time it is realized that who was driving is an issue, the vehicles have been disposed. Nevertheless, the two interior photographs taken do yield some important information. Note in Exhibits 16 and 17 that the steering wheel has been moved to the right. Blood is found on both seats and on the passenger door. Statements by police and fire personnel indicate that occupant B (the one found in the passenger seat) had his arm "pinned in" because of damage to the right door.

Step 2 — Understanding Vehicle Movements

The procedure for determining the relative positions of vehicles in a collision and how they move to their final positions is discussed in Topic 861. That methodology is applied here. The damage to the Ford and Buick is shown in Exhibits 18–21. For such a collision it is usually easier to start with the car with the front-end damage.

The Buick has contact damage across the whole front of the car. The front has been pushed back and has also been pushed from the car's left to right. The direction of thrust that would give this kind of damage to the Buick is shown in Exhibit 22 A.

The damage to the Ford is on its right side from the front wheel back to just in front of the rear wheel. There is more

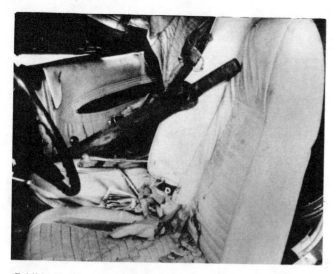

Exhibit 16. *The interior of the Ford is shown in this photograph. Often, poor data is available for interior damage analysis.*

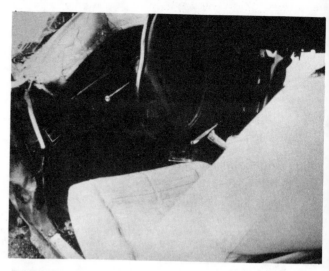

Exhibit 17. *A second interior-damage photograph was taken of the Ford. Use of fill-in flash can help in showing interior damage to a car. This was not done in this case.*

Exhibit 18. *Exterior damage to the Ford is shown here.*

Exhibit 19. *An additional photograph of the exterior Ford damage was taken. Note the considerable collapse to the side of the car.*

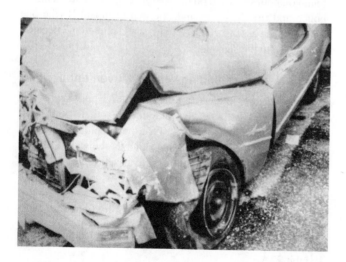

Exhibit 20. *Damage to the front of the Buick is shown in this photograph.*

Exhibit 21. *An additional photograph of the Buick was taken. Note that the front of the Buick is not only pushed rearward but is also pushed sideways.*

collapse in the front part of the contact damage than in the rear part. The direction of thrust that would give this is shown in Exhibit 22B.

Both vehicles would rotate clockwise as a result of the collision. The force on the Buick is slightly more eccentric than that on the Ford. Thus, more rotation would be expected on the Buick than on the Ford, because both cars are approximately the same size.

The final positions of the vehicles are known from the data collected by the police at the scene. The vehicles' final positions are shown in Exhibit 23. Based on the known positions of the vehicles at maximum engagement (see Exhibit 22C), an estimate of the vehicles' first contact positions can be made. Recall from Topic 861 that colliding vehicles move relative to each other as they move from first contact to maximum engagement. Using this analysis approach, the vehicles' first contact positions are established as shown in Exhibit 24. The vehicle movements from first contact can then be easily envisioned. The data suggests that the Ford simply made an abrupt left turn in front of the oncoming Buick.

Step 3 — Occupant Motion Relative to the Vehicles

The primary effect of the collision on the Ford was to stop its forward motion while the Buick pushed it sideways. The thrust on the Ford was a combination of the two illustrations shown in Exhibits 10 and 11. The force on the Ford was closer to the sideways force shown in Exhibit 11, but there was also a rearward component. Thus, the primary movement of the front-seat occupants was to the car's right.

Because both the driver and front-seat passenger would have moved to the car's right as a result of the collision and neither of the occupants came out of the car, you would expect the occupant in the car at rest on the right side to be the passenger and the occupant on the left side to be the driver: the forces exerted on both driver and passenger would not have allowed the passenger to move to his left and the driver to move to his right. However, it has been suggested in cases similar to this one that the driver stiffened his arms and "pole vaulted" to his right, while the passenger moved under the driver to the left. It has been found that braking and muscular reactions have a minimal effect on the path of an occupant's travel.[7] This did not happen in this case, because there was no outside force moving the passenger to the left. Therefore, both driver and passenger had to move to the right.

The passenger would be expected to have serious injuries to his right side because of his proximity to the collapsed door, and because of his shorter stopping distance. The driver would mainly strike the passenger, thus lessening injuries to his right side by hitting a softer object. The passenger could have some injury to his left side by being struck by the driver.

Step 4 — Injury Data and How They Match

Occupant B (found in the right seat) had several injuries. His right forearm was pinned in the damage. He had a flailed-chest injury on his right side and double fractures of the fifth, sixth, seventh and eighth ribs on that side.

Occupant A (found in the left seat) also had several serious injuries: fractures of his fifth, sixth and seventh ribs and a hemothorax on the right side.

Clearly, both occupants moving to the right relative to the car could have sustained the injuries described above. Occupant B's arm, pinned in the damage, supported the right side of his body as it contacted the right interior of the car.

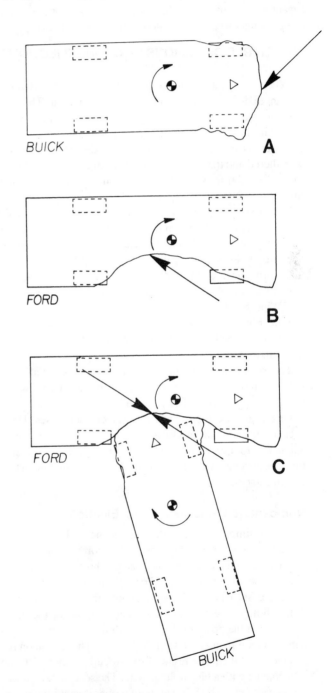

Exhibit 22. The resulting directions of thrust and rotations on the Ford and Buick are shown. Their relative positions at maximum engagement are thus known by lining up the thrust lines.

Step 5 — Check Injuries Against Occupant Motion Conclusions

The occupant motion analysis (Step 3) is supported by the injury data and by the interior damage to the car. The general conclusion is that the occupants moved forward and to the car's right as a result of the collision. This is clearly supported by the damaged steering wheel (moved to the right) and the injuries. Thus, the driver was Occupant A, who was found farthest to the left. The injuries, coupled with the occupant motion analysis, refute any suggestion that the driver and passenger switched positions during the collision.

5. VEHICLE COLLISIONS INVOLVING EJECTIONS

When occupants are found outside vehicles, it is often important to determine how and when they came out. The term *ejection* is often used to indicate that occupants came out of the vehicle. As discussed earlier, it is not so much that occupants were ejected (or thrown out) as that the vehicle's motion was altered and the occupants kept traveling in essentially the same direction in which they were going before the vehicle impact.

The basic procedures to determine occupant motion for vehicle ejection cases begin the same way as for cases where the occupants stayed inside the vehicle. First, a thorough vehicle inspection should be made. Look for the possible apertures through which the bodies could have left the vehicle:

- Open or broken side windows
- Windshields
- Rear hatch or back window
- Doors forced open as a result of the collision
- Sun roof

The remaining steps of the analysis are essentially the same as those applicable to occupant motion cases where there was no ejection. The case studies discussed in the following pages are typical non-rollover ejection cases. However, do not assume that any of these examples are exactly applicable to a case you may be working on. Each collision must be evaluated in the context of its own unique set of circumstances.

Non-centered Pole Impact with Ejection

A very simple case that illustrates some of the points discussed is shown in Exhibits 25–30. It involves a single vehicle that went into a yaw, left the road and hit a pole. The yaw-mark is shown in Exhibit 25. (For a discussion of yawmarks, see Topic 817.) The car's right side hit the pole (see Exhibit 26), behind the rear wheel. The final positions of the body, the car, and the pole are shown in Exhibit 28. An after-accident situation map is shown in Exhibit 29. The person on the ground was killed as a result of electrocution when he came into contact with a high-voltage wire. The second person was found walking outside the car, with no significant injuries; he stated that he was still inside the car when it came to rest. The right-side door was found open when the police arrived.

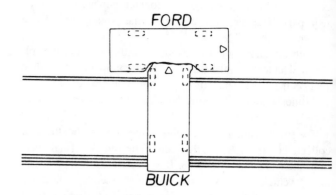

Exhibit 23. *The final positions of the Ford and Chevrolet are known from measurements taken by the police.*

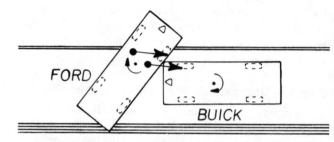

Exhibit 24. *The first contact positions and the resulting unrestrained occupant motions are shown above. The relative occupant final positions should be near where they were before the collision.*

For this case, all five steps will not be discussed in detail. The issue is who was the driver. When the vehicle was inspected, no windows were down or broken. The only opening for occupants to exit the car was the right door. The at-scene investigator stated that the right door would not stay closed because the latch mechanism was damaged. To burst a door open takes a fairly high load. Severy[1] suggests a load of 1,000 lbs. (4,450 N) is required to have door bowing and/or to open the door by overloading the latch mechanism. Multiple occupants being forced into the door can help considerably to reach this loading.

The occupant motion resulting from the collision with the pole is shown in Exhibit 30. The person coming out the right side door is consistent with the occupant motion and final positions. The driver did not come out of the car, because the car rotated considerably before he came into contact with it. The area of the driver's impact with the car is more forward, while the passenger's motion was more sideways (relative to the car). This is because the passenger had only a short distance to travel before hitting the door, and came out almost immediately.

The injuries to the passenger (found outside the car) are primarily to his right side. The cause of death was electrocution when a power line came into contact with the body. The injuries to the driver (person inside the car) were insignificant except for general soreness.

Exhibit 25. *Yawmarks made by the accident vehicle are shown in the above photograph.*

Exhibit 26. *Damage on the right side of the car came from striking a utility pole.*

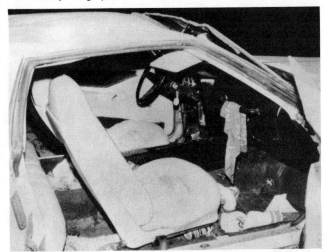

Exhibit 27. *The interior of the car shows little damage relative to other parts of the car.*

Exhibit 28. *The final positions of the vehicle and pole are shown above.*

Single-Vehicle Centered Collision into a Pole

The photographic data available for this case is somewhat limited. However, the information that can be obtained from the three photographs shown in Exhibits 31, 32, and 33 is considerable. By inspecting the photographs it is obvious that the car has moved sideways into the pole. To fully decipher the vehicle position relative to the pole from the photographs, you need to diagram the damaged vehicle relative to the pole and median. This has been done in Exhibit 34B. The diagram based on the photographs showing the final position of the car is somewhat different from the investigating officer's diagram (Exhibit 34A). The police report diagram certainly suggests that the car was in a yaw as it came into the pole. A tire mark is obvious on the median in Exhibit 31, which is consistent with this assumption.

Inspecting the photographs of the vehicle and the police report yields several important pieces of information. The police report states that the driver's door had to be pried

open. Thus, the condition of the door shown in Exhibit 33 is *not* how it looked right after the car came to rest. Exhibit 31 shows that the windshield is still attached to the car. The right side door has been pushed nearly into the middle of the car (see both Exhibits 31 and 32). The photograph of the rear shows that the back hatch is gone. Exhibit 33 shows a steering wheel that has been bent up from the bottom. The seat back has been bent backward.

The issue in this case is who was the driver. One occupant was found outside, behind the car. The other occupant was found inside the car as shown in Exhibit 33. The police report says that the occupant found in the car "was pinned." The behavior of the car as it approached the pole should now be considered. The force on the car from the pole was centered. The front and rear parts of the car did not separate, but rotated about the pole. The curved tire marks observed by the police and recorded on their diagram indicate that the car was in a yaw. (See Topic 817 for a further discussion of

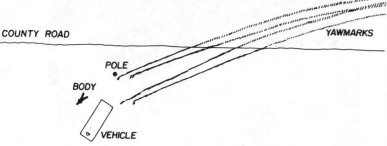

COUNTY ROAD

YAWMARKS

POLE

BODY

VEHICLE

Exhibit 29. *A summary of the photographic data is shown in this after-accident situation map.*

ROADWAY

POLE

LAST CONTACT

APPROACH

FIRST CONTACT

BODY

MAXIMUM ENGAGEMENT

FINAL REST

Exhibit 30. *The sequence of the collision and the resulting occupant motion are shown in this exhibit.*

Exhibit 31. *The front of the car is shown in this photograph. Note its position relative to the raised concrete median.*

Exhibit 32. *The rear of the car is shown in this photograph. Note that its rear hatch is missing.*

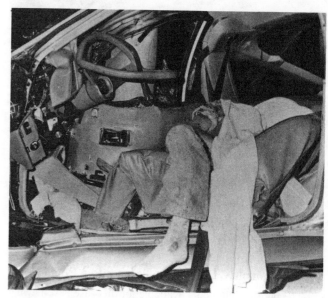

Exhibit 33. *The inside of the car is shown here. Note that the steering wheel has been bent up.*

yaws). Therefore, based on the yaw marks and the vehicle damage, we can assume the car moved toward the pole as shown in Exhibit 35.

Before the car struck the pole, it was traveling nearly sideways. Thus, it should have been decelerating at a rate close to the coefficient of friction (about 0.5 g's). The occupants would have tended to slide toward the right side of the car. As the car first contacted the concrete median, their movement toward the right became more pronounced. As the car hit the median, this tended to make the car start to roll about its longitudinal axis. However, before much roll could take place, the car started to contact the pole. The car, as it contacted the pole, decelerated very quickly. The passenger in the right

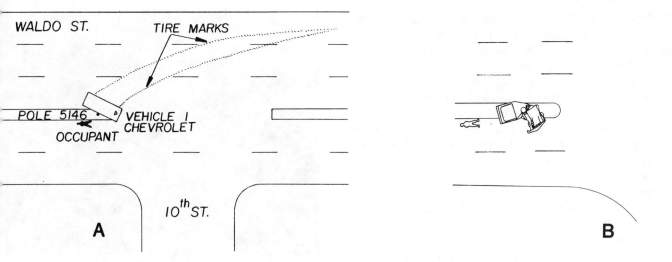

WALDO ST.

TIRE MARKS

POLE 5146

OCCUPANT

VEHICLE I
CHEVROLET

10th ST.

A

B

Exhibit 34. *The police sketch made by the investigating officer is shown in 34A. Note that the shape of the car is different in the map shown in 34B. The map in 34B was based on photographic data only.*

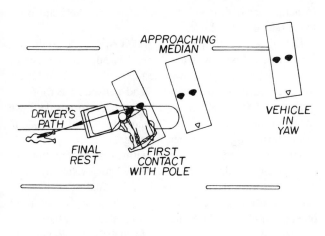

APPROACHING
MEDIAN

DRIVER'S
PATH

FINAL
REST

FIRST
CONTACT
WITH POLE

VEHICLE
IN
YAW

Exhibit 35. *The path of the driver is shown in this exhibit. Note how the driver continues to travel in essentially the same direction he was going before the collision with the pole. The passenger cannot keep moving because of his impact with the pole/door.*

front seat immediately struck the inside right door as it was stopped by the pole. The driver of the car continued moving in the direction in which he was going before the collision — toward the rear of the car as the rear end bent around the pole. Damage to the car supporting this conclusion includes the bent-up steering wheel, the seat back that is bent back, the missing rear hatch, and what appears to be a cassette tape lying on the pavement. All of these items suggest a rearward movement of the driver out the back hatch. This is also consistent with the final position of the occupant behind the car.

Analyzing the occupant motion indicates that significant injuries would be expected for the occupant found in the car, and that injuries to the person found outside the car would be less serious. The impact of the passenger on the pole would

result in a load applied to the body that would be expected to be fatal.

The injuries to the two occupants were summarized as follows:

The person inside the car was killed and had the following injuries: broken neck, multiple fractures of both legs, five-inch laceration of right anterior pelvis, and a skull fracture. The person found outside the car survived the accident with the following injuries: fracture of the left pubic bone, tenderness in paravertebral cervical muscles and lacerations of face, neck and hand. From the occupant motion analysis it was predicted that the injuries to the passenger (found inside the car) would be quite severe. The fractures could certainly be attributed to the intrusion of the pole into the car. The action of the pole simply pushed the passenger toward the driver's seat. The laceration could have been caused by some part of the car as the body was pushed over. The driver (found outside the car) was predicted to have less severe injuries due to the collision. This generally would be attributed to the condition of having a greater distance to decelerate to zero (as compared with the passenger) and that he would hit softer material. The pubic bone injury may have occurred as the driver left the seat and struck the bottom of the steering wheel. The neck and face injuries could have resulted as the driver exited via the rear hatch.

Car-Truck Partial Impact with Multiple Ejections

A difficult problem to resolve for "who was driving" cases often occurs when several people are found outside a vehicle. This can happen in cases involving convertibles with the top down, where it is relatively easy for unrestrained occupants to exit the vehicle. Another easy-exit situation is when a whole side is removed as a result of the collision. Exhibit 36 shows a car that collided with a tractor and semi-trailer. A partial collision resulted, in which no significant part of the damaged car attained a common velocity with a damaged part of the truck. One obvious result is that the whole right side was "opened up," and the unrestrained occupants had nothing to hold them in the car.

Without going into a great deal of background for this case, consider the post-collision motion of the car as shown in Exhibit 37. As the car moved away from the collision at point A, the car was moving mainly backwards, with little drag between its tires and the road surface. If three people were in the front bench seat, they would already have hit the front dash of the car and would have been accelerated backward. The three people would have attained the velocity of the car at that point. As the car moved to point B, it decelerated at a faster rate because the tires were sliding more from the more broadside movement of the car. At point C the car is nearly sliding sideways and is now decelerating at a rate near the coefficient of friction.

Consider now what is happening to the three passengers in the front bench seat. They are not wearing seat belts; the only thing that seems to be holding them in is the friction between their clothes and the seat. Thus, as the deceleration increases on the car, the available friction to keep the bodies inside the car is no longer enough. Obviously the first person out would be the one seated farthest to the right. If the others came out, the sequence would be the center passenger and then the driver.

We now need to consider the expected final positions of the three people. When the bodies first came out, they did not immediately hit the ground and stop: when they first left the car, they were simply traveling through the air. Thus, they traveled at an essentially constant velocity as they fell to the ground. Then the bodies decelerated at a rate determined mainly by the friction between their bodies and the surface they were sliding on. Obviously, if the last person out of the car was the driver, you would expect that he would be the closest to the final position of the car. The second person out would be the next-closest to the final position of the car. Injuries to the driver would be expected to be less severe than injuries to the passengers because of the former's distance from the damaged part of the vehicle. Also, the driver would have been traveling at a slower velocity at the moment of ejection.

6. VEHICLE ROLLOVERS AND OCCUPANT MOTION

In rollover cases when there are several unrestrained occupants, it is often much more difficult to determine the seating positions of the occupants. It may be equally likely that a right-side occupant or a left-side occupant was ejected. The subject of occupant motion in rollovers has been addressed by others.[2,7] In many cases, the occupants do not move far from their initial seating positions, even if they are unrestrained. Orlowski[2] did several rollover tests with two front-seat dummies. In one case, one of the dummies was ejected.

Exhibit 36. *The damage to the right side of this car has opened the side of the car, so nothing is there to hold in unrestrained occupants.*

In actual accident cases, unrestrained occupants are often found outside the vehicle.

Exhibit 38 shows a car that rolled over as a result of a right-angle collision with another car. The driver's head came out of the left-side window. The top of the car, as it hit the pavement, crushed the driver's head between the roof and pavement. Exhibit 39 shows a body under an upside-down car that rolled over as a result of having gone off the road in a yaw, furrowing in, and then flipping.

The general procedure for evaluating occupant motion in a rollover case is the same as that used for evaluating other cases: you must have a thorough understanding of how the vehicle moved as a result of the collision (or as a result of other possibilities). After that, try to evaluate how the occupants would have moved relative to the vehicle. Review injuries and contact points with the vehicle interior to evaluate your conclusions.

Roof Contact with the Ground

Moffatt[3] suggests some considerations that should be made in rollover cases. Consider the two cases shown in Exhibit 40. Because, in the rollover, the car had rotation about its longitudinal axis, the impact with the ground in Part A of Exhibit 40 would tend to increase the roll velocity, while the case depicted in Part B would slow the roll velocity. The number of rolls, the manner in which the vehicle struck the ground, and the probable injury mechanisms become more difficult to analyze for occupant seat positions. It may be just as likely that a right-side occupant was ejected as it is that a left-side occupant was ejected.

After a rollover collision, there is sometimes considerable damage to the roof, as shown in Exhibit 41. The damage is often thought of as having been caused by the roof's being pushed down. Actually, it would be correct to think of the damage as having resulted from the rest of the car's continuing to move toward the ground after the roof stopped mov-

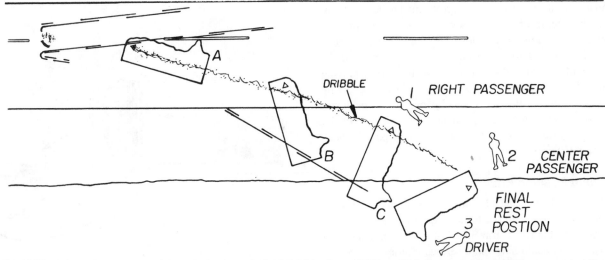

Exhibit 37. *The post-collision motion of the vehicle shown in Exhibit 36 is shown in this exhibit. Front-seat occupants come out of the car one after the other and come to rest at various positions. For this case the last person out (the driver) would be expected to be closest to the car.*

Exhibit 38. *The car shown was hit in the side near the rear of the car, causing it to rotate very rapidly. The car then rolled and landed on its top. The driver was partially out the left-side window when the top contacted the pavement.*

Exhibit 39. *This body came out of the car shown in the photograph. The body was found under the upside-down car.*

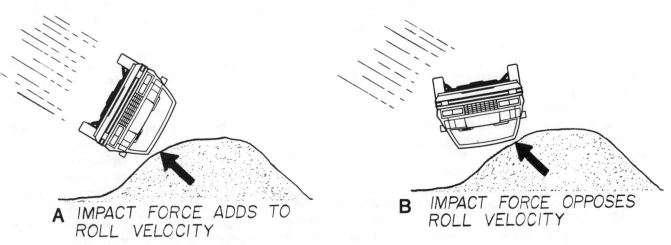

A IMPACT FORCE ADDS TO ROLL VELOCITY

B IMPACT FORCE OPPOSES ROLL VELOCITY

Exhibit 40. *How a car hits the ground in a rollover can increase or decrease its roll velocity.*

ing relative to the ground. Thus, unrestrained occupants contacting the interior of the roof move into the roof (instead of the roof moving into them). However, if the roof damage is extensive, even belted occupants could have contacted the roof. It is important to distinguish between injury occurring because the occupant struck the roof and injury occurring because he rotated through the collision. If the occupant never struck the roof (i.e., the ground), less injury is likely: the occupant was carried by the rolling vehicle past the peak deceleration point.

Occupant Position Effects

Exhibit 41 shows a vehicle starting the rollover and moving toward contact with the ground. Clearly, the person on the outside of the roll is traveling faster than the person on the inside, and could have more serious injuries as a result. Another important consideration in a rollover case is the occupant positions relative to the roof damage. In Exhibit 42 the occupant sitting in the area of maximum roof damage was killed, even though he was wearing a safety belt. In the three cases shown in Exhibit 43, an unrestrained occupant had head impact with the roof right after ground contact, with either maximum roof crush or no crush at all. In all of these cases, the injuries will be similar.

Utility Vehicle Ejection Case

Consider the case described by the after-accident situation map shown in Exhibit 44. A utility vehicle *without doors* was involved in a partial collision with an oncoming vehicle. This occurred at the tiremarks shown at Point A. The collision is classified as a partial, because no parts of the colliding surfaces reached a common velocity. Nevertheless, the collision was severe enough to have detached a wheel from one of the vehicles. Both vehicles continued to move after the collision. The utilitly vehicle rotated very rapidly as a result of the collision and ultimately ended up on its side, as shown in Exhibit 44. The issue for this case is how the driver (sole occupant) came out of the utility vehicle.

There are two possibilities. The first possibility to consider is that the driver came out of the right-side door opening as the vehicle was rolling over. The second possibility is that the driver came out much earlier, out of the left-side door opening.

The first option clearly implies that the driver stayed with the vehicle after the first collision and attained the same post-collision velocity. Then, as the vehicle started to roll over, the driver was "dumped out." If this had been the case, the expected final position would be near the final position of the vehicle. It would be expected that both the vehicle and the driver, as they separated, were moving in the same general direction. Thus, their final positions would be expected to be fairly close. However, the final position of the driver's body is approximately 60 ft (20m) in front of the vehicle. This is inconsistent with his coming out of the vehicle late in the sequence of the collision.

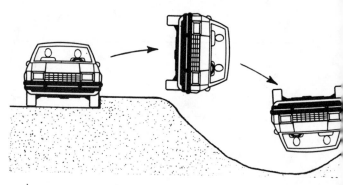

Exhibit 41. *The occupant on the inside of the roll will have less roll velocity than the outside occupant.*

Exhibit 42. *Considerable damage from a rollover has resulted to the roof of this car. The belted occupant in the area of maximum collapse suffered severe injuries.*

The second option, where the driver came out of the left door opening, seems unlikely at first. The following general conditions would have to have occurred: The collision with the oncoming car caused a sudden and severe deceleration of the vehicle. The driver must simply have fallen out through the left-door opening immediately after the collision. This would indicate that the driver and his vehicle were not traveling with a common velocity right after the collision. The vehicle moved out from under the driver. The driver continued to move in the same general direction in which he was going before the collision — definitely not in the same direction as the vehicle was going after the collision. The final position of the body is consistent with this explanation.

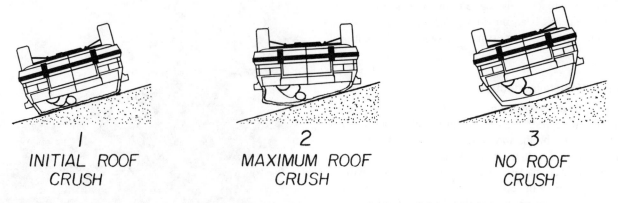

I	2	3
INITIAL ROOF CRUSH	MAXIMUM ROOF CRUSH	NO ROOF CRUSH

Exhibit 43. *In all of these cases the unrestrained occupant will have contact with the roof of the car. Injuries would be expected to be similar in each case.*

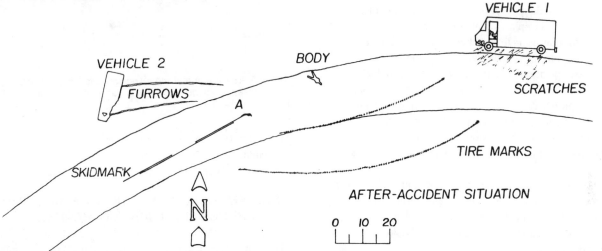

Exhibit 44. *An opposite direction collision occured at A. Vehicle 1 came to rest on its right side. An issue in this case is how the body came out of vehicle 1.*

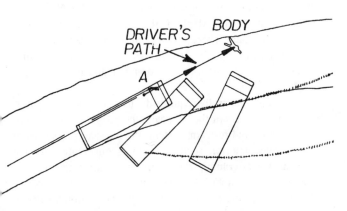

Exhibit 45. *Because the utility van did not have doors, it was relatively easy to have the body go out the left door. This conclusion is supported primarily by the final position of the body. If the body had come out later, it would have been closer to the final position of vehicle 1 as shown in Exhibit 44.*

7. RESTRAINT SYSTEM EFFECTS ON OCCUPANT MOTION AND INJURIES

It is widely known that the change in an unrestrained occupant's speed in a collision can result in injuries. The amount of speed change the vehicle undergoes, called *delta-V,* is determined by the circumstances of the collision. This speed change is nearly complete by the time another collision would occur between the unrestrained occupant and the vehicle's interior (the so-called "second collision"). The vehicle's delta-V occurs over a distance measurable in feet as the vehicle and the object struck are being deformed. The unrestrained occupant undergoes the same change in speed during the time he and the interior surface he strikes are being deformed. This deformation generally is measured in inches. The occupant undergoes the speed change in much less time, thereby increasing the chance of injury. If a restraint system is employed, however, it forces the occupant to change speed while the vehicle is changing speed, thereby lengthening his deceleration time and lessening his chances for injury. Additionally, the restraint system prevents occupant ejection and redirects the collision forces to parts of his anatomy likely to withstand them without serious injury.

The procedure for analyzing restraint-system cases is identical to what has been previously described in Section 2. However, certain other considerations need additional attention.

Internal Vehicle Inspection

Inspection of the anchor points, webbing and hardware associated with a restraint system can reveal certain characteristics caused by the forces acting between the occupant and belt. Typically, if the belt is sufficiently loaded, it may imprint its fabric pattern in the plastic. The signs will be more predominant in severe collisions and with heavier occupants. It is important to note that the absence of evidence does not necessarily mean restraints were not in use.

During the vehicle inspection, note whether any of the restraints are located in places that would preclude their use. It is common for non-users to stuff belts behind and under seats so they do not interfere with vehicle entry and exit.

Check seat position and the length of adjustable belts. Note whether the seat has been jammed. Check the belt retractors for proper operation. When checking the length of adjustable belts, note the position of the "comfort clip." The clip's position changes the tension on the shoulder belt; if adjusted too loosely, the belt might allow the wearer to slip out during a collision.

Note also any foreign matter on the restraint system. Dirt, blood, body materials, glass, and other materials can be deposited on the belt. If the belt is retracted, note whether these deposits are on the area of the belt which should have been stored if not in use.

If the collision forces are sufficient, the anchor points of an in-use restraint system will be deformed. Correlate the direction of deformation with the expected direction of force of the loaded belt. It is important to distinguish this type of deformation from that caused by other forces in the collision.

Inspect the buckles, fasteners and any other hardware coated with plastic. If the belt is loaded, it may have imprinted its fabric pattern onto the plastic. This same phenomenon can be observed on seat edges that are in contact with the belt under severe loads.

Examine both sides of the webbing for signs of abrasion and, if noted, determine what other part it was in contact with. Again, it is important to distinguish between abrasions caused by continuous use and those caused by the belt loading during collisions. Exhibit 46 shows a vehicle with extensive front-end damage. Both front seat occupants were belted. The passenger's side seatbelt is shown in Exhibit 47. Note the characteristic imprint of the belt's fabric pattern in the plastic. The belt and hardware on the driver's side was unremarkable.

Occasionally, a belt will break under a severe load. The location of the break is expected to be near the belt's own hardware attachment points. If the webbing is broken elsewhere, look for signs that it was cut. Cutting the webbing with a knife or other sharp object results in an even cut, with

Exhibit 46. *A severe frontal impact occurred to this car. Damage to one of the seat belts indicated that it was in use at the time of the collision (see Exhibit 47).*

many of the fibers about the same length. If the webbing is broken under a severe load, the fibers are of random lengths. That is, the ends appear frayed and of uneven length.

8. MATHEMATICAL SIMULATION OF OCCUPANT KINETICS AND INJURY MECHANISMS

The mathematical simulators currently available have limited practical value for traffic accident reconstruction. Three models were developed during the 1970's: the Crash Victim Simulator Three-Dimensional (CVS-3D) model developed by Calspan Corporation, and the Motor Vehicle Manufacturers Association's Two-Dimensional (MVMA-2D) Crash Victim Simulator and HSRI3D (H3D), developed at the University of Michigan. There are several more recent variations being used in research. At this writing, most of these simulators require a main-frame computer and input data not easily obtained.

Simulation generally requires the user to supply the physical characteristics of the occupant; the geometry of the vehicle's interior and restraint system; the physical properties of the vehicle's interior, such as stiffness information for the steering wheel/column, dashboard and seat; initial orientation of the occupant's body segments; and a motion history of the vehicle during collision. Obtaining the motion history of the accident vehicle generally requires using the output from other computer programs such as CRASH (Calspan Reconstruction of Accident Speeds on the Highway) and SMAC (Calspan Simulation Model of Automobile Collisions). (See Topic 892 for further discussion of computer-aided accident reconstruction.)

If the required inputs are obtained, the simulators generally will provide as output the vehicle and occupant displace-

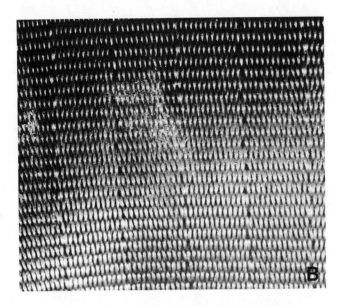

Exhibit 47. *Signs of abrasion/heavy loading of a seat belt is shown in photo A. Abrasions on the webbing are shown in photo B. Damage to the car is shown in Exhibit 46.*

ments, velocities and accelerations, seat belt loads, occupant/vehicle contact forces, and expected occupant injuries. Another output comprises graphs of selected variables and graphical presentation of occupant displacement at various instants. In general, the results are accurate if the input data is good.

9. SUMMARY

In many cases, issues such as who was driving, how people were injured, how occupants were ejected from a vehicle, and other aspects of occupant motion can be answered. Desired information on vehicle damage (both interior and exterior), occupant injuries, final rest positions (vehicles and bodies), marks on the road, and other sources may be available for the analysis. Often it may not be. The data may be fairly sketchy on interior damage. Also, injury data is often very poor in fatality cases. At the time of the accident there may not be much interest in the case and an autopsy often is not done. Nevertheless, in many cases satisfactory conclusions can be developed with less than complete data. In highly complicated cases it may be desirable to have a team of experts evaluating the case from both the occupant motion perspective and the injury mechanism perspective.

10. SOURCES

Authors

Lynn B. Fricke is a traffic engineer specializing in accident investigation. He has been with The Traffic Institute since 1975. In 1981, he became director of the Institute's Accident Investigation Division. He has B.S. and M.S. degrees in engineering.

Kenneth S. Baker is a senior lecturer and consultant at The Traffic Institute. Before coming to the Institute in 1986, he was with the Indiana State Police. Mr. Baker has a B.A. degree from Indiana University.

References

Superscript numbers in the preceding pages refer to the following publications:

1. Severy, D.M., D.M. Blaisdell, and L.S. Horn, "Motorist Head and Body Impact Analysis, Methodologies and Reconstruction" (SAE 850097), Society of Automotive Engineers, Warrendale, Pennsylvania.

2. Orlowski, Kenneth F., R. Thomas Bundorf, and Edward A. Moffatt, "Rollover Crash Tests — The Influence of Roof Strength on Injury Mechanics" (SAE 851734), Society of Automotive Engineers, Warrendale, Pennsylvania.

3. Moffatt, Edward A., "Occupant Motion in Rollover Collisions," *Proceedings of the 19th Conference of the American Association for Automotive Medicine,* 1975.

4. Nyquist, Gerald W., and Everett P. Kennedy, "Accident Victim Interaction with Vehicle Interior: Reconstruction Fundamentals" (SAE 870500), Society of Automotive Engineers, Warrendale, Pennsylvania.

5. Strother, Charles E., and Michael B. James, "Evaluation of Seat Back Strength and Seat Belt Effectiveness in Rear End Impacts" (SAE 872214), Society of Automotive Engineers, Warrendale, Pennsylvania.

6. *Mathematical Simulation of Occupant and Vehicle Kinematics* (Publication P-146), Society of Automotive Engineers, Warrendale, Pennsylvania, May 1974.

7. Habberstad, John L., Roger C. Wagner, and Terry M. Thomas, "Rollover and Interior Kinematics Test Procedures Revisited" (SAE 861875), Society of Automotive Engineers, Warrendale, Pennsylvania.

Exhibits

The following are the sources of the exhibits used in this topic:

Baker, J. Stannard, San Diego, CA
Diagrams: 9-11, 13-15

Baker, Kenneth S., Traffic Institute, Evanston, IL
Photographs: 3, 6, 46, 47

Badger, Joseph, Indiana State Police
Photograph: 2

Cooper, Gary W., Traffic Institute, Evanston, IL
Diagrams: 29, 30, 37

Fricke, Lynn B., Traffic Institute, Evanston, IL
Diagrams: 22-24, 34-35, 38-39
Photographs: 1, 8, 12, 43

Jefferson County Sheriff, KY
Photograph: 3

Manitowoc Police Dept., WI
Photograph: 31-33

Marr, Kimberly, Hamilton County Sheriff, IN
Photograph: 5a

Moffatt, Edward, Warren MI
Diagrams: 42, 44, 45

Nelson, Wilton, Howell MI
Photograph: 4

Owens, Michael, Indiana State Police
Photographs: 25-28

Seward County Sheriff, NB
Photograph: 41

Unknown
Photographs: 7, 16-21, 36, 40

VEHICLE-PEDESTRIAN ACCIDENT RECONSTRUCTION

Topic 877 of the *Traffic Accident Investigation Manual*

by
Lynn B. Fricke

NORTHWESTERN UNIVERSITY TRAFFIC INSTITUTE

VEHICLE-PEDESTRIAN ACCIDENT RECONSTRUCTION

1. TYPICAL ISSUES

Vehicle-pedestrian accidents often result in severe injuries to pedestrians. (Several references on vehicle-pedestrian collisions are listed at the end of this topic; reference 1 gives an extensive bibliography which may be consulted.) As with other types of traffic accidents, there frequently is considerable interest in how the accident occurred. Typical issues that remain unresolved when reconstructing a pedestrian accident include

- First contact positions
- Vehicle speed
- Pedestrian kinematics
- Driver and pedestrian strategy
- Driver and pedestrian tactics
- Possible suicide or homicide

In nearly all car-pedestrian accidents, there is a question raised regarding the positions of the pedestrian and the car when *contact first occurred*. This often suggests culpability on the part of the driver or may indicate poor risk perception on the part of the pedestrian. In some cases it is also important to have an understanding of how the pedestrian was oriented to the car when struck. For example, it may be quite important to know whether the pedestrian was struck from behind, front, left side, or right side.

An issue is nearly always raised regarding the *speed* of the vehicle involved in the collision. This, of course, could suggest culpability or negligence on the part of the driver. Occasionally, the speed of the pedestrian is an issue — that is, whether the pedestrian was running or walking at the time of the accident. In many cases, the issue of vehicle speed may be indeterminate because of poor data collection or because suitable reconstruction techniques are not available.

Pedestrian kinematics, or how the pedestrian moved as a result of the collision, may be important to know in determining vehicle speed or injury mechanisms. Important information for resolving this issue includes the pedestrian's injuries, final rest position and contact points with the ground, as well as damage to the vehicle. By knowing how the pedestrian moved after the collision, it may be possible to resolve issues such as whether the pedestrian was running, walking, attempting suicide, or facing the car.

Driver and pedestrian strategy involves such issues as position on the road and pedestrian conspicuousness. It deals with the decisions drivers and pedestrians make before perceiving any hazard that may influence their chances to avoid an accident. For a detailed discussion of strategy, see Topic 852.

Driver and pedestrian tactics relate to what drivers and pedestrians do when a hazard has been perceived. Proper interpretation and prompt reaction to the hazard may influence the likelihood of accident avoidance. Typical evasive tactics of the driver include braking and steering. A more detailed discussion of tactics is included in Topic 852.

In some pedestrian cases, there may be reason to believe that a *suicide or homicide* may be the reason for the "accident." There are more efficient ways to murder someone than using an automobile; the use of a vehicle in a homicide may be to cover up the murder. The cover-up motive may also be present in a suicide. Both suicide and homicide cases may have insurance motives.

2. INFORMATION FROM THE ROAD, VEHICLE, AND BODY

As in any traffic accident investigation, there is much to be gained from inspecting the road and vehicle(s) involved. In addition, the injuries that may be expected in pedestrian accidents can also be quite helpful in explaining how the accident happened. They are discussed in this topic. Scene documentation techniques for a vehicle-pedestrian accident are the same as for any traffic accident. These are discussed in several topics of the *Manual*, which should be consulted if you are unfamiliar with them. Similarly, vehicle inspections involve essentially the same techniques as for any accident and are also discussed in other topics.

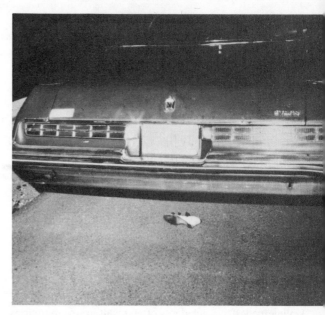

Exhibit 1. *A distinct but inconspicuous friction mark is sometimes left by a shoe.*

Exhibit 2. *The final position of a shoe (even though it has come off the pedestrian) may not indicate accurately the first contact position of the pedestrian. In this case the woman's shoe came off a short time after the initial impact.*

Road Information

The results of a vehicle-pedestrian accident should be documented by measurements and photographs at the accident scene. For pedestrian accidents, take special care to look for signs of the first contact positions. Often, this can be determined from scuff marks of shoes, the shoe position itself, tire irregularities of the motor vehicle, or debris from the vehicle and pedestrian. One of the best indicators of first contact is a mark from a shoe. Exhibit 1 shows a friction mark left by a shoe in a car-pedestrian collision. In some cases, the pedestrian may be lifted out of his shoes. However, the final position of a shoe may not always be a good indication of first contact. Exhibit 2 shows the final position of a woman's shoe after a car-pedestrian accident. In this case the woman was not immediately lifted out of her shoes. The shoe came off in the collision sequence. Vehicle debris can give a clue to the general area of a collision. However, debris from a car can be a considerable distance from the first contact positions. Exhibit 3 shows paint chips from a car that struck a pedestrian. Other debris from a pedestrian other than shoes (Exhibit 4) can be found at an accident scene. However, hats, canes, glasses and other things can be found some distance from the first contact positions.

Another important element of a pedestrian accident that needs to be carefully considered at the scene is evidence of where the pedestrian contacted the ground after vehicle contact. This may be of use in a speed analysis. The example shown in Exhibit 5 clearly shows the path of the pedestrian from the blood path. In this case the pedestrian was separated into two parts because of the collision. For cases where the after-collision travel distance of the body on the ground can be determined, measure the length of travel. Be sure to locate

Exhibit 3. *Debris from a vehicle in a pedestrian collision can be found. In this photograph, paint chips from the striking vehicle (not the one shown in the photograph) were found in front of the parked car.*

the initial ground contact point and the body's final position so an after-accident scale map can be drawn.

All of the data from a car-pedestrian accident should be collected so that an after-accident scale map can be drawn. Be sure to include final positions of vehicles, bodies, the pedestrian's personal items (hats, canes, glasses, purses, watches, etc.), and marks on the road. A typical after-accident situation map of a pedestrian-car accident is shown in Exhibit 6.

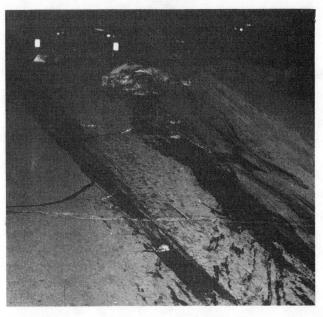

Exhibit 4. *Debris from the pedestrian, such as glasses, hats and canes, can often be found at the scene of a vehicle-pedestrian accident.*

Exhibit 5. *The blood path from a pedestrian severed into two pieces by the impact of the car front is clearly shown in this photograph.*

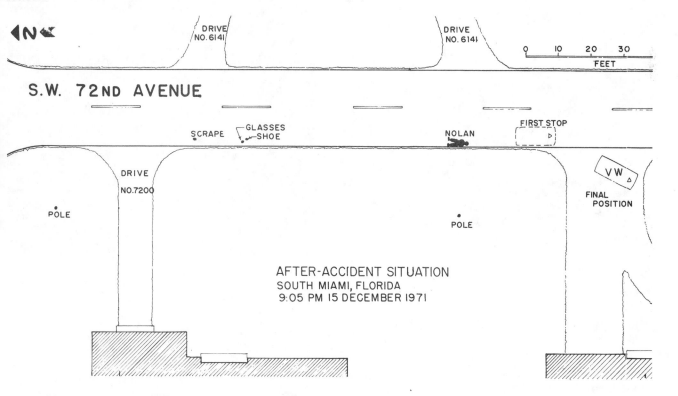

Exhibit 6. *All results of the accident, such as the items shown in this exhibit, along with body and vehicle final positions, should be located by measurements so that a scaled map can be drawn.*

Vehicle Information

The general subject of vehicle examination is discussed in Topic 820. Only the specific parts that apply to pedestrian accidents will be discussed in this topic. Generally, the damage a vehicle receives in a pedestrian collision is quite minor. In some cases, you may have to look very carefully to see any damage. The example shown in Exhibit 7 has very minor damage as compared to the photograph shown in Exhibit 8. Note in Exhibit 8 the damage to both the headlight area and the hood of the car.

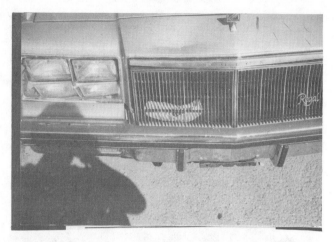

Exhibit 7. *The damage to a vehicle in a pedestrian accident can often be very slight. In this case it is hardly noticeable except for the damage to the fiberglass behind the grill. Notice the shoe found behind the grill. This was a fairly high-speed collision.*

Exhibit 8. *Damage to a car can be somewhat extensive in a vehicle-pedestrian accident. Notice the damage to the headlight area at G and the hood damage at H.*

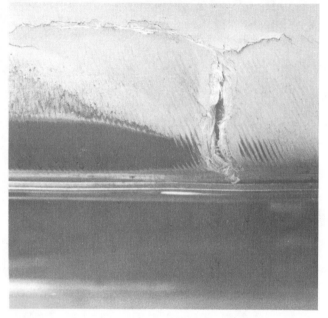

Exhibit 9. *In a few cases the actual imprint of fabric from the pedestrian's clothing can be seen on the vehicle as shown in this photograph.*

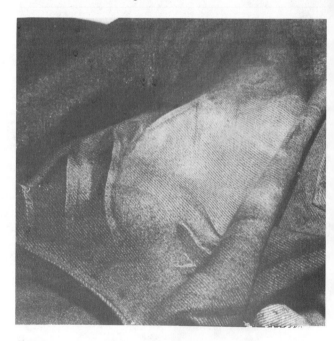

Exhibit 10. *The blue jeans that made the imprint on the car shown in Exhibit 9 are shown in this photograph.*

Imprints and blood from the pedestrian can often be found on the vehicle. Note the imprint of fabric on the car in Exhibit 9. The clothes that left the imprint are shown in Exhibit 10. On the same car, blood left on the trunk lid gives an indication of how the body moved as a result of the collision.

The windshield, fenders, radio antenna, and mirrors can also be damaged in vehicle-pedestrian collisions. Damage to a windshield and fender are shown in Exhibit 11 and 12.

Pedestrian Injury Information

Good data are often not available for injuries to the pedestrian. In many U.S. jurisdictions, autopsies are not conducted when pedestrians are killed in accidents. Later on, if ques-

tions are raised as to how the accident occurred, it may be too late to get injury information.

Injuries from pedestrian-vehicle accidents are discussed elsewhere.[2,3,4] For example, Backaitis[4] summarized injuries for car-cadaver collisions where the tests were performed with the test subject "standing" and being impacted by the center of a forward-moving vehicle into the cadaver's right side. The standing position of the cadaver was maintained by overhead wires that were released immediately prior to impact. The speed of the cars was 25 mi/hr (40 km/hr) at impact. Tests were done with a fairly large car and a small car. As would be expected, fractures of the leg (tibia and fibula) resulted. Head injuries were more severe for the large car.

Exhibit 11. *If the right conditions are met, the pedestrian's body can strike the windshield and even break it. Generally, this requires a fairly high impact speed.*

Exhibit 12. *This off-road vehicle has damage to the fender and hood on its right side. Little other damage was found on the vehicle.*

This is most likely explained by how the head interacted with hard parts of the car. For a more in-depth discussion of pedestrian injuries you should refer to reference 4 and many other reports dealing with pedestrian injuries.

Pedestrian injuries may not just come from impact with the vehicle. If the body falls and/or slides some distance, some of the injuries may result from post-vehicle collision interaction with the road surface.

If you are working on a pedestrian case where there is a question as to how a pedestrian received an injury, it may be useful also to get an opinion from a forensic pathologist. Keep in mind, however, that the pathologist may not have a good understanding of how a pedestrian moves as a result of the vehicle collision. The person doing the reconstruction with the pathologist may provide an excellent team approach to the solution of the questions being raised.

3. PEDESTRIAN MOTION AS A RESULT OF A VEHICLE COLLISION

Any object, if it is struck off-center (that is, by a force that is not directed through the object's center of mass), will rotate as a result of the collision. Consider the body shown in Exhibit 13. The force on the body is above the center of mass. Thus, the body will rotate clockwise as shown. In Exhibit 14 the force on the body is below the center of mass, so the body will rotate in a counterclockwise direction as shown. If a body is struck by a vehicle which imparts a force above the center of mass as in Exhibit 13, then it would be expected that the body would be forced down into the road. However, if the force was as shown in Exhibit 14, you would expect the body to move upward (perhaps onto the hood of a car).

Exhibit 15 shows the results of a large car and small car striking a large cadaver at 20 mi/hr (32 km/hr). Exhibit 16 shows similar results of a smaller car striking a large cadaver at 26 mi/hr (42 km/hr). In all cases the collision force on the body is below its center of mass, which causes it to rotate toward the oncoming car. Ultimately the feet leave the ground. The upper part of the body then strikes the hood and windshield. For the large-car case it could be argued that the head does not make much contact with the windshield. If the vehicle speed is high enough, the body may go over the vehicle. It is also possible that the body may be carried for a short time on the hood of the car.

Car frontal impacts to pedestrians occur in 80 to 90 percent of car-pedestrian accidents.[6,7] As can be seen for frontal impacts in Exhibits 15 and 16, the shape of the car front will affect where the head will hit the car. Another obvious factor is the pedestrian's height. Ashton and others[5] concluded that location of head contact was a function of pedestrian height: the taller the pedestrian, the further back the head contact. Head injury in vehicle-pedestrian accidents has been listed as the highest cause of death[6]. Serious head injuries frequently occur at vehicle impact speeds of 30 mi/hr (50 km/hr) or greater[3]. Severe head/face injuries are more often caused by vehicle contact than by ground contact.

Consider what would happen if a small pedestrian not moving rapidly is struck above his center of mass as shown in Exhibit 17. The car is not braking hard before, during, or after the collision. For the case shown in Exhibit 17, the pedestrian would go under the vehicle because the force is above the body's center of mass. As the body comes into contact with the pavement, it starts slowing with a drag factor equal to the coefficient of friction. Typically on a clean, dry,

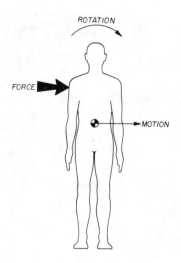

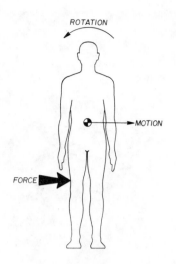

Exhibit 13. *If the collision force applied on a body is above the cen-ter of mass, the body will rotate as shown.*

Exhibit 14. *If the collision force applied on a body is below the cen-ter of mass, the body will rotate as shown.*

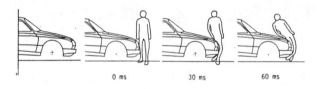

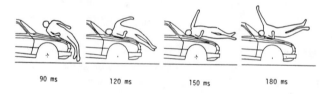

LARGE CAR

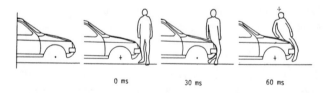

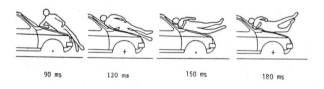

SMALL CAR

Exhibit 15. *Large cadavers are shown here being struck by a small and a large car at 20 mi/hr (32 km/hr). This data came from the study listed as reference 4.*

hard surface a value of approximately 0.5 is found. (Drag factors appropriate for sliding bodies are discussed in more detail later in this topic). If the body is decelerating at a rate of 0.5 g and the car is continuing at a constant velocity, the car passes over the body (unless some part of the pedestrian's clothes catches on the undercarriage of the car).

If a car strikes a pedestrian with a generally centered im-pact, the body will be accelerated to the same speed as the car. The body will drop toward the ground as the force be-tween the body and the car goes to zero. The feet dragging on the ground will also tend to encourage this behavior. If the car is being braked hard (with a drag factor around 0.7), it would be expected that the car will stop at its rest position with the pedestrian in front of it. Consider what is happening in Exhibit 18. The car is being braked at a drag factor of 0.7. The fastest typical deceleration from pedestrian sliding that would normally be expected on a body is around 0.5g as shown in Exhibit 18. Because both car and pedestrian are traveling at the same speed at separation and the car is de-celerating at a higher rate than the pedestrian, the body is found at rest in front of the rest position of the car.

In a car-pedestrian collision it is possible for the body to reach the same speed as the car and stay on the hood. If the driver then brakes with some intensity, for example with a deceleration of 0.7 g, the body will slide off the hood. Pre-sumably, the only thing that holds the body on the hood is the friction between the body and the hood. A typical coefficient of friction would be around 0.3. Thus, if the car decelerated at 0.7 g, then clearly the body would slide off as is illustrated in Exhibit 19.

Occasionally dimemberment takes place in a vehicle-pedestrian accident. For this to happen, a fairly high speed for the car is required. Exhibit 20 illustrates a situation where a body is severed into a top and bottom half. The upper part of the body goes over the car and the lower part is passed over by the car. Exhibit 5 shows a photograph where this described pedestrian motion took place. For this case, the pedestrian clearly will not be accelerated to the same speed the car was traveling. This type of impact is described as a *partial* impact. A partial impact is an impact where none of the colliding surfaces attains a common velocity. This is discussed in more detail in Topic 861.

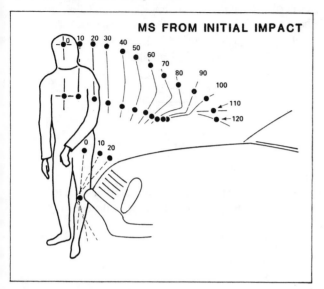

Exhibit 16. *A large cadaver is shown here being struck by a small car at 26 mi/hr (42 km/hr). This data came from the study listed as reference 3. This exhibit is similar to the results shown in Exhibit 15.*

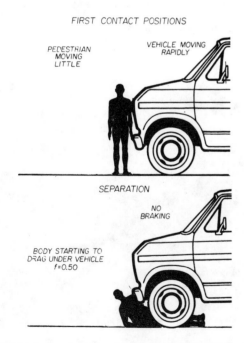

Exhibit 17. *The small pedestrian is hit above his center of mass, causing the top part of the body to rotate toward the pavement. The drag on the body slows it and the car continues over the body without braking.*

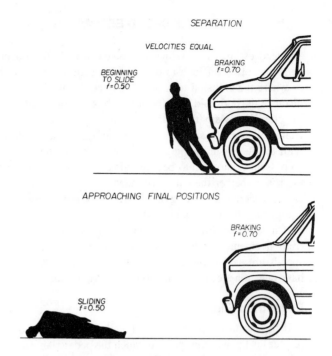

Exhibit 18. *The car is being braked when first contact takes place and continues to brake to a stop. The force on the pedestrian is near his center of mass, accelerating him to nearly the same velocity as the car at first contact. Because the body does not start to decelerate with the full drag factor right after maximum engagement, and because it has a lower drag factor than the decelerating car, the body's final position will be in front of the car.*

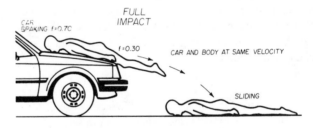

Exhibit 19. *This exhibit shows a pedestrian at one point on the hood of the car. Clearly, this is a full impact because the pedestrian and the car attain the same speed. If the car is braking with a higher drag factor than the coefficient of friction available between the body and car hood, the body will slide off the hood as shown.*

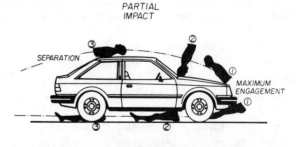

Exhibit 20. *The collision between the body and the car is incomplete because the striking surfaces never attain the same speed. The car essentially "cuts" through the pedestrian. A real case where this has happened is shown in Exhibit 5.*

4. VEHICLE SPEED ESTIMATES

Speed estimates of vehicles involved in pedestrian accidents are often difficult to do. Important information, such as where the collision took place, may not be available. The distance the body slid after the collision is also often difficult to determine. Many times, the vehicle involved in the pedestrian collision does not leave braking skidmarks. Indeed, with the increasing popularity of anti-lock braking systems on passenger cars, it may be impossible to tell from marks on the road whether the car was braked hard (though in some cases, discernable braking tire marks are observed from cars equipped with anti-lock brakes).

If a car leaves braking skidmarks at the scene of a pedestrian accident, the techniques used to determine vehicle speeds are well-known. Refer to Topics 817 and 860 if you have questions regarding speed from braking skids.

Pedestrian Sliding

If the distance a pedestrian slid on the pavement (or other surface) is known, the speed to which the pedestrian was accelerated can be calculated. This speed is nearly always less and never more than the vehicle speed. The reason for this is fairly obvious. In most cases, the collision between the vehicle and pedestrian is not centered (see Exhibits 13 and 14). For these cases, the body is rotated as a result of the collision and does not reach the same velocity as the car. If, however, the body is carried on the car and comes off (for example, as a result of the driver braking – see Exhibit 19), the body would have been accelerated to the same velocity as the car. If the distance the body slid is known, along with the body's rate of deceleration (drag factor, f), then the body's speed can be calculated from

$$v_i = \sqrt{v_e^2 - 2ad}$$

where v_i = initial velocity in ft/sec or m/sec
v_e = end velocity in ft/sec or m/sec
a = acceleration in ft/sec^2 or m/sec^2
d = distance the body slid in ft or m

If the body slid to a stop, then the quantity $v_e = 0$. The value for a is always negative (minus) because the body is slowing. Acceleration, a, is always equal to the drag factor, f, multiplied by the acceleration of gravity, g (32.2 ft/sec^2 or 9.81 m/sec^2).

Typical values for pedestrian drag factors over several surfaces are given in Exhibit 21. These values have been duplicated many times in student projects conducted at The Traffic Institute. As can be seen in Exhibit 21, these values are less than typically seen for rubber tires sliding on clean, dry pavement. The values given in Exhibit 21 were obtained by dragging a person horizontally along a surface. The coefficient of friction was then determined by dividing the horizontal force by the vertical force. The horizontal force was measured when the body was sliding (not at or near static

conditions). A student project to determine drag factor of a pedestrian on grass is shown in Exhibit 22.

Consider the following case, where you have a pedestrian that slid along a level grass shoulder for a distance of 67 ft as a result of a car collision. A low representative value for friction of a pedestrian on grass is 0.45. For this case, the coefficient of friction is equal to drag factor (see Topic 890 if you have a question about this). Therefore, $f = 0.45$. Then acceleration, a, equals fg, or $(.45)(32.2)$, which equals 14.5 ft/sec^2. Initial velocity, v_i, is then calculated

$$
\begin{aligned}
v_i &= \sqrt{v_e^2 - 2ad} \\
&= \sqrt{0^2 - (2)(-14.5)(67)} \\
&= 44 \text{ ft/sec} \\
&= 30 \text{ mi/hr}
\end{aligned}
$$

The 30 mi/hr speed estimate then indicates that the car was traveling at least 30 mi/hr at the time of the collision.

Surface	Range
Grass	.45 - .70
Asphalt	.45 - .60
Concrete	.40 - .65

Exhibit 21. A range in the typical drag factors found for bodies sliding on dry pavement is shown in this exhibit. As can be seen, these values are generally less than what is found for rubber tires on dry pavement.

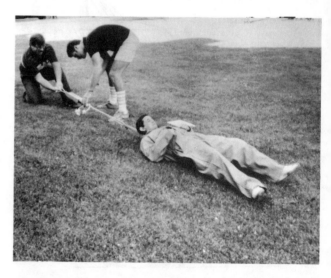

Exhibit 22. This photograph shows a pedestrian being pulled along a grass surface. The horizontal force is being measured. This force, divided by the vertical force (the person's weight), gives the drag factor.

Speed Estimates by Using the Vault Equation

Investigators often try to estimate the velocity of a car by applying the vault equation to the pedestrian. Usually this will not yield acceptable answers, because too many simplifying assumptions are used. Some of the possible errors in assumptions are
- The body takeoff angle is not clearly known;
- The point where the body left the vehicle relative to the ground is not known;
- The point of touchdown of the pedestrian is not known.

Occasionally, the final resting position of the body is assumed to be the point of first touchdown with the ground. The horizontal distance is based on this position. A vault equation calculation may yield an answer of, say, 35 mi/hr (56km/hr). It clearly makes no sense to assume that a body came to a complete stop instantaneously upon first touching the ground at 35 mi/hr as it left the car.

There may be times when using the vault equation is appropriate, but be careful to understand its basic assumptions. If your assumptions are not consistent with those used in its derivation, then you may be making unreasonable speed estimates. Review Topic 890 if you are not familiar with the assumptions made in deriving the vault equation.

Speed Estimates Based on the Fall Equation

If a pedestrian-vehicle collision is a centered, full impact as shown in Exhibit 23, the body will be accelerated to the same velocity as that of the vehicle in a very short distance. When the body and vehicle attain the same velocity, the force between them goes to zero and the body falls toward the ground. The friction between the shoes of the pedestrian and the ground applies a rotational moment to the body, which also contributes to the body motion toward the ground. For the situation depicted in Exhibit 23, the vehicle does not impart any vertical component of velocity to the body. Thus, the body has only horizontal motion right before the body and vehicle separate.

Collins[9] has taken the above-described scenario and applied the fall equation and the slide-to-a-stop equation to develop an initial-vehicle-velocity solution to the case where the initial contact and final pedestrian positions are known but the first touchdown position is not known. Collins suggests an iterative solution technique to arrive at the vehicle speed. Because there are two equations and two unknowns, it is possible to solve for the initial velocity of the vehicle without iterations. The iterative approach, however, can be done very quickly. By using the fall equation

$$v_i = d_f \sqrt{\frac{g}{2(d_f G - h)}}$$

and the slide equation

$$v_i = \sqrt{v_e^2 - 2ad_s}$$

where v_i = initial velocity of the vehicle in ft/sec (m/sec)

v_e = end velocity of the pedestrian (v_e=0) ft/sec (m/sec)

a = rate of slowing of the body sliding (a=$-fg$) ft/sec/sec (m/sec/sec)

g = acceleration of gravity, 32.2 ft/sec/sec (9.8 m/sec/sec)

h = height center of mass falls, h is negative if landing is below take-off position ft(m)

G = percent grade (G=0 for this situation)

d_f = horizontal distance, ft(m), the body traveled while falling

d_s = horizontal distance, ft(m), the body traveled while sliding

In addition, the total distance from first contact to the rest position is

$$d = d_s + d_f$$

By setting the two equations for velocity equal to each other and using the above equation, d_f can be solved. Thus, the general equations to solve for the vehicle velocity at first contact are

$$v = d_f \sqrt{-g/2h}$$

$$v = \sqrt{-2ad_s}$$

where

$$d_f = 2fh - 2h \sqrt{f^2 - df/h}$$

$$d_s = d - d_f$$

The procedure to follow if you have a case like this is to first calculate the fall distance, d_f, and then solve for velocity using either equation. The solution for a simple case follows.

Given: Total distance from first contact to final body position
d=100 ft

Vertical distance the body center of mass fell
h=−2.5 ft

Body drag factor f=0.5

Solution:

$$d_f = 2fh - 2h\sqrt{f^2 - fd/h}$$

$$d_f = 2(.5)(-2.5) - 2(-2.5)\sqrt{(.5)^2 - (.5)(100)/(-2.5)}$$

$$d_f = -2.5 + 5\sqrt{20.25}$$

$$d_f = -2.5 + 22.5$$

$$d_f = 20 \text{ ft.}$$

$$d_s = d - d_f$$

$$d_s = 100 - 20 = 80$$

For fall:

$$v = d_f\sqrt{-g/2h}$$

$$v = 20\sqrt{-(32.2)/(2)(-2.5)}$$

$$v = 50.8 \text{ ft/sec}$$

For slide:

$$v = \sqrt{-2ad_s}$$

$$v = \sqrt{-(2)(-.5)(32.2)(80)}$$

$$v = 50.8 \text{ ft/sec}$$

The velocity calculation for the fall should (and does) equal the slide calculation.

The previous set of equations needs to be considered carefully before they are used. Recall what was said earlier regarding the body movement. The body is accelerated to the speed of the vehicle. The body's only velocity is horizontal, as a result of the collision. Thus, you must have a case similar to that depicted in Exhibit 23. Most cases will *not* be of this type (that is, with a more or less vertical surface striking the pedestrian).

As a result of the acceleration on the body, a large force develops between the vehicle and the body. The acceleration period is short; it lasts only while the body moves forward a few inches (less than the thickness of the pedestrian). The force on the body is centered, so it does not rotate as a direct result of the collision. Once the pedestrian has attained the speed of the vehicle, acceleration of the pedestrian ceases and the force between pedestrian and vehicle decreases to zero.

Then, if the vehicle is slowing, the pedestrian, with only air resistance retarding his motion, continues forward at constant speed, separating from the vehicle. Unsupported by

friction with the vehicle, the pedestrian begins to fall. The pedestrian's feet begin to drag on the road, and the body continues forward. The slight drag of the feet makes the body rotate about a transverse axis – that is, pitch forward. The body then hits the road with whatever side was opposite the impact when struck.

Any movement of the pedestrian across the front of the vehicle before impact is arrested on impact by the large friction forces between vehicle and pedestrian. If the front wheels of the vehicle are sliding at the moment of impact, crosswise movement of the pedestrian may produce some sideslip of the skidding tires and a corresponding slight irregularity in the skidmark. This irregularity may be the best indication of the vehicle's position at first contact.

For the equations developed above, the assumption is that the pedestrian is completely in the air until he hits the road surface and begins to slide. As indicated earlier, the body will tend to pitch forward. However, only a small part of the pedestrian's weight is on the feet at that time. If the fall distance is shortened by the foot drag, then the slide distance is increased. But then the calculated slide distance is shorter than what it may, in fact, be. Hence, the assumption of free fall followed by slide appears to be appropriate, at least when possible errors in assigning values to various variables, such as the height of the pedestrian's center of mass and pedestrian drag factor, are considered.

In practice, locating the body's final position is easy, but locating the place where the pedestrian was struck is difficult. Blood or body tissue is rarely deposited at that point. There may be scuff marks from shoes, but they are difficult to detect. Sometimes glasses, hats, purses, or shoes are left behind to mark the spot. Occasionally, a witness can satisfactorily identify the point of impact. As previously noted, a slight irregularity in a skidmark is probably the best sign of where the vehicle's tires were when the pedestrian was struck.

If the vehicle is not slowing when it strikes the pedestrian, the force between body and vehicle diminishes to zero when the body reaches the vehicle's speed. The two do not separate

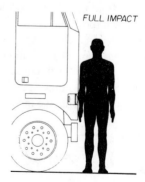

Exhibit 23. *If a standing adult pedestrian is struck by a fairly flat front vehicle such as a van or a bus, he will be accelerated to the same velocity as the vehicle.*

but keep moving forward together. With pressure released between them (because the body is no longer being accelerated), the body falls to the ground in front of the vehicle. Road friction slows the body, but the vehicle keeps on and so runs over the body. Then vehicle speed cannot be estimated by pedestrian fall and slide unless further, usually questionable, assumptions are made.

If the force against the pedestrian is below the pedestrian's center of mass, as when a car hits an adult pedestrian, the impact is usually incomplete, the pedestrian going onto the hood and over the vehicle. The pedestrian's slide can then be used to estimate the speed of the vehicle – but only part of the speed. The pedestrian fall is difficult, if not impossible, to evaluate because one does not know from what height the pedestrian fell.

5. PEDESTRIAN STRATEGY AND TACTICS

Pedestrian strategy deals with such things as choice of which direction to walk (facing or with traffic), selection of sidewalk or roadway, wearing light or dark clothing, crossing at crosswalks or midblock, crossing with or against the traffic signal, and many other choices. Pedestrian strategy often has considerable influence on whether a pedestrian trip will be successfully completed. Poor pedestrian strategy often is a major factor in a traffic accident. For example, walking with traffic and wearing dark clothing is a poor pedestrian strategy. If vehicle speeds are very high, it may be impossible for a driver to see the pedestrian in time if he has to brake to a stop to avoid the collision.

Pedestrian tactics deal with choices the pedestrian can make after he perceives a hazard. This involves such things as continuing to cross a street or waiting, running instead of continuing to walk, and stopping instead of continuing to walk or run. In many cases, the pedestrian has a better opportunity to avoid an accident than does the driver of the vehicle. The reasons for this are fairly obvious. In virtually every case, the vehicle will be traveling at a much greater speed than the pedestrian. It is more difficult to stop even a very small car than it is to stop the forward motion of a pedestrian. It is nearly always more difficult to move a car laterally to avoid an accident than it would be for the pedestrian. Also, the pedestrian is much smaller and would probably not have to move as far. Normally, a pedestrian can see a vehicle much farther away than a driver can see a pedestrian. This gives the pedestrian more time to react to a hazardous situation.

In this section, we will address two areas that relate to pedestrian strategy and tactics. The first is walking speed. In many traffic accidents, pedestrian strategy and tactics are evaluated, and it may be necessary to assume a value for walking speed. In actual accidents, it may be difficult to estimate the correct travel speed of a pedestrian. We will examine some typical examples.

The second area deals with pedestrian visibility: both the possible and the perceived visibility of the pedestrian for a driver of a vehicle. In most cases, the nighttime visibility of a pedestrian is evaluated according to the *driver's* strategy and tactics.

Pedestrian Walking Velocities

The American Association of State Highway and Transportation Officials (AASHTO)[11] states that there is a broad range of walking speeds for pedestrians. Average walking velocities range from 2.5 to 6.0 ft/sec (0.76 to 1.83 m/sec). The *Manual on Uniform Traffic Control Devices* assumes a normal rate of 4.0 ft/sec (1.22 m/sec). AASHTO states that walking rates are faster at midblock than at intersections, are faster for men than for women, and are affected by steep grades. AASHTO also states that age is the best-identified cause for slower walking rates. A walking rate of 3 ft/sec (0.91 m/sec) is suggested for design where there are many older people.

In an actual accident case, it is often difficult to select a walking speed if time and distance calculations are being done. It may be necessary to consider a range of walking rates. For example, if eyewitness testimony indicates that the pedestrian was running not walking, then appropriate values must be considered.

Pedestrian Visibility at Night

The visibility of a pedestrian to drivers at night depends on several factors. The lighter the clothing, the easier it will normally be to see the pedestrian. Reflectors on the clothing (often seen on joggers) can enhance the visibility of pedestrians. The type and intensity of street lighting can affect the nighttime visibility of pedestrians. High-beam or low-beam operation of the headlights and how well they are aimed can help or detract from the visibility of pedestrians, as can the presence or absence of other vehicles.

Allen and others[12] conducted a nighttime visibility study to determine actual pedestrian visibility and the pedestrian's estimate of his own visibility. Actual pedestrian visibility for normal dark clothing was about 175 ft (53 m). The results are typical of values obtained by tests conducted at The Traffic Institute. Only the most pessimistic pedestrian estimated his visibility to be this poor. The average pedestrian thought his visibility was 343 ft (105 m). Actual pedestrian visibility was enhanced to about 790 ft (240 m) by using reflectorized clothing. High-beam headlights will also increase pedestrian visibility.

In pedestrian accident cases, it is usually beneficial to go back to the accident site at night and see how well a pedestrian can be seen. Have someone dress in clothes of the same type, taking particular care to wear the same colors. If, for example, the primary source of lighting at the time of the accident was headlights, position the car at selected distances from the "target pedestrian." Decide when the pedestrian can first be seen. A photographic technique that allows you to record on film what the driver could actually see is discussed in Topic 836, *Traffic Accident Investigation Photography*. This is a useful tool in demonstrating what could be seen by the driver before the collision. Moving-car and moving-pedestrian tests could yield different results. Any test where the observer *expects* to see a pedestrian may give more optimistic results for visibility than an actual accident case, where the driver expectancy is lower.

6. CASE STUDIES

To further illustrate some of the analysis techniques presented in this topic, several case studies have been included. There is always a risk associated with using case studies to illustrate points in training materials. People tend to put their cases into some of the categories they have seen in illustrative material. Each accident case needs to be evaluated on its own merits, although it is not uncommon to have similarities between some cases.

Homicide or Accident

Several pieces of data are available for this particular case. The photographic data are shown in Exhibits 24-27. An after-accident situation map has been drawn, based on measurements and photographs taken at the scene. A tire mark is shown in Exhibit 24. The final positions of the victim's shoes and hat are shown in Exhibit 25. Final positions of the victim's body and coat are shown in Exhibit 26. The front of the car found at the scene is shown in Exhibit 27. A diagram drawn to scale that summarizes the final positions of the evidence is shown in Exhibit 28.

The photograph showing the front of the car (Exhibit 27) does not indicate any apparent damage. The police investigation indicates that there are no signs of any body contact with the front of the car. This suggests that the pedestrian must have been lying down when the car first contacted the body.

Injuries to the body are primarily to the head. The back of the skull has a one-inch hole. Examination of the skeletal system showed no evidence of fractures of the sternal plate, clavicles, or rib cage. All vertebrae appeared intact, with no fractures. The tibiae and fibulae did not show any fractures, nor were any fractures of the forearms found. Pelvic bone is intact. In short, the autopsy revealed that the only fracture was to the back of the skull. This lack of skeletal injury other than the hole in the back of the skull is not typical of a pedestrian-car accident. A further examination of the car was undertaken. The car was reported stolen. Bloodstains and spots throughout the inside of the car, as well as blood on the two front tires and right front hubcap, were found. Bloodstains were also found on the underbody of the car. The presence of blood on the inside of the car is an indication that the victim may have been dead or injured inside the car before the "accident" occurred.

The next issue to determine, from an accident reconstruction perspective, is whether the other data collected at the scene (excluding the blood *inside* the car) indicate an accident or a homicide. Several inconsistencies in the data indicate that this is not a car-pedestrian accident. The car clearly has no damage to the front, and the body has no injuries to indicate that the victim was standing at the time the car hit him. Thus, the possibility is that the person was lying down on the road when the car ran over the body, in which case the tibiae and fibulae would not have been struck by the front of the car. If the pedestrian was supine, then there should be crushing-type injuries to some part(s) of the body. There are none, of course, which supports the conclusion that the pedestrian was not run over by the vehicle. If this was a car-pedestrian accident, would you expect to find the hat, shoe, and dog tags in their final positions? These positions are inconsistent with what would be expected. It is as if someone had once heard that pedestrians are always "lifted" out of their shoes upon impact with cars; so the shoes were taken off and placed in a noticeable position. The tire mark shown in Exhibits 24 and 28 has blood. If this mark is associated with this case, it is inconsistent with this being a car-pedestrian accident.

Other aspects of this case are part of a criminal investigation and, therefore, beyond the scope of this topic.

Suicide or Attempted Suicide

Occasionally, there may be reason to believe that a vehicle-pedestrian collision may be a suicide or attempted suicide. An attempted suicide is certainly suggested by the following case study.

The collision took place on a rural four-lane freeway (two lanes in each direction) and involved an adult male pedestrian approximately 6 ft tall and a tractor and semi-trailer truck. The pedestrian's body was found in the rightmost lane of traffic. The only damage on the truck is to the metal guard shielding the vertical exhaust pipe (muffler) on the right side of the tractor (see Exhibit 29). The only significant injuries to the pedestrian are to the head.

The driver of the truck stated that he was traveling around 65 mi/hr when he first saw the pedestrian walking on the shoulder in the same direction the truck was going. The driver further stated that he started to move over to the left lane as the pedestrian started a fast walk and then ran across the road toward the truck. The driver slowed and continued to move to his left as the person kept running toward the truck. The driver then pulled over to the shoulder and stopped. He walked back and saw the man lying on the pavement. The pedestrian was not killed in the collision, but suffered from brain damage and has no recollection of the incident.

Clearly, this case is not the ordinary type of pedestrian accident. The driver stated that the last time he saw the pedestrian, he was running toward the truck. The only part of the truck that shows contact with the pedestrian is the muffler

Exhibit 24. *This is a photograph showing an alleged car-pedestrian accident scene. Note the final position of the car immediately behind a parked truck.*

Exhibit 25. *The final positions of a hat and a shoe of the alleged accident are shown here near the right front bumper of the car.*

Exhibit 26. *The body's final position is partially under the car. The main part of the body under the car is the head.*

Exhibit 27. *No damage or indication of contact with a body can be found on the front of the alleged accident car.*

shield. The only injury to the pedestrian is to the head. It would be difficult, if not impossible, for the pedestrian to receive only a head injury if the truck ran over him with the front of the truck. This leads to the conclusion that the man moved into the side of the truck. When someone is running, however, his head moves forward of its normal walking position relative to the rest of the body. The injury only to the head, therefore, could only have resulted from the man running *toward* the truck.

Another alternative has been suggested to explain the accident. This theory is that the truck moved close to the pedestrian, who was walking along the shoulder. The large truck created an "aerodynamic effect" in that it caused the pedestrian to be "sucked" into the side of the truck. It is argued that this would account for the pedestrian moving into the truck. There is no reason to believe this is possible. Large vehicles do cause air disturbances. However, no acceleration forces were present to cause the pedestrian to be suddenly

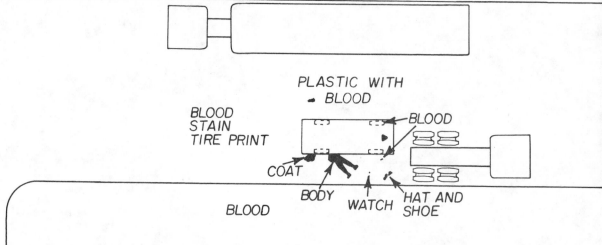

PLASTIC WITH
BLOOD

BLOOD
STAIN
TIRE PRINT

BLOOD

COAT

BODY   WATCH   HAT AND
SHOE

BLOOD

Exhibit 28. *This is a scaled map showing final positions for the alleged car-pedestrian accident.*

sucked into the side of the tractor. Full-scale tests could certainly be done to further evaluate this alleged phenomenon. To date, there are no reported cases of accident investigators (who often work very close to the road edge) having been sucked into the side of a truck.

A further investigation of this case would be warranted to determine whether there was any tendency for the pedestrian to attempt suicide. Other questions need to be addressed, such as why the man was walking on a rural freeway in the first place. The location of his car, and where he lived relative to the accident scene, should also be considered.

Glancing Force on Pedestrian

Occasionally, it must be determined whether the pedestrian walked into the side of a car or whether the car hit the pedestrian. This can be a difficult problem to address. If there are no injuries to indicate that the pedestrian was hit by the front of the car, there is a reason to consider that he ran or walked into the side of the car. The damage to the car would be expected to be very slight, almost nonexistent, unless the body got on the top of the hood. The injuries would not be expected to be as severe as usual in a pedestrian-vehicle collision. It is impossible to determine the vehicle's speed for a case such as this unless the vehicle left braking skidmarks. An estimate based on a fall or vault equation would involve so many assumption that a speed estimate using those equations would have to be considered inappropriate for nearly all situations.

Exhibit 30 shows damage to a vehicle where the pedestrian received a glancing blow. In this case, the pedestrian essentially walked into the side of the moving car. The only sign of contact is the dirt that has been cleaned off the car.

Front Impact Between Vehicle and Child

Exhibits 31-34 show the results of an accident between a child pedestrian and a pickup truck. The driver of the truck

said she applied the brakes hard enough to skid about the time she hit the pedestrian. This is consistent with other eyewitness statements. Exhibit 31 shows braking skidmarks that were clearly left by the pickup truck. Exhibit 32 shows minor damage to the front of the truck. Note the bent lamp. Exhibit

Exhibit 29. *This photograph shows an exemplar vehicle with a muffler shield that was hit in the truck-pedestrian collision described.*

Exhibit 30. *The contact to this car is barely noticeable. Only the cleaning of the dirt from the car indicates that contact has taken place.*

Exhibit 31. *Braking skidmarks were left by a pickup when the driver attempted to avoid hitting a pedestrian.*

Exhibit 32. *Damage to the front of the pickup is barely noticeable except for the bent light mounted on the bumper.*

Exhibit 33. *The final position of the pedestrian is in front of the final position of the pickup. The body's final position is where all the people are standing.*

33 shows the final position of the body relative to the final position of the truck. This is consistent with the earlier discussion relating to Exhibit 18.

The general sequence of the collision is the same as that depicted in Exhibit 18. The body is accelerated forward due to the impact as the truck is being braked hard. The truck decelerates at a faster rate than the pedestrian, and the pedestrian comes to rest in front of the final position of the truck.

A speed estimate can easily be done by measuring the length of the skidmarks and using an appropriate drag factor for the braking truck.

Body Over the Top of a Car

In many cases, eyewitness testimony indicates that a pedestrian was hit very severely, causing the pedestrian to "fly high into the air." Usually there is little reason to believe

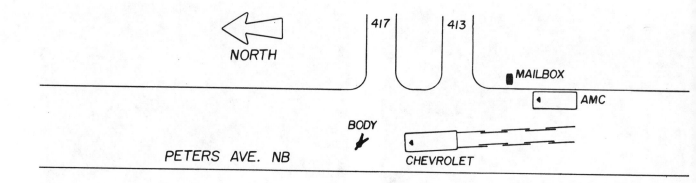

Exhibit 34. *This is a scaled map showing the final positions of the body, pickup and skidmarks that were shown in Exhibit 31-33.*

Exhibit 35. *In this car-pedestrian collision, the body did not make significant contact with the hood of the car, but instead had a considerable impact with the windshield.*

Exhibit 36. *The body in this collision went over the car and had contact with the trunk lid. Notice the blood on the trunk lid.*

that the body went very high into the air as a result of the collision. Clearly, though, as shown in earlier exhibits in this topic, a vehicle that applies a force below the pedestrian's center of mass will cause the pedestrian to rotate toward the striking vehicle. With enough vehicle speed and the right vehicle configuration, the pedestrian can travel over the car, giving the *appearance* to an eyewitness that the body "flew over the car."

A case illustrating the above-described condition is shown in Exhibits 35 and 36. Exhibit 35 shows damage to the front of the car near the right front headlight. Damage to the

windshield can also be seen. Extensive hood damage is not observed. The body was rotated back toward the windshield rapidly enough so that the hood was not hit with much force.

As the body rotated toward the windshield, the top part of the body and head hit the windshield area. The body then continued over the car and had minor contact with the trunk lid. Note the blood left on the rear of the car shown in Exhibit 36.

The body could not have gone very high in the air, or it would not have been able to make contact with the back of the car. In summary, the adult pedestrian was hit by the right

Exhibit 37. *The damage to the front of this van is fairly evident. Because the pedestrian was a full-size adult and the van has a relatively flat front, the body would have been accelerated to the speed of the van.*

Exhibit 38. *The final positions of the body and van are shown. Because the van was braking before the collision and continued to brake to a stop with locked wheels, the body is found in front of the van.*

Exhibit 39. *A scuff from the shoe of the pedestrian is shown in this photograph. This is an excellent indication of the pedestrians first contact position.*

front of the car, which caused the body to rotate backward to the windshield. The major impact to the windshield area was by the head and upper body. The body continued over the car (or the car drove under it) and made an additional contact with the rear trunk lid of the car.

Van and Adult Pedestrian Collision

Earlier in this topic, we discussed a full-impact vehicle-pedestrian collision where the pedestrian was accelerated to the same velocity has that of the vehicle. (See Exhibit 23.) The following case study has similar characteristics. An adult pedestrian is struck by a fairly flat-front full-size van. The van is skidding as it hits the pedestrian more or less in the middle of the van front. The damage to the front of the van is shown in Exhibit 37. The final positions of the body and van are shown in Exhibit 38. The first contact positions of the pedestrian and van are indicated by the shoe scuff shown in Exhibit 39. An after-accident situation map of the accident is shown in Exhibit 40.

In this case, the body was accelerated to the same velocity as that of the van in a very short distance. The van was being braked at the time of the collision, as indicated by the braking skidmarks observed at the scene. The issue in this case is the speed of the van at first braking and at the time the pedestrian is hit.

The police investigation of this case was very good. Measurements were taken so that the after-accident situation map shown as Exhibit 40 could be drawn. The police measurements indicate that the front tires of the van skidded for a total distance of 132 ft. At the point of the shoe scuff mark, indicating the pedestrian's position, the front tires had 29 ft more to skid to the van's final position. Test skids were done with an exemplar vehicle equipped with a bumper gun (pavement spotter). The test vehicle's speed was determined by radar. The test skids yielded a consistent value for drag factor, *f*, to be 0.79.

The initial velocity and the velocity at the pedestrian contact point can be easily calculated. (Similar problems, with examples of how to use the equation, are given in Topic 860.) By using the following equation, the velocities in question can be calculated.

NORTH

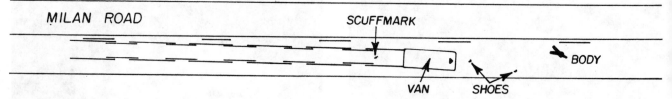

MILAN ROAD

SCUFFMARK

BODY

VAN   SHOES

Exhibit 40. *An after-accident situation map of the case shown in Exhibit 37-39. Note how the body's final position is in front of the final position of the van.*

$$v_i = \sqrt{v_e^2 - 2ad}$$

If the van skidded to a stop, then $v_e=0$. The value for acceleration, a, is given by $a=fg$. Drag factor, $f=0.79$. In USA units $g=32.2$ ft/sec/sec. Because the vehicle is decelerating, a is a negative number. The distance the vehicle skidded is 132 ft. Therefore, substitute back into the equation for initial velocity:

$$v_i = \sqrt{0^2 - 2(-0.79)(32.2)(132)}$$

$$v_i = 82 \text{ ft/sec} = 55.7 \text{ mi/hr}$$

The van's velocity when there are 29 ft left to skid can be done in the same manner. The only value that changes is the value for distance, d.

$$v_i = \sqrt{v_e^2 - 2ad}$$

$$v_i = \sqrt{0^2 - 2(-0.79)(32.2)(29)}$$

$$v_i = 38.4 \text{ ft/sec} = 26 \text{ mi/hr}$$

These equations can be easily done in the metric system. The value for distance needs to be in meters. For calculating a, the value to use for g is 9.81 m/sec/sec. The numbers substituted into the equation to solve for initial skidding velocity follow. The value for d is now 40.2 m (132 ft=40.2 m).

$$v_i = \sqrt{0^2 - 2(-0.79)(9.81)(40.2)}$$

$$v_i = 25 \text{ m/sec} = 89.9 \text{ km/hr}$$

Earlier in this topic we discussed how to calculate speed from a pedestrian fall. Doing so for this particular case would probably yield fairly accurate results. This is because the van was slowing when the body was hit, and the shape of the front of the van would tend only to add horizontal veloc-

ity to the body. The distance the body traveled horizontally during the fall (that is, before the sliding of the pedestrian started) is calculated from

$$d_f = 2fh - 2h\sqrt{f^2 - fd/h}$$

The value used for the pedestrian drag factor, f, was 0.45. The value for the pedestrian's center of mass height, h, was -2.2 ft. The distance the body traveled from first contact to its final position, d, was 72 ft. Substituting these values into the above equation gives the following:

$$d_f = 2(.45)(-2.2) - 2(-2.2)\sqrt{(.45)^2 - (.45)(72)/(-2.2)}$$

$$d_f = 15 \text{ ft}$$

Then the velocity at the beginning of the fall (separation with the van) calculates to be

$$v = d_f\sqrt{-g/2h}$$

$$v = 15\sqrt{-32.2/2(-2.2)}$$

$$v = 40.6 \text{ ft/sec} = 27.6 \text{ mi/hr}$$

The answer obtained using the pedestrian motion is consistent with the skid analysis. However, a word of caution is called for. In *very few* pedestrian cases will you find that data are available to pinpoint the position of first contact as accurately as it could be done in this case. Also, the profile of the van is fairly flat across the front. In very few cases will both of these conditions be met.

7. Sources

Author

Lynn B. Fricke, is a traffic engineer specializing in traffic accident reconstruction. He has been with The Traffic Institute since 1975. In 1981, he became the director of the Institute's Accident Investigation Division.

Exhibits

The following are the sources of the exhibits used in this topic:

Backaitis, S., National Highway Traffic Safety
Administration
Diagram: Exhibit 15
Baker, J. Stannard, San Diego, CA
Diagrams: Exhibits 6, 17 through 20
Booker, O., Fond du Lac Police Dept., WI
Photographs: Exhibits 31 through 33
Cook County Sheriff's Police, IL
Photographs: Exhibits 2, 3, 8
Cooper, Gary W., Traffic Institute, Evanston, IL
Photographs: Exhibits 9 through 11, 30, 35, 36
Diagram: Exhibit 28
Fricke, Lynn B., Northwestern University Traffic Institute,
Evanston, IL
Photographs: Exhibits 22, 29
Diagrams: Exhibits 13, 14, 23
Table: Exhibit 21
Indianapolis Police Dept.
Photograph: Exhibit 12
Kentucky State Police, KY
Photograph: Exhibit 7
Krause, Lyle, Accident Investigation Photography, Union, IL
Photograph: Exhibit 1
Paterson Police Dept, NJ
Photographs: Exhibits 24 through 27
Perkins Township Police Dept., OH
Photographs: Exhibits 37 through 39
Pfanner, R.J., Perkins Township Police Dept., OH
Diagram: Exhibit 40
Pritz, Howard B., National Highway Traffic Safety
Administration
Diagram: Exhibit 16
Strand, Mark, Fond du Lac Police Dept., WI
Diagram: Exhibit 34

References

1. Brook, D., J. Wiechel, M. Sens, and D. Guenther, "A Comprehensive Review of Pedestrian Impact Reconstruction," Society of Automotive Engineers paper 870605, Warrendale, PA.

2. Cesari, D., C. Cavallero, J. Farisse, and J. Bonnoit, "Effects of Crash Conditions on Pedestrian Leg Kinematics and Injuries Based on Cadaver and Dummy Tests," 29th Annual Proceedings, American Association for Automotive Medicine, October 1985.

Production Vehicles," Society of Automotive Engineers paper 830055, Warrendale, PA.

4. Backaitis, S., S. Daniel, D. Cesari, and C. Cavallero, "Comparison Pedestrian Kinematics and Injuries in Staged Impact Tests with Cadavers and Mathematical 2D Simulations," Society of Automotive Engineers paper 830186, Warrendale, PA.

5. Ashton, S.J., D. Cesari, and J. van Wijk, "Experimental Reconstruction and Mathematical Modeling of Real World Accidents," Society of Automotive Engineers paper 830189, Warrendale, PA.

6. Ashton, S.J., and Mike Pereira, "Experimental Development of Pedestrian Head Injury Tolerance Data," Society of Automotive Engineers paper 830056, Warrendale, PA.

7. Brun-Cassan, F., H. Vallee, C. Tarriere, A. Fayon, C. Got, A. Patel, and J. Aureau, "Reconstruction of Actual Car-Pedestrian Collisions with Dummy and Cadavers," Society of Automotive Engineers paper 830053, Warrendale, PA.

8. Greetham, Thomas A., and Dennis A. Guenther, "An Analysis of Head Injuries in Real World Pedestrian Accidents," Society of Automotive Engineers paper 830057, Warrendale, PA.

9. Collins, James C., *Accident Reconstruction*, 1979, Charles C. Thomas, Publisher, Springfield, IL.

10. Pike, J.A., "Biomechanics and Human Tolerance" (continuing education course reference manual), Society of Automotive Engineers, Warrendale, PA.

11. *A Policy on Geometric Design of Highways and Streets*, 1984, American Association of State Highway and Transportation Officials.

12. Allen, Merrill J., Richard D. Hazlett, Herman L. Tacker, and Ben V. Graham, "Actual Pedestrian Visibility and the Pedestrian's Estimate of His Own Visibility," *American Journal of Optometry and Archives of American Academy of Optometry,* January 1970.

13. Hazlett, Richard D., and Merrill J. Allen, "The Ability to See a Pedestrian at Night: Effects of Clothing, Reflectorization, and Driver Intoxication," *Highway Research Record* No. 216.

14. Strickland, J., B. Ward, and M.J. Allen, "The Effect of Low vs. High Beam Headlighhts and Ametropia on Highway Visibility at Night," *American Journal of Optometry and Archives of American Academy of Optometry,* February 1968.

RECONSTRUCTION OF HEAVY TRUCK ACCIDENTS

Topic 878 of the *Traffic Accident Investigation Manual*

by
Kenneth S. Baker

NORTHWESTERN UNIVERSITY TRAFFIC INSTITUTE

RECONSTRUCTION OF HEAVY TRUCK ACCIDENTS
TOPIC 878

In traffic accident reconstruction, perhaps no area of investigation lends itself to more erroneously made assumptions and improper applications of basic dynamics equations than that of articulated vehicles, and in particular, articulated heavy truck accidents. This is due in part to the attempt by some to apply analytical procedures associated with passenger car accident analyses without modification. Additionally, appropriate data is not collected concerning the important vehicle parameters necessary for an accurate reconstruction.

This topic addresses methods and appropriate physical parameters necessary to accurately reconstruct articulated vehicle accidents. In so doing, it discusses basic truck handling characteristics, including acceleration, steering and braking parameters; terminology specific to heavy vehicles; and functions of the various components involved in handling. Specific applications of the various equations used to calculate acceleration, velocity and distances are also discussed.

1. DEFINITIONS

For purposes of this topic, a *heavy truck* will include single unit trucks larger than pickup trucks and articulated vehicles. *Articulated* means jointed or joined together permanently or semipermanently by means of a pivot connection for operating separate segments as a unit. A passenger car towing a utility trailer or a road tractor with semitrailer are examples.

A towing vehicle with a semitrailer is a vehicle with some part of the weight of the towed vehicle carried on the towing vehicle, such as a passenger car with a utility trailer or house trailer, or a road tractor with semitrailer.

A towing vehicle with a full trailer is a vehicle with no part of the weight of the towed vehicle carried on the towing vehicle, such as a truck pulling a trailer that has an axle at each end or a car pulling another car attached by a drawbar. The front wheels of the trailer are steered through the drawbar.

Combination vehicles such as road tractors with both semitrailer and full trailers attached are called "doubles" or "triples" depending on the number of towed vehicles.

This topic discusses heavy articulated vehicles in more detail than passenger vehicles/semitrailers. Some of the same principles apply to both configurations, and are noted where they occur.

2. BRAKING SYSTEMS

Under the National Traffic and Motor Vehicle Safety Act of 1966, the National Highway Traffic Safety Administration (NHTSA) was authorized to issue Federal Motor Vehicle Safety Standards (FMVSS). However, a notice of proposed rule making for air brake systems on trucks and buses was not issued until 1970. Ultimately the FMVSS 121 became effective in March 1975. This standard required trucks to stop from 60 mi/hr on a dry road in 293 feet (0.41 g) and from 20 mi/hr on a wet road in 60 feet (0.22 g).

In 1978, a suit successfully challenged FMVSS 121 on the grounds that it was not a workable standard. The result of this suit was that stopping distance requirements were effectively eliminated from the air brake standard so that, at present, the only federal truck braking standard with a stopping distance requirement is the Bureau of Motor Carrier Safety (BMCS) inservice regulation. This regulation requires trucks, depending on their configuration, to stop from 20 mi/hr in 35-40 feet (0.33 g) on a dry road. In contrast, FMVSS 105, which is the applicable braking standard for passenger cars and other vehicles with hydraulic brakes, requires passenger cars to stop from 60 mi/hr in 216 feet (0.56 g) on a dry road.

In October 1986, Congress passed (and the President signed into law) the Commercial Motor Vehicle Safety Act of 1986. This act has provisions which require that the Federal Highway Administration (FHA) eliminate the front brake exemption. However, many trucks are still being operated with no brakes on the steering axle.

There are four basic types of brakes found on articulated vehicles: surge brakes, electric brakes, engine brakes, and air brakes.

Surge Brakes

Surge brakes are hydraulic brakes for small semitrailers attached to light trucks and passenger vehicles. The brakes are attached at the trailer hitch and are actuated by compression. The towing hitch is normally in tension when car and trailer are in motion, but provision is made for part of it to telescope slightly when the hitch is put in compression. If the towing vehicle applies its brakes or descends a hill, the trailer tends to overrun it. The shortening of the hitch then operates a lever pivoted on the trailer chassis, which applies the brakes by cables. The amount of braking depends on the rate of slowing force between the vehicles. The greater the braking force of the towing vehicle, the greater the braking force of the trailer.

Electric Brakes

Electric brakes are sometimes used on semitrailers for cars. Typically, the brake itself is a cam-actuated, duo-servo brake of normal configuration, except for the means by which the cam is rotated between the shoe tips. The cam is a part of a lever on the end of which is mounted an electromagnet, the connections to which are led out of the brake backplate. The source of electrical energy for the brake is the battery of the towing vehicle, which is connected to the trailer by way of a suitable electrical coupling. Included in the circuit on the towing vehicle is a controller and a variable resistor attached to the trailer. The controller, which can be matched to suit the braking capabilities of the towing vehicle, is operated hydraulically from part of the brake system, or manually to brake the trailer independently. The voltage in the circuit is varied in proportion to the driver's pedal effort; the variable resistor on the trailer allows the braking effort developed to be matched to the loading condition of the trailer.

Engine Brakes

Engine braking, by itself, is insufficient to make a significant contribution to the braking of heavy vehicles on a grade. However, an engine can be made to absorb an increased amount of energy when driven by the vehicle on a down grade. One method is by use of an exhaust brake. This consists essentially of a means of restricting the exhaust flow from the engine so that power is absorbed during each exhaust stroke. Either a butterfly or slide-type valve may be used. An air cylinder is typically employed to operate it when desired. The degree of restriction achieved is chosen so as to ensure that the exhaust valves are not held off their seats at the end of the exhaust stroke. The exhaust brake is integrated with the service braking system so that it is applied by the first movement of the brake pedal.

A more refined way of enhancing diesel engine braking is the "Jake Brake," which is manufactured by the Jacobs Manufacturing Company. This is an engine conversion which causes the exhaust valves to be opened briefly at the end of the compression stroke, so that the energy used to compress the charge of air is lost, instead of being recovered during the succeeding stroke. With each cylinder exhausted at the commencement of the downward stroke, energy is also absorbed. Pairs of cylinders can be activated individually so that the braking effect can be varied in stages.

Engine retarders are of little value for a panic stop, but are important in mountainous terrain. A typical retarder will absorb enough energy to keep an 80,000 pound truck under control without the use of service brakes at 19 miles per hour on a 10 percent grade.

Air Brakes

By far the most complex and common brake system used by heavy vehicles is the air brake system. We will discuss this system in greater detail.

Exhibit 1 shows a typical dual tractor/trailer air brake system. Some of the more important components and their function are as follows:

Air compressors. The air compressor is the source of energy for the entire air brake system. It is driven by the vehicle engine, either by belt or drive gear, and on most vehicles, uses the vehicle lubrication and cooling system.

Governor. The governor operates in conjunction with the compressor unloading mechanism and maintains reservoir air pressure between a predetermined maximum and minimum pressure. Usually the governor is set to keep the pressure in the air tanks between about 90 and 120 psi (pounds per square inch).

Actuators. Brake chambers and slack adjusters convert the energy of compressed air into mechanical force and motion. This actuates the brake camshaft, which in turn operates the foundation brake mechanism, forcing the brake shoes against the brake drum. Brake chambers are available in several sizes, providing a wide range of output forces and strokes. Slack adjusters can either be manually or automatically adjusted. They are set to adjust the push rod travel that ultimately causes the brake shoes to contact the brake drum.

Air system valves. The *safety valve* protects the air brake system against excessive air-pressure buildup. It is installed in the same reservoir to which the compressor discharge line is connected.

The *quick release valve* functions to exhaust air rapidly from the controlled device through the quick release valve, rather than requiring the exhaust air to return and exhaust through the control valve. This decreases release time.

A *ratio valve* is sometimes installed in the front axle delivery line. During normal service brake applications, the valve automatically reduces application pressure to the front axle brakes. As brake application pressure is increased, the percentage of reduction is decreased until at approximately

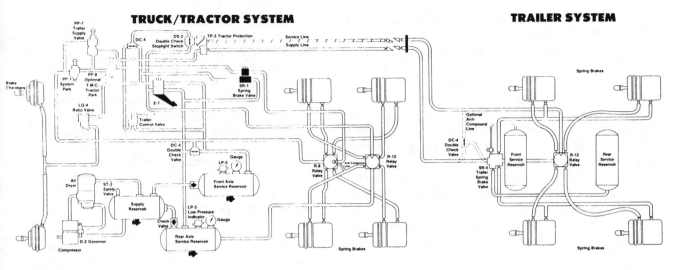

Exhibit 1. *A schematic of a typical dual tractor/trailer braking system.*

60 psi (depending upon the valve design) full pressure is delivered.

Another type of valve mounted on the front axle is the *limiting and quick release valve* which serves two functions. The valve limits front-axle service brake application by 50 percent and serves as a quick release valve for that axle. It is controlled by a valve on the vehicle dash, which allows it to be placed in the 50 percent limiting (slippery road or "wet") position or in the normal ("dry" road) position. In the normal position, it will deliver full application pressure. These valves are common to pre-FMVSS 121 vehicles.

The *spring brake valve* is used in dual-circuit brake systems and serves two functions. During normal operation, it limits hold-off pressure to the spring brakes via a relay valve or quick release valve, generally 90 or 95 psi. Should a loss of pressure occur in the rear service-brake service supply, it will provide a modulated spring brake application proportional to service braking pressure delivered to the front axle.

The *double check valve* is used in the air system when a single function or component must be controlled by either of two sources of pressure. The double check valve will always transmit the higher of the two pressure sources to the outlet port.

The *in-line single check valve* allows air flow in one direction only, preventing the flow of air in the reverse direction.

Reservoir draining devices are installed in air brake reservoirs to allow the accumulation of contaminants collected in the reservoir to be drained off to atmosphere, and can be either manual or automatic.

Inversion valves are air-operated control valves, and unlike most control valves are normally open. The inversion valve is closed by using air pressure from another source and is primarily used in emergency or parking brake systems which operate with air from an isolated reservoir.

Relay valves are primarily used on long-wheelbase vehicles to apply and release rear-axle service or parking brakes.

They are air-operated, graduating control valves of high capacity and fast response. These valves are crucial to the braking efficiency and stability of doubles and triples.

Relay emergency valves are commonly used on pre-FMVSS 121 trailers and in off-highway braking systems. The relay emergency valve is a dual function valve. Under normal braking conditions, it serves the system as a relay valve, applying and releasing the service brakes. The emergency portion of the valve senses supply line pressure; should pressure in the supply line fall below a predetermined minimum, the valve will automatically apply the vehicle service brakes from its own protected reservoir.

Brake valves. The foot-operated brake valve is the control point of the vehicle air brake system. It provides the driver with a means of applying and releasing the brakes on a single vehicle or vehicles in combination. Brake valves are mounted either on the floor or fire wall. The valve is actuated by treadle, pedal, or with a lever/linkage arrangement. The sensitivity of the valve will vary, depending on the method of actuation and the design of the valve. All brake valves are designed to provide a gradual means of applying air in the 5-to-80 psi range, with the capability of delivering full reservoir pressure.

Brake valves can generally be separated into two types: a single-circuit valve and a dual-circuit valve. Generally, pre-FMVSS 121 vehicles employ single-circuit brake systems and later vehicles use the dual-circuit brake systems. The dual-circuit brake valves use two separate supply and delivery circuits for service and secondary braking. The primary circuit portion is mechanically operated through the action of the treadle. The secondary circuit normally operates similarly to a relay valve, with control air delivered from the primary circuit. In the emergency mode (failure of the primary supply), the secondary inlet valve is mechanically opened by a push through mechanical force from the driver's foot via the treadle. Trailer control valves are hand operated, graduating control valves. They are designed to provide graduation of pressure between approximately 5 psi and the end of graduation range. The most common use of the valve is for independent control of trailer service brakes.

Control valves. These valves are used in the air brake system to control various system components and are generally dash-mounted. They are pressure-sensitive, on/off valves which will automatically return to the exhaust position when supply pressure is below the required minimum. They are manually operated to either position when pressure is above the required minimum. A control valve is connected to the *tractor protection valve*. When the switch is in the "normal" position, air passes from the tractor to the trailer to allow operation of the trailer brakes. If the valve is switched to the "emergency" position, the tractor semitrailer protection valve closes and stops the flow of air to the trailer. When this occurs, the trailer brakes will be applied. If no trailer is connected to the tractor, this valve should be in the "emergency" position.

The tractor protection valve is to protect the tractor air brake system under trailer breakaway conditions and/or conditions where severe air leakage develops in the tractor or trailer. In addition, the valve is used to shut off the trailer service and supply lines before disconnecting the tractor from the trailer.

Air reservoirs. The *air reservoir* serves the air brake system as a storage tank for a volume of compressed air. Generally, more than one reservoir is used in the system. When heated air leaves the compressor, it goes into a reservoir (sometimes called the *wet tank*), where cooling causes condensation. Because impurities in the air system will cause malfunctions in the air brake system, the air is passed through a single check valve into the *dry tank*. From here the air is distributed to the various brake valves until it is used by the driver.

Low pressure indicators. Low pressure indicators are pressure-operated, electropneumatic switches designed to warn the driver when air pressure in the service brake system is below a safe minimum for normal operation. This indicator is normally used in conjunction with an audible warning buzzer to warn the driver when the air pressure falls below 60 psi.

Antilock Braking

Recent developments in the manufacture of antilock braking system (ABS) devices will once again make these devices available in heavy-vehicle braking systems. Most systems available monitor wheel speed via a toothed wheel installed on the wheel hub near a fixed, pulse-emitting sensor whose magnetic flux produces an alternating current with frequency proportional to wheel speed. The pulses are transmitted to an electronic control unit which determines the speed, acceleration or deceleration of each wheel, and vehicle reference speed and wheel slip. If a wheel slows more than the others or locks up, a brake control valve is instructed

to release air from the brake chamber for that wheel.

Like conventional braking systems, antilock brakes feature two identical circuits installed in a diagonal pattern controlling half of the vehicle's wheels. If a fault occurs, the driver's warning light is lit, and that segment of the system reverts to normal braking. The other half remains under ABS control, preventing loss of lateral stability on any single axle. At present, units are available for tractor braking systems only.

3. UNIQUE ASPECTS OF TRACTOR-TRAILER BRAKES

No Front Axle Brakes

A significant number of truck operators remove, disconnect, disable or fail to maintain front wheel brakes. Many apparently believe that their vehicles are safer and easier to control without them. This belief may have been supported by the National Safety Council winter tests beginning in 1939 and continuing through 1966[1]. The tests evaluated the stopping performance of two- and three-axle trucks and several combinations on dry concrete and ice with and without front brakes. Most of the tests were done at 10 or 20 mi/hr with and without a load. Reference 1 is a summary of the 1939-66 tests. The data presented indicates that in straight-line stops on both dry and ice-covered concrete with full panic stop brake pressure, the vehicles with front axle brakes always stopped in shorter distances than those without. However, during the 1948 tests run on a 200-foot radius ice curve, the results were mixed. During these tests the brakes were modulated to lock and unlock the wheels. The loaded three-axle truck and all of the combinations tested could stop shorter under better control on an ice curve when the front brakes were not connected. The 1948 test results were the only ones

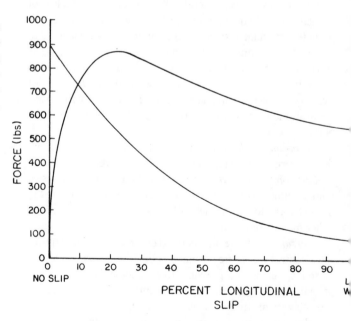

Exhibit 2. *Graph of tire force versus longitudinal slip.*

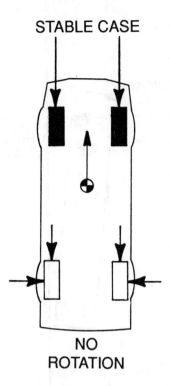

STABLE CASE

NO
ROTATION

Exhibit 3. *Two-axle vehicle with front wheels locked. Lateral forces at the rear tire/road contact patch cause the vehicle to slide straight.*

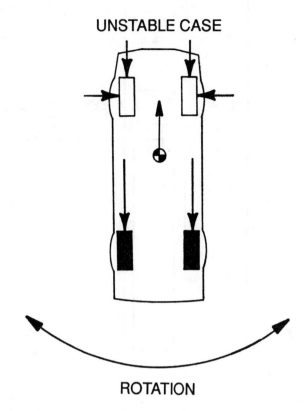

UNSTABLE CASE

ROTATION

Exhibit 4. *Two-axle vehicle with rear wheels locked. Loss of lateral tire forces at the rear tire/road contact patch allows the vehicle to rotate.*

published that indicated better stability and more control. Subsequent testing by the National Safety Council and the U.S. Department of Transportation indicated that in all combinations, drivers were able to stop their vehicles in shorter distances and maintain better control when the vehicle *had* front axle brakes.

Stability of any vehicle is greatly influenced by the relationship of lateral and longitudinal tire forces. While the vehicle's tires are free to rotate and the vehicle is moving parallel to its velocity vector, the longitudinal forces at the tire/road contact patch are minimum and the lateral forces can be at their greatest. Exhibit 2 shows this relationship in graphic form. This phenomenon allows the vehicle to be steered. When the brakes are applied, the longitudinal force increases while the lateral force decreases. This causes the vehicle to slow. If the braking force is large enough to cause wheel lockup, the lateral force will be reduced to such a low level that loss of steering will result. (Consult Topic 872 for additional information on the relationship between steering and tire forces.)

Heavy-vehicle tires have a lower friction value than passenger car tires. Also, heavy vehicles in general have less than ideal brake force distribution and are therefore more likely to have wheel lockup in emergency situations. Exhibit 3 shows a two-axle vehicle with only the front wheels locked. As can be seen, this is a stable situation. Exhibit 4 shows a two-axle vehicle with only the rear wheels locked. The vehicle is very unstable and a small side force from turning, road crown or crosswind will cause a spin-out. This phenomenon

exists whether or not the vehicle is attached to a trailer. The effect is much more complex when a trailer is attached.

Exhibit 5 shows a tractor semitrailer with only the front wheels locked. As in the case of a single-unit vehicle with front wheels locked, the combination tends to travel straight ahead with no steering control available. Exhibit 6 shows a tractor semitrailer with only the tractor tandem wheels locked. The tractor wants to spin and is constrained only by the fifth wheel connection to the trailer. The tractor spins rapidly into the trailer in what is called a "classic" jackknife. Exhibit 7 shows a tractor-semitrailer with only the trailer brakes locked. The trailer wants to spin about the fifth wheel's kingpin connection, and if allowed to continue, the combination will attain the classic jackknife configuration. This phenomenon is usually called "trailer swingout." The trailer swing is much slower than the tractor jackknife situation, because the trailer has a much greater rotational inertia and is therefore easier to control. As more trailers are added to the combination, the possible types of instability increase.

In recent tests conducted at the Vehicle Research and Test Center, East Liberty, Ohio, Radlinski[2] reports a 100 percent increase in stopping distance for road tractors without front brakes, compared to those with full front brakes at 20 mi/hr on dry concrete. Other tests were conducted at the same time using empty and loaded tractor-semitrailer combinations on wet jennite and on wet and dry asphalt. The tests were done in a curve, in lane-change maneuvers, and in straight-line

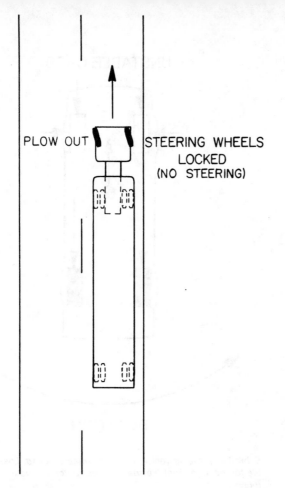

Exhibit 5. *Tractor-semitrailer with steering axle lockup. Lateral forces at the tandem axle tires and semitrailer tires allow the vehicle to slide straight.*

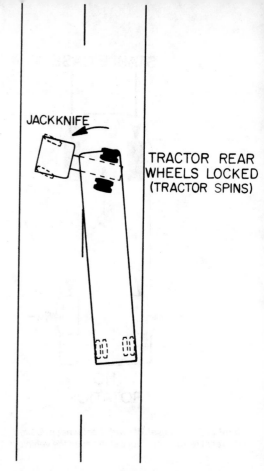

Exhibit 6. *Tractor-semitrailer with tractor tandems locked. Loss of lateral forces allows tractor to rotate causing a jackknife.*

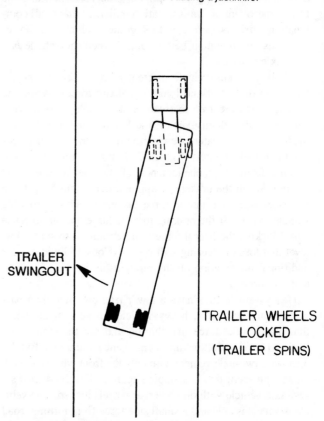

Exhibit 7. *Tractor-semitrailer with semitrailer tandems locked. Loss of lateral forces at semitrailer allows trailer swingout on low friction surfaces.*

stopping from various speeds of 20 to 55 mi/hr. All the vehicle configurations stopped in shorter distances, and drivers maintained better control, when the tractor's front brakes were fully operational.

Time Lag and Brake Force Distribution

For the braking performance of heavy combination vehicles to be optimal, the braking systems on the units that make up the combination must be compatible. The most important factors with respect to compatibility are the braking force of the tractor relative to the trailer, and the brake timing of the tractor relative to the trailer. Braking force distribution can be a significant factor in the ability of the combination to descend grades safely.

There is a time lag between application of brakes and the onset of braking. This time lag may vary from 0.5 to 1.5 seconds, depending on design, mechanical condition, and combination configuration. In an emergency braking situation, when all the brakes are fully applied, the tractor wheels may lock a short time before the trailer wheels. If the tractor does not have front axle brakes, the loss of the lateral force on the tandems could lead to the situation described in Exhibit 6, that is, tractor jackknife. This instability is further emphasized if the combination is in a turn, because the side

78-8

forces on the front tires tend to support the jackknifing action by keeping the tractor front in the intended turn. If the tractor has brakes on all wheels locked in a turn, the same instability results. Large differences in the timing of brake release also cause large directional disturbances in vehicle heading when the vehicle is in a turn. The return of lateral force on some wheels — say, on the tractor tandems before the return of lateral force on the trailer — also leads to instability.

Heavy vehicle owners typically can write purchase specifications for vehicles that determine which brakes and braking components are attached. Additionally, a tractor can be combined with several different semitrailers or trailers, each of which will have its own owner-determined brake components. Also, owner-operators often use trailer brakes in lieu of tractor brakes for routine stops. This leads to situations where the trailer brakes may not be as effective as the tractor brakes.

In long grade descents, brake pressures used are relatively low (approximately in the 10-15 psi range). Typically, at low brake application pressure, the tractor brakes do more work than the trailer brakes. As the braking pressure increases, the braking distribution evens out. In a grade descent, when the trailer brakes are less effective than the tractor brakes, the trailer brakes will run at a relatively low temperature. The tractor's brakes will run relatively hot. It is therefore possible for the tractor's brakes to become so hot that they lose effectiveness and begin to disintegrate or possibly catch fire. Even in the situation where the brake system is completely compatible, the thermal capacity of the brakes is such that these vehicles should proceed at low speed down long, steep grades if they are heavily laden. The cooling rate at which heat can be convected away is a significant factor in situations where the brake is used for minutes at a time. It is insignificant in brake applications lasting for a few seconds, such as in a normal or emergency stop.

Maintenance

The previous discussion involved only relatively new, well maintained vehicles. Braking system performance is significantly affected by maintenance practices.

The braking torque of air-braked heavy vehicles is very sensitive to brake adjustment. Most heavy truck brakes must be manually adjusted. Surveys of heavy-vehicle brake adjustment indicate that the average truck has approximately 30 per cent of its brakes out of adjustment.[12] Automatic slack adjusters are available for air brakes, but relatively few vehicles are so equipped at this time.

Exhibit 8 shows a typical truck air-brake assembly. As the brake lining wears, the pushrod travel must be adjusted at the slack adjuster. Typically, the pushrod travel must be maintained at 1.5 to 2 inches, depending on the size of the brake chamber. The stroke is required to take up slack and deflection in the system. As the brake shoe wears, the stroke increases due to the greater pushrod travel necessary to move the brake shoes out against the brake drum.

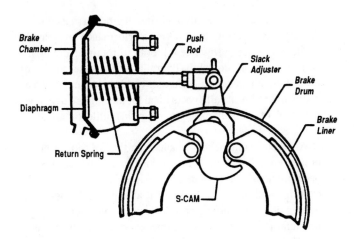

Exhibit 8. *A typical drum brake assembly.*

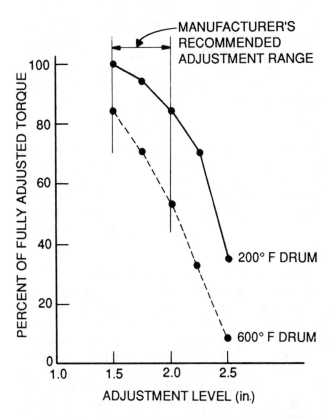

Exhibit 9. *The braking performance of a typical heavy-vehicle brake depends on adjustment level and drum temperature.*

Exhibit 9 shows the brake performance of a typical heavy-vehicle brake as a function of adjustment level and drum temperature.[8] Note that as the adjustment level moves from 1.5 inches to 2 inches, the brake torque falls off to 85 percent for the relatively cool brake. The relatively hot brake, even at 1.5 inches, has only 85 percent torque and drops to 50 percent at the manufacturer's recommended readjustment point. Beyond the adjustment range, the brake torque drop becomes even more pronounced, particularly if the brake is hot.

As noted in the previous section, poorly adjusted brakes

affect the thermal capacity and time lag performance of the vehicle. As a result, the braking performance of a loaded truck can be seriously affected, both in routine slowing maneuvers and in downhill operations. Because maximum brake torque is required when the vehicle is loaded, brake adjustment level is usually not critical for an empty truck unless the level of adjustment is so poor that little or no torque is generated.

Another maintenance problem is that of no front-axle brakes, either by intent or by improper maintenance. This has been previously discussed. Obviously a factor influencing the overall stability during braking, it also places an additional burden on the remaining brakes. Thus, if the other brakes are not adjusted properly, the same overheating problems as noted above occur at a much faster rate.

The type of brake lining materials used to replace those worn by use can adversely affect brake force balance with possible wheel lockup and loss of stability. Additionally, these imbalances affect the grade descent capability. Organic linings, used extensively on drum type air brakes, will fade more at elevated temperatures than will semi- or fully metallic linings. Once the lining temperature exceeds 600°F, a brake's ability to produce torque is appreciably reduced.[3,8]

The pneumatic valves, particularly the relay valves, are an important factor in determining brake force balance at low pressure. The pressure at which these valves start to open (called the "crack" pressure) is the primary determinant of the low-pressure brake balance. As manufactured, these valves are not identified with any markings to assure maintenance personnel that the proper crack pressure for a replaced valve is maintained. Manufacturing variations also affect the crack pressure. As noted before, serious consequences in grade descent capability may result.

The contaminants that collect in air-brake reservoirs consist of water condensed from the air and a small amount of oil from the compressor. This water and oil normally pass into the reservoir in the form of vapor because of the heat generated during compression. Many of the valves used to regulate airflow contain small orifices and passages, and thus are more susceptible to contaminants. If the contaminants are not removed, a system malfunction can occur. It is equally important to prevent freezing. The area affected determines the effect on the braking system.

Other areas of maintenance that can limit braking performance are deteriorated connections, leaking hoses, and foreign matter on the brake linings. The effects of these and other imperfections limit the braking system's performance.

Trailer Brakes Only

Breaking the air hose connection between the tractor and trailer deprives the driver of trailer brake control. Trailers therefore usually have an auxiliary air reservoir and are arranged so that any loss of air supply from the tractor immediately applies the trailer brakes. This configuration is a fail-safe arrangement, but sometimes the trailer brakes may

lock when they should not be locked. Inspecting the connections and associated hoses, as well as checking the roadway carefully for braking tire marks attributable to the trailer, might reveal whether there was a supply line failure.

As described earlier, the trailer brakes can be applied independently of the tractor brakes by using the hand valve. When investigating any accident involving a tractor-semitrailer combination, you need to know whether only the trailer brakes were applied. Slowing with trailer brakes only is not great, especially with an unloaded trailer. Calculations for resultant drag factor (discussed later) are necessary before you can analyze the speed of the combination.

Trailer swingout can occur if trailer brakes are applied in a curve on a relatively slick surface without a load or with a light load. The lower the surface friction and the lower the axle load, the easier it is to lock the wheels, resulting in the loss of lateral force. The trailer can then swing into or across the opposite lane. If an oncoming vehicle is present, it may result in an opposite-direction collision in which the oncoming vehicle passes the tractor but then collides with the side of the trailer or its rear wheels. The tractor driver is usually unaware of what occurred. The force of the collision usually pushes the trailer back into its own lane, so the tractor driver may never see the trailer out of position. Most likely there will be no skidmarks or other evidence of evasive tactics by the driver of the other vehicle, because the driver has no time to react. There may be collision scrubs from the other vehicle's tires, or skidmarks from the trailer (unless the pavement is wet). Most likely there will be gouges from the collision in the approaching vehicle's lane. However, gouges may not occur in cases where the oncoming car essentially does an "underride" into the side of the trailer; there may not be enough downward component (or the force is above the center of gravity). If calculations based on the speed of the vehicles and the available road friction are made, they would show that if the other vehicle passed the tractor, each properly in its own lane, the vehicle could not possibly have swerved sharply enough to strike the trailer if the trailer stayed in its own lane.

Special Axles

On tandem axles, with braking, forward thrust of the vehicle and rearward thrust of the road friction tend to load the front axle and unload the rear, with the result that the front axle does more braking than the rear. Some tandem axles are arranged this way. It is possible to design axles which compensate for this weight shift. Most large tractors and semitrailers with tandem axles are built to compensate for weight shift. Thus, for practical purposes, the tandem axle can be considered as a single axle halfway between the two.

Auxiliary axles are sometimes provided as original equipment on buses, tractors, or trailers. These may have no power and no brakes. They do relieve other axles of some of the load. They are usually designed to carry a limited amount of load. Sometimes the tires on such axles are off the road when the vehicle is traveling unloaded. When in contact with the road, and when the vehicle is in a severe turning maneuver, the wheels on these axles may leave marks which might be confusing if the vehicle is subsequently involved in an accident.

Converter axles are made to change a single-axle tractor to a tandem-axle tractor, thereby enabling it to carry greater loads. This device has a pin which fits into the fifth wheel on the tractor bed, and it carries a fifth wheel, to which the semitrailer is attached. This equipment does not provide driving power, and usually has no brakes.

Pole trailers are used for carrying logs, poles, steel beams, precast concrete beams, steel pipe, and other material. With this arrangement, the load itself connects the trailer bogie (pair of tandem axles) to the tractor. The front end of the load is carried on a pivoted bolster on the tractor, the bolster functioning as the joint or fifth wheel in an articulated vehicle. The rear of the load is carried on a bolster which is part of a bogie. To meet minimum braking requirements, the trailer bogie generally has air brakes connected by air hoses to the brake system of the tractor. The load must be firmly secured to the bolsters. This is usually done by chains cinched with a turnbuckle arrangement.

When investigating an accident where a loaded log truck and trailer fail to negotiate a turn, you should check the crossbeams (called "bunks") for evidence of binding. Logging bunks on a truck and the reach (the long pole or tube which connects the rear axle of the trailer to the tractor) on a logging trailer are generally temporarily fastened in place when the vehicle is not loaded. After the load is on, but before starting out of the woods, the driver must remove the temporary pin. Failure to do so negates the truck's ability to negotiate turns. Binding could also occur if the turn plate is not well lubricated. This type of binding is most likely to occur where the road slope changes in the middle of a curve, and is most dangerous on roads with a low coefficient of friction.

Sometimes the load, air hoses, and wiring for lights are the only connection between the tractor and the trailing bogie. In this case, when traveling unloaded, the trailer bogie and bolster are either hoisted on the tractor as a tractor load or they are connected to the tractor as a semitrailer with a short pintle hitch. Sometimes there is a light tube, adjustable in length, which also connects the trailer to the trailing bogie. This tube can be arranged to steer the rear bogie so that the combination can negotiate sharper turns. With such a trailer (pole or beam), the beam is usually shortened when traveling without load.

4. COLLISION BEHAVIOR

The collision behavior of an articulated vehicle may differ from that of a single vehicle under certain circumstances. The tractor may not rotate in the same way with a trailer attached to it. Therefore, you must be careful in determining

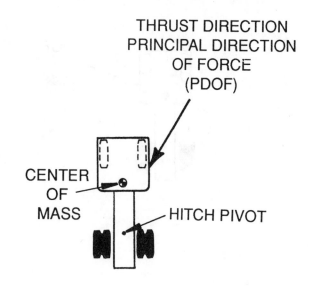

Exhibit 10. *If the principle direction of force passes between center of mass and fifth wheel, the tractor behaves like any single unit vehicle.*

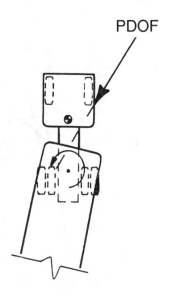

Exhibit 11. *With the same principal direction of force illustrated in Exhibit 10, but the tractor attached to a semitrailer, the tractor will rotate in the opposite direction.*

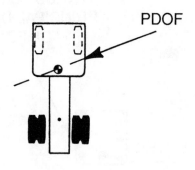

PDOF

Exhibit 12. *Centered force on tractor without semitrailer results in no rotation.*

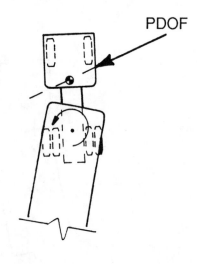

PDOF

Exhibit 13. *A centered force on the tractor attached to a semitrailer results in rotation of tractor about fifth wheel.*

the behavior of an articulated vehicle on the basis of thrust direction derived from an examination of vehicle damage.

Fifth Wheel Effect

Because the articulated vehicle is hinged, or more or less fixed at the hitch or fifth-wheel pivot, it tends to rotate about that point rather than about the tractor's center of mass. This is especially likely when the thrust direction passes behind the tractor's center of mass and ahead of the hitch pivot as illustrated in Exhibits 10 and 11. It may also be significant when the thrust direction is nearly centered on the tractor. Normally such a centered thrust direction causes little or no rotation of the vehicle. But if the rear of the vehicle is held in place by a semitrailer, such a centered force can produce strong rotation as illustrated in Exhibits 12 and 13. Also, if the force on the towing vehicle is toward the hitch pivot, the towing vehicle tends not to rotate.

Behavior of the combination in an articulated vehicle or a vehicle with a full trailer in a collision depends on the tractor's angle to the trailer (articulation angle), the motion of the units, and the load on the trailer hitch. For example, in the case of a car with a small trailer which gives the trailer hitch very little load, the presence of the trailer may have little effect on the behavior of the car in a collision; the trailer does little to stabilize the position of the car at the trailer hitch. On the other hand, a semitrailer with half of its total weight on the fifth wheel may be the predominant factor in the behavior of the towing vehicle in a collision.

Case Study

In an oblique collision with a vehicle considerably lighter than the articulated vehicle, both vehicles may travel to their final rest locations in a manner that may seem to defy the basic laws of motion. Consider the collision and final resting positions of the milk tanker and automobile shown in Exhibits 14 and 15. The tanker was westbound prior to the collision, and the automobile was southbound. After the collision, the tanker initially moved somewhat to the left and then, because of damage to the right side steering axle, turned rapidly to the right, causing the tanker to roll over and rotate 180° before coming to a stop. The automobile, on the other hand, instead of moving off in a southwesterly direction, moved generally to the northeast before striking the guard rail. If this collision had involved similar vehicles, the post-collision directions of travel of both vehicles would have been in a southwesterly direction. Attempting to analyze the collision velocities of either vehicle using linear momentum techniques would be erroneous.

Speed Estimates From Damage

Other topics discuss speed estimates based on the extent of damage incurred by a passenger vehicle in a collision. Little testing has been done to establish a correlation between the damage done to a heavy vehicle during a collision and the ve-

Exhibit 14. *After impact the car rotates clockwise and strikes the guardrail before coming to final rest. Note the path the milk tanker traveled as indicated by the tire marks and the diesel fuel on the roadway. The final rest position of the milk tanker is behind the wrecker and the U.S. 24 sign.*

Exhibit 15. *Note the tiremarks and diesel fuel which describe the path taken by the tractor and the tank trailer. Note the scrapes on the roadway indicating where the tanker was on its side. The wrecker and the sign are the same as depicted in Exhibit 14.*

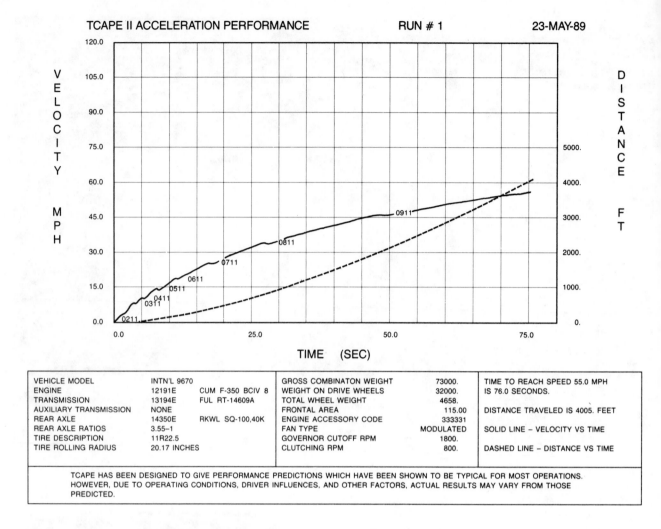

VEHICLE MODEL	INTN'L 9670		GROSS COMBINATON WEIGHT	73000.	TIME TO REACH SPEED 55.0 MPH
ENGINE	12191E	CUM F-350 BCIV 8	WEIGHT ON DRIVE WHEELS	32000.	IS 76.0 SECONDS.
TRANSMISSION	13194E	FUL RT-14609A	TOTAL WHEEL WEIGHT	4658.	
AUXILIARY TRANSMISSION	NONE		FRONTAL AREA	115.00	DISTANCE TRAVELED IS 4005. FEET
REAR AXLE	14350E	RKWL SQ-100,40K	ENGINE ACCESSORY CODE	333331	
REAR AXLE RATIOS	3.55–1		FAN TYPE	MODULATED	SOLID LINE – VELOCITY VS TIME
TIRE DESCRIPTION	11R22.5		GOVERNOR CUTOFF RPM	1800.	
TIRE ROLLING RADIUS	20.17 INCHES		CLUTCHING RPM	800.	DASHED LINE – DISTANCE VS TIME

TCAPE HAS BEEN DESIGNED TO GIVE PERFORMANCE PREDICTIONS WHICH HAVE BEEN SHOWN TO BE TYPICAL FOR MOST OPERATIONS. HOWEVER, DUE TO OPERATING CONDITIONS, DRIVER INFLUENCES, AND OTHER FACTORS, ACTUAL RESULTS MAY VARY FROM THOSE PREDICTED.

Exhibit 16. *Acceleration performance curve for a typical 73,000 lb tractor and semitrailer. Results can be compared by changing the grade and the characteristics of the power unit.*

hicle's speed loss. Therefore, any attempt to apply a passenger vehicle analysis to a heavy truck would be suspect at best, and very likely erroneous.

5. LONGITUDINAL ACCELERATION OF HEAVY TRUCKS

The longitudinal acceleration performance of heavy trucks is considered in designing climbing lanes on long, steep upgrades and in extending sight distances at intersections. In accident situations, longitudinal acceleration performance is useful in determining the maximum velocity and therefore the time required to travel a certain distance from its starting point to the first contact location. This time, then, determines the time-and-distance history of the other vehicle. The aim of this section is to present a concise discussion of the fundamental aspects of acceleration performance.

The ratio of power to weight is the primary determinant of the acceleration capability of vehicles. For loaded heavy trucks with gross vehicle weights in the 60,000-to-80,000-lb. range, the ratio of net engine horsepower to weight is cur-

rently in the vicinity of 0.004 hp/lb.[3]

For some applications, the distance needed to change from one speed to another is an important consideration, and the ratio of weight to power is more convenient to work with. For vehicles in the 60,000-to-80,000-lb. range, the average horsepower is approximately 282. This corresponds to an average weight-to-horsepower ratio of 248 lbs/hp.

The actual acceleration performance of a vehicle depends on the magnitude of the rolling resistance and aerodynamic forces opposing the net propulsive thrust available from the drive system (engine, transmission, rear axle and tires), drive line losses, and the selected transmission gear ratio. Additionally, the type of road surface and whether a grade is present must be considered. At low speeds the aerodynamic drag and rolling resistance are insignificant. However, at 60 mi/hr (95 km/hr), a typical truck has a natural retardation of approximately 0.02 g, which is divided nearly evenly between aerodynamic drag and rolling resistance.

Performance from a standing start may be depicted by curves of velocity and distance versus time. Exhibit 16 shows a typical result.[4]

In actual accident cases, you should try to use an exemplar vehicle to duplicate as closely as possible the situation under consideration. If such an experiment cannot be done, the typical values of acceleration given in Exhibit 17 can be used.

Speed Range	Medium Trucks Normal Acceleration			Big Trucks, Loaded Normal Acceleration		
	ft/sec^2	m/sec^2	f	ft/sec^2	m/sec^2	f
Less than 20 mi/hr (30 km/hr)	3.2	0.98	0.10	1.6	0.48	0.05
Between 20 and 40 mi/hr (30-60 km/hr)	1.6	0.48	0.05	1.0	0.29	0.03
More than 40 mi/hr (60 km/hr)	1.0	0.29	0.03	0.03	0.10	0.01

Exhibit 17. *Typical acceleration rates for medium and heavy trucks on level surfaces.*

6. OFFTRACKING

When a two-axle, four-wheel vehicle with the front wheels turned travels a circular path at zero speed, all wheels travel around the same turn center with zero slip angle. (See Topic 872 for additional information.) During a slow, steady turn, the wheels on the rear axle of such a vehicle track inside the circular paths of the front wheels. This effect is more pronounced when semitrailers and/or trailers are attached. At higher speeds with semitrailers attached, the opposite occurs; that is, the semitrailer tandems track outside the tractor tandems. This difference in the path radii followed by the rear versus front wheels is called the *offtracking dimension*. This becomes important in turning accidents involving pedestrians standing on a curb and in some ramp accidents involving rollover.

Low Speed Offtracking

Exhibit 18 shows a two-axle vehicle traveling a steady-state (the steering angle remains constant), circular path with its front axle center tracking at a turn radius, r_1, and with its rear axle tracking about the same center at a radius, r_2. From the Pythagorean theorem, the length of the path radius, r_2, is given by the equation:

$$r_2 = \sqrt{(r_1^2 - l^2)}$$

where l is the wheelbase of the vehicle. The maximum offtracking dimension of the vehicle is defined as the difference of r_1 and r_2.

For example, if the front wheel of a vehicle follows an arc with a 50 ft radius and the wheelbase of the vehicle is 10 ft, then the radius of the path of a corresponding point at the rear axle is:

$$r_2 = \sqrt{(50^2 - 10^2)}$$

$$r_2 = 49 \text{ ft}$$

The maximum distance, OT, the rear wheels track inside the front wheels is:

$$OT = r_1 - r_2 = 50 - 49 = 1 \text{ ft}$$

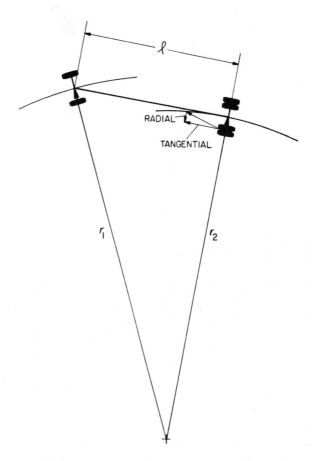

Exhibit 18. *Two-axle vehicle traveling a steady-state circular path.*

If rear wheels are not the same distance apart as the front wheels, if their tires are larger, and especially if there are dual tires, a correction must be made. If the vehicle in the previous example was a truck with a width, l_{tf}, of 6 ft from the outside of one front tire to the outside of the other and an outside width across the rear dual tires, l_{tr}, of 8 ft, the rear wheels would track inside the front ones:

$$OT = r_1 - r_2 + (l_{tr} - l_t)/2$$
$$OT = 50 - 49 + (8 - 6)/2$$
$$OT = 1 + 2/2 = 2 \text{ ft}.$$

When a tractor-semitrailer tracks a steady-state circular trajectory at a very slow velocity, the tractor's rear axle and trailer's rear axle each travel a circular path of differing radii.

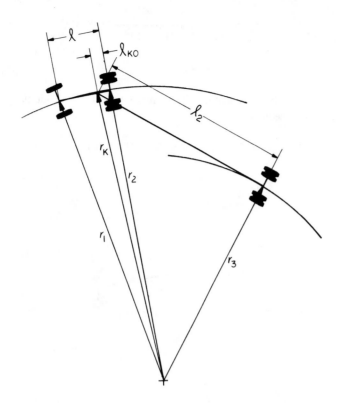

Exhibit 19. *Various radii and length parameters associated with steady state turning for tractor-semitrailer.*

Using the following labels, Exhibit 19 shows the various radii associated with this turning condition: r_1 for the tractor steering axle, r_k for the fifth-wheel kingpin, r_2 for the tractor rear axle, and r_3 for the trailer axle. The total offtracking (OT) is defined by the difference in path radii followed by the centers of the first and last axles of the vehicle, or,

$$OT = r_1 - r_3 = r_1 - \sqrt{r_1^2 + l_{ko}^2 - l^2 - l_2^2}$$

where l_{ko} is the distance the fifth-wheel kingpin is forward of the tractor rear axle; and l_2 is the wheelbase of the semitrailer.

Use a value of 12 ft for the tractor wheelbase, 36 ft for the semitrailer wheelbase, 1.2 ft for the fifth-wheel offset, and a turn radius of 41 ft; calculate the maximum offtracking of the rear axle of the semitrailer.

$$OT = 41 - \sqrt{41^2 + 1.2^2 - 12^2 - 36^2}$$

$$OT = 41 - 15.6 = 25.4 \text{ ft}$$

In the case of a doubles configuration, three additional lengths contribute to the offtracking equation:

l_3, the rearward overhang of the pintle hitch location,
l_4, the length of the dolly drawbar, and
l_5, the wheelbase of the full trailer.

The offtracking by the last axle of a doubles configuration is:

$$OT = r_1 - r_5 = r_1 - \sqrt{(r_1^2 + l_{ko}^2 - l^2 - l_2^2 + l_3^2 - l_4^2 - l_5^2)}$$

Except for configurations using unconventional elements in their design, the maximum zero-speed offtracking can be approximated by using a formula recommended by the Society of Automotive Engineers (SAE)[5]. The variables of the equation are shown in Exhibit 20. The kingpin offset dimension is neglected.

$$OT = r_1 - \sqrt{(r_1^2 - (l_1^2 + l_2^2 - l_3^2 + l_4^2 + l_5^2 - l_6^2 + l_7^2 + l_8^2))}$$

This equation may be used for any conventional vehicle involving any number of trailers by using the pertinent l terms.

As an example for a set of doubles, use a value of 10 ft for the tractor wheelbase, 21 ft for the semitrailer wheelbase, 3 ft for the rearward overhang of the pintle hitch, 6.7 ft for the length of the dolly drawbar, and 21 ft for the trailer wheelbase. Assume a turn radius of 41 ft and calculate the maximum offtracking of the rear axle of the last trailer.

$$OT = 41 - \sqrt{(41^2 - (10^2 + 21^2 - 3^2 + 6.7^2 + 21^2))}$$

$$OT = 41 - 25.8 = 15.2 \text{ ft}$$

The values calculated using the above equations are for a steady-state turn and typically occur when the vehicle has moved through approximately 270°. A lower offtracking value is calculated if a transient (that is, continuously changing from one steady state to another) path is considered through a 90° turn. The more trailing units involved, and the longer the wheelbases, the larger this difference is. If a steady-state assumption is not appropriate for your particular case, you must use care when applying the above equations. Calculations for the transient path of an articulated vehicle require a piecewise solution and the use of a computer.

A measure of the transient offtracking width, called the *swept path,* is illustrated in Exhibit 21. Exhibit 22 shows the numerical results associated with several different combinations.[3] The results show increasing swept-path values, with the increase in length of each unit, while also showing the offtracking benefits of multiple articulations. For example, compare case C3 (tractor-semitrailer) with case G3 (single-axle triples); the triples carry 80% more cargo, yet have the same swept-path dimension. In this chart the swept-path measure describes the width of the path swept by each vehicle combination as it negotiates a right-angle turn in which the outside front tire on the tractor tracks a reference circular arc having a 35 ft radius between entry and exit tangents.

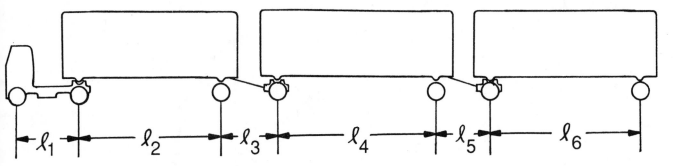

Exhibit 20. *Variables of the SAE equation ignoring the kingpin offset dimension.*

Typical accidents involving the offtracking phenomenon can occur in areas where pedestrians are standing near the roadway edge and are struck by the rear wheels of a turning, single-unit vehicle or a tractor-semitrailer. Additionally, drivers of articulated vehicles typically swing out at a tight-radius, narrow-width turn to compensate for trailer offtracking, thereby creating the false impression for drivers of other vehicles that they can safely pass the turning tractor-semitrailer. Typically, each driver will claim that he had begun his turn or pass before the other had initiated *his*.

Case Study

Consider the vehicle and accident-site photographs in Exhibits 23 and 24. This accident involved a 1976 Mack garbage truck and a pedestrian. The driver of the garbage truck was eastbound on a two-lane street; after making a pickup, he turned left into an alley. During the turning maneuver, the garbage truck struck a pedestrian walking eastbound on the pavement near the north side of the street. The pedestrian was either knocked down or lost her balance, and her legs were run over by the left rear wheels of the garbage truck.

There were no witnesses to the accident. The truck driver stated that prior to the left turn, he stepped out of the right-side steering compartment and looked in back of the truck to see if a vehicle was approaching. The driver then stepped back into the truck and made the left turn from the right side of the street into the alley without observing the pedestrian. Exhibit 25 shows bloodstains on the snow where the pedestrian was run over. Placing the turning path of the truck in relation to the bloodstains indicates how the accident occurred. From the truck's last stop (Exhibit 24) there is only one turning path the truck could have made into the alley, because of the alley's narrowness and obstructions present. As noted in Exhibit 23, the truck is one that can be operated by one driver from both the right and left sides of the cab. On the date of the accident, the operator was positioned on the right side in a standing position to facilitate garbage pickup.

The issue in this case is whether the pedestrian was struck by the front of the truck. Considering the manner in which the truck had to make the turn, it is likely that *if* the pedestrian was struck by the left front bumper of the truck and run over by the left front wheel of the truck, the offtracking of

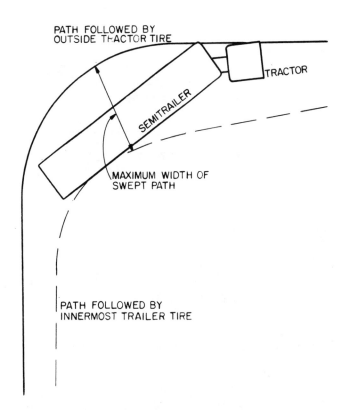

Exhibit 21. *Low speed offtracking in a 90 degree intersection turn.*

the left rear wheels would have run across the pedestrian's upper body. Injuries sustained by the pedestrian did not substantiate this scenario.

High-Speed Offtracking

As mentioned previously, the offtracking problem at low speed is that of trailing units cutting inside the radius followed by the front axle; at high speed, the reverse might occur. That is, the rear axles will follow radii that are larger than the radius traced by the front axle. Obviously, this phenomenon could be significant in analyzing highway ramp accidents. Offtracking can cause the trailer to roll if it moves into a curb. The primary reason high-speed offtracking occurs in the opposite direction is the change in the articulation angle between the towing vehicle and the towed trailer(s) as

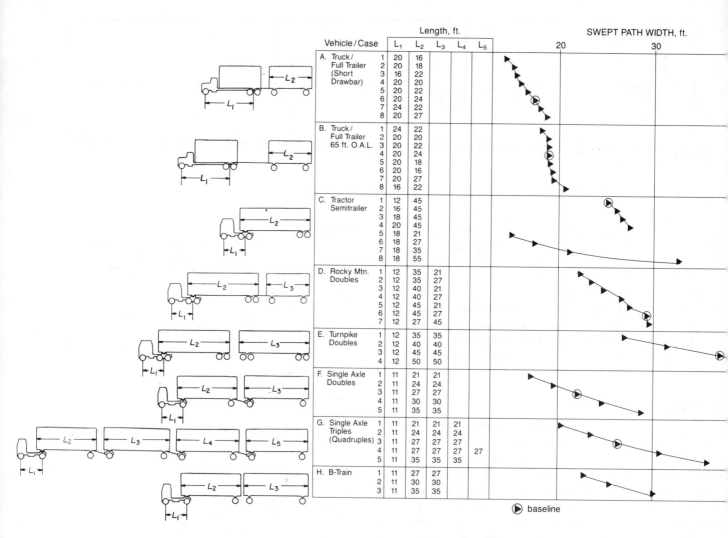

Exhibit 22. Influence of length parameters on low-speed off-tracking.

Exhibit 23. 1976 Mack garbage truck. Note the vehicle is right hand drive.

Exhibit 24. Starting position of garbage truck before collision.

Exhibit 25. *Bloodstains on snow where pedestrian was run over.*

the difference in steering changes with changes in speed. There is some speed at which the articulation angle (which is positive in low-speed turns) becomes negative. Determining this speed is beyond the scope of this topic. However, a discussion of the basic methodology has been presented by Bernard and Vanderploeg.[6] In general, the more articulation points added, the greater the outward offtracking. Thus, a tractor with doubles moves outward a greater distance than a tractor with semitrailer. Ultimately, the primary determinants are the fore and aft locations of the centers of mass of each trailing unit, the cornering compliance of each axle as derived from the axle load, and the cornering stiffness of the tires. Exhibit 26 shows various low- and high-speed offtracking results for several typical combinations.[7]

Offtracking type (Transient)	Tractor & Semitrailer	Truck & Full Trl	Double	Triple
Low speed (ft) 41 ft radius through 90°	+ 14.36	+ 9.71	+ 11.56	+ 15.90
High speed (ft) 1200 ft radius at 55 mi/hr	− 0.73	− 1.36	− 1.29	− 1.92

Exhibit 26. *Typical values for low-speed and high-speed offtracking for various vehicle combinations.*

When investigating rollover accidents on highway exit ramps where evidence suggests the vehicle struck the outside curb, you should consider the possibility of high-speed offtracking as a contributing factor.

7. ROLLOVER

The rollover of a motor vehicle can occur for a variety of reasons. For example, a vehicle leaving the roadway can roll because of irregularities or deformities of the surface (including substantial changes in grade) or by making a cornering maneuver at an excessive speed. Excluding a collision, when a vehicle makes a cornering maneuver on a paved roadway, the lateral traction forces at the tires are the only major contributors to a rollover. This discussion will be limited to a consideration of these forces and will not cover other tripping mechanisms. See Topic 873 for a discussion of flips and vaults.

Some literature indicates that the rollover of a heavy vehicle can be predicted by considering it as a rigid object—that is, an object without suspension, with solid (nonflexible) tires and no movable load, and one which is not in a dynamic lane change. While this method is useful in discussing the basics of the rollover process, it grossly overestimates the basic stability level of the vehicle, and therefore overestimates the speed at which a particular vehicle rolled over.

Consider the rigidly suspended vehicle depicted in Exhibit 27. It can be thought of as an actual vehicle whose tires and suspension springs are infinitely rigid. The following symbols apply to Exhibit 27:

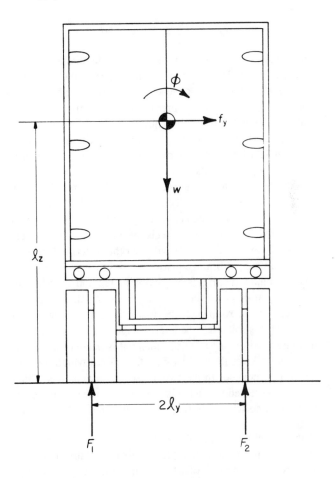

Exhibit 27. *Model showing rigidly suspended vehicle.*

w = vehicle weight,
f_y = steady lateral acceleration in g's,
l_y = 1/2 the vehicle track width,
l_z = height of the center of mass above the ground, and
ϕ = vehicle roll angle in radians

Assuming the vehicle achieves a steady lateral acceleration by means of the lateral tire forces, there are three moments acting on the vehicle. Taking moments about point O and further assuming small roll angles where tan $\phi = \phi$ in radians, the moments are:

$w f_y l_z$ — the major overturning moment, generated by means of a steering maneuver having a lateral acceleration level, f_y;

$(F_2 - F_1) l_y$ — the restoring moment, arising due to a lateral transfer of vertical load between the left and right tires; and

$-w l_z \phi$ — the lateral displacement moment, deriving from the roll motion which displaces the center of gravity laterally toward the outside wheels.

The equilibrium equation is:

$$w f_y l_z = (F_2 - F_1) l_y - w l_z \phi$$

The left side of the equation, the overturning moment, is limited only by the lateral traction capabilities of the tires. The vehicle will become unstable whenever the lateral acceleration level is sufficient to provide an overturning moment which exceeds the net stabilizing moment (the right side of the equation). The term $(F_2 - F_1) l_y$ is maximum when the total vertical load is transferred to the outboard tires and is equal to w_l. When the overturning moment exceeds this maximum, the vehicle begins to roll. As the center of gravity of the vehicle moves laterally as the vehicle rolls, the moment $w l_z \phi$ increases until the center of gravity reaches the point directly over the outboard wheels, beyond which the vehicle is unstable and will roll over without other external forces.

The same equilibrium equation applies to a vehicle which has compliant (nonrigid, or flexible) tires and suspension. However, in this case the restoring moment can only be developed by the rolling of the mass through a greater roll angle. At this roll angle the lateral displacement moment has increased, so the net restoring moment is decreased. Therefore, the rollover threshold value (the ease at which rollover occurs) is reduced. In the case of softer suspensions which must be deflected through a larger value of the roll angle before attaining wheel liftoff, the rollover threshold is reduced further.

Varying the stiffness of the trailer axles and the tractor's rear axles and front axle affects the rollover threshold differently. Reducing the stiffness of the trailer suspension will decrease the rollover threshold. When the stiffness of the tractor's rear axle is increased, the rollover threshold will also decrease. Increasing the stiffness of the tractor's front axle significantly improves the rollover threshold.[3]

The longitudinal and lateral distribution of the load among the axles of a vehicle affects the vehicle's rollover threshold. Moving the load forward, as would occur by adjusting the fifth wheel forward on a tractor, reduces the restoring moment and (therefore) the rollover threshold. Another factor tending to degrade roll stability would be to distribute the trailer load more toward the tractor drive axles, therefore lessening the load on the trailer axles, which would occur by sliding a trailer bogie rearward. Changes in weight regulations which promote a more forward distribution of load on tractors will tend to reduce the roll stability level.[3]

It should be obvious that when the load is offset to one side of the longitudinal centerline of the vehicle, the vehicle's roll stability level in the direction of the offset will be reduced. When the payload weight is large relative to the net weight of the vehicle, the reduction in rollover threshold due to the payload offset approaches the value of the offset divided by the height of the center of mass above the ground (l_z).

In addition to the major factors listed above, fifth-wheel play, stiffness of the tractor and trailer frames, and articulation angle also influence a vehicle's rollover threshold. Except for the case of an extreme articulation angle, these factors have little effect. An extreme articulation angle on the tractor's roll moment tends to reduce the vehicle's effective roll stiffness properties. For example, when the tractor is at a 90° articulation angle, its effective stiffness in response to trailer roll angle is zero, thereby degrading the rollover threshold. This phenomenon (as well as the narrowness of the track width at the fifth-wheel connection) explains why a tractor with semitrailer parked at a large articulation angle (approximately 90°) can easily be rolled over if the driver makes a quick start.

Transient Motions

So far, we have discussed phenomena primarily static in nature. When a maneuver condition involves transient motions (going from one steady state to another), certain conditions serve to modify the vehicle's rollover threshold. Dynamic steering movements can produce rearward amplification of the lateral accelerations in a multiunit train (for example, a set of doubles). In such combinations, the lateral acceleration, and thus the roll moment, experienced by the last trailer in the train can be considerably larger than that of the leading unit or tractor. Relatively moderate lateral acceleration initiated at the tractor can cause a rollover condition in the last trailer. The lateral acceleration of the last trailer can be 1.5 to 2 times that of the tractor in all but a conventional tractor-semitrailer configuration. Because tractors with loaded semitrailers are more resistant to yawing at the semitrailer over all reasonable maneuvering inputs and the semitrailers carry the largest mass, such vehicles may exhibit

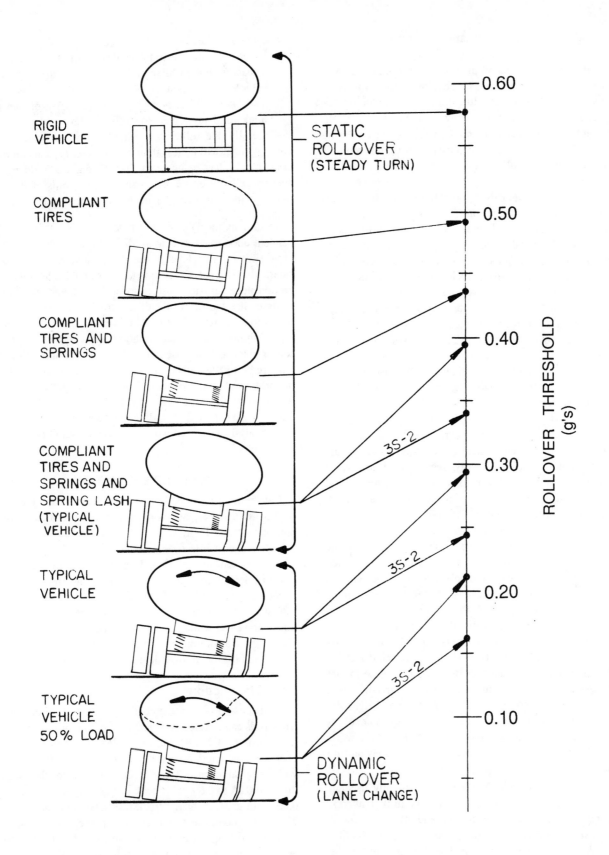

Exhibit 28. Static and dynamic rollover thresholds for idealized and typical gasoline tankers.

78-21

higher rollover thresholds in dynamic rather than steady-state maneuvers.

To reduce the likelihood of the last trailer rolling over, four specific actions can be taken: 1) reducing speed, 2) increasing the wheelbases of the full trailers, 3) reducing the distance from a unit's center of gravity to the pintle hitch installed at the rear of that unit, and 4) increasing the cornering stiffness of the tires.[3] To analyze a particular vehicle requires using a computer simulation (as described in Topic 892) or doing empirical testing.

Both steady-state and dynamic rollover threshold levels can be reduced when the payload is free to move laterally or vertically in response to lateral acceleration. While many types of freight are restrained in such a way that some movement is possible, the commodities usually cited as presenting a shifting load problem are liquids loaded into tank trailers or trucks, hanging meat, and livestock. Motions of the bulk fluid (or hanging meat) during steering maneuvers produce changes in the overturning moments acting on the vehicle, causing the rollover threshold (in certain cases) to go below what would be the full-load case.

A tank filled to anything less than its full capacity allows the liquid to move from side to side, producing a "slosh" load condition. Slosh reduces the vehicle's performance in cornering and rollover, and the motion of the liquid within the tank may exaggerate and thus reduce the rollover threshold.

When a partially loaded tanker is executing a steady-state turn, the liquid displaces laterally, keeping its free surface perpendicular to the combined forces of gravity and lateral acceleration. The liquid's center of mass moves in an arc the center of which is at the center of the tank.

When a partially loaded tanker makes an evasive steering maneuver, such as a lane change, slosh loads introduce the added dimension of dynamic effects. Due to the sudden steering input, the fluid may displace to one side with an overshooting type of behavior, causing a large increase in the lateral acceleration. In general, the amount of time involved in the steering maneuver directly affects the increase in acceleration. Studies done at the University of Michigan Transportation Research Institute (UMTRI)[10] show that drivers in an abrupt lane change maneuver steer at a rate close to that which is conducive to causing rollover of a partially filled tanker. Exhibit 28 shows the estimated static and dynamic rollover threshold for steady state and transient maneuvers for idealized and typical gasoline tankers. Note that the worst case occurs when the tank is loaded to approximately half its capacity.

Transverse (side-to-side) baffles are commonly used in many tanker vehicles (though not in bulk milk haulers). These types of baffles reduce the fore-and-aft movement of the load and in general have little or no effect on preventing lateral slosh. Installing longitudinal baffles minimizes the sloshing effect by reducing the net lateral displacement of the payload's center of mass.

In the case of swinging meat loads, a vehicle's handling properties are affected in two ways:

1. When entering a turn, the load swings to the side, and its impact with the trailer walls causes a disturbance to the vehicle in the transition period.
2. The load's high center of gravity results in greater roll angles and a relatively low rollover threshold.

Generally, the rollover threshold of trailers loaded with hanging meat will be less than that of other typical van trailers, typical values being near 0.20 to 0.25 g's. By reducing the free space between the carcasses and the walls of the container, some improvement in the rollover threshold can be obtained.

To sum up, the rollover threshold of a heavy vehicle is dependent upon several factors. Most of these factors serve to reduce the stability level of the vehicle and so must be considered in any analysis seeking to determine the lateral acceleration necessary to cause rollover. Traditional, rigid-body analyses use the ratio of half the track width of the semitrailer to the height of the load and vehicle's center of mass as typical limits of lateral acceleration. Typical track widths for semitrailers currently used in the highway transportation system are 96 to 108 inches, and typical load and vehicle center of mass heights are 70 to 110 inches. This yields values of 0.45 to 0.80 g's. Experimental values found by UMTRI and others range from 0.25 to 0.45 g's.[3] Clearly, the use of a rigid-body analysis will grossly overestimate the stability level of a heavy vehicle.

8. SPEED ESTIMATION

Determining the speed of a heavy vehicle can be accomplished by using equations of motion as described in Topic 860 and others. First, you must determine the distance the vehicle moved while sliding, its ending velocity, and its rate of acceleration/deceleration. Then use the appropriate equation to calculate the speed. Determining the ending velocity is generally not difficult if the vehicle has come to a stop before striking another vehicle or object. Determining the distance traveled while slowing is generally not difficult. However, determining the rate of acceleration is very involved and is crucial to vehicle motion analysis.

Truck Tire Friction

As discussed before, the coefficient of friction that heavy truck tires can develop is different from that of passenger car tires. Tests by UMTRI and others indicate that the average coefficient of friction on a dry road surface is 0.45 to 0.75, with peak values of 0.70 to 1.0. On wet surfaces the average drops to 0.35 to 0.60, with peak values ranging from 0.55 to 0.80.[9,3] In general, heavy truck tires develop approximately 75% of the coefficient of friction of passenger vehicle tires on a dry road, approximately the same coefficient of friction on a wet surface, and approximately 50% on wet ice (at approximately 30° F). If all wheels are locked and sliding on a level surface, then the acceleration rate is the product of the drag factor and the acceleration of gravity, and no further calculations are necessary.

Generally, heavy trucks do not lock all their brakes. Certain wheels or a combination of wheels may have no brakes, or the brakes may not be able to lock wheels. If all tires do not slide, or if they slide on different surfaces, the drag factor for some wheels will be different from that of others. Wheels with greater drag factors produce the retarding force to slow some of the load carried by wheels with lower drag factors.

Consider a very simple case. The driver of a bobtail (tractor with no semitrailer) locks the rear wheels with the foot brake, but applies no braking to the front wheels because they are disconnected. So the front wheels contribute only rolling resistance to the slowing of the vehicle. Rolling resistance is so slight that, for practical purposes, it has no effect. Virtually all slowing, then, is due to the drag of the sliding rear tires and is determined by the portion of the vehicle's weight on those wheels and by the coefficient of friction. If 40 percent of the vehicle's weight while sliding is on the rear tires and the coefficient of friction is 0.70, the drag factor of the whole vehicle is not 0.70 but $0.70 \times 0.40 = 0.28$. With some wheels rolling free, therefore, and some sliding, the drag factor of the whole vehicle is the same fraction (portion) of the coefficient of friction as the fraction of the vehicle's weight on the sliding wheels. If some wheels have partial braking, then this must be accounted for (see Topic 862).

The matter of total drag factor when individual wheels have different drag factors is complicated, because during braking a vehicle's weight shifts from the rear wheels to front wheels. Braking friction tends to force sliding wheels toward the rear at road level, and inertia tends to force the vehicle forward at the level of the center of mass. Consequently, the vehicle tends to rotate forward (pitch) during braking, the front end down and rear end up.

As a result, a single-unit vehicle with half its weight on the front axle and half on the rear axle when standing may have 60% of its weight on the front and 40% of its weight on the rear when braking. That is one reason for putting stronger brakes on front wheels than on rear ones.

Thus, when slowing, the weight on each axle is the static weight on that axle plus or minus the weight shift to or from that axle. The greater the rate of slowing, the greater the weight shift. But if all axles do not have the same drag factor, the weight shift also depends on the drag factor on each axle, which considerably complicates calculations (see Topics 862 and 890).

Mass Center With Load

Position of the center of mass (center of gravity) of the vehicle also affects weight shift. The center of mass is the point about which an object will balance fore and aft and from side to side. This point would also be directly below the point of suspension if the vehicle or other object were suspended by its front or rear end. How to locate the center of mass of a two-axle vehicle (without load) has been explained in Topic 862 and will not be covered in detail here.

Load must be included in center-of-mass calculations. If the single-unit vehicle is available as loaded, you can determine the longitudinal position of the center of mass by weighing the front and rear axles separately. If the load has been removed from the vehicle or if the vehicle and load are no longer available, you can often obtain a similar vehicle and load it. It should be loaded approximately as the actual vehicle was loaded, for purposes of testing. It is usually impractical, however, to tilt a loaded vehicle to obtain the height of the center of mass. The center of mass of the vehicle and that of the load may be estimated separately and combined by calculations (see Topic 890).

If the load is regular in shape – for example, a full tank of liquid, a rectangular box of granular material, a pile of lumber, or a van loaded to a uniform height with miscellaneous material — then the load's center of mass is at or near its center of volume crosswise, lengthwise, and vertically. Unless the load is obviously lopsided, it can be assumed to be centered right and left on the vehicle, for the purpose of estimating rates of slowing. With some large and special vehicles, engineers locate the vehicle's center of mass by weighing and measuring parts separately and then calculating the location of the center of mass of the entire vehicle.

Calculations for combining the center of mass of an empty vehicle and the center of mass of its load require the following data:

1. Weight of vehicle without load, w_v
2. Weight of load, w_b
3. Height of center of mass of load, l_{zb}
4. Height of center of mass of vehicle, l_{zv}
5. Distance of center of mass of vehicle behind front axle, l_{fv}
6. Distance of center of mass of the load behind the vehicle's front axle, l_{fb}

The equation for the distance of the combined center of mass of the vehicle and the load behind the vehicle's front axle is:

$$l_{fc} = \frac{l_{fb}w_b + l_{fv}w_v}{w_b + w_v}$$

If more than one load is involved, or if parts of a load are treated separately, the product of the weight of each load times the distance of its center of mass behind the front axle is added to the weight of the vehicle times the distance of the vehicle's center of mass behind the front axle; and this sum is divided by the combined weight of vehicle and loads.

The height of the combined center of mass of vehicle and load is obtained in the same way its longitudinal position is determined. The height of the load's center of mass times its weight is added to the height of the vehicle's center of mass times its weight, and the sum is divided by the combined weight of vehicle and load. Thus:

$$l_{zc} = \frac{l_{zb}w_b + l_{zv}w_v}{w_b + w_v}$$

78-23

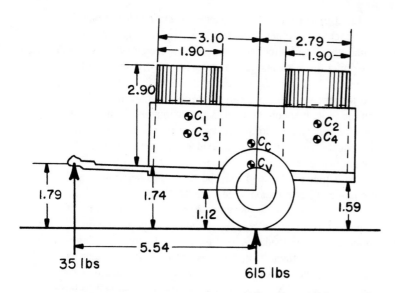

Exhibit 29. Data for example used to illustrate determination of center of mass of utility trailer and its load.

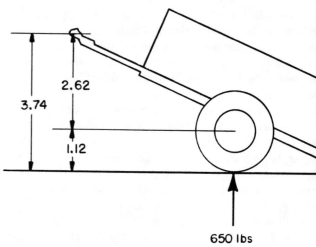

Exhibit 30. The "front axle" of a semitrailer is the trailer hitch. With small semitrailers, the hitch can be lifted to a position at which the trailer balances on its rear axle. Load on the rear axle then equals the weight of the vehicle. The height to which the hitch is hoisted is measured.

If there is more than one load, the product of the weight of each load times the height of its center of mass are all added to the vehicle weight times the height of the vehicle's center of mass, and this sum is divided by the total weight of vehicle and loads. This gives the height of the combined center of mass.

An irregular load can usually be considered as two or more parts. The weight and location of the center of mass of each part is estimated or calculated. Then the parts are treated as separate masses and combined with the vehicle as in the case of more than one load.

Utility Trailer Example

An example will illustrate the calculations for locating the center of mass of vehicle and load. In this example, the vehicle is a utility trailer shown in Exhibit 29. Exhibit 29 gives the dimensions of this vehicle as measured. The load consists of four covered steel drums, each weighing 35 lbs empty. Each drum is filled to within a foot of the top with fingerlings in fresh water from a fish hatchery. Two drums are placed side by side against the front bulkhead, and two are placed side by side against the tailgate.

The longitudinal position of the center of mass behind the trailer hitch (which is the front "axle") is found by substituting values from Exhibit 29 in the appropriate equation:

$$l_f = \frac{w_r l}{w}$$

$$l_f = \frac{615\,(5.54)}{650}$$

$$l_f = 5.24 \text{ ft}$$

This is very close to the rear axle as shown in Exhibit 29.

In some calculations it is simpler to express the location of the center of mass as a decimal fraction, x, of the wheelbase, l. Thus:

$$x_f = \frac{l_f}{l}$$

$$x_f = \frac{5.24}{5.54}$$

$$x_f = 0.946$$

The height of the center of mass of a single-axle trailer can be found rather easily if the trailer, like this one, can be tilted so that it balances over the axle. When the trailer is balanced, the weight on the hitch is zero and the weight on the rear axle is the entire weight of the trailer, 650 lbs. In the balanced position (see Exhibit 30), the front "axle" is 3.74 ft above the ground; the distance it is lifted is this distance above the ground minus the radius of the wheel:

$$h = 3.74 - 1.12 = 2.62 \text{ ft}$$

Using these figures in the equation for the height of the center of mass:

$$l_z = \frac{l\sqrt{(l^2 - h^2)(w_h - w_r)}}{hw} + r$$

$$l_z = \frac{5.54\sqrt{(5.54^2 - 2.62^2)(650 - 615)}}{(2.62)(650)} + 1.12$$

$l_z = 1.68$ ft

The location of the height of the center of mass expressed as a decimal fraction of the wheelbase is:

$$z = \frac{l_z}{l}$$

$$z = \frac{1.68}{5.54}$$

$$z = 0.302$$

The trailer carries four drums or tanks and their four contents, for a total of eight loads. Drums which are side by side can be considered as a single load for longitudinal and vertical positions of centers of mass. Hence, the eight loads can be considered as four.

The center of mass of a drum and its cover is its geometrical center, which is $2.90/2 = 1.45$ ft above the bottom and $1.90/2 = 0.95$ ft from the side. The forward bulkhead is $5.54 - 3.10 = 2.44$ ft back of the front "axle" (hitch). The tailgate is $5.54 + 2.79 = 8.33$ ft behind the front axle. Therefore, the center of mass of the forward two drums is $2.44 + 0.95 = 3.39$ ft behind the front axle and the center of mass of the two rear drums is $8.33 - 0.95 = 7.38$ ft behind the front axle. The center of mass of the two forward drums is $1.45 + 1.74 = 3.19$ ft above the road, and that of the rear pair of drums is $1.45 + 1.59 = 3.04$ ft above the road. The weight of each pair of drums is $(35)(2) = 70$ lbs. The contents of the drums is fresh water which weighs 60 lb/ft^3. The water in the drums is $2.90 - 1 = 1.90$ ft deep. The radius of the drums, previously calculated, is 0.95 ft. The equation for the volume of a drum (right cylinder) is:

$$\text{Volume} = \pi r^2 h$$

Substitute the appropriate values as calculated above:

$$\text{Volume} = (3.141)(0.95^2)(1.90)$$
$$\text{Volume} = 5.387 \text{ ft}^3$$

Therefore, the weight of the contents is $(5.387)(60) = 323.2$ lbs, and a pair of drums weighs $(323.2)(2) = 646.4$ lbs.

The center of mass of the contents of a drum is the same distance from the front axle as is the center of mass of the drum. This has already been calculated. The height of the center of mass of the drum contents above the trailer platform is $1.90/2 = 0.95$ ft. The center of mass in the forward drums is, therefore, $0.95 + 1.74 = 2.69$ ft above the road and that of the rear drums is $0.95 + 1.59 = 2.54$ ft above the road. We now have the weight and the center of mass location of five connected bodies:

1. The trailer, w_v, l_{xv}, l_{zv}
2. Two forward drums, w_{b1}, l_{xb1}, l_{zb1}
3. Two rear drums, w_{b2}, l_{xb2}, l_{zb2}
4. Contents of two forward drums, w_{b3}, l_{xb3}, l_{zb3}
5. Contents of two rear drums, w_{b4}, l_{xb4}, l_{zb4}

To locate the center of mass of the combination, the weight of the vehicle and each part of the load is multiplied by its distance from the front axle. These products are added and divided by the combined weight.

$$l_{xc} = \frac{l_{xv}w_v + l_{xb1}w_{b1} + l_{xb2}w_{b2} + l_{xb3}w_{b3} + l_{xb4}w_{b4}}{w_v + w_{b1} + w_{b2} + w_{b3} + w_{b4}}$$

$$l_{xc} = \frac{5.24(650) + 3.39(70) + 7.38(70) + 3.39(646) + 7.38(646)}{650 + 70 + 70 + 646 + 646}$$

$$l_{xc} = 5.34 \text{ ft}$$

Expressed as a decimal fraction of the wheelbase, $x_{fc} = 5.34/5.54 = 0.964$.

The static (standing) weight on the trailer hitch is:

$$w_f = w_c(1 - x_{fc})$$
$$w_f = 2,082(1 - 0.964)$$
$$w_f = 75 \text{ lbs}$$

The weight on the rear axle is the total weight minus the weight on the trailer hitch: $w_r = w_c - w_f = 2,082 - 75 = 2,007$ lbs.

The height of the combined center of mass is located in the same way:

$$l_{zc} = \frac{l_{zv}w_v + l_{zb1}w_{b1} + l_{zb2}w_{b2} + l_{zb3}w_{b3} + l_{zb4}w_{b4}}{w_v + w_{b1} + w_{b2} + w_{b3} + w_{b4}}$$

$$l_{zc} = \frac{1.68(650) + 3.19(70) + 3.04(70) + 2.69(646) + 2.54(646)}{650 + 70 + 70 + 646 + 646}$$

$$l_{zc} = 2.36 \text{ ft}$$

As a decimal fraction of the wheelbase, this is $z_c = 2.36/5.54 = 0.426$.

Insignificant errors enter into the foregoing estimates, as they do into nearly every engineering calculation. These arise from such minor inaccuracies as the following:

- The total weight of the trailer is only accurate to within 12.5 lbs because the platform scale on which it was weighed measured only to the nearest 25 lbs.
- The height of the hitch with the trailer balanced over the rear axle can be measured to within only about 0.1 ft.
- Additional load compresses springs and tires on the trailer, so that the actual height is perhaps about 0.1 ft below the position calculated.

- The trailer platform is not quite level, so the liquid load in the drums is slightly deeper at the rear of the drums than at the front, and the drums are tilted slightly toward the rear. Hence the position of the center of mass of the liquid in the drums is not quite as calculated.

For practical purposes, these minor errors may be neglected. If you need to do so, you can make more refined measurements and calculations to correct for these variables; but such corrections would not shift the position of the center of mass perceptibly from that shown at C_c in Exhibit 29.

Movable loads are of many kinds, such as:

- Occupants of vehicles
- Horses and other livestock, especially when unconstrained
- Liquids in tanks, especially large tanks without internal baffles
- Machinery and building materials, especially when improperly secured
- Hanging beef or other carcasses

Movable loads cause trouble in two main ways: 1) during strong braking or in collisions, they may shift and come loose or produce a second collision within the vehicle; 2) they may move about enough to change the position of the center of mass and so affect the performance and handling characteristics of the vehicle.

As a rule, the best way to deal with such circumstances is to make calculations assuming extreme or limiting conditions. This will determine what the greatest effect would be and whether more careful estimates may be required. Usually, calculations of limiting conditions are adequate.

Weight shift in slowing is greater if the center of mass is high (a top-heavy vehicle) than if it is low.

Tractor and Semitrailer

Trailers and semitrailers, with or without brakes, introduce more difficulties in obtaining a value for the drag factor of the combination of vehicles. There is a forward or rearward force between the tractor or towing vehicle and the trailer or towed vehicle unless the braking effort on each is exactly proportional to the weight of the vehicle, which is rarely the case. On both towing and towed vehicles, this thrust between units of a combination also produces a weight shift from one axle to another.

The resultant drag factor for a tractor-semitrailer which does not have the same drag factor on each axle can be estimated or computed.

Tractor data needed for such a calculation are:

w = weight of tractor
z = height of center of mass as a decimal fraction of wheelbase
x_f = horizontal distance of center of mass to front axle as a decimal fraction of the wheelbase
x_{rh} = horizontal distance of center of hitch (fifth wheel) ahead of the rear axle (if hitch is behind rear axle, x_{rh} is negative), as a decimal fraction of the tractor wheelbase
z_h = height of the center of the hitch as a decimal fraction of the tractor wheelbase
f_f = estimated drag factor for tractor front axle
f_r = estimated drag factor for tractor rear axle

Semitrailer data needed are:

w' = weight of semitrailer and load

z' = height of combined center of mass as a decimal fraction of wheelbase (wheelbase of trailer is distance from the center of the rear axle to center of hitch)
x_f' = horizontal distance from center of hitch to combined center of mass as a decimal fraction of semitrailer wheelbase
z_h' = height of center of hitch as a decimal fraction of semitrailer wheelbase
f' = estimated drag factor for the semitrailer

The equation for resultant (total) drag factor, f_R, of a tractor and semitrailer is:

$$f_R = \frac{B + Kf_f + f_r(D + w - K)}{w + A - J(f_f - f_r) - Ef_r}$$

In this equation the following abbreviations are used:

$$A = w' \left[1 + \frac{f'(z' - z_h')}{1 + f'z_h'} \right]$$

$$B = \frac{w'f'x_f'}{1 + f'z_h'}$$

$$D = w' \left(1 - \frac{x_f'}{1 + f'z_h'} \right)$$

$$E = \frac{w'(z' - z_h')}{1 + f'z_h'}$$

$$J = wz + Ex_{rh} + Az_h$$

$$K = w(1 - x_f) + D_{xrh} - Bz_h$$

Using the following equations, you can calculate the load on the tractor front axle, w_f; the load on the tractor rear axle, w_r; the vertical load on the trailer hitch, w_f'; and the trailer axle load, w_r':

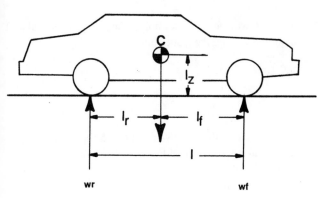

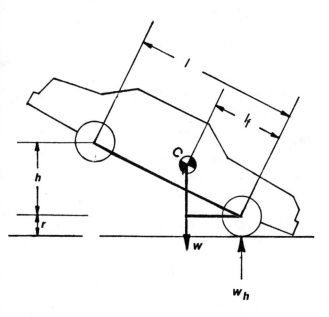

Exhibit 31. *Values involved in estimating resultant drag factor for a unit vehicle when not all axles have the same drag factor.*

$$w_f = f_R J + K$$

$$w_r = f_R(E - J) + w + D - K$$

$$w_r' = \frac{w'x_f'}{1 + f'z_h'} - f_R E$$

$$w_f' = f_R E + D$$

The horizontal force, F_h, between tractor and the semitrailer at the hitch (fifth wheel) can be calculated from this equation:

$$F_h = f_R A + B$$

If F_h is positive, this force will be compression; that is, the semitrailer will be pushing against the tractor. If F_h is negative, the force will be tension; the semitrailer will be pulling back on the tractor.

Car-Trailer Example

As an example, suppose the car illustrated in Exhibit 31 is drawing the trailer illustrated in Exhibit 29. Assume that the trailer hitch on the car is the same height as that on the trailer, 1.79 ft, and is 4.0 ft behind the car's rear axle; that the trailer has no brakes; and that the car slides its wheels on a level roadway with a coefficient of friction of 0.65. Then the values required are:

$$
\begin{aligned}
w &= 3{,}175 \text{ lbs} \\
z &= 0.222 \\
x_f &= 0.449 \\
x_{rh} &= -4.0/9.39 = -0.426 \\
z_h &= 1.79/9.39 = 0.191 \\
f_f &= 0.65 \\
f_r &= 0.65 \\
w' &= 650 + 1{,}432 = 2{,}082 \text{ lbs} \\
z' &= 0.426 \\
x_f' &= 0.964 \\
z_h' &= 1.79/5.54 = 0.323 \\
f' &= 0.02 \text{ (rolling resistance)}
\end{aligned}
$$

Calculate the values for the abbreviated quantities by substituting the established values in the equation for each of those quantities:

$$A = w'\left[1 + \frac{f'(z' - z_h')}{1 + f'z_h'}\right]$$

$$A = 2{,}082\left[1 + \frac{0.02\,(0.426 - 0.323)}{1 + 0.02\,(0.323)}\right]$$

$$A = 2{,}086.3$$

$$B = \frac{w'f'x_f'}{1 + f'z_h}$$

$$B = \frac{2{,}082\,(0.02)\,(0.964)}{1 + 0.02\,(0.323)}$$

$$B = \qquad 39.9$$

$$D = w'\left(1 - \frac{x_f'}{1 + f'z_h'}\right)$$

$$D = 2{,}082\left[1 - \frac{0.964}{1 + 0.02(0.323)}\right]$$

$$D = 87.8$$

$$E = \frac{w'(z' - z_h')}{1 + f'z_h'}$$

$$E = \frac{2,082(0.426 - 0.323)}{1 + 0.02(0.323)}$$

$$E = 213.1$$

$$J = wz + Ex_{rh} + Az_h$$

$$J = 3,175(0.222) + 213.1(-0.426) + 2,086.3(0.191)$$

$$J = 1,012.6$$

$$K = w(1 - x_f) + Dx_{rh} - Bz_h$$

$$K = 3,175(1 - 0.449) + 87.8(-0.426) - 39.9(0.191)$$

$$K = 1,704.4$$

Substitute basic values and values for abbreviations in the equation for resultant drag factor:

$$f_R = \frac{B + Kf_f + f_r(D + w - K)}{w + A - J(f_f - f_r) - Ef_r}$$

$$f_R = \frac{39.9 + 1,704.4(0.65) + 0.65(87.8 + 3,175 - 1,704.4)}{3,175 + 2,086.3 - 1,012.6(0.65 - 0.65) - 213.1(0.65)}$$

$$f_R = 0.422$$

Using the same data, calculate the vertical loads and horizontal force for the car-semitrailer slowing at a rate determined by f_R. Substitute the value for f_R, 0.422, the basic quantities where required, and the values of the abbreviated quantities in the equations for axle loads:

$$w_f = f_R J + K$$

$$w_f = 0.422(1,012.6) + 1,704.4$$

$$w_f = 2,132 \text{ lbs, the load on the car's front axle}$$

$$w_r = f_R(E - J) + w + D - K$$

$$w_r = 0.422(213.1 - 1,012.6) + 3,175 + 87.8 - 1,704.4$$

$$w_r = 1,221 \text{ lbs, the load on the car's rear axle}$$

$$w_r' = \frac{w'x_f'}{1 + f'z_h'} - f_R E$$

$$w_r' = \frac{2,082(0.964)}{1 + 0.02(0.323)} - 0.422(213.1)$$

$$w_r' = 1,904 \text{ lbs, the load on the trailer axle}$$

In the same way, for this example, compute the vertical and horizontal forces on the trailer hitch, w_f' and F_h:

$$w_f' = f_R E + D$$

$$w_f' = 0.422(213.1) + 87.8$$

$$w_f' = 178 \text{ lbs, the downward push of the trailer on the hitch at the back of the car}$$

$$F_h = f_R A + B$$

$$F_h = 0.422(2,086.3) + 39.9$$

$$F_h = 920 \text{ lbs, the forward push of the trailer on the hitch}$$

The total load on the three axles must equal the total weight of the car and trailer. In this case, $2,132 + 1,221 + 1,904 = 5,257$ and $3,175 + 2,082 = 5,257$.

Tractor and Full Trailer

The resultant drag factor for a car or truck with a full trailer when the axles have different drag factors can be estimated. Exhibit 32 shows an example of a towing vehicle with a full trailer.

Data needed for such calculations are, for
Truck or car:

w = weight of the powered vehicle

z = height of the center of mass as a decimal fraction of the wheelbase

x_f = horizontal distance of the center of mass from the front axle as a decimal fraction of the wheelbase

z_h = height of the tongue hitch as a decimal fraction of the wheelbase

f_f = estimated drag factor for the powered vehicle's front axle

f_r = estimated drag factor for powered vehicle's rear axle

Full trailer or towed vehicle:

w' = weight of the towed vehicle

z' = height of center of mass as a decimal fraction of the wheelbase

x_f' = horizontal distance of center of mass from the front axle as a decimal fraction of the wheelbase

z_h' = height of the hitch on the towed vehicle as a decimal fraction of its wheelbase

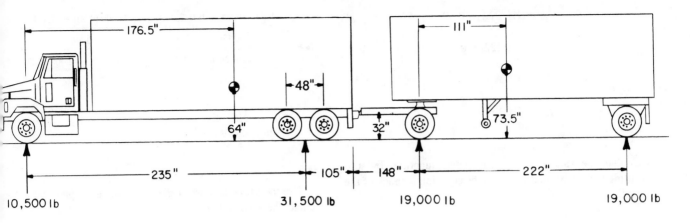

Exhibit 32. *Values involved in estimating resultant drag factor for a loaded truck and full trailer.*

f_f' = estimated drag factor for the front axle of the towed vehicle

f_r' = estimated drag factor for the rear axle of towed vehicle

The equation for the resultant (total) drag factor, f_R, of a powered vehicle and full trailer (towed vehicle) is:

$$f_R = \frac{\dfrac{wx_f - V}{z_h} + \dfrac{w'x_f' - T}{z_h'}}{\dfrac{N + w'z'}{z_h'} + \dfrac{U + wz}{z_h}}$$

In this equation, abbreviations have the following significance:

$$N = \frac{w'(z_h' - z')}{1 - z_h'(f_f' - f_r')}$$

$$T = \frac{w'(x_f' - f_f'z_h')}{1 - z_h'(f_f' - f_r')}$$

$$U = \frac{w(z_h - z)}{1 - z_h(f_f - f_r)}$$

$$V = \frac{w(x_f - f_fz_h)}{1 - z_h(f_f - f_r)}$$

Axle loads during braking with axles on a car or truck with a full trailer having different drag factors are:

$w_f = w - f_R U - V$ (towing vehicle front axle)

$w_r = f_R U + V$ (towing vehicle rear axle)

$w_f' = w' - f_R N - T$ (towed vehicle front axle)

$w_r' = f_R N + T$ (towed vehicle rear axle)

Force on the trailer hitch:

$$F_h = \frac{f_R (N + w'z') + T - w'x_f'}{z_h'}$$

Truck/Full Trailer Example

As an example, suppose the truck and full trailer illustrated in Exhibit 32 have the dimensions and weight indicated below. The truck slides with all wheels locked on a level surface with a coefficient of friction of 0.60. Assume the full trailer has no brakes on the front axle and full brakes on the rear axle. That is, the front axle has a drag factor of 0.02 for rolling resistance and the rear axle has a drag factor of 0.60. The values for the data required are:

Truck:

w = 42,000 lbs

z = 64/235 = 0.272

x_f = 176.5/235 = 0.75

z_h = 32/235 = 0.136

f_f = 0.60

f_r = 0.60

Full trailer:

w' = 38,000 lbs

z' = 73.5/222 = 0.331

78-29

$$x_f' = 111/222 = 0.50$$

$$z_h' = 32/222 = 0.144$$

$$f_f' = 0.02$$

$$f_r' = 0.60$$

Calculate the values of the abbreviated quantities by substituting the established values in the equation for each of the quantities:

$$N = \frac{w'(z_h' - z')}{1 - z_h'(f_f' - f_r')}$$

$$N = \frac{38,000\,(0.144 - 0.331)}{1 - 0.144\,(0.02 - 0.60)}$$

$$N = -6,558$$

$$T = \frac{w'(x_f' - f_f'z_h')}{1 - z_h'(f_f' - f_r')}$$

$$T = \frac{38,000\,(0.50 - 0.02\,(0.144))}{1 - 0.144\,(0.02 - 0.60)}$$

$$T = 17,434$$

$$U = \frac{w\,(z_h - z)}{1 - z_h(f_f - f_r)}$$

$$U = \frac{42,000\,(0.136 - 0.272)}{1 - 0.136(0.60 - 0.60)}$$

$$U = -5,712$$

$$V = \frac{w\,(x_f - f_f z_h)}{1 - z_h(f_f - f_r)}$$

$$V = \frac{42,000\,(0.75 - 0.60\,(0.136))}{1 - 0.136\,(0.60 - 0.60)}$$

$$V = 28,073$$

$$f_R = \frac{\dfrac{wx_f - V}{z_h} + \dfrac{w'x_f' - T}{z_h'}}{\dfrac{N + w'z'}{z_h'} + \dfrac{U + wz}{z_h}}$$

$$f_R = \frac{\dfrac{42,000\,(0.75) - 28,073}{0.136} + \dfrac{38,000\,(0.50) - 17,434}{0.144}}{\dfrac{-6,558 + 38,000\,(0.331)}{0.144} + \dfrac{-5,712 + 42,000\,(0.272)}{0.136}}$$

$$f_R = \frac{25,200 + 10,875}{41,806 + 42,000}$$

$$f_R = 0.43$$

Use the same data as for the preceding examples and calculate the vertical loads:

$$w_f = w - f_R U - V$$

$$w_f = 42,000 - 0.43\,(-5,712) - 28,073$$

$$w_f = 16,383 \text{ lbs, the load on the truck's front axle}$$

$$w_r = f_R U + V$$

$$w_r = 0.43\,(-5712) + 28,073$$

$$w_r = 25,617 \text{ lbs, the load on the truck's rear axle}$$

$$w_f' = w' - f_R N - T$$

$$w_f' = 38,000 - 0.43\,(-6,558) - 17,434$$

$$w_f' = 23,386 \text{ lbs, the load on the trailer's front axle}$$

$$w_r' = f_R N + T$$

$$w_r' = 0.43\,(-6,558) + 17,434$$

$$w_r' = 14,614 \text{ lbs, the load on the trailer's rear axle}$$

In the same way, for the example, compute the horizontal force on the trailer tongue:

$$F_h = \frac{f_R\,(N + w'z') + T - w'x_f'}{z_h'}$$

$$F_h = \frac{0.43\,(-6,558 + 38,000(0.331)) + 17,434 - 38,000\,(0.50)}{0.144}$$

$$F_h = 7,101 \text{ lbs, push by trailer against the truck}$$

The total load on the four axles of the towing and towed vehicles must equal the total weight of the two vehicles. In this example, $16,383 + 25,617 + 23,386 + 14,614 = 42,000 + 38,000 = 80,000$ pounds.

Assumptions for Equations

The foregoing equations for resultant drag factor when not all axles have the same drag factor, are developed for certain assumptions which should be understood when the equations are applied.

The road is level or nearly so. If the slope is more than 1 in 10 (0.10 or 6°) up or down, the error introduced may have to be reckoned with. On ordinary roads, however, slope may be neglected. Calculations correcting for grade are naturally complicated. Corrections must be made in weight distribution between the axles as well as in drag factor for each axle.

Weight on left and right wheels is assumed to be the same or nearly the same. If the vehicle is unusual or the load is exceptionally unbalanced, corrections may be needed for more precise calculations. In general, loads are not off-center enough to make any important difference.

Tandem axles can generally be considered as a "single" axle halfway between the front and rear axles of the pair (bogie) without introducing a bothersome error, provided the axles have normal brakes and are equipped so that load is equally distributed between the axles when braking.

Auxiliary axles have wheels which are off the road when unloaded. Consider vehicles so equipped as having a single rear axle, the loaded one. If the auxiliary or booster axle is carrying load, an approximation can be made. Consider an equivalent axle at a distance back of the forward axle of the tandem as being equal to the distance between the axles times the load on the rear axle divided by the total load on both axles.

Connections between a towing vehicle and a full trailer are assumed to be level. That is, the draw bar (tongue) that connects the two units is the same height at both ends. If the slope of this bar is less than 1 in 10 (0.10 or 6°), as it usually is, the slope makes so little difference that it may be neglected, for most purposes. However, if the slope is considerable, or great accuracy is important, corrections or adjustments in calculations are required for precise results.

Special vehicles may present problems for which usual equations are useful for only approximate solutions. Examples of such vehicles are beam semitrailers on which logs, pipes, or structural members serve to connect a tractor fifth wheel with a pair of axles; a full trailer behind a semitrailer; and a tandem axle with brakes on only one axle.

Any *irregular circumstance* can be ignored in initial computations, which are considered exploratory. Such tentative calculations usually indicate whether more refined calculations need to be considered.

Braking effort is designed to be equal on the two ends of an axle, but may not always be so. For example, a brake malfunction may produce a situation in which there is normal braking on a wheel on one side and more or less than normal braking on the opposite wheel. Such a situation is common for commercial heavy vehicles but is rare for passenger or light trucks. Sometimes unequal braking can be discovered by examining the brake system. Broken parts or lubricants on friction surfaces most commonly indicate unequal braking. On heavy vehicles, lack of, or improper adjustment of push rod travel is very common and should be checked as a source of unequal brake adjustment.

Road surfaces are much more likely than brakes to produce a difference in drag factor between wheels on the right and left ends of axles. Usually this is a matter of braking with one wheel on the pavement and the other on the shoulder. The extreme case of this is when one wheel is on dry, clean pavement and the other is on an adjacent icy area.

A *severe difference in drag factors* between right and left sides of a vehicle can make the vehicle rotate or yaw. It turns or swerves toward the side with the greatest drag factor, a very disconcerting situation for a driver.

If there is reason to believe that the drag factors of wheels on opposite ends of the axle differ, estimate the drag factor for each wheel by whatever means are available. The lower limit for such an estimate is nearly zero, rolling resistance only. The upper limit is that of a sliding tire, or the coefficient of friction of the road surface. Between these limits, you may have to make a crude estimate based on the degree of brake application suggested by the vehicle operator, or on the condition of brakes as revealed by examining them. Further consideration of these difficulties is explained in Topic 862.

If the weight is the same or nearly the same on both wheels of an axle, the drag factor for the entire axle is the average of the drag factors of the two wheels on that axle. For example, if the left wheel is sliding on hard, clear, dry paving with a coefficient of friction of 0.70 and the right wheel is sliding on loose gravel on the shoulder with a coefficient of friction of 0.50, the axle drag factor is $(0.70 + 0.50)/2 = 0.60$.

If the weight is not nearly the same on the wheels on opposite ends of an axle, the difference in load on the two wheels must be considered when estimating the drag factor for that axle. The drag factor for the axle is then the drag factor for one wheel times the fraction of the load on that wheel plus the drag factor for the opposite wheel times the fraction of the axle load on that wheel. Suppose that the left wheel, for some reason, has no brakes, but because of lopsided loading, carries 0.60 (60 percent) of the weight. Then the right wheel carries 0.40 of the weight. If the right wheel is sliding on a surface with a coefficient of friction of 0.70, the drag factor of the axle is $0.60(0) + 0.40(0.70) = 0 + 0.28 = 0.28$.

Case Study

This accident involved a 1977 GMC tractor towing a Datsun automobile traveling northbound on a newly resurfaced, four-lane highway. The driver of this vehicle combination disregarded a traffic signal at an intersection and struck a 1977 Ford Mustang which was attempting to cross from east to west. The GMC struck the Ford at approximately a 90° angle. The issue is the speed of the GMC at the time of first braking and its speed at first contact with the Ford.

Consider the movement of the GMC as it approaches the

Exhibit 33. *Photograph of tiremarks at scene of US31 & SR218 accident.*

collision area. Exhibit 33 shows tire marks made by all four wheels of the tractor but none that can be attributed to the Datsun. Inspection of the Datsun revealed that all wheels were free to rotate and the tractor operator could not apply the Datsun's brakes. The drag factor of the combination must therefore be reduced to compensate for not all axles braking. The procedure for calculating the resultant drag factor of a truck pulling a full trailer was used.

The road surface was new asphalt (less than a week old), and test skids made in the same direction of travel as the tractor at the accident site indicated a drag factor of 0.93 for a passenger vehicle. Using 75% of this value to compensate for the differences between heavy-truck and passenger tires results in a drag factor of 0.70. The following data were also collected for use in the appropriate equation:

Tractor parameters

$$w = 14,700 \text{ lbs}$$

$$z = 0.31$$

$$x_f = 0.46$$

$$z_h = 0.14$$

$$f_f = 0.70$$

$$f_r = 0.70$$

Trailer (Datsun) parameters

$$w' = 2,150 \text{ lbs}$$

$$z' = 0.20$$

$$x_f' = 0.45$$

$$z_h' = 0.22$$

$$f_f' = 0.02$$

$$f_r' = 0.02$$

Calculations

$$N = \frac{w'(z_h{}' - z')}{1 - z_h{}'(f_f{}' - f_r{}')}$$

$$N = \frac{2{,}150\,(0.22 - 0.20)}{1 - 0.22\,(0.02 - 0.02)}$$

$$N = 43$$

$$T = \frac{w'(x_f{}' - f_f{}'z_h{}')}{1 - z_h{}'(f_f{}' - f_r{}')}$$

$$T = \frac{2{,}150\,(0.45 - 0.02\,(0.22))}{1 - 0.22\,(0.02 - 0.02)}$$

$$T = 958$$

$$U = \frac{w\,(z_h - z)}{1 - z_h(f_f - f_r)}$$

$$U = \frac{14{,}700\,(0.14 - 0.31)}{1 - 0.14\,(0.70 - 0.70)}$$

$$U = -2{,}499$$

$$V = \frac{w\,(x_f - f_f z_h)}{1 - z_h(f_f - f_r)}$$

$$V = \frac{14{,}700\,(0.46 - 0.70\,(0.14))}{1 - 0.14\,(0.70 - 0.70)}$$

$$V = 5{,}321$$

$$f_R = \frac{\dfrac{wx_f - V}{z_h} + \dfrac{w'x_f{}' - T}{z_h{}'}}{\dfrac{N + w'z'}{z_h{}'} + \dfrac{U + wz}{z_h}}$$

$$f_R = \frac{\dfrac{14{,}700\,(0.46) - 5{,}321}{0.14} + \dfrac{2{,}150\,(0.45) - 958}{0.22}}{\dfrac{43 + 2{,}150\,(0.20)}{0.22} + \dfrac{-2{,}499 + 14{,}700\,(0.31)}{0.14}}$$

$$f_R = \frac{10{,}290 + 43}{2{,}150 + 14{,}700}$$

$$f_R = 0.61$$

In a case such as this, the principals of conservation of momentum are of no practical use to calculate the speed of the Ford. This is because of the large difference in the weights of the two vehicles. There would have been some speed loss to the tractor and the Datsun during the collision phase. However, it is so small that it can be ignored.

The physical evidence indicated that the tractor slid 130 feet prior to hitting the Ford and then an additional 50 feet to final rest. Using this information and the resultant drag factor calculated above shows the velocity of the tractor at impact to have been 44 ft/sec (30 mi/hr). The velocity at first braking was 84 ft/sec (57 mi/hr).

In this case, there is little difference between the drag factors of the GMC and Datsun, considering no braking from the Datsun versus ignoring the Datsun completely. This is because of the large difference in weights of the towed and towing vehicles. In other cases where the weight of the towed vehicle represents a higher percentage of the total weight of the combination, a considerable difference in drag factors could result.

In this case, the available information concerning each of the vehicles and the scene was more or less complete. In not every instance will this be the case. If the vehicles are not available for examination, other means will be necessary to approximate the location of the mass centers and other pertinent data. If this is the case, it would be desirable to consider a range of values to check the sensitivity of the analysis.

9. OTHER SPEED ESTIMATE TECHNIQUES

Gear Position and Speed

Occasionally, you can make speed estimates based on which gear of a vehicle's manual transmission was being operated. Five pieces of information are required to make a speed estimate:

1. Engine output speed in revolutions per minute (rpm),
2. The selected gear position of the transmission,
3. The ratio of the selected transmission gear,
4. The differential gear ratio, and
5. The loaded diameter of the drive wheel/tire combination.

The equation for determining velocity from gear position is:

$$v = 0.00436RD$$

where

v = the velocity of the vehicle in ft/sec
0.00436 = conversion factor from rpm inches to ft/sec

$$R = \frac{\text{engine rpm}}{(\text{transmission gear ratio})\,(\text{differential gear ratio})}$$

D = drive wheel/tire diameter (inches)

To obtain the information regarding engine speed, you must rely on the statements of the driver or perhaps a passenger witness. Statements such as "I was bumping the governor" narrow the range of engine speed to the governed rpm of the engine. Be careful when verifying the governed speed of the engine. Most likely a range of values would be appropriate – say, from three quarters to full governed rpm.

The selected gear position can also be determined from statements of the driver and, in some cases, by inspecting the vehicle. Again, some verification, perhaps from wrecker operators who towed the vehicle, would be appropriate.

The selected gear ratio can be determined by consulting the manufacturer's specifications for the particular vehicle. Counting the number of gear teeth on the meshing gears also establishes the ratio. If it is possible to turn either the input or output shaft of the transmission, count the number turned by the opposite shaft. For example, if the input is turned 10 times while the output turns three times, the ratio would be 10:3, or 3.3:1.

The differential gear ratio can also be obtained from the manufacturer's specifications, either by counting the number of gear teeth on the meshing gears or by turning either the drive shaft or drive wheel several revolutions and counting the number of revolutions turned by the other.

The loaded diameter of the drive wheel/tire combination must by measured. Remember that this is not the specified radius of the wheel doubled (although twice the radius is a good first approximation).

Gear Speed Example

As an example, assume that a tractor-semitrailer rolled over in a curve. The driver stated he was going the speed limit, which was 30 mi/hr. He further stated that he was sure of this because he was in fourth gear and was "bumping" the governor, getting ready to shift, and 30 mi/hr is the top speed in fourth. Examining the tractor indicated that for this transmission, fourth gear had a ratio of 1.37:1 and the differential had a ratio of 7.17:1; the wheel/tire diameter was measured at 40.4 inches and the governor was set at 3,000 rpm. What was the speed of the truck?

$$R = \frac{\text{engine rpm}}{(\text{transmission gear ratio}) \, (\text{differential gear ratio})}$$

$$R = \frac{3,000}{1.37 \, (7.17)}$$

$R = 305$
$v = 0.00436RD$
$v = 0.00436 \, (305) \, (40.4)$
$v = 53.8$ ft/sec (36 mi/hr)

Thus, based on statements made by the driver, you can conclude that the vehicle was exceeding the 30 mi/hr limit.

This analysis is not limited to heavy trucks. Any type of vehicle equipped with a manual transmission lends itself to this analysis if the needed information can be obtained.

Tachographs

Another, more reliable means of determining the speed of a vehicle is by analyzing a vehicle's tachograph output if it was so equipped. A *tachograph* is a device which makes a continuous record of several vehicle performance parameters. A tachograph can supply any of the following information:

1. Speed of the vehicle (in miles per hour or kilometers per hour)
2. Distance traveled by the vehicle
3. Engine revolutions per minute (rpm)
4. The total number of engine revolutions
5. The times at which the access door of the device was opened and closed
6. Whether the engine was stopped or running, and whether the vehicle was stopped or moving
7. Other optional data

The tachograph is a mechanical device mounted in the vehicle; it records the above-mentioned data on a paper tape or on one or more paper disks by means of a moving pen. The charts are pressure-sensitive, so no ink is needed. The pen presses into the specially coated surface of the chart and traces a line which may be seen from the front, or from the rear when viewed against a light. The pen markings are against a printed background, so no error should ensue because of expansion or shrinkage of the chart.

The period covered by the chart is typically 12 hours to seven days, depending on the instrument. There are also charts showing up to 31 days. A typical chart is shown in Exhibit 34.

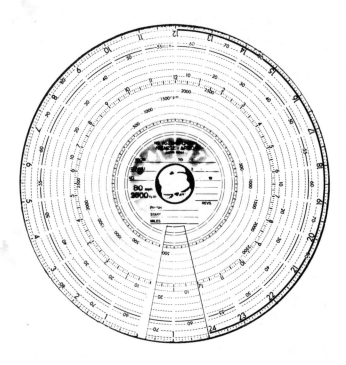

Exhibit 34. A typical 7-day tachograph chart.

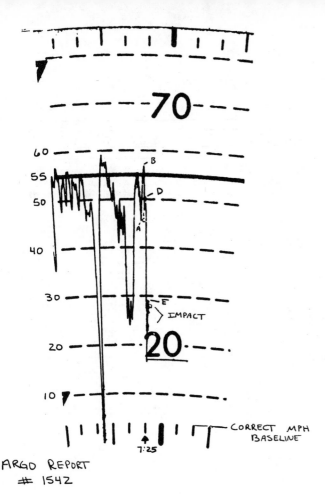

ARGO REPORT
1542

Exhibit 35. *Ten-times enlargement of accident-vehicle tachograph chart.*

The driver can monitor the face of the tachograph from within the cab and observe several of the vehicle's parameters. The chart is inserted inside the instrument and is accessible only by opening an access door. Opening the door causes a mark to made on the chart.

Tachograph charts can be very useful in accident investigation. They can be used to show the speed prior to or at the moment of impact in an accident, as well as the time of the collision. If other evidence is available, such as skidmarks, the chart may be used to compare with calculations of the vehicle's speed from a skidmark analysis.

Exhibit 35 shows a ten-times enlargement of a tachograph from a vehicle involved in a traffic accident at 7:25 p.m. Exhibit 36 shows a linear interpretation, made by an analyst, of the last 6,867 feet (from point A to E) before impact. Both exhibits indicate that 6,867 feet before the fluctuations at point E the vehicle was accelerated from a speed of 49 mi/hr (point A) to 61 mi/hr (point B), covering a distance of 2,501 feet in 31 seconds. Over the following 1,314 feet the vehicle was decelerated to 51 mi/hr (point C), which took 16 seconds. During the next 13 seconds the speed was accelerated to 55 mi/hr (point D), traveling 1,011 feet. The vehicle then decelerated to 32 mi/hr (point E), covering 2,042 feet in 32 seconds. At a speed of 32 mi/hr (point "e"), fluctuations in the normal recording pattern of the tachograph are shown. These fluctuations represent the point of impact. Due to conditions resulting from the accident, the instrument quit recording at 21 mi/hr. Wheel lockup did not occur prior to impact.

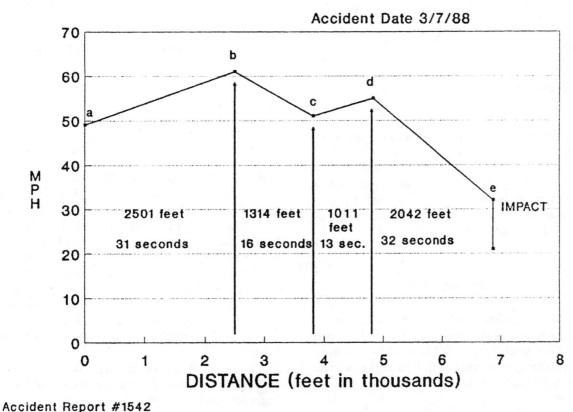

Accident Report #1542

Exhibit 36. *Linear interpretation of Exhibit 35 made by an analyst. The mi/hr stylus in Exhibit 35 was indicating 4 mi/hr slow. All speeds have been adjusted in Exhibit 36.*

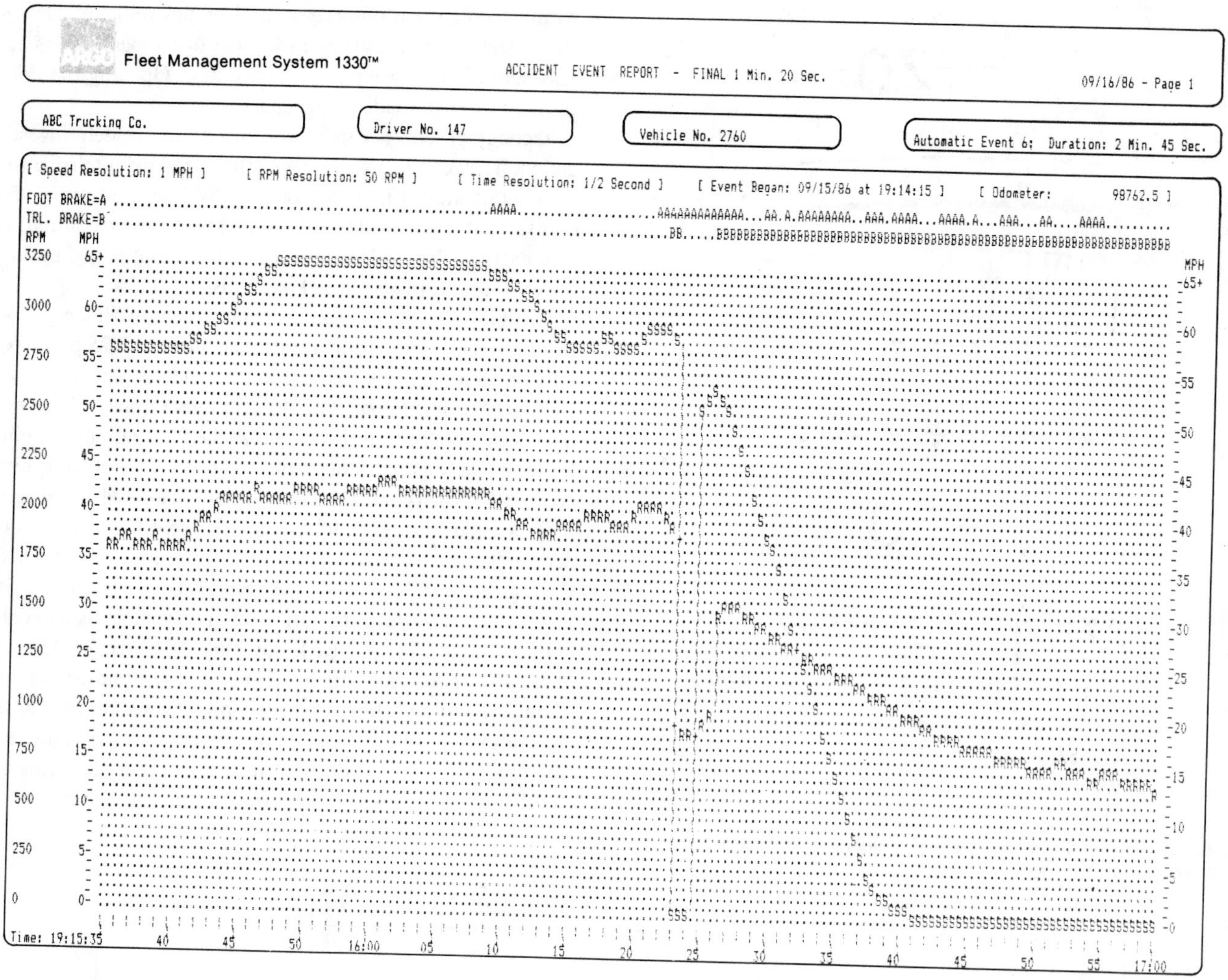

Fleet Management System 1330™   ACCIDENT EVENT REPORT - FINAL 1 Min. 20 Sec.   09/16/86 - Page 1

ABC Trucking Co.   Driver No. 147   Vehicle No. 2760   Automatic Event 6: Duration: 2 Min. 45 Sec.

[Speed Resolution: 1 MPH]   [RPM Resolution: 50 RPM]   [Time Resolution: 1/2 Second]   [Event Began: 09/15/86 at 19:14:15]   [Odometer: 98762.5]

Exhibit 37. Accident event report generated by on-board electronic tachograph.

Electronic tachographs (on-board computers) record data received from sensor-sending units installed throughout the vehicle. The information is stored on a data cartridge which can be read by a separate reader unit that translates and sends data to a personal computer. The personal computer is then used to analyze the information and can either display or print the information. Exhibit 37 shows an accident event report generated from an on-board electronic tachograph.

10. SOURCES

This topic was developed by Kenneth S. Baker, who is a senior consultant and lecturer at the Northwestern University Traffic Institute specializing in traffic accident reconstruction. Before coming to the Institute in 1986, he was with the Indiana State Police. Mr. Baker has a B.A. degree from Indiana University.

References

Superscript numbers in the preceding pages refer to the following publications:

1. Hajela, Gyaneshwar Prased, "Résumé of Tests on Commercial Vehicles on Winter Surfaces 1939-1966," National Safety Council Committee on Winter Driving Hazards, 1968.
2. Radlinski, Richard W., and Flick, Mark A., "Benefits of Front Brakes on Heavy Trucks", Society of Automotive Engineers 870493.
3. Lecture notes from 1988 Engineering summer Conferences, "Mechanics of Heavy-Duty Trucks and Truck Combinations", University of Michigan, Ann Arbor, Michigan.
4. International Harvester. "'TCAPE' and 'TRUKSIM.'" Simulation Programs, Truck Engineering Group, Ft. Wayne, Indiana.
5. "Turning Ability and Offtracking – Motor Vehicles." SAE J695b, SAE Recommended Practice, Society of Automotive Engineers Handbook, 1981.

6. Bernard, J. E. and Vanderploeg, M. "Static and Dynamic Offtracking of Articulated Vehicles." SAE 800151, SP-463, February 1980.

7. "Vehicle Dynamics Handbook for Single-Unit and Articulated Heavy Trucks", University of Michigan, May 1987.

8. Radlinski, Richard W., "Braking Performance of Heavy U.S. Vehicles", SAE 870492, February 1987.

9. "Factbook of the Mechanical Properties of the Components for Single-Unit and Articulated Heavy Trucks", Prepared for National Highway Traffic Safety Administration by University of Michigan Transportation Research Institute, Ann Arbor, Michigan, 1986.

10. "Future Configuration of Tank Vehicles Hauling Flammable Liquids in Michigan." Ervin, R. D., et al., Univ. of Michigan Rept. No. UM-HSRI-80-73-1, December 1980.

11. Hargadine, E. O. and Klein, T. M., "Braking Performance Level of Trucks: 1983," Engineering Economics Systems Group, Mandex, Inc., Vienna, Virginia, Contract Number DTFH61-83-C-00082, September 1984.

12. "General Instructions for Evaluating Tachograph Charts," Argo Instruments, Inc., 1013 Fort Collier Road, Winchester, Virginia, 1989.

13. Baker, J. Stannard, "Estimating Stopping Distance and Time For Motor Vehicles," PN804, 2nd Edition, The Traffic Institute, Northwestern University, Evanston, Illinois, 1981.

14. Baker, J. Stannard, *Traffic Accident Investigation Manual*, 1975, Northwestern University Traffic Institute, Evanston, Illinois.

Exhibits

The following are the sources of the exhibits used in this topic:

Argo Instruments, Winchester, Virginia
    Chart: 34
    Diagram: 35-37

Baker, J. Stannard, San Diego, CA
    Table: 17
    Diagram: 3-7, 10-13, 17, 29-32

Baker, Kenneth S., North Manchester, IN
    Photos: 14-15

Bendix Heavy Vehicle Systems of Allied Signal, Inc.
    Diagram: 1

McCullough, Earl, Logansport, IN
    Photo: 33

Navistar International, Ft. Wayne, IN
    Graph: 16

Radlinski, Richard, National Highway Traffic Safety Administration, Washington, DC
    Graph: 2, 9
    Diagram: 8

University of Michigan, Ann Arbor, MI
    Diagrams: 18, 20
    Tables: 19, 21-22, 26-28

Unknown
    Photos: 23-25

DERIVATIONS OF EQUATIONS FOR TRAFFIC ACCIDENT RECONSTRUCTION

Topic 890 of the *Traffic Accident Investigation Manual*

by
Gary W. Cooper
and
Lynn B. Fricke

NORTHWESTERN UNIVERSITY TRAFFIC INSTITUTE

DERIVATIONS OF EQUATIONS
FOR TRAFFIC ACCIDENT RECONSTRUCTION

1. INTRODUCTION

An equation (formula) is a mathematical statement of equality. It is an expression of a numerical relationship between quantities such as physical measurements. Equations for calculating various quantities have been used in traffic accident investigation/reconstruction for years. In using these equations, it is helpful to know how they originate. This topic will explain the application of basic engineering mechanics to derive various equations used in accident investigation/reconstruction.

The derivations of these equations are manipulations of algebraic relationships to determine the quantity desired. Algebra is simply the use of symbols in a mathematical expression to represent certain quantities. These symbols are called *variables*. The number of variables that exist in an equation indicates the number of different equations that may be formed. The manipulation is simply rearranging the variables and substituting other equivalent expressions for them. This allows different equations to be formed.

The reader is assumed to be more or less acquainted with simple algebraic operations. However, to make these operations more familiar, early derivations in the following explanations are more detailed than later ones. See Topic 856 for a general math review.

Certain principles of geometry, such as the Pythagorean theorem, are used also. The principle of each is stated, but for further explanations, consult textbooks on geometry.

Signs, symbols and abbreviations are needed in all of these equations. The ones used in this topic are listed before each derivation. A complete list of all the symbols used are in Exhibit 1.

In some of the following derivations, the vinculum (horizontal line) above two capital letters is used to indicate the distance between points identified by these letters in the diagram referred to. Thus, $\overline{AB}$ represents the distance between A and B in a geometric diagram. It does not mean A times B.

2. CONSTANT VELOCITY

The quantities used in the equations for an object in motion at a constant velocity are time, distance and velocity.

Time is used to measure a duration within which the motion exists. The symbol for time is t and it has units of seconds (sec,s).

Distance is the change in position of the object in motion with respect to some fixed point. The symbol for distance is d and it has units of feet (ft) or meters (m).

The *velocity* of an object in motion is the rate of motion. The rate of motion is the distance traveled with respect to a certain period of time. The symbol used to represent velocity is v and the units are generally feet per second (ft/sec) or meters per second (m/sec).

The definition of velocity is represented by the equation:

$$v = d/t \qquad (1)$$

Equation (1) can be solved to give the value of d, distance, in terms of time, t, and velocity, v. To solve for d, multiply both sides of equation (1) by t:

$$v = d/t$$

$$t\,v = \frac{d\,t}{t}$$

Cancel the t's on the right half of the equation:

$$v\,t = \frac{d\,\cancel{t}}{\cancel{t}}$$

$$v\,t = d$$

Reverse the equation to make it read:

$$d = vt \qquad (2)$$

To obtain the equation for time, t, divide each side of equation (2) by v thus:

$$d = vt$$
$$d/v = vt/v$$

Cancel the v's on the right side of the equation.

$$d/v = \cancel{v}\, t/\cancel{v}$$
$$d/v = t$$

Reverse the equation to make it read:

$$t = d/v \qquad (3)$$

An equation for changing units of velocity can easily be developed.

Because one mile is 5280 ft, one mile per hour equals 5280 ft/hr. Also, one hour is 3600 sec; one mile per hour equals one mile per 3600 sec. Thus, velocity in feet per second equals the velocity in miles per hour times 5280/3600. Performing the division indicated (5280/3600 = 1.467) gives 1.467.

SYMBOLS USED IN EQUATIONS AND CORRESPONDING QUANTITY ABBREVIATIONS

Quantities (Symbols are in *italics.*)
d = distance in ft or m, mi or km
h = vertical distance in ft or m
l = length of wheelbase between axle of vehicle in ft or m
r = radius of wheel with tire in ft or m
t = time in sec
m = mass (w/g)
N = normal force, force perpendicular to the surface
w = weight in lb or kg
F = force in lb or kg
w_s = weight shifted from rear to front in decelerating in lb or kg
W = work or energy in ft lbs or Nm
KE = kinetic energy in ft lbs or Nm

Ratios (Symbols are in *italics*.)
G = grade or slope (h/d) in ft/ft or m/m
A slope up is $+G$ and a slope down is $-G$
μ = coefficient of friction in lb/lb or kg/kg
f = drag factor (F/w) and (a/g)
z = height of the center of mass as a decimal fraction of the wheelbase
x = horizontal distance of center of mass from axle as a decimal fraction of wheelbase

Rates (Symbols are in *italics*.)
v = velocity (d/t) in ft/sec or m/sec
a = acceleration (v/t) in ft/sec² or m/sec²
Negative acceleration, $-a$, is deceleration.
g = acceleration due to the earth's gravity, 32.2 ft/sec² or 9.81 m/sec²

Locations (Symbols are not in *italics*.)
C = center of mass or center of gravity
P = point on ground directly below axle
Other capital letters indicate other points in various diagrams.

Superscripts indicate what the symbol followed refers to:
′ prime (after)

Subscripts indicate what the symbol followed refers to.
a average velocity
i initial or original velocity or time at the start of acceleration or deceleration
e end or final velocity or time at the finish of acceleration or deceleration
t total
G on a slope or grade of G
v weight of vehicle alone without load
b weight of load alone without vehicle
f front
r rear
R resultant
h vertical distance lifted or slope
s weight shift
sf sliding friction
x longitudinal
y lateral
z vertical
F friction

Exhibit 1. Symbols used in equations and corresponding quantity operations.

This may be expressed by the simple equation:

$$ft/sec = 1.467\,(mi/hr) \qquad (4)$$

or

$$mi/hr = \frac{ft/sec}{1.467} \qquad (5)$$

Likewise, because one kilometer is 1000 m, one kilometer per hour equals 1000 m/hr. Also, because one hour is 3600 sec, one kilometer per hour is one kilometer per 3600 sec. It follows, then, that one kilometer per hour equals 1000 m per 3600 sec. Thus, velocity in meters per second equals velocity in kilometers per hour times 1000/3600. Performing the division indicated, this may be expressed by the equation:

$$m/sec = \frac{km/hr}{3.6} \qquad (6)$$

or

$$km/hr = 3.6(m/sec) \qquad (7)$$

If velocity is constant, the relationships shown in equations (1), (2), and (3) apply exactly. But in slowing (deceleration) or in speeding up (acceleration) velocity is not constant. Then equations (1), (2), and (3) must be modified.

If the vehicle is changing velocity (accelerating or decelerating) at a constant rate, its average velocity, v_a, is half of the sum of the initial velocity, v_i, and end velocity, v_e. Thus:

$$v_a = \frac{(v_i + v_e)}{2} \qquad (8)$$

Equations (1), (2), and (3) are now written:

$$v_a = d/t \qquad (1)$$
$$d = v_a t \qquad (2)$$
$$t = d/v_a \qquad (3)$$

3. EQUATIONS FOR ACCELERATED MOTION

Equations Based on Definition of Acceleration

Acceleration is the rate of change in velocity of an object with respect to time. A *change* in velocity is the *difference* in velocities. Thus the difference between the end velocity, v_e, and the initial velocity, v_i, is $v_e - v_i$. The quantity of time in which the change takes place is t. Because acceleration is the change (difference) in velocity over a time period, acceleration, a, is simply given by

$$a = \frac{(v_e - v_i)}{t} \qquad (9)$$

The units in the numerator of equation (9) are ft/sec or m/sec. The unit for the denominator, t, is sec. Therefore the units of a are *ft/sec/sec* or *m/sec/sec*. Algebraically this is equivalent to ft/sec^2 and m/sec^2.

If the end velocity, v_e, is lower than the initial velocity, v_i, then the object has negative acceleration (deceleration) and has slowed. If the end velocity, v_e, is higher than the initial velocity, v_i, the object has positive acceleration and has speeded up. How quickly the velocity changes during the time it is changing is the *acceleration rate*.

Time in terms of acceleration and velocity change can be derived from equation (9) by multiplying both sides of equation (9) by t and canceling the t's on the right half of the equation:

$$at = \frac{(v_e - v_i)\,\cancel{t}}{\cancel{t}}$$

Divide both sides of the equation by a and cancel the a's on the left half of the equation:

$$\frac{\cancel{a}\,t}{\cancel{a}} = \frac{(v_e - v_i)}{a}$$

$$t = \frac{v_e - v_i}{a} \qquad (10)$$

End velocity in terms of time, acceleration and initial velocity can be obtained by multiplying both sides of equation (10) by a and canceling the a's on the right side of the equation:

$$at = \frac{(v_e - v_i)\,\cancel{a}}{\cancel{a}}$$

$$at = v_e - v_i$$

Add v_i to both sides of the equations and cancel the v_i's on the right side:

$$at + v_i = v_e - \cancel{v_i} + \cancel{v_i}$$

$$at + v_i = v_e$$

Reverse the equation and rearrange it to make it read

$$v_e = v_i + at \qquad (11)$$

Initial velocity in terms of time, acceleration and end velocity can be obtained by subtracting at from both sides of equation (11) and canceling the at's on the right side:

$$v_e - at = v_i + \cancel{at} - \cancel{at}$$

Reverse the equation to make it read:

$$v_i = v_e - at \qquad (12)$$

Equations based on the fundamental distance equation. Distance in terms of time and velocity change can be obtained from equations (2) and (8):

$$d = v_a t \qquad (2)$$

$$v_a = \frac{(v_i + v_e)}{2} \qquad (8)$$

Substitute into equation (2) the value for v_a in equation (8):

$$d = \frac{(v_i + v_e)\,t}{2}$$

Rearranging the equation makes it read:

$$d = \frac{t\,(v_i + v_e)}{2} \qquad (13)$$

Distance in terms of time, acceleration and initial velocity can be obtained by using equations (11) and (13). First, expand equation (13):

$$d = \left(\frac{v_i}{2} + \frac{v_e}{2} \right) t$$

Substitute into the equation the value for v_e from equation (11) and expand:

$$v_e = v_i + at \qquad (11)$$

$$d = \left(\frac{v_i}{2} + \frac{v_i}{2} + \frac{at}{2} \right) t$$

Multiply through the equation by t:

$$d = \frac{v_i t}{2} + \frac{v_i t}{2} + \frac{at^2}{2}$$

Combine the like terms $v_i t$ in the equation and rewrite the $\dfrac{at^2}{2}$ term:

$$d = v_i t + 1/2\,at^2 \qquad (14)$$

90-6

Acceleration in terms of time, initial velocity, and distance can be obtained by solving equation (14) for a, forming a new equation. Subtract $v_i t$ from both sides of equation (14) and cancel the $v_i t$'s on the right side of the equation:

$$d - v_i t = \cancel{v_i t} + 1/2\,at^2 - \cancel{v_i t}$$

Multiply both sides of the equation by 2 and cancel the 2's on the right side of the equation:

$$(d - v_i t)\,2 = (1/\cancel{2}\,at^2)\,\cancel{2}$$

Divide both sides of the equation by t^2 and cancel the t^2's on the right side of the equation:

$$\frac{(d - v_i t)\,2}{t^2} = at^2/\cancel{t^2}$$

Reverse the equation and rearrange it to make it read:

$$a = \frac{2d - 2v_i t}{t^2} \qquad (15)$$

Initial velocity in terms of time, acceleration, and distance can be obtained by solving equation (14) for v_i. Subtract $1/2\,at^2$ from both sides of equation (14) and cancel the $1/2\,at^2$'s on the right side of the equation:

$$d - 1/2\,at^2 = v_i t + \cancel{1/2\,at^2} - \cancel{1/2\,at^2}$$

Divide both sides of the equation by t and cancel the t's on the right side of the equation:

$$\frac{d - 1/2\,at^2}{t} = v_i \cancel{t}/\cancel{t}$$

Expand the left side of the equation and cancel:

$$\frac{d}{t} - \frac{at^{\cancel{2}}}{2\cancel{t}} = v_i$$

Reverse the equation to make it read:

$$v_i = \frac{d}{t} - \frac{at}{2} \qquad (16)$$

Equations Without the Variable Time

Previous equations have had the variable time (t) in them. Often it is useful to have equations where the value for time does not need to be known. These equations are developed in this section.

Distance in terms of acceleration and velocity change can be obtained from equations (10) and (14):

$$t = (v_e - v_i)/a \qquad (10)$$

$$d = v_i t + 1/2at^2 \qquad (14)$$

Substitute into equation (14) the value for t from equation (10):

$$d = v_i\left(\frac{v_e - v_i}{a}\right) + 1/2\,a\,\frac{(v_e - v_i)^2}{a^2}$$

Expand the equation:

$$d = \frac{v_i v_e - v_i^2}{a} + \frac{v_e^2 - 2v_e v_i + v_i^2}{2a}$$

Multiply the term $\dfrac{v_i v_e - v_i^2}{a}$ by 2/2 and add it to the

term $\dfrac{v_e^2 - 2v_e v_i + v_i^2}{2a}$:

$$d = \frac{2v_i v_e - 2v_i^2 + v_e^2 - 2v_e v_i + v_i^2}{2a}$$

$$d = \frac{(v_e^2 - v_i^2)}{2a} \qquad (17)$$

Acceleration in terms of velocity change and distance can be obtained by solving equation (17) for a, multiplying both sides of equation (17) by a/d, and canceling the a's on the right side of the equation and the d's on the left side of the equation:

$$d(a/d) = \frac{(v_e^2 - v_i^2)}{2d}\,\frac{a}{d}$$

$$a = \frac{(v_e^2 - v_i^2)}{2d} \qquad (18)$$

End velocity in terms of acceleration, initial velocity, and distance can be obtained from equation (18). Multiply both sides of equation (18) by $2d$ and cancel the $2d$'s on the right side of the equation:

$$(a)\ 2d = \frac{(v_e^2 - v_i^2)}{2d}\,2d$$

Add v_i^2 to both sides of the equation and cancel the v_i^2 on the right side of the equation:

$$2ad + v_i^2 = v_e^2 - v_i^2 + v_i^2$$

Reverse the equation and rearrange it to make it read

$$v_e^2 = v_i^2 + 2ad$$

Take the square root of both sides of the equation:

$$v_e = \sqrt{v_i^2 + 2ad} \qquad (19)$$

Initial velocity in terms of acceleration, end velocity and distance can be obtained from equation (19). Square both sides of equation (19):

$$v_e^2 = v_i^2 + 2ad$$

and solve for v_i:

$$v_i = \sqrt{v_e^2 - 2ad} \qquad (20)$$

Summary

The twelve equations shown in Exhibit 2 have been proven in the previous paragraphs. Essentially, all of these equations come from the following three equations:

$$a = \frac{v_e - v_i}{t}$$

$$d = v_i t + 1/2\,at^2$$

$$v_e^2 = v_i^2 + 2ad$$

Exhibit 2 simply shows the solution for the five variables: a, v_i, v_e, d, and t.

It can be seen in Exhibit 2 that it is always necessary to know three variables when a problem is worked (center column). By knowing three, the other two variables can always be determined (left column). The equations (right column) are appropriate for either U.S.A. or metric units. In U.S.A. units, velocity is always ft/sec; acceleration is always ft/sec/sec; distance is in ft; and time is in sec. In metric units, velocity is always in meters/sec; acceleration is meters/sec/sec; distance is in meters; and time is always in sec.

4. KINETIC ENERGY

Work

The work, W, done on an object by a force, F, is defined as the product of the magnitude of the force, F, and the distance, d, that the object moves in the direction of the force:

$$W = Fd \qquad (21)$$

TO FIND	WHEN GIVEN	EQUATION TO USE
ACCELERATION a (feet per second^2 or meters per second^2)	$t \quad v_i \quad v_e$	1. $a = \dfrac{v_e - v_i}{t}$
	$t \quad v_i \quad d$	2. $a = \dfrac{2d - 2v_i t}{t^2}$
	$v_i \quad v_e \quad d$	3. $a = \dfrac{v_e^2 - v_i^2}{2d}$
INITIAL VELOCITY v_i (feet per second or meters per second)	$t \quad a \quad v_e$	4. $v_i = v_e - at$
	$t \quad a \quad d$	5. $v_i = \dfrac{d}{t} - \dfrac{at}{2}$
	$a \quad v_e \quad d$	6. $v_i = \sqrt{v_e^2 - 2ad}$
END VELOCITY v_e (feet per second or meters per second)	$t \quad a \quad v_i$	7. $v_e = v_i + at$
	$a \quad v_i \quad d$	8. $v_e = \sqrt{v_i^2 + 2ad}$
DISTANCE d (feet or meters)	$t \quad a \quad v_i$	9. $d = v_i t + \frac{1}{2}at^2$
	$a \quad v_i \quad v_e$	10. $d = \dfrac{v_e^2 - v_i^2}{2a}$
	$t \quad v_i \quad v_e$	11. $d = \dfrac{t(v_i + v_e)}{2}$
TIME t (second)	$a \quad v_i \quad v_e$	12. $t = \dfrac{v_e - v_i}{a}$

NOTE: $a = gf$ where $g = 32.2$ fps^2 in USA and 9.81 mps^2 in metric

Exhibit 2. *Equations for uniformly accelerated motion. Watch closely for positive ($+$) acceleration for increasing velocity and negative ($-$) acceleration for decreasing velocity.*

Work has units of foot-pounds (ft-lbs) or Newton-meters (N-m).

The chief significance of the concept of work is that work represents the amount of energy transformed from one form to another. Therefore, work and energy are different aspects for the same thing, and both work and energy have the same units, *ft-lbs* or *N-m*.

The energy of motion of an object is called *kinetic energy*, or *KE*. In all other equations, variables are represented by one symbol (letter). The symbol may also have a subscript. Kinetic energy is nearly universally referred to by the two letters *KE*. Thus, this convention is used here. To derive an equation for kinetic energy, assume an object is at rest ($v_i = 0$). It is acted upon by a force, *F*, and it moves a distance, *d*. With these assumptions equations (11) and (14) are used:

$$v_e = v_i + at \qquad (11)$$

$$d = v_i t + 1/2at^2 \qquad (14)$$

Because $v_i = 0$, these equations become:

$$v_e = at$$

$$d = 1/2at^2$$

Solve the first equation for *t*:

$$t = \frac{v_e}{a}$$

Substitute this into the second equation:

$$d = 1/2 \frac{av_e^2}{a^2}$$

Simplify:

$$d = 1/2 \frac{v_e^2}{a}$$

Newton's second law of motion states that an unbalanced force, *F*, acting on an object will cause the object to accelerate, *a*, in the direction of the force, *F*. The acceleration is directly proportional to the resultant force acting on the object and inversely proportional to the object's mass, *m*. This can be stated in equation form:

$$a = \frac{F}{m} \qquad (22)$$

or:

$$F = ma \qquad (23)$$

Substitute into equation (21) the value for *F* in equation (23):

$$W = mad$$

Substitute $d = 1/2 \frac{v_e^2}{a}$ into this equation and cancel the *a*'s on the right side of the equation:

$$W = \frac{ma(1/2\ v_e^2)}{a}$$

Rearrange the equation to make it read

$$W = 1/2mv^2 \qquad (24)$$

Because all the work done on the object has accelerated it to a velocity, this work is kinetic energy (the energy due to motion). Thus,

$$KE = W = 1/2mv^2 \qquad (25)$$

To slow the object to a stop (assuming no additional energy is added to the object) requires the same quantity of work that it took to accelerate it to its velocity, *v*.

Mass

An obvious question now is what is mass. Newton's second law of motion:

$$F = ma \qquad (23)$$

is used to explain this. In free-fall the force of an object is its weight, *w*. The acceleration, *a*, is equal to the acceleration of gravity, *g*, Substituting $F = w$ and $a = g$ into equation (23) gives

$$w = mg$$

Solve for *m* by dividing both sides by *g* and cancel the *g*'s on the right side.

$$\frac{w}{g} = \frac{mg}{g}$$

Reverse the equation to make it read:

$$m = \frac{w}{g} \qquad (26)$$

Thus, mass is simply weight divided by the acceleration of gravity.

5. DRAG FACTOR AND COEFFICIENT OF FRICTION

Rate of change of velocity (acceleration or deceleration) of a body free to move depends on the force of the body relative to the body's mass (weight). In terms of common knowledge, a large unbalanced force adds more velocity to an object than a small unbalanced force. Also, the same large force will add more velocity to a small object than to a large object. Essentially, this is Newton's second law of motion.

Drag factor is a non-dimensional (no units) number used to represent acceleration or deceleration of a vehicle or other body. It is defined as the force in the direction of an object's acceleration divided by the object's weight.

$$f = \frac{F}{w} \qquad (27)$$

Then clearly drag factor multiplied by 100 is the percentage of the object's weight.

The force required for a given drag factor can be solved from equation (27) by multiplying both sides by w.

Then
$$wf = \frac{F\cancel{w}}{\cancel{w}}$$

$$F = fw \qquad (28)$$

Recall the following equations:

$$F = ma \qquad (23)$$

$$m = \frac{w}{g} \qquad (26)$$

Substitute into equation (23) the value of m from equation (26)

$$F = \frac{w}{g} a$$

Now substitute the value for F from equation (28)

$$fw = \frac{w\, a}{g}$$

Divide both sides of the equation by w and cancel:

$$\frac{f\cancel{w}}{\cancel{w}} = \frac{\cancel{w}\, a}{g\,\cancel{w}}$$

$$f = \frac{a}{g} \qquad (29)$$

solving for a:

$$a = fg \qquad (30)$$

Hence, every value of drag factor, f, has a corresponding value of acceleration, a, which is represented by these equations. In other words, drag factor is the number of "g's" of

acceleration or deceleration. One g is the acceleration of gravity. This has been determined to be approximately:

$$g = 32.2\, ft/sec/sec = 9.81\, m/sec/sec \qquad (31)$$

If an object has one-half g of acceleration, $a = .5g = (.5)(32.2)\, ft/sec/sec = 16.1\, ft/sec/sec$ or $(.5)(9.81)\, m/sec/sec = 4.9\, m/sec/sec$.

Coefficient of friction, μ (mu), is the force parallel to a surface required to cause an object to slide along a level surface, expressed as a decimal fraction of the force pressing the object against the surface. Therefore, for an object such as a vehicle sliding on a level surface, the coefficient of friction equals the drag factor; but if the surface is not level or if the object is rolling rather than sliding, the coefficient of friction and drag factor are *not* the same.

Drag factor and coefficient of friction often are confused. Many times, vehicles have one wheel or one axle locked and thus sliding when other wheels or axles are free to rotate. Examples include motorcycles, vehicles with trailers, and braked wheels not sliding. In those cases drag factor and coefficient of friction are unequal.

6. DERIVATION OF INITIAL VELOCITY EQUATION USING ENERGY

In addition to that described for equation (20), there is another derivation for the initial velocity in terms of acceleration, end velocity, and distance. Although this alternative procedure is more complicated, it has perhaps been more widely used. The derivation begins with equations (21), (25), (26), (28), and (30):

$$W = Fd \qquad (21)$$
$$KE = 1/2\, mv^2 \qquad (25)$$
$$m = w/g \qquad (26)$$
$$F = fw \qquad (28)$$
$$a = fg \qquad (30)$$

The principle underlying this derivation is that a body in motion will continue in motion until its energy of motion, $1/2mv^2$, is used doing work, Fd. In the case of a sliding vehicle, the energy is dissipated as heat due to friction in sliding. If the vehicle is not sliding, the friction is in brakes or rolling friction rather than between tire and road.

The total energy, W_t, is equal to the initial kinetic energy, KE_i; the initial kinetic energy is equal to the end kinetic energy, KE_e, plus the work done by sliding friction, W_{sf}. This relationship is written:

$$W_t = KE_i = KE_e + W_{sf}$$

where

$$KE_i = 1/2\, mv_i^2$$

$$KE_e = 1/2 \, mv_e^2$$

$$W_{sf} = Fd$$

Substitute these equations into the original:

$$1/2mv_i^2 = 1/2mv_e^2 + Fd$$

Substitute into this equation the value for F from equation (28):

$$1/2mv_i^2 = 1/2mv_e^2 + fwd$$

Substitute into this equation the value for m from equation (26):

$$1/2 \, (w/g) \, v_i^2 = 1/2 \, (w/g) \, v_e^2 + fwd$$

Multiply both sides of this equation by $2g/w$ and cancel:

$$v_i^2 = v_e^2 + 2gfd$$

Substitute into this equation the value for a from equation (30). This will be negative acceleration because of slowing:

$$v_i^2 = v_e^2 - 2ad$$

Take the square root of both sides of the equation:

$$v_i = \sqrt{v_e^2 - 2ad} \qquad (20)$$

7. DRAG FACTOR ON A GRADE

When a road surface is level, the grade, G, is equal to zero; then, if all wheels slide, the drag factor, f, equals the coefficient of friction, μ, on a *level* surface.

When a road is not level, however, a downgrade makes stopping distance greater whether all wheels are locked or not, and an upgrade makes stopping distance less. In other words, a grade increases or decreases drag factor (but not coefficient of friction). Therefore, what is the equivalent drag factor for slowing to a stop on a grade or slope? This adjusted drag factor, f_G, is greater than the drag factor on the level, f, if the slope is up, and less if the slope is down.

A grade or slope is measured by the rise or fall, h, over the horizontal distance, d. A number representing the grade is the feet of rise or fall per foot of level (horizontal) distance. This grade designation is sometimes expressed as the feet of rise or fall per 100 ft of level distance; that is the percent grade. The equation for grade, G, is thus:

$$G = \frac{h}{d} \qquad (32)$$

From equation (32):

$$h = Gd \qquad (33)$$

$$d = \frac{h}{G} \qquad (34)$$

In trigonometric terms, grade is the tangent of the angle, θ, between the slope and a level plane.

Grade is illustrated by Exhibit 3. The horizontal distance is d, the vertical distance is h, and θ is the angle formed. As shown in Exhibit 3, a right triangle is formed with the two sides, h and d, and the hypotenuse, d_G. The Pythagorean theorem states that the square of the hypotenuse of a right triangle is equal to the sum of the squares of the other two sides.

Thus:

$$d_G^2 = d^2 + h^2$$

Substitute into this equation the value for h from equation (33):

$$d_G^2 = d^2 + G^2d^2$$

Collect terms:

$$d_G^2 = d^2 \, (1 + G^2)$$

Take the square root of both sides:

$$d_G = d \sqrt{(1 + G^2)} \qquad (35)$$

Solve for d:

$$d = \frac{d_G}{\sqrt{(1 + G^2)}} \qquad (36)$$

Exhibit 3 also shows the relationship between the weight of a vehicle and the force on a sloped roadway. The vector (vertical arrow) downward from the center of mass, C, indicates the direction and the amount of the force of gravity on the vehicle; that is, the vehicle's total weight, w. The vector through the vehicle's center of mass and perpendicular to the sloped surface indicates the direction and amount of the vehicle's weight, w_z, pressing against the sloped surface. The other vector represents the direction and amount of the vehicle's weight, w_x, that is parallel to the sloped surface. These

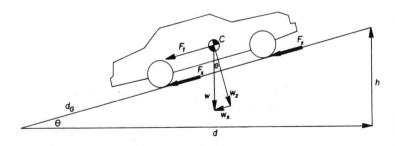

Exhibit 3. Relationships involved in equation for drag factor on a grade.

three vectors form a right triangle with the weight, w, as the hypotenuse. By geometry, the right triangle formed by these vectors is similar to the right triangle formed by the horizontal distance, d, the vertical distance, h, and the distance along the slope, d_G. Therefore, the two angles θ in each triangle are equal.

The total forces acting on the vehicle to slow it are also slown in Exhibit 3. The total force, F_t is equal to the sum of the frictional force in the x direction, F_x, and the weight, w_x, of the vehicle acting parallel to the sloped surface. Therefore:

$$F_t = F_x + w_x \quad (37)$$

The frictional force, F_x, is due to the coefficient of friction for a level surface and the vehicle's weight, w_z, that is pressing it against the sloped surface. This can be written in the form of equation (28):

$$F_x = w_z \mu$$

Substitute into equation (37) the value for F_x from this equation.

$$F_t = w_z \mu + w_x \quad (38)$$

From trigonometry, the relationship of the weight, w; the vertical weight component, w_z; the slope weight component, w_x; and angle θ can be expressed

$$w_z = w \cos\theta$$

$$w_x = w \sin\theta$$

Substitute into equation (38) these values for w_z and w_x:

$$F_t = w\mu \cos\theta + w \sin\theta$$

Divide both sides of the equation by $\cos\theta$ and cancel:

$$\frac{F_t}{\cos\theta} = w\mu \frac{\cancel{\cos\theta}}{\cancel{\cos\theta}} + \frac{w \sin\theta}{\cos\theta}$$

From trigonometry, $\dfrac{\sin\theta}{\cos\theta}$ is equal to $\tan\theta$:

$$\frac{F_t}{\cos\theta} = w\mu + w \tan\theta$$

The grade, G, is the tangent of the angle, θ. Substitute into the equation G for $\tan\theta$:

$$\frac{F_t}{\cos\theta} = w\mu + wG$$

Multiply both sides of the equation by $\cos\theta$ and rearrange to make it read

$$F_t = w \cos\theta\, (\mu + G) \quad (39)$$

From trigonometry, the cosine of angle θ in terms of vertical height, h, distance along the slope, d_G, and horizontal distance, d, is

$$\cos\theta = \frac{d}{d_G}$$

Substitute into this equation the value for d_G from equation (35) and cancel:

$$\cos\theta = \frac{\cancel{d}}{\cancel{d}\sqrt{1 + G^2}}$$

Substitute into equation (39) this value for $\cos\theta$:

$$F_t = \frac{w\,(\mu + G)}{\sqrt{(1 + G^2)}}$$

Divide both sides of the equation by w and cancel:

$$\frac{F_t}{w} = \frac{(\mu + G)}{\sqrt{1 + G^2}} \quad (40)$$

From equation (27)

$$f = \frac{F}{w}$$

where f is the drag factor and F is the force in the direction of acceleration.

From equation (40) F_t is the total force in the direction of acceleration. Therefore, drag factor on a grade where all tires are sliding is given by

$$f_G = \frac{\mu + G}{\sqrt{1 + G^2}} \quad (41)$$

If the grade, G, is small as it is on nearly all road grades, the factor $(1 + G^2)$ is insignificant and, for practical purposes, may be neglected. This makes the drag factor on a grade with all tires sliding equal to the coefficient of friction on the level, plus G, the grade:

$$f_G = \mu + G \quad (42)$$

Note that if the slope is down, G is negative and $f_G = \mu - G$ for tires sliding. Then the combined drag factor is less than it would have been on the level.

The work done in slowing to a stop on a slope is another way of deriving the effective drag factor on a grade. Work done in slowing to a stop on a slope has two parts:

1. The drag force of the vehicle times the distance moved along the surface, as described in equation (21):

$$W = Fd$$

2. The force of gravity, equal to the vehicle's weight, times the vertical distance moved.

For the first part, work done by braking on the sloped surface, consider the force against the surface and the drag factor of the tires on the surface. On a grade, only part of the weight of the vehicle forces the tires against the surface. Exhibit 3 shows the relationship between the weight of a vehicle and the force on a sloped roadway. The vector (vertical arrow) downward from the center of mass, C, indicates the direction and the amount of the force of gravity on the vehicle; that is, the vehicle's total weight, w. A vector through the vehicle's center of mass and perpendicular to the sloped surface indicates the direction and amount of the vehicle's weight, w_z, pressing against the sloped surface. The other vector represents the direction and amount of the vehicle's weight, w_x, that is parallel to the sloped surface. These three vectors form a right triangle, with the weight, w, as the hypotenuse. By geometry, the triangle formed by these vectors is similar to the right triangle formed by the horizontal distance, the vertical distance, and the distance along the slope of the road. They are similar because both are right triangles and each has two sides which are parallel to two sides of the other. Sides of similar triangles are proportional. Then the vector representing the vehicle's weight that is pressing against the sloped surface bears the same relationship to the vehicle's total weight as the horizontal distance, d, bears to the length of the slope, d_G.

Hence:

$$w_z/w = d/d_G$$

Substitute into this equation the value for d_G from equation (35):

$$\frac{w_z}{w} = \frac{d}{d\sqrt{(1 + G^2)}}$$

Cancel the d's on the right side of the equation and multiply both sides by w and cancel:

$$w_z = \frac{w}{\sqrt{(1 + G^2)}} \quad (43)$$

On a level surface, from equation (28), the force required to slide a vehicle along a surface is the coefficient of friction (all wheels slide) times the weight of the vehicle.

$$F = \mu w$$

But on a slope, weight, w, of the vehicle pushing against the slope is w_z, from equation (43). This value (w_z) is less than the vehicle's actual weight. Hence, the total force parallel to the slope required to slide the vehicle along the sloped surface is:

$$F_t = \frac{\mu w}{\sqrt{(1 + G^2)}}$$

The work done (energy transformed) in sliding an object along a surface is given by equation (21). Substitute into equation (21) for F the value for F_t from above, for d substitute d_G, and for W substitute W_G.

$$W_G = \frac{d_G \mu w}{\sqrt{(1 + G^2)}} \quad (44)$$

Equation (44) represents the work done sliding the vehicle along the surface. The second part of the work done in moving the vehicle on the sloped surface is the work, W_h, required to lift the vehicle a vertical distance, h, while moving a distance, d_G, along the slope. The vertical force is the full weight of the vehicle, w. Then, from equation (21):

$$W = Fd \quad (21)$$

Substitute w for F and h for d:

$$W_h = wh$$

Substitute into this equation the value for h from equation (33):

$$W_h = wGd$$

Substitute into this equation the value for d from equation (36):

$$W_h = \frac{d_G wG}{\sqrt{(1 + G^2)}} \quad (45)$$

The total work, W_t, for moving up the slope a distance of d_G is then

$$W_t = W_G + W_h$$

Substitute into this equation the values for W_G and W_h from equations (44) and (45), respectively:

$$W_t = \frac{d_G w \mu}{\sqrt{(1 + G^2)}} + \frac{d_G w G}{\sqrt{(1 + G^2)}}$$

Collect like terms:

$$W_t = d_G w \frac{(\mu + G)}{\sqrt{(1 + G^2)}} \quad (46)$$

Combining equations (21) and (28):

$$W = Fd \quad (21)$$

$$F = fw \quad (28)$$

$$W = dwf$$

Comparing this equation with equation (46) indicates the effective drag factor for a vehicle sliding up a slope is

$$f_G = \frac{(\mu + G)}{\sqrt{(1 + G^2)}}$$

Again as in the previous derivation, the factor $(1 + G^2)$ is insignificant and for practical purposes may be neglected. This makes the equation read

$$f_G = \mu + G \quad (42)$$

8. EQUATION FOR VELOCITY INDICATED BY A FALL

When a vehicle is no longer supported by the ground (pavement, etc.), it travels unsupported through the air. The vehicle tends to keep traveling in a straight line in the direction in which it was headed when it left the ground. But the vehicle's weight (force of gravity) makes it fall toward the ground with increasing vertical velocity. The time it takes to move through the air from where it is no longer supported to where it first contacts the ground (or other fixed object) depends on the initial vertical velocity and the acceleration of gravity.

As a vehicle starts to travel unsupported through the air, it has an initial velocity. If the beginning of the fall occurs to a vehicle that has been traveling on a grade, the initial velocity has both horizontal and vertical components (Topic 856). Exhibit 4A shows this with the angle of the grade exaggerated and given by θ. The vertical velocity component is v_h, the horizontal velocity component is v_d, and the velocity is v_i.

The path of a vehicle moving through the air which was initially traveling on a grade (exaggerated) at takeoff is shown in Exhibit 4B. At the same time that a vehicle is traveling through the air vertically, it continues to move forward horizontally at a constant velocity. The time it takes a vehicle to move through the air vertically is the same time it takes it to move through the air horizontally. The time it would take a vehicle to move a given distance at a constant velocity is given by equation (3):

$$t = d/v \quad (3)$$

For this case d is the horizontal distance, t is the total time the vehicle moves through the air, and v is the horizontal component, v_d, of the initial velocity, v_i. From trigonometry (Topic 856), $v_d = v_i \cos \theta$. Thus equation (3) becomes:

$$t = d/v_i \cos \theta \quad (47)$$

The total time a vehicle moves through the air may be broken down into two segments when considering its vertical motion. The first time segment, t_1, is the time it takes the vehicle to reach the maximum height, h_1, of its trajectory (Exhibit 4B). The second time segment, t_2, is the time required for the vehicle to fall from the maximum height of its trajectory to landing.

The maximum height of a vehicle's trajectory can be found by using equation (14):

$$d = v_i t + 1/2 a t^2 \quad (14)$$

When considering the maximum height, d becomes h_1, t becomes t_1, a becomes $-g$, and v_h becomes $v_i \sin \theta$ (Topic 856):

$$h_1 = (v_i \sin \theta)t_1 - 1/2 g t_1^2 \quad (48)$$

The time required to reach the maximum height (t_1) can be found by using equation (10):

$$t = (v_e - v_i)/a \quad (10)$$

From Exhibit 4B, for the first time segment, equation (10) becomes:

$$t_1 = (v_{he1} - v_{hi1})/a$$

However, $v_{he1} = 0$, $v_{hi1} = v_h = v_i \sin \theta$, and $a = -g$, making the equation:

$$t_1 = v_i \sin \theta/g \quad (49)$$

Combine this equation and equation (48) by substituting the value for t_1 into equation (48):

$$h_1 = (v_i \sin \theta)(v_i \sin \theta)/g - 1/2 g(v_i \sin \theta/g)^2$$

Expand the equation and cancel:

$$h_1 = v_i^2 \sin^2 \theta/g - v_i^2 \sin^2 \theta/2g$$

EXHIBIT 4A

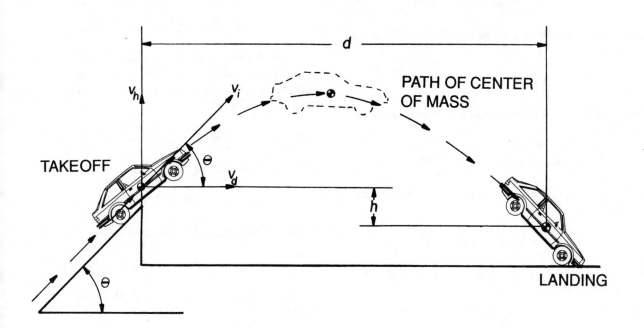

EXHIBIT 4B

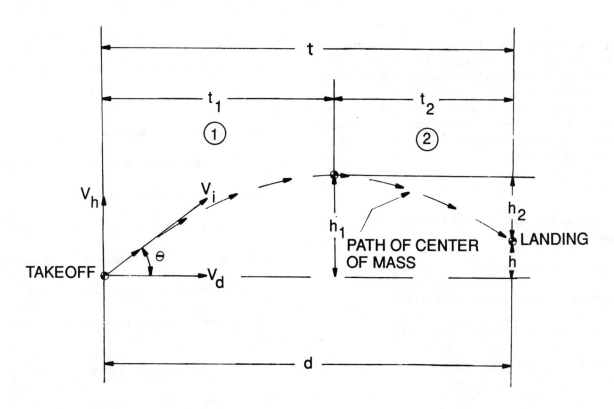

Exhibit 4. *Relationships involved in equation for speed from a fall.*

Simplify:

$$h_1 = v_i^2 \sin^2\theta / 2g \quad (50)$$

The second time segment, t_2, can also be found by using equation (10):

$$t = (v_e - v_i)/a \quad (10)$$

From Exhibit 4B, for the second time segment, equation (10) becomes:

$$t_2 = (v_{he2} - v_{hi2})/a \quad (51)$$

Here, $v_{hi2} = 0$, $a = g$, and v_{he2} is found by using equation (19):

$$v_e = \sqrt{v_i^2 + 2ad} \quad (19)$$

With $v_e = v_{he2}$, $v_i = v_{hi2} = 0$, $a = g$, and $d = h_2$, equation (19) becomes:

$$v_{he2} = \sqrt{2gh_2}$$

Substitute this into equation (51):

$$t_2 = \sqrt{(2gh_2)}/g \quad (52)$$

The distance through which the vehicle falls from its maximum height, h_1, to landing is h_2. The vertical difference between takeoff and landing is h. The vertical difference between takeoff and landing is considered to be negative if the vehicle lands lower than takeoff and positive if it lands higher than takeoff. The distance through which the vehicle falls from the maximum height of its trajectory to landing is given by the equation:

$$h_2 = h_1 - h$$

Substitute the value of h_1 from equation (50) into this equation:

$$h_2 = [(v_i^2 \sin^2\theta)/2g] - h$$

Substitute this equation into equation (52):

$$t_2 = \sqrt{\{2g[(v_i^2 \sin^2\theta/2g) - h]\}}/g$$

Simplify:

$$t_2 = \sqrt{(v_i^2 \sin^2\theta - 2gh)}/g$$

The total time, t, that the vehicle would move through the air vertically would be equal to the time it takes the vehicle to reach its maximum height, t_1, and the time it would take

it to fall from the maximum height to landing, t_2. This is equal to the sum of the above equation and equation (49):

$$t = v_i \sin\theta/g + \sqrt{(v_i^2 \sin^2\theta - 2gh)}/g$$

As stated before, the time it takes the vehicle to move through the air vertically is the same time it takes it to move through the air horizontally. Therefore, set this equation equal to equation (47):

$$d/v_i \cos\theta = v_i \sin\theta/g + \sqrt{(v_i^2 \sin^2\theta - 2gh)}/g$$

Multiply both sides of the equation by g and cancel:

$$dg/v_i \cos\theta = v_i \sin\theta + \sqrt{v_i^2 \sin^2\theta - 2gh}$$

Multiply both sides of the equation by v_i and cancel:

$$dg/\cos\theta = v_i^2 \sin\theta + v_i\sqrt{v_i^2 \sin^2\theta - 2gh}$$

Expand under the radical by multiplying by v_i^2/v_i^2 and simplify:

$$dg/\cos\theta = v_i^2 \sin\theta + v_i^2\sqrt{\sin^2\theta - 2gh/v_i^2}$$

Divide both sides of the equation by v_i^2 and cancel:

$$dg/v_i^2 \cos\theta = \sin\theta + \sqrt{\sin^2\theta - 2gh/v_i^2}$$

Subtract $\sin\theta$ from both sides of the equation and cancel:

$$dg/v_i^2 \cos\theta - \sin\theta = \sqrt{\sin^2\theta - 2gh/v_i^2}$$

Square both sides of the equation:

$$d^2g^2/v_i^4 \cos^2\theta - 2dg \sin\theta/v_i^2 \cos\theta + \sin^2\theta = \sin^2\theta - 2gh/v_i^2$$

Subtract $\sin^2\theta$ from both sides of the equation and cancel:

$$d^2g^2/v_i^4 \cos^2\theta - 2dg \sin\theta/v_i^2 \cos\theta = -2gh/v_i^2$$

Multiply both sides of the equation by v_i^2 and cancel:

$$d^2g^2/v_i^2 \cos^2\theta - 2dg \sin\theta/\cos\theta = -2gh$$

Add $2dg \sin\theta/\cos\theta$ to both sides of the equation and cancel:

$$d^2g^2/v_i^2 \cos^2\theta = 2dg \sin\theta/\cos\theta - 2gh$$

Multiply both sides of the equation by $v_i^2 \cos^2\theta$ and cancel:

$$d^2g^2 = v_i^2 \cos^2\theta [(2dg \sin\theta/\cos\theta) - 2gh]$$

Divide both sides of the equation by $cos^2\theta \, [(2dg \, sin\theta / cos\theta) - 2gh]$ and cancel:

$$d^2g^2 / cos^2\theta \, [(2dg \, sin\theta / cos\theta) - 2gh] = v_i^2$$

Rearrange the equation and take the square root of both sides:

$$v_i = \sqrt{d^2g^2 / \{cos^2\theta \, [2dg \, sin\theta / cos\theta) - 2gh]\}}$$

Simplify under the radical by factoring out $2g$ in the denominator and cancel:

$$v_i = \sqrt{d^2g / \{2cos^2\theta \, [(d \, sin\theta / cos\theta) - h]\}}$$

Further simplify under the radical:

$$v = d\sqrt{g / [2cos\theta \, (d \, sin\theta - h \, cos\theta)]} \qquad (53)$$

For grades that are typically encountered (and the resulting angle θ), $cos\theta$ is approximately equal to 1 and $sin\theta$ is approximately equal to $tan\theta$ which is equal to grade G. Thus equation (53) can be simplified to:

$$v = d\sqrt{g / [2 \, (dG - h)]} \qquad (54)$$

Remember, if you are using U.S.A. units, d is in feet, h is in feet, v is in ft/sec, and $g = 32.2$ ft/sec/sec. In the metric system d is in meters, h is in meters, v is in m/sec and $g = 9.81$ m/sec/sec. Also note that the vertical height difference between takeoff and landing, h, is positive if landing is higher than takeoff and negative if landing is lower.

9. FLIPS AND VAULTS

Vehicles may move through the air not only by falling, but also by leaving the ground in a flip or vault.

If a vehicle moving on a road surface strikes an object which stops forward movement of part of the vehicle at or near the ground, the rest of the vehicle tends to keep going. It can only do this by pivoting on the part that is stopped, usually a wheel. Exhibit 5A shows a vehicle at takeoff in a flip; Exhibit 5B shows a vehicle at takeoff in a vault. Angle θ is the takeoff angle, v_h is the vertical velocity component, v_d is the horizontal velocity component, and v_i is the initial velocity (Topic 856). The relationships between v_h, v_d, v_i, d, h, g, and θ are the same as indicated in the derivation of the fall equation. Therefore, the same algebra can be done to reach equation (53):

$$v = d\sqrt{g / [2 \, cos\theta \, (d \, sin\theta - h \, cos\theta)]} \qquad (53)$$

If $\theta = 45°$, $cos \, 45° \approx 0.707$, and $sin \, 45° \approx 0.707$. Substitute these values into equation (53):

$$v = d\sqrt{g / \{(2) \, (0.707) \, [d \, 0.707 - h \, 0.707]\}}$$

Simplify:

$$v = d\sqrt{g / (d - h)} \qquad (54)$$

Note that the difference in elevation between takeoff and landing, h, is positive if landing is higher than takeoff and negative if it is lower.

In most cases, setting the takeoff angle, θ, equal to 45 degrees will approximate the minimum velocity required to travel the given horizontal distance. However, by using some basic calculus, the takeoff angle, θ, required to minimize the takeoff velocity, v, while maximizing the horizontal distance traveled, d, can be found.

Start with equation (53):

$$v = d\sqrt{g / [2 \, cos\theta \, (d \, sin\theta - h \, cos\theta)]} \qquad (53)$$

Square both sides of the equation:

$$v^2 = d^2g / [2 \, cos\theta \, (d \, sin\theta - h \, cos\theta)]$$

Expand the denominator:

$$v^2 = d^2g / [2 \, (d \, sin\theta \, cos\theta - h \, cos^2\theta)]$$

Multiply both sides of the equation by $2 \, (d \, sin \, cos\theta - h \, cos^2 \, \theta)$ and cancel:

$$2v^2 \, (d \, sin\theta \, cos\theta - h \, cos^2 \, \theta) = d^2g$$

Subtract $2v^2 \, (d \, sin\theta \, cos\theta - h \, cos^2 \, \theta)$ from both sides of the equation, cancel, and rearrange:

$$d^2g - 2v^2 \, (d \, sin\theta \, cos\theta - h \, cos^2 \, \theta) = 0$$

Differentiate d with respect to θ using the product rule:

$$d \, (cos^2\theta - sin^2\theta) + h \, (2 \, sin\theta \, cos\theta) = 0$$

Use the trigonometric identities, $sin \, 2\theta = 2 \, sin\theta \, cos\theta$, $cos \, 2\theta = cos^2 \, \theta - sin^2 \, \theta$, and substitute:

$$d \, cos \, 2\theta + h \, sin \, 2\theta = 0$$

Subtract $h \, sin \, 2\theta$ to both sides of the equation and cancel:

$$d \, cos \, 2\theta = - h \, sin \, 2\theta$$

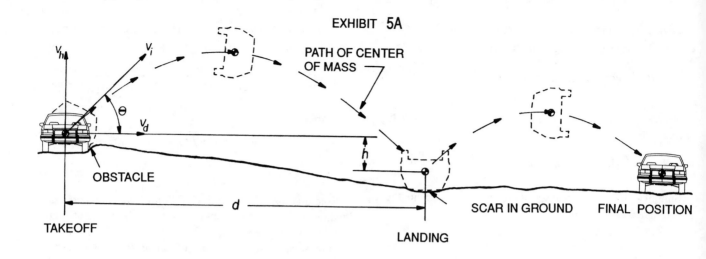

EXHIBIT 5A

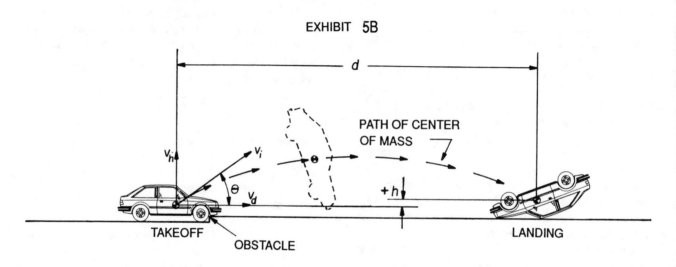

EXHIBIT 5B

Exhibit 5. *Relationships involved in equation for speed from a flip.*

Divide both sides of the equation by $-h\ cos\ 2\theta$ and cancel:

$$d/(-h) = sin\ 2\theta/cos\ 2\theta$$

Substitute $tan\ 2\theta$ for $sin\ 2\theta/cos\ 2\theta$ and rearrange the equation:

$$tan\ 2\theta = d/(-h)$$

Given this relationship, from right-triangle trigonometry and the Pythagorean theorem:

$$cos\ 2\theta = -h/\sqrt{h^2 + d^2}$$

Solve for θ:

$$\theta = 1/2\ cos^{-1} - h/\sqrt{h^2 + d^2} \qquad (56)$$

10. MOVEMENT IN A CIRCLE

Consider what happens when an object, such as an auto, is not moving in a straight line, but is following a curve that is an arc of a circle. From Exhibit 6 assume that it has a constant velocity of v on a circular path that is at a distance r (radius) from the center point Q. At point 1 the direction of motion, that is the velocity v_1, will be tangent to the circular path and at a right angle to the radius, r, at that point.

A short time later, say t sec later, the object will have moved to point 2 on the circle. The *magnitude* of velocity will be the same at point 2 as at point 1. But the *direction* will now have changed to that shown as v_2. The vector diagram in Exhibit 7 indicates the amount of change. With constant motion in a circle, the magnitudes of v_1 and v_2 are the same, but the directions are different. The quantity, v_3, would be the *change* in velocity of the object moving around the circular path from points 1 to 2 (the difference in motion from v_1 to v_2 in time t).

The angle θ between the radius at 1 and 2 is the same as the angle between v_1 and v_2. (This can be demonstrated by geometry.) The triangle between the radius at 1 and that at 2 in Exhibit 6 is similar to the triangle formed by v_1, v_2, and v_3 in Exhibit 7. (This also can be demonstrated by geometry.) From geometry, corresponding sides of similar triangles are proportional.

Then:

$$\frac{v_3}{v_1} = \frac{l}{r}$$

The l in the equation is the chord or straight line between points 1 and 2.

Divide each side of this equation by t:

$$\frac{l}{tr} = \frac{v_3}{tv_1} \qquad (57)$$

If the object moving around the circle goes the distance from point 1 to point 2 on the curved path, b, in t seconds, its velocity along the path will be $\frac{b}{t}$.

But for a short distance along the arc, b is approximately equal to the chord, l. Then the velocity $\frac{b}{t}$ will be approximately equal to the velocity $\frac{l}{t}$ which is equal to v_1.

Therefore:

$$\frac{b}{t} \cong \frac{l}{t} \cong v_1$$

Substitute v_1 for l/t in equation (57):

$$\frac{v_1}{r} \cong \frac{v_3}{tv_1}$$

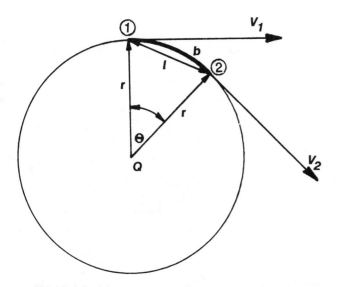

Exhibit 6. Quantities involved in circular motion.

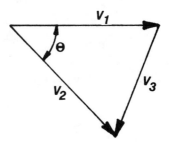

Exhibit 7. Vector diagram showing how velocity changes with circular motion.

The change in velocity v_3 per unit time, t, is v_3/t which is also equal to acceleration, a. Substitute into the equation a for v_3/t:

$$\frac{v_1}{r} \cong \frac{a}{v_1}$$

Multiply both sides of the equation by v_1 and reverse the equation to read:

$$a \cong \frac{v_1^2}{r}$$

As the time, t, gets shorter and shorter, the distance the object will travel will be less and less. Hence the difference between the arc, b, and the chord, l, gets less and less. Then a is essentially equal to v_1^2/r.

As the time, t, becomes infinitely small, that is, as it becomes 0, there will be no difference between arc, b, and chord, l. Then a will exactly equal v^2/r.

Thus, at any instant an object following a circular path is constantly changing its velocity by being accelerated toward the center of the circle. The amount of acceleration is given by:

$$a = \frac{v^2}{r} \qquad (58)$$

When an object, such as a vehicle, is making a turn, it tends to keep on going straight. (Newton's first law of motion.) To make a turn, there must be a force on the vehicle. The force that makes the vehicle turn is a sidewise force toward the center of the curve in which the vehicle is turning. This is called *centripetal* force and is due to the acceleration given in equation (58). Its equal and opposite reaction (Newton's third law of motion) is called the *centrifugal* force. The amount of centripetal force, and hence the amount of centrifugal force, can be calculated from equations (23) and (58):

$$F = ma \qquad (23)$$

$$a = \frac{v^2}{r} \qquad (58)$$

Substitute into equation (23) the value for a in equation (58):

$$F = \frac{mv^2}{r}$$

To simplify this equation, substitute into it the value for m from equation (26):

$$F = \frac{wv^2}{gr} \qquad (59)$$

The sidewise centripetal force that accelerates a vehicle toward the inside of a curve to make it turn a corner or follow the curve is produced by friction between tires and road and, in some cases, the weight of the vehicle. The centrifugal force tending to make the vehicle follow a straight line is produced by its velocity, weight, and radius of the curve. If the centrifugal force is less than the centripetal friction traction force between tire and road, the vehicle will make the turn. If the centrifugal force is greater than the centripetal traction force, the vehicle will start to sideslip and will not follow the curve intended.

The velocity at which the vehicle will just begin to slip is called *critical velocity*. It occurs when centrifugal force just equals the traction force. Exhibit 8 shows the forces on a vehicle rounding a superelevated (banked) curve to the left. In Exhibit 8, the centrifugal force is denoted by F_{cent}, with components $F_{cent\,y}$ for force along the sloped surface and $F_{cent\,z}$ for force perpendicular to the sloped surface. The frictional force is denoted by F_F. The total force pressing the vehicle against the surface is denoted by N. Finally, the total weight of the vehicle is denoted by w, with component w_y for weight along the sloped surface and w_z for weight perpendicular to the sloped surface.

Sum the forces perpendicular to the sloped surfaces:

$$+ \downarrow \Sigma F_z = 0 = F_{cent\,z} + w_z - N$$

Because the vehicle is in equilibrium:

$$N = w_z + F_{cent\,z} \qquad (60)$$

From trigonometry:

$$w_z = w \cos \theta$$

$$F_{cent\,z} = F_{cent} \sin \theta$$

Substitute into equation (60) these values for w_z and $F_{cent\,z}$:

$$N = w \cos\theta + F_{cent} \sin\theta \quad (61)$$

Sum the forces along the sloped surface:

$$\overset{+}{\rightarrow} \Sigma F_y = 0 = F_{cent\,y} - F_F - w_y$$

Because the vehicle is in equilibrium:

$$F_{cent\,y} = F_F + w_y$$

The frictional force, F_F, is due to the coefficient of friction, μ, and the force pressing the vehicle against the surface, N. Substitute into this equation $N\mu$ for F_F:

$$F_{cent\,y} = N\mu + w_y$$

From trigonometry:

$$w_y = w \sin\theta$$

$$F_{cent\,y} = F_{cent} \cos\theta$$

Substitute into equation (62) these values for w_y and $F_{cent\,y}$:

$$F_{cent} \cos\theta = \mu N + w \sin\theta$$

Substitute into this equation the value for N in equation (61)

$$F_{cent} \cos\theta = \mu (w \cos\theta + F_{cent} \sin\theta) + w \sin\theta$$

Rearrange the equation to make it read:

$$F_{cent} \cos\theta = \mu w \cos\theta + \mu F_{cent} \sin\theta + w \sin\theta$$

Divide both sides of the equation by $\cos\theta$ and cancel:

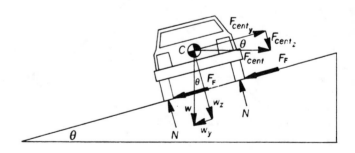

Exhibit 8. Forces on a vehicle rounding a superelevated curve to the left.

$$\frac{F_{cent}\,\cancel{cos\theta}}{\cancel{cos\theta}} = \frac{\mu\,w\,\cancel{cos\theta}}{\cancel{cos\theta}} + \frac{\mu\,F_{cent}\,sin\theta}{cos\theta} + \frac{w\,sin\,\theta}{cos\theta}$$

From trigonometry $\dfrac{sin\theta}{cos\theta}$ is $tan\theta$. Substitute this into the equation and subtract $\mu\,F_{cent}\,tan\theta$ and cancel:

$$F_{cent} - \mu\,F_{cent}\,tan\theta = \mu w + \cancel{\mu F_{cent}\,tan\theta} + w\,tan\theta - \cancel{\mu F_{cent}\,tan\theta}$$

Rearrange the equation to make it read:

$$F_{cent}\,(1 - \mu\,tan\theta) = w\,(\mu + tan\theta)$$

Divide both sides of the equation by $(1 - \mu\,tan\theta)$ and cancel:

$$\frac{F_{cent}\,\cancel{(1 - \mu\,tan\theta)}}{\cancel{(1 - \mu\,tan\theta)}} = \frac{w\,(\mu + tan\theta)}{(1 - \mu\,tan\theta)}$$

Substitute the value for F given in equation (59) into this equation for F_{cent} :

$$\frac{wv^2}{gr} = \frac{w\,(\mu + tan\theta)}{(1 - \mu\,tan\theta)}$$

Multiply both sides of the equation by gr/w and cancel:

$$\frac{\cancel{w}v^2}{\cancel{g}\cancel{r}}\,\frac{\cancel{g}\cancel{r}}{\cancel{w}} = \frac{\cancel{w}(\mu + tan\theta)}{(1 - \mu\,tan\theta)}\,\frac{gr}{\cancel{w}}$$

The tangent of angle θ, $tan\,\theta$, is equal to h/d, which is from equation (32) for grade, G (superelevation in this case). Substitute G into the equation for $tan\theta$:

$$v^2 = \frac{gr\,(\mu + G)}{(1 - \mu\,G)}$$

Take the square root of both sides of the equation:

$$v = \sqrt{\frac{gr\,(\mu + G)}{(1 - \mu\,G)}} \qquad (63)$$

If the superelevation, G, is small, as it is on nearly all curves, the factor $(1 - \mu\,G)$ and G are insignificant. Note G is positive for positive superelevation, the outside of curve higher than the inside, and negative for negative superelevation, the outside of curve lower than the inside of the curve, and zero for a level curve. If the effect of superelevation is completely ignored, the equation becomes:

$$v = \sqrt{gr\mu} \qquad (64)$$

11. GEOMETRIC EQUATIONS

Radius can be calculated from measurements of the chord and middle ordinate. Exhibit 9 shows a circle with radius r, chord l, and middle ordinate h. A right triangle is formed with r as the hypotenuse, $l/2$ as one side, and $r - h$ as the other side. The Pythagorean theorem states that the square of the hypotenuse of a right triangle is equal to the sum of the squares of the other two sides. From Exhibit 9 this is written:

$$r^2 = (l/2)^2 + (r - h)^2$$

Expand $(r - h)^2$:

$$r^2 = (l/2)^2 + r^2 - 2rh + h^2$$

Subtract r^2 from both sides of the equation, add $2rh$ to both sides of the equation and cancel:

$$\cancel{r^2} - \cancel{r^2} + 2rh = (l/2)^2 + \cancel{r^2} - \cancel{2rh} + h^2 + \cancel{2rh} - \cancel{r^2}$$

Divide both sides of the equation by $2h$ and cancel:

$$\cancel{2h}r\,/\,\cancel{2h} = \frac{\dfrac{l^2}{4}}{2h} + \frac{h^2}{2h}$$

Rearrange the equation to make it read:

$$r = \frac{l^2}{8h} + \frac{h}{2} \qquad (65)$$

Tangent offset method is a way to draw an arc with a large radius on a scale diagram. This method requires points to be plotted along the circumference of the circle and connected with a smooth curve. The points are plotted as offsets from a tangent to the curve. The offsets are at right angles to the tangent. The distance of the offsets from the tangent line can be calculated.

Exhibit 9 shows a line parallel to the chord of length x, starting from the intersection of the middle ordinate and the circle. The perpendicular distance from the end of this line to the circle is the offset, y. This distance, y, is equal to the middle ordinate, h, from equation (65):

$$r = \frac{l^2}{8h} + \frac{h}{2}$$

The term $h/2$ is very small, so it is removed to make the equation:

$$r = \frac{l^2}{8h}$$

The distance, x, is equal to half the length of the chord. Substitute into this equation $2x$ for l:

$$r = \frac{(2x)^2}{8h}$$

Multiply both sides of the equation by h/r and cancel:

$$\cancel{x}\frac{h}{\cancel{x}} = \frac{(2x)^2}{8\cancel{h}}\frac{\cancel{h}}{r}$$

Simplify the equation:

$$h = \frac{x^2}{2r}$$

Because h is equal to y, substitute y into the equation for h:

$$y = \frac{x^2}{2r} \qquad (66)$$

By removing the term $h/2$ initially, equation (66) gives only an approximation for the offset distance. A more accurate equation begins with equation (65):

$$r = \frac{l^2}{8h} + \frac{h}{2}$$

Substitute into this equation $2x$ for l and y for h:

$$r = \frac{(2x)^2}{8y} + \frac{y}{2}$$

Multiply both sides of the equation by $2y$ and cancel:

$$(r)\,(2y) = \frac{(x^2)}{2\cancel{y}}\,2\cancel{y} + \frac{(y)}{\cancel{2}}\,2\cancel{y}$$

$$2ry = x^2 + y^2$$

Subtract x^2 and $2ry$ from both sides of the equation and cancel:

$$2\cancel{ry} - 2\cancel{ry} - x^2 = \cancel{x^2} + y^2 - 2ry - \cancel{x^2}$$

$$-x^2 = y^2 - 2ry$$

Complete the square on the right side of the equation (divide the term $2ry$ by $2y$ to get r and square r). Add r^2 to both sides of the equation:

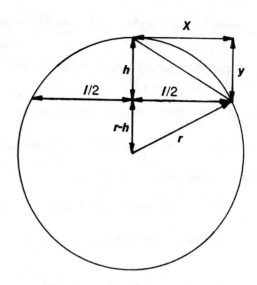

Exhibit 9. *Geometric relationships of a circle.*

$$r^2 - x^2 = r^2 - 2ry + y^2$$

The right side of the equation is now a perfect square:

$$r^2 - x^2 = (r - y)^2$$

Take the square root of both sides of the equation:

$$\sqrt{r^2 - x^2} = \sqrt{(r - y)^2}$$

Add y to both sides of the equation and cancel:

$$\sqrt{r^2 - x^2} + y = r - \cancel{y} + \cancel{y}$$

Subtract from both sides of the equation $\sqrt{r^2 - x^2}$ and cancel:

$$\cancel{\sqrt{r^2 - x^2}} + y - \cancel{\sqrt{r^2 - x^2}} = r - \sqrt{r^2 - x^2}$$

This leaves the equation for the tangent offset:

$$y = r - \sqrt{r^2 - x^2} \qquad (67)$$

12. VEHICLE CENTER OF MASS

There are times when it is important to know the location of a vehicle's center of mass (center of gravity). The center of mass is a point at which the entire mass of a body may be considered concentrated. If a body is supported at the center of mass, it will balance without tipping one way or another. It may be necessary to locate the center of mass longitudinally and laterally. In some cases the height of the center of mass is also of interest.

Longitudinal Position of Center of Mass

To locate the center of mass of a vehicle lengthwise, weigh each axle separately on a level platform. The total weight of the vehicle w is, of course, the sum of the weight on the rear axle, w_r, and the weight on the front axle, w_f.

Then, referring to Exhibit 10, equal moments about the point P_f are clockwise = counterclockwise:

$$wl_f = w_r l$$

Divide both sides of the equation by w and cancel:

$$\frac{\cancel{w}l_f}{\cancel{w}} = \frac{w_r l}{w}$$

This is the equation for finding the distance the center of mass is from the front axle:

$$l_f = \frac{w_r l}{w} \qquad (68)$$

Likewise, with moments about point P_r, where the rear wheels touch the road, the clockwise moments equal the counterclockwise moments:

$$w_f l = w l_r$$

Divide both sides of the equation by w, and cancel. This is the equation for the distance the center of mass is from the rear axle:

$$l_r = \frac{w_f l}{w} \qquad (69)$$

Naturally the total wheelbase is equal to the sum of the two distances, in other words:

$$l = l_r + l_f \qquad (70)$$

In some calculations it is simpler to express the location of the center of mass as a decimal fraction, x, of the wheelbase, l, in the equation. This is expressed by the equations:

$$x_r = \frac{l_r}{l} \qquad (71)$$

$$x_f = \frac{l_f}{l} \qquad (72)$$

Lateral Location

The lateral (transverse, crosswise) position of the center of mass of a vehicle can likewise be determined by weighing the two sides of the vehicle separately and using the track width. Usually, however, the center of mass is so close to the

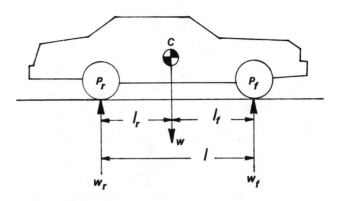

Exhibit 10. *Relationships involved in equation for determining longitudinal position of the center of mass of a vehicle.*

longitudinal (lengthwise) center line of the vehicle that calculations are unnecessary.

Naturally the loading of a vehicle may make the weight on one side or one end more than on the other side or end. In that case, the center of mass of the vehicle as loaded will be different from the center of mass of the vehicle empty.

Height of Center of Mass

In addition to the data w, w_f, and l needed to determine the longitudinal (lengthwise) position of the center of mass of a vehicle, two other measurements are required to determine the height of the center of mass: 1) the weight, w_h, on one axle with the other axle hoisted; and 2) the height, h, to which the other axle is hoisted for this weighing. For the following explanation assume that the *rear* axle is hoisted.

Exhibit 11 is a diagram of a vehicle hoisted for weighing to determine the height of its center of mass. In this diagram, following conventions of geometry, a pair of letters connected by a vinculum, for instance $\overline{AB}$, represent the distance between the two points marked A and B in the geometric diagram. The pair of letters does not represent A times B, the product of the two letters, A and B.

In Exhibit 11, the distance the center of mass is from the line $\overline{AE}$ between the axles is represented by $\overline{CT}$. This distance must be calculated to determine the height of the center of mass above the ground.

In Exhibit 11, note that there are three similar triangles designated by letters at their corners: $\triangle AUE$, $\triangle AGB$, and $\triangle CTB$. The triangles are similar because they have equal angles, one of which is a right angle. In similar triangles, corresponding sides are proportional. Thus, in Exhibit 11, the hypotenuse $\overline{AB}$ of $\triangle AGB$ divided by its long side, $\overline{AG}$, is exactly equal to the hypotenuse, $\overline{AE}$, of $\triangle AUE$, divided by its long side, $\overline{AU}$.

Thus:

$$\frac{\overline{AB}}{\overline{AG}} = \frac{\overline{AE}}{\overline{AU}}$$

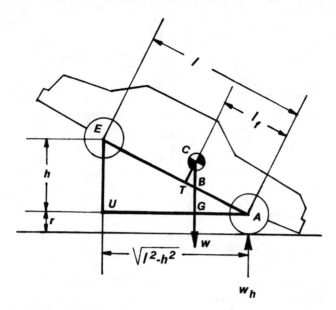

Exhibit 11. *Relationships involved in equation for determining height of the center of mass of a vehicle.*

Multiply both sides of the equation by $\overline{AG}$ and cancel:

$$\overline{AB} = \frac{\overline{AE}\,\overline{AG}}{\overline{AU}} \qquad (73)$$

From Exhibit 11:

$$\overline{AT} = \overline{AB} + \overline{BT}$$

Therefore:

$$\overline{BT} = \overline{AT} - \overline{AB}$$

Substitute into this equation the value for $\overline{AB}$ from equation (73):

$$\overline{BT} = \overline{AT} - \frac{\overline{AE}\,\overline{AG}}{\overline{AU}} \qquad (74)$$

Again from Exhibit 11 and similar triangles:

$$\frac{\overline{CT}}{\overline{BT}} = \frac{\overline{AU}}{\overline{EU}}$$

Multiply both sides of the equation by $\overline{BT}$ and cancel:

$$\overline{CT} = \frac{\overline{AU}\,\overline{BT}}{\overline{EU}}$$

Substitute into this equation the value for $\overline{BT}$ in equation (74):

$$\overline{CT} = \frac{\overline{AU}}{\overline{EU}}\left(\overline{AT} - \frac{\overline{AE}\,\overline{AG}}{\overline{AU}}\right) \qquad (75)$$

The distances represented by the line segments in this equation can be stated in terms of measurements of the vehicle being weighed to determine the height of its center of mass as illustrated in Exhibit 11.

$\overline{AE} = $ the wheel base, l, of the vehicle.

$\overline{EU} = $ the height, h, that the rear axle is lifted.

$\overline{AU} = $ the distance $\sqrt{l^2 - h^2}$ (This is from the Pythagorean theorem applied to $\triangle AUE$ with hypotenuse, l, and one side, h.)

$\overline{AT} = $ the distance from the front axle to the center of mass, l_f, which is equal to $\dfrac{lw_r}{w}$.

$\overline{AG} = $ the distance, $\dfrac{\sqrt{l^2 - h^2}\,(w - w_h)}{w}$,

of the center of mass from the front axle when the vehicle is hoisted. With the rear end hoisted the wheelbase is "shortened" to $\sqrt{l^2 - h^2}$. The weight is increased from w_f to w_h, making the weight on the rear axle $w_r = w - w_h$.

Substitute these values into equation (75):

$$\overline{CT} = \left[\frac{\sqrt{l^2 - h^2}}{h}\right]\left[\frac{lw_r}{w} - l\frac{\sqrt{l^2 - h^2}\,(w - w_h)}{w\sqrt{l^2 - h^2}}\right]$$

Combine terms on the right:

$$\overline{CT} = \left[\frac{\sqrt{l^2 - h^2}}{h}\right]\left[\frac{lw_r\sqrt{l^2 - h^2} - l\sqrt{l^2 - h^2}\,(w - w_h)}{w\sqrt{l^2 - h^2}}\right]$$

Cancel $\sqrt{l^2 - h^2}$ where possible:

$$\overline{CT} = \left[\frac{\sqrt{l^2 - h^2}}{h}\right]\left[\frac{lw_r - l\,(w - w_h)}{w}\right]$$

Rearrange the equation to make it read:

$$\overline{CT} = \left[\frac{\sqrt{l^2 - h^2}}{h} \right] \left[\frac{l\,(w_r - w + w_h)}{w} \right]$$

Because $w - w_r = w_f$, substitute $- w_f$ into the equation for $w_r - w$ and rearrange it to make it read:

$$\overline{CT} = \frac{l\,\sqrt{l^2 - h^2}\,(w_h - w_f)}{hw}$$

Note that $\overline{CT}$ is the distance that the center of mass is above the level of the two axles, not the distance above the ground. The height of the center of mass, above the ground, is l_z. Add the tire-wheel radius, r, to the equation:

$$l_z = \frac{l\,\sqrt{l^2 - h^2}\,(w_h - w_f)}{hw} + r \qquad (76)$$

The height of the center of mass as a decimal fraction of the wheelbase is z. This is expressed in the equation:

$$z = \frac{l_z}{l} \qquad (77)$$

Combined Center of Mass of Vehicle and Load

Referring to Exhibit 12, the center of mass of the venicle, C_v, is the distance, l_{fv}, behind the front axle. The center of mass of the load at C_b is the distance, l_{fb}, behind the front axle. The center of mass of the load can be behind the rear axle if l_{fb} is greater than the wheelbase, l. In Exhibit 12, w_b is the weight of load, w_v is the weight of the vehicle, and w_t is the total weight. From this it can be seen that:

$$w_t = w_v + w_b$$

The combined moments of the vehicle and load about point P_f, the point where the front tires touch the surface, are as follows:

$l_{fb}w_b$ clockwise, therefore positive,
$l_{fv}w_v$ clockwise, therefore positive;
lw_r counterclockwise, therefore negative;

These all sum to zero, therefore:

$$l_{fb}w_b + l_{fv}w_v - lw_r = 0$$

or

$$l_{fb}w_b + l_{fv}w_v = lw_r \qquad (78)$$

But the total weight at the combined center of mass also gives the following moments:

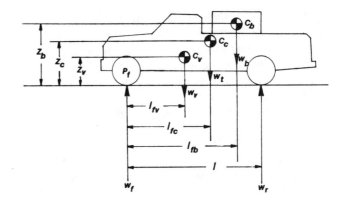

Exhibit 12. *Relationships involved in equation for determining combined center of mass and load.*

$l_{fc}w_t$ clockwise, therefore positive
lw_r counterclockwise, therefore negative

These both sum to zero, therefore:

$$l_{fc}w_t - lw_r = 0$$

or:

$$l_{fc}w_t = lw_r$$

This equation and equation (78) are both equal to lw_r, therefore they are equal to each other:

$$l_{fb}w_b + l_{fv}w_v = l_{fc}w_t$$

Solve this equation for l_{fc} by dividing both sides by w_t:

$$l_{fc} = \frac{l_{fb}w_b + l_{fv}w_v}{w_t} \qquad (79)$$

If more than one load is involved, or if parts of a load are treated separately, the product of the weight of each load times the distance of its center of mass behind the front axle is added to the weight of the vehicle times the distance of the vehicle's center of mass behind the front axle; and this sum is divided by the combined weight of vehicle and loads. That gives the distance that the joint center of mass is behind the front axle.

The height of the combined center of mass of vehicle and load is obtained in the same way as its longitudinal position is obtained. The height of the center of mass of the load times its weight is added to the height of the center of mass of the vehicle times its weight, and the sum is divided by the combined weight of vehicle and load. Thus:

$$l_{zc} = \frac{l_{zv}w_v + l_{zb}w_b}{w_t} \qquad (80)$$

If there is more than one load, the product of the weight of each load times the height of its center of mass are all added to the vehicle weight times the height of the vehicle's center of mass, and the sum so obtained is divided by the total weight of vehicle and loads. This gives the height of the combined center of mass.

The combined center of mass of vehicle and load lies along a straight line between the center of mass of the load and that of the vehicle.

Often the center of mass of an irregular load can best be located by considering the parts of the load as separate loads and combining their centers of mass.

If the load is clearly not centered crosswise of the vehicle, the transverse location of the center of mass and load must be obtained in a similar manner. This is usually unimportant in vehicle-slowing problems but may be important in rollover problems.

13. RESULTANT DRAG FACTOR FOR SINGLE VEHICLE

When all wheels slide, the whole vehicle slides. No part of its weight is carried by rolling wheels. Then the rate of slowing (on a level surface) is determined entirely by the coefficient of friction between the tires and the road surface. The drag factor equals the coefficient of friction.

When not all wheels slide, the drag factor of the sliding wheels is equal to the coefficient of friction of the sliding wheels (if on a level surface); but the drag factors of the wheels which are not locked are not equal to the coefficient of friction of tire and road for those wheels. Thus, when all wheels are not locked, the total retarding force against the vehicle which makes it lose velocity is the sum of the weight or load on each wheel times the drag factor for that wheel. Then the resultant drag factor for the whole vehicle is total retarding force divided by the total weight of the vehicle.

The weight or load on each axle when a vehicle is slowing is not the same as when the vehicle is standing or moving at a constant speed. When the road puts a drag on the vehicle's tires to slow it, the vehicle tends to keep on going. This makes front wheels press down on the road more than when the vehicle is standing. The rear wheels press down on the road less by the same amount; thus, there is a weight shift from rear to front in slowing. There is a corresponding shift from front to rear when the vehicle accelerates. The greater the rate of acceleration, the greater the weight shift.

A general equation is derived for resultant total drag factor when the drag factors of axles differ. This derivation requires consideration of the weight shift in slowing. The road surface is assumed to be level. If there is a slope, each level drag factor is increased or decreased by the amount of the slope.

Symbols for quantities used in this derivation are listed in Exhibit 1. Refer to Exhibit 13 for the arrangement of these quantities relative to the vehicle.

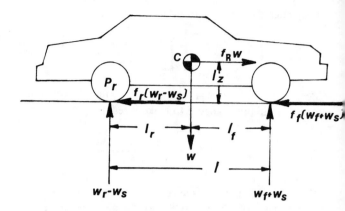

Exhibit 13. *Relationships involved in equations for determining resultant braking when drag factor is different for front and rear axles.*

To compute the total resultant drag factor, f_R, when the drag factor on the front axle, f_f, is different from that on the rear, f_r, the following additional data are needed:

x_r = the horizontal distance of the center of mass from the rear axle as a decimal fraction of the wheelbase of the vehicle given in equation (71):

$$x_r = \frac{l_r}{l} \qquad (71)$$

x_f = the horizontal distance of the center of mass from the front axle as a decimal fraction of the wheelbase of the vehicle given in equation (72):

$$x_f = \frac{l_f}{l} \qquad (72)$$

z = the height of the center of mass as a decimal fraction of the wheelbase of the vehicle given in equation (77):

$$z = \frac{l_z}{l} \qquad (77)$$

The derivation is accomplished by relating two equations:

1) The equation for the weight shift, w_s, from rear to front in slowing; and
2) The equation for total retarding force, $f_R w$, as the sum of the retarding forces on each axle.

The load on each axle has two components: 1) the static (standing) weight on the axle; and 2) the load, w_s, shifted from the rear to the front axle in slowing. Refer to Exhibit 13.

Weight Shift, w_s, is obtained by taking moments about point P_r, the point the rear tires touch the ground, and setting this equal to zero.

$$(w_f + w_s)\, l - wl_r - f_R wl_z = 0$$

Divide both sides of the equation by l:

$$\frac{(w_f + w_s)}{l}\, l - \frac{wl_r}{l} - \frac{f_R wl_z}{l} = 0$$

Cancel and substitute x_r and z where appropriate:

$$w_f + w_s - wx_r - f_R wz = 0$$

Solve the equation for w_s:

$$w_s = wx_r + f_R wz - w_f \qquad (81)$$

From equation (71):

$$x_r = \frac{l_r}{l} \qquad (71)$$

From equation (69):

$$l_r = \frac{w_f l}{w} \qquad (69)$$

Substituting l_r from equation (69) into equation (71) gives:

$$x_r = \frac{\dfrac{w_f l}{w}}{l} = \frac{w_f}{w} \qquad (82)$$

Substitute this value for x_r into equation (81):

$$w_s = \frac{w\, w_f}{w} + f_R wz - w_f$$

Cancel:

$$w_s = f_R wz \qquad (83)$$

This is the amount of weight shift from rear to front in slowing.

Total retarding force, $f_R w$, is the sum of the retarding forces on the axles:

$$f_R w = f_f\, (w_f + w_s) + f_r\, (w_r - w_s)$$

Perform the indicated multiplications

$$f_R w = f_f\, w_f + f_f w_s + f_r\, w_r - f_r w_s$$

Regroup terms containing w_s:

$$f_R w = (f_f\, w_s - f_r w_s) + f_f\, w_f + f_r w_r$$

or

$$f_R w = (f_f - f_r)\, w_s + f_f\, w_f + f_r w_r$$

Substitute the value for w_s from equation (83) into this equation:

$$f_R w = (f_f - f_r)\, f_R wz + f_f\, w_f + f_r w_r \qquad (84)$$

From equation (82):

$$x_r = \frac{w_f}{w} \text{ or } w_f = x_r w$$

Similarly:

$$x_f = \frac{w_r}{w} \text{ or } w_r = x_f w$$

Substitute these values for w_r and w_f into equation (84):

$$w f_R = (f_f - f_r)\, f_R wz + f_f\, x_r\, w + f_r\, x_f\, w$$

Divide both sides of the equation by w:

$$f_R = (f_f - f_r)\, f_R z + f_f\, x_r + f_r\, x_f$$

Subtract from both sides of the equation $(f_f - f_r)\, f_R z$:

$$f_R - (f_f - f_r)\, f_R z = f_f\, x_r + f_r\, x_f$$

Regroup the terms containing f_R:

$$f_R \left[1 - (f_f - f_r)\, z \right] = f_f\, x_r + f_r\, x_f$$

Divide both sides of the equation by $1 - (f_f - f_r)\, z$:

$$f_R = \frac{f_f\, x_r + f_r\, x_f}{1 - z\, (f_f - f_r)} \qquad (85)$$

Because $x_f + x_r = 1$:

$$x_r = 1 - x_f$$

Substitute this into equation (85):

$$f_R = \frac{f_f(1 - x_f) + f_r\, x_f}{1 - z\,(f_f - f_r)}$$

Multiply $(1 - x_f)$ by f_f:

$$f_R = \frac{f_f - f_f\, x_f + f_r\, x_f}{1 - z\,(f_f - f_r)}$$

Rearrange the equation to make it read:

$$f_R = \frac{f_f + f_r\, x_f - f_f\, x_f}{1 - z\,(f_f - f_r)}$$

Combine terms with x_f and rearrange the equation to make it read:

$$f_R = \frac{f_f - x_f\,(f_f - f_r)}{1 - z\,(f_f - f_r)} \quad (86)$$

14. CONSERVATION OF MOMENTUM

The derivation of conservation of momentum can be done by looking at a simple collision. Exhibit 14 shows two bodies before, during and after a collision. The symbols $\triangle P_1$ and $\triangle P_2$ stand for the change in momentum of bodies 1 and 2; m_1 and m_2 stand for the mass of bodies 1 and 2; v_1 and v_2 stand for the velocity before the collision of bodies 1 and 2; and v_1' and v_2' are the after-collision velocities of bodies 1 and 2.

In most collisions the mass is the same after collision as it was before. Therefore, the velocity change is what changes the momentum. The change in momentum for bodies 1 and 2 can be written as follows:

$$\triangle P_1 = m_1 v_1' - m_1 v_1$$

$$\triangle P_2 = m_2 v_2' - m_2 v_2$$

The change in momentum of body 1 was caused by the force of body 2 on body 1 for the time, t, of the collision. Thus:

$$F_{2\text{ on }1}\, t = \triangle P_1 = m_1 v_1' - m_1 v_1 \quad (87)$$

The change in momentum of body 2 was caused by the force of body 1 on body 2 for the time, t, of the collision. Thus:

$$F_{1\text{ on }2}\, t = \triangle P_2 = m_2 v_2' - m_2 v_2 \quad (88)$$

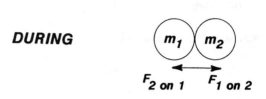

Exhibit 14. Motion of two bodies before, during and after a collision.

The total change in momentum is the sum of the change in momentum of both bodies 1 and 2. Add equations (87) and (88) together:

$$(F_{2\text{ on }1} t) + (F_{1\text{ on }2} t) = \quad (89)$$
$$(m_1 v_1' - m_1 v_1) + (m_2 v_2' - m_2 v_2)$$

According to Newton's third law of motion, these forces are equal and opposite. Thus their sums must be zero:

$$F_{2\text{ on }1} + F_{1\text{ on }2} = 0$$

This makes the left side of equation (89) zero:

$$0 = (m_1 v_1' - m_1 v_1) + (m_2 v_2' - m_2 v_2)$$

Rewritten, this equation becomes:

$$m_1 v_1 + m_2 v_2 = m_1 v_1' + m_2 v_2' \quad (90)$$

For accident reconstruction purposes equation (90) is often rewritten with m being replaced by w. This can be done because from equation (26):

$$m = \frac{w}{g}$$

Substituting into equation (90):

$$\frac{w_1}{g} v_1 + \frac{w_2}{g} v_2 = \frac{w_1}{g} v_1' + \frac{w_2}{g} v_2'$$

Multiply both sides by g to get

$$w_1 v_1 + w_2 v_2 = w_1 v'_1 + w_2 v'_2 \quad (91)$$

Because momentum is a vector quantity, its direction as well as its magnitude must be taken into consideration. Although equations (90) and (91) are correct, they only imply direction. The next derivation will be equations that consider both direction and magnitude directly in momentum problems.

For the momentum equations derived here to work, three rules must be followed:

1) Whichever vehicle is represented by vehicle 1 *must* be on the x-axis. This makes the approach angle of vehicle 1, θ_1, *always* equal to 0° or 180°.

2) All angles must be measured *from* the positive x-axis *counterclockwise*, with the tail of the vectors representing the first contact and after-impact momentum of each vehicle at the origin. Exhibit 15 gives an example of the proper angle measurement. Note that the vectors representing the approach of each vehicle must be moved or the measurement taken at their tail.

3) The equation for the velocity of vehicle 2 at first contact must be solved first. This is because the value is used in the equation for the velocity of vehicle 1 at first contact.

Using Exhibit 15 as a reference, for each vehicle, divide the problem into first contact momentum for the $x-$ and $y-$ direction. The symbol P is used for momentum. In the rest of this topic, P is used to denote the product of weight and velocity. Normally P represents the product of mass and velocity.

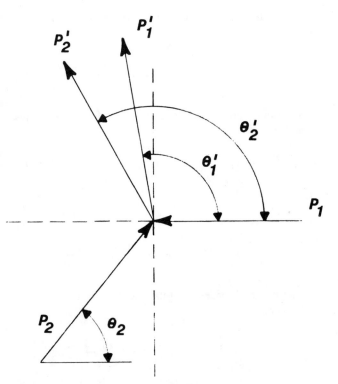

Exhibit 15. *Required coordinate system in order to use the momentum equations.*

Vehicle 1 at first contact:

$x-$ direction $\quad P_{1x} = P_1\,cos\,\theta_1 = w_1v_1\,cos\,\theta_1$ (92)

$y-$ direction $\quad P_{1y} = P_1\,sin\,\theta_1 = w_1v_1\,sin\,\theta_1$ (93)

Vehicle 2 at first contact:

$x-$ direction $\quad P_{2x} = P_2\,cos\,\theta_2 = w_2v_2\,cos\,\theta_2$ (94)

$y-$ direction $\quad P_{2y} = P_2\,sin\,\theta_2 = w_2v_2\,sin\,\theta_2$ (95)

For each vehicle, divide the problem into after impact momentum for the $x-$ and $y-$ directions.

$x-$ direction $\quad P_1'_x = P_1'\,cos\,\theta_1' = w_1v_1'\,cos\,\theta_1'$ (96)

$y-$ direction $\quad P_1'_y = P_1'\,sin\,\theta_1' = w_1v_1'\,sin\,\theta_1'$ (97)

Vehicle 2 at after impact:

$x-$ direction $\quad P_2'_x = P_2'\,cos\,\theta_2' = w_2v_2'\,cos\,\theta_2'$ (98)

$y-$ direction $\quad P_2'_y = P_2'\,sin\,\theta_2' = w_2v_2'\,sin\,\theta_2'$ (99)

The total first contact momentum in the $x-$ and $y-$ directions equals the total after-impact momentum in the $x-$ and $y-$ directions. The total first contact momentum in the $x-$ direction is the sum of equations (92) and (94):

$$P_{1x} + P_{2x} = w_1v_1\,cos\,\theta_1 + w_2v_2\,cos\,\theta_2 \quad (100)$$

The total after-impact momentum in the $x-$ direction is the sum of equations (96) and (98):

$$P_1'_x + P_2'_x = w_1v_1'\,cos\,\theta_1' + w_2v_2'\,cos\,\theta_2'$$

This equation and equation (100) are equal:

$$w_1v_1\,cos\,\theta_1 + w_2v_2\,cos\,\theta_2 = w_1v_1'\,cos\,\theta_1' + w_2v_2'\,cos\,\theta_2'$$

Solve this equation for v_1:

$$v_1 = \frac{w_1v_1'\,cos\,\theta_1' + w_2v_2'\,cos\,\theta_2' - w_2v_2\,cos\,\theta_2}{w_1\,cos\,\theta_1} \quad (101)$$

This is the equation for the velocity of vehicle 1 at first contact. The total momentum at first contact in the $y-$ direction is the sum of equations (93) and (95):

$$P_{1y} + P_{2y} = w_1v_1\,sin\,\theta_1 + w_2v_2\,sin\,\theta_2 \quad (102)$$

The total after-impact momentum in the $y-$ direction is the sum of equation (97) and (99):

$$P_1{'}_y + P_2{'}_y = w_1 v_1{'} \sin\theta_1{'} + w_2 v_2{'} \sin\theta_2{'}$$

This equation and equation (102) are equal:

$$w_1 v_1 \sin\theta_1 + w_2 v_2 \sin\theta_2 = w_1 v_1{'} \sin\theta_1{'} + w_2 v_2{'} \sin\theta_2{'}$$

Solve this equation for v_2:

$$v_2 = \frac{w_1 v_1{'} \sin\theta_1{'} + w_2 v_2{'} \sin\theta_2{'} - w_1 v_1 \sin\theta_1}{w_2 \sin\theta_2} \quad (103)$$

The first contact approach angle for vehicle 1, θ_1, is always $0°$ or $180°$, which has the sine of 0. Therefore, $w_1 v_1 \sin\theta_1$ is equal to zero and cancels from the equation:

$$v_2 = \frac{w_1 v_1{'} \sin\theta_1{'} + w_2 v_2{'} \sin\theta_2{'}}{w_2 \sin\theta_2} \quad (104)$$

This is the equation for the velocity of vehicle 2 at first contact.

15. SAME-DIRECTION IN-LINE COLLISION

In a same-direction in-line collision, the relative velocity or closing velocity is important. The relative velocity is how much faster the rear vehicle is going than the front vehicle. This is represented by:

$$v_c = v_r - v_f \quad (105)$$

Where v_c is the closing velocity, v_r is the velocity of the rear vehicle (faster) and v_f is the velocity of the front vehicle (slower). From momentum equation (91):

$$w_1 v_1 + w_2 v_2 = w_1 v_1{'} + w_2 v_2{'} \quad (91)$$

Change vehicle 1 to the rear vehicle and vehicle 2 to the front vehicle:

$$w_r v_r + w_f v_f = w_r v_r{'} + w_f v{'}_f \quad (106)$$

The nature of this type of collision results in a full impact which means both vehicles attain the same velocity immediately after impact. Therefore:

$$v_r{'} = v_f{'} = v{'} \quad (107)$$

Substitute this value into equation (106) and rearrange it to make it read:

$$w_r v_r + w_f v_f = v{'} (w_r + w_f)$$

Solve this equation for $v{'}$:

$$v{'} = \frac{w_r v_r + w_f v_f}{w_r + w_f} \quad (108)$$

An energy equation similar to the momentum equation (106) can be written:

$$KE_r + KE_f = E_d + KE_r{'} + KE_f{'}$$

Where KE_r and KE_f are the kinetic energies for the rear and front vehicles at first contact, respectively. $KE_r{'}$ and $KE_f{'}$ are the after-impact kinetic energies for the rear and front vehicles, respectively. E_d is the total energy due to damage to both vehicles.

Substitute into this equation the value for KE from equation (25):

$$1/2\, m_r v_r{}^2 + 1/2\, m_f v_f{}^2 = E_d + 1/2\, m_r (v{'}_r)^2 + 1/2\, m_f (v{'}_f)^2$$

Substitute into this equation the value for $v_r{'}$ and $v_f{'}$ from equation (107):

$$1/2\, m_r v_r{}^2 + 1/2\, m_f v_f{}^2 = E_d + 1/2\, m_r (v{'})^2 + 1/2\, m_f (v{'})^2$$

Multiply both sides of this equation by 2:

$$m_r v_r{}^2 + m_f v_f{}^2 = 2E_d + m_r (v{'})^2 + m_f (v{'})^2$$

Rearrange to make the equation read:

$$m_r v_r{}^2 + m_f v_f{}^2 = 2E_d + (v{'})^2 (m_r + m_f)$$

Substitute into this equation the value for m from equation (26):

$$\frac{w_r}{g} v_r{}^2 + \frac{w_f}{g} v_f{}^2 = 2E_d + (v{'})^2 \frac{(w_r + w_f)}{g}$$

Substitute into this equation the value for $v{'}$ from equation (108):

$$\frac{w_r v_r{}^2}{g} + \frac{w_f v_f{}^2}{g} = 2E_d + \frac{(w_r v_r + w_f v_f)^2 (w_r + w_f)}{(w_r + w_f)^2 g}$$

Cancel:

$$\frac{w_r v_r{}^2}{g} + \frac{w_f v_f{}^2}{g} = 2E_d + \frac{(w_r v_r + w_f v_f)^2}{(w_r + w_f) g}$$

Multiply both sides of this equation by $(w_r + w_f) g$ and cancel:

$$(w_r + w_f)(w_r v_r{}^2 + w_f v_f{}^2) = 2E_d g (w_r + w_f) + (w_r v_r + w_f v_f)^2$$

Multiply:

$$w_r^2v_r^2 + w_rw_fv_r^2 + w_fw_rv_f^2 + w_f^2v_f^2 =$$
$$2E_dg\ (w_r + w_f) + w_r^2v_r^2 + 2w_rw_fv_rv_f + w_f^2v_f^2$$

Simplify by cancelling like terms:

$$w_rw_fv_r^2 + w_fw_rv_f^2 = 2E_dg\ (w_r + w_f) + 2w_rw_fv_rv_f$$

Subtract $2w_rw_fv_rv_f$ from both sides of the equation and cancel:

$$w_rw_fv_r^2 - 2w_rw_fv_fv_r + w_fw_rv_f^2 = 2E_dg\ (w_r + w_f)$$

Factor the left side of the equation:

$$w_rw_f\ (v_r^2 - 2v_fv_r + v_f^2) = 2E_dg\ (w_r + w_f)$$

or

$$w_rw_f\ (v_r - v_f)^2 = 2E_dg\ (w_r + w_f)$$

Substitute the value for $(v_r - v_f)$ from equation (105):

$$w_r\ w_fv_c^2 = 2E_dg\ (w_r + w_f)$$

Solve this equation for v_c:

$$v_c = \sqrt{\frac{2E_dg\ (w_r + w_f)}{(w_r\ w_f)}} \qquad (109)$$

Recall from before the equation:

$$w_r\ v_r + w_f\ v_f = v'\ (w_r + w_f)$$

Which came from equations (106) and (107):

From equation (105), $v_c = v_r - v_f$, therefore $v_f = v_r - v_c$.
Substitute this value into the equation:

$$w_r\ v_r + w_f(v_r - v_c) = v'\ (w_r + w_f)$$

Multiply the left side of the equation:

$$w_r\ v_r + w_f\ v_r - w_f\ v_c = v'\ (w_r + w_f)$$

Add $w_f\ v_c$ to both sides of the equation and cancel:

$$w_r\ v_r + w_f\ v_r = v'\ (w_r + w_f) + w_f\ v_c$$

Rearrange the equation to make it read:

$$v_r\ (w_r + w_f) = v'\ (w_r + w_f) + w_f\ v_c$$

Divide both sides of the equation by $(w_r + w_f)$:

$$v_r = \frac{v'\ (w_r + w_f)}{(w_r + w_f)} + \frac{w_f\ v_c}{(w_r + w_f)}$$

Cancel:

$$v_r = v' + \frac{w_f\ v_c}{(w_r + w_f)} \qquad (110)$$

Some words of caution concerning these equations and their use:

1. E_d is the total energy due to damage; i.e., this includes energy "used" in damaging both vehicles.
2. It is assumed that a straight in-line collision occurs; i.e., the cars come together and move off in a straight line.

16. SPECIAL-CASE EQUATIONS

Many equations that have been used in traffic accident reconstruction are limited to only certain situations. For example, equations have been developed that only apply if a vehicle is accelerated from or decelerated to a stop. In many instances these equations are misused because the "to or from a stop" condition did not exist. Other equations have been used that give an answer for speed directly in mi/hr. This result may be used in another equation where the units for velocity (speed) must be ft/sec instead of mi/hr. For the beginning student in accident reconstruction, this can be confusing.

The equations derived thus far in this topic have not been these "special" case conditions. The equations are equally appropriate for metric or U.S.A. units as long as the appropriate units are consistently used. (For example, distance in U.S.A. units is always feet, while in metric units it is always meters). There is, however, some interest no doubt still in these "special" case equations. Generally, the use of these equations is *discouraged* because they create more problems by increasing the number of equations and their limited use. The derivations of a few of these equations are included because of their past use.

Velocity (speed) slide to a stop in mi/hr and km/hr

The following equation can only be used to calculate the velocity of a vehicle if it slid to a stop. The answer is given in miles per hour. Begin with equation (20):

$$v_i = \sqrt{v_e^2 - 2ad} \qquad (20)$$

The vehicle is decelerating, therefore a is negative, making the equation:

$$v_i = \sqrt{v_e^2 + 2ad}$$

The end velocity, v_e, of the vehicle is 0, therefore:

$$v_i = \sqrt{2ad}$$

Substitute into this equation the value for a from equation (30):

$$v_i = \sqrt{2gfd}$$

Substitute into this equation the value for g from equation (31):

$$v_i = \sqrt{(2)(32.2)fd} \qquad \text{U.S.A. units}$$

$$v_i = \sqrt{(2)(9.81)fd} \qquad \text{metric units}$$

Multiply:

$$v_i = \sqrt{64.4\,fd} \qquad \text{U.S.A. units}$$

$$v_i = \sqrt{19.62\,fd} \qquad \text{metric units}$$

Take the square root of 64.4 or 19.62:

$$v_i = 8.02\sqrt{df} \qquad \text{U.S.A.}$$

$$v_i = 4.43\sqrt{df} \qquad \text{metric}$$

Multiply both sides of the equation by equation (5) or equation (7) to get S *(mi/hr or km/hr)*:

$$S = 5.47\sqrt{df} \qquad \text{U.S.A.} \qquad (111)$$

$$S = 15.9\sqrt{df} \qquad \text{metric} \qquad (112)$$

An alternative derivation begins with equation (21):

$$W = Fd \qquad (21)$$

Substitute into equation (21) the value KE in equation (25) for W:

$$1/2\,m\,v^2 = Fd$$

Substitute into this equation the value for m from equation (26):

$$\frac{1/2\,w\,v^2}{g} = Fd$$

Substitute into this equation the value for F from equation (28):

$$\frac{1/2\,w\,v^2}{g} = fwd$$

Multiply both sides of the equation by $\frac{2g}{w}$ and cancel:

$$v^2 = 2gfd$$

Take the square root of both sides of the equation:

$$v = \sqrt{2gfd}$$

Substitute into this equation the value for g from equation (31):

$$v = \sqrt{(2)(32.2)fd} \qquad \text{U.S.A. units}$$

$$v = \sqrt{(2)(9.81)fd} \qquad \text{metric units}$$

Multiply and take the square root:

$$v = 8.02\sqrt{df} \qquad \text{U.S.A.}$$

$$v = 4.43\sqrt{df} \qquad \text{metric}$$

Multiply both sides of this equation by equation (5) or equation (7):

$$S = 5.47\sqrt{df} \qquad \text{U.S.A.} \qquad (111)$$

$$S = 15.9\sqrt{df} \qquad \text{metric} \qquad (112)$$

An equation for f can easily be found by solving equations (111) and (112) for f. Square both sides of the equation:

$$S^2 = 29.9\,df \qquad \text{U.S.A.}$$

$$S^2 = 252.8\,df \qquad \text{metric}$$

Divide both sides of this equation by 29.9d or 252.8d:

$$f = \frac{S^2}{29.9d} \text{ or } f = \frac{S^2}{30d} \qquad \text{U.S.A.} \qquad (113)$$

$$f = \frac{S^2}{252.8d} \text{ or } f = \frac{S^2}{253d} \qquad \text{metric} \qquad (114)$$

An equation for d can be found by solving equations (113) and (114) for d:

$$d = \frac{S^2}{30f} \qquad \text{U.S.A} \qquad (115)$$

$$d = \frac{S^2}{253f} \qquad \text{metric} \qquad (116)$$

Combined Velocities

If a vehicle skids a certain distance, its slide-to-stop velocity for that distance can be estimated. But if the vehicle does not come to a stop at the end of the skidding distance, the velocities must not be added but combined. The combined velocity equation can be derived by writing an energy balance equation:

$$W_t = W_1 + W_2$$

Where W_t is the total energy at the beginning of the skid, W_1 is the energy "used" while sliding and W_2 is the amount of energy left at the end of the sliding. Substitute into this equation the value for work energy from equation (24):

$$1/2 \; m \; v_t^2 = 1/2 \; m \; v_1^2 + 1/2 \; m \; v_2^2$$

Where v_t is the total velocity, v_1 is the velocity for the vehicle as if it slid to a stop and v_2 is the velocity of the vehicle at the end of the slide. Multiply both sides of this equation by $\dfrac{2}{m}$ and cancel:

$$v_t^2 = v_1^2 + v_2^2$$

Take the square root of both sides of the equation:

$$v_t^2 = \sqrt{v_1^2 + v_2^2} \qquad (117)$$

Other Equations

The equations for a fall (54), flip/vault (56) and yaw (64):

$$v = d \sqrt{\frac{g}{2 \, (dG - h)}} \qquad (54)$$

$$v = d \sqrt{\frac{g}{(d - h)}} \qquad (56)$$

$$v = \sqrt{gr\mu} \qquad (64)$$

can be solved for speed, S, in mi/hr and km/hr by substituting the appropriate values for g and v.

17. SOURCES

This topic was developed by:

Gary W. Cooper, who has been on the Traffic Institute staff since 1984 in the Accident Investigation Division. Formerly a member of the Indiana State Police, he graduated from Purdue University with an A.S. degree in Mechanical Engineering Technology.

Lynn B. Fricke, who is a traffic engineer specializing in traffic accident reconstruction. He has been with The Traffic Institute since 1975. In 1981, he became the director of the Institute's Accident Investigation Division.

Exhibits

The following are the sources of tables and diagrams that are used in this topic as exhibits.

Cooper, Gary W., Traffic Institute, Evanston, IL
Tables: 1,2
Diagrams: 3,4,5,6,7,8,9,10,11,12,13,14,15

THE USE OF COMPUTERS IN TRAFFIC ACCIDENT RECONSTRUCTION

Topic 892 of the *Traffic Accident Investigation Manual*

by
Terry D. Day
and Randall L. Hargens

NORTHWESTERN UNIVERSITY TRAFFIC INSTITUTE

THE USE OF COMPUTERS
IN TRAFFIC ACCIDENT RECONSTRUCTION

1. INTRODUCTION

The use of computers has become of major importance to individuals in all walks of life, from balancing the family budget to providing control over the entire launch sequence of a space shuttle. It would seem logical, then, that computers could also be used to reconstruct motor vehicle crashes. Indeed, this is the case.

This topic describes the use of computers in accident reconstruction by practicing accident investigators: persons with a working knowledge of accident investigation and reconstruction. You already know how the equations of motion are applied to vehicular accident reconstruction. You want to benefit from the computer's speed and accuracy. Computers do not replace knowledge; they simply allow those who understand the analysis of motor vehicle crashes to analyze them more quickly and more thoroughly and, therefore, more accurately.

The purpose of this topic is to provide an overview of the use of computers in reconstructing motor vehicle crashes, to discuss various types of programs available (including illustrations), to discuss the admissibility of computer-generated results, and, finally, to describe the process of implementing computers in accident investigation.

2. HISTORY

Crashes are reconstructed for different reasons by different agencies. For example, the federal government reconstructs crashes for statistical purposes, to develop safety standards, and to perform or fund research on behalf of the general public. Vehicle manufacturers analyze crashes to help design safer vehicle structures and restraint systems. Insurance companies use consultants to reconstruct crashes to determine liability. And law enforcement personnel reconstruct crashes to determine if any laws were violated.

Role of Government

As a result of the Federal Motor Vehicle Safety Act of 1966, the National Highway Traffic Safety Administration (NHTSA) was formed as a branch of the U.S. Department of Transportation. The main purpose of NHTSA was to determine how and why traffic accidents occur, and how to reduce the associated death and injury. NHTSA approached its mission by suggesting a statistical study on a large number of accidents. To do this, a large database of accidents was needed, as well as tools to reconstruct these accidents.

In 1966, reconstruction tools for analyzing raw vehicle and accident site data were limited to lengthy calculations performed using a slide rule. No serious study could be performed unless large amounts of data could be analyzed quickly and consistently. Seeing this need, and recognizing the power and capability available in the recently developed digital computer, NHTSA contracted with Cornell Aeronautical Laboratory (now CALSPAN) to develop a suitable computer program. Under the leadership of Raymond McHenry at CALSPAN, several computer programs were developed. This work still stands as the cornerstone for most of the subsequent development in computer programs used for accident investigation.

Since the early seventies, accident statistics have been provided by several studies which use these programs, including the National Crash Severity Study (NCSS),[1] the Fatal Accident Reporting System (FARS),[2] and the National Accident Sampling System (NASS).[3] These studies have helped to shed light on the nation's leading cause of lost human productivity.

Role of MVMA

At the same time NHTSA was developing new standards, vehicle manufacturers developed methods to meet those standards. Funded collectively through the Motor Vehicle Manufacturers Association (MVMA), the manufacturers developed several sophisticated computer programs used in crash research for passenger cars and heavy commercial vehicles. Most of these programs were developed at the University of Michigan Highway Safety Research Institute (now the University of Michigan Transportation Research Institute, or UMTRI).

Role of the Courts

Legal reform during the sixties and seventies resulted in a large increase in civil actions between persons involved in traffic crashes. The need to describe to a jury how the crash occurred, especially in those crashes where there were no independent witnesses, brought about a new need for forensic scientists in the field of accident reconstruction. Lawyers were anxious to use the esoteric, computer-generated results as evidence, although courts usually required the expert witness to demonstrate an understanding of the program before allowing the results to be admitted as evidence. The subject of admissibility is discussed in more detail later in this topic.

Role of Society

Social pressure also played a significant role in the use of computer programs by supporting the general need for accident reconstruction. Considerable public pressure has been placed on prosecuting attorneys to do something about the greatest single cause of death for people between the ages of two and 40: car crashes.[4] The fact that more than half of these deaths involved the abuse of alcohol brought about the desire to reduce these needless deaths by successfully convicting persons charged with vehicular homicide. Conviction not only required proof that the driver was legally drunk, but also that the driving behavior was extraordinarily impaired by the use of alcohol. This resulted in the need to understand the events surrounding the crash — that is, a good, clear accident reconstruction.

Role of the Personal Computer

During the late seventies, the computer tools developed at CALSPAN and UMTRI saw widespread use by the federal government, universities, large research institutions, and a few large engineering firms. Using these programs was limited by one factor: they required a mainframe computer costing more than $100,000.

This all changed when the first personal computer was introduced. As early as 1980, a mainframe program developed at CALSPAN was converted for use on an Apple computer.[5] However, the first major breakthrough in the development of these tools came about as the result of the introduction of the IBM PC in August 1981. This computer was the first to provide large program capacity in a PC environment. The development of PC versions of several mainframe computer programs soon followed.[6]

Program Design

Computer programs have evolved. No longer does a program user need to be a trained computer scientist. No longer does the user have to create the input data using a key punch or general purpose editor.

Today's computer programs provide simple, question-and-answer-oriented and menu-driven input methods with "help" keys and other ways of simplifying them for accident investigation. Compatibility ("My old programs don't work with my new computer!") is no longer a problem, because today's programs can usually work well with various types of computer hardware. Most programs also allow you to save working files for future use or modification — you don't have to start over.

Graphics

The ability to produce graphic images (a pictorial representation) from the results significantly enhances the use of computer programs. Many programs are designed for both graphic input and graphic output. Most of today's programs also reproduce high-resolution, color drawings that can be printed or plotted on most standard computer hardware.

Documentation

An instruction or user's manual describes how to use the program on a particular computer, usually by way of input and output examples and a tutorial section. Some programs include a brief section on theory, although most refer the user to a separate technical reference.

3. PROGRAM TYPES

Reconstructionists now use the computer to perform many types of analyses, ranging from simple to extremely complex calculations that previously required several hours. Many of these calculations were not even possible before the computer became available. Computers are also being used for new purposes never envisioned a short time ago, such as drawing accident sites and obtaining scaled accident site dimensions from photographs. This section of the topic describes several different types of these useful computer programs. Computer programs may be broadly categorized into two types:

- General Calculation Programs
- Sophisticated Analysis Programs

General Calculation Programs

This section of the topic describes a type of computer program that performs general physics calculations easily done by hand. The primary reason for using these programs is their ability to perform these important calculations with speed and accuracy. The equations used by these programs are usually found in the documentation accompanying the program and will not be presented here. Some of the more important calculations are listed below:

CG Location. Compute the longitudinal, lateral, and vertical elevation of the center of gravity (CG) from wheelbase, track width, and weight distribution (elevation requires the front of the vehicle to be lifted to a known height).

Path Radius. Curve data (radius, tangent offset) when field measurements are available.

Coefficient of Friction. Tire/road friction values from test data (vehicle weight and weight distribution, pull force).

Kinematics (distance, velocity and acceleration versus time). General equations of motion for skidding vehicles [velocity when skid distance and drag factor are known, acceleration when velocity, distance and time are known, distance traveled when velocity and time are known (and other rearrangements of these formulas), and critical speed in curves when path radius and drag factor are known].

Flips/Vaults. General equations for airborne vehicles (velocity when grade and distances are known).

Energy. General equations based on the conservation of energy (kinetic energy when velocity and weight are known, skid energy when weight, drag factor and skid distance are known).

Momentum. General equations based on the conservation of linear momentum (impact velocities when separation velocities and path directions are known).

The following example illustrates the use of these programs.

Example 1 – Speed from Skidmarks

A moving vehicle struck a pedestrian. The at-scene investigators measured 105 feet of skidmarks before impact and 35 feet after impact. Then, using a similar car with an accelerometer, a drag factor of 0.72 was obtained when the test car was skidded. The reconstruction required knowledge of the speed before braking and the impact speed. Given 35 feet of post-impact skidmarks and f = 0.72, the impact speed equals 27.61 mi/hr, or 41.2 ft/sec (see Exhibit 1). Next, the deceleration rate (0.72 g, equivalent to -23.2 ft/sec^2), impact velocity (41.2 ft/sec), and pre-impact skid distance (105 ft) were used to determine the speed at the beginning of braking. As shown in Exhibit 2, the car was traveling 81.05 ft/sec (55 mi/hr) when the driver first applied the brakes.

This type of program can also determine the length of time the vehicle skidded before impact. Given the pre-braking speed (81 ft/sec), the impact speed (41 ft/sec) and the deceleration rate (-23.2 ft/sec^2), the vehicle skidded for 1.72 seconds before impact (see Exhibit 3). Finally, if the driver's perception/reaction time is assumed to be 1.5 seconds, the pre-braking speed (81 ft/sec) can be used to determine where the driver's vehicle was located when he perceived a need to react. As shown in Exhibit 4, this location was about 121 feet before the location where the skidding was first observed, or about 226 (121 + 105) feet before impact.

Although these calculations could be done quite easily on a hand-held calculator, the computer program has provided the benefit of an organized, question-answer format to the process, greatly minimizing the chance for error. The results can also be printed for file documentation.

As with any analysis method, you need to understand the equations to properly apply them. When properly applied, these programs are an invaluable tool.

Sophisticated Analysis Programs

Many of the computer programs developed under federal sponsorship at CALSPAN and UMTRI have been significantly refined and enhanced and are now available for use by the general accident reconstruction community. These programs can no longer be considered as a calculation, but rather as a series of calculations. Therefore, they are termed *analysis programs*. Because of the number of individual cal-

```
            COMPUTER-AIDED TRAFFIC ACCIDENT INVESTIGATION
            THE TRAFFIC INSTITUTE, NORTHWESTERN UNIVERSITY

    OPTION 6-7: SPEED FROM SKID MARKS

    REFERENCE EQUATION NUMBER: 6-7                    MEASURE: ENGLISH

                        ENTER SKID DISTANCE (FT):  35

                     ENTER COEFFICIENT OF FRICTION:  .72

        MINIMUM VELOCITY AT BEGINNING OF SKID (MPH):  27.61


                                           ANOTHER RUN (Y/N):

    F1:CANCEL      F2:MAIN MENU      SHFT-PRTSC
```

Exhibit 1. *Output from a general calculation program.[7] This example illustrates the calculation of speed from skidmarks.*

```
            COMPUTER-AIDED TRAFFIC ACCIDENT INVESTIGATION
            THE TRAFFIC INSTITUTE, NORTHWESTERN UNIVERSITY

    OPTION 6-5: INITIAL VELOCITY WHEN ACCELERATION RATE, END VELOCITY,
               AND DISTANCE ARE KNOWN

    REFERENCE EQUATION NUMBER: 6-5                    MEASURE: ENGLISH

                   ENTER ACCELERATION RATE (FT/SEC/SEC):  -23.2
                       ENTER END VELOCITY (FT/SEC):  41.2
                           ENTER DISTANCE (FT):  105

                     INITIAL VELOCITY (FT/SEC):  81.05


                                           ANOTHER RUN (Y/N):

    F1:CANCEL      F2:MAIN MENU      SHFT-PRTSC
```

Exhibit 2. *Output from a general calculation program,[7] initial velocity based on impact velocity, deceleration rate, and skid distance.*

```
            COMPUTER-AIDED TRAFFIC ACCIDENT INVESTIGATION
            THE TRAFFIC INSTITUTE, NORTHWESTERN UNIVERSITY

    OPTION 7-1: TIME REQUIRED WHEN ACCELERATION RATE, INITIAL VELOCITY,
               AND END VELOCITY ARE KNOWN

    REFERENCE EQUATION NUMBER: 7-1                    MEASURE: ENGLISH

                   ENTER ACCELERATION RATE (FT/SEC/SEC):  -23.2
                       ENTER INITIAL VELOCITY (FT/SEC):  81
                         ENTER END VELOCITY (FT/SEC):  41

                                  TIME (SEC):  1.72


                                           ANOTHER RUN (Y/N):

    F1:CANCEL      F2:MAIN MENU      SHFT-PRTSC
```

Exhibit 3. *Output from a general calculation program,[7] calculating the skidding time from deceleration rate and initial and final speeds.*

```
            COMPUTER-AIDED TRAFFIC ACCIDENT INVESTIGATION
            THE TRAFFIC INSTITUTE, NORTHWESTERN UNIVERSITY

    OPTION 5-4: DISTANCE TRAVELED WHEN CONSTANT VELOCITY AND TIME ARE KNOWN

    REFERENCE EQUATION NUMBER: 5-4                    MEASURE: ENGLISH

                   ENTER CONSTANT VELOCITY (FT/SEC):  81
                           ENTER TIME (SEC):  1.5

                     DISTANCE (FT) TRAVELED:  121.50


                                           ANOTHER RUN (Y/N):

    F1:CANCEL      F2:MAIN MENU      SHFT-PRTSC
```

Exhibit 4. *Output from a general calculation program,[7] showing the distance traveled during the perception/reaction phase before braking.*

culations and the amount of built-in flexibility and sophistication, these programs usually go beyond what is practical to perform on a hand-held calculator. However, each of these programs was developed using laws of physics according to well-established engineering principles. Many have also been validated by staged collision studies.

These techniques generally lend themselves to graphics, and are capable of producing drawings as well as numeric results. The graphics are particularly useful because the accident investigator frequently must present his results to lay persons. Graphics also assist the investigator by uncovering facts that might otherwise remain buried in the wealth of data produced by the program.

This section of the topic describes some of the sophisticated analysis programs available to accident investigators.

HVOSM. The HVOSM (Highway-Vehicle-Object Simulation Model) computer program was the first of several programs developed under federal sponsorship by R.R. McHenry at CALSPAN.[8-10] HVOSM can be used to simulate the three-dimensional motion of a four-wheeled vehicle. Two versions of the program were developed: a roadside design version (HVOSM-RD) and a vehicle dynamics version (HVOSM-VD).

HVOSM is used to study how vehicles interact with highway medians, barriers, and other objects (roadside design version) and to study the complicated interaction between the vehicle and its driver (vehicle dynamics version). It remains the only validated computer program capable of analyzing a car which is simultaneously rolling, pitching and yawing, and traveling on an unlevel surface. It is also the only program which can correctly simulate the flight of an airborne vehicle. All this power comes at a great expense, however. HVOSM is a huge mainframe program (not currently available for use on a personal computer) and requires a huge amount of input data describing the vehicle and road. It also calls for considerable technical and computer expertise. As a result of its complexity and the frequent lack of all the necessary input data, it is not used routinely for accident reconstruction, but as a general research tool. An interesting example of the use of HVOSM follows.

Example 2 – Simulating a Stunt

In the James Bond movie *Man with the Golden Gun*, the vehicle Mr. Bond was driving was to be launched airborne during a chase scene. While traveling at high speed, the vehicle was to roll 360 degrees, return to earth, and continue the chase. Instead of using trial and error (at the expense of several stunt drivers and cars), the producers used a computer simulation to determine where to place the ramps, what the ramp angle should be, and how fast the car was to be driven. HVOSM was used to simulate the stunt, and by varying the simulated ramp positions and angles, they were able to determine the correct speed (see Exhibit 5). Back at the movie set, the ramps were placed at the specified locations (strategically behind bushes) and the stunt was properly performed in

COMPUTER PREDICTION

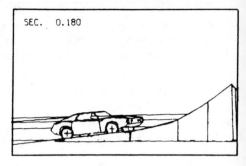

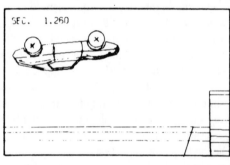

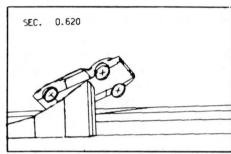

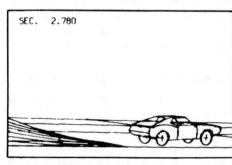

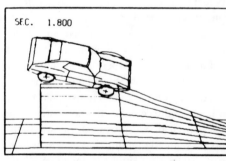

Exhibit 5. Simulating a stunt using HVOSM.[10]

one take. This example does not relate directly to accident reconstruction, but it does illustrate the power of a validated computer simulation.

SMAC. The SMAC (Simulation Model of Automobile Collisions) computer program was developed following HVOSM, again by McHenry while at CALSPAN.[11-15] A PC version of SMAC is available.[16] The SMAC program is used to simulate two-car collisions. It starts with the user's estimates of vehicle speed and position at impact. Based on these initial conditions, SMAC predicts the outcome of the accident — that is, where the vehicles should come to rest and what the vehicle damage pattern should look like.

Unlike HVOSM, the SMAC program cannot be used to study rollover accidents. Like HVOSM, however, the SMAC program produces a time-history of the vehicle motion from the initial conditions until the vehicle comes to rest, making it very useful for animation. You can use SMAC to determine how an accident may have occurred. By repeated adjustments of the initial speeds and directions, you will converge on those which best match the known accident site evidence (rest positions and vehicle damage).

A useful feature of SMAC is the ability to test various possible accident scenarios. This is called a "what-if" analysis. Different impact speeds can be tested and changed to assess the effect on the outcome of the accident. The following example illustrates this application.

Example 3 – Are Witnesses Telling the Truth?

A vehicle was at a stop sign when it was struck from the rear by another vehicle. The four occupants in the struck vehicle, all reportedly seriously injured, stated the other vehicle was traveling at least 40 mi/hr when their vehicle was struck. The vehicles are shown in Exhibits 6 and 7.

SMAC will be used to test the theory that the striking vehicle was traveling 40 mph at impact. The impact positions for both vehicles are selected to provide the proper damage overlap between vehicles. The impact speeds for the struck vehicle (#1) and striking vehicle (#2) are entered as 0 and 40 mi/hr, respectively.

The SMAC results in graphic form are shown in Exhibits 8 and 9. Comparison of the large amount of predicted damage with the small amount of actual damage strongly suggests the impact speed was much slower. The distance the struck vehicle traveled after impact (55 ft simulated versus 22 ft actual) also supports this conclusion. Based on these results, the investigator concluded that the witnesses were not telling the truth!

The SMAC program was originally intended for use as a statistical analysis tool by various NHTSA crash injury studies.[3] However, as a simulation program, SMAC requires estimates of the vehicles' impact speeds. The source of this information was witness statements, or trial and error by the investigator. However, NHTSA soon found these methods were too time-consuming. NHTSA returned to CALSPAN

Exhibit 6. Photograph of Vehicle #1, a Datsun 210, struck in the rear. Damage was relatively minor.

Exhibit 7. Photograph of front of Vehicle #2, a Renault Medalion, which struck the rear of Vehicle #1 (see Exhibit 6).

requesting a computer program to provide initial speed estimates for SMAC. As a result, CALSPAN developed the CRASH program.

CRASH. The CRASH (CALSPAN Reconstruction of Accident Speeds on the Highway) computer program was the third major program developed at CALSPAN under federal sponsorship.[17-20] A PC version of this program is also available.[21] Originally, the CRASH program grew out of the need to provide impact speed estimates for the SMAC program.

The CRASH program is used to reconstruct single- and two-vehicle accidents. The program determines the impact speeds and severity of impact, using information obtained from accident site and vehicle inspections.

The output from CRASH depends on the amount of information supplied. The minimum amount of information is the vehicle weights and a description of vehicle damage, or *damage profile*.

Based on these results alone, CRASH will estimate the severity of impact by computing a quantity called the speed change, or *delta-V* (change in occupant compartment velocity

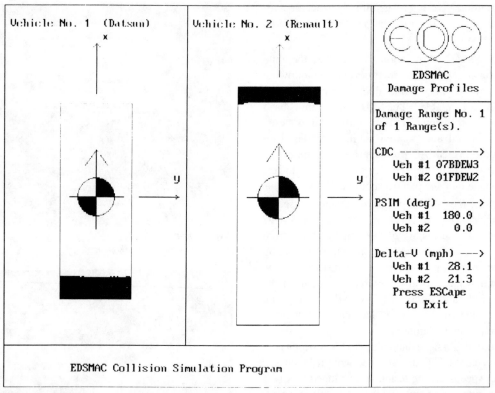

Exhibit 8. *Damage profiles simulated by SMAC program,[16] illustrating what damage would be expected from a 40 mi/hr impact with a stationary vehicle. Comparison with the actual damage (see Exhibits 6 and 7) suggests the impact speed was much lower than 40 mi/hr.*

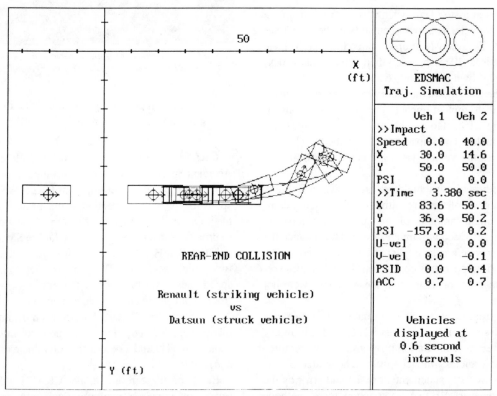

Exhibit 9. *Vehicle trajectories simulated by SMAC,[16] illustrating how far the vehicles would be expected to travel after a 40 mi/hr impact with a stationary vehicle. Comparison of these post-impact path lengths (55 and 35 ft for Vehicles 1 and 2, respectively) with the actual path lengths (22 and 20 ft) suggests the impact speed was much lower than 40 mi/hr.*

SUMMARY OF RESULTS

```
IMPACT SPEED (TRAJECTORY AND DAMAGE)
          TOTAL          FWD.           LAT.          SIDESLIP
VEH #1    0.2 mph        0.2 mph        0.0 mph       0.0 deg
VEH #2   22.1 mph       22.1 mph        0.0 mph       0.0 deg

       SPEED CHANGE (DAMAGE)
          TOTAL          LONG.          LAT.          PDOF
VEH #1   14.2 mph       14.2 mph       -0.0 mph      180.0 deg
VEH #2   10.2 mph      -10.2 mph        0.0 mph        0.0 deg

ENERGY DISSIPATED BY DAMAGE:  VEH #1   17299.8 ft-lb  VEH #2   17918.8 ft-lb
```

```
ENTER:     ESCape          Home     End     or     <RETURN>
```

Exhibit 10. *Output from CRASH program,[21] showing the impact speeds and delta-V's (speed changes) during the rear-end collision. Note the speed of the struck vehicle is estimated at 0.2 mi/hr, very close to the known speed.*

during the impact phase, also approximately the speed at which an unbelted occupant strikes the vehicle interior).[22,23] If accident site measurements (impact and rest positions) and friction values are supplied, CRASH will compute the impact speeds.

For most types of collisions, CRASH uses two independent methods of analysis. One method is based on the damage profile, the other on linear momentum (if accident site measurements are supplied). Because the two methods are independent, the two results can be compared for consistency. This is normally done via built-in warning messages.

The following example illustrates the use of CRASH.

Example 4 – Impact Speed Estimates

This example is a continuation of Example 3. CRASH will be used to estimate the actual speeds of the vehicles involved in the rear-end collision (note that if the results are perfect, the speed computed for the struck vehicle should be exactly zero mi/hr; thus, we have a way to cross-check our results).

This reconstruction requires the vehicle weights, impact and rest positions, the drag factor, and damage profiles. After entering these data, the results for impact speed and speed change (delta-V is synonymous with speed change) are displayed (see Exhibit 10).

The graphic results can also be displayed (see Exhibits 11, 12 and 13). The CRASH analysis reveals the impact speed of the striking vehicle was 22 mi/hr. Note that the speed of the struck vehicle is estimated by CRASH to be 0.2 mi/hr, very close to the known speed, zero mi/hr.

TBST/TBSTT. The TBST and TBSTT (Truck Braking and Steering) programs were developed at the UMTRI by a group of researchers headed by H. Moncartz under sponsorship by the MVMA.[24,25] TBST is a single-vehicle simulator (SVS) and TBSTT is a vehicle-trailer simulator (VTS). PC versions of both of these programs are available.[26,27]

These computer simulation programs are useful for studying the response of a vehicle to braking and steering efforts by the driver.

Although originally developed for studying commercial vehicles, these programs are applicable for studying passenger cars as well. Accident investigators can use these simulation programs to determine how a driver may have lost control of his vehicle as a result of excessive speed, braking, over-correction, and other driver-related errors. By repeated adjustments of the braking and steering input tables, the path of the simulated vehicle will begin to match the accident site evidence. The final result is obtained when a satisfactory match is achieved. These programs can also be used to study the handling effects due to changes in friction, weight distribution, wheelbase, track width, CG height, and other parameters. The following examples illustrate typical program applications.

Example 5 – Simulating Loss of Control

A late-model passenger car with normal handling characteristics has been simulated. The simulation will show how this typical vehicle can spin out in a turn if the rear tires are under-inflated. Low inflation pressure affects a tire's corner-

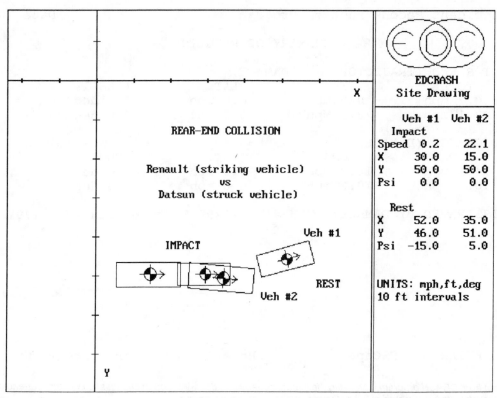

Exhibit 11. CRASH site drawing.[21] This graphic shows the vehicles at their impact and rest positions. Pertinent data, including impact speed, are displayed to the right.

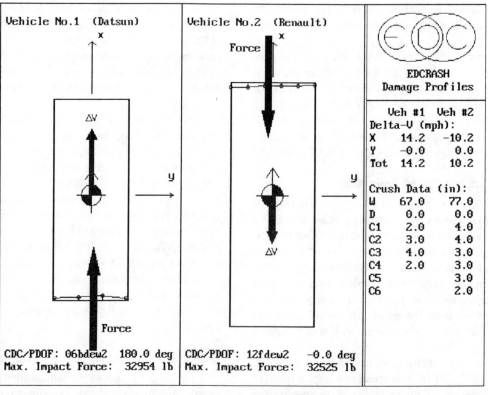

Exhibit 12. Vehicle damage profiles and principal directions of force (PDOF) from CRASH program.[21] These damage profiles are scaled from the actual crush measurements. Compare these actual profiles with those which would be expected from the 40 mi/hr collision, simulated in Exhibit 8.

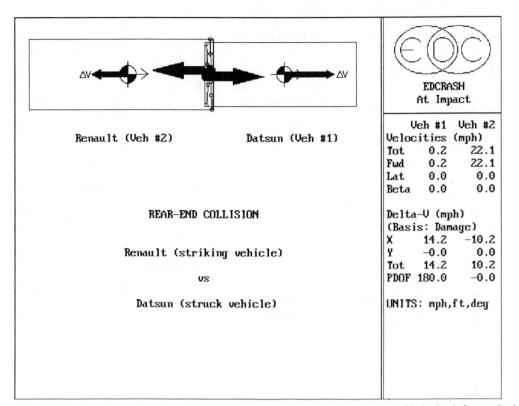

EDCRASH
At Impact

	Veh #1	Veh #2
Velocities (mph)		
Tot	0.2	22.1
Fwd	0.2	22.1
Lat	0.0	0.0
Beta	0.0	0.0
Delta-V (mph)		
(Basis: Damage)		
X	14.2	-10.2
Y	-0.0	0.0
Tot	14.2	10.2
PDOF	180.0	-0.0

UNITS: mph,ft,deg

Renault (Veh #2)   Datsun (Veh #1)

REAR-END COLLISION

Renault (striking vehicle)

vs

Datsun (struck vehicle)

Exhibit 13. *CRASH results showing the configuration at impact.[21] Speeds are also displayed, along with the basis for results (damage).*

	R/F	L/F	R/R	L/R
Normal	131	131	121	121
Reduced	131	131	90	90

Exhibit 14. *Tire cornering stiffness (lb/deg) for normal and reduced inflation pressure.*

Time (sec)	Wheel Force(lb)				Steer Angle (deg)
	R/F	L/F	R/R	L/R	
0.0	0	0	0	0	1.25
1.2	0	0	0	0	
1.3	-384	-384	-256	-256	

Exhibit 15. *Driver braking and steering vs. time for vehicle negotiating a 375 ft radius curve.*

ing stiffness. The tire data for the run with normal inflation pressure and low inflation pressure are shown in Exhibit 14.

All the remaining vehicle data are loaded by the program automatically, according to the vehicle's wheelbase. The only remaining data are the wheel force and steer tables. In this example, the driver had entered a curve too fast and braked moderately, attempting to slow down. The resulting driver input table is shown in Exhibit 15. The program output is both numeric and graphic. Exhibit 16 shows the path taken by the normal vehicle, while Exhibit 17 shows the path taken by the vehicle with under-inflated rear tires. A comparison of Exhibits 16 and 17 clearly shows how under-inflation can cause a vehicle to lose control in a curve.

Similar investigations can be conducted for a tractor-trailer vehicle or a passenger car pulling a trailer. The following example illustrates a potential handling problem for a passenger car and trailer combination.

Example 6 – Simulating an Over-braked Trailer

In this example, a passenger car is pulling a trailer. The heavy-duty trailer is lightly loaded. The simulation illustrates how trailer brakes, which must be designed to stop the trailer when it is fully loaded, can cause the trailer to skid when it is empty (this is a classic design conflict).

All the vehicle data are loaded automatically, according to the vehicle's wheelbase. The trailer dimensions are added separately. Then, the wheel force and steer tables are entered (see Exhibit 18).

The resulting vehicle path is shown graphically in Exhibit 19. Note that when the trailer begins to skid, it loses directional control and begins to slide wide in the curve. This, in turn, pulls the back end of the tow vehicle around. This serious condition will inevitably end up in an accident, regardless of the driver's attempt to regain control of the vehicle by any combination of braking and steering.

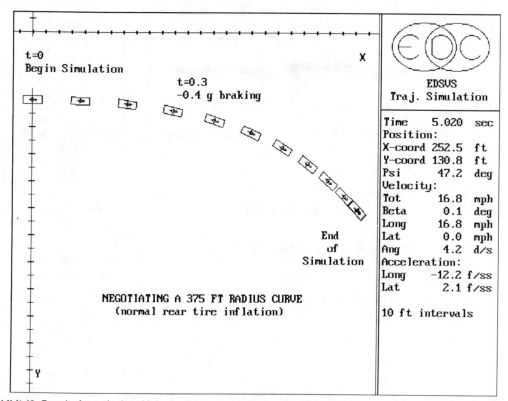

Exhibit 16. *Results from single vehicle simulator program[26] showing the vehicle successfully negotiating the curve.*

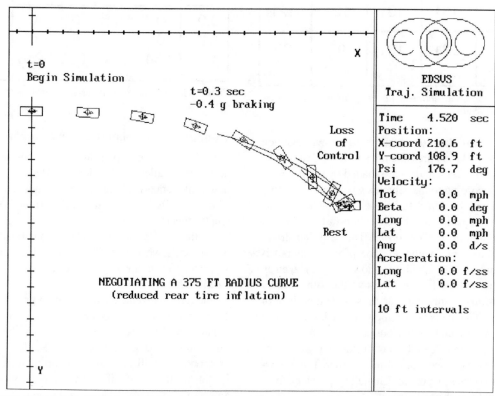

Exhibit 17. *Results from SVS program[26] showing the vehicle with low rear-tire inflation pressure losing control in the curve.*

Time (sec)	Wheel Force (lb)						Steer Angle	
	R/F	L/F	R/R	L/R	R/T	L/T	(sec)	(deg)
0.0	0	0	0	0	0	0	0	0
0.025	-310	-310	-155	-155	0	0	.5	10
0.040	-490	-490	-250	-390	-200	-200		
0.050	-540	-540	-280	-400	-350	-350		
0.060	-545	-545	-300	-390	-440	-440		
0.075	-540	-540	-320	-390	-440	-440		
0.100	-530	-530	-350	-390	-440	-440		
0.150	-530	-530	-380	-390	-440	-440		

Exhibit 18. Driver braking and steering vs. time for passenger car pulling a trailer while braking in a curve.

IMPAC. The IMPAC (Impact Momentum of a Planar Angled Collision) program was developed by Collision Safety Engineering.[28,29] It can be used to reconstruct the impact phase of a two-car collision using the conservation of linear and angular momentum. A PC version of IMPAC is available.

IMPAC requires scene data (position and orientation at impact, estimate of initial velocities) and uses this information to compute the separation velocity. The best solution is obtained by adjusting the initial velocities until the separation velocities match the target velocities obtained from an independent analysis, such as a single-vehicle simulator[26] or general analysis program.[7]

The following example illustrates the use of IMPAC in an angled collision.

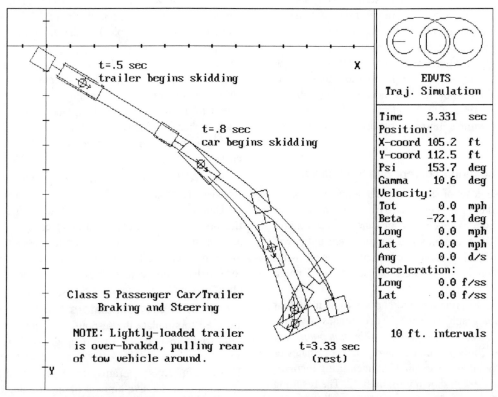

Exhibit 19. Results from vehicle/trailer simulator program[27] showing the trajectory of the passenger car pulling a trailer as it attempts to negotiate a curve while applying the brakes. Note how the trailer wheels begin to slide, then pull the rear of the tow vehicle around, causing it to lose control.

	"Target" Post-Impact Conditions	
	Vel (mph)	Ang (deg)
Veh A	22	0
Veh B	16	19

Exhibit 20. Estimated separation velocities and angles.

Example 7 – Computing Impact Speed from Scene Data

In this example, the separation velocities were estimated from the skid-to-rest paths for each vehicle using one of the general programs described earlier. Next, the separation angles were estimated from scene measurements transferred to a scaled accident site diagram.[41] These target post-impact conditions are displayed in Exhibit 20. Finally, several trial sets of impact speed estimates for both vehicles were entered until a set resulting in the target separation velocities and angles was obtained. As shown in Exhibit 21, these impact speeds for vehicles A and B were 48 and 26 mi/hr, respectively.

Photogrammetry

Photogrammetry is defined as the use of photographs in making maps. The process involves transforming dimensions scaled directly in a photograph to the actual dimensions of the objects or scenery portrayed in the photograph.

Photogrammetry is extremely useful in accident investigation because it allows you to locate information, particularly skidmarks and debris visible in accident site photographs but not measured at the time of the accident.

The following example illustrates the use of computerized photogrammetry.

Example 8 – Locating Accident Site Skidmarks

In this example, a set of skidmarks was found at the accident site, believed to have been caused by one of the vehicles involved. The skidmarks were not measured at the time of the accident, so their locations and lengths were unknown. However, a good-quality photograph clearly showed them, along with four points which were measured (see Exhibit 22).

The first step in locating the skidmarks is to identify four points in the photograph whose X,Y coordinates *were* (or can be) measured. These points, called *calibration points,* are shown in Exhibit 23. Next, the photographic coordinates of each calibration point are determined by measuring them directly off the photograph shown in Exhibit 22. The resulting photographic coordinates for each calibration point are also shown in Exhibit 23.

The calibration points and their matching photographic coordinates are fed into the photogrammetry program, labeled as points REF1, REF2, REF3, and REF4 (see Exhibit 24).

The photogrammetry program uses these points to calculate a special matrix, called a *transformation* matrix. This matrix has a very important property: when it is multiplied by a new set of photographic coordinates (in this example, the start and end coordinates of the skidmark), it will calculate the actual accident-site X,Y coordinates of the skidmark!

The next step is to measure the photograph to determine the coordinates at the start and end of the skidmarks. Once these points are entered, the program calculates the actual coordinates, in feet, for the skidmarks. For reference, these points have been labeled SKID1 through SKID6 (see Exhibit 24). Because we now know where the skidmarks begin and end, we can draw them on our scaled accident site diagram. These skidmarks, in turn, can be used for further analysis and reconstruction of the accident.

Other Sophisticated Programs

Several other programs have also been developed. Although not currently in widespread use by accident reconstructionists, many are powerful tools, and commercially available versions are under development. These programs are described below.

PHASE4. The Phase4 program is the culmination of a major effort undertaken at the University of Michigan.[31] This program is a vehicle dynamics simulator (VDS) used to simulate the response of a single vehicle or vehicle-trailer combination (up to triples) to driver braking and steering. The program has very elaborate methods for studying tires, suspensions, and anti-lock braking systems. It also requires a substantial amount of input data. Because the simulated vehicle is not constrained to a flat highway, the program is well suited to analyses beyond the scope of simpler programs. Such applications include the study of truck rollovers at highway off-ramps having a grade, super-elevation, and spiral curve.

EES-ARM. The EES-ARM (Equivalent Energy Speed Accident Reconstruction Method) program was developed by Daimler-Benz and is used by European accident investigators. It employs a combination of conservation of energy and linear and angular momentum to reconstruct the impact phase of a crash. The post-impact phase must be handled separately; it has been described in the literature,[35,36] but applications in North America are not common.

Human Impact Simulators (HIS). These programs are used to simulate the response of human occupants and pedestrians to impact. Several programs have been developed, including MVMA-2D,[37] CVS-3D,[38,39] and H3D.[30] These mainframe programs are large, extremely complex, and require a massive amount of input data. User-friendly, personal computer versions of these programs are under development.[40]

IMPACT MOMENTUM OF A PLANAR ANGLED COLLISION.   ex3
Exercise 3 -- Example Reconstruction of an Angled Frontal Collision

Vehicle A:	PROGRAM IMPAC - INPUT	Vehicle B:
Medium car		Small car
3531.0 lbm	Vehicle mass	2860.0 lbm
54.0 inches	Radius of gyration	49.0 inches
74.4 inches	Impulse center, fwd from veh CG	80.4 inches
31.2 inches	Impulse center, lat from veh CG	-24.0 inches
30.0 degrees	Vehicle heading at impact	-110.0 degrees
48.0 mph	Forward speed at impact	26.0 mph
.0 mph	Lateral speed at impact	.0 mph
3.0 deg/sec	Pre-impact rotational velocity	-15.0 deg/sec
80. millisec	Time duration of impulse	
.0 deg	Angle of slip plane (relative to vehicle A)	
.0 % slip	Slip velocity, % of approach vel along slip plane.	
24.0 inches	Selected point-1, fwd from CG	24.0 inches
18.0 inches	Selected point-1, lat from CG	18.0 inches
24.0 inches	Selected point-2, fwd from CG	24.0 inches
-18.0 inches	Selected point-2, lat from CG	-18.0 inches
		version: R88L02W08

Exercise 3 -- Example Reconstruction of an Angled Frontal Collision

A: Medium car	PRE-IMPACT CONDITIONS B:	Small car
30.0 deg	Vehicle Heading‑	-110.0 deg
48.0 mph ⓐ 30.00 deg	CG Velocity	26.0 mph ⓐ-110.00 deg
3. deg/sec	Rotational Velocity	-15. deg/sec
271962. 3.ft-lb	Linear & Rotational KE	64631. 51.ft-lb

	IMPACT CONDITIONS	
30.8 mph ⓐ-129.00 deg	Crash Severity Index (^V)	38.1 mph ⓐ 51.00 deg
-4635. lbf-sec	Longitudinal Impulse	-4694. lbf-sec
-1779. lbf-sec	Lateral Impulse	1617. lbf-sec
3.8 inch ˚ 20.07 deg	Collision Radius(h); PDOF	4.9 inch -19.97 deg
	Approach Velocity - CG's	69.9 mph ⓐ 43.82 deg
	Separation Velocity- CG's	8.7 mph ⓐ -35.92 deg
	Impulse Duration	80 milli-sec
	Approximate Mutual Crush	4.11 ft
3.7 ft & 1.4 ft	X & Y Impact Motion of CG	.4 ft & -1.1 ft
Approach Vel ⓐ IC: 68.6	mph tangential & 14.7 mph normal to slip plane.	
	Slip Velocity along plane	.0 mph ⓐ 30.92 deg
	Crush Energy of Collision	252884. ft-lbf

	POST-IMPACT CONDITIONS	
31.8 deg	Vehicle Heading ⓐ runout	-108.1 deg
22.2 mph ⓐ .08 deg	Runout velocity	15.9 mph ⓐ 18.90 deg
43. deg/sec	Runout rotational speed	64. deg/sec
16.6 ft	Runout Work / Weight	8.8 ft
19.5 mph ⓐ 6.13 deg	Velocity ⓐ impulse-center	19.5 mph ⓐ 6.13 deg
21.0 mph ⓐ 1.41 deg	Velocity ⓐ point-1	17.8 mph ⓐ 18.79 deg
22.3 mph ⓐ 3.37 deg	Velocity ⓐ point-2	16.5 mph ⓐ 12.56 deg
57946. 633.ft-lb	Linear & Rotational KE	24273. 911.ft-lb

Collision Safety Engineering

Exhibit 21. *Output from IMPAC.[28] Top portion shows input data, while lower portions show computed pre-impact and post-impact conditions. Note the computed conditions (22.2 mi/hr and .08 deg for Vehicle A and 15.9 mi/hr and 18.9 deg for Vehicle B) are very close to the target conditions (see Exhibit 20).*

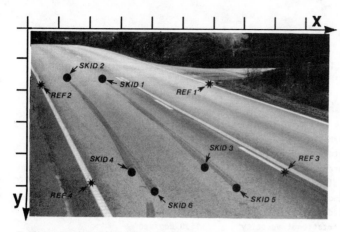

Exhibit 22. *Photograph of accident site showing skidmarks. The locations of four points, REF 1-4, were measured at the site. However, the starting and ending points of the skidmarks, SKID 1-6, were not measured. Photogrammetry can be used to determine their locations.*

	Calibration Points			
	Acc. Site		Photo	
	X_r	Y_r	X_p	Y_p
	(feet)		(millimeters)	
REF 1	0	0	73	16
REF 2	0	22	5	16
REF 3	76	11	104	49
REF 4	76	22	24	49

Exhibit 23. *Table of calibration points and matching photographic coordinates. The accident-site X, Y coordinates of points REF 1 through REF 4 were measured during inspection of the accident site. Their photographic counterparts were measured directly from Exhibit 22.*

```
Source File: FIGURE24     EDITING TRANS4 DATA POINTS                 OVERTYPE

Date 10/24/88   By TDD  Case EX. 9    Roll A   Frame 21  Run 2   Plot P  0.50L
COMMENTS:        Photo Units mm       +/-  0.500      Real Units feet

Locating skidmarks from photgraphic Exhibit 22.

  C1=-2.5202070E+02   C2= 0.0000000E+00   C3= 1.5751300E+01   C4= 0.0000000E+00
  C5= 1.1917100E-01   C6= 1.8038860E+01   C7=-9.4041450E-01   C8= 3.1632130E+00
                        DIGITIZER NOT ALIGNED
  Pt.           MEAS, - PHOTO      MEAS. - REAL      COMPUTED REAL COORDINATES
  No.  NAME      Xp      Yp        Xr      Yr        Xc       Yc      Dx    Dy
  BP   REF1    73.00   16.00     0.00    0.00      0.0      0.0      2.7   0.6
  BP   REF2     5.00   16.00     0.00   22.00      0.0     22.0      2.7   0.2
  BP   REF3   104.00   49.00    76.00   11.00     76.0     11.0      0.5   0.2
  BP   REF4    24.00   49.00    76.00   22.00     76.0     22.0      0.5   0.1
   5   SKID1   31.00   16.00     0.00    0.00      0.0     13.6      2.7   0.3
   6   SKID2   17.00   16.00     0.00    0.00      0.0     18.1      2.7   0.2
   7   SKID3   72.00   48.00     0.00    0.00     75.0     15.2      0.5   0.1
   8   SKID4   43.00   49.00     0.00    0.00     76.0     19.4      0.5   0.1
   9   SKID5   85.00   56.00     0.00    0.00     82.1     15.0      0.4   0.1
  10   SKID6   52.00   58.00     0.00    0.00     83.6     19.3      0.4   0.1


1HEADER 2BASE P 3INVERS 4 SAVE  5ABANDN 6ADD LN 7DEL LN 8 HELP  9DIGTZR 0 CALC
```

Exhibit 24. *Example from TRANS4 photogrammetry program.[32] The first four data points, labeled REF1 through REF4, are the calibration points. The last six data points, labeled SKID1 through SKID6, were computed by the program. These are the actual X, Y coordinates (in ft) of the beginning and end of the skidmarks found at the accident site. (See also references 7, 33, 34, 41.)*

Human impact simulators use several geometrical shapes to simulate the human body, and several contact surfaces to simulate the vehicle interior (dash, floorboard, seat) or exterior (bumper, grille, hood). Each of these surfaces is assigned physical properties defining its size, initial location, and how hard or soft the surface is.

Various programs use varying numbers of masses to model the human body. Programs with a large number of masses (MVMA-2D has nine masses for the head, neck, upper and lower torso, hips, upper and lower arm, and upper and lower leg; see Exhibit 25) require significantly more

input information than do programs with fewer masses (H3D has three masses for the head, torso and legs). Programs with a larger number of masses and contact surfaces (see Exhibit 26) provide more detailed information about occupant injuries, at the expense of several hours of computer calculation time. Programs with fewer masses and contact surfaces provide less specific information about occupant motion and injuries, but require substantially less calculation time.

Human impact simulators can be either two- or three-dimensional. The former requires less input data and simulates motion only in a single plane (i.e., side view or front view),

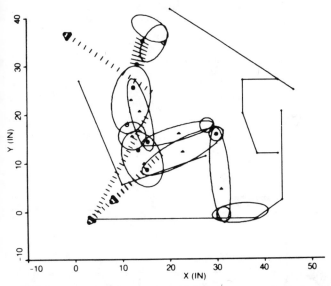

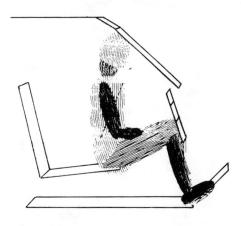

Time = 80 MSEC

Exhibit 25. *Example of output from MVMA-2D,[37] a two-dimensional computer program used for studying occupant injury. This program uses nine masses to model the human body.*

Exhibit 26. *Example output from CVS-3D,[38] another program used to study occupant injury. This program simulates three-dimensional motion of occupants and pedestrians.*

while the latter requires more input data, but simulates motion in all three directions.

Accident investigators can use these programs to determine how vehicle occupants and pedestrians are injured during impact. Occupant injury studies may include the effect of interior design, the use (or non-use) of restraint systems, and the effectiveness of headrests. For pedestrian collisions, human impact simulators can be used to determine throw distances from impact speed, as well as to study how injuries relate to vehicle exterior design. These programs are not normally useful for determining who was driving in a complex rollover accident. As their use by reconstructionists increases, however, human impact simulators may become an important tool for illustrating the conditions causing injury during a crash.

Presentation Tools

An accident reconstructionist is always faced with the need to present his results to others, whether in the form of a report or courtroom exhibits. An ineffective presentation will make even the most thorough reconstruction useless. To meet the presentation need, the reconstructionist prepares a scaled diagram of the accident scene, showing the highway, vehicles and highway evidence. Until recently, these drawings were prepared by hand, using the same techniques a draftsman would use for preparing building plans.

The newest application for computers is the preparation of drawings. This grew out of the high-technology industries, such as aerospace, which use the computer to design components and prepare final design drawings. These programs are ideal for preparing accident site diagrams.

An accident site drawing program is actually a mapping program. It must have some special features that distinguish it from a program for drawing building design plans. As a

mapping program, it must use the same coordinate system other programs use. As with all drafting programs, it should also have a built-in library of frequently-used objects (in this case, highways, intersections, cars, road signs, etc.).

Drawing programs can be lumped into two major categories: CAD (computer-aided drafting) programs and paint programs. Both types of programs are described below, along with examples.

CAD. CAD programs are drafting programs designed to draw lines according to an established scale. Each line, therefore, is positioned according to real-world coordinates, making it easy to locate lines and other objects precisely, using accident site measurements. Thus, it is also easy to produce scale diagrams, an essential part of a reconstruction. A typical CAD accident site drawing is shown in Exhibit 27.

A CAD program essentially replaces a ruler and pencil. The investigator uses CAD to draw a scale diagram for purposes of analysis. Then, if necessary, the same drawing can be enhanced or rescaled on the computer for preparing report or courtroom exhibits.

PAINT. Paint programs are designed to be used as an artist's tool. As such, paint programs work by keeping track of points on the computer's screen rather than using real-world measurements. This makes it very easy to draw and erase lines and circles, or even portions of lines and circles. It also is very easy to produce multiple copies of certain areas on the screen. These same features, however, place restrictions on their use in accident reconstruction, because it is usually not possible to place an object at a known coordinate location or produce scale diagrams using paint programs except by trial and error. A typical accident site drawing using a paint program is shown in Exhibit 28.

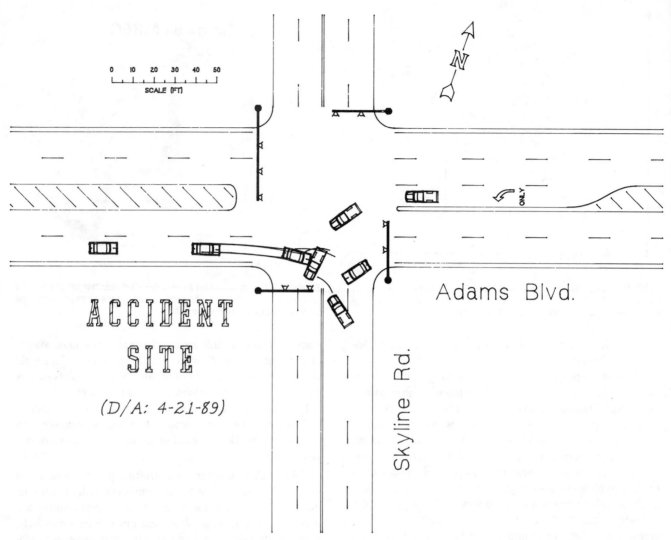

Exhibit 27. *An example of a scaled accident-site drawing using a CAD program.*[41] *The vehicles, trees, north direction indicator and scale are all part of a built-in accident site template.*

4. ADMISSIBILITY

An investigator who understands the calculations performed by a computer program seldom has any difficulty getting his results admitted in a court of law. However, any good lawyer will challenge an analysis, whether it was done using a hand calculator or a computer. This section provides an overview of the things you should remember when using a computer analysis as part of your testimony.

The computer is just one tool. You will seldom base all your conclusions on only one source of information. In every investigation, several methods of analysis are used. These methods include experience, other supporting calculations, and comparison with independent eyewitnesses. It is important to realize when testifying that the computer is just one of several tools at your disposal. It is even likely that more than one computer program will be used on a particular accident.

Computers are not mysterious. Any computer program is simply a pre-programmed series of calculations. In the case of accident reconstruction programs, the calculations represent the solution to a physics problem – nothing more, nothing less. It is inappropriate to label the results as accurate just because they were produced by a computer. The calculations are only as correct as the input data that produced them. The saying "garbage in, garbage out" applies to all calculation methods, including computer programs. However, a good computer program will provide you with warning messages alerting you to data inconsistencies. You should simply use and present the computer as a technical tool in your investigation.

Remember the history. Experience has shown that courts are much more willing to admit scientific evidence produced by an independent engineering analysis tool than scientific evidence produced by a tool specifically developed for litigation. All the sophisticated programs described in this topic were specifically developed as tools to improve traffic safety. Their application in litigation is a by-product of that important purpose.

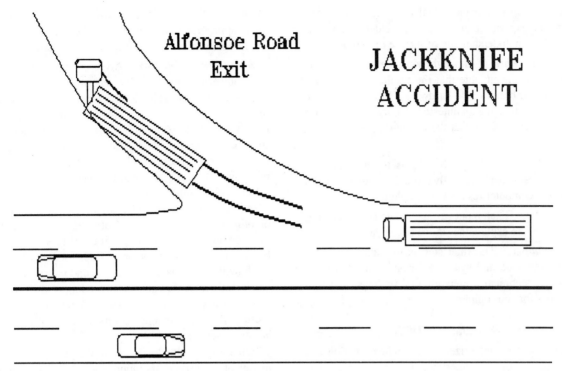

Exhibit 28. *An example of a scaled accident site drawing using a paint program.*[42]

As a result of their development by NHTSA for improving highway safety, all of the analysis tools described in this topic have been tested for validity (see References). While a validation study cannot prove the accuracy of every reconstruction, it does provide a valid basis for the program's use.

You don't need to be a programmer. As an accident investigator using a computer program, you need not understand each and every line of computer language in the program. Indeed, it would be wise to state at the outset of your testimony that this is not the case; you did not write the program and are not familiar with every line of code. Rather, you are a user of the program, just as hundreds of others are, and understand the procedures extremely well. As an investigator, however, you can and should expect to be questioned on the procedures used by the program.

Stay within the scope of analysis. When used properly, computer programs usually work quite well. It is essential to use the program only for its intended purpose. A program may provide a solution for an unintended purpose; but if this other purpose is untested, the investigator cannot be certain of the results — and those results will be subject to scrutiny.

Understand the assumptions and limitations. All computer programs incorporate certain basic assumptions and limitations. To properly apply the program, you must understand what they are. These are normally listed in the documentation.

You make assumptions as well, and must be prepared to defend those assumptions. A basic understanding of the program points toward the need for adequate training.

One of the advantages of computer analysis is the organization it provides. You can always review your input to see exactly what information was used. But so can others! Therefore, be ready to defend the input. An understanding of how the program works is essential.

Do not exaggerate the accuracy. Lastly, do not exaggerate the importance or accuracy of the results, just because they were generated by a computer. Go back to the basics: a computer program is simply a pre-programmed series of calculations. The program may display the speed of a vehicle as 53.54 mi/hr, but the true accuracy is not quite that good. Always perform a series of analyses using a range for important variables, such as friction and impact positions. The resulting range in speed estimates is much more important (and believable) than showing you can determine the speed of a vehicle with two-decimal-place accuracy.

The above concepts provide a basis for using computer programs in accident reconstruction. If you are to present your results in court, you must be prepared for the qualification process. This is a five-step process:

- Qualify the Expert
- Qualify the Hardware
- Qualify the Software
- Qualify the Input
- Qualify the Output

Each of these steps is described below.

Qualify the Expert. Using the computer does not make you an expert. In fact, it places additional demands on your expertise. Qualifications for expert testimony vary from state to state, and it is up to the individual to demonstrate a true knowledge and experience in the field of accident reconstruction, as well as an understanding of the use of computers.

Qualify the Hardware. Although not generally necessary, it does no harm if you state that the results were obtained using recognized brand-name hardware. However, if the results were obtained using an untested prototype computer, it will be necessary to show that the computer produces valid results.

Qualify the Software. The third step is to show that the computer program is valid, usually through the use of a study comparing the computer results with actual test data.

Qualify the Input. Each input variable is subject to scrutiny. You must be able to explain the source of the data.

Qualify the Output. The final step is to explain how the results were obtained and what they mean. This step is required for any technical presentation of findings, and provides the basis for your opinions.

5. IMPLEMENTATION

The benefits of computerized accident investigation can only be realized if the computerization is implemented correctly. To properly implement the system requires a general understanding of four major areas:

- Management Support and Encouragement
- Software Selection
- Hardware Selection
- Training

Each area is necessary for the overall implementation; skipping any of these four will guarantee an incomplete system and the risk of failure. Computer systems (whether in accident investigation or other fields) that have failed can be attributed to one of the four basic areas of successful implementation. Each of these important areas is described below.

Management Support and Encouragement. The first step in implementation is to gain the support and encouragement of management. This usually involves a cost vs. benefit analysis and an overall implementation plan. Although management may not need to know the technical aspects of the hardware or software, they do need to know the system capabilities and general requirements.

Gaining management support should start by illustrating the need for computerizing. This means comparing the present method of operation with how accident investigation might be improved by computerizing. Lost opportunities can also be equated with lost time and revenue.

One method of presenting and reviewing computer alternatives with management is called an *options comparison*. An options comparison lists the advantages and disadvantages of each alternative. Many of the advantages can be summarized from the benefits of the cost/benefit analysis. Other advantages may be less tangible. Where possible, try

to quantify the advantages or disadvantages in dollars. The most appropriate system usually becomes apparent after weighing the costs and benefits of each alternative.

Software Selection. After reviewing the alternatives and comparing the costs and benefits, you should select the software. This should be done *before* selecting hardware. Although the typical software program may cost less than the total hardware costs, the total costs to the company resulting from choosing the wrong software will far exceed the hardware costs. These may be costs resulting from additional manpower, procedures, or lost revenue directly traceable to selecting the wrong software.

In selecting software, be aware of the effects it might have on other aspects of your accident investigation practice. Ask for a demonstration of the program(s) to see what you are buying. Knowing how the program is used and actually seeing how the information is entered and the results displayed will greatly increase your understanding of the program and how well it will meet your needs. A demonstration is also useful when confirming compatibility with a potential hardware selection.

Hardware Selection. Hardware selection is simply a matter of identifying the appropriate computer and devices to effectively run the selected software. The options available can be obtained from the software vendor. Other items that should be considered when selecting hardware are:

- *Compatible equipment* (sometimes called clones). Although these devices might represent significant savings and be advertised as a "true compatible," subtle differences may cause problems now or in the future — after the software is updated. It can be stated categorically: there is no such thing as a true 100% compatible.

If you do purchase a clone, you may incur additional costs in the future (such as product updates, lost time spent on troubleshooting problems, or additional software costs).

- *Other business needs.* Depending on the size of the company or agency, other business functions can be automated and used on the same computer. Keeping in mind the original cost/benefit analysis, this should only be done if it does not hinder the original objectives.

- *Future needs and capabilities.* Hardware "expandability" is critical in today's market of ever-expanding hardware technology. Purchasing a "close-out sale" computer guarantees obsolescence and eliminates the possibility of future expansion. Computer hardware can generally be classified into one of three categories:

- Mainframes
- Minicomputers
- Microcomputers

Although the distinction among these has become less clear-cut with the advancements in hardware technology, historically the differences have been due to computer size,

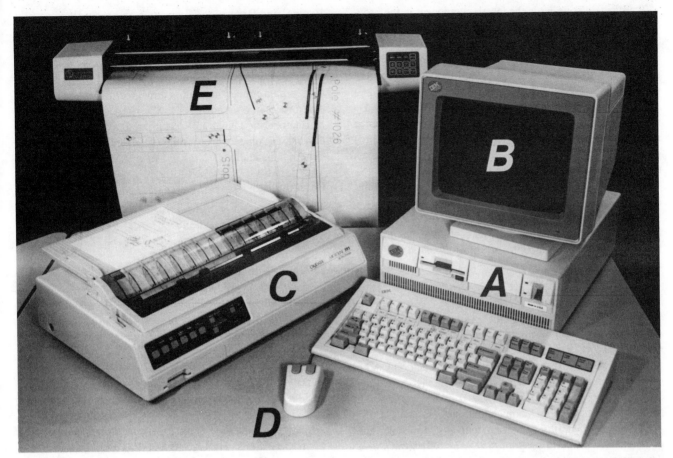

Exhibit 29. *An example of a complete computer hardware system. The system includes (a) the microcomputer with keyboard and disk storage, (b) the display, with high-resolution graphics option, and (c) the dot-matrix printer. This system also includes some enhancements useful for many accident reconstruction programs. These enhancements include (d) a mouse and (e) a plotter. Also, not visible inside the computer is a math coprocessor, which greatly increases the calculation speed.*

single or multiple processors, number of terminals, and processing speed. Unless otherwise noted, the software referenced in this topic was developed for microcomputers.

In selecting microcomputer hardware, you should be familiar with the basic components and optional attachments. Exhibit 29 identifies the primary components of a microcomputer system. Other devices that can be added to enhance the system are also included in Exhibit 29. These devices provide easier methods of input, and improved output, processing, or storage. They include the following:

Graphics display and adapter. These devices allow the computer to produce graphic images or pictures, as well as text. They are usually required for accident reconstruction software. Besides offering different colors, they also may offer varying screen resolution which determines the amount of detail the screen can display.

Math coprocessor. This optional chip can be added to the computer to increase the speed of performing math functions. Most simulation programs can benefit from adding a math coprocessor, since they are calculation-intensive. However, not all software was developed to take advantage of the

math coprocessor, and not all hardware has the capability of adding the chip.

Mouse. A mouse simplifies the input process and locating data on the screen. It's a pointing device for directing a set of crosshairs on the screen. Buttons on the mouse assist in selecting the desired item. A mouse is very helpful when using presentation software.

Digitizer. A digitizer provides another method of entering data. It is an electronic tablet used to enter the coordinates of specific points of graphic information into a computer. Like the mouse, it lets you point to the location on a known map, drawing, or picture with a stylus or cursor, and the coordinate data is automatically sent to your computer. Certain photogrammetry and presentation software programs are greatly enhanced by this device.

Plotter. A plotter uses one or more pens to draw graphic images on paper or transparencies. Since standard "dot-matrix" printers use several small wire pins to form characters, they can be programmed to produce graphic images as well. But diagonal lines in dot-matrix output sometimes appear jagged, as opposed to plotter output, which is smooth and continuous. (For an example of the latter, see Exhibit 27).

Training. Training is the fourth component in the process of computerizing. Perhaps the most overlooked, training can be the most important component in implementing a successful system. This is especially true in a technical field such as accident reconstruction, where the engineering aspects and terms must also be known.

The most popular form of training is self-learning. By reading the program tutorial and other available reference materials, an investigator can frequently learn to use the program satisfactorily. However, this type of training takes time, and mistakes usually occur along the way.

The alternative to self-learning is a one-week training seminar. These seminars are usually given several times a year at particular locations or on-site. They usually focus on the use of a specific program. Seminars offer the opportunity to learn the greatest amount of information in the least amount of time.

6. SUMMARY

There are two primary benefits in using computers for accident reconstruction. The first is speed. By programming a computer to perform the necessary calculations, an analysis normally requiring several hours of hand calculation can be done in seconds. Not only does the analysis take less time, but also a whole series of possible scenarios can be analyzed, resulting in a much more thorough analysis.

The second benefit is freedom from mistakes. Once the equations are properly programmed, they will always give the correct answers to the given equations. This is of major importance in a complicated analysis, where hundreds or thousands of separate calculations are required.

There are additional benefits. The computer only works as a logical extension of the user. As a result, it forces you into using a logical procedure. (Some may think of this as a disadvantage!) The output from a well-written computer program is neat and well designed, allowing you to quickly find important data.

Finally, the use of computers can also provide a learning experience, because in the normal process of studying a crash, the investigator typically gains a tremendous amount of knowledge about accident reconstruction. As a direct result, the investigator's ability to communicate his findings to others, whether a district attorney, trial lawyer, insurance adjuster, jury, or another investigator, is vastly improved. The end result is a better understanding of what causes accidents. And that, after all, is the primary reason for accident reconstruction.

7. SOURCES

Authors

Terry D. Day, P.E., is a mechanical engineer and a member of the Accident Investigation Practices subcommittee of the Society of Automotive Engineers. Mr. Day is president of Engineering Dynamics Corporation and has written several technical articles on the use of computers for accident reconstruction.

Randall L. Hargens, a computer scientist, has been developing computer programs for over 21 years. He has a certificate in data processing and is a member of several national data processing organizations. Mr. Hargens is a co-founder of Engineering Dynamics Corporation, and has written several articles on data processing, computer selection, and system implementation.

References

1. Ricci, Leda L., "NCSS Statistics: Passenger Cars," DOT-HS-805-531, June 1980.
2. *Fatal Accident Reporting System 1986*, DOT-HS-807-245, NHTSA, March 1988.
3. *National Accident Sampling System: Accident Investigation Procedures Manual*, DOT, NHTSA, 1980.
4. Petrucelli, E., "The USA and Safety Belt Use: A Prognosis for the Remainder of the '80s," SAE Paper No. 840324, Society of Automotive Engineers, Warrendale, PA, 1980.
5. Hess, R.L., "Microcomputer Programs Useful for Aspects of Accident Reconstruction," SAE Paper No. 800174, Society of Automotive Engineers, Warrendale, PA, 1980.
6. Day, T.D., and R.L. Hargens, *Engineering Dynamics Vehicle Analysis Package* (EDVAP), Engineering Dynamics Corporation, Lake Oswego, OR, 1984/1986/1988.
7. *A-I-CALC Program User's Guide*, Northwestern University Traffic Institute, Evanston, IL, 1987.
8. McHenry, R.R., and N.J. DeLeys, "Vehicle Dynamics in Single Vehicle Accidents – Validation and Extensions of a Computer Simulation," CAL Report No. VJ-2251-V-3, Cornell Aeronautical Labs, Buffalo, NY, 1968.
9. Segal, D.J., "Highway-Vehicle-Object Simulation Model," FHWA-RD-76-162, Federal Highway Administration, Washington, DC, 1976.
10. McHenry, R.R., "The Astro Spiral Jump – An Automobile Stunt Designed Via Computer Simulation," SAE Paper No. 760339, Society of Automotive Engineers, Warrendale, PA, 1976.
11. Solomon, P.L., "The Simulation Model of Automobile Collisions (SMAC) Operator's Manual," U.S. DOT, NHTSA, Accident Investigation Division, Washington, DC, 1974.
12. McHenry, R.R., "Development of a Computer Program to Aid the Investigation of Highway Accidents," DOT HS-800 621, December 1971.
13. McHenry, R.R., D.J. Segal, J.P. Lynch, and P. Henderson, "Mathematical Reconstruction of Highway Accidents," DOT HS-800 801, January 1973.
14. Bartz, J.A., D.J. Segal, and R.R. McHenry, "Mathematical Reconstruction of Highway Accidents – Analytical

and Physical Reconstruction of Ten Selected Highway Accidents," DOT HS-801 150, March 1974.

15. Jones, I.S., J.P. Lynch, and R.R. McHenry, "Mathematical Reconstruction of Highway Accidents – Scene Measurement and Data Processing System," DOT HS-801 405, February 1975.

16. *Vehicle Analysis Package – EDSMAC Program Manual, Version 2*, Engineering Dynamics Corporation, Lake Oswego, OR, 1989.

17. McHenry, R.R., "Extensions and Refinements of the CRASH Computer Program Part II, User's Manual for the CRASH Computer Program," DOT HS-801 838, February 1976.

18. Jones, I., and A. Baum, "Research Input for Computer Simulation of Automobile Collisions, Vol IV – Staged Collision Reconstructions," DOT HS-805 040, December 1978.

19. Campbell, K., P. Cooley, R. Hess, R. Scott, and C. Winkler, "Training Materials for Accident Investigation, Volume 1 – Reference Manual," DOT HS-801 968, May 1979.

20. *CRASH3 User's Guide and Technical Manual*, US DOT, NHTSA, 1981.

21. *Vehicle Analysis Package – EDCRASH Program Manual*, Engineering Dynamics Corporation, Lake Oswego, OR, 1986.

22. Day, T.D., and R.L. Hargens, "An Overview of the Way EDCRASH Computes Delta-V," SAE Paper No. 870045, Society of Automotive ¡Engineers, Warrendale, PA, 1987.

23. Day, T.D., and R.L. Hargens, "An Overview of the Way EDSMAC Computes Delta-V," SAE Paper No. 880069, Society of Automotive Engineers, Warrendale, PA, 1988.

24. Moncartz, H.T., J.E. Bernard, and P.S. Fancher, "A Simplified, Interactive Simulation for Predicting the Steering and Braking Response of Commercial Vehicles," University of Michigan, UM-HSRI-P-75-8 August, 1975.

25. Bernard, J.E., "A Computer-Based Mathematical Method for the Prediction of Braking Performance of Trucks and Tractor-Trailers," SAE Paper No. 730181, Society of Automotive Engineers, Warrendale, PA, 1973.

26. *Vehicle Analysis Package – EDSVS Program Manual*, Engineering Dynamics Corporation, Lake Oswego, OR, 1988.

27. *Vehicle Analysis Package – EDVTS Program Manual*, Engineering Dynamics Corporation, Lake Oswego, OR, 1988.

28. Woolley, R.L., "IMPAC User's Guide and Technical Manual," Version R84L12W03, Collision Safety Engineering, Orem, UT, 1985.

29. Woolley, R.L., "The IMPAC Computer Program for Accident Reconstruction," SAE Paper No. 850254, Society of Automotive Engineers, Warrendale, PA, 1985.

30. Robbins, D.H., R.O. Bennett, and V.L. Roberts, "HSRI Three-Dimensional Crash Victim Simulator: Analysis, Verification and User's Manual, and Pictorial Section," University of Michigan, DOT HS-800 551, June 1971.

31. MacAdam, C.C., P.S. Fancher, G.T. Hu, and T.D. Gillespie, "A Computerized Model for Simulating the Braking and Steering Dynamics of Trucks, Tractor-Semitrailers, Doubles, and Triples Combinations - User's Manual," University of Michigan, UM-HSRI-80-58, Ann Arbor, MI, September 1980.

32. *TRANS4 Photogammetry Programs for Accident Investigation*, Kinney Engineering, Inc., and MC2, Inc., Corvallis, OR, 1988.

33. Brelin, J.M., *FOTOGRAM*, GM Technical Center, General Motors Corporation, Warren, MI, 1986.

34. Brelin, J.M., W.G. Cichowski, and M.P. Holcomb, "Photogrammetric Analysis Using the Personal Computer," SAE Paper No. 861416, Society of Automotive Engineers, Warrendale, PA, 1986.

35. Das EES – Unfallrekonstruktions-program, DEKRA-Hauptverwaltung, Postfach, 810207, 7000 Stuttgart 80.

36. Zeidler, F., H. Schreier, and R. Stadelmann, "Accident Research and Accident Reconstruction by the EES-Accident Reconstruction Method," SAE Paper No. 850256, Society of Automotive Engineers, Warrendale, PA, 1985.

37. Bowman, B.M., R.O. Bennett, and D.H. Robbins, "MVMA Two-Dimensional Crash Victim Simulation, Version 4, Volume 2," University of Michigan, UM-HSRI-79-5-2, Ann Arbor, MI, June 1979.

38. Fleck, J.T., and F.E. Butler, "Validation of the Crash Victim Simulator, Volume 3, User's Manual," Calspan Corp. Report No. ZS-5881-V-3, NHTSA Contract No. DOT-HS-6-01300, February 1982.

39. Digges, K.H., "Reconstruction of Frontal Accidents Using the CVS-3D Model," SAE Paper No. 840869, Society of Automotive Engineers, Warrendale, PA, 1984.

40. *Vehicle Analysis Package – EDHIS Program Manual*, Engineering Dynamics Corporation, Lake Oswego, OR (under development).

41. *Vehicle Analysis Package – EDCAD Program Manual*, Engineering Dynamics Corporation, Lake Oswego, OR, 1988.

42. *Microsoft Paintbrush User's Guide*, Microsoft Corporation, Redmond, WA, 1986.

ACKNOWLEDGMENTS

The authors wish to thank the following people for their assistance and contributions to this topic:

Dr. Ronald L. Woolley, Collision Safety Engineering

Ms. Janet M. Brelin, General Motors Corporation

Dr. J. Rolly Kinney, Kinney Engineering, Inc.

Mr. Lynn B. Fricke, Northwestern University Traffic Institute

TRADEMARKS

PC Paintbrush is a trademark of ZSoft Corporation. Microsoft is a registered trademark of Microsoft Corporation.

EDVAP, EDSVS, EDVTS, EDCRASH, EDSMAC and EDCAD are trademarks of Engineering Dynamics Corporation.

IBM is a registered trademark of International Business Machines Corporation.

INDEX AND GLOSSARY

All topics have two-part page numbers. Their parts are separated by a hyphen. The first number identifies the topic, the second one the page in the topic. Topics in this volume are arranged sequentially so that it is easy to locate a particular page from an index reference.

A glossary is combined with the index so that the meanings of important terms can be found without further reference.

A

this marking with care is permitted only as a left-turn maneuver. It is frequently used as a channelizing line in advance of an obstruction which must be passed on the right, and to form a channelizing island separating traffic in counter directions.

Bicycle, a two-wheeled pedalcycle.

Bituminous concrete, concrete cemented with a bituminous material such as tar or asphalt.

Body type, the general configuration or shape of a vehicle distinguished by characteristics such as number of doors, seats or windows, or by roof line; hardtop, convertible, etc.

Braking distance, the distance through which brakes are applied to slow a vehicle; the shortest distance in which a particular vehicle can be stopped by braking from a specified speed on a particular surface; the distance from application of brakes to collision.

Braking systems

Braking time, time required to traverse the braking distance.

Bus, any motor vehicle designed for carrying more than 10 passengers and used for transporting persons; any motor vehicle, other than a taxicab, designed and used for transporting persons for compensation.

C

Car, any vehicle, except motorcycles and motor-driven cycles, designed for carrying 10 or fewer passengers and used for transporting persons.

Carelessness – see **negligence**.

Cause analysis, the effort to determine, from available information, why the accident occurred — that is, the complete combinations of factors that caused the highway transportation system to malfunction at the time and place of the accident with resultant injury and damage; the fifth and final level of traffic accident investigation. Cause analysis has been referred to as determining "indirect" or condition factors.

Causes of traffic accidents

Centered thrust, a thrust directed toward the center of mass of the vehicle or other object in collision.

Center of mass

Centrifugal force, the force of a body in motion which tends to keep it continuing in the same direction rather than following a curved path.

Chip, a short, deep gouge; a hole in pavement made by a strong, sharp, pointed metal object under great pressure, usually without striations.

Chop, a broad, shallow gouge, even and regular on the deeper side and terminating in scratches and striations on the opposite, shallower side; a depression in pavement made by a strong, sharp metal edge moving sidewise under heavy pressure.

Chord, a straight line connecting the ends of an arc or two points on a curve. A chord is never greater than the diameter of a circle of which the arc is a part.

Coefficient of friction, a number representing the resistance to sliding of two surfaces in contact; the drag factor of a vehicle or other object sliding on a roadway or other level surface; the force parallel to a level surface required to keep an object sliding on that surface; the force parallel to a surface required to keep an object sliding on that surface in motion, divided by the force of the object against that surface; measured in pounds per pound; often designated by the Greek letter mu (μ). See **friction force**.

Coefficient of restitution

Collision 68-5

Collision scrub, a short, usually broad skidmark or yawmark made during engagement of collision vehicles. A collision scrub may be connected to skidmarks or yawmarks made before or after collision, but has characteristics that differentiate it from such marks.

Complex reaction, a choice between two or more possible reactions to an unexpected hazard. See **reaction**. 64-12

Computer programs

Computer systems

Computer use history

Concrete, a paving material consisting of an aggregate of stones of assorted sizes held together with a cement or binder; bituminous concrete; portland cement concrete.

Condition factors, deficiencies in basic attributes of roads, vehicles or people, as related to highway transportation and permanently or temporarily modified, that contribute to operational factors.

Conservation of energy, the principle of physics stating that the amount of energy in a closed system is constant regardless of the changes in the form of that energy. Used in accident investigation in estimating vehicle speed from the distance required to slide to a stop and other applications, such as speed from damage. See **momentum**.

Conservation of momentum, the principle of physics stating that the total momentum of two bodies colliding with each other is the same before collision as after collision.

Contact damage, deformation or defacement resulting from direct pressure of another object or surface in an impact; direct damage. Compare with **induced damage**.

Coordinate measurements, a method of locating any spot in an area by taking two measurements from the nearest point to the spot on a specified reference line: 1) the distance and direction from that point to the spot, and 2) the distance and direction from that point to a specified reference point on the reference line.

Coordinate system

Courtroom admissibility

Critical velocity, a velocity above which a particular highway curve, or a curve demanded by the driver, could not be negotiated by a motor vehicle without yaw; the speed at which the centrifugal force of a vehicle following a specific curve exceeds the traction force of the tires on the surface. See **yaw**. 72-31

Crook, an abrupt change of direction of a tire mark due to collision forces. The crook often indicates the position of a tire at first contact.

D

Damage

Debris, loose material strewn on the road as the result of a traffic accident, such as dirt, liquids, vehicle parts, clothing, etc.

Deceleration, rate of slowing; negative acceleration.

Decision, determination of what action to take after perceiving a situation; choice of driving strategies or evasive tactics.

Deposit – see **imprint**.

Deposition, pretrial questioning of a witness, under oath, subject to cross examination for the purpose of discovering evidence or perpetuating testimony; the document in which this is recorded.

Discriminatory reaction, a reaction to perceiving an unfamiliar hazard or other situation which requires information in addition to that immediately available to make a decision or which presents several choices of possible evasive tactics. Time required is 1.5 sec or more, possibly much more. 64-15

Drag factor, a number representing the acceleration or deceleration of a vehicle or other body as a decimal fraction of the acceleration of gravity; $f = a/g$; the force needed to produce acceleration in the same direction, divided by the weight of the body to which the force is applied. When a vehicle slides with all wheels locked on a level surface, the coefficient of friction and the drag factor have the same value.

Dribble, liquid debris, from a vehicle or its cargo, that drops to the ground, often leaving a trail (if the vehicle is moving) from a spatter area to a puddle.

Driver, any person who drives or who is in physical control of a vehicle.

Dropoff, the edge of pavement where it is more than about 2 in. (about 5 cm) higher than the abutting shoulder.

E

Eccentric thrust, a thrust which is not toward the center of mass of the vehicle or the center of mass of the other object in collision.

Edge line, a line indicating the edge of the roadway.

Energy, ability to do work or produce an effect such as damage; a unit of force operating through a unit of distance; half of the mass or weight, times velocity squared; force times distance; measure in foot-pounds (ft lb); $wv^2/2g$.

Equations

Evasive steering maneuver

F

Factor, any circumstance contributing to a result without which the result could not have occurred; an element which is necessary to produce the result but which is not, by itself, sufficient; operational factor; condition factor.

Fall, a downward and onward movement in the air under the force of gravity after forward momentum carries an object beyond its supporting surface; rotation during a fall is gradual and the object usually lands right side up. Compare with **flip**.

Field sketch, a freehand map of the scene or site of an accident or road configuration, usually for the purpose of recording measurements.

Final position, the exact location of a vehicle or body after a traffic accident.

First contact point (FCP), the exact point on a vehicle, pedestrian, or other object touched in a collision; the place on the road or ground closest to the first contact between colliding objects. Sometimes called **point of impact** or **collision point**.

First harmful event, the first occurrence of injury or damage.

Flat-tire mark, a scuffmark made by an overdeflected tire; a mark made by a tire which is seriously underinflated or overloaded.

Flip, a sudden upward and onward movement off the ground when an object's horizontal movement is obstructed below its center of mass by an obstacle on the surface supporting the object. Rotation during a flip is rapid and the object usually lands upside down. Sometimes called **vault**. Compare with **fall**.

Force, that which influences motion or tends to do so; pressure, thrust; a vector quantity measured in pounds (lbs), newtons or kilograms (kg).

Centrifugal 72-9, 90-19
Centripetal 72-9, 90-19
Cornering 72-15, 72-19
Rectangular components 56-19
Tire cornering 72-5

Friction force – see **coefficient of friction**.

ABS-equipped cars 62-7
ABS-equipped motorcycles 74-12
Dynamic and static 62-5
Friction circle 62-9
Lateral force 62-9
Longitudinal force 62-9
Related to sliding area 62-6
Related to weight 62-4
Temperature effects 62-7
Velocity effects 62-6

Friction mark, a tire mark made when a slipping or sliding tire rubs the surface of the road or other surface.

Full impact, an impact during which motion momentarily ceases between some areas of the colliding objects while they are in contact with each other. If the colliding objects do not separate after collision, the impact is complete. 61-5

G

Gap skid, a braking skidmark which is interrupted by release and reapplication of brakes, or which terminates by release of brakes before collision. Compare with **skip skid**.

Geometry, plane

Law of Pythagoras 56-9
Parallel lines 56-10
Parallelograms 56-10
Principles of 56-9
Radius of a curve derivation 90-21
Similar triangles 56-10

Gore, the area immediately behind the bifurcation of two roadways, bounded by the edges of those roadways; the angle between two roadways where one roadway divides into two.

Gouge, a pavement scar deep enough to be easily felt with the fingers; chip, chop, or groove.

Grade, the change in elevation in unit distance in a specified direction along the center line of a roadway or along the path of a vehicle; the difference in level of two points divided by the level distance between the points. Grade is designated in feet per foot (meters per meter) of rise or fall per foot (meter) of level distance, or in rise or fall as a percent of the level distance. Grade is positive (+) if the surface rises in the specified direction, and negative (-) if it falls in that direction.

Groove, a long, narrow, pavement gouge; a channel in the pavement made by a small, strong, metal part being forced some distance along the surface while under great pressure.

H

Hatching, shading consisting of closely spaced parallel lines in a drawing.

Highway, the entire width between the boundary lines of any publicly maintained way when any part thereof is open to the public for vehicular travel; a street; a publicly maintained trafficway.

Homicide 77-3
In vehicle-pedestrian collisions 77-14

I

Identification, designation of a road location, a vehicle, a person, or a traffic accident in such a manner as to positively distinguish it from all others of the same description. Identification is often accomplished by a unique number, such as a vehicle identification number, registration number, or driver's license number.

Identifying numbers, numbers (and letters, if any) on a vehicle designated for the purpose of identifying the vehicle; VIN. Not the registration number.

Impact, the striking of one body against another; a collision of a vehicle with another vehicle, a pedestrian, or some other object.

First contact 61-4, 61-13
Full impact 61-5
Full impact of pedestrian 77-12
Maximum engagement 61-4, 61-13
Partial impact 61-5
Partial impact for pedestrian 77-9
Separation 61-5, 61-13

Imprint, a mark on the road or other surface made without sliding by a rolling tire or a person's foot. An imprint usually shows the pattern of the tire tread or shoe that made it.

Impulse

From the graphic momentum solution 68-18
In a collision 68-15

Induced damage, damage to a vehicle other than contact damage. Often indicated by crumpling, distortion, bending, and breaking. Induced damage includes damage done by another part of the same vehicle. Compare with **contact damage**.

Informant, any person who communicates information; not an informer.

Information, any knowledge received concerning a particular matter, such as a traffic accident, from any source, regardless of the reliability of that knowledge.

Injuries

Pedestrian accidents 77-6
Restraint system effects 76-19
To vehicle occupants 76-11

Intended course, the path that would have been followed by a traffic unit as a normal part of its trip had the situational hazard not led to evasive tactics or accident.

Interchange, a system of interconnecting roadways in conjunction with one or more grade separations, providing for traffic movement between two or more roadways on different levels. Compare with **intersection** and **junction**.

Interrogation, formal examination of a suspect by questioning.

Intersection, the area embraced within the prolongation or connection of the lateral curb lines; or, if none, then the lateral boundary lines of the roadways of two highways which join one another at, or approximately at, right angles; the area within which vehicles traveling on different highways joining at any other angle might come in conflict. When a highway includes two roadways 30 ft or more apart, then every crossing of each roadway of such divided highway shall be regarded as a separate intersection. In the event such intersecting highway also includes two roadways 30 ft or more apart, then every crossing of two roadways of such highways shall be regarded as a separate intersection. Compare with **junction**.

J

Junction, the general area where two or more highways join or cross, within which are included the roadway and roadside facilities for traffic movement in the area. A junction may include several intersections of roadways.

K

Kinematics, see **occupant motion** and **pedestrian motion**.
> Basic three equations 60-2
> Equation to calculate time 60-11
> Equations for 60-3
> Equations for initial velocity 60-6
> Equations to calculate distance 60-8
> Equations for end velocity 60-7
> Example problems 60-11
> Five basic quantities 60-2
> Motorcycle occupants 74-16

Kinetic energy – see **energy**.
> Definition 70-4
> Derivation of 90-7
> Equation for 70-4
> Equation for skid speed 70-5

L

Lane line, a line separating two lanes of traffic traveling in the same direction.

Last contact, the final touching of objects in a collision before separation; the time and place on a traffic unit or trafficway where this touching occurs. If colliding objects do not separate, there is no last contact.

Liquid debris, debris consisting of liquids from a vehicle or its cargo; spatter, dribble, puddle, runoff, or soak-in.

M

Mass
> Equation for 90-9

Maximum engagement, greatest penetration of one body, such as a vehicle, by another during collision; instant of greatest force between objects in collision; time and place of this occurrence; position of the bodies with respect to each other at this instant. 61-22

Median, that portion of a divided highway separating the roadways for traffic in opposite directions. If the median is more than about 100 ft (30 m), the area is usually considered as roadside.

Metal marks
> From motorcycles 74-5
> Motorcycle sidestand 74-5

Middle ordinate, the perpendicular distance between an arc and its chord at the middle of the chord.

Momentum, mass times velocity. Momentum is a vector quantity. See **conservation of momentum**.
> Angle collisions 68-7
> Case study 68-28
> Collinear collision example 68-5
> Components of 68-21
> Definition of 68-3
> Equations for 68-27
> Law of conservation of 68-3
> Sensitivity analysis 68-11
> Simple example 68-4
> Standard angle definitions 68-23
> Units of 68-3
> Using a personal computer 68-27

Motorcycle
> Abrasion mark 74-5
> Accident scene 74-4
> Braking 74-8
> Case study 74-20
> Cornering 74-15
> Drag factor 74-11
> Maneuverability 74-14
> Operator/passenger kinematics 74-16
> Sliding on its side 74-12
> Speed from damage 74-16
> Speed from skids 74-10
> Tire marks 74-4
> Types 74-7

N

Negligence – see **carelessness**.
> Definition 52-16

Newton's laws of motion
> 56-17

Nomograph, a chart on which three or more scales are arranged so that a straight line drawn through values on any two will cross the third at a corresponding value; nomogram; a graphic calculator.

O

Operational factor, functional failure of the highway transportation system that contribute to the cause of a traffic accident. The failures may be malfunctions of perception, decision or performance in trip planning, driving strategy, or evasive tactics.

Opposite-direction collision, a collision between two traffic units moving in opposite directions on the same roadway. Sometimes called **head-on collisions**.

Overdeflected, a condition of a tire in which the pressure on the road is greater at the edges of the tread than in the middle; an overloaded or underinflated tire condition.

Overreaction, a driver's excessive reaction to a hazardous situation that produces another, or additional, hazard. Overreaction is usually a matter of too much steering at high speeds, and often results in yaw.

Oversteer, a characteristic of a motor vehicle as loaded that results in a tendency to swerve toward the inside of a curve, especially at high speed. Motor vehicles with more weight on the rear wheels than on the front, and with too little pressure in the rear tires, are likely to oversteer. 72-14

P

Partial impact, an impact in which motion is continuous between the parts of colliding objects which are in contact with each other; sideswipe. Compare with **full impact**. 61-5

Passenger, any person in or on a vehicle involved in an accident, other than the driver.

Pedalcycle, a vehicle operated solely by pedals, and propelled by human power.

Pedestrian, any person afoot; any person not in or upon a motor vehicle or other road vehicle.

Perception, the general process of detecting some object or situation and comprehending its significance.

Perception delay, the time from the point of possible perception to actual perception.

Performance, the degree to which reaction corresponds to a decision relating to evasive tactics or driving strategy; how well the decision is executed. Performance is not necessarily the success of reaction, because an excellent performance of a bad decision may have an unfortunate result.

Perspective grid, a parallelogram (usually square or rectangle) of known size placed on a flat surface so as to appear in a photograph as a basis for locating marks or points which also show in the photograph of the surface.

Photogrammetry, the use of photographs for making maps.

Point of possible perception, the place and time at which the hazard could have been perceived by a normal person. It precedes actual perception and is the beginning of perception delay.

Point of collision – see **first contact point**.

Point of impact – see **first contact point**.

Point of tangency, the point on a curve where a tangent touches it; PT; on a roadway, usually the point where a curve begins or ends.

Pole trailer, any vehicle without motive power designed to be drawn by another vehicle and attached to the towing vehicle, and ordinarily used for transporting long or irregularly shaped loads, such as poles, pipes or structural members, which are generally capable sustaining themselves as beams between the supporting connections. See **truck**.

Portland cement concrete, a concrete made with portland cement.

Potential energy
    Elastic energy 70-6
    Gravitational energy 70-6
    Hooke's Law 70-7

Principal direction of force – see **thrust**.
    Related to impulse 68-15
    In collision 61-6

Primary cause, a misnomer loosely applied to the most obvious or easily explained factor in the cause of an accident or the most easily modified condition factor.

Print, an imprint of liquid or fine dust picked up by a tire or shoe sole at one place and left at another, usually showing the pattern of the tire or shoe that made it.

Professional reconstruction, the effort to determine, from available information, how the accident happened. Reconstruction is the fourth level of traffic accident investigation. It involves studying results of the accident, considering other circumstances, and applying scientific principles to form opinions relative to events of the accident which are otherwise unknown or are a matter of dispute.

Puddle, a wet area on the road or roadside where dribble accumulates after a vehicle has come to rest. A puddle often marks the final position of a vehicle after an accident.

R

Radius of a curve
    Derivation of equation for 90-21
    Methods to determine 72-24

Reaction, a person's voluntary or involuntary response to a hazard or other perceived situation; the response to a sensory stimulus. Reactions may be reflex, simple, complex, or discriminatory.
    Complex 64-12
    Definition 64-6
    Discriminatory 64-15
    Distance 52-6
    Elements of simple reaction 64-8
    Factors affecting response time 64-9
    Measuring 64-7
    Mental 64-6
    Muscular 64-6, 64-9
    Numerical values 64-17
    Reflex 64-14
    Simple 64-7

Reaction distance, the distance moved or traveled by a vehicle or other traffic unit during reaction time.

Reaction time, the time required from perception to the start of vehicle control for tactical or strategic operations.

Recklessness – see **carelessness**. 52-16

Reference line, a line, often the edge of a roadway, from which measurements are made to locate spots, especially spots along a roadway.

Reference point, a point from which measurements are made to locate spots in an area; sometimes the intercept of two reference lines; RP. A reference point is described in terms of its relation to permanent landmarks.

Reflex reaction, an involuntary response to a stimulus; an instinctive act resulting from perception of an imminently hazardous situation. Time: 0.2 sec, more or less. 64-14

Reporting, basic data collection to identify and classify a motor vehicle traffic accident and the persons, property, and planned movements involved. Only strictly factual information is wanted, no opinions. Reporting is the first level of traffic accident investigation.

Restitution – see **coefficient of restitution**.

Road, the part of a trafficway which includes both the roadway, which is the traveled part, and any shoulder alongside the roadway. Where there are unmountable curbs, the road and roadway are the same. If there is a guard rail, the road is considered to extend to the guard rail.

Roadway, the part of the road intended for vehicle travel. It does not include paved or otherwise improved shoulders or what is sometimes called a "berm" or "breakdown lane."

Roll, the motion of a vehicle which has been retarded at ground level while the remainder of the vehicle continues moving forward without leaving the ground; rollover.

Rolling resistance, horizontal force required to keep a vehicle in motion on a level surface, with the engine disconnected from the wheels and with no brake application; drag factor produced by friction within the vehicle and deformation of the tires and road surface.

Rotation
    From collision 61-6

Runoff, rivulets of liquid debris from a puddle area downhill toward soak-in at the edge of the pavement; frequently the source of tire prints after a collision.

Rut, a depression in soft or loose material, such as snow or dirt, made by a rolling tire.

S

Same-direction collision, a collision between two traffic units moving in the same direction on the same roadway. Sometimes called **rear-end collision**.

Scar, any sign that the road, roadside, or a fixed object has been damaged or marred by a traffic accident.

Scene, the location of a traffic accident while people and vehicles involved are still there. Compare with **site**.

Scrape, a broad area of a hard surface covered with many scratches or striations made by a sliding metal part without great pressure.

Scratch, a light and usually irregular scar made on a hard surface, such as paving, by a sliding metal part, without great pressure.

Scuffmark, a friction mark on a pavement made by a tire which is both rotating and slipping; acceleration scuffs, yawmarks, flattire marks.

Semitrailer, any vehicle with or without motive power, other than a pole trailer, designed for carrying persons or property and for being drawn by a motor vehicle, and so constructed that some part of its weight and that of its load rests upon or is carried by another vehicle. See **truck**.

Shoulder, that portion of the road contiguous with the roadway for accommodating a stopped vehicle, for emergency use, and for lateral support of the roadway structure. The line between the roadway and the shoulder may be a painted edge line, a change in surface color or material, or a curb.

Sidewalk, that portion of a street between the curb lines, or the lateral lines of a roadway, and the adjacent property lines, and intended for use by pedestrians.

Significant figures 56-4

Skidding vehicle speed
Motorcycle skids 74-10
Nomograph in km/hr 62-19
Nomograph in mi/hr 62-18
Speed equation 62-13
Table in km/hr 62-17
Table in mi/hr 62-16
Tables and nomographs 62-15

Simple reaction, a preplanned reaction to an expected hazard or other stimulus. Time: 0.5 sec, more or less. 64-7

Site, the location of a traffic accident after vehicles and people involved have gone. Compare with **scene**.

Situation hazard, a circumstance that more or less endangers a traffic unit on a trip and which must be avoided to prevent an accident.

Skidmark, a friction mark on a pavement made by a tire that is sliding without rotation. Sliding of wheels may be due to braking, to collision damage, or, rarely, to other circumstances.
From motorcycle 74-4
Locating by photogrammetry 92-14

Skip skid, a braking skidmark interrupted at frequent regular intervals; the skidmark made by a bouncing wheel on which brakes keep the wheel from turning. Compare with **gap skid**.

Slave flash, a supplementary photo-flash placed at a distance from the master flash to increase the illuminated field in a photograph and fired by a photoelectric device actuated by light from the master flash.

Soak-in, an area on the shoulder or roadside saturated with liquid debris either at the end of runoff or as a puddle marking the rest position of a vehicle after a collision.

Spatter, the collection of marks on the road made by liquid from the vehicle or its cargo squirted from containers on the vehicle by force of collision. Spatter areas are irregular in shape and often consist of many small spots.

Speed, rate of progress, usually without regard to direction; distance divided by time (if speed is constant).

Speed estimates – see **falls**, **flips**, **vaults**, **conservation of momentum**, **velocity** and **pedestrian accidents**.
From gear position 78-33
From tachographs 78-34

Speed from damage
Equivalent barrier speed 70-20
For trucks 78-12
Motorcycles 74-16
Stiffness coefficients 70-17

Stabilized accident situation, the condition prevailing after motion and other action constituting the events of an accident have ceased and no further harm will ensue unless a new series of events is initiated by some means.

Standard symbols
Table of 56-23

Steering
Ackermann principle 72-10
Neutral steer 72-14
Oversteering 72-14
System geometry 72-11
Understeer 72-14

Strategy, adjusting speed, position on the road, and direction of motion, giving signals of intent to turn or to slow, or any other action in situations involving potential hazards; any maneuvers while on a trip which make evasive tactics easier or increase the chance of success in avoiding an actual hazard. 64-3, 52-9
Laws relating to 52-10
Pedestrian 77-3, 77-13
Reconstruction inferences 50-3

Striations, narrow, light, parallel stripes or streaks usually made by friction or abrasion on the roadway or on vehicle parts.

Suicide 77-3
In vehicle-pedestrian collisions 77-14

Superelevation, the degree to which the outside edge of a roadway is higher than the inside edge at a specified point on a curve; the change in elevation per unit distance across the roadway from the inside of a curve to the outside edge; bank.

Symbols
Table of 90-4

T

Tactic, action taken by a traffic unit to avoid a hazardous situation; steering, braking, accelerating, etc., to avoid a collision or other accident. Often called **evasive action**.

Tangent, a line that touches a curve at only one point and that is perpendicular to the radius at that point; a term used to describe a straight section of a roadway.

Technical follow-up, collection of additional facts from any source and organization and preliminary study of all available data relating to an accident; level 3 of accident investigation.

Testimony, evidence given by a competent witness under oath or affirmation.

Thrust, the force against a traffic unit considered to be concentrated on a particular point on that unit at any instant during a collision. See **principal direction of force**.

Tire

Tire friction mark, a tire mark made when a slipping or sliding tire rubs the road or other surface; skidmarks; yawmarks; acceleration scuffs and flat tire marks.

Tire mark, a mark made on a road or other surface by a tire on a vehicle: tire friction mark, imprint.

Track, the distance on the ground between the center of the tire tread on one side of the vehicle, and the center of the tire tread on the opposite side.

Tracking, marks made when tires roll through puddles, runoff or spatter and, becoming wet, leave tire prints on the pavement as they roll on.

Traffic, pedestrians, ridden or herded animals, motor vehicles, street cars, and other conveyances either singly or together while using any highway for travel.

Traffic accident reconstruction

Traffic unit, an element of traffic; a person using a trafficway for travel or transportation; vehicle, pedalcycle, pedestrian, etc.

Trafficway, the entire width between property lines, or other boundary lines, of every way or place of which any part is open to the public for vehicular travel as a matter of right or custom. All highways are trafficways, but trafficways also also certain areas on private property, such as shopping centers.

Trailer, any vehicle with or without motive power, other than a pole trailer, designed for carrying persons or property and for being drawn by a motor vehicle, and so constructed that no part of its weight rests upon the towing vehicle.

Tread, that part of a tire designed to come in contact with the ground.

Triangulation, a method of locating a spot in an area by measurements from two or more reference points, the locations of which are identified for future reference. Compare with **coordinates**.

Trigonometry

Truck, any motor vehicle designed, used, or maintained primarily for transporting property.

Truck tractor, any motor vehicle designed and used primarily for drawing other vehicles and not so constructed as to carry a load other than part of the weight of the vehicle and load so drawn.

U

Uncontrolled final position, a final position reached by a traffic unit after an accident without conscious human intervention.

Underbody debris, debris consisting of mud, dust, rust, paint, snow, or road tar loosened by collision from the underside of the vehicle body, fenders, and other parts.

Understeer, a characteristic of a motor vehicle as loaded that results in a tendency to swerve toward the outside of a curve. Motor vehicles with more weight on front wheels than on rear wheels, or with too little pressure in front tires, are likely to understeer at high speed. 72-14

Uniform Vehicle Code, a specified set of motor vehicle laws, designed and advanced as a comprehensive guide or standard for state motor vehicle and traffic laws.

V

Vault, an endwise flip.
Data needed 66-15
Derivation of equation 90-17
Equations 66-16
Principles 66-15
Speed table in km/hr 66-15
Speed table in mi/hr 66-14

Vector, a quantity that has both magnitude and direction, such as force, velocity, acceleration, momentum; represented graphically by an arrow indicating direction and, by its length, magnitude.

Vector addition
By parallelograms 56-12
By trigonometry 56-16
Momentum analysis 68-8
Principles of 56-11

Vehicle, any device in, upon, or by which any person or property is or can be transported or drawn upon a highway, excepting devices moved by human power or those used exclusively upon stationary rails or tracks.

Vehicle damage
Interior inspection 76-4
Systematic procedure 61-15

Vehicle identification number (VIN), the number assigned to the vehicle by the manufacturer, primarily for identification and registration purposes.

Vehicle kinematics
Data required 61-3
Example of angle impact 61-20
Examples of 61-7
Opposite direction example 61-18
Related to damage 61-10
Systematic approach 61-3

Velocity, time rate of change of position in which direction and rapidity are elements; distance divided by time (if velocity is constant); a vector quantity measured in feet per second (ft per sec) or meters per second (m per sec); v = d/t.
Circular 90-18
Closing 68-6
Constant 90-3
Initial velocity equation derivation 90-10
Units for 60-5

Visibility
Amount of 64-16
Of pedestrians 77-13
Vehicle lights 64-16
Visual acuity 64-16

W

Weight shift
Lateral 72-22
Longitudinal 72-22

Wheelbase, the distance from the center of the front wheels to the center of the rear wheels or, if there is a tandem axle, the distance to the midpoint between the two tandem axles.

Wind resistance, the force of the atmosphere against a moving vehicle; atmospheric drag factor; a combination of forces produced by motion of the vehicle through the air and motion of the air itself. Under certain circumstances, wind may assist rather than resist the motion of the vehicle.

Work
Definition 70-3
Definition of 90-7
Equation form 70-3
Relationship to energy 70-4

Y

Yaw, a sidewise movement of a vehicle in turning; movement of a vehicle in another direction than that in which it is headed; sidewise motion produced when centrifugal force exceeds traction force. Often the result of overreaction or exceeding the critical speed. Sometimes revealed by tiremarks on the roadway.

Yawmark, a scuffmark made while a vehicle is yawing; the mark made on the road by a rotating tire which is slipping in a direction parallel to the axle of the wheel. 72-23

Yaw velocity
Basic equations for 72-41
Computer analysis 72-49
Considering side slip angle 72-35
Considering side slip angle and braking 72-37
Considering special conditions 72-41
Data needed 72-23
Empirical studies 72-44
Equations for 72-27